4th Edition

MEDIA TODAY

An INTRODUCTION to MASS COMMUNICATION

Praise for *Media Today*, 4th Edition

"*Media Today* is the best textbook to understand the organization, economics, and emerging trends within the U.S. media sector. Its institutional focus and the level of detail and updated knowledge it provides in this regard makes it the best textbook for an introductory media course."

Gisela Gil-Egui, Fairfield University

"What makes *Media Today* especially stand out is the extra attention to the dynamics of the ever-changing media industries. Joe Turow's book offers a nuanced, comprehensive and accessible treatment of how economic incentives and current trends in media matter for us and our democracy."

Matt McAllister, Pennsylvania State University

"*Media Today* engages students and serves as a helpful guide to our new media-saturated world. The writing is lively and concise, and the colorful illustrations are full of zest. Turow's dry wit engages students in a conversational narrative that prompts them to connect what they read to their own experience of contemporary media trends."

Edward M. Clift, Woodbury University

"*Media Today* skillfully weaves together all the core components needed for an introductory media course: basics of media literacy and criticism, details about a wide range of the most current media, and an uncommonly thorough integration of the functioning of media industries. Accessible and smart in its writing style and full of useful illustrations and tables, *Media Today*, is not only up-to-date in its information, but its perspective prepares the future of media studies."

Amanda Lotz, University of Michigan

4th Edition

MEDIA TODAY

An INTRODUCTION to MASS COMMUNICATION

JOSEPH TUROW

Routledge
Taylor & Francis Group

NEW YORK AND LONDON

Senior Acquisitions Editor: Matt Byrnie
Senior Development Editor: Nicole Solano
Freelance Development Editor: Kristen Desmond LeFevre
Senior Editorial Assistant: Stan Spring
Editorial Assistant: Carolann Madden
Production Editor: Alf Symons
Project Manager: Nicola Haig
Marketing Manager: Joon Won Moon
Text Design: Alex Lazarou, Alf Symons, and Keystroke
Copy-editor: Deborah Bennett
Proofreader: Emma Needs
Indexer: Jim Henderson
Graphics: Integra and Laserwords
Cover Design: Mathew Willis
Composition: Rhiannon Miller
Companion Website Designer: Leon Nolan

Published 2011
by Routledge
270 Madison Avenue, New York, NY 10016

Simultaneously published in the UK
by Routledge
2 Park Square, Milton Park, Abingdon, Oxon OX14 4RN

First edition published in 1999 by Houghton Mifflin Company
Second edition published in 2003 by Houghton Mifflin Company
Third edition published in 2009 by Routledge

Routledge is an imprint of the Taylor & Francis Group, an informa business

© 2011 Taylor & Francis

Typeset by Prepress Projects Ltd, Perth
Printed and bound in India by Replika Press Pvt Ltd

Library of Congress Cataloging-in-Publication Data
Turow, Joseph.
  Media today: an introduction to mass communication / Joseph Turow. – 4th ed.
  p. cm.
  Includes bibliographical references and index.
  1. Mass media. I. Title.
  P90.T874 2010
  302.23_dc22

2010023865

ISBN13: 978-0-415-87607-0 (hbk)
ISBN13: 978-0-415-87608-7 (pbk)
ISBN13: 978-0-203-83651-4 (ebk)

For Judy

About the Author

Joseph Turow is the Robert Lewis Shayon Professor of Communication at the University of Pennsylvania's Annenberg School for Communication. He has been described by the *New York Times* as "probably the reigning academic expert on media fragmentation." He holds a Ph.D. in communication from the University of Pennsylvania, where he has taught since 1986. He has also served on the faculty at Purdue University and has lectured at many other universities in the United States and around the world. For 2010, he was awarded an Astor Visiting Lectureship by Oxford University. He is a Fellow of the International Communication Association and was named a Distinguished Scholar by the National Communication Association.

Turow has authored eight books, edited five, and written more than 100 articles on mass media. Among those books, in addition to *Media Today*, are *Playing Doctor: Television, Storytelling, and Medical Power* (University of Michigan Press, 2010), *Niche Envy: Marketing Discrimination in the Digital Age* (MIT Press, 2006), *Breaking Up America: Advertisers and the New Media World* (University of Chicago Press, 1997), and *The Hyperlinked Society* (co-edited with Lokman Tsui, University of Michigan Press, 2008). He has also written about media and advertising for the popular press, including *The Washington Post*, the *Los Angeles Times*, *The Boston Globe*, and the *San Francisco Chronicle*.

Turow has received two departmental Best Teaching Awards, along with numerous conference-paper awards. He served as elected Chair of the Mass Communication Division of the International Communication Association for four years. Turow edits "The New Media World" book series for the University of Michigan Press and currently serves on the editorial boards of the *Journal of Broadcasting and Electronic Media*, *Poetics*, and *New Media & Society*.

Brief Contents

Detailed Contents

Part 1
Understanding the Nature of Mass Media 2

Part Two
Media Giants and Cross-Media Activities   154

Part Three
The Print Media   **224**

Part Four
The Electronic Media

Part Five
Advertising and Public Relations   524

Feature Topics

TECH & INFRASTRUCTURE

WORLD VIEW

MEDIA RESEARCH

MEDIA PROFILE

IS IT ETHICAL?

Preface

Welcome to *Media Today: An Introduction to Mass Communication*, Fourth Edition. *Media Today* stems from my concern that students in the introductory course need to be exposed to a fuller, more realistic view of the exciting, changing world of media in the new century. **With updated content, examples, and case studies throughout, and completely revamped companion website material**, this leading-edge new edition reveals the forces that guide the creation, distribution, and exhibition of media systems; places the internet and digital media as organic parts of those media systems; and actively challenges students to see and hear their favorite media products in genuinely new ways.

A Cutting-Edge, Real-World Approach to Studying Mass Communication

Media Today is the product of over three decades of teaching the introductory course, talking to colleagues around the country about course trends and issues, and writing about mass media industries and issues in the scholarly and popular press. The hope is that readers will become critical, media-literate consumers of mass media and, if they go on to work in mass media industries, more alert, sensitive practitioners. The book presents a cutting-edge, real-world approach to the contemporary media system and its issues without wrenching the instructor from the familiar flow of topics in the basic course.

    Media Today, Fourth Edition is built around four distinct concepts:

- A media systems approach
- Unique insights into media trends
- Emphasis on the centrality of digital convergence
- A media literacy goal

    Let's take a look at each:

A Media Systems Approach

Unlike other texts for the introductory course, *Media Today* takes a media systems approach out of the conviction that the best way to engage students is to reveal the forces that guide the creation, distribution, and exhibition of news, information, entertainment, education, and advertising with media systems. Then, once they begin to understand the ways these systems operate, students will be able to interact with the media around them in new ways.

    The key to this unique approach is this: What fundamentally separates mass communication from other forms of communication is neither the size of the audience (it could be large or small) nor the use of technology (mediated communication can be mass or interpersonal). Rather, what distinguishes mass communication is the industrialized, or mass production, process that is involved in creating and circulating the material. It is this industrial process that generates the potential for reaching millions (even billions) of diverse anonymous people at around the same time (say, through televising the repercussions of BP's oil spill in the Gulf of Mexico). *Media Today* uses this production-based approach to scrutinize the media, in order to show students how the industrial nature of the process is central to the definition of mass communication.

The text introduces the media as an interconnected system of industries—not as totally separate from one another. Of course, an introductory text can't begin with a sophisticated exploration of boundary blurring. Students have to first understand the nature of the mass communication process. They must become aware that taking a mass communication perspective on the world means learning to see the interconnected system of media products that surrounds them every day in new ways.

Chapters 1 through 4 introduce this notion of interconnected news as they explore the nature of the mass communication process, the business of media, society's formal and informal controls on media, and research on media effects and culture. Chapters 7 through 16 emphasize this industrial process, beginning with an overview of each industry, and then moving through production, distribution, and exhibition, taking time to discuss relevant issues and controversies along the way.

Unique Insights Into Media Trends

Chapter 5: A World of Blurred Media Boundaries is unique among introductory media texts, and introduces students to the general media environment by taking a close look at the six trends that are guiding today's media environment:

- Media fragmentation
- Audience segmentation
- Distribution of products across media boundaries
- Globalization
- Conglomeration
- Digital convergence

Chapter 6: Understanding the Strategies of Media Giants builds upon students' new understanding of these six guiding trends through vivid case studies that examine how three of the largest media firms—News Corporation, Disney, and Google—are responding to these trends across media, and how their strategies are influencing all media industries. Students are then equipped with the media literacy skills and knowledge about the "big picture" to consider and explore eleven individual media industries—from books (Chapter 7) to public relations (Chapter 16).

Emphasis on the Centrality of Digital Convergence

This new edition of *Media Today* takes full account of one of the most important developments of our time: the rise of digital media, including the internet, iPads, and the rise of tablets, video games, MP3 players, and mobile phones, and their convergence—that is, their interconnection and blurring—with each other and with traditional mass media such as newspapers, magazines, and digital television. It used to be that an introductory mass communication text could nod to new media developments by concentrating them in a chapter on the internet and maybe one on video games. That is no longer enough.

It is today simply impossible to write about workings of the newspaper, television, magazine, recording, movie, advertising, and public relations industries without taking into account fundamental changes being wrought by websites, blogs, email, MP3 files, and multimedia streams. Consequently, the reader will find that every chapter incorporates digital media developments into the main flow of the material.

Chapter 1: Understanding Mass Media and the Importance of Media Literacy announces from its very first line—"Your TV is ringing"— that this book will cover a wide variety of media in ways that highlight the clash between the new and the old. Chapter 2: Making Sense of the Media Buisness's introduction to the business aspects of the media shows how internet activities—such as those involved with broadcast television and newspapers—can be illuminated through the categories of production, distribution, and exhibition. Chapter 3: Controls on Media Content's discussion of formal and informal controls on media content, and Chapter 4: Making Sense of Research on Media Effects and Media Culture's discussion of the history of media research on key social issues, cover topics related to the internet and other digital vehicles alongside topics relating to traditional media. Chapter 5: A World of Blurred Media Boundaries' introduction to the blurring of media boundaries and Chapter 6: Understanding the Strategies of Media Giants' close examination of the cross-media strategies of major media firms place digital changes at the center of corporate activities—developments that Chapter 6 underscores with a section devoted to Google's activities on the Web and across many other platforms.

This emphasis on the centrality of digital convergence is carried through each of the ten chapters on the individual media industries (Chapters 7 through 16). Chapter 8: The Newspaper Industry introduces students to the opportunities and challenges of the online, on-mobile, 24/7 organizational environment that has been emerging. Similarly, much of Chapter 10: The Recording Industry centers on the transformation that is taking place around digital music. Chapter 14: The Internet and Video Game Industries describes unique characteristics of the Web domain and of the digital gaming environment.

A Media Literacy Goal

The overarching goal of the Fourth Edition of *Media Today* is to help students become media-literate members of society. Being media-literate involves applying critical thinking skills to the mass media, and finding meanings beneath the surface of movies, ads, and other types of content. It also involves reasoning clearly about controversies that may involve the websites students use, the mobile devices they carry, the TV shows they watch, the music they hear, the magazines they read, and much more. It means becoming a more aware and responsible citizen—parent, voter, worker—in our media-driven society.

The aim of *Media Today* is to help students become critical consumers who seriously examine the mass media's roles in their lives and in the greater culture, without making them totally cynical and distrustful of all mass media. The text helps students think in an educated manner about the forces that shape the media and their relationships with them so that they will become media-literate citizens who are:

■ Knowledgeable about the influences that guide media organizations
■ Up-to-date on political issues relating to the media
■ Sensitive to the ethical dimensions of media activities
■ Knowledgeable about scholarship regarding media effects

Media Today encourages and develops these skills and attributes as it presents students with a realistic, cutting-edge picture of the changing media world in the new century. It reinforces and develops students' media literacy skills in every chapter of the text, through unique chapter-ending sections applying media literacy to the issues of the chapter.

Media Today's Updated Features

A number of valuable features—including updated boxes and end-of-chapter materials—appear in each chapter to enhance students' exploration and enjoyment of the Fourth Edition of *Media Today*.

Engaging, Up-to-Date Feature Boxes Provide Students Perspective and Interest

These eighty-six boxed features have been completely updated throughout the book to address the latest issues, trends, and developments in today's media environment. Topics include media convergence and the aftermath of the earthquake in Haiti (Culture Today box, Chapter 1), the controversial move by Google to add the Buzz feature to all active Gmail accounts (Critical Consumer box, Chapter 6), the role of social media campaigns in the box office success of *Paranormal Activity* (Culture Today box, Chapter 12), the tactic of getting ads banned from the Super Bowl to gain customer attention (Culture Today box, Chapter 15), and much, much more.

CULTURE TODAY BOXES explore current, often controversial issues in today's media-rich environment. Boxes encourage a media literacy approach by asking students to consider the role that mass media plays in shaping and reflecting our culture.

CRITICAL CONSUMER BOXES challenge students to think critically about controversies they encounter in the films and TV shows they watch, the music they listen to, and the books, newspapers, and magazines they read. Boxes prompt students to explore the effects and implications of mass media on individuals and on society as a whole.

TECH & INFRASTRUCTURE BOXES help students demystify mass media technologies by explaining how they work, helping students understand their role in the production, distribution, and exhibition of content across media outlets and around the world.

WORLD VIEW BOXES focus on the global aspects of mass media systems and provide an up-to-date, international perspective on the availability and social implications of media throughout the world.

IS IT ETHICAL? BOXES use vivid, current real-world examples to discuss issues of ethics in increasingly competitive industry environments.

MEDIA PROFILE BOXES   take an in-depth look at biographies of media people—both historical and current—with a special emphasis on diversity. Boxes feature profiles of media practitioners, critics, institutional leaders, and others.

MEDIA RESEARCH BOXES   introduce students to practical aspects of real-world media research and discuss the impact of research findings. Emphasis is placed on the importance and influence of historical and ongoing media research.

Rich and Diverse Chapter-Ending Materials and Exercises Give Students an Opportunity to Test and Explore What They've Learned

These valuable end-of-chapter materials are designed to challenge students to think critically and to build their media literacy skills.

QUESTIONS FOR CRITICAL THINKING AND DISCUSSION   ask students to consider the "big picture" impact of what they've learned in each chapter and to apply their knowledge to contemporary debates about the media.

QUESTIONS FOR CONSTRUCTING MEDIA LITERACY   invite students to think about how *they* use the media.

CASE STUDIES   ask students to research the media they consume regularly in their everyday lives (say, for instance, a magazine of their choosing), exploring in-depth how mass media moves through the production, distribution, and exhibition processes.

ONLINE CHAPTER REVIEW AND STUDY GUIDES   provide students with a way to recap what they've read in a chapter, or to review for an upcoming exam.

INTERNET RESOURCES   connect students to relevant websites to guide them in their further research into the topics discussed in each chapter.

KEY TERMS   highlight the important terms introduced in each chapter, which can also be found in the marginal glossary, or reviewed through interactive flash cards on the Media Today student website.

Media Today's Updated Ancillary Package

A full array of newly enhanced ancillary materials supplementing these book-based features—including a companion DVD and completely revised and improved online resources for instructors and students—make teaching the course, and being a student in it, especially rewarding.

For Students

Student website at **http://www.routledge.com/textbooks/mediatoday4e**

The student website features content-rich assets to help students expand their knowledge, study for exams, and more! Features include:

- **UPDATED! DYNAMIC SELF-QUIZZES FOR EACH BOOK CHAPTER:** help students test their knowledge and prepare for exams.
- **UPDATED! INTERACTIVE KEY TERMS FLASHCARDS:** provide students with a fun way to review important terms and definitions.
- **UPDATED! CHAPTER SUMMARIES AND STUDY GUIDES:** recap the key points and themes of each chapter.
- **NEW! ONLINE VIDEO RESOURCES:** enable students to view videos keyed to each chapter that offer unique and exciting insights into the media literacy topics and ideas discussed in the text, from issues of censorship to race and gender stereotypes in popular media.
- **UPDATED! STUDY PODCASTS AUDIO CHAPTER SUMMARIES:** allow students to recap each chapter and study *on the go!* These free podcasts can be downloaded directly from the *Media Today* website and are playable on any MP3 audio device.
- **UPDATED! *MEDIA TODAY* INTERNSHIP AND CAREER GUIDE:** offers students information and job listings to get started in a career in media.
- **UPDATED! LINKS TO FURTHER RESOURCES:** direct students to key media websites for further study and the latest news on media industries.
- **UPDATED! REGULARLY UPDATED AUTHOR BLOG *MEDIA TODAY AND TOMORROW*:** connects students to the most recent developments, controversies, and trends in mass media, and offers a forum for critical discussion with the author.

For Instructors

Instructors website at **http://www.routledge.com/textbooks/mediatoday4e**

The password-protected instructor site provides completely updated instructor support materials in the form of:

- **UPDATED! COMPLETE, ONLINE, AND DOWNLOADABLE INSTRUCTOR'S MANUAL REVISED FOR THIS UPDATE:** written by Chenjerai Kumanyika of Penn State University, it summarizes key learning objectives of each chapter and provides instructors with discussion starters to help build a dialogue in the classroom.
- **UPDATED! EXTENSIVE EXPANDED TEST BANK:** provides multiple choice, true–false, and fill-in-the-blank questions as well as new short-answer questions for exams for each chapter.
- **UPDATED! FULLY REVISED POWERPOINT PRESENTATIONS:** offer lecture outlines for each chapter, along with a set of slides for every figure in the text.
- **UPDATED! REGULARLY UPDATED AUTHOR BLOG *MEDIA TODAY AND TOMORROW*:** suggests new lecture starters and classroom discussion topics pulled from today's media headlines.
- **NEW! SAMPLE SYLLABI:** to help instructors plan their courses around semester and trimester schedules.
- **NEW! INTERACTIVE STUDENT ACTIVITIES:** to help students actively participate with new material and enhance their learning experience.

Key Readings in Media Today
(ISBN 13: 978–0–415–99205–3)

Edited by Brooke Erin Duffy and Joseph Turow, this exciting student-friendly anthology brings together thirty-two of the most important historical and contemporary writings on media, technology, and culture to help students make sense of the rapidly changing media environment. Designed to supplement *Media Today* and enrich students' understanding of key issues and controversies in twenty-first-century media, *Key Readings in Media Today* presents works of media criticism drawn from the academic and popular press on each of the media industries profiled in *Media Today*. This anthology can be packaged with *Media Today* or purchased separately.

Acknowledgments

A book such as this is impossible to create alone, and so there are several people to thank. My wife Judy has been very supportive with her encouragement and smart advice. At the University of Pennsylvania's Annenberg School for Communication, a number of graduate students helped with research and editorial work. Special thanks go to Brett Bumgarner and Nora Draper for their work on this edition. Sharon Black, the great Annenberg librarian, has always been ready to help with the best references available.

At Routledge, I'm indebted to Matt Byrnie, whose enthusiasm for the project and helpful suggestions were an important incentive. Kristen Desmond LeFevre, the supervisory editor, has been enormously influential to this project. Her ideas and hard work shine through on every page. In addition, thanks go to the professional insights and efforts of development editor Nicole Solano, editorial assistant Stan Spring, marketing director Amy Lee, marketing manager Joon Won Moon, project manager Nicola Haig, production editor Alf Symons, copy-editor Deborah Bennett, and proofreader Emma Needs.

I would also like to thank the following academic reviewers whose (anonymous) suggestions during the reviewing process helped me greatly as I prepared the fourth edition:

Aje-Ori Agbese, *University of Texas, Pan-American*

Daren C. Brabham, *University of Utah*

Larry Burris, *Middle Tennessee State University*

Edward Clift, *Woodbury University*

John Couper, *Idaho State University*

Richard Craig, *San Jose State University*

Greg Downey, *University of Wisconsin-Madison*

Samuel Ebersole, *Colorado State University—Pueblo*

Joan Erben, *New Mexico State University at Grants*

Emily Erickson, *Louisiana State University*

Connie Fletcher, *Loyola University*

Bradley C. Freeman, *Nanyang Technological University*

Peter Galarneau, *West Virginia Wesleyan College*

Gisela Gil-Egui, *Fairfield University*

Eunice Goes, *The American University in London*

David Gudelunas, *Fairfield University*

Harry W. Haines, *Montclair State University*

Sharon Hollenback, *Syracuse University*

Patricia A. Holmes, *University of Louisiana at Lafayette*

Junhao Hong, *State University of New York at Buffalo*

Kelli Lammie, *State University of New York at Albany*

Teresa Mastin, *DePaul University*

Deb Merskin, *University of Oregon*

Steve Miller, *Rutgers University*

Merrill Morris, *Gainesville State College*

Siho Nam, *University of North Florida*

David D. Perlmutter, *University of Kansas*

Deborah Petersen-Perlman, *University of Minnesota Duluth*

Mihaela Popescu, *California State University, San Bernardino*

Elli Lester Roushanzamir, *University of Georgia, Athens*

Marshel Rossow, *Minnesota State University, Mankato*

Jeremy Sarachan, *St. John Fisher College*

Joseph W. Slade, *Ohio University*

Cathy Stablein, *College of DuPage*

Jane Stokes, *University of East London*

Susan Weill, *Texas State University*

Scott Weiss, *St. Francis College*

Bob Williams, *Lindenwood University*

Janice Xu, *Cabrini College*

A Visual Tour of *Media Today*

Discussion Quotes
Compelling quotes from media figures draw attention to key ideas and spark discussion.

1 Understanding Mass Media and the Importance of Media Literacy

After studying this chapter, you will be able to:

1 Discuss the differences between interpersonal communication and mass communication

2 Explain why an unorthodox definition of mass communication makes the term especially relevant in today's media environment

3 Explain the meaning and importance of culture's relationship with the mass media

4 Analyze the ways in which the mass media affect our everyday lives

5 Explain what the term "media literacy" means

6 List the key principles involved in becoming media literate

7 Discuss the importance of developing media literacy skills for the classroom and beyond

8 Explain current and future trends in mass communication

"Whoever controls the media controls the culture."
— ALLEN GINSBERG, POET

"Information is the oxygen of the modern age."
— RONALD REAGAN, U.S. PRESIDENT

MEDIA TODAY

"Your TV is ringing."

The first time you saw apps on an iPhone or another "smartphone" you might have said, "cool," or "I want that" about virtually everything. The nearly 134,000 free and paid programs include ways to play games, read the news, find out where your friends are, tweet to them, find a cheap airline ticket, learn when your plane is leaving, search for restaurants, watch sports, view a television show, and a whole lot more.[1]

It's certainly an exciting time to study mass communication. None of the activities described above could have been attempted on a telephone just a few years ago, but now they have become standard for many mobile phones. The developments raise questions about the impact that these and other technologies will have on us, our society, and the content of TV, movies, video games, music, newspapers, magazines, websites, and advertisements.

Consider the mass media menu that Americans have today. Instead of three or four TV channels, most Americans receive more than fifty and a substantial number receive 150 and more. Radio in urban areas delivers dozens of stations; satellite radio brings in hundreds more, and music streaming on the web—sometimes called internet radio—is carried out by countless broadcast and nonbroadcast entities. Desktop computers, laptops, netbooks, e-readers, video game consoles, CD players, and DVDs have brought far more channels into our lives than ever before. So has the internet—allowing us to interact with information, news, and entertainment from all over the nation and the world.

Research indicates that Americans spend an enormous amount of time with mass media.[2] Think about your own media habits. How close do you come to the average thirty-two hours a week (about 4.5 hours a day) of television that Americans view on the traditional TV set as well as online? What about radio? Studies suggest that Americans listen to around fifteen hours a week of radio in the regular broadcast mode, via satellite channels, or from their online feeds. Do you do that, or do you instead listen to recorded music on your iPod or on your MP3 or CD player? Studies show that Americans spend an average of about 3.5 hours a week with recorded music (although college students undoubtedly do more of it). And what about the time you spend reading books, newspapers, and magazines? Data show that on average Americans spend about eight hours a week with one or another of these, both their printed versions and their websites.

Just a few years ago, media such as television, radio, books, and newspapers seemed pretty separate. It was clear what content from each medium looked or sounded like, and it would have been foolish to suggest that newspaper articles and television programs would show up on the same channel. But because of the rise of computer technologies that we will explore in the coming pages, this "foolishness" is exactly what has happened. The access the internet gives us to content from different types of media is part of a process called convergence. Convergence takes place when content that has traditionally been confined to one medium appears on multiple media channels.

The media of mass communication are an integral part of our lives, occurring in a wide variety of settings. In this chapter, we will explore and define communication, media, and culture, and we will consider how the relationships among them affect us and the world in which we live. We will also consider why the term "mass communication" remains relevant in the twenty-first century, contrary to what some writers say. In fact, the changes taking place in the media system actually make a rethought and redefined version of the term more important than ever.

convergence when content that has traditionally been confined to one medium appears on multiple media channels

Learning Objectives
Each chapter begins with a set of clearly defined goals to make the point of the chapter clear to students from the outset.

Chapter Opening Vignettes
Engaging stories connect students' daily interactions with media to key concepts introduced and issues raised in each chapter.

CRITICAL CONSUMER
HOW MUCH AM I WORTH?

individuals. Customers can access infoUSA's databases online through their Sales Genie service, which costs between $75 and $180 per month. Another company,

CULTURE TODAY
ADVERTAINMENT

Advertainment refers to content that blurs the line between advertisement and entertainment. It has become an increasingly important tactic in a world so saturated by commercial con... novative for their p... popular online vide... important site for th...

Some of the most... ing videos in which... the viewer is surpri... As one marketing d... as an advertising pl... play and the oppor... and become an onl... tion for other sites t...

After releasing th... Oscars, Apple put th... it quickly became c... number of corporati... ing Porsche, Sony, a... made, there is little f... the ad on their onlin...

There is substantial risk that goes along with posting advertisements on YouTube. Viewers can comment on ads and often make negative statements about the video

MEDIA RESEARCH
THE PEW INTERNET AND
AMERICAN LIFE PROJECT

The rise of the internet has led to a host of questions regarding its impact on society. Although it is agreed that the internet affects the way people live and interact, it is an ongoing process to understand the nature(s) of this influence. The Pew Internet and American Life Project (http://www.pewinternet.org) produces reports that examine the impact of the internet on a variety of aspects of American life. The project covers the following eleven areas: demographics; E-Gov and E-Policy; education; family, friends and community; health; internet evolution; major news events; online activities and pursuits; public policy; technology and media use; and work. According to its mission statement, "The Project aims to be an authoritative source on the evolution of the internet through collection of data and analysis of real-world developments as they affect the virtual world."

Utilizing nationwide random telephone surveys and online surveys, the project collects both quantitative and qualitative data to aid research initiatives throughout the country and the world. Both individual and group use is tracked through the surveys, painting detailed portraits of the internet in its many forms and functions. The Pew Internet and American Life Project is a project

of the Pew Research Center, a nonpartisan "fact tank" that provides information on the issues, attitudes, and trends shaping America and the world. (http://www. pewresearch.org). Funding is provided by the Pew Charitable Trust, an independent nonprofit organization dedicated to improving public policy, informing the public, and stimulating civic life.

Source: http://www.pewtrusts.org.

Informative Boxed Features
Boxed features enhance students' exploration and enjoyment of every chapter by examining current, and sometimes controversial, trends and issues in the media world today.

Critics have pointed out that a disadvantage of the embeds was the tendency for them to be highly sympathetic to the troops with whom they lived and on whom they depended for survival. These critics argue that self-censorship was sometimes the result. To meet these criticisms, the military allowed other journalists to work as **unilaterals**—to travel through the war zone by themselves.

CLEAR AND PRESENT DANGER The U.S. Supreme Court has long held that speech can be limited before it is distributed if the result of that speech is likely to pose a threat to society. But what determines whether that speech (or media content) poses a threat? The answer has varied over the decades, with more recent Supreme Court decisions making it difficult to restrain speech based on the clear and present danger test.

The earliest justification for imposing prior restraint because of social threats involved the **bad tendency test**. Under this rule, the government could restrain media material if it had any tendency to cause social evil. This rule has the potential to cover a lot of territory; for example, a speech by a labor organizer that holds even a small chance of creating a disturbance could be open to prior restraint. The bad tendency test was eventually ruled unconstitutionally vague and hasn't been used since the early 1900s.

Taking its place is the **clear and present danger test** set forth by Supreme Court Justice Oliver Wendell Holmes. The difference between the clear and present danger test and the bad tendency test is that Holmes' approach suggests the importance of the social evil being *likely* to happen (not just that it might happen) and that it would happen imminently (that is, soon after the material is released).

The case that Holmes used to put forth his idea centered on two socialists who distributed anti-draft pamphlets during World War I, and who were convicted of violating the Espionage Act of 1917. When the Supreme Court heard their appeal in the 1919 case *Schenck* vs. *United States*, Holmes wrote for the majority of justices that the socialists could be convicted. Ordinarily, Holmes wrote, the pamphlets would be protected by the First Amendment. But in this case, distributing the pamphlets during wartime was similar to the kind of danger created by "crying fire in a crowded theater." His point was that the government has a right to restrict the speech of anyone (or any organization) whose words might clearly cause social harm in particular circumstances.

unilaterals reporters who receive permission from the military to travel across the battlefield without military escort

bad tendency test materials that may be restricted because they are distributed in a time of war, domestic unrest, or riot, even though they do not meet the level of clear and present danger

clear and present danger test as stated by Justice Oliver Wendell Holmes, "expression can be limited by the government when the words are used in such circumstances and are of such a nature as to create a clear and present danger that they will bring about the substantive evils that Congress has a right to prevent"

Marginal Glossary
Provides key terms where students need them—next to their discussion in the text.

Engaging Images

Illustrative tables and figures give students a visual key to unlock difficult concepts and theories, while dynamic photos and illustrations enrich students' understanding of the ideas discussed in each chapter.

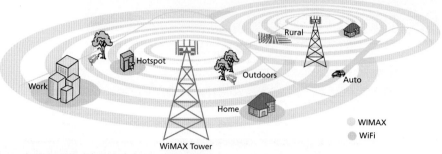

WiMAX will blanket large areas to deliver broadband internet access that moves with you beyond WiFi hotspots.

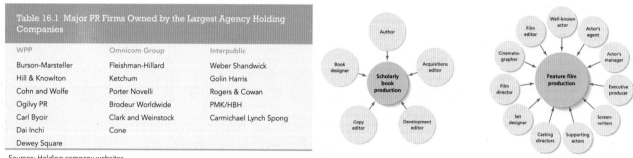

Table 16.1 Major PR Firms Owned by the Largest Agency Holding Companies		
WPP	**Omnicom Group**	**Interpublic**
Burson-Marsteller	Fleishman-Hillard	Weber Shandwick
Hill & Knowlton	Ketchum	Golin Harris
Cohn and Wolfe	Porter Novelli	Rogers & Cowan
Ogilvy PR	Brodeur Worldwide	PMK/HBH
Carl Byoir	Clark and Weinstock	Carmichael Lynch Spong
Dai Inchi	Cone	
Dewey Square		

Sources: Holding company websites.

Meaningful End-of-Chapter Materials

These valuable end-of-chapter resources and exercises go beyond standard chapter reviews to challenge students to think critically and to build their media literacy skills.

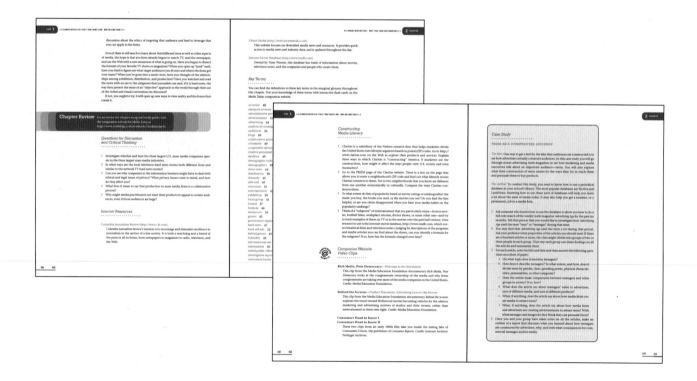

Companion Website

http://www.routledge.com/textbooks/mediatoday4e

The website features fully updated and enhanced material to help students expand
their knowledge, study for exams, and more! Features include:

- NEW! Online video resources for each chapter
- UPDATED! Dynamic self-quizzes for each chapter
- UPDATED! Interactive vocabulary flash-cards
- UPDATED! Chapter summaries and study guides
- UPDATED! Downloadable chapter summary podcasts
- UPDATED! Author's blog *Media Today and Tomorrow* connects the text to the latest issues in the media
- UPDATED! All new instructors' materials – including a revised *Instructor's Manual*, brand new test bank materials, and much more!

Media Today video resources

Now available free online to all students through the companion website, and on DVD to qualifying instructors, the *Media Today* video resources, completely updated for the Fourth Edition, are keyed to each chapter of the book.

- Historical clips—including early sound recordings, silent films, and television—provide rich context
- Excerpts from documentaries about the media produced by the Media Education Foundation show students media literacy in action

To the Student

I hope that you'll find *Media Today* fun to read, helpful for understanding the media-saturated world around you, and (if you're so inclined) useful for thinking about a future career in mass media. More likely than not, you've grown up with all or at least most of the media we cover in this book. Your family has probably had newspapers, books, magazines, CDs, radios, and a television set in your home from the time you were born. It's likely, too, that you have also had a computer and the internet in your home from the time you were small. In one sense, then, you're already an "expert" at mass media: you've seen a lot of it, you know what you like, and you know what you don't like. At the same time, there's probably a lot about the content mass media present, the industries behind them, and their roles in society that you haven't considered yet.

The purpose of *Media Today* is to introduce you to these ideas, with the expectation that they will help you think about the media you think you already know in entirely new ways. To get the most out of this text, use all the bells and whistles that come with it. The chapter objectives, the marginal glossary, the art and photo selections, and the boxed features have all been created with an eye toward making the text itself as clear and relevant as possible. The companion website accessible at **http://www.routledge.com/textbooks/mediatoday4e** will also be of enormous value for helping you learn more about book topics, studying for exams, learning about careers in mass media, quizzing yourself, and more. Get to know all these learning aids, and let us know what you think of them.

Media Today

Part 1

Understanding the
Nature of Mass Media

Mass media circulate words, sounds, and images that surround us. Too often, we immerse ourselves in media materials without asking where they come from, what meanings they might have, and what their consequences might be.

This section introduces media literacy and applies it to some basic but crucial questions. What is mass communication and how does it work? What roles do governments, businesses, academic researchers, members of the public, advocacy organizations, and culture play in what we read, see, and hear? This section—and the sections that follow— aim to help you become a critical consumer by encouraging you to ask questions—and get answers—about the media you use.

THE CHAPTERS

1. Understanding Mass Media and the Importance of Media Literacy

2. Making Sense of the Media Business

3. Controls on Media Content: Government Regulation, Self-Regulation, and Ethics

4. Making Sense of Research on Media Effects and Media Culture

1 Understanding Mass Media and the Importance of Media Literacy

After studying this chapter, you will be able to:

1 Discuss the differences between interpersonal communication and mass communication

2 Explain why an unorthodox definition of mass communication makes the term especially relevant in today's media environment

3 Explain the meaning and importance of culture's relationship with the mass media

4 Analyze the ways in which the mass media affect our everyday lives

5 Explain what the term "media literacy" means

6 List the key principles involved in becoming media literate

7 Discuss the importance of developing media literacy skills for the classroom and beyond

8 Explain current and future trends in mass communication

"Whoever controls the media controls the culture."
— ALLEN GINSBERG, POET

"Information is the oxygen of the modern age."
— RONALD REAGAN, U.S. PRESIDENT

MEDIA TODAY

"Your TV is ringing."

The first time you saw apps on an iPhone or another "smartphone" you might have said, "cool," or "I want that" about virtually everything. The nearly 134,000 free and paid programs include ways to play games, read the news, find out where your friends are, tweet to them, find a cheap airline ticket, learn when your plane is leaving, search for restaurants, watch sports, view a television show, and a whole lot more.[1]

It's certainly an exciting time to study mass communication. None of the activities described above could have been attempted on a telephone just a few years ago, but now they have become standard for many mobile phones. The developments raise questions about the impact that these and other technologies will have on us, our society, and the content of TV, movies, video games, music, newspapers, magazines, websites, and advertisements.

Consider the mass media menu that Americans have today. Instead of three or four TV channels, most Americans receive more than fifty and a substantial number receive 150 and more. Radio in urban areas delivers dozens of stations; satellite radio brings in hundreds more, and music streaming on the web—sometimes called internet radio—is carried out by countless broadcast and nonbroadcast entities. Desktop computers, laptops, netbooks, e-readers, video game consoles, CD players, and DVDs have brought far more channels into our lives than ever before. So has the internet—allowing us to interact with information, news, and entertainment from all over the nation and the world.

Research indicates that Americans spend an enormous amount of time with mass media.[2] Think about your own media habits. How close do you come to the average thirty-two hours a week (about 4.5 hours a day) of television that Americans view on the traditional TV set as well as online? What about radio? Studies suggest that Americans listen to around fifteen hours a week of radio in the regular broadcast mode, via satellite channels, or from their online feeds. Do you do that, or do you instead listen to recorded music on your iPod or on your MP3 or CD player? Studies show that Americans spend an average of about 3.5 hours a week with recorded music (although college students undoubtedly do more of it). And what about the time you spend reading books, newspapers, and magazines? Data show that on average Americans spend about eight hours a week with one or another of these, both their printed versions and their websites.

Just a few years ago, media such as television, radio, books, and newspapers seemed pretty separate. It was clear what content from each medium looked or sounded like, and it would have been foolish to suggest that newspaper articles and television programs would show up on the same channel. But because of the rise of computer technologies that we will explore in the coming pages, this "foolishness" is exactly what has happened. The access the internet gives us to content from different types of media is part of a process called convergence. Convergence takes place when content that has traditionally been confined to one medium appears on multiple media channels.

The media of mass communication are an integral part of our lives, occurring in a wide variety of settings. In this chapter, we will explore and define communication, media, and culture, and we will consider how the relationships among them affect us and the world in which we live. We will also consider why the term "mass communication" remains relevant in the twenty-first century, contrary to what some writers say. In fact, the changes taking place in the media system actually make a rethought and redefined version of the term more important than ever.

convergence when content that has traditionally been confined to one medium appears on multiple media channels

Introducing Mass Communication

To understand why some writers suggest that the term "mass communication" doesn't connect to what's going on in today's world, we have to look at how the term has traditionally been used. Over the past hundred years, people who wrote about mass communication tended to relate it to the size of the audience. That made a lot of sense back then. From the mid-nineteenth century onward, new technologies such as high-speed newspaper presses, radio, movies, and television provided access to the huge "masses" of people. Not only were those audiences very large, they were dispersed geographically, quite diverse (that is, made up of different types of people), and typically anonymous to the companies that created the material. The essential reason newspapers, radio, television, and other such media were considered different from other means of communication had to do with the size and composition of the audience.

This perspective on mass communication worked well until recently when the key aspects of the traditional definition of mass communication as reaching huge, diverse groups no longer fit. The reason is that the arrival of media channels—including the growing number of radio and TV stations, the rise of the VCR, the multiplication of cable networks, and the rise of the Web—led to **audience fragmentation** (see Figure 1.1). That is, as people watched or read these new channels, there were fewer people using any one of them. Because these new media channels do not necessarily individually reach large numbers of people—the "masses"—some writers suggested that we can abandon the term "mass communication."

audience fragmentation the process of dividing audience members into segments based on background and lifestyle in order to send them messages targeted to their specific characteristics

mass production process the industrial process that creates the potential for reaching millions, even billions, of diverse, anonymous people at around the same time

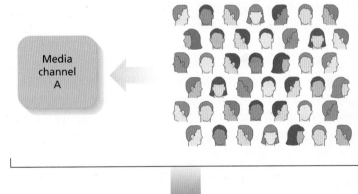

Figure 1.1 Audience Fragmentation
The arrival of the diverse array of media channels has had a fragmenting effect on audiences—as audience members move to watch, read, or listen to a new channel, fewer people use any single channel.

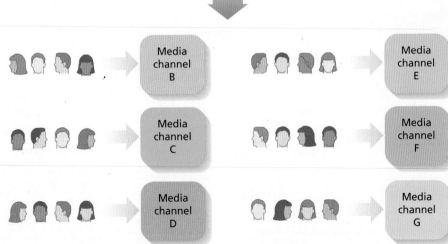

The traditional notion of the audience as a large mass of anonymous individuals has given way beneath the fragmenting of audiences to reveal smaller, specially targeted media audiences made up of individuals who are segmented by any number of characteristics

However, the view in this book is that mass communication is still a critically important part of society. As we will see, what really separates mass communication from other forms of communication is not the size of the audience—it can be large or small. Rather, what makes mass communication special is the way the content of the communication message is created.

Mass communication is carried out by organizations working together in industries to produce and circulate a wide range of content—from entertainment to news to educational materials. It is this industrial, **mass production process** that creates the potential for reaching millions, even billions, of diverse, anonymous people at around the same time. And it is the **industrial nature** of the process—for example the various companies that work together within the television or internet industries—that makes mass communication different from other forms of communication even when the audience is relatively small and even one-to-one. To help you understand how mass communication relates to other forms of communication, let's take a closer look.

industrial nature what distinguishes mass communication from other forms of communication is the industrialized—or mass production—process that is involved in creating the message material. This industrial process creates the potential for reaching billions of diverse, anonymous people simultaneously

The Elements of Mass Communication

Communication is a basic feature of human life. In general, the word **communication** refers to people interacting in ways that at least one of the parties involved understands as **messages**—collections of symbols that appear purposefully organized (meaningful) to those sending or receiving them.

When you signal your needs or thoughts to others, the signals you send are both verbal and nonverbal. When Jane shouts excitedly to her friend Jack and leaps with joy into his arms after she wins a tennis match, that's a form of communication. It's likely that Jack, whose arms she almost broke, realizes that she wants to tell him something. People who study communication would typically call the interaction just described **interpersonal communication**, a form that involves two or three individuals signaling to each other using their voices, facial and hand gestures, and other signs (even clothes) that they use to convey meaning. When you talk to your parents about your coursework, discuss a recent movie over dinner with friends, or converse with your professor during her office hours you are participating in the interpersonal form of communication.

communication refers to people interacting in ways that at least one of the parties involved understands as messages

messages collections of symbols that appear purposefully organized (meaningful) to those sending or receiving them

interpersonal communication a form of communication that involves two or three individuals signaling to each other using their voices, facial and hand gestures, and other signs (even clothes) that they use to convey meaning

mediated interpersonal communication a specialized type of interpersonal communication that is assisted by a device, such as a pen or pencil, a computer, or a telephone

medium part of a technical system that helps in the transmission, distribution, or reception of messages

Mediated interpersonal communication can be described as interpersonal communication that is assisted by a **medium**—part of a technical system that helps in the transmission, distribution, or reception of messages. It helps communication take place when senders and receivers are not face-to-face. The internet is an example of a medium, as are the radio, CD, television, and DVD. (Note that the term "medium" is singular; it refers to one technological vehicle for communication. The plural is media.) When you write a thank you note to your grandmother, send an email to your graduate teaching assistant, or call a friend on the phone, you are participating in the mediated form of interpersonal communication.

Although interpersonal, mediated interpersonal, and mass communication have their differences, they have a central similarity: they involve messages (see Table 1.1). Eight major elements are involved in every interaction that involves messages. These elements are the source, encoder, transmitter, channel, receiver, decoder, feedback, and noise.

source the originator of the message, which may be a person, several people, or an organization

SOURCE   The **source** is the originator of the message. In mass communication, the source is an organization—such as a company—not a single person. For example, think of Jon Stewart delivering his version of the news on Comedy Central's *The Daily Show*. If Jon were in the same room as you telling you about what he just read in the paper, he—as an individual—would be a source. But when you watch him do his monologue on *The Daily Show*, Jon is no longer the source. That's because behind him is an organization that is creating the news satire for him to present. Sure, Jon is reading the messages, and so it may seem that he should be called "the source." But the writing team of *The Daily Show* helped him write the script, produced and edited the videos he introduces, and prepared his set for the broadcast. Moreover, the photos and clips he satirizes sometimes come from news firms, such as ABC News. So Jon is really just the most visible representative of an organizational source.

CULTURE TODAY
WHERE DOES THE TERM "MEDIA" COME FROM?

Until the "Roaring" 1920s, to most Americans a medium was a fortune teller or palm reader, not a publication, and as for media—well, there was no such thing. The term "media" was just an obscure Latin plural of the word "medium."

Then came modern advertising and a sense of media that had nothing to do with psychics. Advertisers began to speak of placing ads in different media.

The original means of mass communication were print—magazines, journals, and newspapers—and their collective name was already in place: publications. Then radio and television were added to the mix, and the term "publications" would not stretch to fit. Needing a term that would encompass all these means of communication, writers borrowed "media" from the advertising people and have used it ever since to accommodate these and even newer means of communication, such as the internet.

"Welcome to 'All About the Media,' where members of the media discuss the role of the media in media coverage of the media."

Table 1.1 Differences in Types of Communication

	Interpersonal Communication	Mediated Interpersonal Communication	Mass Communication
Message	Uses all the senses	Typically verbal and/or visual	Typically verbal and/or visual
Source	An individual	An individual	One or more organizations
Encoding	By an individual's brain	By an individual's brain and technology	By an organization and technology
Channel	The air	The air, technology	The air, technology
Transmitter	A person's vocal cords	Technology and vocal cords	Technology and vocal cords
Receiver	A few individuals in the same location	A few or many individuals in the same location	Typically, many people in different locations
Decoding	By an individual's brain	By technology and an individual's brain	By technology and an individual's brain
Feedback	Immediate and direct	Immediate or delayed; generally direct	Immediate or delayed; generally indirect
Noise	Environmental, mechanical, and semantic	Environmental, mechanical, and semantic, with environmental sometimes caused by organizations	Environmental, mechanical, and semantic, sometimes caused by organizations

ENCODING   **Encoding** takes place when a source translates a message in anticipation of its transmission to a receiver. When the source is a person, encoding goes on inside the brain. When the source is an organization, encoding takes place during the creation of the message. For example, *The Daily Show*'s creators prepare the program with the knowledge that it will be recorded on a stage for presentation to a cable audience during a preset time for a particular number of minutes on a particular day. These basic realities are among the many factors that shape the way they prepare their program for its transmission.

encoding the process by which the source translates the thoughts and ideas so that they can be perceived by the human senses—primarily sight and sound, but may also include smell, taste, and touch

TRANSMITTING   The **transmitter** performs the physical activity of actually sending out the message. Imagine an employee meeting with his supervisor to apologize for missing a day of work. The employee's entire body will transmit the words, tone, and gestures that the supervisor will see, hear, and understand as meaningful. Now, picture this same employee apologizing to his supervisor by email. In this case, a second type of transmitter operates along with his body—the computer, which turns the clicks from his keyboard into digital signals that travel across the internet into the supervisor's digital mailbox.

transmitter performs the physical activity of distributing the message

In mass communication, however, transmission is too complex to be accomplished by an individual or even a few people. That is because transmission involves distributing the material to several locations and presenting the material (that is, exhibiting it) at those locations. Instead of a few individuals, a number of organizations (usually large ones) are typically involved in the process.

Think of our *Daily Show* example again. When Jon reads the script on *The Daily Show*, his vocal cords transmit the words into a microphone; however, transmission of Jon on Comedy Central involves a number of further steps. First the show is sent to a satellite company that the network uses to send its programs to cable TV systems around the country. The cable systems, which themselves are complex organizations, receive those messages and send them to "head-end" transmission centers that they own. These centers send out the program through coaxial cables that eventually connect to television sets in locations (homes, bars, hotels) where subscribers have paid to receive the signal. In this way, millions of people around the country can watch *The Daily Show* at the same time.

The creation and transmission of mass media messages—of news articles, television programs, and recorded music, for example—are the result of decisions and activities by many people working together in companies that interact with other companies.

channels the pathways through which the transmitter sends all features of the message, whether they involve sight, sound, smell, or touch

CHANNEL   All communication, whether mediated or not, takes place through **channels**. Channels are the pathways through which the transmitter sends all features of the message, whether they involve sight, sound, smell, or touch. When a man on the street walks up to you and shouts at you in a way that you can hardly understand, the channel is the air through which the sound waves move from the man's vocal cords. If your roommate sends you a text message asking to meet up for lunch, the channel is the electromagnetic frequency band through which the message travels.

receiver the person or organization that gets the message

RECEIVER   As suggested above, the **receiver** is the person or organization that gets the message. Sometimes the source's message will reach its intended receiver; sometimes it reaches another receiver altogether. But even if someone other than the intended receiver receives the message, communication has still taken place. Say, for example, that you assume that by putting a message on your friend Brad's Facebook "wall," only Brad will see it. Turns out, though, that Brad's privacy settings are such that everyone in the world can see what you wrote: oops. Even if it turns out that Brad didn't go to his Facebook page and read (receive) the message you sent him, but instead his girlfriend, Keiko, did, the episode can still be considered mediated interpersonal communication: your message was encoded, transmitted via your keystrokes to the computer and internet service provider, sent through the channel of the internet, decoded by the receiver (although not the one you intended), and received.

decoding the process by which the receiver translates the source's thoughts and ideas so that they have meaning

DECODING   Before a receiver can make sense of a source's message, the transmitted impulses must be decoded—converted to signs that the brain can perceive as meaningful. It is the opposite of the encoding process—**decoding** is the process

The broadcasting of *The Daily Show* is a complex process that involves writers, producers, editors, and cameramen, not to mention the cable channel Comedy Central.

by which the receiver translates the source's thoughts and ideas so that they have meaning.

In interpersonal communication, the decoder is the human brain. When two people communicate via mediated interpersonal communication, however, for example over the telephone, the electrical impulses that travel through the phone lines must be decoded into sound waves before they can be decoded by the brain. In fact, all media require this sort of decoding. For example, televisions decode the electrical impulses from the air or cable and convert them into the programs you watch.

FEEDBACK **Feedback** occurs when the receiver responds to the message with what the sender perceives as a message. When Keiko, your friend's girlfriend, tells you, "I never knew you felt that way about me, you jerk," that is feedback. In fact, this sort of feedback continues the interpersonal communication process. As Figure 1.2 shows, two people continue their communication by continually receiving and responding to each other's messages. The communication "episode" between the two ends when one of them sends no more feedback to the other (the person walks away, the parties hang up the phone).

In mass communication, feedback from all the receivers is often impossible because of the number of people involved. (Think of the millions of people watching a TV program.) Even when feedback does happen, the people in the organization who created the message in the first place will typically not get it. Someone else who is specifically appointed to deal with feedback will generally receive your message.

Consider the following comparison. You meet Jon Stewart in a movie line and have a leisurely conversation with him about current events in New York City where he lives. Jon nods in response to your comments and answers your questions. By contrast, a week later you see a satirical piece about New York City on *The Daily Show* that angers you. Moved to complain, you phone Comedy Central in New York to speak to Stewart or a producer. Instead, you get an operator who will politely take down your

feedback when the receiver responds to the message with what the sender perceives as a message

Figure 1.2 A Model of Interpersonal Communication
In this model of interpersonal communication, information moves from a starting point at the source through the transmitter, via the channel, to the receiver for decoding.

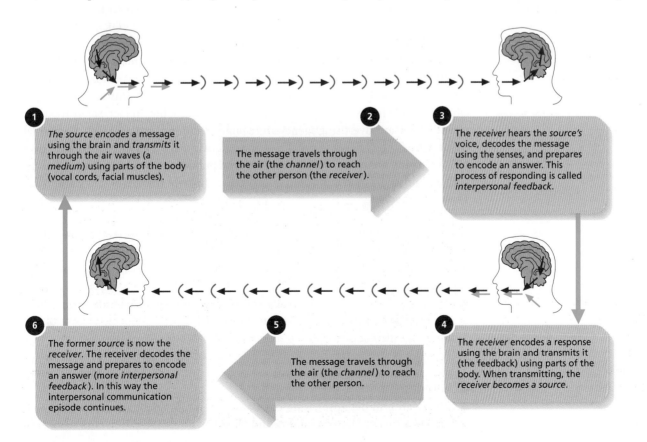

1 *The source encodes* a message using the brain and *transmits* it through the air waves (a *medium*) using parts of the body (vocal cords, facial muscles).

2 The message travels through the air (the *channel*) to reach the other person (the *receiver*).

3 The *receiver* hears the *source's* voice, decodes the message using the senses, and prepares to encode an answer. This process of responding is called *interpersonal feedback*.

6 The former *source* is now the *receiver*. The receiver decodes the message and prepares to encode an answer (more *interpersonal feedback*). In this way the interpersonal communication episode continues.

5 The message travels through the air (the *channel*) to reach the other person.

4 The *receiver* encodes a response using the brain and transmits it (the feedback) using parts of the body. When transmitting, the *receiver becomes a source*.

comments, send you to a voicemail service that will record them, or suggest that you provide feedback through the program's website. If you write to Jon Stewart or one of the show's producers, chances are that staff members whose job it is to summarize complaints for production executives will intercept it. That is typical of mass media organizations. *The Daily Show* gets thousands of letters and emails, and its principals are too busy to attend to all audience letters and phone calls themselves.

NOISE   **Noise** is an environmental, mechanical, and semantic sound in the communication situation that interferes with the delivery of the message. Environmental noise comes from the setting where the source and receiver are communicating. Mechanical noise comes from the medium through which the communication is taking place. Say there is static on the phone—that would be mechanical noise that would add to the environmental noise.

A hypothetical comparison of interpersonal and mass communication will help to explain the differences in sender, transmitter, feedback, and noise. Meet Antwaan Andrews, a self-employed independent insurance agent. Using a list of potential clients that he has compiled from friends, acquaintances, and other clients, Antwaan sends postal or email letters to ten people a night for two months to tell them about his service. He develops his sales pitch himself and tailors it to each person. Each note contains his name, postal address, phone number, and email address, along with the assurance that he will reply quickly to their messages.

Note that Antwaan's audience—the receivers of his letters and email messages—is limited in number by the people he can learn about from others and contact personally. Note, too, that any feedback goes straight to Antwaan. Potential customers either speak to him directly or they leave a message on his voicemail or email. (Of course, if a potential client doesn't return his message at all, Antwaan may take that as feedback that the person is not interested in buying life insurance.) One example of unwanted noise might be a problem Antwaan sometimes has with retrieving his voicemail. (It's a pain in the neck, he says, but it generally works OK and he doesn't want to spend money upgrading his service.)

Contrast Antwaan's mediated interpersonal work with the mass communication activities of SafetyTrust Mutual, one of the insurance companies Antwaan represents. SafetyTrust is mounting its own campaign to help agents like Antwaan attract specific groups of clients that they have identified as profitable. In fact, SafetyTrust has recently hired an advertising agency and a public relations agency to attract potential clients who fit the following profile: young parents with a combined income of over $75,000 a year. Members of the advertising and public relations teams have come up with a multimedia marketing plan built around the twin themes of safety and trust. Their plan involves:

■ Creating commercials and airing them on two or three TV series that rate highly with young married couples

■ Creating print ads and buying space for those ads in upscale newspapers and magazines

■ Attempting to place SafetyTrust's young and photogenic president on NBC's *Today Show* and ABC's *Good Morning America* to speak about new government insurance regulations

■ Paying a custom-magazine firm to create and mail a glossy new magazine for young, upscale SafetyTrust clients

■ Advertising during a VH1 cable series

■ Paying an internet advertising company to send an email ad to 30,000 people on a list the company bought of individuals who fit the profile and who have

noise an environmental, mechanical, and semantic sound in the communication situation that interferes with the delivery of the message. Environmental noise comes from the setting where the source and receiver are communicating. Mechanical noise comes from the medium through which the communication is taking place. Semantic noise involves language that one or more of the participants doesn't understand.

CRITICAL CONSUMER
JON STEWART AND AGENDA SETTING

In recent years there has been a good deal of popular and academic interest concerning the role that "fake news" or "infotainment" shows are playing in the journalistic landscape. Such shows take a satirical or humorous approach to political affairs and world news. *The Daily Show* with Jon Stewart and *The Colbert Report* are the two most prominent examples of infotainment shows in the United States.

There is some evidence to suggest that Americans, and particularly young Americans, are increasingly turning to infotainment shows as their primary news source. A 2009 *Rasmussen Report* states that "Nearly one-third of Americans under the age of 40 say satirical news-oriented television programs like *The Colbert Report* and *The Daily Show* with Jon Stewart are taking the place of traditional news outlets." There is also evidence to suggest that tuning into such shows does not negatively affect political knowledge. A Pew Research Center report suggests that regular viewers of *The Daily Show* and *The Colbert Report* have among the highest levels of public knowledge. For a substantial number of people, then, these programs help set the agenda about what public issues are important.

Jon Stewart, host of *The Daily Show*, maintains that his is a fake news show and, therefore, does not need to live up to the journalistic standards of objectivity and tough questioning of people in power to which mainstream news outlets are often held. Everything on *The Daily Show*, from the format to the host himself, is designed to poke fun at the perceived inadequacies of the media industry. In an appearance on CNN's *Crossfire*, Stewart chastised the hosts for their part in creating a media theater instead of engaging in civilized discourse. Interestingly, Stewart sidesteps his own role in creating this arena for civilized discourse noting that his show is run on Comedy Central. When the *Crossfire* hosts asked why he doesn't ask tougher questions when important political figures appear on his show, Stewart countered: "If your idea of confronting me is that I don't ask hard-hitting enough news questions, we're in bad shape, fellows."

Jon Stewart has never claimed to be a professional journalist. However, he does host a television show that reports on political and current affairs, no matter how satirically. Moreover, many Americans turn to his show as their primary source for news—and so, for an agenda about what to attend to in the world beyond their immediate knowledge. In light of these facts, some suggest he should be held to journalistic standards regarding the agenda he sets for his audience. What do you think?

Sources: *Rasmussen Reports*, "Nearly One-Third of Younger Americans See Colbert, Stewart As Alternatives to Traditional News Outlets," March 25, 2009. http://www.rasmussenreports.com/public_content/lifestyle/entertainment/march_2009/nearly_one_third_of_younger_americans_see_colbert_stewart_as_alternatives_to_traditional_news_outlets (accessed August 1, 2010); *Pew Research Center for People and the Press*, "Public Knowledge of Current Affairs Little Changed by News and Information Revolutions: What Americans Know: 1989–2007," April 15, 2007. http://people-press.org/report/319/public-knowledge-of-current-affairs-little-changed-by-news-and-information-revolutions (accessed August 1, 2010).

indicated that they would be interested in learning about how to save money on insurance

■ Reworking a website where customers can learn about their plans and send responses to the company

Note that although these messages reach millions of people, getting feedback from them is difficult. Typical feedback would include phone responses to an 800 number in the TV commercials and print ads, but this would probably include only a tiny percentage of the people who saw the messages. SafetyTrust might also pay a company to conduct research to estimate the number of people who viewed the materials and what they thought about them.

These methods would often yield delayed feedback from potential customers. SafetyTrust executives are particularly proud of the plan for the website, because it customizes the message and encourages immediate feedback. The site changes its sales pitch and look based on information that the person types in at the site. For example, whenever a potential customer goes to the company's homepage at http://www.safetytrust.com, that person is asked a number of questions about their age, salary, marital status, and educational background, among other things. Based upon the potential customer's responses (and a computer program's evaluation of those responses) he or she will be able to view a custom-tailored site—helping SafetyTrust to best explain its products and sell its services. At the same time, the feedback helps tailor the message so as to minimize semantic noise that might drive some potential customers away.

Additionally, users of the website may choose to email SafetyTrust at any time with questions, concerns, or requests for more information. This feedback doesn't reach a real agent at SafetyTrust. Instead, it is collected and analyzed daily by "consumer response specialists," who may eventually contact people who are good prospects. Their conversations may not be the careful discussions that individual agents like Antwaan carry out when they call back each person who has left messages on their voicemail. Still, SafetyTrust finds that its approach is quite efficient, as it can quickly weed out people who the company considers to be high insurance risks. But just in case a person who comes to the site wants to speak to an agent near his or her home, SafetyTrust has links to those of its agents who have websites. Antwaan is one of these agents with his own content, and he finds that many of the best prospects who come to his home page are referred through the SafetyTrust site.

With his much smaller operation, Antwaan couldn't possibly do what SafetyTrust is doing with its website and feedback from prospective customers. In fact, even if he had thought of all of SafetyTrust's marketing activities, Antwaan could never implement them without adding enormously (and unrealistically) to his staff and overhead costs. After all, SafetyTrust—a large insurance company with millions of dollars in its marketing budget—hired an advertising agency and a public relations agency to help it create its messages to potential customers. It also used large organizations (NBC, ABC, VH1, and an internet access firm) to help distribute its messages.

The difference between mediated interpersonal and mass communication, then, can be seen as a difference between personal, hand-crafted production on the one hand, and mass production on the other (see Table 1.2 for an illustration of these differences as they relate to Antwaan and SafetyTrust). Put another way, SafetyTrust's work is part of an industry process. An **industry** is a grouping of companies that use technology to work together in a regularized way to produce and distribute goods and services. It is this industrial approach that makes it possible for SafetyTrust to get its messages out to its intended audiences.

industry a grouping of companies that use technology to work together in a regularized way to produce and distribute goods and services

Mass Communication Defined

And so we come at last to the definition of mass communication that we have been building: mass communication is the industrialized production and multiple distribution of messages through technological devices. The industrial nature of the process is central to this definition of mass communication, as shown in Figure 1.3.

mass media the technological vehicles through which mass communication takes place (note that the term "mass media" is plural; it refers to more than one vehicle; the singular version is mass medium)

As the definition suggests, mass communication is carried out by mass media industries. Think, for example, of the movie industry, in which many different companies—from production studios, to film providers, to catering firms—work to make and circulate movies. **Mass media** are the technological instruments—for example, newsprint, the internet, televisions, radio (both traditional and satellite)—through which mass communication takes place. **Mass media outlets** are companies that send out messages via mass media—for example, *Time* magazine, foxnews.com, and the NBC television network.

mass media outlets companies that send out messages via mass media

Mass communication's power allows media consumers to share the materials they are reading and listening to with millions of people. This sharing is made possible, of course, because of the industrial nature of the activity and its technology of production and distribution. When complex organizations comprising many workers join together to use the latest technology to produce media, those organizations have the potential to distribute the same message to huge numbers of people.

Consider the typical television broadcast of the Grammy Awards, the ceremony in which the recording industry honors its most successful talent. It is transmitted via satellite from Los Angeles to broadcast television production facilities in New York, then distributed "live" to every corner of the United States, as well as to many parts of the world.

Or consider a typical presidential news conference. It is covered by dozens of newspaper reporters and television and radio news crews. Snippets of the event will commonly end up confronting Americans around the country in many different forms during that day and the next on the national TV news, on internet news and blog sites, on the local news, in the morning papers, and throughout the day on hourly radio news reports.

As a third, and slightly different, example, consider a mega-hit film such as one of the *Twilight* movies. Millions of people around the world saw it in theaters within a few months of its release. In addition, word of the movie's popularity sped around the globe as Summit Entertainment, its U.S. distributor and its distributor in many regions outside the United States, revved up a publicity and advertising machine. It peppered as many media outlets as possible with word of the high-octane action and head-lopping digital effects.

Twilight, the presidential news conference, and the Grammy Awards represent only three examples of activities that happen all the time in industrialized countries such as the United States. Linking large numbers of people to share the same materials virtually instantly has become standard practice for the broadcast television,

Table 1.2 Comparing Antwaan's Approach to SafetyTrust's Approach

	Antwaan's Approach (Mediated Interpersonal)	SafetyTrust's Approach (Mass Communication)
Message	A postal mail and email sales pitch tailored to what he knows about the potential customer	TV commercials, newspaper and magazine ads; public relations activities on *Today* and *Good Morning America*; a custom magazine for upscale clients; sponsorship of a VH1 cable program to reach young adults; a website
Source	Antwaan himself	SafetyTrust's advertising agency and public relations agency
Encoding	Antwaan's creation of his phone messages	The activities by the advertising and public relations agencies that create the messages
Channel	The postal mail, the Internet, and (sometimes) telephone answering machine	Broadcast and cable television networks, newspapers, magazines, the Web
Transmitter	Postal trucks and machines, electrical and phone lines	Postal trucks and machines, electrical and phone lines
Receiver	The dozens of individuals that Antwaan contacts over the phone	The millions of people who see or read SafetyTrust's ads, custom magazine, public relations activities, or website
Decoding	The individuals who read email or postal messages	Members of the target audience who see SafetyTrust ads or visit the website
Feedback	The returned phone calls and emails of individual potential customers—or their failure to contact Antwaan	Letters from listeners, messages sent from the SafetyTrust website, research indicating the number of people who read/watched the ads
Noise	Hums on Antwaan's answering machine	Messages that use language certain types of potential customers wouldn't understand

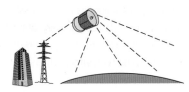

1 The *source*, a media organization, creates a *message* in words and/or images. Often working with other organizations in its industry, it encodes the image for *transmission* (that is, *distribution*) through a *medium*. Let's say that in this case the organization is a TV network news division, the message is a news report, and the media are both television and a website.

2 The electronic impulses travel from ground transmitters owned by the network to satellites (*media channels*) leased by it and from there to TV stations (*mass media outlets*) around the country and the world. The stations, in turn, send the impulses to other transmitters that broadcast them through the air (another media channel) to millions of televisions. After the TV transmission, a version of the report is placed on the TV network's website through high speed cable lines.

3 The *receivers* are millions of people who receive the electronic impulses on their TV sets (more media). The TV sets decode the impulses back into video and commentary, which the viewers themselves decode as messages.

6 Network employees—not those directly involved with the original news report or website discussions —receive the messages and send summaries of them to the news and marketing staff and to website designers. The marketing staff uses this *indirect feedback* to convince advetisers of the involvement of viewers in site. Web designers use some of the comments to alter the site's look. Encouraged by responses to the Web activity and by telephone surveys that reveal general audience interest in the topic, executives in the news organization decide to air more stories on the topic and expand their website discussions about it. In this way, the feedback influences the network's mass communication activities.

5 The responding individuals are now sources in mediated communication with an organization. Their individual messages are transmitted across phone and cable lines to reach the TV network's website.

4 In many cases, there is no response from viewers—no *feedback*. in this example, though, assume that several thousand of these viewers later go to the TV network's website to find out more about the report and participate in a poll. They are involved in feedback to the station on a *delayed basis*.

Figure 1.3 A Model of Mass Communication

In this model of mass communication, the elements (source, message, transmission, etc.) are all marked by the industrial production and multiple distribution by mass media organizations.

internet, radio, cable TV, and satellite television industries. Just as significant is the sharing that takes place relatively more slowly when newspapers, magazines, books, movies, billboards, and other mass media release their messages. Because of mass media industries and their abilities to mass produce media content, millions of people within the United States and around the world can receive the same messages within a fairly short time. Think about it—here are huge numbers of people who are physically separated from one another, have no obvious relationship with one another, and most often are unknown to one another. Yet on a daily basis they are watching the same news stories, listening to the same music, and reading the same magazine articles.

Mass Media, Culture, and Society

How Do We Use the Mass Media in Our Daily Lives?

Mass media materials speak to the most personal parts of our lives, and connect us to the world beyond our private circumstances. As a result, mass media industries are a major force in society. To understand what this means, we have to dig deeper into how people use the media and what they get out of them.

Scholars have found that individuals adapt their use of mass media to their own particular needs.[3] Broadly speaking, people use the media in four ways: for enjoyment, companionship, surveillance, and interpretation. Let's examine these uses one at a time.

ENJOYMENT   The desire for enjoyment is a basic human urge. Watching a television program, studying the Bible, finishing a newspaper crossword puzzle, networking on Facebook, or even reading an advertisement can bring this kind of gratification to many people.

News stories, daytime soap operas, sports, and primetime sitcoms can ignite everyday talk with friends, relatives, work colleagues, and even strangers. During the mid-1990s, for example, many local television stations around the United States were advertising their morning talk programs with the phrase "We give you something to talk about." This process of using media content for everyday interpersonal discussions is called using media materials as **social currency** or coins of exchange. "Did you hear Jay Leno's monologue last night?" someone might ask around the water cooler at work. "No, I watched Letterman," might be one reply, triggering a chain of comments about late-night TV comedy that brings a number of people into the conversation.

social currency media content used as coins of exchange in everyday interpersonal discussions

Of course, another way people can bring mass media material into friendly conversation is by experiencing the content together. If you have attended Super Bowl parties, you have an idea of how a televised event can energize friends in ways that have little to do with what is taking place on the screen. In this way, the media provide us with the enjoyment we seek as a basic human need.

COMPANIONSHIP   Mass media bring a sense of camaraderie to people who are lonely and those who are alone. A chronically ill hospital patient or a home-bound senior citizen may find companionship by viewing a favorite sports team on TV, or listening to the music of days gone by on the radio. A *Grey's Anatomy* fan might feel part of a community by reading the blogs written by the show's writers.

Sometimes, media can even draw out people who feel troubled and in need of friends. The term **parasocial interaction** describes the psychological connections that some people establish with celebrities they learn about through the mass media—typically feeling a sense of bonding with those celebrities. Facebook pages and Twitter tweets created by an actor's publicity firm around their screen personality might lead fans to feel a special knowledge of and relationship with the person. You might know someone who gets so involved with media images of rock or rap

parasocial interaction the psychological connections that some media users establish with celebrities who they learn about through the mass media

stars that they sometimes act as if they know them well. In a few publicized cases, this feeling has gotten out of control, leading individuals to stalk, and even harm, the media figures who were the objects of their adulation. In 2009, for example, a man was arrested for trying to get in to a vehicle with *American Idol* host Ryan Seacrest, while possessing a knife. A month later he was arrested for attempting to approach the star in his workplace. A judge therefore forbade him from coming within 100 yards of Seacrest, his home, car, and places of employment.[4]

surveillance using the media to learn about what is happening in the world around us

SURVEILLANCE   **Surveillance** users of the media employ them to learn about what is happening in the world. We all do this every day, often without realizing it. Do you turn on the radio or TV each morning to find out the weather? Do you check the stock listings to find out how your investments are faring? Have you read classified ads in print or online to look for a job, concert tickets, or used furniture? Have you ever called or logged on to Fandango or Moviefone to find out where and when a film is playing? All these activities are illustrations of using the mass media for surveillance. Of course, our surveillance can be more global. Many people are interested in knowing what is going on in the world beyond their immediate neighborhood. Did the flooding upstate destroy any houses? Will Congress raise taxes? What's going on with the negotiations for peace in the Middle East?

interpretation using the media to find out why things are happening—who or what is the cause—and what to do about them

INTERPRETATION   Many of us turn to the media to learn not only what is going on, but also why and what, if any, actions to take. When people try to find reasons why things are happening, they are looking for **interpretation**. We may read newspaper editorials to understand the actions of national leaders and come to conclusions about our stand on an issue. We know that financial magazines such as *Money* and *Barron's* are written to appeal to people who want to understand how investment vehicles work and which ones to choose. And we are aware that libraries, bookstores, and some websites such as http://www.howstuffworks.com specialize in "how to" topics ranging from raising children, to installing a retaining wall, to dying with dignity. Some people who are genuinely confused about some topics find mass media the most useful sources of answers. Pre-teens, for example, may want to understand why women and men behave romantically toward each other but they may feel embarrassed to ask their parents. They may be quite open to different opinions—in the *Twilight* films, on *Oprah*, in Justin Timberlake's music, or in *CosmoGirl* magazine—about where sexual attraction comes from and what the appropriate behavior is.

But how do people actually use the explanations they get from the mass media? Researchers have found that the credibility people place in the positions that mass media take depends on the extent to which the individuals agree with the values they find in that content.[5] For example, a person who is rooted in a religiously conservative approach to the Bible would not be likely to agree with a nature book that is based on the theory of evolution; a political liberal would probably not be persuaded by the interpretations that politically conservative magazines offer about ways to end poverty. Keep in mind, however, that in these examples, these people would probably not search out such media content to begin with. Unless people have a good reason to confront materials that go against their values (if they will be engaging in a debate on the ideas, for example), most people stay away from media that do not reflect (and reinforce) their own beliefs, values, or interests. And if they do come across materials that go against their values, they tend to dismiss them as biased.

MULTIPLE USE OF MASS MEDIA CONTENT   The example of a pre-teen seeking interpretations of romance from four very different outlets—a movie series, a television talk show, a musical record, and a magazine—raises an important point

about the four uses that people make of the mass media: the uses are not linked to any particular medium or genre. If we take television as an example, we might be tempted to suggest that enjoyment comes from certain sitcoms or adventure series, that companionship comes from soap operas, that surveillance is achieved through network and local news programs, and that interpretation can be found in Sunday morning political talk shows such as *Meet the Press*, as well as from daily talk fests such as *Oprah* and *The View*. In fact, we may divide many kinds of content in these ways. Communication researchers point out, however, that individuals can get just about any gratification they are seeking from just about any program—or any kind of mass media materials.[6]

You might find, for example, that you use the *NBC Nightly News* for enjoyment, surveillance, and interpretation. Enjoyment might come from the satisfaction of watching reporters' familiar faces day after day (is a little parasocial interaction working here?); surveillance might be satisfied by reports from different parts of the globe; and interpretation might flow from stray comments by the reporters and those they interview about what ought to be done to solve problems.

How Do the Mass Media Influence Culture?

When we use the term **culture**, we are broadly talking about ways of life that are passed on to members of a society through time and that keep the society together. We typically use the word **society** to refer to large numbers of individuals, groups, and organizations that live in the same general area and consider themselves connected to one another through the sharing of a culture.

What is shared includes learned behaviors, beliefs, and values. A culture lays out guidelines about who belongs to the society and what rules apply to them. It provides guideposts about where and what to learn, where and how to work, how to eat and

Mass communication's power allows media consumers to share the materials we are reading and listening to with millions of people. Consumers around the world saw *Twilight* in theaters within a few months of its release and joined in the media craze surrounding it.

culture ways of life that are passed on to members of a society through time and that keep the society together

society large numbers of individuals, groups, and organizations that live in the same general area and consider themselves connected to one another through the sharing of a culture

sleep. It tells us how we should act toward family members, friends, and strangers, and much, much more. In other words, a culture helps us make sense of ourselves and our place in the world.

A culture provides people with ideas about the kinds of arguments concerning particular subjects that are acceptable. In American culture, people would likely feel that on certain topics (vegetarianism, for example) all sorts of positions are acceptable, whereas on other topics (cannibalism, incest) the range of acceptable views is much narrower. Moreover, American culture allows for the existence of groups with habits that many people consider odd and unusual but not threatening to the more general way of life. Such group lifestyles are called **subcultures**. The Amish of Pennsylvania who live without modern appliances at home represent such a subculture, as do Catholic monks who lead a secluded existence devoted to God.

subcultures groups with habits that many people consider odd and unusual but not threatening to the more general way of life

For better or worse, it is not always easy to find direct evidence of who belongs and what the rules are by simply looking around. The mass media allow us to view clearly the ideas that people have about their broad cultural connections with others, and where they stand in the larger society. When mass media encourage huge numbers of people who are dispersed and unrelated to share the same materials, they are focusing people's attention on what is culturally important to think about and to talk and argue with others about. In other words, mass media create people's common lived experiences, a sense of the common culture, and the varieties of subcultures acceptable to it.

The mass media present ideas of the culture in three broad and related ways: they help us (1) identify and discuss the codes of acceptable behavior within our society, (2) learn what and who counts in our world and why, and (3) determine what others think of us, and what people "like us" think of others. Let's look at each of the ways separately.

IDENTIFYING AND DISCUSSING CODES OF ACCEPTABLE BEHAVIOR   A culture provides its people with notions about how to approach life's decisions, from waking to sleeping. It also gives people ideas about the arguments concerning all these subjects that are acceptable. If you think about the mass media from this standpoint, you'll realize that this is exactly what they do. Newspapers continually give us a look at how government works, as do internet sites such as *Wonkette* and *Huffington Post*. TV's CSI series act out behavior the police consider unacceptable and open up issues in which the rules of police and "criminal" behavior are contested or unclear. Magazine articles provide ideas, and a range of arguments, about what looks attractive, and how to act toward the opposite sex. We may personally disagree with many of these ideas. At the same time, we may well realize that these ideas are shared and possibly accepted broadly in society.

LEARNING WHAT AND WHO COUNTS IN OUR WORLD . . . AND WHY   Mass media tell us who is "famous"—from movie stars to scientists—and give us reasons why. They define the leaders to watch, from the U.S. president to religious ministers. News reports tell us who these people are in "real life." Fictional presentations such as books, movies, and TV dramas may tell us what they (or people like them) do and are like. Many of the presentations are angrily critical or bitingly satirical; American culture allows for this sort of argumentation. Through critical presentations or heroic ones, though, mass media presentations offer members of the society a sense of the qualities that we ought to expect in good leaders.

Fiction often shows us what leaders ought to be like—what values count in the society. Actor Denzel Washington excels at playing law enforcement officers or other social protectors who are courageous, smart, loyal, persevering, strong, and handsome; think, for example, of the movies *Déjà vu*, *Inside Man*, and *The Story of Eli*.

Sometimes, mass media discussions of fiction and nonfiction merge in curious ways. During the election of 2000, for example, several mass media commentators noted that President Bartlett of the then-popular *West Wing* TV drama would be a better choice than any of the real candidates because of his better leadership qualities.

DETERMINING WHAT OTHERS THINK OF US . . . AND WHAT PEOPLE "LIKE US" THINK OF OTHERS   Am I leadership material? Am I good-looking? Am I more or less religious than most people? Is what I like to eat what most people like to eat? Is my apartment as neat as most people's homes? How do I fit into the culture? Mass media allow us, and sometimes even encourage us, to ask questions such as these. When we read newspapers, listen to the radio, or watch TV we can't help but compare ourselves to the portrayals these media present. Sometimes we may shrug the comparisons off with the clear conviction that we simply don't care if we are different from people who are famous or considered "in." Other times we might feel that we ought to be more in tune with what's going on; this may lead us to buy new clothes or adopt a new hairstyle. Often, we might simply take in ideas of what the world is like outside our direct reach and try to figure out how we fit in.

At the same time that the mass media get us wondering how we fit in, they may also encourage feelings of connection with people whom we have never met. Newscasters, textbooks, and even advertisements tell us that we are part of a nation that

CULTURE TODAY
MAD MEN'S TWITTER CAMPAIGN

Around the time cable network AMC's critically lauded drama *Mad Men* was set to debut its second season, a strange thing started to happen: the show's characters started posting on Twitter. "Drinking a scotch with Roger so he doesn't feel like an alcoholic," tweeted antihero Don Draper. "So many deadlines this week," lamented copywriter Peggy Olson. Before long, dozens of the show's characters had Twitter accounts, including a golden retriever and the office photocopier.

Though the employees of fictional advertising agency Sterling Cooper didn't have access to cellphones or Twitter back in the show's setting of 1960s Manhattan, that didn't keep them from continuously posting their thoughts. The posts were so in character that one could almost envision Don Draper typing away at his blackberry over a three-martini lunch. As the show's characters developed a steady group of followers, they started to interact with fans on Twitter, responding to questions, doling out advice, and expressing well wishes to what eventually amounted to thousands of followers among themselves.

Speculation abounded as to who was behind the tweets of these very fictional characters. Was it a savvy Web 2.0 marketing ploy on the part of AMC and their Web marketing agency, Deep Focus? Was it the actors themselves, tweeting in character? In actuality, however, the Twitter accounts turned out to be the creation of a large network of devoted fans creating a new genre

of fan fiction. Though AMC expressed concern that the use of its characters violated its copyright, resulting in Twitter initially suspending the fan-generated accounts, the value of allowing the audience to engage with the show in a unique way became apparent. The fans behind the Twitter accounts were later permitted to continue posting as the show's characters.

Traditionally, imagined links between fans and fictional characters or media personalities have been labeled parasocial relationships. However, the characters of *Mad Men* offered a new twist on this old phenomenon. Through Twitter, fans of the show were able to actually communicate with or pose as the show's characters, lending a component to the parasocial relationship rooted in actual interaction. In the process, AMC has unintentionally embarked upon innovative forms of audience engagement, ones in which their product can be both mass and interpersonal communication at the same time.

Sources: "Don Draper (don_draper) on Twitter," Twitter.com. https://twitter.com/don_draper (accessed March 26, 2010); Keith O'Brien, "Brand Hijacking is Both Obstacle and Opportunity for Companies," *PR Week*, September 1, 2008, Opinion, p. 11; "Peggy Olson (PeggyOlson) on Twitter," Twitter.com. https://twitter.com/PeggyOlson (accessed March 26, 2010); Anna Pickard, "I Wanna be your Blog," *Guardian*, February 7, 2009, The Guide, p. 4.

extends far beyond what we can see. We may perceive that sense of connection differently depending on our personal interests. We may feel a bond of sympathy with people in a U.S. city that the news shows ravaged by floods. We may feel linked to people thousands of miles away who a website tells us share our political opinions. We may feel camaraderie with Super Bowl viewers around the country, especially those rooting for the team we are supporting.

Similarly, we may feel disconnected from people and nations that mass media tell us have belief systems that we do not share. U.S. news and entertainment are filled with portrayals of nations, individuals, and types of individuals who, we are told, do not subscribe to key values of American culture. Labels such as rogue nation, Nazi, communist, and Islamic extremist suggest threats to an American sense of decency. When mass media attach these labels to countries or individuals, we may well see them as enemies of our way of life, unless we have personal reasons not to believe the media portrayals.

CRITICISMS OF MASS MEDIA'S INFLUENCE ON CULTURE   Some social observers have been critical of the way mass media have used their power as reflectors and creators of culture. One criticism is that mass media present unfortunate prejudices about the world by systematically using **stereotypes**—predictable depictions that reflect (and sometimes create) cultural prejudices—and **political ideologies**—beliefs about who should hold the greatest power within a culture, and why. Another is that mass media detract from the quality of American culture. A third criticism, related to the first two, is that the mass media's cultural presentations encourage political and economic manipulation of their audiences.

Criticisms such as these have made people think deeply about the role that mass media play in American culture. These criticisms do have their weak points. Some might note that it is too simplistic to say that mass media detract from the quality of American culture. Different parts of the U.S. population use the mass media differently and, as a result, may confront different kinds of images. Related to this point is the idea that people bring their own personalities to the materials they read and watch. They are not simply passive recipients of messages. They actively interpret, reshape, and even reject some of them.

Nevertheless, the observations about stereotypes, cultural quality, and political ideology should make us think about the power of mass media over our lives. Many people—most people at one time or another—do seem to see the mass media as mirroring parts of the society and the world beyond it, especially parts they do not know first-hand. Most people do accept what the mass media tell them in news—and even in entertainment—about what and who counts in their world and why. Many seem to believe that the mass media's codes of acceptable behavior accurately describe large numbers of people, even if the codes don't describe their own norms. And they accept the mass media's images as starting points for understanding where they fit in society in relation to others and their connection with, or disconnection from, others. They may disagree with these images, or think that they shouldn't exist. Nevertheless, the media images serve as starting points for their concerns about, and arguments over, reality. We will have more to say about critical views on the effects of media in Chapter 4.

stereotypes predictable depictions that reflect (and sometimes create) cultural prejudices

political ideologies beliefs about who should hold the greatest power within a culture

Media Literacy

The aim of this book is to help you learn how to seriously examine the mass media's role in your life and in American life. The goal is not to make you cynical and distrustful of all mass media. Rather, it is to help you think in an educated manner about the

CULTURE TODAY
MEDIA CONVERGENCE AND HAITI

Celebrities used their clout to raise donations for the "Hope For Haiti Now: A Global Benefit For Earthquake Relief" telethon on January 22, 2010 in Los Angeles

Media coverage of the 2010 Haitian earthquake stands as a testament to both the media's role in guiding public attention toward specific events and topics and the multitude of ways a message can reach us through the media. Whether messages reach us through the realm of news or the realm of entertainment, the interweaving structures of the media often converge to allow text, sounds, and pictures to quickly disseminate across a global population. In times of crisis, this can mean all the difference in the world.

Following the catastrophic magnitude 7.0 earthquake that shook Haiti on January 12, 2010, the world turned toward the small Caribbean country. With Haiti's death toll climbing well past 200,000 and the country's political, financial, and cultural capital of Port-au-Prince in shambles, Haiti was completely debilitated. Searches for survivors began as humanitarian aid flocked to the country, which was already the poorest in the Western hemisphere.

A flurry of news coverage of the devastating aftermath commenced immediately, and news of the disaster became nearly unavoidable. Social networking sites Twitter and Facebook also became sources of news for a shocked and horrified public, as reports of witnesses to the disaster communicating with friends and family through social media poured into newsrooms.

Media coverage was not simply relegated to the news, either. Actor George Clooney partnered with MTV networks to host a two-hour live charity telethon event airing across dozens of networks and viewable online through websites such as Hulu, YouTube, and Yahoo, among others. Over 100 celebrities, ranging from Ringo Starr to Taylor Swift, Lady Gaga to Tom Hanks, manned the phones, taking donations, ultimately garnering over 83 million viewers and raising over $61 million. Then, debuting during the opening ceremonies of the 2010 Winter Olympics in Vancouver was the charity single "We Are the World 25 for Haiti," performed by eighty-five artists, including Miley Cyrus, Jaime Foxx, Barbara Streisand, and Lil Wayne. The single also served as a twenty-fifth anniversary remake of the 1985 hit single, written by Lionel Richie and Michael Jackson in an effort to aid famine-struck regions of Africa. Fans could download the song, video, or both for a small donation to Haitian relief funds.

Here was a case of media convergence with a strong humanitarian bent.

Journalists rushed to provide first-hand accounts of the earthquake and its aftermath in Haiti

Sources: *Associated Press*, "Haiti Raises Earthquake Toll to 230,000," February 9, 2010; Johua Gillin, "Stars Remake the 'World'," *St. Petersburg Times,* February, 2010; Kramer, Staci D., "Haiti Telethon Will Stretch Across Platforms, Countries; Paste Tries Different Approach," paidContent.org, January 19, 2010; Ben Rayner, "We Are the World all Over Again, This Time for Haiti," *Toronto Star*, January 22, 2010.

forces that shape the media and your relationships with them so that you will better evaluate what you see and hear. The aim is to give you the tools you need to become media literate.

A media-literate person is:

- Knowledgeable about the influences that guide media organizations
- Up to date on political issues relating to the media
- Sensitive to ways of seeing media content as a means of learning about culture
- Sensitive to the ethical dimensions of media activities
- Knowledgeable about scholarship regarding media effects
- Able to enjoy media materials in a sophisticated manner

Being media literate can be satisfying and fun. For example, knowing movie history can make watching films fascinating because you will be able to notice historical and technical features of the films that you wouldn't have otherwise noticed. Having a comparative understanding of different forms of news can help you think more clearly about what you can expect from journalism today and how it is changing. Understanding the forces that shape formulas and genres, and the social controversies around stereotyping and violence, can make your daily use of the media jumping-off points for thinking critically about yourself in relation to images of others in society. All these and other media activities can also start important conversations between you and your friends about the directions of our culture and your place in it. That, in turn, can help you become a more aware and responsible citizen—parent, voter, worker—in our media-driven society (see Figure 1.4).

Principles of Media Literacy

literacy the ability to effectively comprehend and use messages that are expressed in written or printed symbols, such as letters

media literacy the ability to apply critical thinking skills to the mass media, thereby becoming a more aware and responsible citizen—parent, voter, worker—in our media-driven society

When we speak about **literacy**, we mean the ability to effectively comprehend and use messages that are expressed in written or printed symbols, such as letters. When we speak about **media literacy**, however, we mean something broader. To quote the National Leadership Conference on Media Literacy, it is "the ability to access, analyze, evaluate and communicate messages in a variety of forms."[7]

Much of what we know about the world comes from what we see and hear in the media. Beyond simply mirroring what our world looks like, the media interpret, alter, and modify our reality. To develop media literacy skills and become responsible, media-literate consumers who can critically examine the way the media work in our lives, we first need to understand some basic principles about mass media materials—principles that help us engage in and understand the media's role in our daily lives.

PRINCIPLE 1: THE MEDIA CONSTRUCT OUR INDIVIDUAL REALITIES   Along with our observations and experiences, media materials help us to create our own individual notions of reality. Much of what we see as reality comes from the media we've experienced, and it is sometimes difficult to distinguish between our personal experiences and the world of the media. When we read newspapers, watch TV, and surf the Web we need to be aware that what we are seeing and hearing is not reality—even so-called reality TV. Rather, media materials are created with specific purposes in mind. They are constructions—that is, a human creation that presents a kind of script about the culture. Even when media materials appear to be particularly "natural" or reflective reality, many different business decisions and constraints have contributed to the way they are constructed.

PRINCIPLE 2: THE MEDIA ARE INFLUENCED BY INDUSTRIAL PRESSURES   We have already noted in this chapter that mass media materials are produced by organizations that exist in a commercial setting. The need to bring in revenues, often to sell advertising, is foremost in the minds of those who manage

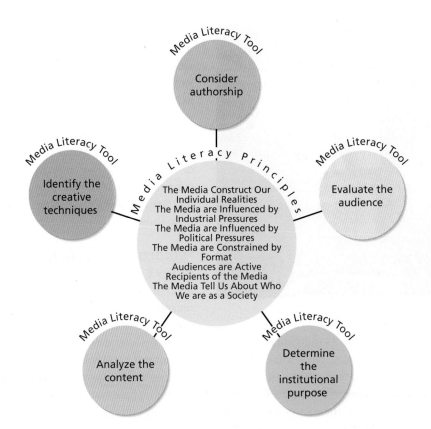

Figure 1.4 Constructing Media Literacy
Steps to becoming a media-literate citizen.

these organizations. As such, when you decode the media, you need to ask yourself: Who paid for this? What economic decisions went into creating this product? What financial pressures affected the distribution and exhibition of this product?

As we'll see in forthcoming chapters, mass media's industrial implications also involve ownership. If the same company owns a record company, a movie studio, a cable service, network television, and book and magazine publications, it has a powerful ability to control what is produced, distributed, and therefore seen.

PRINCIPLE 3: THE MEDIA ARE INFLUENCED BY POLITICAL PRESSURES Politics refers to the way a society is governed. When it comes to mass media, the term refers to a variety of activities. These range from the specific regulations that governments place on mass media, to decisions by courts about what restrictions the government can place on the media, to the struggle by various interest groups to change what media do (often using government leverage). For many media observers, being aware that media operate within a political environment leads to the idea that this environment deeply influences the media content itself. To them, it means being aware that the ideas in the media have political implications—that they are ideological.

PRINCIPLE 4: THE MEDIA ARE CONSTRAINED BY FORMAT Media scholar Patricia Aufterheide and others note that every medium—the television, the movie, the magazine—has its own characteristics, codes, and conventions; its own ways of presenting cultural reality.

Although you probably haven't thought about it, it's a good bet that you recognize the differences between the way these media do things. A report of a presidential press conference looks different depending on whether it was written for a newspaper or a magazine, presented on TV as news, described on a website's blog, or put together for the big screen. You probably also recognize, though, that mass media are

In a nearby Marriott ballroom, over 300 accredited journalists watched as golfer Tiger Woods publicly responded to the scandal of his marital infidelity. Early in his career, Woods had been marketed as a child prodigy, a fierce competitor, and the successful face of multiracial America. News of his fall from grace shocked many who believed in his wholesome public persona.

similar in some of their approaches to presenting the world—they organize the world into a number of basic storytelling forms that we recognize as entertainment, news, information, education, and advertising. As a media-literate person, you should ask yourself: What about the format of this medium that influences the content? What about the format that limits the kind of content that is likely to be shown?

PRINCIPLE 5: AUDIENCES ARE ACTIVE RECIPIENTS OF THE MEDIA The process of making meaning out of media is an ongoing interaction between the reader and the materials. As individual audience members, we filter meaning through our unique experiences: our socio-economic status, cultural background, gender, etc. However, emphasizing the input of the individual does not take away from the broad social importance of the media. Because so many people share mass media materials, large segments of the society see mass media as having cultural importance for the society as a whole.

PRINCIPLE 6: THE MEDIA TELL US ABOUT WHO WE ARE AS A SOCIETY People may like what they see about their society or they may complain about it. They may want people to view media images about themselves and others, or they fear that others will be influenced negatively by certain products (for example, stereotypes and violence). Even with an active audience, then, mass media hold crucial importance for society's visions of itself.

A media-literate person does not complain that something is biased; he or she searches out the bias, the assumptions, the values in everything that's made through the production, distribution, and exhibition processes.

Media Literacy Tools

To be a critical consumer in a mediated society, you need to equip yourself with tools that enable you to distinguish between different media forms and know how to ask basic questions. From the media literacy principles we discussed above flow a series of five basic categories of questions that you can use to begin to take apart and explore any media message. Typically you would apply this questioning process to a specific media "text"—that is, an identifiable production or publication, or a part of one: an episode of *The Hills*, an ad for Pepsi, an issue of *Esquire* magazine, a billboard for Budweiser beer, photos and articles about a bank robbery on the front page of a newspaper, the Super Bowl telecast. Sometimes a media "text" can involve multiple formats. A new animated Disney film, for example, involves not only a blockbuster movie released in thousands of theaters but also a whole campaign of advertising and merchandising—character dolls and toys, clothes, lunchboxes, etc.—as well as a website, storybooks, games, and, perhaps eventually, a ride at one of the Disney theme parks.

Let's take a look at these skill-building categories one at a time. They all involve asking questions about the media. Don't worry if you don't feel comfortable about answering them now. You'll feel much more able as you move through this book.

CONSIDER AUTHORSHIP   Ask yourself: "Who created this message and why are they sending it?" To explore the idea of "authorship" in media literacy is to look deeper than just knowing whose name is on the cover of a book or all the jobs in the credits of a movie. Companies make media texts just as buildings and highways are put together. Lead companies make the plans, they call on a variety of firms to make the products and do the work, the building blocks are brought together and ordinary people get paid to do various jobs. Whether we are watching the nightly news, passing a billboard on the street, or reading a political campaign flyer, the media messages we experience are created, distributed, and exhibited by various organizations in which individuals (and often teams of individuals) have written the words, captured the images, and worked the technical marvels.

Be aware, too, that in this creative process *choices are made*. If some words are spoken, others are edited out. If one picture is selected, dozens may have been rejected. If an ending to a story is written one way, other endings may not have been explored. However, as the audience, we don't get to see or hear the words, pictures, or endings that were rejected. We only see, hear, or read what was accepted! Rarely does anybody ever explain why certain choices were made. Rarely, too, do creators bring up alternative ways to interpret the world we see through our media channels. It is up to us to consider the constructed nature of our media realities and, when possible and important to us, to look for a variety of perspectives on the same realities.

EVALUATE THE AUDIENCE   This proposition involves two broad questions. The first is "Who are the intended targets of these media materials?" The second is "How might different people understand these materials similarly and differently?"

Thinking about the intended targets gets us back to the point that industries typically construct media materials to make money. As we will see, that often means deciding what types of people would want certain kinds of content and creating products designed to fit these interests. As straightforward as this idea sounds, we will see that it is really quite complex. Entire companies revolve around helping firms describe lucrative target audiences and evaluate their interests, and figure out how to reach them. Other firms make money evaluating whether the audiences that were targeted actually attended to the messages. "Audience research" is, in fact, a big business that is increasingly important to all media industries from books and newspapers to the internet and video games. The more you learn about it, the more you will understand the multitude of factors that lead to the sometimes different media worlds that different people encounter.

Of course, if two people receive different media materials—say you receive a different ad from me when we visit the same website—they will necessarily understand them differently. As we will see, that kind of variation can certainly happen in the highly fragmented, targeted media world in which we live. But even if people share the same TV shows, movies, or Web pages, they might interpret them differently because of their different personalities or interests, or other factors. (Chapter 4 covers this topic in some detail.) That insight leads to the second, very different question about the audience—about how people interpret media materials. There are two opposing strains here. First, people who live in a society and learn similar curricula in schools do share many aspects of the same culture. But, second, people at the same time experience media through the lenses of their ethnic, religious, income, racial, gender, age, or other characteristics. So although people may experience some

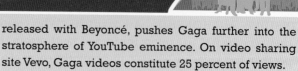

MEDIA PROFILE
LADY GAGA

Lady Gaga (born Stefani Joanne Angelina Germanotta)

Every once in a while, a celebrity will come along who transcends one level of fame—as a recording artist, actor, or marketing guru—and ascends to a level of stardom so ubiquitous it cannot be ignored. Madonna, Beyoncé, and Justin Timberlake achieved this position at one point in their careers. Today perhaps no one personifies this breed of celebrity better than media sensation Lady Gaga.

Lady Gaga's ascent to fame began in September 2008, and she rose so rapidly that in under a year and a half her digital singles surpassed 20 million and album sales broke 8 million (and all at a time when album sales are in steep decline among youth). Not only is Gaga the first recording artist to score consecutive number one singles from a debut album, she also is the first artist to reach 1 billion YouTube views, with the combined hits of her videos "Just Dance," "Poker Face," and "Bad Romance." "Telephone," her most recent single that she

released with Beyoncé, pushes Gaga further into the stratosphere of YouTube eminence. On video sharing site Vevo, Gaga videos constitute 25 percent of views.

Gaga has also become a savvy marketer. After quickly signing Virgin Mobile as a sponsor for her tour, Gaga has released her own line of Heartbeats headphones through the record label Interscope, unveiled a brand of lipstick through Mac Cosmetics, and signed on as the creative director of Polaroid. Unlike celebrities who merely endorse products, Gaga actually creates her designs.

How did Lady Gaga achieve all this in under eighteen months, before even turning 24? "Two words," says *Advertising Age*'s Andrew Hampp. "Social media." As of March 2010, Gaga has nearly 6 million Facebook fans and well over 3 million followers on Twitter—just behind Barack Obama and Oprah. Gaga's celebrity has emerged so swiftly and so forcefully thanks in no small part to this sharing through social media.

In a time when there are a seemingly infinite number of media options and when audiences seem to be broken up into thousands of niche fragments sharing little of the same media, the Gaga phenomenon has become one thing that audiences can undoubtedly share in. Whether you find her brilliant, obnoxious, or simply perplexing, you most likely have noticed her. In doing so, you've shared in a phenomenon with millions of people the world over.

Sources: Samuel Axon, "Lady Gaga First Artist with One Billion Online Video Views," *Mashable*, March 24, 2010. http://mashable.com/2010/03/24/lady-gaga-billion/ (accessed August 1, 2010); Andrew Hampp, "Gaga, Oooh La La: Why the Lady is the Ultimate Social Climber," *Advertising Age*, February 22, 2010. http://adage.com/digitalalist10/article?article_id=142210 (accessed March 25, 2010); "Lady Gaga," Facebook.com. http://www.facebook.com/ladygaga (accessed March 25, 2010); "Top User Rankings and Stats," Twitterholic.com. http://twitterholic.com/ (accessed March 25, 2010).

aspects of a movie, song, or TV show in similar ways, they may also interpret other aspects of the movie, song, or TV show quite differently from one another.

It's fascinating to consider how and when such differences work and what they mean. The next time you go to a "gross out" comedy film, consider the parts where virtually everyone is laughing at the same time. What is behind that similarity in "getting" the humor? Is it the same cultural sense of what embarrassing activities are funny? Is it the collective understanding of that humor by the movie's target age group? Is it mostly a male preoccupation with that kind of humor? Try to see who isn't laughing in the theater when so many others find it hilarious. Also think about the kinds of people who wouldn't go to a film like that because the entire notion is offensive. (Perhaps you're one of them.)

As we will see, the companies that produce, distribute, and sponsor media materials often have certain ideas in mind about what certain audiences will share as funny, sad, repulsive, scary, and exhilarating. Even though they contend that these notions are based on research, they may also be rooted in social stereotypes. Thinking about audience when you confront media materials will force you to dive in to some of the most interesting questions about their creation and the roles they play in society.

DETERMINE THE INSTITUTIONAL PURPOSE   Ask yourself: "Why is this content being sent?" This question flows from the previous questions about the audience. We noted that much of the world's media were developed as moneymaking enterprises and continue to operate today as commercial businesses. Chapters 8 and 9, for example, will discuss how newspapers and magazines decide how much space they can devote to different kinds of material based on the amount and kinds of advertisements they sell. What's really being sold through commercial media is not just the advertised products to the audience—but also the audience to the advertisers! Moreover, we will see in Chapter 16 that the selling takes place not only through obvious advertisements but also through much less obvious product integrations. These are activities through which media platforms from printed magazines to television shows to websites present goods, people, and ideas as natural parts of the program, movie, or article when the production firm actually put them there for a fee.

We will see in Chapter 4 that some scholars argue that examining the "purpose" of media content also means confronting issues of ownership and the structure and influence of media institutions in society. To them the overall "purpose" of media content created by huge corporations is to reinforce the power of those companies by continuing to keep them rich and powerful politically. To these media critics, these corporations have little interest in encouraging social controversy or economic challenge to their power. As a result, the critics say, mainstream media material is often propaganda for the political and social status quo. But there's also another side of the media system. Commentators have noted that the internet has become an international platform through which a variety of forces with hateful political and social views have easy access to powerful tools that can tell persuasive stories in favor of their anti-establishment points of view. The politics in both kinds of storytelling make clear the importance of knowing how to think about the institutional purposes behind the media we use, to verify sources, and insist on openness from creators and sponsors of the material.

ANALYZE THE CONTENT   Ask yourself, "What values, lifestyles, and points of view are represented in (or omitted from) this message?" Because all media messages are constructed, choices have to be made. These choices inevitably reflect the values, attitudes, and points of view of the ones doing the constructing. The decision about a character's age, gender, or race mixed in with the lifestyles, attitudes, and behaviors that are portrayed, the selection of a setting (urban? rural? affluent? poor?), and the actions and re-actions in the plot are just some of the ways that values become "embedded" in a TV show, a movie, or an ad. As we will discuss in Chapter 2, even the news has embedded values in the decisions made about what stories go first, how long they are, what kinds of pictures are chosen, and so on.

Our discussion of scholarly media research in Chapter 4 will provide you with a variety of tools for analyzing content. There, as well as throughout this book, we will address two major complaints that many people have about the widespread mass media: (1) less popular or new ideas can have a hard time getting aired, especially if they challenge long-standing assumptions or commonly accepted beliefs; and (2) unless challenged, old assumptions can create and perpetuate stereotypes, thus further limiting our understanding and appreciation of the world and the many possibilities of human life. If we have the skills to question and rationally identify both overt and latent values in a mediated presentation, whether from the news, entertainment, or, now especially, the internet, we are likely to be much more astute in our evaluation of the materials and thinking about what views of the world it might be presenting to its audiences.

IDENTIFY THE CREATIVE TECHNIQUES   Ask yourself, "What creative techniques are being used to attract my attention?" This question relates partly to the need to identify the ways that media materials provide clues to their institutional purpose and choices made. You should think about how a message is constructed to connect with its intended audience: the creative components that are used in putting it together—words, still images, moving images, camera angle, music, color, movement, and many more. Apart from the issue of targeting, understanding the creative techniques of mass media will enhance your appreciation of the artistry involved. All forms of communication—whether magazine covers, advertisements, or horror movies—depend on a kind of "creative language." For example, use of different colors creates different feelings, camera close-ups often convey intimacy, scary music heightens fear. As we will see, learning the history of a medium involves learning the ways that companies have organized words and images to draw and captivate audiences. Go beyond what you learn here to immerse yourself in the creative languages of media that you love—whether they are comic books, romance novels, hip-hop recordings, cowboy films, daily newspapers, sci-fi video games, or other elements of media culture. What you learn will undoubtedly be fascinating, and it will make your everyday interactions with those media extremely interesting.

The Benefits of a Media-literate Perspective

Armed with the principles of media literacy and the tools to evaluate any media message, you are on your way to developing a media-literate perspective. For those who adopt this perspective, the power held by the mass media raises a host of social issues, including:

- Do media conglomerates have the ability to control what we receive over a variety of media channels? If so, do they use that ability?
- Are portrayals of sex and violence increasing in the new media environment, as some critics allege? Do media organizations have the power to lower the amount of sex and violence? Would they do it if they could?
- Does the segmentation of audiences by media companies lead to groups that those firms consider more attractive getting better advertising discounts and greater diversity of content than groups that those firms consider less important? If so, what consequences will that have for social tensions and the ability of parts of society to share ideas with one another?
- What (if anything) should be done about the increasing ability of mass media firms to invade people's privacy by storing information they gain when they interact with them? Should the federal government pass laws that force companies to respect people's privacy, or should we leave it up to corporate self-regulation? What do we know about the history of corporate self-regulation that would lead us to believe that it would or wouldn't work in this situation?

■ Should global media companies adapt to the cultural values of the nations in which they work, even if those values infringe upon free press and free speech?

Our exploration of these and related questions will take us into topics that you may not associate with the mass media business—for example, mobile telephones, toys, games, and supermarkets. It will also sometimes take us far beyond the United States, because American mass media companies increasingly operate globally. They influence non-U.S. firms around the world and are influenced by them. As we will see, their activities have sparked controversies in the United States and abroad that will likely intensify as the twenty-first century unfolds.

Chapter Review For an interactive chapter recap and study guide, visit the companion website for *Media Today* at http://www.routledge.com/textbooks/mediatoday4e.

Questions for Discussion and Critical Thinking
. . . .

1 What are the similarities and differences between different forms of communication?
2 Give an example of a way that a mass media production firm has purposefully used "noise."
3 Why is it useful to see an audience as "constructed" rather than as objectively real?
4 As newspaper companies cut staff in order to keep up their profits, some observers believe that the investigative report is one genre of journalism that will get less attention. Why would they think that? What might that mean for journalism and for journalism's role in society?
5 Of the forms of funding when production is already complete, advertising is the most common. Why do you think that is?

Internet Resources
. . . .

Action Coalition for Media Education (http://acmecoalition.org)
A network of educators, students, health professionals, journalists, media-makers, parents, activists, and other citizens joined as a member-supported, independent, nonprofit, continental, educational coalition.

Center for Media Literacy (http://www.medialit.org)
A pioneer in its field, the Center for Media Literacy is a nonprofit educational organization that provides leadership, public education, professional development, and educational resources nationally.

Media Awareness Network (http://www.media-awareness.ca/english/)
The Media Awareness Network is home to one of the world's most comprehensive collections of media education and internet literacy resources.

Media Education Foundation (http://www.mediaed.org)

> The Media Education Foundation produces and distributes documentary films and other educational resources to inspire critical reflection on the social, political, and cultural impact of American mass media.

Key Terms

. . . .

You can find the definitions to these key terms in the marginal glossary throughout this chapter. Test your knowledge of these terms with interactive flash cards on the *Media Today* companion website.

audience fragmentation 6
channels 10
communication 7
convergence 6
culture 19
decoding 10
encoding 9
feedback 11
industrial nature 7
industry 14
interpersonal communication 7
interpretation 18
literacy 24
mass media 14
mass production process 6
media literacy 24

mediated interpersonal
  communication 8
medium 8
messages 7
noise 12
parasocial interaction 17
political ideologies 22
receiver 10
social currency 17
society 19
source 8
stereotypes 22
subcultures 20
surveillance 18
transmitter 9

Constructing Media Literacy

. . . .

1 Can you think of entertainment (as opposed to news) content that you have used for surveillance or interpretation?

2 What are some ways in which the mass media have given you a sense of connection with or disconnection from others in the United States or in the rest of the world?

3 Do you agree or disagree with the criticisms of the mass media? Why or why not?

4 In view of the "foundation principles" of media literacy presented in this chapter, how media literate do you think you are at present? Explain your answer.

Companion Website Video Clips

. . . .

San Francisco Celebrating VE Day (1918)

> This newsreel footage captures the celebration of the end of World War I in San Francisco in 1918. Credit: Internet Archive/Prelinger Archives.

Case Study

. . . .

THE MEDIA AS SOCIAL CURRENCY

The idea How much do media really influence what people discuss with you? This study will help you begin to find out by tracking how often people bring up media-related topics with you over the course of a day.

The method The challenge will be to get some sense of a day's media-related conversations that people initiate with you. The trick will be to keep a record of what people talk to you about from the media, but without encouraging them to do it and without making them so self-conscious that they will stop right away or refrain from doing it again during the day. Here are suggestions about how to go about it:

1   Prepare a small notebook that you can carry in your pocket or pocketbook. On each page write the following categories, leaving space underneath each one: Time, Who, Topic, How Long?

2   Go through your day normally. Each time a person (or people) brings up a topic that in some way or other relates to something they clearly say they saw or heard in the media (for example, in the news or in an ad), or that they clearly think you saw or heard in the media, pay particular attention. Involve yourself in the conversation as you normally would. When the conversation has ended and the others involved have left (or if you can absent yourself for a bit) get out your notebook and fill in the topics on the page: What time did the media-related conversation start? Who was involved as speaker(s) and listener(s)? What did they talk about, and for how long? Remember that listeners can also be speakers, and that a conversation can have far more than a single media-related topic.

3   For the purpose of this study, you should note only media-related conversations that people initiate with you. The reason is that you might go out of your way to initiate such activities and that would make the results hard to generalize. Make sure, though, to include mediated conversations—for example, phone calls, Skype calls, text messages, and email—that people use to discuss media with you or to direct you to websites or other media.

4   You might also write notes about topics of conversation that you think originated from the media but when the speaker did not clearly note the connection. A person might talk about the war in Iraq, for example, but not say that he or she learned about it from the media. In fact, the story may have come from a friend who saw it on TV.

5   The next day, pull out your notebook, and make a table that notes each occurrence and what you wrote about each one. Separate the clear cases from the ones that aren't explicit. Write a short (two-page) essay summarizing the findings. What might this mean about media's role in the way people interact with you? Compare your findings with the findings of others in the class, and try to figure out why they are similar or different.

2 Making Sense of the Media Business

After studying this chapter, you will be able to:

1 Recognize how mass media personnel consider the audience an integral part of business concerns

2 Describe the primary genres of the materials created by various mass media industries

3 Identify and discuss the process of producing, distributing, and exhibiting materials in mass media industries

4 Explain the way media firms finance the production, distribution, and exhibition of media materials

5 Harness your media literacy skills to evaluate what this means to you as a media consumer

"If anyone said we were the radio business, it wouldn't be someone from our company. We're not in the business of providing news and information. We're not in the business of providing well-researched music. We're simply in the business of selling our customers' products."

— LOWRY MAYS, CLEAR CHANNEL CEO

MEDIA TODAY

Understanding the changing media system and the issues surrounding it can help us to be responsible citizens—parents, voters, workers—in our media-driven society. If you know how news is created, you might be able to read a paper or watch a TV news magazine with a much keener sense of what's going on. If you know how TV entertainment shows get on the air, and how and why the firms that produce them are changing, you may be able to come up with strategies for influencing those changes that will benefit social groups that you care about. If you are aware of the strategies of media conglomerates, you may have a better understanding of why certain companies want to move into certain businesses, and be able to decide whether the government officials you voted for are doing the right thing by allowing or not allowing them to do that.

The difficulty with getting up to speed on these topics is that understanding the mass media industry can be a bewildering experience. Let's say, for example, that community leaders in the neighborhood where you live have begun to complain about billboard advertising because of the overwhelming number of signs featuring sexual images or advertising beer. In order to help a community group petition billboard company executives to change their companies' ad policies, you decide you must learn about the billboard business. You quickly find that billboards are part of a large and growing "outdoor advertising" industry. Moreover, you learn that mass media conglomerates own some of the biggest companies in the industry. These conglomerates also run several radio stations and other media outlets in your city.

You are faced with a number of crucial questions here. First, how do you begin to get enough of a grasp on the outdoor advertising industry to learn about the factors that affect its policies for accepting ads and how those policies can be changed? Second, is the local radio business tied to some of the goals of the outdoor firms, and, if so, does that make it harder or easier to influence ad policies? Third, in terms of your interest in changing outdoor advertising policies, is it relevant that the mass media conglomerates own both the outdoor firms and the radio stations? If so, how?

You want to learn as much as possible about the outdoor advertising industry to understand how its policies on beer and sex can be changed. But should you also learn about the radio industry and the conglomerates? If so, what should you learn? And where do you start? Must you conduct research on each industry separately, as if the activities in one industry cannot help you understand the activities in another? If that's the case, you may find yourself thinking that it's not worth the time and effort.

This chapter aims to assure you that becoming knowledgeable about the business of mass media is not as intimidating as it may sound. By learning a small number of general points about the mass media business, you will understand particular conglomerates and mass media industries much better than if you started from scratch every time.

Identifying An Audience for Mass Media Content

In its 2009 *Communications Industry Forecast*, consulting firm Veronis Suhler Stevenson (VSS) estimated that 2008 spending on media was $882.61 billion.[1] That number will give you one sense of the large overall size of the media business. As we move through this book, we will see that the revenues of individual media industries come to tens of billions of dollars, and sometimes far more. Table 2.1 gives you another sense of the media economy by presenting the revenues of the five biggest media firms. As the table notes, those five companies alone brought in almost $97 billion in 2005.

audiences the people to whom a media product is directed

No media business can exist (or continue to take in revenues) without content that attracts consumers, or **audiences**—the people to whom mass media firms are directing their products. **Media practitioners**—the people who select or create the material that a mass media firm produces, distributes, or exhibits—are keenly aware that their content must be attractive to audiences if money is to flow their way instead of to their competitors. In fact, audiences pose enormous risks as well as great opportunities for success for media practitioners. To best manage these risks and increase their chances of success, they must carefully consider the following questions:

media practitioners the people who select or create the material that a mass media firm produces, distributes, or exhibits

1   How should we think about our audience? How should we define our audience?
2   Will the material we are thinking of creating, distributing, or exhibiting to attract that audience generate adequate revenues?
3   Were the people we thought would be attracted to our products in fact attracted to our products? Why or why not?

Defining and Constructing a Target Audience

Executives who are charting the direction of media firms do not think about the members of their audience in the same way that they think about themselves. Take, for example, Kaya. She thinks of herself in a number of ways—as a hard worker who juggles her communication studies major with her twenty-hour-a-week job at a local restaurant; as a daughter who visits her parents twice a week; as a moderate church-goer (about two Sundays a month); as a girlfriend who makes time for her boyfriend, Omar; as a loyal friend who tries to keep up with high school classmates by phone and email.

Table 2.1 The Top Five Largest U.S. Media Companies by Revenue, 2008			
Rank	Media Company	Headquarters	Revenue
1	Comcast Corp	Philadelphia	$29,026
2	Time Warner	New York	20,533
3	Walt Disney Co.	Burbank, Calif.	18,599
4	DirecTV Group	El Segundo, Calif.	17,310
5	Time Warner Cable	New York	15,581

Note: Dollars are in millions.

Source: *Advertising Age*. http://adage.com/datacenter/datapopup.php?article_id=139407 (accessed August 1, 2010).

Now consider how executives at a magazine that Kaya gets—say, *Time*—think of her. Of course, they are not really thinking specifically about Kaya at all. Instead, *Time* executives focus on the characteristics that they can use to show potential advertisers the types of people they can reach through their magazine. *Time* gets some of its data from a questionnaire that Kaya filled out after she received a student discount to the periodical. Other data came from lists that the magazine bought from companies that bring together information about millions of people and sell to media firms.

To *Time*, Kaya is (among other things) in the 18–34 age group, female, a student, a small-car owner, unmarried, childless, an apartment renter, an earner of $30,000 a year, the possessor of two credit cards, an avid moviegoer, not a big TV watcher, and someone who has taken at least three airplane trips in the past two years. The major reason that *Time* collects this information it does have about Kaya is because these are some of the characteristics that major advertisers consider when they think about buying space in magazines. A car manufacturer who is thinking of advertising in the magazine doesn't care how many times a month Kaya goes to church, or whether she visits her parents. The car manufacturer *does* care about her age, her gender, her income, and the kind of car she presently owns, because it believes this information predicts the likelihood that she will buy its brand. Kaya's age and student status make her attractive to advertisers such as car manufacturers, even though she doesn't make a lot of money; they believe these factors indicate that she will make a lot more some day.

Because *Time* magazine gets at least half of its revenue from advertising, its executives want to keep subscribers who are attractive to advertisers, so they use the information they have about Kaya and subscribers like her, and about other groups of subscribers that they have identified as being attractive to advertisers, to help them decide what kinds of materials in the magazine will keep these people as subscribers. These identified and selected population segments, then, become the desired audience for *Time*. Once the magazine's executives have identified the target segments, they try to learn things about those segments that will lead to an increase in sales. That, in turn, leads to more research to understand the groups. Figure 2.1 illustrates this process by focusing on Kaya. The example assumes that *Time* marketers are attracted by what they know about Kaya and want her to be part of their audience. If they didn't find Kaya and people with characteristics like hers attractive as consumers, they would produce content that would speak to different interests and that might drive Kaya away, rather than encourage her to renew her subscription.

Thinking about the audience, then, means learning to think of people primarily as consumers of media materials and other products. For media professionals, thinking about people in this way requires a combination of intuition and solid knowledge of the marketplace. As the example of Kaya and *Time* magazine suggests, when advertisers contribute all or part of a firm's revenue stream, the firm's executives have two challenges: they have to create content that will attract audiences, and they must also make sure that the content and the audience it brings in will be attractive to advertisers so that money flows its way, instead of to its competitors. To do this, they need to decide whether enough advertisers want to reach that audience in order to provide **adequate revenue**—enough cash to allow the enterprise to pay for itself and give the owners or bankers who put up the money the desired return on their investment.

Sometimes, in fact, media executives reverse the order of the questions. They first ask which audiences advertisers want to reach, and then look for ways to attract those audiences. ABC television network executives know, for example, that advertisers covet viewers in the 18–34 age group from 8 to 11 p.m. That basic premise guides much of their thinking about the programming decisions. All of the production firms working with the network know that they must come up with ideas that will

adequate revenue enough cash to allow the enterprise to pay for itself and give the owners or bankers who put up the money the desired return on their investment

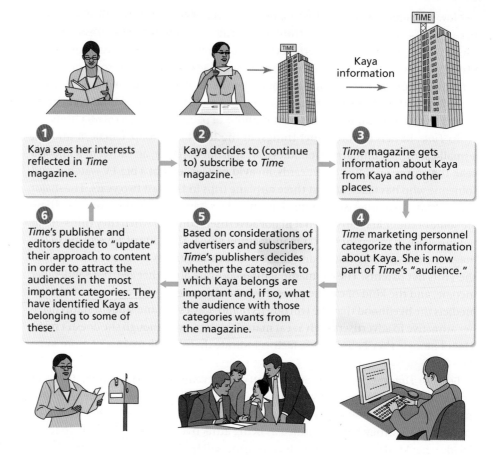

① Kaya sees her interests reflected in *Time* magazine.

② Kaya decides to (continue to) subscribe to *Time* magazine.

③ *Time* magazine gets information about Kaya from Kaya and other places.

⑥ *Time*'s publisher and editors decide to "update" their approach to content in order to attract the audiences in the most important categories. They have identified Kaya as belonging to some of these.

⑤ Based on considerations of advertisers and subscribers, *Time*'s publishers decides whether the categories to which Kaya belongs are important and, if so, what the audience with those categories wants from the magazine.

④ *Time* marketing personnel categorize the information about Kaya. She is now part of *Time*'s "audience."

Figure 2.1 Kaya and the Constructed Audience
The ways in which executives at *Time* view their readers and the way in which *Time*'s readers view themselves are very different.

be a magnet to that age group. (Think *Grey's Anatomy* and the rest of ABC's Thursday night schedule to get a concrete sense of what this means.)

The most important questions executives ask are often quite basic. Say, for example, a greeting card company president wants his firm to create a new **line**—a new assortment of products with a particular, predetermined format. Should the company aim the line at everybody? That plan probably wouldn't work out well, since in recent years the lines offered by greeting card companies have been quite **targeted**: they have been written and drawn to appeal to particular segments of society rather

line an assortment of products with a particular, predetermined format

targeted created to appeal to particular segments of society rather than the population as a whole

Sometimes magazines create multiple covers for special issues in order to appeal to a wider array of targeted audiences as shown here by *Time* magazine.

than to the population as a whole. Well, then, what segments should be the targets? Women or men; the rich, the middle class, or the poor; Asians, Latinos, whites, or blacks; people who live in the eastern United States or those who live in the Midwest—or some combination of these and other categories?

Many companies spend a lot of energy deciding which audiences they should pursue, what those audiences' characteristics are, and what those audiences like and don't like. Executives try to verify their intuitions and control their risks with research. In conducting this research, they think about the types of people who make up their audience—that is, they construct their audience—in three broad ways: through demographics, psychographics, and lifestyle categories.

demographics characteristics by which people are divided into particular social categories

DEMOGRAPHICS   **Demographics**—one of the simplest and most common ways to construct an audience—refers to characteristics by which people are divided into particular social categories. Media executives focus on those characteristics, or factors, that they believe are most relevant to understanding how and why people use their medium. **Demographic indicators** include such factors as age, gender, occupation, ethnicity, race, and income (see Figure 2.2).

demographic indicators factors such as age, gender, occupation, ethnicity, race, and income

PSYCHOGRAPHICS   Media organizations also differentiate groups by **psychographics**, or categorizing people on the basis of their attitudes, personality types, or motivations. Consider the management of an interior design magazine that wants advertisers to understand its readership beyond the familiar demographics of "high

psychographics a way to differentiate among people or groups by categorizing them according to their attitudes, personality types, or motivations

CRITICAL CONSUMER
HOW MUCH AM I WORTH?

Have you ever considered how much your name is worth? Of course, to us, our name is our identity, it's who we are and how people know us. When we meet someone new, we can freely give that person our name as a sign of friendship. But we can also withhold our name, or information about ourselves, if we don't want to talk to that person again.

Information about who you are is worth a lot of money to marketers. InfoUSA, a database marketing firm, has collected information on more than 210 million

individuals. Customers can access infoUSA's databases online through their Sales Genie service, which costs between $75 and $180 per month. Another company, CAS Marketing Solutions, sells lists of consumer information for as little as $35 per thousand names.

For these database companies, your name, along with your accompanying information, is a commodity. These corporations have assembled massive databases to store knowledge about you from the purchases that you have made, information you have given out, or even which sites you visit on the Web.

CAS Marketing Solutions claims to have "psychographic data that defines the lifestyle characteristics, behavior and product interests of individuals" based on social roles, interests, and hobbies. For example, they may classify you based on the type of music you like, the books you read, the pets you own, even the type of food you like to eat.

Information like this is valuable to a wide range of marketers for it can give them a strong idea of who you are and what you are likely to buy in the future.

Your name can be bought and sold, just as you buy and sell a CD or a car. Such transactions occur without your knowing that people are making money off your name.

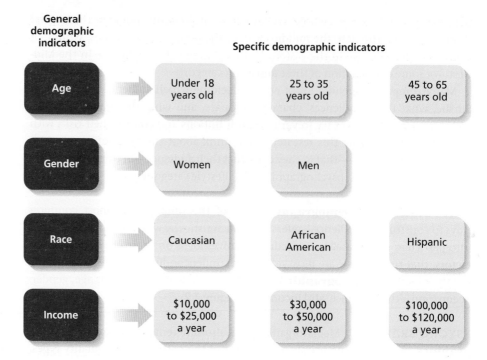

Figure 2.2 Demographic Indicators
Demographic indicators, like those shown in this figure, help media executives group individuals into categories that will be most attractive to their target advertisers.

income," "age thirty and up," and "homeowners." The magazine executives hire a research firm to interview a large number of subscribers and create psychological profiles of them. The researchers find that the readers can be divided into three psychographic types: comparers (20 percent of subscribers), who like to read the magazine to see how their furniture stacks up against the pieces on the pages; idea hunters (40 percent of subscribers), who read it to help them with their own decorating; and art lovers (40 percent), who subscribe because they love the beautiful furniture that appears in the magazine each month. The researchers also find that the three psychographic categories differ in terms of the length of time people remain subscribers. Those readers who are classified as art lovers stay the longest time (an average of five years), while those classified as idea hunters stay the shortest time (two years), with the comparers in the middle (three years). The magazine executives can use this construction of the audience to shape their articles to appeal to the comparers and art lovers and to find advertisers that are interested in any of the groups (see Figure 2.3).

Figure 2.3 Psychographic Indicators
Psychographic indicators can help media executives further shape their product to attract the audience members their advertisers seek.

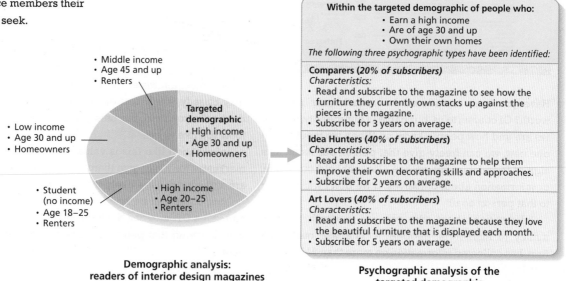

Demographic analysis: readers of interior design magazines

Psychographic analysis of the targeted demographic

LIFESTYLE CATEGORIES   We can also describe media audiences using **lifestyle categories**—finding activities in which potential audiences are involved that mark them as different from others in the audience or in the population at large. Suppose, for example, that the interior design magazine conducts another research study that finds that its readers go to restaurants, own expensive cars, and travel outside the United States far more than the average for the U.S. population. In this way, the magazine's employees are categorizing readers from a lifestyle point of view.

Keep in mind that what media professionals learn about their audiences through research is relevant only if it relates to making money by attracting advertisers or by keeping them as audience members. The lifestyle characteristics that our fictional interior design magazine found are terrific—just the sort that will attract major automobile, airline, hotel, and restaurant advertisers. The demographics and psychographics are also useful for getting sponsors as well as for thinking about the kind of content that will keep particular groups as part of the audience.

Creating Content to Attract the Target Audience

A key challenge for mass media firms is knowing what kind of content to present to their target audiences, and how to present it. Although this may seem straightforward, it actually involves quite a bit of selection, thought, and risk.

Suppose you are in charge of programming for CBS; that is, setting the television schedule for the coming year. Your job is to set up the menu of shows that the owners of CBS hope will attract tens of millions of viewers to their airwaves every day. Quite a daunting task, isn't it? For one thing, you must try to get a thorough understanding of the audiences your company wants to attract—who they are and what they like. For another, you have to have a strong grasp of the kinds of materials that may be available to meet audience interests at different times of the day. What will grab people's attention? Who can create it? How do you even begin to determine whether the ideas that potential creators pitch to you will succeed?

Sometimes the answers to these questions are based on the intuitions and experiences of the executives in charge. To lower their risk, they may choose creators with good **track records**—that is, a history of successes. They may also choose to produce material that is similar to other material that has recently been successful. For example, if a comedy/horror movie aimed at young adults has recently been successful at the box office, executives might search for another film of the same type, hoping that lightning will strike twice.

When a lot of money is at stake (and it usually is), executives often turn to **research and development (R&D)** activities to systematically investigate potential sources of revenue. These activities involve learning about the leisure habits of different audiences through a number of tools, including surveys, focus groups, or the analysis of existing data.

In **surveys**, a certain number of carefully chosen people are asked the same questions individually over the phone, via the internet, or in person. A **focus group** is an assemblage of eight to ten carefully chosen people who are asked to discuss their habits and opinions about one or more topics. The **analysis of existing data** involves systematic investigation of the potential audience for certain kinds of content (who they are, where they are, how much they like the idea, how much they will pay for it) and the competitors (who they are, how similar their products are, how powerful they are). Based on these results, executives must decide what kinds of materials to create and how—and whether their proposed budget is adequate to create the product and market it successfully against the competition.

---

lifestyle categories activities in which potential audiences are involved that mark them as different from others in the population at large

track record the previous successes or failures of a product, person, or organization

research and development (R&D) departments within companies that explore new ideas and generate new products and services, systematically investigating potential sources of revenue through surveys, focus groups, or the analysis of existing data

surveys a research tool that seeks to ask a certain number of carefully chosen people the same questions individually over the phone or in person

focus group an assemblage of eight to ten carefully chosen people who are asked to discuss their habits and opinions about one or more topics

analysis of existing data a systematic investigation into the potential audience for the material (who they are, where they are, how much they like the idea, how much they will pay for it) and the competitors (who they are, how similar their products are, how powerful they are)

CULTURE TODAY
BETTY WHITE

At an age when most actors are long retired, actress and comedienne Betty White is having one of the busiest times of her career. White, best known for her roles as the man-eating Sue Ann Nivens on *The Mary Tyler Moore Show* and the sweet-but-dim Rose Nylund on *The Golden Girls*, as well as for her recurring appearances on the game shows *Password* and *Match Game*, is experiencing a career resurgence at nearly 90 years old.

Betty White hosted *Saturday Night Live* on May 8, 2010.

After starring in Sandra Bullock's hit romantic comedy *The Proposal*, having a cameo in a popular Super Bowl Snickers commercial, and winning a Screen Actors Guild lifetime achievement award, White was tapped to host NBC's popular sketch comedy *Saturday Night Live*. Perhaps most interesting is what prompted *SNL* to contact White as a potential host: Facebook.

In December 2009, Betty White fan David Matthews created the Facebook group "Betty White to Host SNL (please?)!" "Betty White has been doing television since *before I Love Lucy*! What a way to honor her career, her comedic timing, and her life than by inviting her to host *Saturday Night Live!!!*" wrote Matthews for the group's profile. Through word of mouth, the group rapidly accumulated over half a million fans, and, in the process, caught the attention of the mainstream media, White, and *SNL* producer Lorne Michaels. It didn't take long for Michaels to respond by scheduling White as the host for their Mother's Day episode.

Though the audience has always possessed the ability to pressure media producers to adapt to their desires, never before has their ability to do so been so readily accomplished. Audiences are now more capable of taking on an active role in shaping media content intended for their consumption. While media production has hardly become democratic, the Betty White for *SNL* movement illustrates the changing role of the audience in relation to media production industries.

Sources: *Radio Business Report/Television Business Report*, "Betty White Takes Over 'Saturday Night Live'," March 13, 2010. http://www.rbr.com/tv-cable/tv-programming/22303.html (accessed March 26, 2010); "Betty White to Host SNL (please?)!" Facebook.com. http://www.facebook.com/pages/Betty-White-to-Host-SNL-please/266442514828 (accessed March 26, 2010); Gary Levin, "Yes Betty White will host 'SNL'," *USA Today*, March 11, 2010, Life, p. 1D.

Black Entertainment Television (BET) provides an example. In the 1990s, BET executives were aware that African-Americans tend to watch television substantially more than other Americans. They also learned that African-Americans accounted for about 20 percent of the audience for HBO, the major cable movie channel supported by monthly subscriber fees. African-Americans' presence in that audience was more than 7 percentage points higher than their presence in the general population. These figures were among the data that led BET to embark upon a new pay-cable service aimed specifically at the African-American audience.

MEASURING THE CONTENT'S SUCCESS WITH THE TARGET AUDIENCE   You might think that the degree to which mass media content will find success with its audience would become clear when the material is created and released. This all depends, however, on the mass medium and the exact questions being asked. At its simplest, measuring success may involve counting the sales—how many magazines or movie tickets were sold. In cases in which sales are not involved, such as with radio, broadcast television, and the Web, ratings companies conduct regular surveys to count audiences to help executives determine how many people watched particular programs. As we will see later in the text, however, neither counting sales nor conducting ratings surveys is really a simple activity.

Nevertheless, counting sales and audiences is a lot easier than determining *why* a media product succeeded or failed. Executives often try to find out what went wrong—or what went right—so that they can avoid future mistakes and/or repeat past successes. That sometimes involves conducting focus groups or surveys to gauge the intended audience's opinions. Often, though, executives discuss their failures and successes with one another.

Baldwin Hills is a reality television show on the BET channel featuring wealthy African-American teenagers.

They try to figure out which elements led to success and which led to failure. This is not at all "scientific," but it's often the best that people whose business it is to select or create mass media content can do.

Determining a Genre for Mass Media Content

When media practitioners try to determine how to choose or produce content that is appropriate for the audiences they want to reach, they must do so with an understanding of the major categories of content from which they can build their material. Major categories of media content are called **genres**—categories of artistic composition, as in music or literature, marked by a distinctive style, form, or content.[2] The primary genres that media practitioners discuss are entertainment, news, information, education, and advertising. Let's first take a look at each.

genres major categories of media content

Entertainment

The word **entertainment** derives from the Latin *tenere*, which means "to hold or keep steady, busy, or amused." The notion of making money by keeping an audience steady, busy, or amused remains central to those in the business of entertainment. Media practitioners, then, define entertainment as material that grabs the audience's attention and leaves agreeable feelings, as opposed to challenging their views of themselves and the world. However, this doesn't mean that people who work in the entertainment business always stay away from informing or persuading. Many movies that are categorized under "entertainment" by their production firms have been written and produced with the intention of making a political point (think of *2012*, *Religulous*, or *W*) or an educational point (like *Schindler's List*, *Invictus*, or *Letters from Iwo Jima*). When media practitioners label a product as "entertainment," though, they are signaling to their audiences that their primary concern should be with enjoyment, not with any other messages that may be included.

entertainment material that grabs the audience's attention and leaves agreeable feelings, as opposed to challenging their views of themselves and the world

SUBGENRES OF ENTERTAINMENT One way to understand entertainment is to see it as consisting of four **subgenres**—festivals, gaming, drama, and comedy. We can see each of these subgenres, in turn, as having still more subcategories nested

subgenres subcategories of media content genres

within it. Consider, for example, the subgenre gaming, which may include sports (*Monday Night NFL Football*), quiz shows (*Deal or No Deal*), and newspaper crossword puzzles, among other forms. Similarly, the subgenre comedy may include situation comedies (*Two and a Half Men*), stand-up comedy routines (*Dane Cook*) and their ancillary products (Cook's CD/DVD *Isolated Incident*), certain radio talk shows (*The Howard Stern Show*), and joke lists (Michael Kilgarriff's *1000 Knock-Knock Jokes for Kids*), among other forms. We can even go further and think of a more specific level—subgenres of these subgenres. We can break situation comedies into school sit-coms (*Glee*), workplace sitcoms (*The Office*), family sitcoms (*Family Guy*), and buddy sitcoms (*Men of a Certain Age*). In turn, people who are specialists in sitcoms might be able to create still further subgenres of these categories. Workplace sitcoms might be divided into hospital sitcoms (*Scrubs*) and office sitcoms (*The Office, 30 Rock*). Take a look at Figure 2.4 for an illustration of these relationships.

ENTERTAINMENT FORMULAS   You may have noticed that there are key elements that make up various subgenres: the family situation comedy, the hospital drama, the baseball broadcast, or any other subgenre. This specific combination of elements is called a **formula**—a patterned approach to creating content that is characterized by three major features:

formula a patterned approach to creating content that is characterized by the use of setting, typical characters, and patterns of action

■ Setting
■ Typical characters
■ Patterns of action[3]

setting the environment in which content takes place

The **setting** is the environment in which content takes place. A football program such as *Monday Night NFL Football* takes place in a stadium and in an announcer's booth. A doctor show such as *Grey's Anatomy* takes place in a hospital.

typical characters those who appear regularly in the subgenre

The **typical characters** are those who appear regularly in the subgenre. In the football program, the announcers, the athletes, the referees, and the coaches are typical characters. Doctor shows such as *Grey's Anatomy* are populated by (you guessed it) doctors, patients, nurses, and medical technicians.

patterns of action the predictable activities associated with the characters in the settings

The **patterns of action** are the predictable activities associated with the characters in the settings. The football program's patterns of action center on the rules of the game, which are bounded by the clock (sixty minutes plus time-outs and half-time) and the field (the playing zones). The patterns of action in doctor shows aren't as clearly based on rules. Nevertheless, each episode does have its plot patterns, revolving around issues of life and death.

When it comes to reality shows, you can probably suggest different forms of the subgenre depending on whether you are discussing *Amazing Race, Dancing with the Stars*, or *Survivor*. *Survivor* might be called an "isolation" reality show subgenre, along with such series as *The Apprentice, The Biggest Loser*, and *Project Runway*. They contain similar formula elements:

■ Setting: a location that isolates a group with minimal interference from the "outside" world
■ Typical characters: good-looking individuals of diverse ethnic backgrounds who have certain expected character profiles—selfish or generous, gregarious or loner, crafty or naïve
■ Patterns of action: challenges that the producers set up that often set members of the group against one another and lead to individuals being chosen to leave

Keep in mind, too, that formulas can and do change. Media practitioners who use these formulas to create stories for movies, television, video games, or other media

Genre	ENTERTAINMENT			
Subgenre	**Festival**	**Drama**	**Gaming**	**Comedy**
Second-level subgenre	Parades	Workplace	Sports	Situation comedy
Third-level subgenre	Secular parades	Dramas about professionals	Professional sports	Work-based sitcoms
Fourth-level subgenre	Nonrecurring secular parades	Hospital dramas	NFL football	Hospital-based sitcoms

are often steeped in their history. Writers and producers in all mass media often "borrow" plot elements, characters, and settings from previously successful stories. Their hope is that the basic elements of the formula will stay popular and that they can reshape these elements to fit what they believe are the interests of contemporary audiences.

Examples are all around us, but you have to know something about the history of a mass medium to notice them. Perhaps you've seen the remakes of classic horror movies that appeared in movie theaters over the past few years—for example, *Friday the 13th* (2009), *The Echo* (a 2009 remake of the Philippine film *Sigaw*), *The Wolfman* (2009), and *Halloween* (2007). If you go back to the originals, you will see how the writers borrowed settings, characters, and plot elements from the originals and then changed them to fit their idea of what audiences of the 2000s would like. Watching TV, going to the movies, reading novels, and even playing video games will take on a whole new dimension.

Apart from updating genres, writers and producers are also eager to find new ways to mix entertainment subgenres to entertain their target audiences. The term **hybrid genres** can be used to describe mixed genres; the process of mixing genres within a culture and across cultures is called **hybridity**. Hybrid genres are all around us. Consider, for example, the music of T-Pain, which consciously blends rhythm and blues influences with sounds and sensibilities of rap. Hybridity can also take place across cultures. Think of attempts by U.S. producers and writers to mix plots, settings, and characters of Indian "Bollywood" films with traditional Hollywood plots, characters and settings. For example, *Bride and Prejudice* is a 2004 movie that inserts an Indian family into the basic plot of the Jane Austen novel *Pride and Prejudice* and follows them through Indian, U.K., and U.S. locales. The advertising tagline for the movie, which was filmed in India, the United Kingdom, and the United States, trumpeted this hybridity: "Bollywood meets Hollywood . . . and it's the perfect match."[4]

Beyond combining specific entertainment subgenres, some producers and writers try to get people's attention by blending the rules associated with drama (serious) and comedy (funny) into what some media practitioners call a **dramedy**. Dramadies have shown up fairly frequently on U.S. television in recent years. Think of *Desperate Housewives*, *Psych*, *Monk*, *Ugly Betty*, and *Californication*. These programs don't have laugh tracks, and they can veer from an hilariously funny scene to one that tugs strongly at viewers' heartstrings. *New York Daily News* TV critic David Hinckley zeroed in on that quality in *Monk* when commenting on the series' final episode. The closing drama brings Adrian Monk (Tony Shalhoub) back to the show's original launching point: the unsolved murder of his wife, Trudy. As Hinckley noted,

Figure 2.4 Entertainment Genres and Subgenres
Here, entertainment is divided into subgenres of festival, gaming, drama, and comedy. One subgenre under each is extended two levels to illustrate how these categories contain subcategories. You might be able to break these down into even more specific categories. For example, people who write hospital-based sitcoms might be able to describe various subgenres of these sitcoms.

hybrid genres a term used by some academic writers to describe mixed genres

hybridity the process of mixing genres within a culture and across cultures

dramedy a subgenre that blends the rules associated with drama (serious) and comedy (funny)

"Last week on 'Top Surgeon' Erica won immunity, while Carl was sent home for killing his patient during routine gallbladder surgery."

Trudy's death gave the show a bed of tragedy and Monk a terrible sadness that passing seasons did not diminish. It also left him with a nightmare of phobias, quirks and general obsessive compulsion. He was afraid of germs, of closed areas, of pretty much anything involving people. But the show's genius, and Shalhoub's, was that all this somehow honed his skills. He solved case after case even as he couldn't crack the one he most cared about.

The finale carried these features to a conclusion that combined formula-driven TV with a wonderful understanding of the program's characters. Hinckley wrote that "it's so well-written and so true to the wonderfully tragicomic tone of the whole show that you won't even mind the fact that the actual plot wrapup is pretty formulaic."[5]

News

News, like entertainment, involves the telling of stories. We often don't think of news in this way, but it is useful to pause and consider this point. When you watch the *CBS Evening News,* in one sense news anchor Katie Couric is telling you a tale with a beginning, a middle, and an end. Of course, Couric reads most of the story and shows short video clips of the accompanying action, whereas other storytelling media genres (such as a sitcom) continuously illustrate the story through acting. The tales that Katie Couric tells during her newscast, however, may not be that different from the sitcom you will be viewing just two hours later on the same network. In fact, many of the ideas for non-news television programming are generated from news. NBC's *Law & Order,* in fact, used to boast that its plots are "ripped from the headlines." The program's ads stopped saying that out of the producers' fear they might be sued for libel by the people whose news stories they adapted. Nevertheless, even casual viewers of *Law & Order* and its spinoff *Law & Order: SVU* would notice that the program draws on news stories.

journalist an individual who is trained to report nonfiction events to an audience

Reporters, directors, editors, producers, and other people who work in the news business are called **journalists**. A journalist is someone who is trained to report nonfiction events to an audience. Their reporting can be in print (newspapers, magazines) or electronic media (radio, TV, the Web). Historically, newspapers have been central to the circulation of news in America. But as we'll see in later chapters, big changes are taking place that are eroding the presence and power of newspapers in people's lives. Today's journalists are learning that they must present news in many media, including audio and video reports on the Web.

SUBGENRES OF NEWS   How would these people explain the difference between what they produce and other storytelling genres, such as entertainment? They would undoubtedly argue that there is one clear distinction: news stories are constrained by facts, whereas entertainment stories are not. The writer of the screenplay for a TV show that is "based on a true story" or "ripped from the headlines" can decide whether a character who is accused of rape is guilty or innocent. The reporter of the real-life news event, however, should never make such a judgment. Building on this basic distinction, news workers divide news broadly into four subgenres:

■ Hard news
■ Investigative reports

- Editorials
- Soft news

Hard News

Hard news is what most people probably think of as news. It is the first-hand report-age of a battle, the coverage of a congressional bill's passage, the details of a forest fire. News workers use four guidelines when they try to decide what is and what isn't hard news. An event that fits only one of these guidelines will probably not be considered hard news. Additionally, the more of these guidelines that apply to an event, the more likely news workers are to cover it.

- *Timeliness* A hard news event must have happened recently—typically within the past day or so. A murder that happened yesterday might deserve coverage. A murder that happened last year would not, unless new information about it has been released or discovered.
- *Unusualness* Hard news events are those that most people would consider unu-sual. To use the classic example, "Dog Bites Man" is not news, whereas "Man Bites Dog" is.
- *Conflict* Conflicts—struggles between opposing forces—often lie at the center of hard news stories. Often these struggles are physical; they can be wars or bar-room brawls. Sometimes the conflicts involve wars of words, as between members of Congress. Other times they pit humans against nature (a fire or other natural disaster).
- *The closeness of the incident* An event is more likely to be seen as hard news if it happens close by than if it takes place far away. Note, however, that closeness carries two meanings: it can mean geographically close (physically near to the audience), or it can mean psychologically close. An incident is psychologically close when members of the audience feel a connection to it even though it takes place far away. Because of Boston's large Irish population, for example, newspaper editors in Boston may consider certain happenings in Ireland to be hard news, whereas editors in areas of the United States with small Irish populations would not cover those events.

Once they have decided that something is hard news, news workers must decide how to present it. Journalists use the word **objectivity** to summarize the way in which news ought to be researched, organized, and presented. Most journalists would agree that it is impossible to present a *totally* objective view of an event, if that means a view which is the absolute truth with no personal viewpoints inserted. The fact is that no two people will see the same thing in exactly the same way. Most jour-nalists would say that what they mean by an objective report is a report that presents a fair, balanced, and impartial representation of the events that took place.

Over the decades, journalists have agreed upon certain characteristics that an objective story will have. These characteristics give a reporter the tools to describe an incident efficiently in ways that his or her editor (or any other editor) will consider fair and impartial. Here are four major characteristics of an objective story, particu-larly with regard to print news:

- It should be written in a form that journalists call an inverted pyramid. This means that the reporter should place in the first paragraph (the lead paragraph) a concise recounting of the entire story. Typically that means "leading" with the six Ws—who did it, what they did, to whom (or with whom), where they did it, when they did it, and why (see Figure 2.5). This is the most general statement of the story—the base of the pyramid. In the paragraphs that follow, the reporter

hard news a news story marked by timeliness, unusualness, conflict, and closeness

objectivity presenting a fair, balanced, and impartial representation of the events that took place by recounting a news event based on the facts and without interpretation, so that anyone else who witnessed the event would agree with the journalists' recounting of it; the way in which news ought to be researched, organized, and presented should give increasingly specific information about the material in the lead paragraph. (The ever more specific information supposedly corresponds to the increasingly narrow pyramid.)

■ An objective story should be told in the third person. That means writing as if the journalist is a novelist telling the tale but is not involved in it. So, for example, an objective report of a riot can state, "The crowd ran wildly around the square breaking store windows." It would not be objective for the reporter to write, "I saw the crowd run wildly around the square breaking windows."

■ An objective story should report at least two sides of a conflict. If a politician is accused of corruption, the objective report must also note the politician's denial of the charges.

■ An objective story uses quotes from those involved or from experts on the topic to back up statements.

These characteristics can be used in creating objective news stories for any medium. If you watch television news programs carefully, however, you may note that reporters also convey the idea of objectivity in a visual way. Here are three camera rules for an objective story:

■ There should be a title on the screen telling the viewer who the reporter is interviewing.

■ The camera should film the reporter or a person being interviewed from the height of a normal person, not from the ground staring up at the person or from above the person staring down.

■ The camera should give as much time to a person representing one side of the conflict as it does to a person representing the other side. Anything less would be considered biased.

accuracy reporting factually correct information

In addition to being objective, hard news reports are also held to strict standards of accuracy. **Accuracy** means reporting factually correct information. Many news organizations expect their reporters to check "facts" with at least two sources before they use them in stories, and many news-oriented magazines employ fact checkers who review stories for accuracy before they are released to the public.

Investigative Reports

investigative reports in-depth explorations of some aspects of reality

Investigative reports are in-depth explorations of some aspects of reality. This news subgenre shares the same standards of objectivity, accuracy, and fairness or balance with hard news. However, a major difference between hard news and investigative

Figure 2.5 The Inverted Pyramid
The inverted pyramid approach to reporting the news begins with the most general statement of the story and grows increasingly more specific.

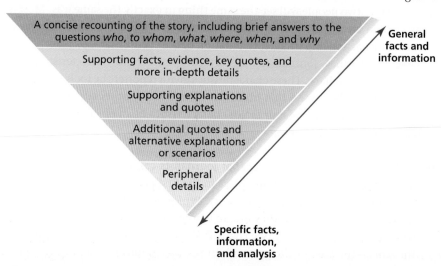

A concise recounting of the story, including brief answers to the questions *who, to whom, what, where, when,* and *why*

Supporting facts, evidence, key quotes, and more in-depth details

Supporting explanations and quotes

Additional quotes and alternative explanations or scenarios

Peripheral details

General facts and information

Specific facts, information, and analysis

reports is the amount of time journalists can devote to the project. When it comes to hard news, journalists typically work on tight schedules; their time limit (**deadline**) for the completion of an assignment is often only a few hours after they begin it. In contrast, journalists who work on investigative reports have quite a bit more time to do their research, interview their sources, and write their script. Their deadlines can be days or weeks from the time they begin, or even longer.

Investigative reporters often seek to uncover corruption or other problems in government or business, and the tone of the report resembles that of a detective story. A few television news series, such as *60 Minutes*, *Dateline NBC*, and *20/20*, present this type of material.

60 Minutes is a television news series that specializes in investigative reports. Here, Katie Couric traveled to Afghanistan with Secretary of Defense, Robert Gates.

Editorials

Opinions regarding hard news are usually reserved for editorials. Unlike hard news and investigative reports, an **editorial** is a subgenre of news that expresses an individual's or an organization's point of view. Some editorials are written in the name of (and express the point of view of) the person who wrote the piece, whereas others are written in the name of the entire news organization—for example, the newspaper that printed the piece or the television station that aired it.

News organizations may also allow their reporters and knowledgeable people who do not work for their firm to present editorial comments. **Columnists** are individuals who are paid to write editorials on a regular basis—usually weekly, monthly, or daily. Editorials by the most famous columnists, such as Dave Barry, Peggy Noonan, and Anna Quindlen, are carried by many news outlets across the United States and even around the world. On the Web, columnists may show up within journalistic websites (such as http://www.cnn.com or http://www.slate.com) or on **blogs**, online sites written in the style of journal entries, often in reverse chronological order. A well-known example is the Huffington Post group of political opinion blogs. They include regular columns by Arianna Huffington, humorist Harry Shearer, and Congressman John Conyers, as well as opinion pieces from invited celebrities such as actor John Cusack and political comedian Bill Maher.

Soft News

Whereas news workers generally consider hard news reporting a place for objective, accurate, and balanced reporting with little (if any) editorial commentary, they consider another news category, **soft news**, to be an area in which the reporter's opinions and biases can show through. As you may be able to tell by its name, soft news (also known as the human interest story) is the kind of story that news workers feel may not have the critical importance of hard news, but nevertheless would appeal to a substantial number of people in the audience. Cooking spots, articles on the best ways to shovel snow without injuring your back, video clips highlighting

editorial a subgenre of news that concentrates on an individual's or organization's point of view

columnist an individual who is paid to write editorials on a regular basis—usually daily, weekly, or monthly

blogs journalistic websites or opinion sites in which writings are in the style of journal entries, often in reverse chronological order

soft news the kind of news story that news workers feel may not have the critical importance of hard news, but nevertheless would appeal to a substantial number of people in the audience

local students in community plays or recitals—these are topics that news workers consider soft rather than hard news.

Information

information the raw material that journalists use when they create news stories

One way to understand the difference between news and information—a difficult distinction to draw for some—is to say that **information** is the raw material that journalists use when they create news stories. On the most basic level, a piece of information is a fact, an item that reveals something about the world. Generally, we must bring together many pieces of information in order to draw conclusions about a person, place, thing, or incident.

All of us use pieces of information as tools in our personal and professional lives. Students gather information as part of paper-writing assignments. Accountants bring together the facts of a client's expenses and wages to fill out the client's tax return. Professors compile information to prepare (it is hoped interesting) lectures. Similarly, journalists often stitch together facts when they create a news story.

Sometimes searching for relevant facts means speaking to individuals (as reporters might), looking at old bills (as accountants might), or reading scholarly books (as professors might). Often, however, people find the information they want in special collections of facts called databases. Journalists search motor vehicle records, collections of trial transcripts, gatherings of old newspaper articles, and city real-estate files. Students, too, use databases: computerized and manual library catalogs are databases; so are dictionaries, LexisNexis, Factiva, and the *Reader's Guide to Periodical Literature*.

Information is a widely used and lucrative mass media commodity—bringing together facts and packaging them in a multitude of ways. A trip to any library's reference collection reveals an extensive array of categorized facts on an enormous number of subjects that are waiting to be used for papers, dissertations, books, or just to settle arguments.

But although a major library's collection of databases may appear quite impressive, it is merely the tip of a huge iceberg of information that mass media firms collect and offer for sale. The information industry creates and distributes much of its product for companies, not individual consumers.

www.huffingtonpost.com. The Huffington Post is a popular political-opinion blog.

INFORMATION GATHERING AND DISTRIBUTING One major segment of the information industry aims to help businesses find, evaluate, and understand their current customers. For example, Trans Union Credit Information Company and Equifax hold collections of information about the income and debts of hundreds of millions of people worldwide. These firms are in the business of selling selected segments of that information to banks, insurance companies, and other organizations that are interested in the creditworthiness of particular individuals.

Information activities affect you directly when you are approved (or turned down) for a loan or a credit card. This part of the information business also provides lists of names to the marketers who send you postal mail or email—or phone you (often in the middle of dinner) with "great" offers. Catalog companies, too, often rely on information companies to help them find new customers.

INFORMATION RESEARCH AND RETRIEVAL   Another major segment of the information industry focuses on providing quick retrieval of data for people whose work requires them to get facts quickly. Consider the services provided by LexisNexis, for example. The Nexis information service, owned by publishing giant Reed Elsevier of the Netherlands, enables journalists, professors, students—in fact, researchers of all kinds—to search for and retrieve virtually any fact in more than 2.5 billion searchable documents. Lexis, a sister service, enables attorneys and paralegals to find, analyze, and validate information from countless legal documents by keywords via computer networks. For example, through Lexis' database, legal professionals can retrieve background information on public and private companies, find information about individuals, identify an organization's assets, and research judges, expert witnesses, and opposing counsel, among other things.

The subscription for services such as those offered by Reed Elsevier, News Corporation (for example, Factiva), and other similar firms in the information business can be costly. Information industry executives tie their high prices to the expense of collecting the data, trying to ensure their accuracy, storing them and protecting them from hackers, preparing print or computer retrieval methods, and distributing the data to clients. But the high price of information is also based on the realization that certain types of information can be extremely valuable, allowing companies to make (or save) millions of dollars. Quick access to the right information helps businesses and governments go about their work efficiently.

Education

When it comes to genres of media, **education** means content that is purposefully crafted to teach people specific ideas about the world in specific ways. Education is a large segment of the media marketplace. In fact, spending for "instructional materials" by elementary and high schools reached $8.2 billion in 2008.[6] Spending on instructional materials for traditional private and state colleges hit $9.2 billion.[7] Much of this money was spent on textbooks, the medium that most of us conjure up when we think of instructional materials for schools.

But the genre of education extends far beyond textbooks and other types of printed materials. Consider for a moment the wide variety of media that you've encountered in your long trek through school. Textbooks, workbooks, course packs, wall maps, flash cards, software, and online services—these and more account for the almost $10 billion of spending in the educational media marketplace.

In addition, there is a vast amount of educational media material that is produced primarily for home use. When you were a child, your parents might have set you in front of the TV to view *Sesame Street* or *Reading Rainbow*. Perhaps you watched *Bill Nye, the Science Guy*, or *Where in the World is Carmen San Diego?* when you got a bit older. Maybe your parents gave you the *Math Blaster*, *Fraction Fever*, *LeapFrog*, or *Jump-Start* computer programs for a birthday present. These are just a few of the products that media companies have explicitly designed to teach basic skills.

education content that is purposefully crafted to teach people specific ideas about the world in specific ways

Advertisements

advertisement a message
that explicitly aims to direct
favorable attention to certain
goods and services

An **advertisement** is a message that explicitly aims to direct favorable attention to certain goods and services. The message may have a commercial purpose or be aimed at advancing a noncommercial cause, such as the election of a political candidate or the promotion of a fundraising event.

As we will see in Chapter 15, advertising involves far more than explicit messages. People who work in the advertising industry help their clients with a range of activities from package design to coupon offers. A broad definition of advertising even includes **product placement**, which is the paid insertion of products into TV shows and movies in order to associate those products, often quietly, with certain desirable characters or activities.

product placement the
process by which a
manufacturer pays—often
tens of thousands of dollars
and sometimes far more—a
production company for the
opportunity to have its product
displayed in a movie or TV
show

SUBGENRES OF ADVERTISEMENTS   No matter what the medium, advertising practitioners speak about three broad subgenres of advertisements:

■ Informational ads
■ Hard-sell ads
■ Soft-sell ads

Informational Advertisements

informational ads
advertisements that rely
primarily on the recitation of
facts about a product and the
product's features to convince
target consumers that it is
the right product for them to
purchase

Informational ads rely primarily on a recitation of facts about a product and the product's features to convince target consumers that it is the right product for them to purchase. An advertisement in *Stereo Review Magazine* that carefully details the specifications and capabilities of a set of Bose speakers would be informational in nature. Similarly, a television announcement aired during PBS's *This Old House* noting the program's support by Home Depot is another example of an informational ad.

Hard-Sell Advertisements

hard-sell ads messages that
combine information about
the product with intense
attempts to get the consumer to
purchase it as soon as possible

Hard-sell ads are messages that combine information about the product with intense attempts to get the consumer to purchase it as soon as possible. For example, a TV commercial in which a car salesman speaks a-mile-a-minute about the glories of his dealership, shouts about a two-day-only sale, and recites the address of the dealership four times before the spot ends is a hard-sell ad.

Soft-Sell Advertisements

soft-sell ads advertisements
that aim mostly to create good
feelings about the product or
service by associating it with
desirable music, personalities,
or events that the creators of
that product or service feel
would appeal to the target
audience

Soft-sell ads aim mostly to create good feelings about the product or service by associating it with music, personalities, or events that the creators of that product or service feel would appeal to the target audience. Television commercials for a wide variety of products, including soft drinks, beer, and athletic footwear, are soft-sell ads. Remember the "Got Milk?" ads for milk producers, the "Whassup" commercials for Budweiser, or the "Mac vs. PC" ads for Apple? These are classic examples of ads that aim to create a "hip" feeling about a product that will lead consumers to want to be identified with it.

It is important to note that these three types of ads—informational, hard-sell, and soft-sell—mainly differ in the amount of stress they place on facts about the product, the intensity of the sales pitch, and the emotional connection between the consumer and the product. There are, however, circumstances in which much longer ads are created, and the advertisers can then combine informational, hard-sell, and soft-sell tactics. If you watch TV shopping channels such as HSN, you might see this mix. A hostess may provide a demonstration of a gold necklace that mixes specific information about the necklace ("beautiful 14-karat gold, thirty inches long, with

The ad men of AMC's hit show, *Mad Men*, specialize in soft-sell advertisements.

a sturdy lock, as you can see . . .") and hard-sell encouragement ("these necklaces are going so fast that if you don't call us right now, we might run out of them") with soft-sell tactics that include joking around by people on the set and an attempt to build an entertaining environment for selling.

Mixing Genres

You have probably noticed that soft-sell advertising sometimes shows up as part of entertainment-oriented TV shows. When the Lifetime cable network paraded L'Oreal products as part of the action on *Project Runway*, that was a clear case of mixing genres. Clearly, L'Oreal executives believed that audiences would get a favorable feeling for their stores if they saw their products pop up within a popular entertainment program. As we will discuss in depth in Chapter 15, hybridity involving advertising and entertainment is becoming increasingly common. It is not, however, the only blending of advertising with other genres. Think of a political commercial that runs in a report on the evening news; an informational ad that becomes part of a database for consumers trying to find out about a product; and an elementary school math text that teaches students addition and subtraction by using the names of real products whose companies paid for the inclusion. (Some math textbooks are including real products in the name of realism, though to date no advertiser seems to have paid for inclusion.) A media literate who understands the mixing of genres and the reasons for it will be alert to the practice and know to ask whether it is happening and why.

Of course, advertising is not the only genre that mixes with other genres. Media practitioners who work in the fields of entertainment, information, and education explore the value of hybridity in order to attract and hold audiences. Media practitioners involved in education and advertisements often borrow comedic, dramatic, festival, and gaming elements to attract and hold audiences. Writers for *Sesame Street*, for example, often deliver their educational messages in segments that resemble situation comedies, game shows, and musical variety programs. Think, too, of programs such as *The Daily Show* and *The Colbert Report* on the Comedy Central cable channel, which use the setting and even the character types of news interview programs to create humorous imitations of the styles of those news shows—that is, to create **parodies**—which intend to entertain as well as make serious political points amid the laughter.

parody a work that imitates another work for laughs in a way that comments on the original work in one way or another; a subgenre of entertainment

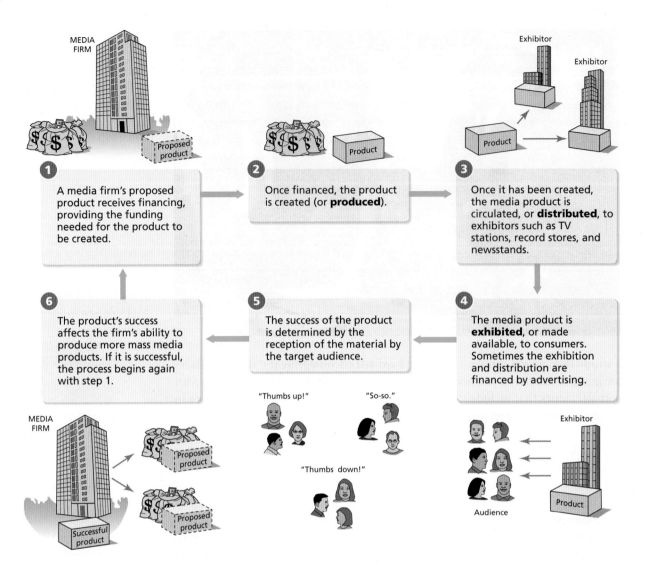

Figure 2.6 The Business of Mass Media
Production, distribution, and exhibition, central to the functions of all media organizations, must first secure financing before they can proceed.

Knowing how to use genres and their formulas to create materials that are popular with carefully targeted audiences is a highly valued skill in mass media industries. But there's a lot more to trying to get a work valued by audiences than just thinking it up. All mass media organizations must also be concerned with six primary business activities:

- Production
- Distribution
- Exhibition
- Audience research
- Finance

As Figure 2.6 shows, production involves creating the content. Distribution involves circulating the material to exhibitors (for example, music stores, TV stations). The exhibitors, in turn, make it available to consumers. Let's examine these steps, which lie at the heart of what goes on in mass media industries, one at a time.

Production of Mass Media Content

production the creation of mass media materials for distribution through one or more mass media vehicles

Production is the beginning of the chain of events that brings mass media content to audiences. **Production** for the mass media means the creation of materials for distribution through one or more mass media vehicles.

Media Production Firms

A **mass media production firm** is a company that creates materials for distribution through one or more mass media vehicles. The Washington Post Company, which publishes *The Washington Post*, is a production company. So is Routledge, the publisher of this book, and its parent company, Informa. So are Time Inc. magazine company (a division of Time Warner), which creates *Time* magazine; Comcast's NBC Universal, which produces *NBC Nightly News*; and http://www.myspace.com (a division of News Corporation), a Web platform for sharing all sorts of print, audio, and audiovisual materials.

WHO DOES THE WORK?   The making of all these media products requires both administrative personnel and creative personnel. **Administrative personnel** make sure the business side of the media organization is humming along. They must thoroughly understand that the media business they are in, and their daily jobs—in, for example, accounting, law, marketing—have much to do with the success of the organizations for which they work. Their work does not, however, relate directly to the creation of their firm's media materials. **Creative personnel** do that. They are the individuals who get initial ideas for the material or use their artistic talent to put the material together.

In all media industries, working on the creative side of a production firm can be done in two ways, on-staff or freelance. An **on-staff worker** has secured a full-time position at a production firm. For example, most, though not all, art directors in advertising agencies are on-staff workers. They work for the same agency all the time; the projects they work on may change, but the company that issues their paycheck remains the same. **Freelancers**, on the other hand, are workers who make a living by accepting and completing assignments for a number of different companies—sometimes several at one time. Most movie actors work as freelancers, for example; when they finish one film, they look for work on another film, which may be made by a different company.

Although freelancing can be highly lucrative for some (we are familiar with the names of well-paid freelance creatives such as the novelist John Grisham or the film actor Tom Cruise), historically freelancing has been a difficult road for many creatives. Even when salaries are high (and they frequently are not), many freelance creatives do not work as often as they would like because of the heavy competition for desirable assignments. Historically, this competition has given tremendous power to the production companies that hire these freelance creatives. Freelancers, from actors, to book editors, to ghost writers, to cinematographers, have reported that production companies have used this power to "borrow" innovative ideas discussed in job interviews, force them to work unusually long hours, and withhold their due credits when the assignment is completed.

To establish a power of their own, many freelance creatives have banded together to create talent guilds. A **talent guild** is a union formed by people who work in a particular craft; consider, for example, the Writers Guild of America, Screen Actors Guild, and Directors Guild of America. These guilds negotiate rules with major production firms in their industries regarding the ways in which freelance creatives will be treated and paid.

The administrative and creative personnel of mass media production firms recognize that the previous successes of individual freelance creators—their positive track records—can help reduce the risk that a project will fail. In an effort to manage their risks, movie companies typically will not allow high-budget movies to be made unless a high-profile actor (such as Matt Damon or Robert Downey, Jr.) signs on.

mass media production firm a company that creates materials for distribution through one or more mass media vehicles

administrative personnel workers who oversee the business side of the media organization

creative personnel individuals who get the initial ideas for the material or use their artistic talents to put the material together

on-staff workers workers who have secured a full-time position at a production firm

freelancers workers who make a living by accepting and completing creative assignments for a number of different companies—sometimes several at one time

talent guild a union formed by people who work in similar crafts to help negotiate rules with major production firms in their industries regarding the ways in which freelance creatives will be treated and paid

CULTURE TODAY
SILICON FREELANCERS

Tales of Hollywood agents busily wheeling and dealing with powerful movie studios for celebrity freelancers such as actors and directors are nothing new to anyone who has even a cursory knowledge of the entertainment industry. But did you know that such power brokers also exist in the computer software industry?

It's common knowledge in high-tech circles that a programmer with the talent to write concise, elegant code quickly and dependably is hard to find. With the proliferation of the internet, software development cycles have quickened so drastically that talented programmers can make a lot more money moving among firms that desperately need their services than by staying in one place.

Many of the industry's most famous products such as Acrobat and the original Apple Macintosh operating system were designed by freelance programmers. They hire agents who act as high-tech power brokers, getting huge rewards for them while bringing the freelancers nearly triple their previous full-time salaries and supplying the companies with top temporary talent.

Software talent brokers act much like Hollywood talent agents for their freelance clients by building relationships over long periods of time with the production companies and code writers. Agents often fill a vital middle role in a fast-paced industry, in which lean and mean firms want immediate results and software writers are famously shy of the nasty haggling that sometimes goes with bagging a six-figure salary.

Similarly, book publishing firms have been known to pay popular writers quite a lot for the rights to their next work. In 2006, various firms agreed to pay $7 million for books to Warren Buffett's ghostwriter, more than $8 million to former U.S. Federal Reserve head Alan Greenspan, and over $10 million to evangelist Joel Osteen. The economic downturn of the late 2000s made it harder for publishers to make these levels of upfront payments. Word in the trade was that book publishers like reality TV hosts because of their high name recognition and built-in following but also because they tend to accept advances in the mid five-figure to low six-figure range, far lower than other celebrities watched by millions every week.[8] Nevertheless, in 2008 the Dutton publishing company agreed to pay "in the millions" for a novel by Anthony Zuiker, creator of TV's highly popular action series, *CSI*, that leads people from the hard-copy book to online motion picture and interactive elements.[9]

HOW DOES PRODUCTION TAKE PLACE?   The personal vision of an actor, novelist, or scholar can sometimes make it to the screen or the page. Inserting such a personal vision into a work is called authorship. Generally, however, production in media industries is a **collaborative activity**, in which many people work together to initiate, create, and polish the end material. The collaborative nature of production holds true for every mass media product, from movies to scholarly books. Some types of production require more creative hands than others. When there are many creators, the "author" of the work may not be a person, but rather a group or company.

collaborative activity an activity in which many people work together to initiate, create, and polish the end material

Compare the production of a scholarly book with that of a typical commercial movie starring a well-known actor (see Figure 2.7). In addition to the writer, a scholarly book requires an acquisitions editor, who finds the author and might help with the initial plan for the work; a few readers (usually other scholars or development editors) who suggest ways in which the writer can improve the book; a copy-editor, who helps with the manuscript's style; and design personnel, who craft the look of the book and perhaps its jacket.

Now consider the film. The well-known actor is chosen by an executive producer or studio head, with the assistance of the actor's business representatives. In addition, the film will need screenwriters to write and rewrite the script; other actors to work with the star; a casting director with assistants to choose the other actors; a set

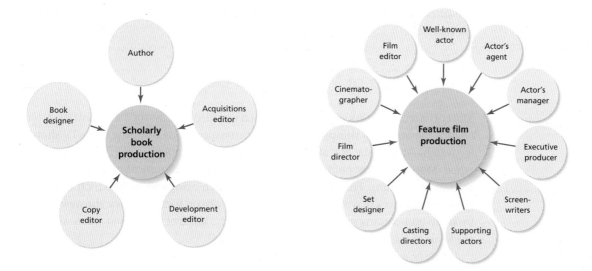

Figure 2.7 Individuals Involved in Two Types of Media Production
The mass media production process is almost exclusively a collaborative process.

designer and assistants to plan the backdrops; a director and assistants to organize the filming; a cinematographer and assistants to photograph the scenes; an editor and assistants to put the scenes together into a finished movie; and many more. Although individual authorship of the scholarly book may be fairly clear, the same cannot be said of the movie. Because so many people are involved on the creative side, it is often very difficult to argue that the final version of a Hollywood film is one person's vision.

We commonly regard the results of production in terms of individual items—a particular movie, book, magazine, TV show. Actually, though, it is possible to find many cases in which what is produced is not an individual item, but rather a stitching together of already-existing products that, taken together, comprise a whole. Take ABC television as an example. ABC creates many, but not all, of the programs that it airs. It leases some programs from other production companies, which grant the network the right to sell time between parts of the shows to advertisers. ABC then sends these shows to TV stations in cities and towns via satellite, and they, in turn, broadcast the shows to the public.

But if you look at ABC's work another way, you will realize that the company could be considered to be heavily involved in TV production even if it didn't actually produce any of its shows. That conclusion comes from seeing production not in terms of individual programs but in terms of the **schedule**, or the pattern in which the programs are arranged. ABC employs programmers who create regular schedules for different parts of the day. The goal of these schedules is to attract viewers to ABC and to keep them watching ABC's shows and commercials for a number of hours. During the late 2000s, for example, ABC fielded a successful Thursday evening schedule (*Grey's Anatomy, Private Practice*) from 8 to 11 p.m. Clearly, the product that ABC programmers were creating was not an individual show but a flow of shows, put together with a particular audience-attracting goal in mind.

In mass media industries, "format" is the term commonly used to describe the rules that guide this flow. A **format** is the patterned choice and arrangement of elements that make up specific media material. The material may be a flow of programs, such as ABC's schedule, or it may be an arrangement of video, audio, or text presentations that people upload to a website, such as MySpace.com, YouTube.com, and Facebook.com. Most radio stations use formats that convey their personalities by combining certain types of songs, disc jockeys' sounds, and jingles that identify the station. The concept of format applies to magazines, too. *Time*'s creative personnel are involved not only in the production of individual articles that appear in the periodical, but also in choosing the topics of the articles to begin with and arranging

schedule the pattern in which media programs are arranged and presented to the audience

format the rules that guide the flow of products that are put together with a particular audience-attracting goal in mind; a formula that describes a particular media product

the articles in a flow that is designed to convey an image and entice readers through the magazine.

Distribution of Mass Media Content

Most of us tend to think of production when we think of mass media industries. After all, it is the output of this production—the newspapers we read, the cable TV shows we watch—that grabs our attention, that makes us happy or angry, interested or bored. Moreover, most public discussion about mass communication tends to center around production. The latest gossip about which actor will be in which film, the angry comments a mayor makes about the violence on local TV news, the newest CD by an up-and-coming music group—these are the kinds of topics that are most often the focus of our attention when we discuss media.

However, media executives and media-literate citizens know that production is only one step in the arduous and risky process of getting a mass media idea to an audience, and that distribution is just as important as production. **Distribution** is the delivery of the produced material to the point where it will be shown to its intended audience; it is an activity that takes place out of public view.

We have already mentioned that ABC acts as a distributor when it disseminates television programming to TV stations via satellite. When Philadelphia Media Holdings delivers its *Philadelphia Inquirer* to city newsstands, when Twentieth Century Fox moves its movies to the Regal Cinema Theaters, and when Sony Music sends its newest releases to http://www.apple.com to be sold over the iTunes website, they are each involved in distribution to exhibitors.

Note that these firms—Philadelphia Media Holdings, Twentieth Century Fox, and Sony Music—use their own distribution divisions rather than rely on other independent distribution firms to do the job. This background ought to underscore for you the importance of successful distribution in the world of media business. Some executives argue that while "content is king," distribution ought to share the crown. The reason is simple: without a distributor, a production firm's media product would literally go nowhere. It would stack up in the warehouse or on a computer, eventually to be destroyed. To get a feel for the power in distribution, consider that you could "publish" a book quite easily. That is, you could take any work of art you've created— some doodles, a love poem, notes to this book—and get it photocopied and bound at the nearest photocopy store, like Kinko's. Say you splurge and print five hundred copies. For a bit more money than you'd spend in the copy shop, you could put a fancy binding on the product, so that it would look like a "real" book.

Of course, now that you have printed the book, the trick is to sell it. You might try to get the university bookstore to carry it, but chances are the store won't. Borders or Barnes & Noble Booksellers probably won't touch your book with a ten-foot pole. It's likely, in fact, that no legitimate bookstore will carry it. This is not necessarily because your writing is bad; your book might actually be a true work of art. The real reason that your chances of getting your book into a bookstore are so poor is that your book does not have a powerful book distributor behind it. If, however, you could persuade a major publishing company to allow its distribution sales force to pitch your book to bookstores, especially large chain bookstores, you might have a pretty good chance to get your book on to bookstore shelves.

Production, then, is useless without distribution. Without a powerful distributor, the material that a production firm's executives believe could be tremendously successful will have much less chance of achieving its potential. Some people believe that the internet reduces the importance of distribution, because just about anyone can post—that is, distribute—just about anything online for very little cost. But

distribution the delivery of the produced material to the point where it will be shown to its intended audience

putting something on a personal website or even on a backwater page of a popular exhibition site such as MySpace or YouTube does not ensure that anyone but your friends will go to it. Perhaps you will get lucky, and the clip you posted to YouTube will become a popular "viral video" viewed by millions. In most cases, however, the key is to have the clout to place the content in a position where many people have a good chance of seeing it. That means getting the attention of a powerful distributor.

What makes a **powerful distributor**? Simply put, a distributor's power is measured in terms of the firm's ability to ensure that the media products it carries will end up in the best locations of the best exhibitors to the best audience. To understand what that means, we have to look at exhibition.

the power of a distributor the firm's ability to ensure that the media products it carries will end up in the best locations at the best exhibitors to the best audience

Exhibition of Mass Media Content

The exhibition of mass media material is closely linked to the distribution in the sense that both are steps in bringing the content to the audience. Sometimes the same company carries out both activities. Because exhibition is quite a different business from distribution, though, it often involves different firms.

Exhibition is the activity of presenting mass media materials to audiences for viewing or purchase. When media executives speak about the importance of exhibition, they often mention shelf space. **Shelf space** is the amount of area or time available for presenting products to consumers. Think of video stores with their long rows of shelves and racks. As large as typical chain stores are today, production firms want to rent and sell more types of DVDs than will fit in the racks of even the biggest stores. As a result, store executives must decide which categories of products, and which company's products within those categories, are carried and which get more room than others.

Consequently, video distributor firms that rely on stores to present their products to consumers must compete furiously for shelf space. The distributors that wield the most power are those with products that the stores need to have because consumers demand them. These distributors will have more ability to negotiate shelf space for new products than will distributors of goods that are not so important to the stores.

The same is true elsewhere in the media business. Magazine and book producers must compete for shelf space in bookstores, on newsstands, and in supermarket aisles. Moreover, some spots in stores and on newsstands are more valuable than others. The area toward the front of a bookstore is most valuable because all customers pass through it. Racks on a newsstand that are at eye level are more valuable than those at floor level because consumers are likely to look at the racks at eye level first.

For cable TV, movies, broadcast TV, radio, the Web, mobile phones, and other media, the concept of shelf space has to be stretched just a bit, but it applies just the same. Executives think of the limited number of channels of a cable system as its shelves. Similarly, some broadcast television executives see the twenty-four hours in a day as their stations' shelves, because time limits what they can air. In cable, radio, and broadcast TV, certain time slots and channels (or stations) are more valuable than others. The same goes for high-traffic pages on websites such as http://www.auto.com and space on the starting areas (the "decks") of cellphones that provide a limited selection of links to areas of the Web. These are the more prominent positions in the electronic "store."

Now imagine a particular case: feel the tension that Marisol Durán, a salesperson for a newly formed independent book distribution firm, experiences as she waits to speak to a purchasing executive at a large bookstore chain such as Barnes & Noble. Marisol represents small publishing firms specializing in science fiction. Because of their small size, these firms don't have the money to hire their own salespeople. She

exhibition the activity of presenting mass media materials to audiences for viewing or purchase

shelf space the amount of area or time available for presenting products to consumers

knows that Barnes & Noble's shelves hold many books, but she also knows that the number of books published each year alone would take up far more space than those shelves can hold. She has been successful in placing many of the titles she carries in bookstores that specialize in the science fiction genre. She has ambitions beyond these small stores, however. A chance to catch the eyes of science fiction readers who shop at Barnes & Noble or at Borders would, she believes, surely result in a strong increase in sales.

She knows, however, that she would get a better hearing at Barnes & Noble—and would place more books there—if she worked for the distribution arm of a publishing house such as Random House or Simon & Schuster, two giants of the book business. One reason is that such publishing giants can afford to advertise and promote their titles to the public better than her struggling publishers can, and such publicity can strongly affect sales.

The large publishers may also be better able than smaller ones to offer **trade incentives**—payments in cash, discounts, or publicity activities that provide a special reason for an exhibitor to highlight a product—that could influence large stores like Barnes & Noble to carry their books. To make sure that a bookstore chain exhibits key titles at the entrances to its stores, for example, a publisher might have to offer—through its distributor—to pay the bookstore chain a sum of money for taking up that space. Bringing the author in for special book readings and book signings and helping to pay for ads in newspapers (a practice called **cooperative advertising**) might also be part of the deal.

As this hypothetical experience suggests, linking up with a powerful distributor is of great benefit to producers in every mass media industry. Not surprisingly, the major production companies either own or are otherwise strategically linked to the major distribution organizations. In these cases, it is important to keep in mind that power over production and distribution is self-reinforcing: creative personnel with strong track records are attracted to the production firm in part because it has powerful distribution; in turn, the company has powerful distribution in part because its production arm attracts creative personnel with strong track records.

In some industries, major firms consolidate their strength by owning not only the distribution organizations, but the major exhibition firms as well. Television networks like NBC, CBS, and ABC, for example, have production divisions that create fiction, sports, and news programs. They also own broadcast TV networks that distribute their programs and broadcast stations in key cities that exhibit them. This control of the entire process from production through distribution to exhibition is called **vertical integration**, and it represents yet another way in which media companies try to reduce the risk that their target audiences won't even have an opportunity to choose the material that competitors create (see Figure 2.8).

Financing Mass Media Content

As you can probably guess, the production, distribution, and exhibition of mass media materials requires a lot of money. Starting a publishing company, even a very small one, costs hundreds of thousands of dollars. Creating a one-hour television program costs more than a million dollars. Starting a new magazine can cost even more. Want to buy a radio station? Despite the recent slowdown of growth in radio advertising, stations still go for tens, even hundreds, of millions of dollars.

The cash coming into a mass media firm can be divided into two categories:

trade incentives payments in cash, discounts, or publicity activities that provide a special reason for an exhibitor to highlight a product

cooperative advertising advertising paid for in part by media production firms or their distributors in order to help the exhibitor promote the product

vertical integration an organization's control over a media product from production through distribution to exhibition

■ Money to fund new production

■ Money to pay for already completed products

We'll explore each in detail.

Funding New Production

Executives in mass media enterprises may need to raise funds to expand into new areas, or they may want to build up areas in which they are already operating. A movie exhibition chain may want to expand by building new theaters in Europe. A publishing firm might want to start a new unit to create oversized coffee-table books. A company might want to buy an AM radio station. In such cases, executives may not want or be able to use the company's current revenues to cover the costs of the new venture.

A company generally has two ways to get money in anticipation of production: it can take out loans and/or it can encourage investments in the company.

TAKING OUT LOANS   A **loan** is money that is borrowed from an organization, usually a bank, for a certain price (a percentage of the loan called an interest rate). To get a loan, executives must persuade the lending organization that their plans will realistically bring in the cash they expect so that the firm will be able to repay the amount of the loan (its principal) plus the interest in a timely way. The lender will also want to be sure that it has a claim on some of the current value (assets) of the firm—for example, the real estate of an exhibition chain or the current holdings of a radio station owner—in case the firm does not pay back the loan.

Investment banks are companies that arrange to lend millions, even tens and hundreds of millions, of dollars to companies, and also arrange stock offerings. Some investment banks specialize in particular industries, and the executives of these investment banks feel that they understand quite well the risks involved. Large investment banks hire experts in particular industries to guide the banks' lending activities in their areas of expertise. These investment bankers assess the firms that want loans and put together the terms of agreement. When very large amounts of money are involved, the investment banker will organize a **syndicate**, a group of banks that agree to share the risks and rewards of the lending deal. Because it takes

loan money borrowed from a company, usually a bank, for a certain price (a percentage of the loan called an interest rate)

investment banks companies that arrange to lend millions, even tens and hundreds of millions, of dollars to companies, and also arrange stock offerings

syndicate a group of banks that agree to share the risks and rewards of a lending deal, organized by investment banks when very large amounts of money are required

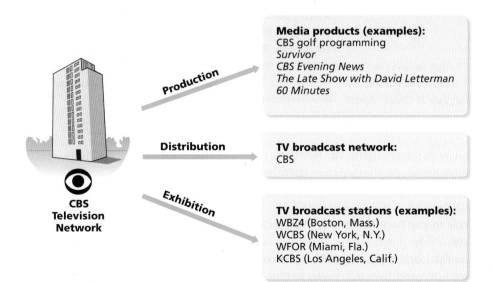

CBS Television Network

Production → **Media products (examples):**
CBS golf programming
Survivor
CBS Evening News
The Late Show with David Letterman
60 Minutes

Distribution → **TV broadcast network:**
CBS

Exhibition → **TV broadcast stations (examples):**
WBZ4 (Boston, Mass.)
WCBS (New York, N.Y.)
WFOR (Miami, Fla.)
KCBS (Los Angeles, Calif.)

Figure 2.8 Vertical Integration
CBS—which owns production divisions, distribution channels, and exhibition venues—is a successful example of vertical integration.

CULTURE TODAY
NETWORK DEMANDS

The conflict over *The Tonight Show* and a spinoff illustrates just how many demands a television network must juggle when producing and distributing television programming: ratings, advertisers, talent, local stations (the exhibitors), and, of course, the bottom line. It also shows just what happens when all these demands collide.

Established in 1954, *The Tonight Show* has become a long-standing tradition of NBC programming, airing weekday nights around 11:30 p.m. After venerable host Johnny Carson stepped down in 1992, Jay Leno took over as host. Despite solid ratings, in 2004 NBC asked Leno to step down as host of *The Tonight Show* five years down the line so that the increasingly popular Conan O'Brien, host of *The Late Night Show* immediately following Leno, could become the new host. Come 2009, however, NBC was reluctant to lose the ratings Leno brought in, or to have him compete with O'Brien at another network.

Conan O'Brien hosting one of his last episodes at the helm of *The Tonight Show.*

NBC's solution was to create *The Jay Leno Show*, airing weekdays at 10 p.m., a slot traditionally held by hour-long dramas such as *E.R.* and *Law & Order.* Apart from wanting to keep Leno, a major factor in the decision was the cost of production, as an entire week of *The Jay Leno Show* was cheaper to produce then just one episode of an hour-long drama. O'Brien became the host of *The Tonight Show*, with network affiliates' local news sandwiched in between.

The move has been widely considered a colossal failure. Ratings for both Leno and O'Brien suffered. Perhaps most important, the local stations that exhibit the shows saw a decline in the ratings for their all-important local news programs. They held *The Jay Leno Show* responsible because of its shortcomings as a lead-in.

Struggling to rectify the situation, NBC offered to move Leno to the 11 p.m. slot, bumping local news to 11:30 p.m. and *The Tonight Show* all the way into the next day at 12:05 a.m. O'Brien refused the deal. "I believe that delaying *The Tonight Show* into the next day to accommodate another comedy program will seriously damage what I consider to be the greatest franchise in the history of broadcasting," he said, subsequently accepting a $40 million buyout from NBC to walk away from what had long been his dream job.

Not only did commentators portray the imbroglio as a public relations disaster for NBC, the episode cost the network millions of dollars and loss in prime time and local news ratings that remain to be regained.

Sources: Tim Arango, "NBC's Slide from TV's Heights to Troubled Nightly Punch Line," *The New York Times,* January 17, 2010, Section A, p. 1; Bill Carter, "Conan O'Brien Says He Won't Host 'Tonight Show' After Leno," *The New York Times*, January 12, 2010. http://mediadecoder.blogs.nytimes.com/2010/01/12/ conan-obrien-says-he-wont-do-tonight-show-following-leno/ (accessed March 30, 2010); Bill Carter, "Fingers Still Pointing, NBC and O'Brien Reach a Deal," *The New York Times*, January 22, 2010, Section A, p. 3; Meg James and Joe Flint, *Los Angeles Times*, January 16, 2010, Part B, p. 1; Jill Sergeant, "NBC's Talk Show Wars Seen as PR Disaster for All," *ABC News*, January 15, 2010. http://abcnews.go.com/Entertainment/ wireStory?id=9575927 (accessed March 30, 2010).

on more responsibility, the lead bank (the bank that organizes the syndicate) makes more money on the deal than the others.

ENCOURAGING INVESTMENTS   While bankers worry that firms will not be able to pay back the money they have borrowed, executives of those firms worry about how much money the loans are costing them. That is, paying the interest on the loans requires cash that the company could use for other purposes. Consequently, executives may prefer to raise money through **stock offerings**. A share of

stock offering selling units of ownership in the company, or shares of stock, to organizations and individuals

stock is a unit of ownership in a company. All corporations, whether they are owned by only a few people or millions of people, issue stock. When a company engages in a stock offering, it sells these units of ownership to organizations and individuals.

For example, let's say that DigitalDynamics, a media organization that creates specialized sites on the internet, wants to expand. One of its computer engineers has just created a device that executives believe will revolutionize the industry and make the firm a leader.

The three founders of the company still own all the stock; as there is no public market for the stock, the value of each of their holdings equals the assets of the firm divided by three. The founders (who also run the firm) are concerned that taking out loans in addition to the loans they already have would make the interest payments too high for the firm to afford, as they don't expect the new device to be profitable for at least a year. They decide to open up ownership of the company to people other than themselves.

Working with the company's accountants and with outside specialists, the company's founders determine the value of the company. That amount includes the worth of its equipment and also its goodwill—that is, the value of its reputation among its clients and potential clients in the online world. The founders decide that the company should issue six million shares; each of the founders will keep one million of those shares, and DigitalDynamics will offer the other three million at $2 each. Consequently, if the company is able to sell all of the nonpartners' shares, it will receive $6 million, which will be enough to expand the venture.

In view of its small size, DigitalDynamics will probably sell its stock to **venture capitalists**. Venture capitalists are individuals or companies that invest in startup or nonpublic firms in the hope that the firms' value will increase over time. These people and firms are in the business of assuming the high risks of investing in such firms in the hope of receiving high rewards. In the case of DigitalDynamics, they are assuming that the company's earnings will increase because its new device will bring in more business. That increase in earnings would make the company more valuable, and so each share will be worth more than the amount the venture capitalists paid for it. If the company were then sold, the venture capitalists would get substantially more money than they invested.

venture capitalists individuals or companies that invest in startup or nonpublic firms in the hope that the firms' value will increase over time

There are other ways in which DigitalDynamics can raise more money. Assume, for example, that after the sale of stock to the venture capitalists, DigitalDynamics' board of directors (which now includes some of the venture capitalists) decides upon an **initial public offering (IPO)** of the company's stock. The board needs to convince an investment banker that the company's future is so great that investment companies and individual investors would buy five million new shares of the company's stock at $10 a share. The investment bank agrees to manage (or underwrite) the offering for a fee. Because five million new shares will be created, the shares that already exist will represent a smaller percentage of the ownership than they did before the IPO. Still, the market value of the early stockholders' shares has gone from $2 to $10 a share. DigitalDynamics, meanwhile, has $50 million more to chew on.

initial public offering (IPO) the offering for sale to the general public of a predetermined number of shares of stock of a company that previously were owned by a limited number of individuals and the listing of the company's shares on a stock exchange

Funding When Production is Already Complete

A primary indicator of the health of any company is its **profits**—the amount of money brought in by the completed products minus expenses. Even if a company is run efficiently and its expenses are low, it still needs to bring in ever-increasing amounts of revenue in order to increase its profits and satisfy its investors and lenders. In mass media firms, there are several ways to bring in revenues.

profits the amount of money brought in by the completed products minus expenses

direct sales a strategy to gain revenue in which the consumer pays the producer, distributor, or exhibitor for the item and can use it in any way she or he sees fit

license fees a strategy to gain revenue in which a person or organization pays the producer for the use of a product but the producer has ultimate control over the way it is used

rentals a strategy to gain revenue in which a producer, distributor, or exhibitor charges for employing (reading, viewing, or hearing) a mass media product for a certain period of time, and then gets it back

usage fees a strategy to gain revenue in which the producer, distributor, or exhibitor charges for a mass media product based on the number of times it is employed

subscriptions a strategy to gain revenue in which the producer, distributor, or exhibitor charges for continually providing a media product or service

advertising a strategy to gain revenue in which a company buys space or time on a mass medium (a page in a magazine, thirty seconds on a radio station) in exchange for being allowed to display a persuasive message (an advertisement) for a product or service

DIRECT SALES   The purchaser pays the producer, distributor, or exhibitor for the item and can use it in any way she or he sees fit—keep it forever, throw it away, give it to someone else, or even resell it. In college textbook publishing, for example, most of the money comes from sales to consumers (the students).

LICENSE FEES   A person or organization pays the producer for the use of a product, but the producer has ultimate control over the way it is used. For example, a toy company may pay Warner Brothers for the right to use the image of Bugs Bunny on toy banks for five years. Similarly, if you have Microsoft Word on your computer, what you have actually bought is a license to use it. (Remember the package telling you that if you unwrap the disk, you are accepting the "license agreement"? One consequence is that, according to the agreement, you are prohibited from reselling the software to someone else.)

RENTALS   A producer, distributor, or exhibitor charges for the right to employ (read, view, or hear) a mass media product for a certain period of time, and then gets the product back. For example, with movie rentals, the store typically buys the video from the production firm and tries to make a profit by renting it to you and many others.

USAGE FEE   The amount the producer, distributor, or exhibitor charges for a mass media product is based on the number of times the product is employed. For example, an internet database of articles may charge you for the number of articles or "page views" you print.

SUBSCRIPTIONS   The producer, distributor, or exhibitor charges for regularly providing a media product or service. (Think of a magazine subscription, a subscription to a cable system, and a subscription to a company that provides you with internet service.)

ADVERTISING   A company buys space or time on a mass medium (a page in a magazine, thirty seconds on a radio station) in which it is allowed to display a persuasive message (an advertisement) for a product or service. We will have a good deal to say about the workings of the advertising industry in Chapter 15. What is important to remember here is that the advertising industry is the dominant support system for the mass media. If advertising did not exist, the amount you pay for magazines, newspapers, internet content, and cable television, not to mention broadcast television and radio, would skyrocket. Reliable estimates suggest, for example, that because of advertising people on average pay half of what they would otherwise pay for magazines, and substantially less than half for newspapers.

The mention of magazines and newspapers brings up another important point about the sources of cash in mass media industries. Many companies in these industries benefit from what economists call a dual revenue stream. That is, they take in money from two sources: advertisers and consumers. Magazine and newspaper firms, for example, both sell ads and ask consumers to pay for each issue. Local TV broadcasters, on the other hand, live overwhelmingly off only a single revenue stream, advertiser support; viewers do not have to pay them. This revenue stream happens to be quite an outpouring: in 2008, local TV stations took in $23.9 billion from advertisers.[10] But as competition tightens in the television industry, as costs go up, and as advertisers have the option of placing ads in other media if the local stations raise their advertising rates, the single revenue stream does not look as lucrative as it once did. That is why the stations are demanding that cable systems pay them for carrying their signals to their customers (what is called a **retransmission fee**). The stations are also trying to make money via advertising on their websites.

By now, the complexity of trying to navigate the mass media environment should be quite clear. But wait—there's more! Not only do media practitioners have to worry about production, distribution, exhibition, and finance, they also have to concern themselves with **government regulation**. Government regulation involves a wide variety of activities and laws through which elected and appointed officials at local, state, and federal levels exercise influence over media firms. The different forms of regulation are so important to what media firms can and cannot do when it comes to production, distribution, exhibition, advertising, and finance that we devote the entire next chapter—Chapter 3—to them.

Media Literacy and the Business of Mass Media

At this point, you may be asking yourself two questions: How does knowing about the business of media help me to be a more aware consumer of mass media materials? And what difference might being an aware consumer make in my life? The questions speak, of course, to the important topic of media literacy, which we introduced in Chapter 1.

Think back to the billboard scenario that began this chapter. Remember that the premise was that community leaders in the neighborhood where you live had begun to complain about billboard advertising featuring beer and sex, and you wanted to help these community leaders influence billboard executives to change their ad policies. At the beginning of this chapter, most of what you could do was list what you didn't know. Now (after reading the chapter), you ought to know enough to help your community deal with billboard (or "outdoor") firms.

- To begin with, you know that billboard companies are the exhibition point of a chain of events that often also involves companies that create the ad ideas and other firms that actually make the posters and distribute them to the billboard owners. Your community group will try to persuade the exhibitors to change their policies—but if they refuse, you now know that there may well be two other levels of firms to which you can bring your demands. You might put pressure on the ad agencies that thought up the ads, or on the companies that manufactured them and delivered them to the billboard firm. The ad agencies may be more sensitive to organized pressure and anger than the billboard company.
- You now bring to your talk with company executives a basic understanding of the advertising genre that will give you credibility with them and help you make your arguments. You know, for example, that sex and violence are often used in soft-sell advertising. The issue here is twofold: whether the practice is ethical when it is used for selling beer and whether it is ethical in areas where there are children who might consider the ads attractive and hip and so consider the combination (sex and beer) attractive and hip.
- Our discussion of the way media firms think about audiences and the importance of segmentation and targeting to today's media should sensitize you to the issues that outdoor firms consider when they put their billboards up and that advertisers think about when they decide to place their ads on the billboards. By examining the locations of the most objectionable billboards, you might be able to show the billboard firms that you know that their supposed targets—adults—are not their only targets. You might, for example, find several of the objectionable billboards within a few blocks of high schools. That can get you into an interesting

retransmission fee amount a cable system or satellite firm pays to a broadcaster for the right to pick the broadcaster's signal off the air and send it to cable or satellite subscribers

government regulation a wide variety of activities and laws through which elected and appointed officials at local, state, and federal levels exercise influence over media firms

discussion about the ethics of targeting that audience and lead to leverage that you can apply to the firms.

Even if there is still much to learn about this billboard issue as well as other aspects of media, the hope is that you have already begun to watch TV, read the newspaper, and use the Web with a new awareness of what is going on. Have you begun to dissect the formats of your favorite TV shows or magazines? When you open up "junk" mail, have you tried to figure out what target audiences you fit into and where the firms got your name? When you've gone into a music store, have you thought of the relationships among exhibition, distribution, and production? Have you watched and read the news with an eye to the subgenres that journalists use and, if it is hard news, the way they present the sense of an "objective" approach to the world through their use of the verbal and visual conventions we discussed?

If not, you ought to try; it will open up new ways to view reality and the forces that create it.

Chapter Review

For an interactive chapter recap and study guide, visit the companion website for *Media Today* at http://www.routledge.com/textbooks/mediatoday4e.

Questions for Discussion and Critical Thinking

. . . .

1   Investigate whether and how the three largest U.S. mass media companies operate in the three largest mass media industries.
2   In what ways are the local television hard news stories both different from and similar to the network TV hard news stories?
3   Can you see why companies in the information business might have to deal with ethical and legal issues of privacy? What privacy issues come to mind, and how do they affect you?
4   What does it mean to say that production in mass media firms is a collaborative process?
5   Why might media practitioners not want their products to appeal to certain audiences, even if those audiences are large?

Internet Resources

. . . .

Columbia Journalism Review (http://www.cjr.com)
> *Columbia Journalism Review*'s mission is to encourage and stimulate excellence in journalism in the service of a free society. It is both a watchdog and a friend of the press in all its forms, from newspapers to magazines to radio, television, and the Web.

I Want Media (http://www.iwantmedia.com)

> This website focuses on diversified media news and resources. It provides quick access to media news and industry data, and is updated throughout the day.

Internet Movie Database (http://www.imdb.com)

> Owned by Time Warner, this database has loads of information about movies, television series, and the companies and people who create them.

Key Terms

· · · · · · · · · · · · ·

You can find the definitions to these key terms in the marginal glossary throughout this chapter. Test your knowledge of these terms with interactive flash cards on the *Media Today* companion website.

Constructing
Media Literacy

1   Claritas is a subsidiary of the Nielsen research firm that helps marketers divide the United States into lifestyle segments based on postal (ZIP) codes. Go to http://www.claritas.com on the Web to explore their products and services. Explain three ways in which Claritas is "constructing" America. If marketers use the constructions, how might it affect the ways people view U.S. society and even themselves?

2   Go to the PRIZM page of the Claritas website. There is a box on the page that allows you to enter a neighborhood's ZIP code and find out what lifestyle stories Claritas connects to them. Put in two neighborhoods that you know are different from one another economically or culturally. Compare the ways Claritas constructs them.

3   To what extent do lists of popularity based on survey ratings or rankings affect the music you buy, the books you read, or the movies you see? Do you find the lists helpful, or are you often disappointed when you base your media habits on the popularity rankings?

4   Think of a "subgenre" of entertainment that you particularly enjoy—horror movies, football films, workplace sitcoms, doctor shows, or some other one—and try to track examples of these on TV or in the movies over the past half century. (One resource to use is the internet movie database, http://www.imdb.com, which covers theatrical films and television series.) Judging by descriptions of the programs and maybe articles you can find about the shows, can you identify a formula for the subgenre? If so, how has the formula changed over time?

Companion Website
Video Clips

Rich Media, Poor Democracy—Welcome to the Revolution

This clip from the Media Education Foundation documentary *Rich Media, Poor Democracy* looks at the conglomerate ownership of the media and why fewer conglomerates are taking over more of the media companies in the United States. Credit: Media Education Foundation.

Behind the Screens—Product Placement: Advertising Goes to the Movies

This clip from the Media Education Foundation documentary *Behind the Screens* explores the trend toward Hollywood movies becoming vehicles for the ulterior marketing and advertising motives of studios and their owners, rather than entertainment in their own right. Credit: Media Education Foundation.

Consumers Want to Know I
Consumers Want to Know II

These two clips from an early 1960s film take you inside the testing labs of Consumers Union, the publishers of *Consumer Reports*. Credit: Internet Archive/ Prelinger Archives.

Case Study

. . . .

TEENS AS A CONSTRUCTED AUDIENCE

The idea One way to get a feel for the idea that audiences are constructed is to see how advertisers actually construct audiences. In this case study you will go through recent advertising trade magazines to see how marketing and media executives talk about an important audience—teens. You will also explore what their construction of teens means for the ways they try to reach them and persuade them to buy products.

The method To conduct this study, you need to know how to use a periodical database in your school's library. The most popular databases are Factiva and LexisNexis. Knowing how to use these sorts of databases will help you learn a lot about the state of media today. It may also help you get a summer, or a permanent, job in a media firm.

1 Ask someone who knows how to use the database to show you how to do a full-text search of the weekly trade magazine *Advertising Age* for the past six months. Tell that person that you would like to investigate how *Advertising Age* used the term "teen" or "teenager" during that time.
2 You may find that *Advertising Age* used the term a lot during that period. Ask your professor what proportion of the articles you should read. If there are a hundred articles or more, the class might divide into groups of two or three people in each group. That way each group can share findings on all the articles and summarize them.
3 For each article, note the title and date and then answer the following questions on a sheet of paper:
    a On what topic does it mention teenagers?
    b How does it describe teenagers? To what extent, and how, does it divide teens by gender, class, spending power, physical characteristics, personalities, or other categories?
    c Does the article make comparisons between teenagers and other groups in society? If so, how?
    d What does the article say about teenagers' value to advertisers, uses of different media, and uses of different products?
    e What, if anything, does the article say about how media firms create media to attract teens?
    f What, if anything, does the article say about how media firms and advertisers are creating advertisements to attract teens? With what messages and images do they think they can persuade them?
4 Once you and your group have taken notes on all the articles, make an outline of a report that discusses what you learned about how teenagers are constructed by advertisers, why, and with what consequences for commercial messages and for media.

3 Controls on Media Content: Government Regulation, Self-Regulation, and Ethics

After studying this chapter, you will be able to:

1 Explain the reasons for and the theories underlying media regulation

2 Identify and describe the different types of media regulation

3 Analyze the struggle between citizens and regulatory agencies in the search for information

4 Discuss the internal and external ways media organizations self-regulate

5 Identify and evaluate ethical dilemmas facing media practitioners today

6 Harness your media literacy skills to comprehend how media regulation affects you as a consumer

MEDIA TODAY

On May 10, 1933, the Nazi-led government of Germany organized several book burnings at universities around the country. One took place in Berlin at Wilhelm Humboldt University. Guided by top-level politicians, students from the university selected books to destroy from their university library. They chose to burn books by Jewish and Marxist authors and by other authors that the Nazi government found disreputable, including such world-famous thinkers as Heinrich Heine, Sigmund Freud, Thomas Mann, Erich Maria Remarque, Albert Einstein, Walter Benjamin, Karl Marx, Jack London, and Margaret Sanger.

The students took the books to the Franz Joseph Platz, a large plaza next to the school. Denouncing the authors and their ideas, they tossed thousands of books into a bonfire. German newspapers, which were allied with the government, triumphantly reported that Germany was beginning to eliminate so-called corrupters of the German spirit. Many newspapers and magazines outside Germany responded with surprise and shock; in the United States, journalists and authors expressed outrage. A study of American reaction to this and other book burnings that took place during the 1930s concluded that the American public generally was upset about these incidents, even though they took place so far away.[1] What was especially shocking to many Americans in 1933—and remains shocking even today—is the idea that a government could command so much direct, destructive power over mass media content. In addition to orchestrating book burnings throughout the rest of the 1930s, the Nazis controlled German newspaper reaction to

Book burnings were one of the means Nazis used to control media during World War II.

those book burnings.

American schoolchildren are taught that such government control over "the press" is contrary to this nation's democratic ideals. Yet many Americans sometimes wish that the government would do something about what they consider media that are out of moral control. They complain about sex, violence, racism, sexism, and other aspects of media content. They cry out for some sort of government action to stop the objectionable images and words.

To what extent can U.S. government officials respond to their concerns? To what extent should they respond? What influence does the U.S. government exert over the mass media? What are the legal limits on government intervention? These are among the questions that we address in this chapter.

How Do Governments Regulate The Media?

regulation with regard to mass media, laws and guidelines that influence the way media companies produce, distribute, or exhibit materials for audiences

When we talk about the **regulation** of mass media, we mean the laws and guidelines that influence the way media companies produce, distribute, or exhibit materials for audiences. Government regulation of mass media covers a wide range of territory. It can mean regulation by federal, state, county, or city government. Such regulation is carried out for different reasons, and in different ways, in different countries.

Four Models of Media Regulation by Governments

Figure 3.1 illustrates four models of government regulation of the media—from high levels of control to low levels of control. Those four models are:

- Authoritarian
- Communist
- Libertarian
- Social responsibility

Let's take a look at each.

authoritarian model approaches to media regulation that require the owners of mass media firms to be avid supporters of the authoritarian regime, with workers who are willing to create news and entertainment materials that adhere strictly to the party line; typically adopted by dictators who want to keep themselves and the elite class that supports them in direct control over all aspects of their society

THE AUTHORITARIAN MODEL   In the **authoritarian model** of media regulation, a government controls what the population sees, reads, and hears through media outlets. This model is typically adopted by dictators who want to keep themselves and their supporters in full control of society. Authoritarian rulers may claim to be rescuing their people from past evils that the society may have experienced. They justify their strict control in the name of unifying the public and spreading truth.

The authoritarian model does not require that all the media outlets be owned by the government, but it *does* require that the owners of mass media firms support the government and its leaders, with workers who are willing to create news and entertainment materials that adhere to the party line. Dissenters are barred from making reports or speaking against the government. In addition, it is illegal for people to read or listen to media materials from other countries that the government doesn't sanction.

Versions of the authoritarian approach were proudly practiced by the regimes of fascist Germany and Italy before and during World War II. The governments of Burma and Uzbekistan today can be described as among those operating under this philosophy of strict government control of the media. According to a 2007 Radio Free Europe/Radio Liberty report about Uzbekistan, "truly independent newspapers, radio, and television stations are almost nonexistent in Uzbekistan, [and] the government has turned its attention to the internet, blocking news websites and creating

Figure 3.1 Approaches to Government Regulation of the Media

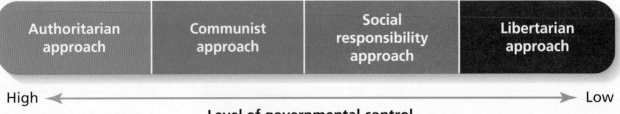

| Authoritarian approach | Communist approach | Social responsibility approach | Libertarian approach |

High ⟵——————————————————⟶ Low

Level of governmental control

pro-government sites that cover events from the government's viewpoint."[2] In 2009, conclusions from Human Rights Watch suggested that nothing had changed.[3]

THE COMMUNIST MODEL   Like the authoritarian model, under a **communist model** the government strictly controls what the population sees, reads, hears, and experiences through media outlets. The communist model follows the writings of Vladimir Lenin, a leader of the Russian communist revolution. Lenin argued that the purpose of communist society was to help create a nation (and eventually a world) in which the common people share everything. In this ideal society, there would be no rich or poor classes. People would be paid what they needed in order to live comfortably, no matter what kind of job they held.

Lenin believed firmly that the mass media were important vehicles for teaching people the values of communism. The media system of a communist society, he said, should be considered part of its educational system. Countries with communist governments—North Korea and Cuba, for example—teach their creators of news and entertainment that they must learn how to see the world through the eyes of communist beliefs. Armed with these understandings, their goal is to convey these beliefs in everything they produce for public consumption.

THE LIBERTARIAN MODEL   On the other end of the spectrum from authoritarian and communist models of media control is the **libertarian model**. It comes down to opposing views of human nature—people who endorse the authoritarian or communist model of regulation of the media have little regard for the individual in society; libertarians, in contrast, operate under the belief that individuals are capable of making sound decisions for themselves.

Libertarians believe that government restrictions placed on the dissemination and expression of ideas infringe upon the rights of the individual. In their view, government should intervene only in those rare circumstances in which society cannot be served by people going about their own business. For example, according to libertarians, a government should intervene to provide a military force, since individuals would be unlikely to coordinate such an activity on their own. In the libertarian view, a government should not regulate the mass media, because individuals and companies can readily create mass media materials without government help.

Moreover, say libertarians, in a free-flowing media system individuals will be able to make their own decisions about what is true and what is false. Libertarians get this notion from English writer and philosopher John Milton. In his 1644 pamphlet, *Areopagitica*, Milton called for a **marketplace of ideas** in which different opinions would compete for public approval. Milton felt that truth would always win out in such a contest.

"Where is this model practiced?" you might ask. The answer is: nowhere. That is because in democratic societies (where it might be practiced) critics consider the libertarian model unrealistic. They say that giving media companies total freedom to do as they like would lead to control of the media by a few huge corporations. There would not be any real struggle for "the truth" to come out because there would not be enough different viewpoints presented. As such, political democracies tend to choose the social responsibility model of government regulation—to which we now turn—over the libertarian one.

THE SOCIAL RESPONSIBILITY MODEL   Like the libertarian model, the **social responsibility model** of government regulation of the media is marked by belief in the importance of the individual and the marketplace of ideas. However, supporters of the social responsibility model believe that the competition of ideas that

communist model approaches to media regulation that hold that the government should determine what the population sees, reads, hears, and experiences through media outlets in order to convey communist beliefs in everything the media produce for public consumption

libertarian model approaches to media regulation that hold that individuals are capable of making sound decisions for themselves and that government should intervene only in those rare circumstances in which society cannot be served by people going about their own business; the mass media do not represent such an area, since individuals and companies will create mass media materials without prodding from the government

marketplace of ideas the belief, asserted by John Milton in *Areopagitica*, that in a free-flowing media system, individuals will be able to make their own decisions about what is true and what is false, because media competition will allow different opinions to emerge and struggle for public approval (as in a market), and in the end the true opinion will win out

**social responsibility
model** approaches to media
regulation that agree with
the libertarian belief in
the importance of the individual
and the marketplace of
ideas, but hold that the real
competition over ideas
will never happen without
government action to
encourage companies to
be socially responsible by
offering a diversity of voices
and ideas, and also argue
that sometimes things that
individuals or companies
want to publish—for example
child pornography—might be
harmful to a large number of
people in the society

libertarians seek could never happen without government action—to encourage companies to offer a diversity of voices and ideas, and to bar companies from publishing material that might be harmful to society (child pornography, for example). According to the social responsibility model, the government's role is to make sure that companies allow—and even encourage—social responsibility in the media system so that a diverse marketplace of voices and ideas can flourish.

Keep in mind that definitions of social responsibility will vary among societies, and even within societies. The ideal in social responsibility approaches is to strike a balance among the needs and rights of the individual, of media organizations, and of the society as a whole. That balance may be struck by passing laws aimed at forcing private media companies to pay attention to their social responsibilities. In the United States, for example, the government encourages this balance by providing public funding to the Corporation for Public Broadcasting, a nonprofit, private organization that distributes money to public broadcasters. The United Kingdom strikes the balance differently—supporting the state-owned British Broadcasting Corporation (BBC) with a tax on its citizens

The differences among the four approaches are shown in Figure 3.2. The categories may look quite distinctive in the illustration, but sometimes in real life things get ambiguous. Where, for example, should we put China? China is not really a "communist" state anymore; despite the name of its ruling party, capitalism is making headway there. Some parts of the social responsibility model do apply to China: the Chinese government allows private print and broadcast media to exist, and it has loosened some of its restrictions on criticizing government activities such as corruption.

Chinese government officials might even argue that China espouses the social responsibility model of media. They might claim that the Chinese government seeks a balance between government and private control over media in order to establish social harmony and national security. But does China truly espouse the social responsibility model? Critics of media regulation by China's government argue that the government's claim of regulation in the interest of social harmony and diversity is merely a cover to apply anti-democratic media controls. Although the government allows private internet companies to operate, it enforces many rules about what websites citizens can visit and what topics they can discuss online. It even blocks websites that it says incite social unrest. Although many media companies accept these anti-democratic restrictions as the price of doing business in the world's largest marketplace, Google made the decision in 2010 to pull its search engine business out of the country. The company contended that China-sponsored attackers had been trying to hack into its servers to take, among other information, email belonging to Chinese human rights advocates.

www.chinaview.cn, the English language website of China's official government news agency

These four regulatory models do not describe all situations. Societies may fall between these types, and it might be best to see the authoritarian, communist, social responsibility, and libertarian models as starting points for analyzing the media structures of different societies rather than as absolute categories that can accommodate every situation.

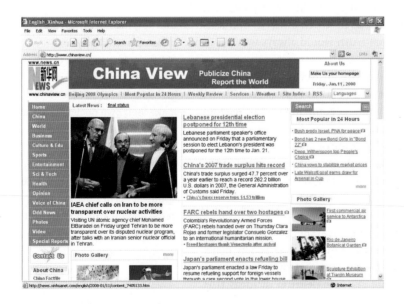

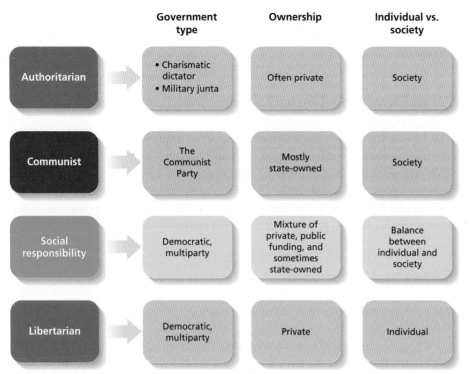

	Government type	Ownership	Individual vs. society
Authoritarian	• Charismatic dictator • Military junta	Often private	Society
Communist	The Communist Party	Mostly state-owned	Society
Social responsibility	Democratic, multiparty	Mixture of private, public funding, and sometimes state-owned	Balance between individual and society
Libertarian	Democratic, multiparty	Private	Individual

Figure 3.2 Differences Among the Regulatory Approaches
The four regulatory approaches typically reflect (1) different types of government, (2) different attitudes toward media ownership, and (3) different attitudes toward whether the media should care about society's or the individual's needs and interests.

Influences on Media Regulation by Governments

Even when countries have the same approach to government regulation of the media—whether the approach is authoritarian, communist, social responsibility, or even libertarian—the actual laws that they pass may be quite different. Political, economic, and/or cultural factors may help to explain the differences in the ways countries translate the same approach into actual regulation. Let's take a look at each.

POLITICAL INFLUENCES **Political influences** refer to the types of power that officials can exert. The leaders of some countries have more power to impose their will over their nation's institutions than do the leaders of other countries. A dictator with a strong army to enforce his orders will typically be able to exert more direct control over his country's television stations and newspapers than a dictator who does not yet feel strong enough to pull every aspect of his society under his control.

political influences the types of power that government officials have to impose their will over the nation's institutions, including the media

ECONOMIC INFLUENCES **Economic influences** are involved in the cost of carrying out certain types of regulation. For example, some governments may find media controls to be too expensive, while the governments of other countries may not be bothered by such costs. A country that adopts the social responsibility approach may use tax money to maintain an active educational TV broadcasting system (a costly option), whereas another country may force privately owned TV stations to devote a certain number of hours a day to education (a less costly option). Similarly, some nations may pass laws mandating the use of government funds to help schools get connected to the internet, whereas other countries can't afford such costly efforts.

economic influences the costs associated with carrying out certain types of government regulation

CULTURAL INFLUENCES **Cultural influences** center on the historical circumstances that lead societies to accept a certain media system over another. For example, in an attempt to protect the nation from repeating its horrific Nazi past, laws in Germany make it illegal for any mass media outlet in the country to speak in

cultural influences the historical and social circumstances that lead societies to accept certain media systems and government regulations

favor of Nazi ideology or to deny Germany's intentional destruction of Europe's Jews during World War II. Such laws would undoubtedly be considered unconstitutional in the United States.

How Does the United States Regulate the Media?

The United States has a tradition with respect to limits on the press that is different from the situations that exist in Germany, England, and many other countries. That difference is rooted in the U.S. Constitution—the basis for the authority of the country's government and courts. The legal foundation for government's regulation of the press is the First Amendment to the Constitution. It is one of a group of ten amendments collectively known as the Bill of Rights.

The First Amendment

The First Amendment to the Constitution reads:

> Congress shall make no law respecting an establishment of religion, or prohibiting the free exercise thereof; or abridging the freedom of speech, or of the press, or of the right of the people peaceably to assemble, and to petition the Government for a redress of grievances.

The First Amendment's statement that "Congress shall make no law . . . abridging freedom of speech, or of the press" seems to rule out any type of government interference in journalistic organizations ("the press"), and even in media that present content other than news. The country's Founders were determined that, in the new nation, no one would need the government's permission to communicate ideas to a wide public.

The reality of lawmaking has been quite different, however. Over the decades, the federal government has been involved in regulating media firms, raising continuing debate about the precise meaning of the First Amendment. The U.S. Supreme Court has repeatedly sorted out fights between government agencies that seek to curtail mass media content and companies interested in protecting and extending it.

WHAT DOES THE FIRST AMENDMENT MEAN BY "NO LAW," AND WHERE DOES IT APPLY? From the time the First Amendment was passed, lawmakers and lawyers have understood that its phrase "make no law" means that the federal branches of government could not make laws abridging press freedoms. They debated, however, whether the First Amendment applies to the states as well. The issue is an important one. Imagine you are the publisher of a newspaper that prints controversial

A visitor looks at a copy of the Constitution of the United States, set between the Bill of Rights and the Declaration of Independence.

views about politicians throughout the United States. You would like to be sure that the Constitution protects your work, no matter which politicians object to it. If the legislature of the state in which you work has the right to stop you from publishing your views, your newspaper would likely go out of business.

In 1925, this question was resolved by the Supreme Court in the case of *Gitlow* vs. *New York*. Socialist agitator Benjamin Gitlow published a circular called *The Left Wing Manifesto*, calling for an uprising to overthrow the government. This upset local authorities, and Gitlow was convicted in the state of New York for the statutory crime of criminal anarchy. Gitlow then appealed his case to the U.S. Supreme Court. His lawyers argued that the Constitution (and therefore the First Amendment) should override any state law that contradicts it.

The U.S. Supreme Court agreed with Gitlow and his lawyers, ruling that the First Amendment's phrase "Congress shall make no law" should be interpreted as "government and its agencies shall make no law," regardless of the location or level of government. The Court reasoned that in the Fourteenth Amendment, Congress had ensured that fundamental personal rights and liberties could not be trampled by the states.

WHAT DOES THE FIRST AMENDMENT MEAN BY "THE PRESS"?   When the Founders wrote that "Congress shall make no law . . . abridging the freedom of speech, or of the press," how did they define the term "press"? The Founders could not have possibly imagined the complex world of media messages and channels in which we currently live. So which segments of the media are included under the First Amendment's definition of the press?

If only news companies fell under the protection of the First Amendment, then book publishers, magazine firms, websites, movie companies, and advertising firms would be open to government interference. This, in turn, might place a chill on the creation of entertainment and fiction, as companies would fear getting in trouble with federal and state governments. In recent decades, court decisions and political interpretations of what precisely the First Amendment means by *the press* have expanded the definition to include all types of mass media, not just the journalistic press.

Film

The Supreme Court established the First Amendment's protection of movies in 1952, in the case of *Burstyn* vs. *Wilson*. In its ruling, the Court declared:

> Expression by means of motion pictures is included within the free speech and free press guaranty of the First and Fourteenth Amendments. It cannot be doubted that motion pictures are a significant medium for the communication of ideas. Their importance as an organ of public opinion is not lessened by the fact that they are designed to entertain as well as to inform.
>
> (*Burstyn* vs. *Wilson*, 343 U.S. 495, Supreme Court of the United States, 1952)

This ruling overturned the Court's long-standing 1919 decision in *Mutual Film Corp* vs. *Ohio Industrial Commission*, which had ruled that films were not a protected form of expression, because of their nature as novelty and entertainment pieces.

TV and Radio

TV and radio's protection under the First Amendment was established by the Supreme Court in 1973, in the case of *CBS* vs. *Democratic National Committee*. In preparing the Court's decision, Justice William Douglas wrote:

TV and radio stand in the same protected position under the First Amendment as do newspapers and magazines. The philosophy of the First Amendment requires that result, for the fear that James Madison and Thomas Jefferson had of government intrusion is perhaps even more relevant to TV and radio than it is to newspapers and other like publications. That fear was founded not only on the specter of a lawless government but of government under the control of a faction that desired to foist its views of the common good on the people.

(*CBS* vs. *Democratic National Committee*, 412 U.S. 94, Supreme Court of the United States, 1973)

Other Forms of Entertainment

The Supreme Court established the protected status of entertainment content in its 1967 ruling in the case of *Time Inc.* vs. *Hill*. The Court reversed a New York Court of Appeals decision that, because the purpose of a *Life* magazine article was entertainment and marketing, the article wasn't protected by the First Amendment. In explaining the Court's reasoning, Justice William Brennan quoted two previous Supreme Court decisions, *Winters* vs. *New York* (1948) and *New York Times Co.* vs. *Sullivan* (1964), declaring that all sorts of materials, not just news, enjoy First Amendment protection:

> The guarantees for speech and press are not the preserve of political expression or comment upon public affairs, essential as those are to healthy government. One need only pick up any newspaper or magazine to comprehend the vast range of published matter which exposes persons to public view, both private citizens and public officials . . . The line between the informing and the entertaining is too elusive for the protection of . . . [freedom of the press].
>
> (*Winters* vs. *New York*, 333 U.S. 507, 510, Supreme Court of the United States, 1948)

The Supreme Court has also ruled that mistakes in entertainment that might make politicians angry are not less likely than mistakes in public affairs materials. In both types of material, incorrect statements that were created simply out of innocent ignorance or even sloppiness (negligence) "must be protected if the freedoms of expression are to have the 'breathing space' that they 'need . . . to survive'." (*New York Times Co.* vs. *Sullivan*, 271–272 , Supreme Court of the United States, 1964).[4]

Advertising

In 1976, the Court ruled that even advertising and other forms of commercial speech are included in the First Amendment's definition of "the press" and therefore enjoy protection. In *Virginia State Board of Pharmacy et al.* vs. *Virginia Citizens Consumer Council* a majority of the justices found that a state law making it illegal for pharmacists to advertise their prices was unconstitutional. Judge Harry Blackmun bluntly expressed the Court's position:

> What is at issue is whether a State may completely suppress the dissemination of concededly truthful information about entirely lawful activity, fearful of that information's effect upon its disseminators and its recipients . . . . Reserving other questions, we conclude that the answer to this one is in the negative.[5]

When it comes to regulation of what is and what is not considered "the press," under the First Amendment, certain types of media expressions are protected more than others (see Figure 3.3). Moreover, we must also recognize that regulation is not limited to the content level. Government decisions that affect the economic health of a company or industry can also be thought of as an abridgment of "the press" because such decisions often affect the media products that the companies produce, distribute, and exhibit.

WHAT DOES THE FIRST AMENDMENT MEAN BY "ABRIDGING"? The term **abridge** means "to cut short" or "to curtail." In fact, the Supreme Court has often approved government restrictions on speech or the press that place limits on the time, place, and manner of an expression. Such restrictions are legal as long as those limits:

abridge to reduce in scope, to diminish

- Are applicable to everyone
- Are without political bias
- Serve a significant governmental interest
- Leave ample alternative ways for the communication to take place

The issue has come up a lot in the area of outdoor advertising. Over the decades, communities upset about both the clutter that billboards bring and the content of some of them—sexual images and unwholesome products—have tried to create laws regulating them. Based on the points above, courts have ruled that any laws restricting outdoor advertising have to apply to all business and cannot reflect any prejudice toward any particular lawful business. That approach satisfies the four criteria above. Following this logic, federal courts have ruled that liquor ads could not be singled out for a ban on highways on the presumption that teen drivers would be influenced by them. The reasoning is that free speech should be protected as long as there are other ways to warn teenagers about the dangers of drinking and driving.

Anti-cigarette activists argue that outdoor cigarette advertising ought to be an exception to this approach. At this point, cigarette companies have stopped using large billboards as part of a "voluntary" agreement with the federal government to limit commercial messages for the product that, although it harms people, can still be bought legally.

Three Types of Media Regulation Practiced by the U.S. Government

Certain kinds of media regulation have been found constitutional numerous times by the Supreme Court. We can divide these types of governmental regulation into three categories:

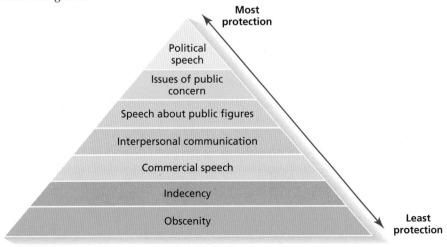

Figure 3.3 Levels of Protected Communication in the United States
The level of protection that the U.S. government provides depends upon the type of speech—from constitutionally valueless speech (no protection), to speech given intermediate protection (some protection), to fully protected speech (full protection).

- Regulation of content before it is distributed
- Regulation of content after it has been distributed
- Economic regulations

Let's look at each of these three types separately.

Regulating Content Before Distribution

prior restraint government restriction of speech before it is made

When the government restricts speech before it is made, it is engaging in **prior restraint**. Since the 1930s, the U.S. Supreme Court has consistently ruled that the practice of regulating or restricting speech before it is made violates both the spirit and the letter of the First Amendment. At the same time, however, the Court has held that in some rare, specific circumstances prior restraint is in the interest of the public good.

To understand the importance of the Supreme Court's approach, consider the landmark 1931 case of *Near* vs. *Minnesota*, in which the Court struck down a Minnesota law that gave judges the authority to allow police to halt the distribution of "malicious, scandalous or defamatory publications." Such authority was granted against anti-Semitic newspaper publishers Jay Near and Howard Guilford who wrote in their *Saturday Press*, "every snake-faced gangster and embryonic yegg in the Twin Cities is a JEW," and accused the Minneapolis police chief of turning a blind eye to Jewish crime.

injunction a court order requiring a person or organization to perform or refrain from performing a particular act

The trial court declared the paper a nuisance and issued an **injunction**—a court order requiring a person or organization to perform or refrain from performing a particular act—that said if Near and Guilford printed such "defamatory" and "scandalous" comments again, they would be punished for being in contempt of court. Near appealed against the injunction, and although the Minnesota Supreme Court upheld the trial court, the U.S. Supreme Court reversed the state decision and allowed the *Saturday Press* to continue publication.

Writing for the majority, Chief Justice Charles Hughes argued that, even though the articles were despicable, the main purpose of the First Amendment is to prevent prior restraint on publication. Hughes added that he agreed that charges of government scandal might cause a public scandal. But, he said, "a more serious public evil would be caused by authority to prevent publication."

In writing his decision in the Near case, Chief Justice Hughes cited instances in which prior restraint would be acceptable. And, in fact, over the years, the Court followed Hughes' suggestions, allowing the regulation of content before publication in some cases involving:

- Obscenity
- National security
- Military operations
- Clear and present danger to public safety
- Copyright
- Courtroom proceedings
- Education
- Commercial speech

Let's take a brief look at each of these special cases in which prior restraint may be allowed.

OBSCENITY AND PORNOGRAPHY The Supreme Court has ruled that obscene materials are not protected by the First Amendment. The term "obscene" means "offensive to accepted standards of decency or modesty." One problem, of course, is that different people may have different standards of what constitutes obscenity; books such as D. H. Lawrence's *Lady Chatterley's Lover*, Walt Whitman's *Leaves of Grass*, and J. D. Salinger's *Catcher in the Rye* may not be acceptable to some in the society, but may be considered genuine works of art by others. Of course, the same holds with respect to images on television and websites. In 2009, the conservative Parents Television Council (PTC) objected to a forthcoming episode of the CW series *Gossip Girl* in which three major characters engaged in a "multiple-partner sex scene." The PTC fired off a letter to the network's affiliates asking them not to air the episode, calling it "reckless and irresponsible" and warning that stations could be liable for Federal Communications Commission (FCC) fines if the government agency decides the show violates decency laws. CW's president, undoubtedly happy for the publicity, countered with the claim that the story "is organic to the characters and it's handled in a responsible way."[6] Related to these disagreements about obscenity is the dilemma that the public's collective standards of what is obscene and what is not obscene change and shift almost constantly. Communities that deemed a book or film obscene in the 1970s might not agree with that assessment today.

The Saturday Press stood at the center of the precedent-setting case of *Near* vs. *Minnesota* (1931).

In 1957, the U.S. Supreme Court made a significant advance in the freedom of expression with regard to sex. It held that:

> Sex and obscenity are not synonymous. **Obscene material** is material which deals with sex in a manner appealing to prurient interest. The portrayal of sex in art, literature and scientific works, is not itself sufficient reason to deny material the constitutional protection of freedom of speech and press. Sex, a great and mysterious motive force in human life, has indisputably been a subject of absorbing interest to mankind through the ages; it is one of the vital problems of human interest and public concern.
>
> (*Roth* vs. *United States*, 354 U.S. 476, 1957)

obscene material material that deals with sex in a manner appealing to prurient interest

Additionally, the Court made it clear that a media product must be considered in its entirety, and not just in excerpt, ruling, "The standard for judging obscenity, adequate to withstand the charge of constitutional infirmity, is whether, to the average person, applying contemporary community standards, the dominant theme of the material, taken as a whole, appeals to prurient interest" (*Roth* vs. *United States*, 354 U.S. 476, 1957). It also made it clear that the standard to be used must be community-based; that is, what is deemed obscene in Bloomington, Indiana, may be seen as merely pornographic in Boston, Massachusetts, and may be judged as purely artistic in Los Angeles, California.

The word "obscenity" is often linked to the word **pornography**, which can be defined as "pictures, writing, or other material that is sexually explicit." Pornographic materials are not subject to prior restraint unless they are declared obscene. According to a three-part rule devised by the U.S. Supreme Court in the 1973 case of *Miller*

pornography the presentation of sexually explicit behavior, as in a photograph, intended to arouse sexual excitement

vs. *California*, a mass media product—whether it is pornographic in nature or not—would be declared obscene if it meets all three of the following tests:

- First, an *average person*, applying current standards of the community, would have to find that the work as an entirety reflects an obsessive interest in sex.
- Second, the work has to portray in a *clearly offensive manner*—in pictures or writing—certain sexual conduct specifically described as unallowable by state law.
- Third, a *reasonable person* has to agree that the work lacks serious literary, artistic, scientific, or political usefulness.

It is important to note that, even if pornographic materials do not meet these tests of obscenity, they can still be restricted under import regulations, postal regulations, zoning ordinances, and other laws. For example, child abuse laws have been used to bar materials that feature nude children.

national security one of the circumstances that permits government censorship via prior restraint; an example is the right to restrain speech about military activities during times of war

NATIONAL SECURITY   The U.S. Supreme Court has consistently ruled that the government has a right to censor using prior restraint when the **national security** of the United States is at stake. For example, a newspaper can be stopped from disseminating the names of U.S. intelligence agents, or a television station from broadcasting the numbers and names of soldiers heading to the front, or of ships leaving a port when the nation is on a war footing.

The Court has made it clear, however, that the term "national security" should be defined narrowly. In 1971, the federal government tried to justify prior restraint by applying a very broad interpretation of national security in the case of the *Pentagon Papers*. Government researcher Daniel Ellsberg investigated U.S. policy in Vietnam and subsequently prepared a detailed Pentagon study on the subject. Ellsberg believed that the American public was entitled to an inside look at Pentagon decision-making, so he copied the top-secret study and handed it over to Neil Sheehan, a reporter for *The New York Times*. Government officials were alarmed when the *Times* began publishing excerpts from the study, which became known as the *Pentagon Papers*.

Claiming harm to national security, the Nixon administration got a district court to order the *Times* to halt the series. The *Times*, however, refused and instead turned to the U.S. Supreme Court. In its argument before the Court, the government claimed that publication of the *Pentagon Papers* had put national security at risk—but that claim proved to be weak and without merit. The Court ruled that the government could not stop publication of the *Pentagon Papers*. In the Court's decision, Justice Hugo Black wrote:

The Supreme Court ruled that the government could not halt the publication of the *Pentagon Papers* despite the government's claim that publication had put national security at risk.

Only a free and unrestrained press can effectively expose deception in government. And paramount among the responsibilities of a free press is the duty to prevent any part of the government from deceiving the people and sending them off to distant lands to die of foreign fevers and foreign shot and shell. In my view, far from deserving condemnation for their courageous reporting, *The New York Times*, *The Washington Post*, and other newspapers should be commended for serving the purpose that the Founding Fathers saw so clearly. In revealing the workings of government that led to the Vietnam War, the newspapers nobly did precisely that which the Founders hoped and trusted they would do . . .

(*New York Times* vs. *United States*, U.S. Supreme Court, 403 U.S. 713, 1971)

Despite the government's defeat in this case, the Court held that it could conceive of circumstances in which the national security of the United States could override First Amendment guarantees against prior restraint. The ruling thus upheld prior cases in which the Court had held that the government would be within its rights in restraining reports on troop movement and other military activities in wartime if those reports constituted a "clear and present danger" to U.S. national security.

MILITARY OPERATIONS   The regulation and control of media content during times of war has taken place since the Civil War. At times, media personnel have been required to submit their scripts and stories for governmental review before distribution.

During World War I, Congress passed the Espionage Act (1917) and the Sedition Act (1918), which together formalized wartime censorship of the press by preventing "disloyal" publications from being mailed via the U.S. Postal Service. During World War II, the Espionage Act was again put into effect—allowing the government to control broadcasting from 1941 until 1945. During this time, the Office of Censorship had the power to censor international communication at its "absolute discretion." With a staff of more than 10,000 censors, the office routinely examined mail, cables, newspapers, magazines, films, and radio broadcasts. Its operations constituted the most extensive government censorship of the media in U.S. history and one of the most vivid examples of the use of executive emergency powers.

In cases in which the United States is involved in a military operation but has not officially declared war, the government may seek to control access to information, rather than officially censoring that content. When U.S. troops were sent to the Caribbean island of Grenada in 1983, the Pentagon took control of all transportation to and from the island, and refused to transport reporters to the island to cover the conflict. Journalists protested this military news "blackout." In 1989, when U.S. troops were sent to Panama, the Pentagon instituted a system of **pool reporters**— selected members of the media who are present at a news event and share facts, stories, images, and firsthand knowledge of that event with others. Journalists were skeptical about the system, and, as it turned out, their skepticism was well founded. Reporters in the press pool were held in a briefing room at a military post and were given briefings that consisted of little more than history lessons on the relationship between the United States and Panama. As a consequence, journalists soured on the idea of a specially chosen pool of reporters, and the practice faded.

pool reporters selected members of the media who are present at a news event and share facts, stories, images, and first-hand knowledge of that event with others

In the Iraq War that began in 2004, as well as in the parallel, continuing Afghanistan conflict, the military allowed **embeds**—reporters who received permission to travel with a military unit across the battlefield. The Defense Department required all embeds to agree not to break military information embargos, not to report on ongoing missions without clearance, and not to reveal deployment levels below large numbers such as troop corps and carrier battle groups. Nevertheless, some news outlets such as CNN and the UK's ITN pushed the limits of these requirements, and they were periodically threatened with losing the right to have embeds. Despite the restrictions, many of the embeds in Iraq were able to report the battlefield in great detail; one book calls the initial U.S. invasion of Iraq "the most covered war in history."[7] According to one reporter who studied the embed approach, journalists who were embedded in Iraq "experienced a freedom to do their jobs that journalists had not had since the Vietnam War."[8]

embeds reporters who receive permission from the military to travel with a military unit across the battlefield

Critics have pointed out that a disadvantage of the embeds was the tendency for them to be highly sympathetic to the troops with whom they lived and on whom they depended for survival. These critics argue that self-censorship was sometimes the result. To meet these criticisms, the military allowed other journalists to work as **unilaterals**—to travel through the war zone by themselves.

CLEAR AND PRESENT DANGER   The U.S. Supreme Court has long held that speech can be limited before it is distributed if the result of that speech is likely to pose a threat to society. But what determines whether that speech (or media content) poses a threat? The answer has varied over the decades, with more recent Supreme Court decisions making it difficult to restrain speech based on the clear and present danger test.

The earliest justification for imposing prior restraint because of social threats involved the **bad tendency test**. Under this rule, the government could restrain media material if it had any tendency to cause social evil. This rule has the potential to cover a lot of territory; for example, a speech by a labor organizer that holds even a small chance of creating a disturbance could be open to prior restraint. The bad tendency test was eventually ruled unconstitutionally vague and hasn't been used since the early 1900s.

Taking its place is the **clear and present danger test** set forth by Supreme Court Justice Oliver Wendell Holmes. The difference between the clear and present danger test and the bad tendency test is that Holmes' approach suggests the importance of the social evil being *likely* to happen (not just that it might happen) and that it would happen imminently (that is, soon after the material is released).

The case that Holmes used to put forth his idea centered on two socialists who distributed anti-draft pamphlets during World War I, and who were convicted of violating the Espionage Act of 1917. When the Supreme Court heard their appeal in the 1919 case *Schenck* vs. *United States*, Holmes wrote for the majority of justices that the socialists could be convicted. Ordinarily, Holmes wrote, the pamphlets would be protected by the First Amendment. But in this case, distributing the pamphlets during wartime was similar to the kind of danger created by "crying fire in a crowded theater." His point was that the government has a right to restrict the speech of anyone (or any organization) whose words might clearly cause social harm in particular circumstances.

unilaterals reporters who receive permission from the military to travel across the battlefield without military escort

bad tendency test materials that may be restricted because they are distributed in a time of war, domestic unrest, or riot, even though they do not meet the level of clear and present danger

clear and present danger test as stated by Justice Oliver Wendell Holmes, "expression can be limited by the government when the words are used in such circumstances and are of such a nature as to create a clear and present danger that they will bring about the substantive evils that Congress has a right to prevent"

More than 600 reporters and photographers traveled alongside coalition troops as "embedded journalists" to report on the U.S. military presence in Iraq and Afghanistan. Critics worried that the journalists would lose their objectivity as they relied on the troops for their safety, but other observers welcomed increased public access to the battlefield.

In the 1957 case *Yates* vs. *United States*, the Supreme Court interpreted "clear and present danger" in a narrower, more literal way when it overturned a conspiracy conviction because the danger was too far removed (that is, not imminent and perhaps not even likely). Similarly, in a 1969 case, the Court ruled that even a speech by the Ku Klux Klan is protected unless it is specifically directed toward producing imminent lawless action. These cases set a legal precedent: although the government can still impose prior restraint because a media product will likely cause imminent social harm, it's rare to find cases that fit these criteria.

COPYRIGHT   When we speak about **copyright**, we mean the legal protection of an author's right to a work. According to the U.S. Constitution, the purpose of copyright is "to promote the progress of science and the useful arts." The framers of the Constitution believed that only if people could profit from their work would they want to create materials that could ultimately benefit the nation as a whole. At the same time, the framers wanted lawmakers to strike a balance between the rights of authors to gain personally from their work, and the right of the society to draw on the information.

> **copyright** the legal protection of an author's right to a work

The hesitancy of government agencies to stop the press from circulating content does not apply to copyright violations, for two reasons. The first is that authors ought to be able to control how their work—their *intellectual property*—is used. The second is that authors should be *paid fairly* for the use of their work.

The **Copyright Act of 1976** lays out the basic rules as they exist in the United States today. The law, as later modified (in 1978 and again in 1998), recognizes the rights of an individual creator (in any medium) from the time he or she has created a work, and protects a creative work for the lifetime of its author plus seventy years.

> **Copyright Act of 1976** a law that recognizes the rights of an individual creator (in any medium) from the time he or she has created a work, and protects a creative work for the lifetime of that author plus seventy years

As an example, let us say that Hector, an English student, writes a poem. From the moment Hector finishes the poem, he holds an automatic copyright on the poem for his lifetime plus seventy years. He may, if he decides, send the poem to the U.S. Copyright Office to register it for a small fee. Even if he does not do this, however, he is protected as long as he can prove that he wrote the poem before anyone else did. (In order to prove when a work was created, some people mail a copy of the work to themselves and do not open it. The cancellation by the post office serves as proof of the date the material was sent. Let's say that Hector does that with his poem.)

Hector is proud of his poem, and he sends it to his friend Paloma, a former classmate in a summer poetry workshop. Now let's say that Paloma is envious of Hector's poem. She submits the poem to a literary journal as her own, and the journal accepts it, pays her a small honorarium, and publishes it under her name, not Hector's. At this point, Paloma has violated U.S. copyright law, and she can be prosecuted if Hector pursues the case, since she falsely passed herself off as the poem's true author.

But even if Paloma had not lied about the poem's authorship—let's say she submitted it to the journal under Hector's name to surprise him—Paloma (and the journal) probably would not be allowed to publish the poem—or even parts of it. Apart from not asking Hector's permission to publish the poem, Paloma has also violated the second proposition of copyright law—that authors must be paid fairly for the use of their works. Sometimes, even a line of a poem or a song may be considered crucial to the work's value. As you can see, Paloma and the editors of the literary journal would have to think hard before they printed all or part of Hector's poem without getting his permission.

The copyright rules for musical compositions are similar to those for poems. If a magazine or website wants to publish selected words or music from a tune by Paul McCartney, it needs the permission of his publisher. Copying parts of copyrighted musical material from someone else who had paid for it is also not legal. For decades, while businesses paid attention to this law, individuals ignored it. Friends would often lend records to their friends so that they could copy them onto tapes or CDs. If recording industry executives minded, they generally didn't make noise about it. One reason might be that the taped copies were not as good in sound quality as the originals. As we will see when we discuss the recording industry in Chapter 10, their perspective has changed drastically. With the advent of perfect digital copies and the ability to share them over the internet, recording industry officials started hauling into court people who shared copyrighted music without the publisher's permission. We will review the pros and cons of this activity in Chapter 10, but here it is relevant to note what those officials have not emphasized: even copying part of a song without permission can make one a copyright violator. The same is true regarding movies, which, we will see in Chapter 12, have also become a target for illegal uploading and sharing.

Fair Use

Although Congress has generally supported the right of copyright holders over the desire of individuals to copy their material, one exception involves writers or academics who want to quote from copyrighted material in order to carry out critical analyses. A poet, artist, or novelist might charge an exorbitant rate for use of their works that would make it impossible for a scholar to share critical responses to it. To get around these problems, the law provides **fair use regulations**. Generally, they indicate that a person or company may use small portions of a copyrighted work without asking permission. Nonprofit, educational purposes have more leeway than for-profit ventures.

Another important consideration in fair use decisions is the commercial damage that copying may cause to the copyright material. A third criterion in favor of fair use is the transformative use of the copyrighted material. A use is **transformative** when it presents the work in a way that adds interpretations to it so that some people might see it in a new light. So, for example, a magazine essay on John Updike's novels that quotes various passages from them to show how his views of suburbia have changed over time would likely be considered fair use. By these criteria, when scholarly critiques of popular culture quote from copyright materials to make their points, that is almost surely fair use.

Despite fair use regulations, college copy shops must contact publishers and get permission when they want to use entire articles in "bulk packs" for classes. And you may not know it, but photocopying a work for your own pleasure is normally not fair use. One curious exception to fair use guidelines relates to the videotape recorder. The Supreme Court ruled in 1984 that homeowners may record copyrighted TV shows for their personal, noncommercial use. A majority of the justices reasoned that taping was legal because people use the tapes for *time shifting*—that is, taping for later viewing what they would have watched anyway.

Today, time shifting is a way of life for many people who record TV shows and movies on digital video recorders (DVRs). Although the practice is legal, it has brought interesting headaches to media companies and their advertisers, as people view the programs they copied but not the commercials that support them. Even greater headaches have come with the rise of digital technologies that make it simple for people to copy all sorts of copyrighted materials (including music and movies) in circumstances that do not fall within the fair use rules. Some copyright owners call these behaviors "piracy" and demand that audiences stop doing it. The activities raise important legal and ethical issues that we will explore in chapters to come.

Parodies

A **parody** is a work that imitates another work for laughs in a way that comments on the original work in one way or another. A number of major court cases have ruled

fair use regulations provisions under which a person or company may use small portions of a copyrighted work without asking permission

transformative when use of copyrighted material presents the work in a way that adds interpretation to it so that some people might see it in a new light

parody a work that imitates another work for laughs in a way that comments on the original work in one way or another

that when artists add new perspective to a copyrighted material, in the process critiquing it and encouraging people to see it in different ways, that is fully legal. Supreme Court Justice David Souter even suggested that parodies have stronger rights than other kinds of fair use material in that the creator of a parody "may quite legitimately aim at destroying [the original] commercially as well as artistically."[9] The problem with parodies from a legal standpoint, though, is that the line between them and copyright violation is sometimes hard to figure out.

For one thing, not all comically altered versions of songs are fair use. That may explain why Weird Al Yankovic is so conservative when it comes to using his musical parodies. Weird Al is a performer who has based his professional career on writing and recording parodies of popular songs. Pieces such as "My Bologna" (a take on the Knack's "My Sharona"), "I Love Rocky Road," "Another One Rides the Bus," "Eat It," "Like a Surgeon," "I Think I'm a Clone Now," and "Smells Like Nirvana," have given him long-term popularity with a huge number of fans around the globe. Yet Weird Al is actually pretty conservative regarding his parodic creations. His lawyers may have pointed out to him that, although his lyrics are funny, they don't really criticize the originals; nor does his musical take on the originals vary much from them. Perhaps as a result, Weird Al notes he always seeks permission from the artists and writers of the songs before he puts his spin on them. "The parodies are all in good fun and good taste," he says, "and most of the artists normally take it that way. I prefer to have them on my team and I like to sleep well at night."[10]

Weird Al Yankovic has built a career around writing and recording parodies of popular songs

EDUCATION   Prior restraint in education—especially with regard to primary and secondary education—involves newspapers created by students as part of their schoolwork. In 1988, in the case of *Hazelwood School District* vs. *Kuhlmeier*, the Supreme Court held that a principal's decision to remove two articles from a high school newspaper—one describing students' experiences with pregnancy, and another discussing the impact of divorce on students at the school—was perfectly legal. The newspaper was written and edited by a journalism class, as part of the school's curriculum.

Following school policy, the teacher in charge of the student newspaper submitted page proofs to the school's principal, who objected to the pregnancy story because the pregnant students, although not named, could easily have been identified from the text, and because he believed that the article's references to sexual activity and birth control were inappropriate for some of the younger students.

The Court held that, "A school need not tolerate student speech that is inconsistent with its basic educational mission, even though the government could not censor similar speech outside the school." The Court reasoned that, because the school newspaper was part of the school's educational curriculum (it was open only to students taking journalism courses), it was not entitled to First Amendment protection. The wording seems to grant freedom of the press to school newspapers that are not part of the curriculum; college newspapers would seem to fit into this protected category.

COMMERCIAL SPEECH   Yet another area in which the courts have allowed prior restraint over mass media content is what the legal profession calls **commercial speech**. Advertisements make up a large part of this domain, but it also includes all kinds of messages that are designed to sell you products or services, from straightforward TV and magazine ads, to internet pop-up ads, to phone calls that try to convince you to buy stocks. Over the decades, the U.S. Supreme Court has made clear its view

commercial speech
messages that are designed to sell you products or services

CRITICAL CONSUMER
PRIOR RESTRAINT AND STUDENT
JOURNALISM ON THE WEB

Freedom of the press, issues of security, and concerns about school image are bumping into one another as more and more high school journalism classes publish their papers online. School administrators that have allowed their students a lot of leeway when producing paper-bound news work are having second thoughts when the students turn to cyber-journalism.

Most of the restrictions have to do with publishing the last names of students, or their names next to their photos. Administrators worry that the wide reach of the internet means that some stalkers may collect the names and photos with the intention to do harm. They also argue that the Federal Education Records Privacy Act, enacted in 1974, limits what Web newspapers may reveal about students online because of the internet's reach far beyond the school.

Some champions of student journalism worry that school administrators will go beyond concerns about privacy to limit what Web newspapers can write about. Administrators are quite aware that Web editions make student views available to alumni and legislators who live away from the community. Worried about their image and the politics of funding, administrators may use their right to exercise prior restraint as a way to keep students' critical comments from being widely circulated.

Such was the case at California's La Serna High School, where, in 2006, student journalists were banned from publishing the June issue of their newspaper *The*

Freelancer. According to students, the ban was a form of retribution for their May issue, which included a feature on students' attitudes toward sex. Some students considered pursuing legal action under a California law protecting student journalists, yet nothing has been filed to date. In a similar vein, during the spring of 2007, the student newspaper at St Francis High School in Minnesota was taken offline after it published a photo of a student destroying an American flag. Administrators said they feared the photo might be offensive to the veterans in the area. By the end of the summer, the administration still had not backed down.

Gene Policinski, vice president and executive director of the First Amendment Center, criticizes cases like these that overlook students' rights to "exercise control rooted in good journalistic considerations." Instead, he argues, we should "consider the benefits of a healthy student press, staffed by young, educated journalists and advised by trained professional educators."

Sources: Dave Orrick, "Outcome of Minnesota Censorship Case Remains Unclear," National Scholastic Press Association. http://www.studentpress.org/nspa (accessed March 6 2008); Lisa Napoli, "Schools' Online Publications Face Curbs of their Own," *The New York Times*, May 7, 1999. http://www.ny-times.com (accessed August 1, 2010); Gene Policinski, "Why We Need a Strong Student Press," American Press Institute, February 12, 2007. http://www.americanpressinstitute.org (accessed August 1, 2010).

that the Constitution allows the government a level of control over commercial speech that it does not tolerate when noncommercial content is involved.

Sometimes, government officials don't know of a false ad until it is released, but because of their prior restraint powers they can immediately stop an ad that is false and deceptive. In a classic case, in the 1970s the Campbell Soup Company's ad agency put marbles in the bottom of a bowl of soup to emphasize the soup's chunkiness by making it look as if it contained many big pieces of meat and vegetables. Responding to complaints from competitors, the Federal Trade Commission (FTC), which oversees much of the commercial speech domain, forced the company to withdraw the ad. In the 2000s, the FTC has stopped what it considers to be false or unsubstantiated claims by more than sixty dietary-supplement and weight-loss advertisers across all kinds of media.

Children's advocacy groups have claimed that ads aimed at children under the ages of 8 or 12 years are by their very nature deceptive, as kids have a hard time understanding that they are being manipulated. In 2009, these advocates together with groups concerned about a variety of health issues wrote a letter to the new chairman of the Federal Communications Commission calling on the agency to limit the placements of brands relating to junk food, alcohol, tobacco, pharmaceutical drugs, or gambling into certain shows (a practice called product placement or embedded advertising) as deceptive. They argued that a prominently placed can of Coke, cigarette pack, or bottle of whisky influences people, especially children, because they view the items as endorsed by the actors or show, not as paid ads. "When the product itself is potentially unhealthful, harmful or addictive . . . the deceptive nature of embedded advertising poses additional risks to public health" wrote the group that included the Salvation Army, American Academy of Pediatrics, Public Citizen, and U.S. Public Interest Group (PIRG)."[11]

Regulating Information After Distribution

With respect to some areas of content, the courts have stated that authorities must wait until after distribution to press charges of illegal activity. Unlike regulating content before distribution, which usually involves a conflict between the government and the media, regulating content after it has already been distributed—through libel and privacy law, for example—often involves a conflict between an individual and the media.

DEFAMATION, LIBEL, AND SLANDER   A **defamation** is a highly disreputable or false statement about a living person or an organization that causes injury to the reputation that a substantial group of people hold for that person or entity. Libel and slander are two types of defamation.

Libel is written communication that is considered harmful to a person's reputation. Some words and expressions are always considered libelous—false printed accusations that an individual is "incompetent," or that an organization is "disreputable," for example, are considered by courts as statements that, on their face, defame and are called **libel per se** (see Table 3.1 for a list of "red flag" words and expressions that courts have generally considered libelous per se).

Some words, expressions, and statements that seem, on their face, to be innocent and not injurious may be considered **libel per quod** in their actual contexts. In other words, statements that aren't defamatory on their own may become libelous when one knows other facts. For example, saying that Bradley is married to Marisol doesn't sound libelous, but if you know that Bradley is married to Nadia, being married to Marisol would make him a bigamist. And that statement is libelous. Related to libel is **slander**, or spoken communication that is considered harmful to a person's reputation.

Although libel and slander are both forms of defamation, they are controlled by different laws. What is important to remember is that when either libel or slander

defamation a highly disreputable or false statement about a living person or an organization that causes injury to the reputation that a substantial group of people hold for that person or entity

libel written communication that is considered harmful to a person's reputation

libel per se words and expressions that are always considered libelous

libel per quod words, expressions, and statements that, at face value, seem to be innocent and not injurious, but may be considered libelous in their actual contexts

slander spoken communication that is considered harmful to a person's reputation

Table 3.1 Libel Per Se

Listed below are some "red flag" words and expressions that courts have generally considered libelous per se:

ignoramus	rascal	amoral
bankrupt	slacker	unprofessional
thief	sneaky	incompetent
cheat	unethical	illegitimate
traitor	unprincipled	hypocritical
drunk	corrupt	cheating
blockhead		

(or both) occurs, a person's reputation and character are damaged in some way. An example everyone agrees is libel is a former entry in the Web encyclopedia Wikipedia about the retired newspaper editor John Siegenthaler Sr. The elderly Siegenthaler is a hero to those who know his role in encouraging and writing about civil rights in the 1960s. Yet someone added horrible statements to his biography on the collectively created Web encyclopedia. The passage claimed that Siegenthaler was connected to the assassinations of both Robert Kennedy and President John F. Kennedy. When Siegenthaler protested the libelous entry, it was pulled from Wikipedia, as were echoes of the claims that had appeared on the websites http://www.reference.com and http://www.answers.com. Later, the author of the malicious entries came forward, apologized profusely, and said he was playing a joke on what he thought was a prankster website. Clearly, by then, the reputation-damaging contentions had spread through the Web. Siegenthaler didn't sue the blogger for libel, though he certainly could have done so.

It is also important to recognize that there are two categories of libel plaintiffs: public figures and private persons. A **public figure** may be an elected or appointed official (a politician) or someone who has stepped (willingly or unwillingly) into a public controversy (for example, movie stars and TV stars, famous athletes, or other persons who draw attention to themselves). A **private person** may be well known in the community, but he or she has no authority or responsibility for the conduct of governmental affairs and has not thrust himself or herself into the middle of an important public controversy. Because the claim about Siegenthaler related to a time in his life when he did put himself in the midst of an important public controversy, he might well be considered a public figure with respect to the law.

In 1964, the case of *New York Times* vs. *Sullivan* profoundly altered libel law, and set legal precedent that is still in effect today. On March 29, 1960, a full-page advertisement titled "Heed Their Rising Voices" was placed in *The New York Times* by the Committee to Defend Martin Luther King Jr. and the Struggle for Freedom in the South. The ad criticized police and public officials in several cities for tactics used to disrupt the civil rights movement and sought contributions to post bail for the Reverend Martin Luther King Jr., and other movement leaders. The accusations made in the advertisement were true for the most part, but the copy contained several rather minor factual errors. L. B. Sullivan, police commissioner in Montgomery, Alabama, sued *The New York Times* for libel, claiming that the ad had defamed him indirectly. He won $500,000 for damages in the state courts of Alabama, but the U.S. Supreme Court overturned the damage award, reasoning that Alabama's libel laws violated *The New York Times'* First Amendment rights.

In issuing its opinion, the Supreme Court said that the U.S. Constitution (First and Fourteenth Amendments) protected false and defamatory statements made about public officials only if the false statements were not published with actual malice. The Court defined **actual malice** as reckless disregard for truth or knowledge of falsity. Note that actual malice considers a defendant's attitude toward truth, not the defendant's attitude toward the plaintiff. This differs from **simple malice**, which means hatred or ill will toward another person. By his own admission that he concocted the anti-Siegenthaler story, the blogger might be said to have written his piece with actual malice. Yet his claim that he thought the site was for pranksters (and therefore not believable) might make it difficult to have the "reckless" charge stick. If Siegenthaler had sued him for libel, the particulars would be up to a court to decide.

In general, because actual malice is difficult to prove, this ruling makes it difficult for a public official to win a libel suit. Additionally, the Supreme Court has broadened the actual malice protection to include public figures as well as public officials. The Court's reasoning is simple: the actual malice test sets a high bar, but it does so

public figure a person who is an elected or appointed official (a politician), or someone who has stepped (willingly or unwillingly) into a public controversy

private person an individual who may be well known in the community, but who has no authority or responsibility for the conduct of government affairs and has not thrust himself or herself into the middle of an important public controversy

actual malice reckless disregard for truth or knowledge of falsity

simple malice hatred or ill will toward another person

to protect the First Amendment rights of the media. At the same time, however, it allows media outlets to pursue legitimate news stories without the constant fear of being sued by the subjects of news stories. In the end, concern for the First Amendment takes precedence over libel laws as they relate to media.

Supreme Court decisions have also made it hard for a person who is neither a public figure nor an official to sue a media firm for libel. The Court has ruled that the First Amendment requires proof of **simple negligence**—lack of reasonable care—even when private persons sue the mass media for libel.

In order to win a libel suit, a plaintiff—whether a public figure or a private person—must prove that five activities occurred. The jury must be convinced that all of these five elements apply to the case in order for the First Amendment to be set aside in favor of an individual's right.

1 *The defamatory statements were published.* The term "publication" does not necessarily mean printing, as in a magazine or a newspaper. For the purposes of a court deciding a libel case, **publication** occurs when one person—in addition to the plaintiff and the defendant—sees or hears the defamatory material. You can "publish" something by making and circulating a video on the internet, for example.

2 *The defamatory statements identified the plaintiff (although not necessarily by name).* Some courts have ruled that it only takes one person to recognize and identify the plaintiff from a likeness, a description, or a story in context; the plaintiff does not have to be identified by name. Say, for example, that Joachim creates a DVD in which a character who looks and acts like his next-door neighbor is depicted as a person who regularly steals from Joachim's garage.

3 *The defamatory statements harmed the plaintiff.* A plaintiff in a libel case can prove that he or she suffered **harm** by showing that the defamatory statements led to loss of income (actual financial loss) or physical and emotional discomfort. Continuing with our example, say that Russell distributes a hundred DVD copies of the video throughout the neighborhood. He also posts the DVD on the "bulletin board" area of the local Neighborhood Club's website. His neighbor shows the court that people in the area have continually asked him if he is a thief. He argues that his local business has suffered because of the video. The man's lawyer brings forward the man's psychiatrist, who attests that the man's marriage and family life have suffered because of the stress Russell's video has caused.

4 *The defendant was at fault.* In order to win a libel suit, a plaintiff must prove **fault**, but how this is proven can vary from case to case. Depending upon the circumstances, fault may be established according to three factors: (a) who has brought the lawsuit, (b) the nature of the lawsuit (what it is about), and (c) the applicable state laws.

5 *The defamatory statements were false.* Proving **falsity** in a libel case is a question of the burden of proof— who has to prove that the defamatory statements are false? If the plaintiff is a public figure, he or she must prove that the defamatory statements are not truthful or accurate. If the plaintiff is a private person, however, he or she must prove that defamatory statements are untrue only if those statements are regarding a matter of public concern. If the defamatory statements are of a private nature, then the burden of proof shifts to the defendant, who must prove that the defamatory statements are indeed true. In our example, then, it is Joachim who must prove that what his video depicts about his neighbor his true.

Defenses to libel come in three forms: truth, privilege, and fair comment and criticism.

simple negligence lack of reasonable care

publication in libel law, a process that occurs when one person—in addition to the plaintiff and the defendant—sees or hears the defamatory material in question

harm in libel law, loss of income (actual financial loss) or physical and emotional discomfort

fault in libel law, a condition that may be established according to who has brought the lawsuit, the nature of the lawsuit, and the applicable state laws

falsity in libel law, untruth; one party or the other (either the defendant or the plaintiff) must prove that the defamatory statements are either true or untrue, and who must bear this burden of proof depends on whether the plaintiff is a public figure or a private person

truth an absolute defense against charges of libel; to prove that a statement is true, and therefore not defamatory, the evidence presented in court must be both direct and explicit, and the statement must be substantial truth—it doesn't have to be entirely true, but the part that "stings" must be true

privilege a defense to libel that holds that, although the public's right to know takes precedence over a person's right to preserve his or her reputation, certain professions (doctors, lawyers, psychologists) or individuals (chiefly a spouse) can maintain privilege; if any nonprivileged third party was part of the communication, the privilege is broken

fair comment and criticism a defense against libel in which the defendant claims, and proves, that the defamatory statement in question was part of the defendant's fair comment and criticism of a public figure who has thrust himself or herself into the public eye or is at the center of public attention; this defense is good only when it applies to an opinion, not to an assertion of a fact

equal time rule an order of Congress that requires broadcasters to provide equal amounts of time during comparable parts of the day to all legally qualified candidates for political office

1 *Truth*. Claiming and subsequently proving the **truth** of the defamatory statement in question is an absolute defense against a charge of libel. But how do you prove that the statement is true? The evidence presented in court must be both direct and explicit; that is, it must go to the heart of the libelous charge. Additionally, it must be substantial truth; the statement doesn't have to be entirely true, but the part that "stings" must be true. The real test is whether the proven truth leaves a different impression of the plaintiff in the minds of the jury than that left by the falsehood. Because truth can be so very hard to prove, this defense is rarely used.

2 *Privilege*. U.S. courts have held that the public's right to know takes precedence over a person's right to preserve his or her reputation. However, certain materials such as grand jury indictments, arrest warrants, and judicial proceedings are considered **privileged**. If a defendant claims, and subsequently proves, that the defamatory statement in question was privileged (and thus is not public), he or she has presented a valid defense against charges of libel. Only certain professions (doctors, lawyers, psychologists) or individuals (chiefly a spouse) can maintain that privilege; if any nonprivileged third party was part of the communication, the privilege is broken.

3 *Fair comment and criticism*. The third defense is claiming, and proving, that the defamatory statement in question was part of the defendant's **fair comment and criticism** of a public figure who has thrust himself or herself into the public eye or is at the center of public attention. This defense is good only when it applies to an opinion, not an assertion of a fact. There's a world of difference between saying "I think he's a crook" and saying "He's a crook."

THE FCC AND CONTENT REGULATION   The basic principles of freedom of speech and of the press apply in electronic media just as they do in print media. From the early days of broadcasting, Congress has viewed it as different from print because the available wavelengths for radio and TV signals were limited (or scarce). According to Congress, this wavelength scarcity justified the creation of an agency such as the Federal Communications Commission to oversee the distribution of frequencies and to ensure competition of ideas over the airwaves.

Congress' notion of wavelength scarcity applies to broadcasting only—not to cable or satellite television. That has sometimes put Congress and the FCC in the strange position of announcing content regulations for broadcasters that do not apply to hundreds of cable and satellite channels. For example, in 1996 the FCC announced that each week broadcast TV stations must air three hours of educational television programs aimed at children aged sixteen and under that serve their "intellectual, cognitive, social, and emotional needs." Broadcasters complain that it is unfair that they alone, not cable or satellite networks, are required to spend the time and money on such programming. They also say that the requirement is outdated in an era of specialized children's channels such as Nickelodeon and the Disney Channel. Supporters of the rule argue that broadcasters should have greater obligations than other media firms because broadcasters are using valuable public airwaves that reach virtually everyone. The rule's supporters also claim that broadcasters do not always mount programs that match the spirit of the FCC rule. In the case of Univision, the country's largest Spanish-language broadcaster, the Commission agreed. In 2007 it forced Univision to pay a record $24 million fine for airing telenovelas (soap operas) with children during the time it claimed it was fulfilling the children's educational requirement from 2004 to 2006.[12]

A much older requirement of broadcasters, one originating from Congress but enforced by the FCC, is the **equal time rule**. It requires broadcasters to provide equal amounts of time during comparable parts of the day to all legally qualified candidates for political office. Carrying this idea further, in the late 1940s the FCC enacted the **Fairness doctrine**. This rule required broadcasters to provide some degree of balance in the presentation of a controversial issue. Say, for example, a broadcaster aired an editorial supporting one side of a controversial issue—such as the closing of an expensive "magnet" school in a city. The broadcaster would then have to make time (in a new story or by providing or selling the group advertising) for those who disagree.

Fairness doctrine a rule implemented by the FCC in the late 1940s that requires broadcasters to provide some degree of balance in the presentation of controversial issues

CRITICAL CONSUMER
WEB USER BEWARE

Keeping control over important personal information can be tricky in today's digital world, and laws don't always help. Many people know that federal law prohibits their doctors and health firms from releasing information about them to marketers who want to send them advertisements. They may not know, however, that this law covers only a small segment of companies that can learn about their health information. And Madison Avenue really wants to know what is in your medicine cabinet. Drug companies spend as much as $18 billion annually on advertising and education, according to a 2005 report in the *Journal of the American Medical Association*. They'd just love to find more effective ways to target customers. What better way than to gain up-to-the-minute access to everyone's health records?

The idea of a central repository of health information that can help health professionals has great appeal. So does the idea of making it easier for us to see our medical records. The devil, however, is in the details. On sites such as WebMD and Revolution Health, setting up a personal health record is "free"—supported by advertising. This should raise alarm bells, because Madison Avenue has a long tradition of covertly trolling for consumers' personal information for marketing.

Every day, people unwittingly disclose personal health information when they use coupons for prescription drugs, subscribe to disease-based magazines, register at websites, or complete surveys seeking personal information. Often the real motive behind these activities is to compile profiles on individuals and households. Check the diabetes box, and your health condition appears permanently in the marketer's file. List sellers offer contact information on millions of individuals by disease profile. Companies that buy these names offer magazine subscriptions, raise funds, and sell medical products and services.

Commercial repositories of personal health records increase the stakes for consumer privacy several-fold. Companies that charge consumers little or nothing for storing those records will profit by allowing marketers

to use far more information about consumers than traditional lists could. Existing regulations do not cover personal health record firms unless they also are healthcare providers or health plans. Once a consumer consents to the disclosure of medical records to a personal health records company, those records lose the protection of federal health privacy rules.

Companies may say that they will not share individually identifiable information with advertisers or others without consent. Unfortunately, it is too easy for a consumer to unknowingly give consent. A pre-checked box may be unobtrusively included on a Web page that a consumer must click through. Marketers expect that most consumers will not notice or bother to uncheck the box.

Companies may claim to respect your privacy. For example, a personal health records site may sell marketers the ability to advertise to diabetics, and you may be one of them. When you go to your personal record, you will see ads, discount coupons, and articles targeted to diabetics. The marketers who pay for them will not know your name—or they won't until you make a common mistake. To obtain your identity, advertisers will try to entice you to click onto their websites. Once there, your personal information may end up anywhere. One click can result in an irretrievable revelation of your medical status to another company that profits by reselling personal data.

No administrative or legislative responses are on the horizon. Consumers must fend for themselves. Read the labels: Who is funding these services and who profits? And be careful in giving out information about yourself.

Sources: Joseph Turow, Robert Gellman, and Judith Turow, "Why Marketers Want Inside Your Medical Cabinet," *San Francisco Chronicle*, March 5, 2007, p. D9; Joseph Turow, Robert Gellman, and Judith Turow, "Personalized Marketing of Health Products the 21st Century Way," *AMA Virtual Mentor*, 2007, 9: 206–209. http://virtualmentor.ama-assn.org/2007/03/pfor1-0703.html (accessed March 6 2007).

As you might imagine, many broadcasters disliked the Fairness doctrine because it threatened to take away their control over "their" airwaves. By the mid-1980s, they argued to the FCC that new electronic media—for example cable—were creating so many electronic choices that the requirement should be abolished. In the deregulatory climate of the day, the FCC suspended (though it didn't repeal) the Fairness doctrine. Even so, because the Fairness doctrine was not repealed, it could someday be revived by a more activist commission, and the equal time rule still remains in effect.

privacy the right to be protected from unwanted intrusions or disclosures

PRIVACY **Privacy**—the right to be protected from unwanted intrusions or disclosures—is a broad area of the law when it comes to media industries. Almost every state recognizes some right of privacy, either by statute or under common law. Most state laws attempt to strike a balance between the individual's right to privacy and the public interest in freedom of the press. However, these rights often clash.

personal tort behavior that harms another individual

Invasion of privacy is considered a **personal tort**, or behavior that harms another individual. The law is aimed at protecting the individual's feelings. Courts often describe these feelings as "reasonable expectations of privacy." Only a person can claim a right of privacy; corporations, organizations, and other entities cannot.

Public figures have a limited claim to a right of privacy. Past and present government officials, political candidates, entertainers, and sports figures are generally considered to be public figures. They are said to have voluntarily exposed themselves to scrutiny and to have waived their right of privacy, at least regarding matters that might have an impact on their ability to perform their public duties.

Although private individuals can usually claim the right to be left alone, that right is not absolute. For example, if a person who is normally not considered a public figure is thrust into the spotlight because of her participation in a newsworthy event, her claims of a right of privacy may be limited.

There are four areas of privacy:

false light invading a person's privacy by implying something untrue about him or her

- False light
- Appropriation
- Intrusion
- Public disclosure

Let's look at them one at a time.

False Light

distortion a type of false light privacy invasion that involves the arrangement of materials or photographs to give a false impression

Publishing material that puts an individual in a **false light** has been considered an invasion of personal privacy by the courts. Suppose a TV station is creating a news report about the growing use of heroin by middle-class residents of your city. To illustrate the idea that "average" citizens are increasingly involved in the problem, the producer films footage of people walking down the streets of the city; you happen to be one of them. Turning on the local news one evening, you see a report that shows you quite clearly walking down the street just as the narrator notes that average residents are becoming hooked on heroin. You are angry that the station has placed you in a "false light" and invaded your privacy when you walked down the street. You consider suing the station on the grounds that the story made it appear that you were a heroin user.

embellishment a type of false light privacy invasion in which false material added to a story places someone in a false light

fictionalization a type of false light privacy invasion in which reference is made to real people or to thinly disguised characters that clearly represent real people in supposedly untrue stories

False light can take place in a number of ways. The example above constitutes **distortion**, which is the arrangement of materials or photographs to give a false impression. Another type of false light is **embellishment**, in which false material added to a story places someone in a false light. Yet a third way is **fictionalization**, which involves making reference to real people or presenting thinly disguised characters that clearly represent real people in supposedly untrue stories.

The courts do not particularly favor false light cases because very often they conflict with freedom of speech. Decided by the U.S. Supreme Court in 1967, *Time* vs. *Hill* set out the modern standard for false light privacy cases. According to the Supreme Court's decision in that case, a plaintiff is required to prove "by clear and convincing evidence" that the defendant knew of the statement's falsity or acted in reckless disregard of its truth or falsity. Using this standard, it would be difficult for a person who is deemed a public figure—an NBA basketball player who makes extra money by licensing his name on products—to win a case. The "public nature" of the athlete's activities gives writers and broadcasters considerable leeway to report on his or her affairs.

Appropriation

Appropriation means the unauthorized use of a person's name or likeness in an advertisement, poster, public relations promotion, or other commercial context. The law protects individuals from being

In Alfred Eisenstaedt's famous photograph, a sailor kisses a nurse in New York's Times Square on August 14, 1945, the day of victory over Japan, which marked the end of World War II.

exploited and harmed by others for their exclusive benefit. As with libel, a person's entire name need not be used. If the person could reasonably be identified, the appropriation claim will most likely be valid.

Courts have continuously interpreted the law in a way that enables news organizations to use a person's name or likeness when publishing a newsworthy story. They have even extended this privilege when the news organization is a private, for-profit organization that derives income from advertising. However, almost all courts have held that the use of the name and likeness must be newsworthy. The issue came up, for example, with regard to a famous photograph of a sailor kissing a nurse in Times Square. A U.S. district court held that the initial publication of the photograph in *Life* magazine was appropriate to illustrate a newsworthy event, but that *Time*'s subsequent sale of reprints to the public without permission from the man and woman pictured was not.

Courts have been quite clear that the exception allowing the use of such images is limited to newsworthy purposes. They have explicitly denied exceptions even for charitable or informational purposes. For example, courts have ruled that photographs of living cancer survivors could not be exhibited for public informational and educational purposes without the individuals' prior written consent.

Public Disclosure

The term **public disclosure** refers to truthful information concerning the private life of a person that a media source reveals and that both would be highly offensive to a reasonable person and is not of legitimate public concern. Courts have ruled that this is an invasion of privacy. For example, revealing private, sensational facts about a person's sexual activity, health, or economic status can constitute an invasion of privacy under the law of public disclosure.

appropriation an invasion of privacy that takes the form of the unauthorized use of a person's name or likeness in an advertisement, poster, public relations promotion, or other commercial context

public disclosure truthful information concerning the private life of a person, revealed by a media source, that would be highly offensive to a reasonable person and is not of legitimate public concern is considered to be an invasion of privacy

CULTURE TODAY
WOODY ALLEN VS. AMERICAN APPAREL

Two billboard advertisements for the clothing company American Apparel sprang up along the roadsides of New York and Los Angeles in May of 2007. Both sported a photo of Woody Allen dressed as an Orthodox Jew, a still from the film Annie Hall. In Yiddish, the sole text read "the High Rabbi." Within a week the billboards had disappeared. The reason why? Allen had never authorized the use of his image in the advertisements and had demanded that they be taken down.

What ensued was a lawsuit, one pitting legendary writer, director, and actor Allen against American Apparel founder and controversial business and fashion icon Dov Charney. Seeking $10 million in damages, Allen asserted that the use of his image without his permission constituted a breach of his right to privacy and implied that Allen endorsed the Los Angeles-based company. Although courts recognize the right for an organization to use a person's likeness for newsworthy items, courts have generally ruled that consent must be obtained before using another's likeness for commercial purposes.

Charney insisted that the purpose of the billboard was not to sell clothes, but instead to "inspire dialogue" by drawing a comparison between Charney and Allen—both of whom have found themselves at the center of sex scandals. However, lawyer Jonathan Faber of RightofPublicity.com voiced doubts over the legal viability of Charney's claim. "You can't make associations with famous individuals without their permission," he said. "There's a value to it." American Apparel, forced to settle by the company's insurer, ultimately paid Allen $5 million in damages.

Image-appropriation law remains an uncertain and frequently challenged area, one where the law must balance the rights of free speech with the rights of control over one's own image. To what extent do you think celebrities should have a say in their likeness is used?

Sources: Christopher Palmeri, "American Apparel Settles with Woody Allen," *Business Week*, May 18, 2009. http://www.businessweek.com/bwdaily/dnflash/content/may2009/db20090518_942184.htm (accessed March 27, 2010).

How the information was obtained and its *newsworthiness* often determine liability in cases of public disclosure. If a journalistic organization obtains information unlawfully—whether or not the information is truthful—the organization may be held liable for invasion of privacy under the rules of public disclosure. Additionally, courts may consider several factors in determining whether information that is published is newsworthy, including the social value of the facts published, how deeply the article intruded into the person's private affairs, and the extent to which the person voluntarily assumed a position of public notoriety. For example, in a 1951 case, a woman who had been involved in a car accident sued a reporter who revealed that she was living with a man who was not her spouse. That fact was not pertinent to the story, which was otherwise newsworthy, and the reporter was held liable.

More recently, however, courts have made it difficult to win a public disclosure suit against journalists. Just as concerns for the First Amendment have given mass media firms a great deal of latitude when it comes to libel and appropriation, First Amendment considerations have tended to grant media businesses the right to reveal information about individuals. Consider a Florida rape victim's 1989 case against the *Florida Star*, a Jacksonville newspaper. A reporter-trainee for the paper had learned the full name of a rape victim whose initials were in a county sheriff's report. The *Star* published the name, even though a Florida law prohibited an "instrument of mass communication" from making public the identity of rape victims. The victim sued the paper for emotional distress and won. However, the U.S. Supreme Court reversed the decision. The justices said that the government is allowed to punish a paper for publishing lawfully obtained, truthful information only if the government can show that the punishment is "narrowly tailored to a state interest of the highest order."

Intrusion

Intrusion takes place when a person or organization intentionally invades a person's solitude, private area, or affairs. The invasion can be physical (for example, sneaking into a person's office) or non-physical (such as putting an electronic listening device outside the office but in a position to hear what is going on inside). Intrusion claims against the media often center on some aspect of the news-gathering process. This tort may involve trespassing or the wrongful use of tape recorders, cameras, or other intrusive equipment.

Defenses against allegations of privacy invasion are fairly straightforward. If a person *consents*, there can be no invasion of privacy. However, the reporter should be sure that the subject has not only consented to be interviewed, but also consented to having the interview or photographs published or aired. When minors or legally incompetent people are involved, the consent of a parent or guardian may be necessary. A written release is essential for the use of pictures or private information in advertising or other commercial contexts.

Truth can be a defense, but only in false light cases. A litigant claiming false light invasion of privacy who is involved in a matter of public interest must prove that the media intentionally or recklessly made erroneous statements about him or her. However, truth is not a defense to a claim based on publication of private facts.

If the public has a legitimate interest in the story as it was reported, *newsworthiness* can be a defense to the charge of invasion of privacy. But if a report that is of legitimate public interest includes irrelevant private information, publication of those private facts may warrant legal action.

Economic Regulation

Economic regulations placed on media organizations greatly affect the ways in which those organizations finance, produce, exhibit, and distribute their products. Two types of media economic regulation are most common: antitrust laws and direct regulation by government agencies.

ANTITRUST LAWS   One way to expand the marketplace of ideas without directly making rules about content is to limit excessive market control by mass media corporations. **Excessive market control** is behavior by one company or a few companies that makes it nearly impossible for new companies to enter the marketplace and compete. For example, a production company might gain this kind of power by buying up competitors and making sure that exhibitors do not deal with any new competitors. Distributors and exhibitors might do the same thing: a few bookstore chains might swallow up their retail competition to the point that all publishers must deal primarily with them. When it comes to mass media, the excessive control over the market might directly affect consumers or advertisers, or both.

Control of the market by one firm is called **monopoly**. Control by a select few firms is called **oligopoly**. Great concern over train and steel monopolies and oligopolies in the late 1800s led U.S. legislators to begin to take special actions with respect to these activities, in order to maintain competition. These laws came to be known broadly as **antitrust policies**, and in the following decades they were carried out in three ways:

- Through the passage of laws
- Through enforcement of the laws by the U.S. Department of Justice and by state attorneys general

intrusion an invasion of privacy that takes place when a person or organization intentionally invades a person's solitude, private area, or affairs

excessive market control behavior by one company or a few companies that makes it nearly impossible for new companies to enter the marketplace and compete

monopoly control of the market by a single firm

oligopoly control of the market by a select few firms

antitrust policies policies put in place to maintain competition in the U.S. economy, carried out through the passing of laws, through enforcement of the laws by the U.S. Department of Justice and by state attorneys general, and through federal court decisions that determine how far the government ought to go in encouraging competition and forcing companies to break themselves up into a number of smaller companies

TECH & INFRASTRUCTURE
PRIVACY IN THE DIGITAL AGE

Concern about media organizations and government agencies searching for personal details has grown with the enormous rise in the use of computers to collect and combine data about individuals from many sources. Responding to these fears, Congress has passed laws that limit the ability of companies and government agencies to use and share data without the knowledge of the individuals involved.

Clearly, much of this concern with privacy is not tied specifically to the creation and circulation of mass media content. It does, however, affect activities within mass media industries because government actions to limit or broaden a company's ability to deal with information about individuals can affect how a mass media organization approaches its audiences and the profits it can make from them.

The **Cable Telecommunications Act of 1984** provides an example. The lawmakers who wrote it were sensitive to concerns by various privacy protection groups about new "interactive" cable technologies that deliver programs to homes without subscribers' knowledge in order to learn what they watch and how they live. That could happen if cable companies provided subscribers with keyboards and invited them to order products directly on screen, to participate in TV games that ask about their recreational activities, or to answer polls that require information about their voting behaviors and beliefs. This sort of information about every subscriber could then be requested by a government agency or sold to marketers or other media firms, who could merge the data with more information about the person from other places.

To satisfy some of the privacy protection groups' concerns, the Cable Telecommunications Act requires cable companies to report to their subscribers what personal information is collected about them and how it is used. The Act further prohibits the cable operators from releasing to the government or other companies "personally identifiable information" without subscribers' consent. The Act does not prohibit the cable firm from using the information it gathers. It might, for example, send advertisements for upcoming romantic pay-per-view films to teenage girls in its system who have boyfriends, while targeting ads for financial news programs at politically conservative men who are over the age of fifty. The act also does not prohibit a cable firm from selling its information to other firms as long as it does not tell the other parties the specific names involved. For example, a greeting card company might ask the cable firm to send ads about its Valentine's Day cards to the teenage girls who have boyfriends. As long as the cable firm does the actual mailing, it is not doing anything illegal.

As limited as it might be in protecting privacy, because of this feature of the 1984 Cable Act, cable firms are restricted far more than companies that create and distribute mass media materials by way of other media. The only other laws that specifically prohibit media firms from sharing information about their audiences are the **Video Privacy Protection Act (or VPPA) of 1988** and the **Children's Online Privacy Protection Act (or COPPA) of 1998**. The VPPA prevents disclosure of personally identifiable rental records of "prerecorded video cassette tapes or similar audio visual material."[13] Congress enacted the law out of anger at the disclosure of Supreme Court nominee Robert Bork's video rental records in a newspaper, presumably in an attempt to embarrass the Yale University professor.

COPPA states that, if a website wants to get information from children under thirteen years old, it must receive parental permission. (The law requires the Federal Trade Commission to create rules covering how permission can be granted, and the FTC has done that.) Moreover, the parent must be able to tell the website not to give the information to marketers and to ask the site to delete the data in the future.

But these rules are exceptions. The fact is that most firms that create and distribute mass media materials consequently have few direct constraints when it comes to protecting privacy. Companies both offline and online increasingly have the ability to silently and secretly gather information about people using their services. In Chapter 14, we will discuss how much of the Web's commercial activity is based on serving particular ads to individuals based on the demographic and psychographic information that sites have about the people; where they have been on the Web; and even their offline media activities. In other chapters we will see how traditional media are using data about their audiences, too. Magazine firms, for example, can buy information about you from other sources and use it to attract advertisers interested in reaching people like you. Or consider mass media firms that invite you to phone 800 numbers. Did you know that they can learn the telephone number (and usually the ZIP code and neighborhood) from which you are calling even if you have placed a block on your line to stop caller identification (Caller ID) technology? The law allows telephone companies to derail Caller ID blocking for calls to 800 numbers.

■ Through federal court decisions that determine how far the government ought to go in encouraging competition and forcing companies to break themselves up into a number of smaller companies

Over the years, regulators and the courts have ruled that certain activities by firms involved in mass communication represent excessive market control. Typically, they have involved the use of vertical integration by a few firms to control an industry. We will note the most important of these cases when we deal with particular industries in the chapters to come.

DIRECT REGULATION BY GOVERNMENT AGENCIES   The **Federal Trade Commission** and the **Federal Communications Commission** are the two most important federal agencies involved in regulating the mass media.

The first thing to remember when comparing the two agencies is that the FTC's coverage can include any of the mass media—print or electronic—as long as the issue involved is related to the smooth functioning of the marketplace and consumer protection in that sphere. By contrast, the FCC is specifically mandated by Congress to govern interstate and international communications by television, radio, wire, satellite, and cable.

The FTC describes its overall mission in the following manner:

> The Federal Trade Commission enforces a variety of federal antitrust and consumer protection laws. The Commission seeks to ensure that the nation's markets function competitively, and are vigorous, efficient, and free of undue restrictions. The Commission also works to enhance the smooth operation of the marketplace by eliminating acts or practices that are unfair or deceptive.
>
> In general, the Commission's efforts are directed toward stopping actions that threaten consumers' opportunities to exercise informed choice. Finally, the Commission undertakes economic analysis to support its law enforcement efforts and to contribute to the policy deliberations of the Congress, the Executive Branch, other independent agencies, and state and local governments when requested.[14]

Implied in this mission statement are three responsibilities that very much relate to media today: creating technical order, consumer protection, and encouraging competition.

Creating Technical Order
Many of the FTC's most important activities are aimed at simply creating *technical order* in an electronic environment that could become chaotic without some kind of regulation. It is through the FCC that radio stations get licenses that allow them to broadcast on specific wavelengths (the numbers we associate with the stations). The FCC is also in charge of allocating the frequency spectrum among various other technologies, including satellites and cellular phones. Although some of these technical activities have nothing to do with mass media, many of them do. Most major news organizations use satellites and cellphones for their work. Many consumers pay to get TV programming via satellite. Increasingly, too, consumers are even getting news, information, and advertisements through their mobile phones. FCC decisions about how much and how to allocate spectrum space helps to define which and how many companies can afford to get into this business in different parts of the country. That, in turn, affects the number of companies consumers have to consider and how much they will pay.

Cable Telecommunications Act of 1984 a law that requires cable companies to report to their subscribers what personal information is collected about them and how it is used, and prohibits the cable operators from releasing to the government or other companies "personally identifiable information" without subscribers' consent

Video Privacy Protection Act (VPPA) of 1988 a law that prevents disclosure of personally identifiable rental records of "prerecorded video cassette tapes or similar audio visual material"

Children's Online Privacy Protection Act (COPPA) of 1998 a law that applies to the online collection of personal information from children under the age of thirteen; it spells out what a website operator must include in a privacy policy, when and how to seek verifiable consent from a parent, and what responsibilities an operator has to protect children's privacy and safety online

Federal Trade Commission (FTC) a federal agency whose mission is to ensure that the nation's markets function competitively; its coverage can include any mass media—print or electronic—as long as the issue involved is related to the smooth functioning of the marketplace and consumer protection in that sphere

Federal Communications Commission (FCC) a federal agency specifically mandated by Congress to govern interstate and international communication by television, radio, wire, satellite, and cable

Consumer Protection

In the area of *consumer protection*, the Federal Trade Commission is involved in issues ranging from combating deceptive advertising to protecting children's privacy on the Web. As we have noted, the FTC was placed in charge of implementing and administering the Children's Online Privacy Protection Act. To implement the Act, the FTC had to create rules that specified exactly what websites were covered by the Act, exactly what rules should apply to them, and when the rules would go into effect. To administer the Act, the FTC had to create a system for monitoring websites on a regular basis to make sure that they were adhering to COPPA.

Encouraging Competition

Encouraging competition means enforcing federal antitrust laws. As we have seen, these are laws designed to prevent one or a few companies from controlling such a large percentage of an industry that they can dictate high prices and so harm the consumer.

It was with this responsibility in mind that the FTC decided to review the announcement by Google in 2009 that it would like to purchase the firm AdMob for $750 million. AdMob tracks people's mobile phones and serves ads to them based on location and data about their Web use. The FTC contacted Google for more information about the deal, possibly out of concern that it might deter future competition in the mobile space. Reinforcing this perspective was a joint letter sent to the Commission by two advocacy groups, Consumer Watchdog and the Center for Digital Democracy. They argued that Google is buying its way to dominance in the mobile advertising industry by diminishing the competition "to the detriment of consumers." According to a press release by the organizations, the letter asserted that "The mobile sector is the next frontier of the digital revolution. Without vigorous competition and strong privacy guarantees this vital and growing segment of the online economy will be stifled." The two groups added that the deal raises substantial privacy concerns because both companies gather tremendous amounts of data about consumers.[15]

The Struggle with Government over Information Gathering

Although opportunities for prior restraint on speech by governments are rather limited under the U.S. Constitution (as we have noted), government officials have tried to prevent journalists from gaining access to certain types of information in other ways. Over the decades, press organizations have worked to reduce these obstacles.

Gathering Information on Government Documents and Meetings

The government can limit speech—especially speech about the workings of the government—by restricting access to government documents. Documents about the military or foreign policy are often kept from public scrutiny because they may jeopardize important security matters. But sometimes secrecy is aimed at covering government officials' mistakes, or evading public accountability about decisions they have made. Consider, for example, the number of contractors and subcontractors of different nationalities working at U.S. and Iraqi military bases during the Iraq War. In response to demands from Congress, in 2006 the U.S. Central Command began a census of the number of civilian "contractors" working on U.S. and Iraqi bases to determine how much food, water, and shelter was needed. But Congress didn't release that information publicly, perhaps partly because the large number—more than 180,000—exceeded the number of combat troops and might have encouraged new levels of debate on the resources the United States was spending on the war. As we will see below, it took special journalistic enterprise under a special law called the Freedom of Information Act for a reporter to learn that number.[16]

Gathering Information on News Events

During breaking and continuing news stories, journalists seek access to the people and locations that are central to the news event at hand. But instances of breaking news aren't the only times when journalists need access to people, places, and events that are newsworthy. Journalists also need access to government meetings—at the federal, state, and local levels—where important decisions about how to run government and how to spend taxpayer money (among other things) are made. Historically, however, many government organizations have maintained strict closed-meeting policies.

Journalistic coverage of public meetings is critically important to the democratic process. Imagine deliberations by a county government about where to locate a new landfill—a controversial issue in any community. Media coverage of the deliberations would be important to citizens of the area who would worry about the location of the landfill, the nature of the material to be buried there, and the effect the landfill would have on their family's health and the value of their property. Having journalists present at the proceedings might enable people in the community to discuss the landfill plans, and might encourage local officials to guide the process more openly and honestly than they otherwise would.

Gathering Information from Confidential Sources

There are some important and powerful news stories that would never be written if the journalists who reported the information were forced to reveal their sources. Perhaps the source is too afraid to speak without the promise of anonymity; perhaps the source fears retaliation if his or her identity is made public. The result of such a source remaining quiet might be that valuable information goes unheard, harming the public good. In such cases, the journalist may claim an **evidentiary privilege**, which is a journalist's right to withhold the identification of confidential sources.

evidentiary privilege a journalist's right to withhold the identification of confidential sources

Just because a journalist claims evidentiary privilege, however, does not mean that he or she will be granted that privilege by the courts. For example, in 1972 the U.S. Supreme Court decided that the First Amendment offers reporters no protection from grand jury subpoenas.

Allowing Information Gathering

Beyond their struggles to keep sources confidential, journalists also work to uncover information that government agencies have tried to keep secret. During the past few decades, the federal Freedom of Information Act (FOIA), along with local and state sunshine and shield laws, has helped journalists to learn information that is important for the public's understanding of social policies but which might otherwise have remained out of view.

Freedom of Information Act (FOIA) an act passed by Congress in 1967 that allows citizens to request government records and reports that have not yet been made public, so long as these records and reports do not relate to nine specific areas: national security, agency interpersonal activities, statutory exemptions, trade secrets, some intra-agency and inter-agency memos, issues involving personal privacy, police investigations, protection of government-regulated financial institutions, and information about oil and gas wells

sunshine laws regulations that ensure that government meetings and reports are made available to the press and to members of the public

Government-in-the-Sunshine Act a federal act passed by Congress in 1977 that requires more than fifty governmental agencies, departments, and other groups to open their meetings to the public and the press (except under specific conditions)

shield laws laws passed in thirty states and the District of Columbia that afford the media varying degrees of protection against being forced to disclose information about their sources

FREEDOM OF INFORMATION ACT   Congress passed the **Freedom of Information Act** in 1967, allowing citizens to request government records and reports that have not yet been made public, so long as those reports and records do not involve nine specific areas:

- National security
- Agency interpersonal activities
- Statutory exemptions
- Trade secrets
- Some intra-agency and inter-agency memos
- Issues involving personal privacy
- Police investigations
- Protection of government-regulated financial institutions
- Information about oil and gas wells

Government agencies have sometimes tried to use these nine sensitive areas as barriers to prevent reporters and others from gaining access to other types of information. So the struggle for access to government information continues. Still, the work of many journalists has benefited from the Freedom of Information Act.

SUNSHINE LAWS   Over the past forty years, the alliance between journalism and advocacy organizations has persuaded many states to pass **sunshine laws**—regulations that ensure that government meetings and reports are made available to the press and to members of the public. The extent of openness varies from state to state, but a journalist's ability to explore the workings of government is much improved compared with earlier in the century.

The federal **Government-in-the-Sunshine Act**, which took effect in 1977, requires more than fifty government agencies, departments, and other groups to open their meetings to the public and the press, except under specific conditions.

SHIELD LAWS   The U.S. Supreme Court has ruled that the First Amendment doesn't give journalists the right to protect their sources. Nevertheless, press organizations have managed to convince legislators in thirty states and the District of Columbia to pass **shield laws** that afford the media varying degrees of protection against being forced to disclose information about their sources.

These laws vary greatly from state to state. In many states without shield laws, state courts have recognized some form of qualified privilege. In others, the state constitution may include "free press" provisions, which are similar to the First Amendment and afford qualified protection. States such as Hawaii and Wyoming, however, do not recognize any privilege to protect unpublished sources of journalistic information.

Media Self-Regulation

There are a number of media industry pressures—both external and internal—aimed at ensuring that media professionals operate in an ethical manner—including pressure from members of the public, advocacy groups, and advertisers. These outside pressures directly influence the internal self-regulation mechanisms that industries create. Let's start with external pressures and then move inside media industries.

A basket of notes sits next to a picture of *NY Times* reporter Judith Miller at the National Press Club in Washington. Miller served a sentence for refusing to testify before a grand jury about the leaking of the name of CIA officer, Valerie Plame.

External Pressures on Media Organizations to Self-Regulate

Every public squabble over what media firms should or shouldn't do involves parties at interest, called **stakeholders**. These are parties outside of media industries who care particularly about an issue, and use their economic and political power to influence the outcome to their benefit. Such stakeholders include members of the public, public advocacy organizations, and, perhaps most importantly, advertisers.

PRESSURE FROM MEMBERS OF THE PUBLIC When individuals are disturbed about media content, they may contact the production firms involved to express their displeasure and demand alterations in the content. Pick any topic—from racism to religion, from politicians to business people—and you will probably find that some sector of society is concerned about the portrayal of that topic in the mass media. People who see the mass media as a series of windows on the world often want to see the people, behaviors, and values that they hold dear portrayed in the media products they use.

As we noted in Chapter 2, media executives understand that they must think of their audiences as consumers who buy their products or whom they sell to advertisers. The complaining individual might be successful in getting the content changed or even removed if he or she convinces the media executives that they might otherwise lose a substantial portion of their target market. But an individual's concern

stakeholders parties outside media industries who care particularly about an issue and may try to use their economic and political power to influence the outcome to their benefit

103

will garner little attention if it is clear that the person does not belong in the target audience. The editors from *Cosmopolitan* magazine, which aims at twenty-something single women, for example, are not likely to follow the advice of an elderly sounding woman from rural Kansas who phones to protest what she feels are demeaning portrayals of women on covers of the magazine that she sees in the supermarket. Yet the magazine staff might well act favorably if a *Cosmo* subscriber writes with a suggestion for a new column that would attract more of the upscale single women they want as readers.

PRESSURE FROM ADVOCACY ORGANIZATIONS   Individuals who are particularly outraged about certain media portrayals may try to find others who share their concerns. They might join or start **advocacy organizations or pressure groups**, which work to change the nature of certain kinds of mass media materials.

Some advocacy organizations are specific to media—such as the Center for Media Education, which concentrates on children and television; the Committee for Accuracy in Middle East Reporting in America (CAMERA), which is devoted to promoting its view of accurate coverage of Israel in the media; and the Center for the Study of Commercialism, a critic of advertising and marketing. Other advocacy organizations pay attention to media as part of more general concerns, such as People for the American Way, which supports politically liberal approaches to social problems; Gay & Lesbian Alliance Against Defamation; and the conservative American Family Association, which monitors all aspects of society for attacks on its image of the family.

Representatives of these organizations may try to meet with the heads of media firms, start letter-writing campaigns, or attempt to embarrass media firms by attracting press coverage about an issue. If their target is an advertiser-supported medium, they may threaten to boycott the products of sponsors. They may also appeal to government officials for help.

PRESSURE FROM ADVERTISERS   Advertisers are a powerful force in pressuring the media to make changes in their content. Many advertisers like to buy space for their commercial messages within media content that reflects well on their products. Companies such as Hallmark and Procter & Gamble, which spend enormous amounts of money on advertising, sometimes have the clout to persuade media firms to tone down certain kinds of portrayals that don't fit their brand image.

Consider, for example, efforts by marketers to generate more "family-friendly" programming to sponsor during prime time on television networks. In 1998, such advertising giants as Johnson & Johnson, AT&T, Bristol-Myers Squibb, Coca-Cola, Ford Motor Company, General Motors, Gillette, IBM, Kellogg's, McDonald's, Procter & Gamble, and Unilever United States became concerned that the increased level of sex and violence on TV was angering many of their customers. The standard TV programming was also making it difficult for them to reach both parents and children at the same time.

In response, the marketers created the **Family Friendly Programming Forum**. It seeks to stimulate the production of shows meant to appeal to broader, multigenerational audiences and suitable to run between 8 and 10 p.m. (Eastern and Pacific times). "We want to sit and watch TV with our families and not be embarrassed," explained Steve Johnston, vice president for advertising and brand management at Nationwide Mutual Enterprises in Columbus, Ohio.

Critics of this coalition fear that it wants to create programs that romanticize a kind of fictional nuclear family. The advertisers insist, however, that it is possible to be both contemporary and family-friendly. "We have to be realistic; families may not be gathered around one TV anymore, and they're not your traditional families," said

advocacy organizations or pressure groups collections of people who work to change the nature of certain kinds of mass media materials

Family Friendly Programming Forum a forum created by a coalition of marketers in order to stimulate the production of shows meant to appeal to broader, multigenerational audiences and suitable to run between 8 and 10 p.m. (Eastern and Pacific times)

Susan Frank, executive vice president and general manager of the Odyssey Network in Studio City, California, a cable channel owned by Hallmark Cards that focuses on family-oriented programming. "But there are times you can bring family members together with content that's thought-provoking, done in a good, quality way," she added. "You have to be relevant to the way people live today."

By 2009, the group had come directly under the wing of the Association of National Advertisers (ANA) and changed its name to the ANA Alliance for Family Entertainment. The name change reflected a broadened mission to reflect the changing media environment "ensuring that there are family entertainment choices on broadcast and cable networks, as well as on the internet, mobile devices, and gaming platforms." To emphasize it was building on success, the Alliance noted on its website that it had "played a significant role in bringing 20 primetime programs to air, including hits *The Gilmore Girls*, *Chuck*, *Everybody Hates Chris*, and *Friday Night Lights*."[17] Although this project has itself created controversy, it does show how powerful advertisers can respond to concerns they perceive in their target audience and act to influence media.

Media-literate consumers should ask themselves whether or not it is ethical to pressure mass media organizations to alter their activities. Given the importance of freedom of the press and the dangers of censorship, we might consider any attempt to interfere with the media to be an unethical infringement of that freedom—a kind of censorship.

Some mass media executives add that they are already responsible to the most important pressure consumers can place on them: the pressure of the marketplace. These executives argue that if their target audiences don't like certain products, they won't buy those products and the content will be discontinued. Pressures from outside this relationship, if they continue, are unfair to the creators and the audience.

Internal Pressures on Media to Self-Regulate

To maintain their credibility with the public at large (and their target audiences in particular), and to avoid pressures from government and other outside entities interfering with their firms' activities, media executives set up self-regulation policies and

Adam Lambert performs onstage at the 21st Annual GLAAD Media Awards held annually in Los Angeles, CA. GLAAD recognizes and honors the media for their fair, accurate, and inclusive representations of the lesbian, gay, bisexual, and transgender community and the issues that affect their lives.

editorial standards written statements of policy and conduct established by media organizations as a form of self-regulation

policy books guidelines for fairness, accuracy, and appropriateness of station content, etc., adopted by media organizations in the interest of self-regulation

operating policies policies, most often used by print media organizations, that spell out guidelines for everyday operations, such as conflicts of interest, acceptable advertising content, boundaries of deceptive information-gathering practices, paying sources for news stories, etc.

editorial policies policies, most often used by print media organizations, that identify company positions on specific issues, such as which presidential candidate the paper supports, and whether the paper is in support of certain governmental policies

ombudsperson an individual who is hired by a media organization to deal with readers, viewers, or listeners who have a complaint to report or an issue to discuss

codes. This internal self-regulation can take a number of forms, including editorial standards and ombudspersons at the level of individual organizations, and professional codes of ethics, content ratings, press councils, and journalism reviews at the industry level.

EDITORIAL STANDARDS   Most media organizations have established **editorial standards**—written statements of policy and conduct. In the case of the network television industry, these policies are maintained and enforced by a department known as *Standards and Practices*, which makes difficult decisions regarding the acceptability of language in scripts, themes in plot lines, and images used in visual portrayals. At the local television station level, policy and conduct are most often guided by **policy books**, which help to lay down guidelines for fairness, accuracy, and appropriateness of station content, among other things.

Newspapers and magazines are most often guided by two kinds of editorial standards. The first, **operating policies**, spell out guidelines for everyday operations, such as conflicts of interest, acceptable advertising content, boundaries of deceptive information-gathering practices, and paying sources for news stories, among other things. The second, **editorial policies**, identify company positions on specific issues, such as which presidential candidate the paper supports and whether the paper is in support of certain governmental policies.

OMBUDSPERSONS   An **ombudsperson** is hired by a media organization to deal with readers, viewers, or listeners who have a complaint to report or an issue to discuss. Although an ombudsperson is employed directly by a media organization, his or her role is to act as an impartial intermediary between the organization and the public.

PROFESSIONAL CODES OF ETHICS   One of the oldest approaches to self-regulation is the professional code of ethics. These codes are often administered by societies or associations that represent an industry's interests to the outside world, to establish internal standards of professionalism.

Examples of such organizations are the Society of Professional Journalists, the American Society of Newspaper Editors, the Radio-Television News Directors Association, the American Advertising Federation, and the Public Relations Society of America. Each has an established code of ethics—that is, a formal list of guidelines and standards that tell the members of the profession, in this case media practitioners, what they should and should not do. See Figure 3.4 for the code of ethics adopted by the Society of Professional Journalists in 1996.

CONTENT RATINGS AND ADVISORIES   Another way in which media organizations regulate themselves is through the adoption of ratings systems, like those of the film, television, and computer media industries. These ratings are often controversial. Some people believe that they are not informative enough; still others believe that the ratings allow companies to place all the responsibility on the audience by creating whatever violent or sexually explicit materials they want and then simply slapping a rating on the material.

Film

A voluntary film rating system was adopted by the Motion Picture Association in 1968 and revised in 1990. The ratings place films into one of five categories:

Code of Ethics

Preamble

Members of the Society of Professional Journalists believe that public enlightenment is the forerunner of justice and the foundation of democracy. The duty of the journalist is to further those ends by seeking truth and providing a fair and comprehensive account of events and issues. Conscientious journalists from all media and specialties strive to serve the public with thoroughness and honesty. Professional integrity is the cornerstone of a journalist's credibility.

Members of the Society share a dedication to ethical behavior and adopt this code to declare the Society's principles and standards of practice.

Seek Truth and Report It

Journalists should be honest, fair and courageous in gathering, reporting and interpreting information.

Journalists should:

▶ Test the accuracy of information from all sources and exercise care to avoid inadvertent error. Deliberate distortion is never permissible.

▶ Diligently seek out subjects of news stories to give them the opportunity to respond to allegations of wrongdoing.

▶ Identify sources whenever feasible. The public is entitled to as much information as possible on sources' reliability.

▶ Always question sources' motives before promising anonymity. Clarify conditions attached to any promise made in exchange for information. Keep promises.

▶ Make certain that headlines, news teases and promotional material, photos, video, audio, graphics, sound bites and quotations do not misrepresent. They should not oversimplify or highlight incidents out of context.

▶ Never distort the content of news photos or video. Image enhancement for technical clarity is always permissible. Label montages and photo illustrations.

▶ Avoid misleading re-enactments or staged news events. If re-enactment is necessary to tell a story, label it.

▶ Avoid undercover or other surreptitious methods of gathering information except when traditional open methods will not yield information vital to the public. Use of such methods should be explained as part of the story.

▶ Never plagiarize.

▶ Tell the story of the diversity and magnitude of the human experience boldly, even when it is unpopular to do so.

▶ Examine their own cultural values and avoid imposing those values on others.

▶ Avoid stereotyping by race, gender, age, religion, ethnicity, geography, sexual orientation, disability, physical appearance or social status.

▶ Support the open exchange of views, even views they find repugnant.

▶ Give voice to the voiceless; official and unofficial sources of information can be equally valid.

▶ Distinguish between advocacy and news reporting. Analysis and commentary should be labeled and not misrepresent fact or context.

▶ Distinguish news from advertising and shun hybrids that blur the lines between the two.

▶ Recognize a special obligation to ensure that the public's business is conducted in the open and that government records are open to inspection.

Minimize Harm

Ethical journalists treat sources, subjects and colleagues as human beings deserving of respect.

Journalists should:

▶ Show compassion for those who may be affected adversely by news coverage. Use special sensitivity when dealing with children and inexperienced sources or subjects.

▶ Be sensitive when seeking or using interviews or photographs of those affected by tragedy or grief.

▶ Recognize that gathering and reporting information may cause harm or discomfort. Pursuit of the news is not a license for arrogance.

▶ Recognize that private people have a greater right to control information about themselves than do public officials and others who seek power, influence or attention. Only an overriding public need can justify intrusion into anyone's privacy.

▶ Show good taste. Avoid pandering to lurid curiosity.

▶ Be cautious about identifying juvenile suspects or victims of sex crimes.

▶ Be judicious about naming criminal suspects before the formal filing of charges.

▶ Balance a criminal suspect's fair trial rights with the public's right to be informed.

Act Independently

Journalists should be free of obligation to any interest other than the public's right to know.

Journalists should:

▶ Avoid conflicts of interest, real or perceived.

▶ Remain free of associations and activities that may compromise integrity or damage credibility.

▶ Refuse gifts, favors, fees, free travel and special treatment, and shun secondary employment, political involvement, public office and service in community organizations if they compromise journalistic integrity.

▶ Disclose unavoidable conflicts.

▶ Be vigilant and courageous about holding those with power accountable.

▶ Deny favored treatment to advertisers and special interests and resist their pressure to influence news coverage.

▶ Be wary of sources offering information for favors or money; avoid bidding for news.

Be Accountable

Journalists are accountable to their readers, listeners, viewers and each other.

Journalists should:

▶ Clarify and explain news coverage and invite dialogue with the public over journalistic conduct.

▶ Encourage the public to voice grievances against the news media.

▶ Admit mistakes and correct them promptly.

▶ Expose unethical practices of journalists and the news media.

▶ Abide by the same high standards to which they hold others.

Sigma Delta Chi's first Code of Ethics was borrowed from the American Society of Newspaper Editors in 1926. In 1973, Sigma Delta Chi wrote its own code, which was revised in 1984 and 1987. The present version of the Society of Professional Journalists' Code of Ethics was adopted in September 1996.

Figure 3.4 The Society of Professional Journalists' Code of Ethics

Source: Copyright © Society of Professional Journalists: http://www.spm.org. Reprinted with permission.

G: *General audience—all ages admitted.* This is a film that contains nothing in theme, language, nudity and sex, violence, etc., that would be offensive to parents whose younger children view the film.

PG: *Parental guidance suggested—some material may not be suitable for children.* This is a film that needs to be examined or inquired into by parents before they let their children attend.

PG-13: *Parents strongly cautioned—some material may be inappropriate for children under thirteen.* This is a film that goes beyond the boundaries of the PG rating in theme, violence, nudity, sensuality, language, or other content, but does not quite fit within the restricted R category.

R: *Restricted—under seventeen requires accompanying parent or adult guardian.* This is a film that definitely contains some adult material, possibly including hard language, tough violence, nudity within sensual scenes, drug abuse, or a combination of these and other elements.

NC-17: *No one under seventeen admitted.* This is a film that most parents will consider patently too adult for their youngsters under seventeen. No children will be admitted.

The basic mission of the rating system is a simple one: to give parents advance information about movies so that they can decide what movies they want their children to see and what movies they don't want their children to see.

Film ratings are determined by a full-time Ratings Board, located in Los Angeles, California. The board is made up of eight to thirteen people who are not specially qualified in any way, other than the fact that they all have "parenthood experience." When a film is submitted to the Ratings Board, each member estimates what most parents would consider to be an appropriate rating for the film. The criteria the board considers are theme, violence, language, nudity, sensuality, and drug abuse, among other elements. After a group discussion, the board votes on the film's rating, which is decided by a majority vote.

The MPAA produces promotional items such as this poster to guide movie consumers on how to best use the film rating system.

The Ratings Board stresses that there is no requirement that films be submitted to it. Any producer, filmmaker, or distributor who does not want to participate in the ratings process can send his or her film to the free market without any rating at all. This appears quite voluntary, doesn't it? But as a media-literate consumer (or aspiring producer), can you see what's wrong with this picture? If producers of a film refuse to submit it for rating, it will be extremely difficult (if not impossible) to persuade theater companies to show the picture. Some newspapers and websites may not even accept ads for the film. That is an invitation to lose money. So unless the film is pornography (and so moves through a very different production-to-distribution system), working with the Ratings Board is really a requirement.

Television

Far more than 3,000 hours of television are available in many American homes each day. To help parents sort through this huge volume of material and choose programs they want their young children to see—or not to see—the television industry has developed TV parental guidelines. The parental guidelines are modeled after the familiar movie ratings, and consist of the following six categories:

TV-Y: *All children.* This program is designed to be appropriate for all children, including children ages two to six.

TV-Y7: *Directed to older children.* This program is designed for children age seven and above.

TV-G: *General audience.* Most parents would find this program suitable for all ages. It contains little or no violence, no strong language, and little or no sexual dialogue or situations.

TV-PG: *Parental guidance suggested.* This program contains material that parents may find unsuitable for younger children. The theme itself may call for parental guidance and/or the program contains one or more of the following: moderate violence (V), some sexual situations (S), infrequent coarse language (L), or some suggestive dialogue (D).

TV-14: *Parents strongly cautioned.* This program contains some material that many parents would find unsuitable for children under fourteen years of age. This program contains one or more of the following: intense violence (V), intense sexual situations (S), strong coarse language (L), or intensely suggestive dialogue (D).

TV-MA: *Mature audience only.* This program is specifically designed to be viewed by adults and therefore may be unsuitable for children under seventeen. This program contains one or more of the following: graphic violence (V), explicit sexual activity (S), or crude indecent language (L).

The networks and producers of each show determine the show's parental guidelines. A monitoring board formed by the National Association of Broadcasters works to achieve accuracy and consistency in applying the parental guidelines by examining programs with inappropriate guidelines and reviewing programs that have been publicly criticized.

Electronic Software and Video Games

As a result of threatened federal intervention in the early 1990s, the gaming industry created an independent rating system of its own. The Entertainment Software Rating Board (ESRB)—which assigns ratings, enforces advertising guidelines, and helps ensure responsible online privacy practices for the interactive entertainment software industry—was established in 1994. Its ratings are designed to give consumers information about the content of an interactive video. ESRB ratings and their definitions are listed below:

EC: *Early childhood.* May be suitable for children ages three and older. Contains no material that parents would find inappropriate

E: *Everyone.* May be suitable for persons ages six and older. These titles will appeal to people of many ages and tastes. They may contain minimal cartoon, fantasy, or mild violence and/or infrequent use of mild language. This rating was formerly known as Kids to Adult (K–A).

These parental guidelines icons represent the television industry's rating system.

TV RATINGS

| ALL CHILDREN | DIRECTED TO OLDER CHILDREN | DIRECTED TO OLDER CHILDREN - FANTASY VIOLENCE | GENERAL AUDIENCE | PARENTAL GUIDANCE SUGGESTED | PARENTS STRONGLY CAUTIONED | MATURE AUDIENCE ONLY |

CULTURE TODAY
THIS FILM IS NOT YET RATED

Filmmakers Kirby Dick and Eddie Schmidt attend a DVD signing for *This Film Is Not Yet Rated*.

The Motion Picture Association of America (MPAA) has long been responsible for reviewing and assigning ratings to films based on their level of age-appropriateness. However, when Kirby Dick released his critically lauded documentary *This Film Is Not Yet Rated* in 2006—an exposé on the inner workings of the MPAA rating system—the MPAA found itself under review.

The MPAA—a nonprofit trade association—created its rating system in the 1960s to ward off potential government censorship by allowing studios to voluntarily submit their films to the MPAA for review. The express purpose of the ratings is to inform parents of films' contents so they can decide whether or not films are suitable for their children's viewing. For each film, approximately eight board members—all supposedly typical parents of minors—view, discuss, and vote on an appropriate rating. The identities of these board members are withheld from the public.

Dick skewered the MPAA rating system from a number of angles, in particular criticizing the MPAA for biases against sexual content. Dick juxtaposed clips from films garnering an R rating to those receiving an NC-17 rating to illustrate a bias against homosexual content as opposed to heterosexual content and male nudity as opposed to female nudity.

The difference between an R and an NC-17 or unrated film can mean tens of millions of dollars. Almost all major theaters refuse to screen films that are either unrated or have received the MPAA's most severe rating of NC-17. (The only widely released NC-17 success was the commercial failure *Showgirls*.) Subsequently, unrated and NC-17 films perform poorly at the box office, with NC-17 films taking in less than $4 million on average and unrated films taking in less than $1 million on average.

However, Dick primarily took aim at the MPAA for what he perceived as a lack of transparency in the rating system. With the identities of the board members undisclosed and the lack of clear guidelines on what constitutes each rating, Dick claims that the MPAA's rating system is left unaccountable and vulnerable to the whims and biases of the board.

Since the film's release, the MPAA has instituted a series of reforms in the name of transparency, including releasing guidelines on the organizations website as to what constitutes each rating and the demographic makeup of the review board. Dan Glickman, the MPAA head at the time, commented, "If there's any perceptions that the system is secret, I don't want those out there."

Sources: Scott Bowles, "R rating under review," *USA Today*, April 10, 2007; David M. Halbfinger, "Hollywood Rethinks its Ratings Process," *The New York Times*, January 28, 2007; Pamela McClintock, "PAA, NATO Reform Ratings System," *Variety*, January 17, 2007.

E10+: *Everyone ten and older*. May be suitable for ages ten and older. Titles in this category may contain more cartoon, fantasy, or mild violence, mild language, and/or minimal suggestive themes.

T: *Teen*. May be suitable for ages thirteen and older. Titles in this category may contain violence, suggestive themes, crude humor, minimal blood, simulated gambling, and/or infrequent use of strong language.

M: *Mature*. May be suitable for persons ages seventeen and older. Titles in this category may contain intense violence, blood and gore, sexual content, and/or strong language.

AO: *Adults only*. Should only be played by persons eighteen years or older. Titles in this category may include prolonged scenes of intense violence and/or graphic sexual content and nudity.

Each ESRB rating is based on the consensus of at least three specially trained raters who review content based on numerous criteria. Raters must be adults and typically have experience with children through previous work experience or education, or by being caregivers themselves. Each rater reviews written submission materials and DVDs or videotapes provided by the publisher, capturing all pertinent content in the game. The ratings are then compiled and a consensus is drawn from the three ratings. Finally, ESRB staff review the final rating and issue a certificate to the game's publisher with the official rating assignment. When the game is ready for release to the public, publishers must send final copies of the product to the ESRB where the packaging is reviewed for accuracy.

Ratings systems such as these are an increasingly common form of self-regulation. Media executives favor these systems of self-regulation because they allow the industry to shift the burden of responsibility for content to parents and other members of the audience. Government officials also like them because it takes some of the public pressure off them to force companies to change their content.

> ESRB ratings, introduced in 1994, are designed to give consumers information about the content and age-appropriateness of computer and video games.

PRESS COUNCILS   A **press council** is an independent group of people who monitor complaints from media consumers, including complaints about unbalanced coverage, inadequate coverage, and erroneous coverage.

One of the most active press councils in the United States is the Minnesota News Council, founded nearly thirty years ago. The council is made up of thirteen media professionals and thirteen members of the public. The Minnesota News Council aims to promote fairness in the news media by giving members of the public who feel that they have been damaged by a news story an opportunity to hold the news organization accountable. The council's role has been expanding in recent years to include reaching out to the media and the public to create awareness that will reduce the reasons for complaints.

The Minnesota News Council makes it clear, however, that it has no authority—and wants none—to order any news organization to do, or not to do, anything. It exists in order to help the public and the media create a moral force for fairness. People who come to the council with complaints are not interested in recovering money damages (if they were, they would sue); they are interested in vindication. To qualify for a hearing, one must waive the right to sue.

> **press council** an independent group of people who monitor complaints from media consumers, including complaints about unbalanced coverage, inadequate coverage, and erroneous coverage

JOURNALISM REVIEWS   **Journalism reviews**—publications that report on and analyze examples of ethical and unethical journalism—are yet another internal force that helps the media to self-regulate. These reviews include publications such as *Quill*, *Columbia Journalism Review*, and *American Journalism Review*. Take a look at the print copies of these journals or their counterparts on the Web. What you'll see are vehicles that explore the realities of the news business and stand up for the values of journalism and for the rights of journalists around the world.

> **journalism reviews** publications that report on and analyze examples of ethical and unethical journalism

The Role of Ethics

ethics a system of principles
about what is right that guides
a person's actions

Ethics is a system of principles about what is right that guides a person's actions. Let's look a bit more carefully at the topic of ethics and the way in which it relates to business requirements.

Making Ethical Decisions

Every day you will find yourself in situations in which ethical decisions need to be made—whether those situations involve the mass media or not. How will you make these decisions? What sort of moral reasoning process should you follow—not only as a media consumer but, more importantly, as a good citizen?

Bob Steele, a senior faculty member at the Poynter Institute, outlines a model that media literates and professionals alike can use to evaluate and examine their decisions and to make good ethical decisions. Steele is concerned specifically with journalism, but the ethical-thinking process that he suggests can work for all sorts of media practitioners and consumers. Steele says, ask yourself these ten questions:

1 What do I know? What do I need to know?
2 What are my ethical concerns?
3 What is my journalistic (or informational, entertainment, advertising, or educational) purpose?
4 What organizational policies and professional guidelines should I consider?
5 How can I include other people, with different perspectives and diverse ideas, in the decision-making process?
6 Who are the stakeholders—those affected by my decision? What are their motivations? Which are legitimate?
7 What if the roles were reversed? How would I feel if I were in the shoes of one of the stakeholders?
8 What are the possible consequences of my actions in the short term and in the long term?
9 What are my alternatives to maximize my truth-telling responsibility and minimize harm?
10 Can I clearly and fully justify my thinking and my decision to my colleagues, to the stakeholders, and to the public?

Try to answer these questions for yourself. Where do you stand?

Ethical Duties to Various Constituencies

Combined with larger philosophies of ethics, Bob Steele's questions can help media practitioners think about their day-to-day responsibilities and prepare for events that raise grave ethical dilemmas. Ethical dilemmas often come about because we are torn in a number of directions over an issue. The perspective that media-ethics scholars Clifford Christians, Mark Fackler, and Kim Rotzoll[18] bring to this topic can help bring a sharper focus to the topics Steele raises when it comes to knotty ethical situations. In order to reach a responsible decision, these scholars write, an individual must clarify which parties will be influenced by a decision and which ones the person feels particularly obligated to support.

Consider yourself, for a moment, as a media practitioner trying to carry out an important assignment—writing a news story, directing a film, writing a TV movie, or any of a myriad of other activities. Fackler and his colleagues stress that, as we carry out these activities, we have obligations to five parties, or constituencies. These five parties are ourselves, the audience, the employer, the profession, and society. To these five, we will add one more: the people to whom we've made promises, such as publics and sources.

- *Duty to self.* As a media practitioner, you clearly feel a duty to make sure your actions do not harm yourself. In fact, a key goal of your work is to make yourself look good—to shine in your job—and to act in ways that allow you to feel ethically correct.
- *Duty to audience.* As a media practitioner, you also have a duty to make sure that what you do takes the nature and expectations of the audience into consideration.
- *Duty to the employer.* The company that pays your salary is also an important consideration. At the very least, a practitioner owes the firm good work—a product that meets the expectations that caused the person to be hired in the first place.
- *Duty to the profession.* Most practitioners feel an allegiance to their profession. Movie scriptwriters feel an obligation to keep up the reputation and pay of the people who ply that craft. Similarly, reporters feel a responsibility to help other journalists who are in trouble and to make sure that their profession is taken seriously by editors and publishers.
- *Duty to promise holders.* If you made promises to people during the course of covering a news story, putting a movie together, or making an ad, you may (and should) feel an obligation to those people when you move forward with your

IS IT ETHICAL?
THE BAN ON PHOTOS OF SOLDIERS' COFFINS

When is it ethical for a news outlet to show images of the dead? This question resurfaced in 2009 when the Obama administration lifted an eighteen-year-old ban on photographing the coffins of dead American soldiers as they returned home to the United States.

The Pentagon issued the ban after television networks broadcast split-screen images of then-president George H. W. Bush joking with reporters alongside images of a military honor guard unloading coffins. Two years later, the ban was put into effect. The ban was later renewed under George W. Bush's presidency. Under the new rules, the surviving families have the right to decide whether or not photographing the coffins will be permitted—rules similar to those guiding funerals at Arlington National Cemetery.

Ostensibly the debate revolved around themes of respect and privacy. Did it memorialize America's fallen soldier's to photograph their flag-draped coffins? Or did it invade the privacy of the dead and their grieving families? Below the surface of the debate, however, the potential political impact of the images on public

opinion drove a large portion of the controversy. "What is the need to show these caskets other than to try to inflame controversy?" asked John Ellsworth, president of Military Families United.

While proponents of the ban such as Ellsworth argued that the photographs could be used as anti-war propaganda, free-speech advocates countered that the ban sanitized the war, hiding its consequences from the American public. "The public has a right to see and to know what their military is doing," said Associated Press photographer Santiago Lyon. "They have a right to see the cost of that military action."

What do you think? Should the ban have been lifted? And where should government policy mark the boundary between rights to free speech and rights to privacy?

Sources: Elisabeth Bumiller, "Defense Chief Lifts Ban On Pictures of Coffins," *The New York Times*, February 27, 2009, Section A, p. 13; Andrea Stone, "Ban on Photographing U.S. Troops' Coffins Lifted," *USA Today*, February 27, 2009, p. 1A.

work. If a source requested anonymity, you can't divulge the name even if your editor thinks the article would be better if it were there. If you promised a young TV talk show host the first interview about your new film, you are obligated to give that show the first interview, even though Jay Leno wants you first.

■ *Duty to society.* Many practitioners also feel an obligation to society at large. You live in a real world, with neighbors, children, stores, churches, and governments. If you produce recordings, edit movies, write sitcoms, or illustrate children's books, you may feel that what you produce should have a positive social impact. At least, you may say, what you produce should not have a negative social impact.

Forming Ethical Standards for the Mass Media

If you think about these ethical systems, about Bob Steele's ten questions and about the constituencies that Mark Fackler and his colleagues discuss, you will see that ethical standards for the mass media often involve at least three levels:

■ The personal level
■ The professional level
■ The societal level

Most media practitioners find that they cannot exist on one level only. How their standards develop at each level has to do with their values and ideals. From these two sources come their principles—the basis for their ethical actions at every level.

values those things that reflect our presuppositions about social life and human nature

Values are those things that reflect our presuppositions about social life and human nature. Values cover a broad range of possibilities, such as aesthetic values (something is harmonious or pleasing), professional values (innovation and promptness), logical values (consistency and competency), socio-cultural values (thrift and hard work), and moral values (honesty and nonviolence).

ideals a notion of excellence, a goal that is thought to bring greater harmony to ourselves and to others

Ideals are a notion of excellence, a goal that is thought to bring about greater harmony to ourselves and to others. For example, American culture respects ideals such as tolerance, compassion, loyalty, forgiveness, peace, justice, fairness, and respect for persons. In addition to these human ideals, there are institutional or organizational ideals, such as profit, efficiency, productivity, quality, and stability.

principles those guidelines we derive from values and ideals that are precursors to codified rules

Principles are those guidelines we derive from values and ideals and are precursors to codified rules. They are usually stated in positive (prescriptive) or negative (proscriptive) terms. Consider, for example, the motto "Never corrupt the integrity of media channels"—a principle derived from the professional value of truth-telling in public relations—or the statement "Always maximize profit"—a principle derived from belief in the efficacy of the free enterprise system. The ideals, values, and principles of the media will differ according to the differing goals and loyalties of each.

Media Literacy, Regulation, and Ethics

The high risks involved in today's highly competitive media environment often create pressure on individuals to conform to organizational activities that, although legal, might be considered unethical. An individual's duty to the media organization may conflict with his or her duty to society; an individual's personal values may conflict with the organization's values.

For example, consider the use of graphic violence in TV dramas, in local TV news programs, in ads, and in music recordings. Many of the distributors and exhibitors of the material, and even its creators, may personally abhor some elements of what they are doing. In their business lives, though, they may feel they have to use those elements. Why? Because they "work"—that is, they seem to sell the product to the right audience in a manner that supports the organization and brings paychecks to its members. A well-paid writer of TV movies once yelled at the author of this textbook for asking him questions that implied respect for his craft. "I write junk!" he shouted. He added that he knew he used violence and sex as props to advance his plots and that he wrote according to the most blatant pop-cultural formulas. "I do it because I have a family to support and a big mortgage to pay off for this house in Brentwood! I do it, but I know it's junk. Don't forget that!"

Whereas this writer may condemn his own scripts as contributing to the violent and mediocre nature of popular culture, the producers of the programs that were based on these scripts might argue that they were handsome creations that explore issues of good and evil in ways that are accessible to large audiences.

There may also be ambiguity regarding how to apply the ethical principles. Ethical criteria may seem straightforward, but they are not always so. Take the principle of not misleading people—a notion that most people would agree is a basic ethical principle. Look at the Campbell Soup case, noted earlier, in light of this principle. When the company's ad agency used marbles in the soup to boost the soup's chunkiness, was that "misleading"? Campbell's argued that the company was trying to emphasize a genuine feature of its soup that the camera couldn't easily reflect without the marbles. The Federal Trade Commission disagreed, but that doesn't mean that Campbell's employees felt that they were acting unethically—do you?

Sometimes, though, executives do acknowledge that the business competition leads them to act unethically. One way to guard themselves and their competitors from improper behavior is by encouraging rules that prohibit it. From one point of view, then, media laws and regulations can be seen as a way to formally enforce agreed-upon norms of behavior by government officials with respect to media practitioners and by media practitioners with respect to the government and the society as a whole. The First Amendment, Freedom of Information Act, and Video Privacy Protection Act are, for people who agree with them, rules that reflect ethical values regarding the government's relation to media, information, and the public. Similarly, antitrust laws, laws against deceptive advertising, and self-regulatory ratings voice norms about how media firms and media practitioners ought to behave.

Media Regulations and the Savvy Citizen

Thinking about the rules that guide the media is crucial as a media-literate consumer. You can undoubtedly think of many examples of anger against the media. Activists who believe in women's right to choose abortions might be deeply offended by the portrayals of teen pregnancies in a TV movie shown by one of the networks. They might feel that doing nothing about these portrayals invites further support of the anti-abortion position by the producers when they work on other shows. They might also believe that the portrayals will reinforce in the audience unfortunate images of, and actions toward, teen abortions in society. So they might mobilize to prevent the network from repeat showing of that film and to force the network to air a film or series that is more sympathetic toward teenagers who choose abortions.

However, at the same time that the activists are voicing their complaints, groups that find any portrayal of abortion to be reprehensible might make totally opposite demands to the network. They might argue that such portrayals encourage children and others to think that abortion is acceptable in society, and that that would erode family values—the very values that define American society. Consequently, they might demand that the network never portray any abortions.

Three points about these opposing groups and their demands deserve attention here. One point is the similarity in their approach: although they are far apart ideologically, their concern about the media comes not so much from a worry about how the members of their immediate groups will react to the movie as from concern about how members of society who are less informed on the subject—especially children—will relate to the material. This type of concern is common among media activists. Arguments with media firms are often based on fear about the media's effect on other segments of society.

A second point is that the two groups are divided on the question of what it is ethically correct for the media to do in this case. One side has notions of ethically proper images that involve certain positive portrayals of abortion. The other side considers any portrayals that depict abortion as playing a legitimate part in mainstream society to be unethical.

Finally, it should be clear that this is an ethical conflict that cannot be resolved by government regulation. As we have seen, the First Amendment protects the creators of media materials, including most forms of entertainment, from government interference. The First Amendment would apply in the abortion fight. In other circumstances, however, other laws might take precedence, and a concerned citizen would need to understand that it is appropriate to ask the government to intervene. We have seen, for example, that the libel of a nonpublic figure in a TV entertainment program would likely allow the person who was insulted to have her or his day in court.

Knowing the laws that relate to particular media in particular circumstances is critical to understanding the rights and responsibilities that apply to you, media firms, and government when it comes to materials you like or don't like. In many cases, you will find that no governmental law will help you to force certain media organizations to act in what you believe is an ethical manner. You will also find out that there are few easily agreed-upon media ethics in a nation as complex and varied as the United States. Of course, people who care about media ethics should not give up trying to persuade media organizations to alter their notions of proper behavior. However, persuading media organizations to do things involves much more than simply insisting on the ethical value of one person's or one group's suggestions; as we have seen, there may be others who insist on the ethical value of totally opposite actions. So it is also necessary to understand the following: controversial proposals will not likely be accepted by media organizations as a result of social debate unless the party making the proposal is able to exercise economic and political power.

Chapter Review

For an interactive chapter recap and study guide, visit the companion website for *Media Today* at http://www.routledge.com/textbooks/mediatoday4e.

Questions for Discussion and Critical Thinking

1 In what ways do the authoritarian and libertarian philosophies of media systems represent opposing views of human nature?
2 How has the meaning of "the press" in the First Amendment changed over the course of U.S. history?

3 From a legal standpoint, what is the difference between obscenity and pornography?

4 What does it mean to say that using part of a copyright work is fair use because the use is transformative?

5 "Media laws and regulations can be seen as a way to formally enforce agreed-upon norms of behavior by government officials with respect to media practitioners and by media practitioners with respect to the government and the society as a whole." Explain this statement and bring two examples to support it.

Internet Resources
. . . .

University of Iowa's list of internet resources on media law (http://bailiwick.lib. uiowa.edu/journalism/mediaLaw/)

> This is a useful annotated collection of materials about law, for experts and non-experts, available around the Web.

Court decisions regarding freedom of speech in the United States (http://www. bc.edu/bc_org/avp/cas/comm/free_speech/decisions.html)

> From Boston College Law School, this series of links is arranged in historical and thematic order.

Journal of Mass Media Ethics (http://jmme.byu.edu/)

> According to its website, "the *Journal of Mass Media Ethics* is devoted to explorations of ethics problems and issues in the various fields of mass communication. Emphasis is placed on materials dealing with principles and reasoning in ethics, rather than anecdotes, orthodoxy, dogma, and enforcement of codes."

The Reporters' Committee for Freedom of the Press (http://www.rcfp.org/)

> Based in Arlington, Virginia, RCFP is a nonprofit organization dedicated to providing free legal help to journalists and news organizations since 1970.

Key Terms
. . . .

You can find the definitions to these key terms in the marginal glossary throughout this chapter. Test your knowledge of these terms with interactive flash cards on the *Media Today* companion website.

Constructing
Media Literacy
· · · · · · · · · · · · · · · · ·

1 Why do you think many people get upset about the burning of books? Can you find modern counterparts to the Nazi book burnings?

2 If you were a judge in a murder trial, would you allow cameras into your courtroom? Why or why not?

3 The Children's Online Privacy Protection Act (COPPA) requires websites to get parents' permission if they want to get identifiable personal information (for example, full name, email address, phone number) from children under the age of thirteen. When the bill was first introduced to Congress, many privacy advocates wanted to raise the age to seventeen or under, or at least older than thirteen. Do you agree that this should have happened? Why do you think it didn't?

4 If it were up to you, would you reinstate the Fairness doctrine? Why or why not?

Companion Website
Video Clips
· · · · · · · · · · · · · ·

Consuming Kids—Under the Microscope and The Floodgates Open
These clips from the Media Education Foundation documentary *Consuming Kids* considersthe practices of a multi-billion dollar marketing campaign aimed at children and their parents, raising questions about the ethics of children's marketing and its impact on the health and well-being of kids. Credit: Media Education Foundation.

Freedom of Expression—Fair Use and Free Speech
This clip from the Media Education Foundation documentary *Freedom of Expression* looks at intellectual property laws and how they affect creativity and the expression of ideas. Credit: Media Education Foundation.

Outfoxed—Interview Footage
This clip features original footage from the documentary *Outfoxed: Rupert Murdoch's War on Journalism,* produced and directed by Robert Greenwald. Credit: *Outfoxed: Rupert Murdoch's War on Journalism*, produced and directed by Robert Greenwald.

Case Study
· ·

JOURNALISTS AND ETHICAL DILEMMAS

The idea Reading about the ethical dilemmas that media practitioners experience is not the same thing as experiencing them first hand. You might be able to understand these dilemmas and the ways media practitioners and their organizations deal with them better by talking directly to them about it.

The method Interview a local journalist about an ethical dilemma that he or she confronted during his or her career. Come prepared with questions, and take notes during the interview, or ask the journalist for permission to record it. To get the journalist to be most honest, you may have to promise that when you write your essay about the interview you will not reveal his or her name.

Ask what the dilemma was. With whom did the journalist share the dilemma inside and outside of his/her media organization? How did the journalist resolve the dilemma? Why? How did it affect the story that the journalist wanted to tell?

In writing an essay about the interview, ask yourself if the resolution the journalist found for the dilemma fits with one or more of the ethics models described in this chapter. Also consider whether you would have resolved the dilemma in the same way or in a different way.

Making Sense of Research on Media Effects and Media Culture

4

After studying this chapter, you will be able to:

1 Identify and explain what mass media research is

2 Recognize and discuss the mainstream approaches to mass media research

3 Recognize the shift from mainstream approaches to critical approaches

4 Recognize and discuss the critical approaches to mass media research

5 Recognize and discuss the cultural studies approaches to mass media research

6 Harness your media literacy skills regarding media research and effects to understand and evaluate the media's presence and influence in your life

MEDIA TODAY

Imagine a communication major, Jessica, who is a junior at a college near a large U.S. city. Jessica works on the Culture and Arts beat for the school's daily newspaper, which means that companies send her free tickets to plays, movies, and concerts because they want her to write reviews about them for the paper. Jessica works late into the night at the newspaper office, trying to finish her reviews for the paper's website and its print edition. In the office, three flat screens bracketed to the wall are constantly tuned to the three major network stations in the area, and as she writes her reviews Jessica can't help but pay attention to what they are showing about the city: mostly stories of murder, robbery, and fires.

"Why don't they cover the great plays and concerts happening all around the city?" Jessica wonders. She is worried that viewers are getting the wrong impression, and that the local news is fostering a sense of fear. As the days go by, she decides that these sensational stories are problematic—both for what they show and for what they don't show. The news programs, she realizes, are ignoring the efforts of the mayor, the city commissioners, the school board, and the many other departments that keep the city working—or, sometimes, not working.

"It's hard to believe someone intelligent would watch this stuff," she tells her boyfriend Jim one day over lunch. "Well," Jim offers, "loads of people around here pay attention to those shows. They may watch for the sports summary or the weather. The crime and violence just come along for the ride."

"But why?" Jessica presses him as she finishes her iced tea. "Why would stations put this junk on? And why would intelligent people not get angry and complain? Showing people stories about violence and fires every day without giving them a sense of how the city works and the good things that are going on is dangerous. It can make people afraid, hopeless, and even wanting to leave. And anyway, why should sensational murder stories push out stories about concert series, art exhibits, and city government that can have an impact on viewers' lives?"

Jessica finds that a number of friends at the paper share her concerns about the local news. One friend, a campus anti-poverty activist and criminology major, confides that four months earlier he had met with the news directors of the three major television stations in the city. They listened politely to his complaints, he says, but in the end they did nothing. "The need to attract large numbers of viewers for advertisers obviously exceeds their desire to be publicly responsible," he suggests. But Jessica is determined to go beyond what her friend has done. She decides to start a public advocacy group to put public pressure on the stations to change local news.

But how should she start? Jim suggests that she start with the basics: "You need to research the effects of TV and how local TV news operates. If you go out there and start complaining publicly with no knowledge, you may come off looking foolish. And the people who run the stations will have had their way." Jim suggests that her first step might be to talk to her advisor. "Get his input into how this all works, what effects these sorts of images might have, and the best ways to influence the companies that put them on the air," he says.

Jessica decides to give it a try, so she shares her concerns with her advisor, communication professor Dave Berg. "It's an interesting topic," Professor Berg says. "In fact, it's an issue I would love to pose to the graduate students in my Media Theory class. Why don't you come to the class next week and I'll get the students to help you brainstorm?" Jessica tells him that's a great idea, but she secretly worries that the grad students might be more inclined to think about "ivory tower" concepts and not about her concerns about the local news. Nevertheless, she shows up in the graduate class to find that she has hit on a hot-button topic with a substantial proportion of the grad students, who are eager to express their viewpoints and link them to scholarly research.

The Nature of Mass Media Research

mass media research the use of systematic methods to understand or solve problems regarding the mass media

Research is the application of a systematic method to solve a problem or understand it better than in the past. **Mass media research** involves the use of systematic methods to understand or solve problems regarding the mass media.

The research we are concerned with in this chapter tries to answer questions that relate to society's bottom line, not to a company's bottom line. This type of research asks about the role mass media play in improving or degrading the relationships, values, and ideals of society, and the people who make up that society.

The Early Years of Mass Media Research in the United States

Nearly a hundred years ago, two major media issues preoccupied the thinkers of the day. The first was the media's role in helping to keep a sense of American community alive. The second was the media's role in encouraging bad behavior among children—an issue that faded rather quickly, only to reappear many years later.

MEDIA RESEARCH
TOOLS FOR EVALUATING MEDIA RESEARCH

A question you should consider asking as a media-literate consumer is this: How does anyone know whether these experiments or surveys or content analyses or historical studies reflect reality? And how can anyone be sure that the research they read or that they help people conduct is worth serious attention? The answers are not simple. Everyone who is concerned about the social implications of media—researchers, policy-makers, media executives, and members of the public—has to think critically about research. Over the decades, researchers have developed a variety of ways for trying to think about the drawbacks of research findings. Here are some topics to think about when you read about research:

The Nature of the Sample

If the study has used a sample (of people or of content), how representative is it of the group about which the researcher is drawing conclusions? If a researcher studies teenagers and claims that his findings apply to the entire U.S. population, that's a problem. If a researcher studies situation comedies and claims that her findings apply to all of TV programming, that's a problem. These samples simply don't seem to be applicable to the larger group.

The Size and Collection Methods of the Sample

Statisticians have determined how many people must be studied if a survey is to be reflective of a larger population. They have also devised methods for determining which people should be included in and excluded from samples. Similarly, researchers who conduct experiments have developed systematic ways of choosing subjects. Does the research you are reading discuss these issues?

The Design of the Study

Consider the way the study was set up. If it is a qualitative study, evaluate the way the researcher posed the issues and went about gathering evidence for answers. If it is a quantitative study—a survey, an experiment, or a content analysis, for example—evaluate the questions asked and consider whether they were leading questions. Leading questions imply the answers the researcher wants in the way the questions are posed. For example, if a researcher asks you, "Do you like to watch shows that are terribly violent?" you may feel that saying that you like violent shows will cast you in a bad light. You might therefore say "no" even though you like violent shows. Research based on leading questions is not persuasive because its impossible to know whether people's responses were sincere or not.

Searching for Community: Early Critical Studies Research

The early twentieth century was a time of enormous social change in American society. The industrial revolution was in full swing, and factories were turning out machine-made consumer products at low cost in numbers that had never been seen before. Many of these factories were located in cities, and they drew millions of workers who streamed out of farming communities in order to take advantage of the higher salaries and better opportunities of urban life.

Even more numerous than the workers who came to the cities from U.S. farms were the immigrants from central and eastern Europe who were teeming into American ports looking for a piece of the American dream. For many, the dream was a bit of a nightmare, at least at first. A large number of the newcomers, poor and not knowing the English language, led a difficult, even hand-to-mouth, existence that contrasted dramatically with the lives of the wealthy urban industrialists of the day and the relatively modest, yet still quite comfortable, situation of most nonimmigrants.

Social observers in this period considered this a very serious situation. It wasn't just the poverty that concerned them. They also worried that this new urban, often non-English-speaking population who knew little of American values would endanger the small-town democratic community that they believed had characterized

The Reliability of the Study

When a study is called reliable, the results can be reproduced by repeating the conditions in the study. In other words, another survey asking the same questions and achieving a sample the same way would yield basically the same findings, even though the specific people participating in the sample differed. If a study's methods are unclear, or if the answers to its questions depend greatly on the person asking the questions, most people would consider the study too ambiguous to be a reliable reflection of real-world conditions.

The Soundness of the Analysis

When we evaluate a researcher's analysis of his or her empirical data, we should ask whether the way the researcher is analyzing the data makes sense from the standpoint of basic logic—for example, whether a conclusion about a group's use of television is really justified by the numerical findings. We should also ask whether the researcher has analyzed the data well enough to understand truly what is going on. For example, after dividing certain TV viewing data between men and women, the researcher may conclude that gender is the great divider. A closer look at the data, however, might disclose that the real difference is not men and women in general but specifically between the Latino men and Latina women. Of course, as a reader you wouldn't have the ability to examine the researcher's data to find that out. But you should ask yourself what types of analysis the researcher should have done and be suspicious if they haven't been carried out.

The Validity of the Study

Validity refers to the extent to which the study accurately describes the circumstances that exist in the real world. Determining this is often more difficult, and more controversial, than it may sound. Consider a researcher who wants to determine whether violent cartoons encourage children to commit violence. The researcher decides to set up an experimental situation in which children are exposed to cartoon characters hitting each other and are given the opportunity soon afterwards to hit dolls that look like those cartoon characters. Another group of children, a control group, is shown a nonviolent cartoon but is presented with the same dolls soon after seeing their video. The researcher's findings show that the children in the experimental group are far more likely to hit the dolls and to hit each other while hitting the dolls than are the children in the control group.

Assume that the researcher conducts all her work impeccably. The nature of her sample, its size, the way it's collected, the design of the study—all these elements make for a study that's elegant, with results that are reliable. But a media-literate consumer must still ask, are the results valid? That is, can we believe that what the researcher has found in her experimental situation has any relationship to what children would do in the real world? The answers are not straightforward. Critical consumers of research may disagree about the validity of research even when they agree that the research has passed all the other criteria for good work.

American society before the late nineteenth century. Could the traditional sense of community—that shared sense of responsibility that people felt toward their neighbors and their nation—be sustained in cities where so few people knew or cared about one another? Could the torrents of immigrants be brought into the mainstream of American society so that they considered its values their own?

Now you may not agree that the questions these social observers asked were the correct ones. You may feel that these people were romanticizing small-town communities. Or you might argue that those who already lived in the United States did not have the right to impose their "American" values on the new immigrants. These are quite legitimate objections, but at the turn of the twentieth century many people saw U.S. society's biggest problems as preserving a sense of small-town community and making sure immigrants "assimilated."

The pessimists among them concluded that there really was no hope; that urban society, and especially immigrant urban society, would destroy the connectedness that they associated with small-town America. Drawing upon late nineteenth-century European writings on the dangers of the "crowd" (or the "masses" as they were sometimes called), the prejudiced among them saw these urban crowds as having dangerously irrational tendencies. There was, they felt, a good reason to keep immigrants away from U.S. shores.

A group of prominent sociologists at the University of Chicago argued publicly and in their scholarly writings that it was precisely because of the mass media that the situation in "mass society" was not nearly as bleak as some thought. Professors Robert Park, John Dewey, and Charles Cooley suggested that the widespread popularity of newspapers and magazines in the early twentieth century allowed for the creation of a new type of community (see Figure 4.1).

These researchers argued that the media brought together large numbers of geographically separated, diverse individuals who would otherwise be disconnected from one another and from a common notion of society, and allowed them to share ideas about the society without assembling in the same geographic area. They said that, if media firms acted responsibly, Americans could learn ideas that were essential to their democracy from their messages. Robert Park conducted a study of the immigrant press in the United States and concluded that, far from keeping the foreigners in their own little ethnic worlds, the immigrant newspapers were helping people (over time) to acclimate to American society. Immigrants, he said, were using their foreign-language media to learn how to be good citizens.

Cooley and Dewey were social philosophers. Their work tended to be conceptual rather than empirical. Park, a former newspaper reporter, was more empirically oriented. All three were the most prominent members of what became known as the Chicago School of Sociology. Many of their ideas are fresh and interesting even today. Not everyone agreed with them then (and not everyone agrees with them now). Nevertheless, they were among the first U.S. academics to show how systematically presented ideas and research about the mass media could feed into important social issues.

Media researchers study the effects of a media message on its intended audience. The message of this cartoon from 1921 is critical of the arrival of so many immigrants who fail to assimilate into the national "melting pot" of the United States.

Fearing Propaganda: Early Concerns About Persuasion

At about the same time that Cooley, Dewey, and Park were writing about ways the mass media could help society maintain an informed democratic public, other researchers were expressing strong concerns

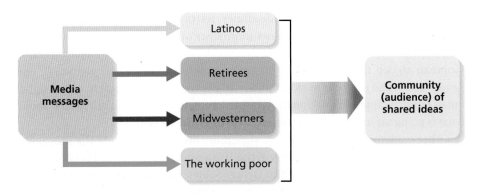

Figure 4.1 A New Type of Community
The media has the power to bring disparate individuals together by broadcasting the same notions of society to large numbers of people who might otherwise never interact—thereby creating a new type of community.

about unethical rulers using the power of the mass media to reach huge numbers of people for undemocratic ends.

University of Chicago political science professor Harold Lasswell saw mass media organizations as powerful weapons of persuasion because they reached enormous numbers of geographically dispersed people in very short periods of time. Never before in history had this been possible, Lasswell and other researchers pointed out. They feared that powerful interest groups in a society would use mass media as **propaganda**—messages designed to change the attitudes and behavior of huge numbers of otherwise disconnected individuals on controversial social issues. Under the right conditions, they feared, such propaganda would enable rulers to spread lies through the media and manipulate large numbers of people to support their views (see Figure 4.2). Those in the society who opposed these rulers would be at a substantial disadvantage.

propaganda messages designed to change the attitudes and behavior of huge numbers of otherwise disconnected individuals on controversial social issues

One reason that such fears abounded in the United States had to do with the successful manipulation of newspaper reports and photographs by both the Allies and the German government during World War I. The head of the U.S. propaganda effort, George Creel, wrote a popular book, *How We Advertised America* (1920), in which he boasted that expertly crafted messages—on billboards, on records, and in movies—had moved huge numbers of people to work for the war effort. In addition, *The Brass Check* (1919), a book by the social critic Upton Sinclair, alleged that major advertisers demanded favorable coverage of their products in newspapers in exchange for ad space purchases. Many liberal thinkers of the day saw these activities as fundamentally threatening to democracy, as citizens often had no idea of the intentions behind the messages they were seeing and hearing.

Some writers, like journalist Walter Lippmann, argued that the most important culprits hindering U.S. newspapers' objective portrayal of the world were not propaganda forces.[1] Rather, said Lippmann, the culprits were U.S. journalists themselves. Because they were mere mortals with selective ways of seeing things, and because

Figure 4.2 The Hypodermic Needle or Magic Bullet Approach has been used by researchers as a punching bag to illustrate what they believe is a simplistic view of media effects.

they worked in organizations with deadlines, restrictions on story length, and the need to grab readers' attentions, news journalists often portrayed predictably patterned (stereotyped), limited views of the world. In his book *Public Opinion* (1922), Lippman argued that the news media are a primary source of the "pictures in our heads" about the external world of public affairs that is "out of reach, out of sight, out of mind."[2] Lippman's notion that the media create "the ideas in our heads" about what is going on in the world is referred to as **agenda setting**.

agenda setting the notion that the media create "the ideas in our heads" about what is going on in the world

Other academic thinkers of the era were more likely to emphasize the propagandistic aspect of the press. Academics of the 1920s and 1930s, such as Leonard Doob, Alfred McLung Lee, Ralph Casey, and George Seldes, saw the importance of systematically exploring the forces guiding media companies, and the value of analyzing media content. They felt that by letting people know how media firms operate, they could help citizens to protect themselves from the undue power of those firms. They called the activity **propaganda analysis**, a type of content analysis that systematically examines mass media messages designed to sway the attitudes of large populations on controversial issues. In their propaganda analysis studies, specially trained coders examined messages (articles, movies, radio shows) for elements that the researchers believed to be significant.

propaganda analysis the systematic examination of mass media messages that seem to be designed to sway the attitudes of large populations on controversial issues

For example, analysts in the late 1930s were concerned that U.S. newspapers were negatively portraying the communist Soviet Union and potentially harming the chances for a U.S.–Soviet collaboration against Hitler's Germany. To find out what influential newspapers were doing, the researchers might systematically examine two years of articles about the Soviet Union in major U.S. newspapers. The researchers would be trained (and tested on their ability) to note a variety of topics included in the coverage of that country, from music, to crime, to politics. After analyzing the findings, the researchers would be able to come to quantitative conclusions about the messages about Russia that major press outlets were presenting to large numbers of Americans.

Some writers on the history of mass communication research have suggested that propaganda analysts took a **magic bullet or hypodermic needle approach** to mass communication (see Figure 4.2). By this, they mean that the propaganda analysts believed that messages delivered through the mass media persuaded all people powerfully and directly (as if they had been hit by a bullet or injected by a needle) without the people having any control over the way they reacted. For example, critics say that propaganda analysts believed that a well-made ad, an emotionally grabbing movie, or a vivid newspaper description would be able to sway millions of people toward the media producers' goals.

magic bullet or hypodermic needle approach the idea that messages delivered through the mass media persuade all people powerfully and directly (as if they were hit by a bullet or injected by a needle) without the people having any control over the way they react

But the terms "magic bullet" and "hypodermic needle" are too simplistic to describe the effects that propaganda analysts felt the media had on individuals. For one thing, the propaganda analysts certainly did not believe that all types of messages would be equally persuasive. (They stated, for example, that audiences would more likely accept messages that reinforced common values than messages that contradicted common values.) For another, they emphasized that propaganda is more likely to work under circumstances of media monopoly than when many competitive media voices argue over the ideas presented. They believed, too, that people could be taught to critically evaluate (and so not be so easily influenced by) propaganda.

Nevertheless, propaganda analysts of the 1920s and 1930s tended to focus more on media producers and their output than they did on members of society. They assumed that most members of the society shared similar understandings of media messages and didn't focus on the possibility that individual audience members might interpret messages in different ways. However, another way of seeing media influence—one that suited very different social questions—was developing.

Kids and Movies: Continuing Effects Research

By the mid-1920s, large numbers of parents, social workers, and public welfare organizations were worried about whether specific films might be negatively affecting youngsters. Invented just a few decades earlier, the movies had become very much a part of Americans' leisure activities by the 1920s. As children and teenagers became accustomed to moviegoing, adults fretted that the violence, sexual suggestiveness, and misrepresentations of reality in many of the films they watched might bring about a slew of problems in their lives. Among the ills suggested were bad sleep patterns, improper notions of romance, and violent conduct.

These ideas may sound very modern to have been around as early as the 1920s. You may know (and we'll note later in the book) that in recent years television programs, comic books, video games, sports programs, the internet, songs—as well as movies—have all been accused of encouraging these same problems among U.S. youth.

These early controversies over movies marked the first time that social researchers carried out systematic research to determine whether these accusations had any basis in reality. The most important of these projects, formally known as Motion Pictures and Youth, is more commonly referred to as the Payne Fund Studies because a foundation called the Payne Fund paid for the project. The research effort was led by Professor W. W. Charters of Ohio State University and was conducted by the most prominent psychologists, sociologists, and educators of the day. The studies, published in 1933, look at the effects of particular films on sleep patterns, knowledge about foreign cultures, attitudes about violence, and delinquent behavior.

The researchers used a range of empirical techniques, including experiments, surveys, and content analysis. One especially interesting survey was qualitative: a sociologist interviewed female college students about the extent to which and ways in which movies had affected their notions of romance. A noteworthy experiment

When is propaganda *really* propaganda? The critical, media-literate consumer must learn to recognize that even persuasive material circulated by those who seem to be "in the right" are pieces of propaganda all the same. These American (left) and German (right) propaganda posters from World War II show that both sides used persuasive, even manipulative, messages to garner support for their side and anger toward the opposition.

This sequence of images, which appeared in *Look* magazine in 1963, re-opened the floodgates of public concern over the effects of media-depicted violence. Media researcher Dr. Albert Bandura shot this series of photos during what is often referred to as his "Bobo doll research," in which children in a laboratory setting were observed behaving violently with a blow-up Bobo doll after watching a film of people behaving violently.

IS IT ETHICAL?
WHEN POLITICS MEET SOCIAL RESEARCH

In 2003, a terrorism prevention project under works by the Department of Defense surfaced in the press. The project involved creating a "futures market" in which users could buy and trade contracts on the likelihood of certain political events in the Middle East transpiring, such as the assassination of Palestinian leader Yasser Arafat or a terrorist attack on Israel. The rationale behind the project—officially known as the Department of Defense's "Policy Analysis Management" project—was that markets can be highly accurate predictors by aggregating the collective intelligence of many. A futures market such as this could aid the Department of Defense in predicting and preventing potential terrorism.

However, once the project came to light in the media, the Department of Defense was met with unrelenting moral outrage, with the project dubbed as a "terrorist futures market." One concern was that the futures market would be an avenue for terrorists to spread misinformation, while another was that traders could ensure an event they bet on occurred by carrying it out themselves, such as by assassination. However, the most vocal backlash was more ethical than pragmatic, arising from the idea that betting on and profiting from the occurrence of terrorism—and, with that, the lives of others—was distasteful.

Putting aside whether the project's potential to prevent terrorism and save lives outweighed any concerns over its distastefulness, the project illustrates a constant ethical dilemma among social scientists. How should social scientists react when approached to conduct research with a questionable ethical underpinning? In this case, what ethical considerations should have been taken into account by these social-networks researchers when accepting military funding?

Many government agencies and corporations rely on the research of social scientists for their operations, and these agencies and corporations fund a large amount of social scientific research. This research is not without consequence, as policies, campaigns, and business strategies are formulated around these research findings. Social scientists thus may find themselves torn in different directions—toward the pursuit of knowledge, toward concerns over the ethical consequences of their findings, and, of course, toward the need for financial sponsorship.

Do social scientists have an ethical responsibility—to the academic community and the general public—to ensure that the research they conduct causes no harm once the findings are in someone else's hands? Or does the pursuit of knowledge and understanding justify such research? How would you weigh the ethics of your own research if accepting funding from a government agency or corporation?

Sources: Rebecca Goolsby, "Ethics and Defense Agency Funding: Some Considerations," *Social Networks* 27, 2 (May 2005), pp. 95–106; Steven Weber and Philip Tetlock, "New Economy: The Pentagon's Plan for Futures Trading Might Have Been a Good Test of the Internet and the Markets," *The New York Times*, August 11, 2003.

was aimed at determining whether children who have seen violent films sleep more restlessly than those who have seen only nonviolent films. The children in the experiment were shown a movie featuring a lot of fighting, whereas those in the control condition saw a film with no combat at all. To determine the effects of the films on sleep, the researchers had the children sleep where they could observe them. Among other aspects of the children's sleep, the researchers measured their "restlessness" by attaching equipment to their beds that would note how often they moved and turned. They found that the children who had viewed the violent film tossed and turned more than the ones who had not.

Some popular commentators in the 1930s suggested that the results showed that individual movies could have major negative effects on all children—a kind of hypodermic needle effect. Most of the Payne Fund researchers themselves, though, went out of their way to point out that youngsters' reactions to movies were not at all uniform. Instead, these reactions very much depended on specific social and psychological differences among children. A sociologist in the group, for example, concluded that a particular film might move a youngster to want or not want to be a criminal. The specific reaction, the sociologist found, depended to a large extent on the social environment, attitudes, and interests of the child.

The psychologists in the group, for their part, pointed out that the way children reacted to films often depended on individual differences in mental or cognitive ability. So, for example, two researchers looked at children's emotional reactions to a film by hooking them up to instruments that measured their heartbeat and the amount of sweat on their skin. They found that children varied widely in emotional stimulation, and suggested that differences in response to specific scenes were caused by varied abilities to comprehend what they saw on the screen.

Social Relations and the Media

At Columbia University's sociology department in the early 1940s, a new contribution to this emphasis on people's different reactions to media materials emerged. It was the idea that **social relations**—interactions among people—influence the way individuals interpret media messages. For example, when people watch movies, read newspapers, listen to the radio, or use any other medium, they often talk with other people about what they have seen or heard, and this can affect their opinions about what they have seen or heard. To understand how media content affects one person differently from another, then, we might want to know more about who people speak to about what they've seen, read, or heard in the media.

It wasn't until the early 1940s that researchers began to think of placing social relations alongside individual social and psychological differences as a major factor in helping determine the different understandings that people draw from the media. Paul Lazarsfeld and his colleagues at Columbia were the first to make this discovery, and their research started in a large-scale survey of the voting attitudes and activities of people in Erie County, Ohio, about the 1940 presidential election.

Lazarsfeld and his colleagues interviewed four similar samples of approximately 600 people about their use of

social relations interactions among people that influence the way individuals interpret media messages

Paul Lazarsfeld and his colleagues found that social relations play a significant role in how people understand news from media. Here, a group of miners in Harlan, Kentucky, listen to the news report in 1943.

panel survey asking the same individuals questions over a period of time in order to find out whether and how the attitudes of these people change over time

radio and newspapers as it related to the election. The researchers split the people up in this way because they were using a technique called a **panel survey**. In a panel survey, the same individuals are asked questions over a period of time. The purpose is to see whether and how the attitudes of these people change over time. In the early 1940s, panel surveys were an innovative design. Lazarsfeld wanted to find out whether asking people questions once a month during the election campaign (May to November) would lead to their answering questions differently from the way they would answer if the investigators asked them questions a few times during the period, only once during the period, or only at the end of the period. After comparing the answers given by the four samples, Lazarsfeld concluded that surveying people every month did not affect their answers. The good thing about surveying them every month, however (despite its expense), was that the researchers could track the changes in the people's opinions regarding the candidates.

When the Columbia researchers concentrated on the roles that radio and newspapers played in individuals' decisions regarding the campaign, they found that news about the race seemed to change few people's voting intentions. However, when Lazarsfeld and his colleagues turned away from the issue of direct media influence to knowledge about the election, they got a surprise. The researchers were struck by the importance of voters' influence on one another. In short, voters who participated in the survey reported that instead of being exposed to the election through news coverage, they learned what was going on through discussions with friends and acquaintances.

two-step flow model a model, developed by Paul Lazarsfeld and his colleagues, that states that media influence often works in two stages: (1) media content (opinions and facts) is picked up by people who use the media frequently, and (2) these people, in turn, act as opinion leaders when they discuss the media content with others, who are therefore influenced by the media in a way that is one step removed from the actual content

Building from their data in a somewhat shaky manner, Lazarsfeld and his colleagues offered the **two-step flow model** (see Figure 4.3). This model states that media influence often works in two stages: (1) media content (opinions and facts) is picked up by people who use the media frequently, and (2) these people, in turn, act as opinion leaders when they discuss the media content with others. The others are therefore influenced by the media in a way that is one step removed from the actual content.

As an everyday example, think of a friend whose taste in movies is similar to yours and who is much more likely than you to keep up with the latest news about films. When the movie companies put out new releases, he not only reads newspaper and magazine reviews, but also checks the Web and reads the trade press. At least once a week, over lunch, you and that friend talk about the new releases and discuss the possibility of seeing "the best one" that weekend. Clearly, media discussions of the new movies are influencing you through your friend. The two-step flow is first from the various media to your friend and then to you.

Paul Lazarsfeld, his colleague Robert Merton, a graduate student named Elihu Katz, and other members of Columbia's sociology department went on to conduct several other studies on the relationship between opinion leaders, the two-step flow,

Figure 4.3 Model of the Two-Step Flow of Media Influence
Through their social relations research, Lazarsfeld and his colleagues found that media messages often move in two distinct stages—from media organizations to opinion leaders, and then from opinion leaders to opinion followers, through discussion and interaction.

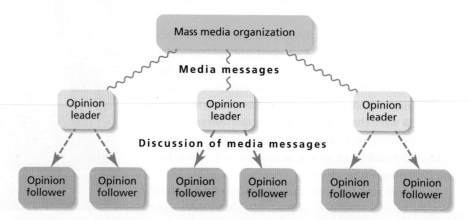

and the mass media. In addition to these important works, the Columbia program also conducted research that examined the relationship between the media and their audiences—research that emphasized the idea of the active audience. By **active audience**, they meant that people are not simply passive recipients of media messages. Rather, they respond to content based on their personal backgrounds, interests, and interpersonal relationships.

The best-known aspect of this research, which came to be known as **uses and gratifications research**, studies how people use media products to meet their needs and interests. The aim of this research was to ask (and answer) questions about why individuals use the mass media. Underlying these studies is the belief that it is just as important to know what people do with media as it is to know what media do to people. You may remember that in Chapter 1 we discussed why people use the media and raised such topics as enjoyment, companionship, surveillance, and interpretation—all are ideas that sprang from scholarly writings about the uses and gratifications people make of and get from the mass media.

Uses and gratifications research typically employs two research methods. One method involves interviewing people about why they use specific media and what kinds of satisfactions (gratifications) they get from these media. Often such research involves a small population so that the research can be conducted in depth. The second research method involves surveys that try to predict what kinds of people use what media, or what certain kinds of people do with particular media.

Consider a researcher who is interested in whether computers in nursing homes can enrich the lives of seniors. He might want to use both of these methods. One way to start such a project would be to go to nursing homes that provide internet access and interview residents about the extent to which they use the internet and what they get out of it. You might object that such a small-scale study is not clearly generalizable to other situations. You're right about that, but the researcher might sacrifice getting a representative sample of the population in return for the ability to really learn the habits and ideas of these people. He then might test what he learns in other circumstances or through large-scale surveys. In fact, the researcher might want to use the survey technique to canvass nursing homes with Web access around the country. One goal might be to find out whether certain characteristics of seniors—their age, their health, or their attitudes about the future, for example—predict the kinds and extent of their Web use.

The Limits of Propaganda: Limited Effects Research

Amidst all this interest in how difficult it is for media to change people's attitudes and behaviors, even propaganda research was turned on its head. Remember how powerful the propaganda analysts of the 1920s and 1930s considered the mass media to be? Well, in the 1940s, social psychologists were pointing out that even media materials specifically designed to persuade people would succeed only under limited circumstances and with only certain types of people.

The issue was by no means just a theoretical one. Propaganda became an important tool during World War II in the 1940s and during the height of the cold war with the Soviet Union in the 1950s and 1960s. During World War II, military officials became especially interested in the ability of movies, filmstrips, and other media to teach soldiers about the reasons for the war and to increase their motivation to serve. Research on the power of these media was carried out as part of a wide investigation called *The American Soldier*.

Because a soldier's duty is to do what he or she is told, a team of social psychologists under the leadership of Carl Hovland conducted careful naturalistic

active audience the idea that people are not simply passive recipients of media messages; they respond to content based on their personal backgrounds, interests, and interpersonal relationships

uses and gratifications research research that studies how people use media products to meet their needs and interests; it asks (and answers) questions about why individuals use the mass media

naturalistic experiment a study in which randomly selected people are manipulated in a relatively controlled environment (as in an experiment) without knowing that they are involved in an experiment

experiments with large numbers of people, a task that is typically difficult to accomplish. A **naturalistic experiment** is a study in which randomly selected people are manipulated in a relatively controlled environment (as in an experiment) without knowing that they are involved in an experiment. Some (who make up the experimental group) see the media message that is being evaluated, while others (the control group) do not. Researchers ask both groups the same questions at different points in time. The researchers take care to separate the questionnaire from the viewing so that the subjects don't suspect the relationship between the two. The before/after answers of the two groups are then compared. This approach is typically more like "real life" than a typical experiment, in which groups of randomly chosen subjects know that they are involved in an experiment and often participate in a laboratory setting.

Hovland and his colleagues used a variety of techniques with different subjects, but all were shown movies explaining America's reason for entering World War II. The 4,200 soldiers involved in the study were not told they were involved in an experiment. Instead, they were told they were being given a general opinion survey; the questionnaires they were given before seeing the film were different from those they received a week after seeing the film to disguise the real purpose of the questionnaire. Some of the experimental groups were also given questionnaires nine weeks after seeing the movie to study the long-term effects of the film. Control groups did not see the movies, but they were given questionnaires to fill out to see if changes happened without their having viewed the movies.

Hovland's naturalistic experiments showed how difficult it is to change an individual's opinions. As an example, consider the researchers' findings when they evaluated the effects of *The Battle of Britain* (a short film that explored in vivid detail how Britain fought bravely against the Nazis, why the United States went to war to help Britain, and why it was necessary to fight to win) on men enrolled in the military. The team found that the movie had strong effects on what men learned about the battle; how much they learned depended on their educational background. When it came to convincing the men in the study that the British and French were doing all they could to win, however, the film had much less effect; few soldiers who were suspicious of the French and British before they saw the film changed their opinion.

American servicemen answering questionnaires in Carl Hovland's *American Soldier* research.

The film was also ineffective in strengthening the overall motivation and morale of the soldiers. Specifically, one item on the questionnaire given after the experimental group saw the film asked whether the soldiers preferred military service at home or joining the fighting overseas. Only 38 percent of the control group said they wanted to fight. For the film group—supposedly fired up by the film—the comparable figure was 41 percent, not a significant difference. Even Hovland (who later went on to run the influential Program of Research on Communication and Attitude Change at Yale University) agreed that

the findings did not contradict what by the 1950s was the mainstream verdict about media influence: under normal circumstances, in which all aspects of the communication environment could not be equal, the mass media's ability to change people's attitudes and behavior on controversial issues was minimal.

Consolidating the Mainstream Approach

The seeds planted by the Columbia School, the Yale School, and to a lesser degree the Payne Fund Studies bore great fruit in the 1950s and beyond, as researchers in many universities and colleges built upon their findings. We can divide these later approaches into three very broad areas of study: opinion and behavior change, what people learn from media, and why, when, and how people use the media. Let's look at these one at a time.

Studying Opinion and Behavior Change

Many researchers have been interested in understanding why some people's opinions or behaviors are influenced by certain types of content, and others are not. Some of these researchers became involved in the most contentious issues involving media in the second half of the twentieth century—those centering on the effects of TV violence on children and the effects of sexually explicit materials (pornography) on adults.

In general, researchers seem to agree that the ways in which most adults and children react to such materials depend greatly upon family background, social setting, and personality. At the same time, they also agree that consistent viewing of violent television shows or movies may cause some children to become aggressive toward others regardless of family background. Researchers have come to similar conclusions about violent sexual materials, the kind in which men hurt women or vice versa. There is mounting evidence that, for some viewers, irrespective of their background or initial attitudes, heavy exposure to such materials may desensitize them to the seriousness of rape and other forms of sexual violence. For example, in one study, viewers of sexual violence had less concern about the supposed victim of a violent rape than the control group viewers who hadn't seen such materials. Because most of these findings are based on lab experiments, though, there is a significant amount of debate about whether they apply to the real world.

"Sorry, this block is closed for filming a gritty, hard-edged tale of passion and violence."

Studying What People Learn from Media

A large number of researchers have been interested in who learns what from mass media material, and under what conditions. There are many facets to this study area, but two particularly important ones stand out. The first is whether media can encourage children's learning of educational skills. The second looks at who in society learns about current national and world affairs from the media.

CAN MEDIA ENCOURAGE LEARNING SKILLS IN CHILDREN?   *Sesame Street*, which made its TV debut in 1969, has been the subject of a great deal of research into what children learn from it. Researchers have found that the program can teach boys and girls from different income levels their letters and numbers, and can be credited with improving the vocabulary of young children.

Professor Ellen Wartella, an expert on this topic, summarizes other findings on children's learning of education skills this way:

> Since the success of *Sesame Street*, other planned educational programs, such as *Where in the World is Carmen Sandiego, Bill Nye the Science Guy, Square One Television, Reading Rainbow, Gullah Gullah's Island, Blue's Clues* and *Magic School Bus*, have been found both to increase children's interest in the educational content of programs and to teach some of the planned curriculum. In addition, other children's shows, which focus less on teaching cognitive skills but more on such positive behaviors as helping others and sharing toys, can be successful. The most important evidence here comes from a study of preschool children's effective learning of such helping or pro-social behaviors from watching *Mister Rogers' Neighborhood*.[3]

WHICH INDIVIDUALS LEARN ABOUT NATIONAL AND WORLD AFFAIRS FROM THE MASS MEDIA?   Researchers who examine what people learn about national and world affairs from the mass media would probably argue that they, too, are looking at pro-social learning, but of a different kind. The basic belief that guides their work is that a democratic society needs informed citizens if public policies are to be guided by the greatest number of people. Some of their questions center on Walter Lippman's agenda-setting theory that we discussed earlier in this chapter.

Agenda-setting scholars agree with the mainstream position that differences among individuals make it unlikely that the mass media can tell you or me precisely what opinions we should have about particular topics. They point out, however, that by making some events and not others into major headlines, the mass media are quite successful at getting large numbers of people to agree on what topics to think about. That in itself is important, these researchers argue, because it shows that the press has the power to spark public dialogue on major topics facing the nation.

Professors Maxwell McCombs and Donald Shaw at the University of North Carolina, Chapel Hill, demonstrated this agenda-setting effect in research for the first time in a 1970 article. They surveyed Chapel Hill voters about the most important issues in the presidential campaign. They also conducted a content analysis of the attention that major media outlets in Chapel Hill paid to issues in the presidential campaign. McCombs and Shaw showed that the rankings

Just how much do children learn from what they see and hear in the media?

of the importance that voters placed on certain issues in the presidential election campaign were related not to the voters' party affiliation or personal biases but to the priorities that the media outlets in Chapel Hill presented at the time.

That one study on the influence of the media agenda on the public agenda led to more than 200 others. The agenda-setting power of the press has generally been shown to operate in both election and nonelection studies across a variety of geographic settings, time spans, news media, and public issues. Researchers have also described an effect called *priming* as a "close cousin of agenda-setting."[4]

Priming means the process by which the media affect the standard that individuals use to evaluate what they see and hear in the media. The idea is that the more prominent a political issue is in the national media, the more that idea will prime people (that is, cue them in) that the handling of that issue should be used to evaluate how well political candidates or organizations are doing their jobs.

But the power of agenda setting and priming is by no means the entire story. Researchers have found that mass media agenda setting has the ability to affect people's sense of public affairs priorities, and that mass media coverage primes people with respect to the criteria they use to evaluate particular issues. Nevertheless, researchers emphasize that individual backgrounds and interests weaken these effects—that is, they bring about a lot of variation in what issues people pick up as important, how they prioritize these issues, and whether or not they use these issues as evaluation criteria. The weakening of these effects occurs primarily because people's differences lead them to pay attention to different things in the media. As with the Yale studies described earlier, the strongest agenda-setting effects have been found in experimental studies. That suggests that a major condition for obtaining these effects is attention, because in experiments subjects are essentially forced to pay attention, whereas under naturalistic conditions some people do and others don't, based on their interest in what is going on.

If it is sometimes difficult to get people to pay attention to current events via the headlines, imagine how difficult it is to get them to pay attention to less obvious aspects of our political culture. In fact, in the decades since World War II, researchers have found a wide variation in what individuals learn from the mass media. Education has consistently been a major factor that is positively associated with differences between those who pick up knowledge of public affairs and those who do not. It seems that people are more likely to remember the events and facts that media present if they have frameworks of knowledge from schooling that can help them make sense of the news events they see or hear.

In the late 1960s, Professors Phillip Tichenor, George Donahue, and Clarice Olien of the University of Minnesota came upon a sobering survey finding that relates to the difference in the amount of current events information that different people learn from the media. They found that in the development of any social or political issue, the more highly educated segments of a population know more about the issue early on and, in fact, acquire information about that issue at a faster rate than the less educated segments. That is, people who are information rich to begin with get richer faster than people who are information poor, and so the difference in the amount of knowledge between the two types of people will grow wider.

Professors Tichenor, Donahue, and Olien concluded that this growing **knowledge gap** was dangerous for society in an age in which the ability to pick up information about the latest trends is increasingly crucial to success (see Figure 4.4). Because the information rich in society were often the well schooled and well off financially, a growing knowledge gap might mean that the poorer segments of society could not participate meaningfully in discussions of social issues. It also might mean that they would not know about developments that would help them prepare for, and get, better jobs.

priming the process by which the media affect the standard that individuals use to evaluate what they see and hear in the media

knowledge gap a theory developed by Tichenor, Donahue, and Olien that holds that, in the development of any social or political issue, the more highly educated segments of a population know more about the issue early on and, in fact, acquire information about that issue at a faster rate than the less educated ones, and so the difference between the two types of people grows wider

Studying Why, When, and How People Use the Media

Some of the most basic questions that researchers ask about mass media in society center on who uses them, how, and why. As we noted earlier, it was a group of scholars at Columbia University who created the first notable research program that went beyond basic factual descriptions of the numbers of newspaper readers and radio listeners to ask what motivated people to use certain kinds of content.

They asked, for example, "Why do people like such programming as radio soap operas and quiz shows?" This question may have gotten sneers from some of their elitist colleagues. Nevertheless, over the decades, this uses and gratifications research has received a lot of attention. The focus is on when, how, and why people use various mass media or particular genres of mass media content.

True to the spirit of the mainstream approach, uses and gratifications research has at its core a belief in the active audience. The term means that individuals are not just passive receivers of messages. Rather, they make conscious decisions about what they like, and they have different reasons for using particular media, depending on different social relationships as well as on individual social and psychological differences. Moreover, people are physically active when they use media. When it comes to TV, for example, studies have shown that people do not sit quietly, transfixed by the tube, as some cartoon stereotypes would have it. Rather, they move around, do other things, and talk to friends and family.

A huge amount of literature explores how people use a variety of media and why. Some very interesting work connects uses and gratifications research with effects

MEDIA RESEARCH
A WORLD CLASS IDEA

In 1970, an eleven-page article by three professors at the University of Minnesota appeared in the journal *Public Opinion Quarterly*. "Mass Media Flow and Differential Growth in Knowledge," by Phillip Tichenor, George Donahue, and Clarice Olien, presented the idea that a knowledge gap exists between socio-economic classes. The idea was that those who are information rich are able to gather new information faster than those who are information poor. Both groups gain information, but there is a difference in the rate at which they gather it. Tichenor, Donahue, and Olien supported their contention that there is a growing knowledge gap through a study of people's understanding of newspaper and scholarly journal articles. Now, more than thirty years later, scholars have accepted that the notion of a knowledge gap holds for other media as well. Hundreds of articles have been written on knowledge gap issues with topics ranging from health communication to interactive media.

Although the original study was carried out in Minneapolis, the knowledge gap theory has expanded to cover activities of people all over the world. Scholars have used the knowledge gap in dealing with such diverse topics as leprosy in India, democratic education in Argentina, vaccination knowledge in the Philippines, European information policy, AIDS education in Norway, mental health images in Canadian newspapers, migration in Thailand, earthquake predictions in Japan, and knowledge of voters in municipal elections in Sweden. The theory has captured the imagination of academics throughout the planet.

Tichenor, Donahue, and Olien emphasize that, rather than having an equalizing effect by making information widely and inexpensively available, mass media may actually widen the gap between the information rich and the information poor. This conclusion demands attention, as it causes us to pause and reflect on the dark side of information dissemination in our mediated society.

Source: Phillip Tichenor, George Donohue, and Clarice Olien, "Mass Media Flow and Differential Growth in Knowledge," *Public Opinion Quarterly* (Summer 1970), pp. 159–170.

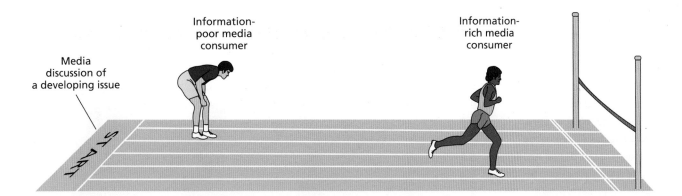

Media discussion of a developing issue

Information-poor media consumer

Information-rich media consumer

START

research, linking how or why people use media content with the extent to which it changes their opinions, actions, or ideas about the world.

Much of this work is interesting and important in its own right. It is useful to know, for example, what percentage of poor families have been connecting to the internet compared with the percentage of middle-class and wealthy families. The findings that there are sharp differences in income between families that are online at home and those that are not has sparked discussion of a **digital divide** in the United States—a separation between those who are connected to "the future" and those who are being left behind (see Figure 4.5). That, in turn, has led to efforts by governments and corporations to place Web-linked computers with instructors in libraries and community centers that are within easy reach of people who cannot afford the internet at home.

Activists argue that there is a lot more to do in this area. Of particular concern are economically disadvantaged children in the United States and elsewhere in the world who are falling behind in their ability to be part of the modern world. More than a few of their advocates point out that, although providing them with new technology is a beginning, it is not enough. Teaching them how to use the technology in ways that will benefit them and their societies is a critical part of bridging the digital divide.

The Rise of Critical Approaches

As you can see, the **mainstream approaches**—the research models that developed out of the work of the Columbia School, the Yale School, and the Payne Fund Studies—have led to valuable work that helped many researchers contribute to society's most important debates. At the same time, however, other researchers insist that the questions asked by mainstream approaches are not really the most important ones when it comes to understanding the role of mass media in society.

Moving from Mainstream Approaches to Critical Approaches

According to critics of the mainstream approach, there are two major problems with even the best mainstream research. One problem is its stress on *change* rather than *continuity*. The other is its emphasis on the active role of *the individual*—the active audience member—in the media environment and not on the power of *larger social forces* that control that media environment.

Let's look at the first problem. By a stress on change over continuity, critics of mainstream research mean that much of this research focuses on whether a change will occur as a result of specific movies, articles, or shows. Critics say that this approach ·

Figure 4.4 The Knowledge Gap

In the development of any social or political issue, people who are information rich to begin with will become information richer much more quickly than people who are information poor to begin with. For this reason, the difference in the amount of information between the information rich and the information poor grows exponentially wider.

digital divide the separation between those who have access to and knowledge about technology and those who (perhaps because of their level of education or income) do not

mainstream approaches the research models that developed out of the work of the Columbia School, the Yale School, and the Payne Fund Studies

Figure 4.5 The Digital Divide
Now, more than ever, the gap between those people and communities who can make effective use of information technology and those who cannot is widening. While a consensus does not exist on the extent of this digital divide (and whether this digital divide is growing or narrowing), researchers are nearly unanimous in acknowledging that some sort of divide exists at this point in time, as this figure shows.

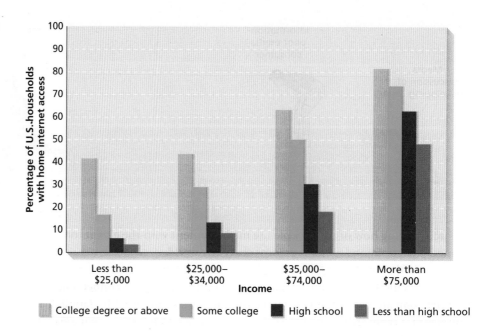

ignores the possibility that the most important effects of the media have to do not with changing people but with encouraging them (or reinforcing them) to continue certain actions or perspectives on life.

Mainstream researchers might focus, for example, on whether a girl will hit her little brother after watching the violent antics of a *Three Stooges* film or whether a woman will learn about politics from a website or TV news program. Now, there's nothing wrong with such questions, the critics allow. But, they add, fascination with these questions of change often hides the importance of the media in encouraging the reinforcement of actions and beliefs among many in society.

Mainstream researchers emphasize that most people's opinions and behaviors don't change after they view television or listen to the radio. What the researchers don't emphasize, the critics point out, is that the flip side of change—reinforcement—may well be a powerful consequence. In fact, the critics argue, reinforcement is often the major consequence of mass media messages. Media may repeat for us values that we have come to love, ideas about the world that we have come to trust, social class relationships that we have come to accept, and beliefs about the way people who are not like us look and act that we have come to accept. These are the ideas that hold a society together, the critics say, so it is a shame that the mainstream people have played them down.

But the critics often go further. They argue that mainstream research has placed so much emphasis on the individual's relationships to media—the second major problem we identified—that it has ignored social power. It has neglected to emphasize that there are powerful forces that exert control over what media industries do as part of their control over the society.

What really ought to be studied, say the critics, is the way these powerful groups come to influence the most widespread media images in ways that help them stay in power. From this perspective, agenda setting and the digital divide are not just phenomena that point to what people learn and how differently they learn. They are phenomena that help the powerful classes in the society retain their power.

Clearly, we have here a major difference of opinion about how to look at mass media, where their powers lie, and which of their aspects should be studied. Many critics of the mainstream approach prefer an avenue of research that recalls the most sophisticated of the propaganda analysts. Like the propaganda analysts, contemporary critical scholars emphasize the importance of systematically exploring the forces guiding media companies. They also place great value on analyzing media content to reveal the patterns of messages that are shared broadly by the population. Like the propaganda analysts, their aim is often to expose to public light the relationship of media firms to powerful forces in the society. They want to publicize their findings in order to encourage public understanding and, sometimes, to urge government regulations that would promote greater diversity among creators of media content and in the content itself.

The "critical" label describes a wide variety of projects relating to the mass media. Three prominent perspectives that guide critical researchers are the critical theory of the Frankfurt School, political economy research, and cultivation studies.

THE DEEP POLITICAL INFLUENCE OF THE MEDIA: THE FRANKFURT SCHOOL'S CRITICAL THEORY   The Frankfurt School is a shorthand name for a group of scholars who were associated with a place called the School for Social Research during the 1930s and 1940s. This shorthand name comes from the original location of the institute in Frankfurt, Germany. The researchers who made significant contributions to this school of thought are Theodor Adorno (philosopher, sociologist, and musicologist), Walter Benjamin (essayist and literary critic), Herbert Marcuse (philosopher), and Max Horkheimer (philosopher, sociologist). Each of these philosophers shared the basic view of capitalism set forth by the nineteenth-century philosopher Karl Marx. According to Marx, **capitalism** is the ownership of the means of production by a ruling class in society. Marx insisted that, in societies that accept this economic approach, capitalism greatly influences all beliefs. He further insisted that capitalism and the beliefs it generates create economic and cultural problems. They exploit the working class and celebrate that exploitation in literature and many other aspects of culture. Marx believed that the direction of history was toward labor's overthrow of the capitalist class and the reign of workers in a society in which everyone would receive what he or she needs.

The Frankfurt School focused on the cultural aspect of this issue, and its members were pessimistic about it. Marxist and Jewish, they were exiled from Germany to the United States because of the rise of Nazism during the 1920s and 1930s. In New York (where they established the New School for Social Research), the members of the Frankfurt School explored the relationship between culture and capitalism in an era in which economic depression, war, and mass exterminations made it difficult to be optimistic about the liberating potential of culture. Their writings about the corrosive influence of capitalism on culture came to be known as **critical theory**. Writings by Adorno stress the power of "the culture industry" to move audience members toward ways of looking at the world. Writings by Marcuse suggest to researchers how messages about social power can be found in all aspects of media content, even if typical audience members don't recognize them. For example, **co-optation** is a well-known term that Marcuse coined to express the way capitalism takes potentially revolutionary ideas and tames them to express capitalist ideals. For an example of co-optation, consider how advertisers take expressions of youthful rebellion such as tattoos and colored hair and turn them into the next moneymaking fads. Marcuse would say that this sort of activity shows how difficult it is for oppositional movements to create symbols that keep their critical meanings.

Many media scholars today feel that the members of the Frankfurt School tended to overemphasize the ability of mass media to control individuals' beliefs. Nevertheless, over the decades, the philosophies collectively known as critical theory have influenced many writings on mass media.

POLITICAL ECONOMY RESEARCH   **Political economy** theorists focus specifically on the relationship between economics and the culture. They look at when

capitalism as defined by Karl Marx, the ownership of the means of production by a ruling class in society

critical theory the Frankfurt School's members' theories focusing on the corrosive influence of capitalism on culture

co-optation a term coined by Marcuse to express the way in which capitalism takes potentially revolutionary ideas and tames them to express capitalist ideals

political economy an area of study that focuses specifically on the relationship between the economic and the cultural, and looks at when and how the economic structures of society and the media system reflect the political interests of society's rich and powerful

Author and media critic Ben Bagdikian is the winner of almost every top prize in American journalism, including the Pulitzer, and is one of the most respected media critics in the United States.

and how the economic structures of society and the media system reflect the political interests of society's rich and powerful. In this vein, professor and media activist Robert McChesney examined ownership patterns of media companies in the early 2000s. He concluded in his 2004 book *The Problem of the Media* that we have reached "the age of hyper-commercialism," where media worry far more about satisfying advertisers and shareholders than providing entertainment or news that encourages people to understand their society and become engaged in it.[5] McChesney blames government legislators and regulators for allowing the rise of huge media conglomerates that control large portions of the revenues of particular media industries for the purposes of selling advertising time and space. One alarming consequence, he contends, is a journalistic system that focuses more on attracting the attention of audiences than on trying to build an informed society like that imagined by Jefferson and Madison. As alarming to McChesney is the notion that, because U.S. media firms are so powerful internationally, this commercially driven perspective on journalism is spreading through the world. He and political economist Edward Herman put that idea succinctly in a 1997 book called *The Global Media*:

> Such a [global] concentration of media power in organizations dependent on advertiser support and responsible primarily to shareholders is a clear and present danger to citizens' participation in public affairs, understanding of public issues, and thus to the effective workings of democracy.[6]

Another writer from a political economy perspective, Ben Bagdikian, points out in his book *The Media Monopoly* that huge media firms are often involved in many businesses outside of journalism. Comcast, the main parent of NBC News, owns many cable systems, for example. Disney owns theme parks around the world as well as ABC News. News workers who are employed by these firms may be afraid to cover controversies that involve those operations; in fact, corporate bigwigs may keep them from doing so (see Figure 4.6).

The problem is not just theoretical: when ABC News investigative reporter Brian Ross was putting together a report on child abuse issues in theme parks, he was ordered by executives of the Walt Disney Company, which owns ABC News, not to report on possible problems with childcare in Disneyland. ABC officials denied that the corporate linkage influenced their decision to pull an investigative report on allegations involving Disney. *Disney: The Mouse Betrayed*, a *20/20* segment produced by Brian Ross, alleged, among other things, that Disney World in Florida fails to perform security checks that would prevent the hiring of sex offenders and has problems with Peeping Toms. According to an ABC spokeswoman, news president David Westin's killing of the story had nothing to do with any network reluctance to criticize its parent company. "The fact that this particular story involved Disney was not the reason it did not make air," claimed ABC officials.

The work by McChesney, Herman, and Bagdikian looks into the economic relationships within the media system and tries to figure out their consequences for issues of social power and equity. It is concerned with looking at how institutional and organizational relationships create requirements for media firms that lead the employees of those firms to create and circulate certain kinds of material and not others. These scholars might explore, for example, whether (and how) major advertisers' relationships with television networks affect programming. They would look at the extent to which advertisers' need to reach certain audiences for their products causes networks to signal to program producers that shows that aim at those types of people will get preference.

The topics political economists choose vary greatly. Some, like Herbert Schiller, explore global issues. An example is the study of factors that encourage the spread of Western (often U.S.) news and entertainment throughout the world. These political scientists consider such activities to be cultural colonialism. **Colonialism** means control over a dependent area or people by a powerful entity (usually a nation) by force of arms. England and France practiced colonialism in places such as India and Vietnam for many years. **Cultural colonialism** involves the exercise of control over an area or people by a dominant power, not so much through force of arms as by surrounding the weaker countries with cultural materials that reflect values and beliefs supporting the interests of that dominant power. The political economists who explore cultural colonialism argue that, by celebrating values such as commercialism and immediate gratification, the cultural colonizers encourage markets for goods that reflect those values and so help their own country's business interests.

Other political economists focus on the concerns of media in individual countries. They look, for example, at the extent to which ethnic or racial minorities can exert some control over mainstream media. Their fear is that social minorities often do not get to guide their own portrayals in their nation's main media. The result is underrepresentation and stereotyping of these groups by producers who are insensitive to their concerns. These political scientists urge changes so that minority producers and actors can have input regarding their groups' depictions.

colonialism control over a dependent area or people by a powerful entity by force of arms

cultural colonialism the exercise of control over an area or people by a dominant power, not so much through force of arms as by surrounding the weaker countries with cultural materials that reflect values and beliefs supporting the interests of that dominant power

CULTIVATION STUDIES   Cultivation researchers are also interested in depictions, but in a different way. Such studies are different from political economy studies in that they focus not on industry relationships but on the information about the world that people pick up from media portrayals. You might object that this sounds very much like what many mainstream effects researchers do. On the surface it does. Where cultivation researchers differ is in the perspective they bring to the work and how they interpret their findings. **Cultivation studies** emphasize that when media systematically portray certain populations in unfavorable ways, the ideas about those people that mainstream audiences pick up help certain groups in society retain their power over the groups they denigrate. Stereotypes, they believe, reinforce and extend ("cultivate") power relationships.

Cultivation work is most associated with Professor George Gerbner and his colleagues at the University of Pennsylvania's Annenberg School for Communication from the 1960s through the 1980s. Gerbner began his work with the perspective that all mass media material—entertainment and news—gives people views of the world. Those views, he said, are mass-produced output of huge corporations. These corporations have a vested interest in perpetuating their power along with the power of established economic and cultural approaches in U.S. society. Their power is seen especially in the way violence is used in television entertainment, the most widely viewed entertainment medium in the United States.

Across all channels on the tube, argues Gerbner, TV violence is a kind of ritual ballet that acts out social power. Although TV violence may sometimes encourage aggression, most of the time it cultivates lessons about strength and weakness in society. For example, Gerbner contends that the "hidden curriculum" of TV violence tells us that women and blacks, who tend to be the objects of violence, are socially

cultivation studies studies that emphasize that, when media systematically portray certain populations in unfavorable ways, the ideas about those people that mainstream audiences pick up help certain groups in society retain their power over the groups they denigrate

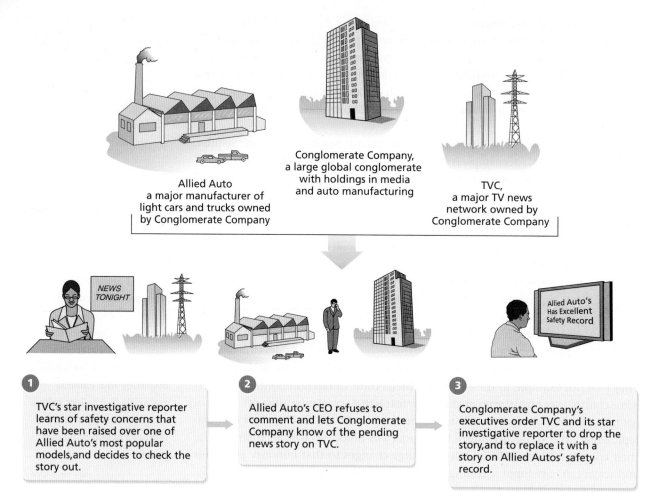

Allied Auto
a major manufacturer of
light cars and trucks owned
by Conglomerate Company

Conglomerate Company,
a large global conglomerate
with holdings in media
and auto manufacturing

TVC,
a major TV news
network owned by
Conglomerate Company

1 TVC's star investigative reporter learns of safety concerns that have been raised over one of Allied Auto's most popular models, and decides to check the story out.

2 Allied Auto's CEO refuses to comment and lets Conglomerate Company know of the pending news story on TVC.

3 Conglomerate Company's executives order TVC and its star investigative reporter to drop the story, and to replace it with a story on Allied Autos' safety record.

Figure 4.6 Covering Controversies: A Hypothetical Example

A conflict of interest can arise when conglomerates with a direct stake in businesses outside of journalism own many of the media outlets through which the public is informed. In this hypothetical example, Conglomerate Company, which has holdings in TV news and in the auto industry, orders its news arm to "kill" a negative story about the safety ratings of the cars it produces. What are the ethical implications of Conglomerate Company's actions? What about harm to the public good? How often do you think this sort of situation takes place in the real world? To what extent is it possible to find out?

weak. White males, who tend to be perpetrators of violence (including legal violence by the police or military), are socially strong.

Moreover, Gerbner argues, the overall message of TV violence is that we live in a scary, mean world. He and his colleagues found support for this view through a two-pronged research design. First, they conducted a content analysis of many hours of television entertainment programming, using a careful definition of violence and noting who is violent to whom and under what conditions. Next, they conducted a telephone survey of a random sample of the U.S. adult population and asked the people questions about how violent the world is and how fearful they are. They found that heavy viewers of television are more fearful of the world than light viewers. Over time, these viewers also engage in more self-protective behavior and show more mistrust of others than do light viewers.

Gerbner maintains that, although this phenomenon affects the individual, it also has larger social implications. The message of fear helps those who are in power because it makes the heavy viewers (a substantial portion of the population) more likely to agree to support police and military forces that protect them from that scary world. Not incidentally, those police and military forces also protect those in power and help them maintain control over unruly or rebellious groups in society.

Gerbner's cultivation research and the critical approaches of political economists and the Frankfurt School helped to add another dimension to the way U.S. scholars looked at the mass media. In the past couple of decades, a third broad avenue of inquiry has added to the mix of ideas about media power and consequences. This avenue is widely known as cultural studies.

CRITICAL CONSUMER
"FRAMING" GAY MARRIAGE

Whereas the agenda-setting function of the press tells us what issues to think about, the way the press "frames" an issue tells us how to approach it. Frames set the terms for a debate, emphasizing certain elements and downplaying others. With almost any political issue, there is a contest over what frames dominate discussion of the issue.

Consider gay marriage. Within the last decade, it has become one of the most heated topics of debate in the United States. Since the introduction of gay marriage into several states and the ban of gay marriage in several others, news coverage of the controversy has become nearly unavoidable. But is the debate one over family values? Or is it one over equality? The way you answer that question is a prize over which both opponents and proponents of gay marriage alike are competing.

Those opposed to gay marriage frequently stress family values, emphasizing the moral elements of marriage. By contrast, gay rights advocates emphasize legal discrimination against gays and situate the debate as one of fairness. To people on both sides of the issue, it is important how key news media frame it. Do they accept one way of thinking about the debate, or is there a balance of frames?

A recent study at the Syracuse University's Newhouse School of Public Communications examined coverage of same-sex marriage by newspapers around the United States. The researchers performed quantitative content analysis to analyze stories from February 2004 and February 2005 about gay marriage from daily papers and wire services. They also performed qualitative textual analysis of marriage in stories published in the states with anti-same-sex marriage ballot initiatives.

The findings reveal a complex picture. The researchers discovered that the newspapers' use of terms such as "threatens" and "in jeopardy" gave the impression that gay marriage posed risks to traditional marriage. However, the other side got its frame in as well. The researchers stated that news coverage generally portrayed gay marriage as an issue of equality, with homosexual couples lacking the same civil rights as heterosexual couples.

Still, the authors consistently found that opponents of gay marriage set the terms of the debate by defining what "normal" marriage is: between one man and one woman. "What this suggests is that same-sex marriage, as an institution, has no definition of its own separate from heterosexual marriage," wrote the authors. "Rather, it is presented as a reflection, a shadow, or outgrowth of that institution."

The next time you are reading a news article about a particularly contentious political issue, try to pinpoint what frames the article is employing. Ask yourself who might be trying to put forth these frames, and how they could affect the way you approach that issue.

Source: Carol M. Liebler, Joseph Schwartz, and Todd Harper, "Queer Tales of Morality: The Press, Same-Sex Marriage, and Hegemonic Framing," *Journal of Communication* 59, 4 (2009), pp. 653–675. doi: 10.1111/j.1460–2466.2009.01451.x.

Cultural Studies

Let's say that you accept the importance of emphasizing the connection between mass media and social power, but you're a bit uncomfortable with what you feel is the too-simplistic perspective of the political economy and cultivation theorists. "Media power isn't as controlling as they would have it," you say. "I don't believe that everybody in the society necessarily buys into the images of power that these systems project. People have minds of their own, and they often live in communities that help them resist the aims of the powerful."

If that's your perspective, you would probably find one of the many approaches within cultural studies to be up your alley. The approach taken by cultural studies was developed in Europe and had been used there for many years before it attracted a large following in the United States, which it did during the 1980s. Writings in this area often tie media studies to concepts in literature, linguistics, anthropology, and history. **Cultural studies** scholars often start with the idea that all sorts of mass media, from newspapers to movies, present their audiences with technologies and texts, and that audiences find meaning in them. Major questions for these scholars

cultural studies studies that start with the idea that all sorts of mass media, from newspapers to movies, present their audiences with technologies and texts and that audiences find meaning in them; scholars then ask questions that center on how to think about what "making meaning" of technologies and texts means and what consequences it has for those audiences in society

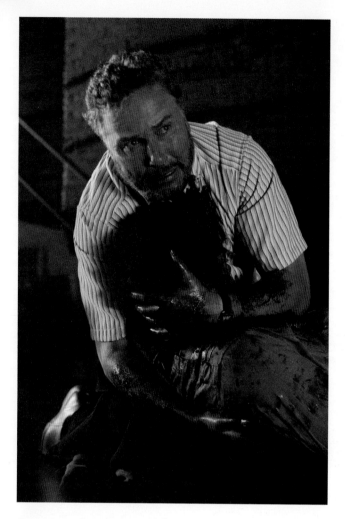

Media researchers have found that heavy television watchers tend to be more fearful of the world than light viewers, a possible result of the violence frequently portrayed in crime shows.

center on how to think about what "making meaning" of technologies and texts means and what consequences it has for those audiences in society. As you might imagine, there are many ways to answer these questions.

Historical Approaches to Cultural Studies

One way is to answer them from a historical perspective. Professor Lynn Spigel, for example, explores the expectations that men and women have had for audiovisual technologies in the home and how those expectations have tied into larger social issues. She points out, for example, a historical relationship between home TV use and social fear:

Communications technologies have promised to bring the outside world into the home since the late 19th century. At the time of industrialization, when urban centers were linked to the first suburban towns, there were endless speculations about the joys and potential pitfalls of a new design for middle-class living which would allow people to be joined together in an electrical public space without ever going outside. Middle-class families could, in this way, enjoy social encounters while avoiding the elements of urban space—such as labor unrest or ethnic immigration—which made them feel most threatened.[7]

Anthropological Approaches to Cultural Studies

Another way to look at what technologies mean in the context of social class and social power is to take an anthropologist's approach and closely examine the way people use media. Cultural studies researchers tie people's uses of the media to their class, racial, or gender positions within the society. Here, for example, is Professor Ellen Seiter writing in 1997 on differences in the use of television and computers between men and women in the home:

Television sets and computers introduce highly similar issues in terms of placement in domestic space, conflicts among family members over usage and control, value in the household budget, and we can expect these to be articulated with gender roles in the family. Some research on gendered conflicts over computers (Giacquinta; Murdock; Haddon) reproduces themes of family-based studies about control of the television set. Already researchers have noted a strong tendency for men and boys to have more access to computers in the home. Television studies such as Ann Gray's, David Morley's and my own work suggest that women in nuclear families have difficulty watching a favorite television show (because of competition for control of the set from other family members, and because of shouldering the majority of childcare, housework and cooking). If male family members gravitate towards the computer as hobbyists, the load of chores relegated to female family members will only increase, and make it more difficult for female members to get time on the home computer. Computers require hours of trial and error experimentation, a kind of extended play demanding excess leisure time. Fully exploring the internet needs time for lengthy downloading, and patience with connections that are busy, so much so that some have dubbed the World Wide Web the World Wide Wait.[8]

Linguistic and Literary Approaches to Cultural Studies

You probably found the paragraphs by Ellen Seiter and Lynn Spigel quite straightforward and easy to understand. The same can't be said typically for the areas of cultural studies that apply linguistic and literary models to the meaning of media texts. They tend to use the complex phraseology of linguistics and the jargon of literary analysts to make their points. That is unfortunate, because some of the scholars involved in this area often proclaim that their goal is to encourage viewers and readers to "resist" the dominant models of society that are suggested in the text.

Moreover, these discussions are actually quite interesting and important, once you cut through the language. A major topic of discussion is just where the meaning of a text lies. Is it preset into the written or audiovisual material (the book, the TV show), is it in the way a person using the material understands it, or is it in some relationship between the two? That may sound like an odd question, but it is significant because it speaks to the power of the media to guide people's understanding of the world.

At one extreme are scholars who believe that a text is open to multiple meanings (they say that it is **polysemous**) because people have the ability to subject media content to endless interpretations based on their critical understanding of the world. So, for example, Professors Elihu Katz and Tamar Liebes interviewed people in Israel and Japan to find out how they understood the popular 1980s U.S. TV series *Dallas*. They found that Japanese viewers, Israeli viewers from Morocco, and Israeli viewers from Russia had quite different interpretations of the program and its relevance to their lives. According to such findings about multiple interpretations, people in this camp have a clear idea of where they should apply their public interest energies. They would say, for example, that trying to limit the power of media conglomerates is not nearly as important as teaching people how to interpret media critically, in ways that resist any support of the dominant system.

polysemous open to multiple meanings

Against this notion of a program or book being open to multiple meanings is the opposite idea that the meaning is in the text itself. Scholars with this view argue that the shared culture of the society leads individuals to share the basic meaning of the text. To them, firms that create agendas in news and entertainment have enormous power that cannot be overcome simply by teaching criticism. Active work to limit the power of these conglomerates is also necessary.

Philosophically, most scholars take a position between these two extremes. They accept the notion of polysemy but they argue that most people's interpretations of media texts are very much shaped by the actual texts themselves and by the industrial and social environments in which these texts are created. They stress that texts are likely to "constrain" meaning in directions that benefit the powerful. That is, because of the way the text is created, viewers or readers notice the "preferred" meaning, the meaning that members of the establishment would likely find most compatible with their own thinking. Certainly, audience members can disagree with this take on the world. Even if they do, however, they may get the strong idea that most other people would not disagree with the text's approaches to racial, gender, ethnic, and religious stereotypes; tales of who is strong and who is weak; or portrayals of what the universe is like, how we (as Americans and humans) fit in, and how we should act toward it. Such scholars might be likely to enthusiastically support media criticism as well as public actions to limit the power of huge media conglomerates.

Using Media Research to Develop Media Literacy Skills

We now return to the story of Jessica. She has heard those grad students discuss everything that you've read in the past several pages, as they present ways of looking at the issues about local news that she has brought to them. Each student gives her a thumbnail summary of the history and nature of different aspects of mass communication research. Jessica's head is spinning from the variety of ways to look at the same media material, the hundreds of questions it is possible to ask.

You may feel the same way she does. But if you think about it a bit more, you'll see that understanding the history of mass media research provides tools with which to figure out three key ideas that a media-literate person must know. One is where you stand with respect to the effects of media on society. A second is how to make sense of the discussions and arguments about media effects. A third is how to get involved in research that can be used to explore concerns you might have about mass media.

CULTURE TODAY
BINGE DRINKING PSAS

We frequently encounter public service announcements (PSAs) that aim to modify our behavior for the greater public good. Common PSAs encourage us to conserve water, stop smoking, and prevent forest fires. Clearly, the creators hope the messages will have their desired impact. Unfortunately for the makers of one PSA, evidence has surfaced that the effect might be the opposite of the one they intended.

The Saskatchewan Ministry of Health recently released a series of PSAs aiming to reduce binge drinking. "This isn't what they meant by 'on-campus accommodation'," reads one of the ads, accompanied by a picture of a woman passed out on a bathroom floor. Another ironically reads "Best night of my life," and depicted a woman slumped over a toilet bowl. But the PSAs may have actually increased the problem, according to a study in the *Journal of Marketing Research*. Researchers Nidhi Argawal and Adam Duhachek designed an experiment wherein over a thousand undergraduates were primed to feel either shame or guilt, exposed to ads modeled after the Canadian PSAs, and then administered surveys measuring their attitudes toward drinking.

The problem with the PSAs, according to Argawal, a marketing professor at Northwestern University's Kellogg School of Management, is that they rely on inducing feelings of guilt and/or shame in order to effect behavioral change. However, viewers are prone to resist these messages and resort to "defensive processing" in order to lessen the negative feelings the ads mean to produce. As a result, this tactic may lead to a boomerang effect, wherein the ads lead to more binge drinking amongst the viewing population. "There's a lot of money spent on these ads that could be put to better use," said Argawal.

Argawal suggested PSA makers emphasize to viewers how to avoid situations that can lead to binge drinking and its ramifications as opposed to shaming them for their behavior. Argawal also noted that PSAs placed in more positive environments—such as in a sitcom—may have a better chance of succeeding. "It's important that the messages be toned down and as positive as possible," she contended.

Sources: Jeremy Mullman, "Why Binge Drinking PSAs May Leave Some Reaching for Another Drink," *Advertising Age*, March 3, 2010. http://adage.com/article?article_id=142459 (accessed March 26, 2010); Nidhi Agrawal and Adam Duhachek, "Emotional Compatibility and the Effectiveness of Antidrinking Messages: A Defensive Processing Perspective on Shame and Guilt," *Journal of Marketing Research* 47 (2010), pp. 263–273.

Where Do You Stand with Respect to Media Effects?

While reading this chapter, it's likely that you found yourself agreeing with some of the media approaches and disagreeing with others. Maybe you dismissed political economy as a lot of baloney, but you felt that uses and gratifications research and some aspects of cultural studies really make sense. That's fine; part of becoming media literate involves taking an informed stand on why the media are important. Learning about the ways in which people have grappled with concerns about the mass media over the decades can help you sort out your concerns. You personally may be more convinced that the individual interpretations and uses of the media are what make a difference for people. You may not be convinced by those who emphasize social issues, such as political economists, cultivation researchers, and even people involved in studying agenda setting.

It's really important, though, that you do not close your mind to all of these possibilities. New ideas keep coming up; your ideas about life keep changing as well. You can keep up with what media researchers are saying by reading press articles about them, or maybe even going to journals such as the *Journal of Communication, Critical Studies in Media Communication, Journalism and Mass Communication Quarterly*, or the *Journal of Broadcasting & Electronic Media*. What you have learned here and what you learn in the future may well affect how you relate to the media yourself, how you introduce your children to different media, and what you tell parents who ask your opinion on how to think about the media's consequences for their children.

How to Make Sense of Discussions and Arguments About Media Effects

When you do read about research in the popular press or in academic journals, think back to this chapter to help you place the work in perspective and critique it. Here are some questions you should ask yourself:

- *Are the questions the researcher is asking interesting and important?* Think of the issues you have learned about in this chapter. How important are the ones dealt with in the study you are considering? Do you wish the researchers had devoted their energies to other topics that you consider more relevant to your life or the life of the country?
- *Into what research tradition does the study fall?* Is it a study of priming, an example of cultivation research, a study of message persuasion, or a representation of another one of the streams of work that we have discussed (see Table 4.1)?
- *How good is the research design?* Whereas journal articles lay out the method used in research quite carefully, press reports of research often don't give you a lot of information about how the work was carried out. Even in the popular press, however, you can often find some of the specific questions the investigators used and some details about the method. When you think about the research design, be skeptical. Think about the type and size of the sample. If the study was an experiment, how realistic was it?
- *How convincing is the analysis?* If the researcher is claiming that the media caused something to happen, are there any other explanations for the findings? Does it appear that the researcher thought about reliability? How valid does the study seem in terms of the real world? These and other questions should roll around in your head as you decide whether or not to accept the conclusions of the researchers or others who are quoted.

Table 4.1 Comparing Media Research Theories

Theory/Research Study	Approach	Participating Researchers	Aim	Example
Chicago School	Early philosophy and sociology of media	Dewey, Cooley, Park	Searching for community	The immigrant press
Propaganda analysts	Early concerns about media persuasion	Lasswell, McClung, Casey	The activities of media producers and the resulting content	Content analyses of newspapers
Payne Fund Researchers	Early research on children and movies	Charters	Explorations of media effects via multiple methods	How violent movies affect children's sleep patterns
Columbia School	The media and social relations	Lazarsfeld, Katz, Merton	Research on how interpersonal relations intervene in media effects	The "two-step flow" influence of radio and newspapers during a presidential election campaign
American Soldier propaganda research	The limits of propaganda	Hovland	Movies, learning, and persuasion	An evaluation of the effects of *The Battle of Britain*
Yale Program of Research on Communication and Attitude Change	The limits of propaganda	Hovland	Research on the conditions that encourage audience persuasion	Experiments to determine whether and when fear appeals were more persuasive than appeals not using fear
Various	Mainstream effects research		Studying behavior and opinion change	
Various	Mainstream effects research		Can television encourage learning skills in children?	Research on what youngsters learn from *Sesame Street*
Various	Mainstream effects research	McCombs and Shaw Tichenor, Donahue, and Olien	Which individuals learn about national and world affairs from mass media?	Research on agenda setting; research on the knowledge gap
Various	Mainstream effects research		Why, when, how people use the media	Investigations of the active audience; research on the digital divide
Frankfurt School	Critical approaches to mass media	Adorno, Marcuse, Horkheimer	The relationship between capitalism and culture	Critical theory about the culture industry
Various	Critical approaches to mass media	Bagdikian, Schiller	Political economy research	Research on media monopolies
Annenberg School	Critical approaches to mass media	Gerbner	Cultivation studies	Research on TV violence and perceptions of a mean world
Various	Cultural studies	Spigel	Historical approaches	Historical relationship between home TV use and social fear
Various	Cultural studies	Seiter, Murdock, Haddon	Anthropological approaches	Differences between men and women in use of TV and computers
Various	Cultural studies	Katz and Leibes	Literary and linguistic approaches	Research on polysemous meanings

■ *What do you wish the researchers would do next in their research?* Asking this question, involving whether or not you like the research, will encourage you to think more deeply than you otherwise might about the role of media in society. Talking with your friends about especially interesting or problematic research is another way to play out some of the meanings that the research holds for you and for others in society.

How to Explore Your Concerns About Mass Media

What are the implications of the research for your personal life as well as for public policy? For example, a well-done study of attitudes toward the Web and uses of the Web by people over the age of seventy might have great meaning to you if you work in a senior center and want to get seniors engaged with the internet. The study might inform members of Congress who are thinking of providing funding to connect senior centers to the Web. The study might also be relevant if you have a parent or grandparent over that age and you have wondered whether and how to introduce email and other Web-related technologies to her or him.

A desire to learn the implications of research for her personal life and public policy, you'll remember, is what brought communication major and student journalist Jessica to Professor Berg's graduate seminar. She now understands that all the research perspectives that the students have presented, from mainstream effects and uses and gratifications research to cultivation research to political economy and cultural studies, can be relevant to understanding local news in her city.

"There are so many possible important approaches to this issue that I almost feel paralyzed just worrying which to choose," she says to the assembled group. "Where should I begin? How should I begin?"

As they continue discussing her concerns, though, Jessica realizes that she must choose the approach to mass media that best fits the concerns she personally has about the media and the specific questions that she is asking. She goes home convinced that what she has had all along is a critical studies take on the issue.

Jessica suggests to her friend, who is a criminology major and anti-poverty activist, that they get a group together to conduct a systematic content analysis of local news in the city with the help of one of the professors. Their goal is to find out exactly how much emphasis on violence and sex and how little attention to government issues and city arts activities there is in the city's morning and evening newscasts. After the content research is completed, the group will interview local TV reporters and executives to try to understand the economic and organizational considerations that lead the local news stations to cover the city in certain ways. Jessica also enlists a journalism graduate student to prepare a review of agenda-setting and cultivation literature, to make the point that the TV station's systematic presentations of a violent city and their ignoring of government can have a real impact on the way adults and children perceive their surroundings. When all that is done—Jessica estimates it will take five months—she and her group will present their material to the TV stations, and also to newspaper reporters and city leaders. Their hope is that the work will encourage citizens, city officials, and maybe even some local advertisers to place pressure on station heads to tone down the violence and play up the role of government in people's lives. "Maybe I'm quixotic," Jessica tells her group, "but I really do think it can be done."

Jessica's story is not an unusual one. Every day, all sorts of mass communication research, from all sorts of perspectives, is brought to bear on a multitude of public issues. Local, state, and federal governments draw on the results of mass communication research, and they often commission it. Of course, scholars don't always carry out research with specific public policy questions in mind. Nor, it should be emphasized, do they "cook" their results to conform to their particular political points of view. Nevertheless, as we have seen in this chapter, over the past century academics have asked questions not from the irrelevance of an ivory tower but as human beings concerned with the best ways to think about some of the most important topics of their day. As you read the rest of this book, consider that the topics and issues raised are all subject to systematic investigation from one or more of the perspectives sketched above. You might find carrying out such an inquiry fascinating and rewarding.

Chapter Review

For an interactive chapter recap and study guide, visit the companion website for *Media Today* at http://www.routledge.com/textbooks/mediatoday4e.

Questions for Discussion and Critical Thinking

1 Explain what is meant by the statement, "the best scholarly empirical research is guided by concepts."
2 In what ways do the early concerns of communication researchers—the ability of the media to communicate cultural values to diverse audiences, or the use of propaganda through the media to rally support for the positions of those in power—play out in the contemporary media environment?
3 What kinds of educational effects might mass communication channels have on child and/or adult audiences?
4 What might a political economist like Robert McChesney or Ben Bagdikian say about the issue of television violence and children?
5 In what ways, if at all, do practices like priming and agenda setting on the part of the media limit our perspectives on issues and events in the world?

Internet Resources

Association for Education in Journalism and Mass Communication (http://www. aejmc.org/)

> The AEJMC exists to promote the highest possible standards for education in journalism and mass communication, to encourage the widest possible range of communication research, to encourage the implementation of a multicultural society in the classroom and curriculum, and to defend and maintain freedom of expression in day-to-day living.

Center for Research on the Influences of Television on Children (http://www.utexas. edu/research/critc/)

CRITC, the Center for Research on the Influences of Television on Children, studies the impact of various kinds of television viewing on children's behavior and development. It has conducted studies of how children decode the medium of television; how they understand its forms and formats, as well as its content.

Center for Media and Public Affairs (http://www.cmpa.com/)

The Center for Media and Public Affairs (CMPA) is a nonpartisan and nonprofit research and educational organization that conducts scientific studies of news and entertainment media. CMPA has emerged as a unique institution that bridges the gap between academic research and the broader domains of media and public policy.

Critical Studies in Media Communication (http://www.tandf.co.uk/journals/ titles/07393180.asp)

Critical Studies in Media Communication provides a home for scholarship in media and mass communication from a cultural studies and critical perspective. It particularly welcomes cross-disciplinary works that enrich debates among various disciplines, critical traditions, methodological and analytical approaches, and theoretical standpoints.

Journal of Communication (http://www.blackwell-synergy.com/loi/jcom)

The Journal of Communication is the flagship journal of the International Communication Association and an essential publication for all communication specialists and policy-makers. The *Journal of Communication* concentrates on communication research, practice, policy, and theory, bringing to its readers the latest, broadest, and most important findings in the field of communication studies.

Journal of Broadcasting and Electronic Media (http://www.tandf.co.uk/journals/HBEM)

The Journal of Broadcasting and Electronic Media is the scholarly journal published quarterly by the Broadcast Education Association. Considered one of the leading publications in the communication field, the journal contains timely articles about new developments, trends, and research in electronic media written by academics, researchers, and other electronic media professionals.

Media Effects Research Laboratory at Pennsylvania State University (http://www. psu.edu/dept/medialab/)

The Media Effects Research Laboratory at the College of Communications in the Pennsylvania State University is a facility dedicated to conducting empirical research on the psychological effects of media content, form, and technology. Several experimental studies involving hundreds of subjects have been conducted in the lab since its opening in 1997.

Key Terms

. . . .

You can find the definitions to these key terms in the marginal glossary throughout this chapter. Test your knowledge of these terms with interactive flash cards on the *Media Today* companion website.

Constructing Media Literacy

. . . .

1 Which of the perspectives on media effects do you find most interesting? Why?

2 To what extent have you seen polysemy work when you and a friend go to the movies? Give an example.

3 Scholars point out that the digital divide may show itself differently in relatively wealthy countries such as the United States and the United Kingdom compared with poor countries such as Bangladesh or the Sudan. Using newspaper or magazine articles, bring some examples of such differences.

4 How do you think your ideas of romance have been shaped by movies and popular songs?

5 Have you ever gotten angry at media portrayals? What, if anything, did you do about it? Do you think that you would go so far as to do what Jessica did? Why or why not? What realistic steps could you/did you take?

Companion Website Video Clips

. . . .

The Mean World Syndrome—"It's Like the Fish in the Water . . ."
This clip from the Media Education Foundation documentary *The Mean World Syndrome* is based on the late George Gerbner's groundbreaking analysis of media influence and media violence. Credit: Media Education Foundation.

Peace, Propaganda, and the Promised Land—Defining Who is Newsworthy
This clip from the Media Education Foundation documentary *Peace, Propaganda, and the Promised Land* explores the U.S. and international coverage of the crisis in

the Middle East, specifically the Israeli–Palestinian conflict. Credit: Media Education Foundation.

Stuart Hall: The Origins of Cultural Studies—Introduction and a Point of Disturbance

In this clip from the Media Education Foundation video of Stuart Hall's 1989 lecture, Hall traces the social, intellectual, and institutional environment from which cultural studies emerged. Credit: Media Education Foundation.

200

This 1976 animation by Vincent Collins is a tribute to the U.S. bicentennial and it was produced by the U.S. Information Agency, the government's propaganda agency. Credit: Internet Archive.

Case Study
. . . .

EVALUATING A SCHOLARLY ARTICLE

It takes some training to evaluate a scholarly article. The main thing to remember is that just because a study has been published in an academic journal doesn't mean that it is perfect. Sometimes published articles have many flaws as well as good points. Hone your scholarly reading skills in the following manner:

1. Read an article about an empirical study that is published in a scholarly journal such as the *Journal of Communication*, *Journal of Broadcasting and Electronic Media*, *Critical Studies in Media Communication*, or *Journalism and Mass Communication Quarterly*.
2. Write a summary of the main points of the article in a page or less, focusing on the major questions, the theory the authors are working with to help understand or address those questions, the method used to carry out the study, the major findings, and the authors' conclusions about what the study means.
3. Then evaluate what you like and don't like about the study from the standpoint of the features discussed in this chapter: the nature of the sample, the size of the sample and the way it's collected, the design of the study, the reliability of the study, the soundness of the analysis, and the validity of the study.
4. In general, do you think the topics or questions that the author addressed are important? Why or why not? How convinced are you that the way the authors addressed those topics sheds an important light on the topics or questions?

The point here is not to scare you, but to alert you to what it means to be a literate consumer of mass media research. If you understand the basics of evaluating research and you get an overview of the kinds of concerns media researchers have had over the decades, you will be able to ask the right questions and critically evaluate the answers to those questions.

Part Two

Media Giants and
Cross-Media Activities

We live in an age of media giants—large companies with major businesses that influence several media areas. Firms such as Disney, News Corporation, Time Warner, Google, and Sony are setting a pattern for twenty-first-century operations. That pattern is global and requires an ability to control content across media boundaries.

In this section, we examine the strategies of media giants and their impact on the media system. We also introduce concerns by media critics that a small number of media conglomerates have too much influence over the news, entertainment, information, and even education materials that surround us in our daily lives.

THE CHAPTERS

5 A World of Blurred Media Boundaries

After studying this chapter, you will be able to:

1 Identify and discuss the six guiding trends shaping the world of mass media

2 Analyze and discuss media fragmentation's impact on media organizations and their consumers

3 Recognize and evaluate the audience segmentation strategies of media organizations

4 Identify and explain the benefits and challenges of distributing products across media boundaries

5 Analyze and discuss the impact of digital convergence on media organizations and their consumers

6 Recognize the trend toward globalization in the mass media and evaluate its consequences

7 Recognize the trend toward conglomeration in the mass media and evaluate its consequences

8 Harness your media literacy skills by taking a critical view of the six trends discussed in this chapter

MEDIA TODAY

If you flip through the pages of this book, you'll notice that in the chapters to come we look at mass media industries individually. You'll see, for example, that there are separate chapters on the book, newspaper, film, and internet industries—with good reason. Each industry has its own way of doing things, its own approaches to production, distribution, and exhibition.

Yet, if we want to understand how the mass media work today, there is also a good reason for thinking of the mass media industries as related rather than separate. Top media executives certainly think of them as related. Those executives point out that the boundaries of media industries are becoming increasingly blurred. That is, it is getting more and more difficult to know where the movie industry ends and the television industry begins; where the internet industry ends and the newspaper industry begins; where the advertising industry ends and the public relations industry begins, and so on. Materials that are created for one mass media industry are increasingly showing up in others in one form or another. The *Harry Potter* series, for example, has moved from its original format as a book to the advertising poster, the movie screen, the website, the soundtrack, the action figure, the DVD, and the television, among other things.

"Wait!" you may hear yourself saying. "These kinds of cross-media connections have been going on for decades. Instead of *My Little Pony* and *Wubbzy*, my parents and grandparents had *Howdy Doody* and *Bullwinkle* stuff that crossed media: from TV to movies and toys and lunch boxes, comic books, and posters. Has anything really changed? Hasn't this always been a standard part of the mass media world?" Good question. A glance back in time does reveal that media industries have always interacted. Still, what is happening at the start of the twenty-first century represents a major change. Within the past fifteen years, the quick movement of all sorts of materials across a variety of mass media industries has become critical to the financial health of virtually all types of media firms.

The aim of this chapter and the one that follows is to help you critically examine these cross-media activities. How do they work? What effects might they have on society and on you as a consumer? It is useful to address these questions before you study individual mass media industries. Being sensitive to the cross-media picture will help you be better able to think about the way the individual industries we discuss operate in the larger media system.

Six Guiding Mass Media Trends

Six related trends describe the mass media world at the beginning of the twenty-first century:

- Media fragmentation
- Audience segmentation
- Distribution of products across media boundaries
- Globalization
- Conglomeration
- Digital convergence

Mass media executives see media fragmentation and audience segmentation as special challenges that force media producers to move materials across media outlets in search of profits. And they see digital convergence, conglomeration, and globalization as potential solutions to the difficulties of cross-media distribution while also adding to their ways of maximizing profit. Media critics worry that these activities pose serious dangers to a democratic society. They are especially concerned about ill effects of globalization and conglomeration. To understand why, we must first understand what's going on in all these activities. Let's start with media fragmentation.

Media Fragmentation

media fragmentation the increase in the number of mass media and mass media outlets that has been taking place during the past two decades

As we discussed in Chapter 1, the term **media fragmentation** refers to the increase in the number of mass media and mass media outlets that has taken place during the past two decades (see Figure 1.1 on page 6). Over the past thirty years, mass communication growth has skyrocketed via cable TV, UHF TV, VCRs, the personal computer, telemarketing, DVDs, out-of-home media such as smartphones, and the internet. The number and variety of particular media outlets in the United States have skyrocketed as well—including more than a hundred cable networks, tens of independent television stations, and millions of personal computers with technology connecting them to the outside world.

The process is ongoing as companies continue to find even more ways to distribute and exhibit news, information, advertising, and entertainment in as many places as possible. For leaders of long-standing firms, the changing world poses major challenges.

Audience Erosion

audience erosion a decrease in the percentage of the population using a particular mass medium or a specific media outlet

The most far-reaching of these challenges is audience erosion. **Audience erosion** refers to a decrease in the percentage of the population using a particular mass medium (such as newspapers in general) or a specific media outlet (such as a specific newspaper). Audience erosion happens for a number of reasons, but when media executives talk about audience erosion they usually mean erosion that is taking place because of media fragmentation. The dramatic increase in the number of media and media outlets has given people more choices for news, entertainment, information, and education, leading to smaller audiences overall.

The most important erosion of magazine audiences began as a result of the introduction of television in the 1940s. Erosion of AM radio audiences began with the

TECH & INFRASTRUCTURE
CAN THE INTERNET AND
TELEVISION CO-EXIST?

In 2010, Nielsen ratings showed that, contrary to the popular belief that the internet was siphoning away television viewers, the amount of time Americans spend watching television while on the internet was actually increasing. The report from the fourth quarter of 2009 found a 35 percent rise in the time Americans spent using the internet and television simultaneously when compared with the same quarter in 2008.

Matt O'Grady, Nielsen's media product leader, suggested that this should allay fears that the internet was taking over traditional television: "The initial fear was that internet and mobile video and entertainment would slowly cannibalize traditional TV viewing, but the steady trend of increased TV viewership alongside expanded simultaneous usage argues something quite different."

To some professional observers, findings such as these suggest that soon it will no longer be valuable to draw a distinction between the internet and television. In early 2009, Eric Schmidt, Google CEO, predicted that, in five years, there would be no distribution distinctions between TV and the Web. Schmidt forecast that the wall separating these two competing platforms would cease to exist.

Already, internet users can watch television online through sites such as Hulu and Surf the Channel. High-end television sets have the ability to connect users to Facebook, email, and news. Set-top boxes are increasingly allowing access to similar features. Google has announced intentions to enter into the field of internet television. The internet powerhouse announced that it had partnered with Sony and Intel to launch Google TV. The technology is designed to allow television viewers to download Web applications, run internet searches, and stream video from YouTube and Hulu directly onto their TV screen.

How useful is the internet–TV distinction in your current use of media?

Sources: Marshall Kirkpatrick, "Google's Eric Schmidt on What the Web Will Look Like in 5 Years," *Read Write Web*, October 27, 2009. http://www.readwriteweb.com/archives/google_web_in_five_years.php (accessed August 2, 2010); Jill Serjeant, "TV and Internet Use Together Growing," *Reuters*, March 23, 2010. http://www.reuters.com/article/idUSTRE62L4UB20100323?type=technologyNews= (accessed August 2, 2010); Nick Bilton, "Google and Partners Seek TV Foothold," *The New York Times*, March 17, 2010. http://www.nytimes.com/2010/03/18/technology/18webtv.html?ref=technology (accessed August 2, 2010).

introduction of FM radio in the 1960s. Movie producers have also noticed that the number of tickets sold at theaters in the United States has been unchanged for many years, even though the population has grown substantially.

Since the 1980s, media and advertising practitioners have noted that the audiences for all media are eroding at an increasing pace. Much of that erosion is due to the dramatic splintering of audiences for broadcast television. From the late 1940s until the early 1980s, fully 90 percent of all those watching television were tuned to either ABC, CBS, or NBC, according to the Nielsen audience ratings company. By the mid-2000s, though, the three networks' "share" had slid to about 51 percent—that's a 54 percent drop (see Figure 5.1). According to Nielsen, the missing population could be found at the relatively new Fox network (which had about 13 percent of the audience); at the smaller, newer broadcast networks (for example, CW and Univision); and at cable networks, DVDs, and video games.

For today's media executives, the goal is not to try to attract "everybody," but to define and hold an audience niche—to earn the loyalty of specific portions of the population and hold onto them while other companies in the fragmenting media world try to attract other groups. As media executives think about their desired audiences more and more carefully, they engage in what is known as audience segmentation.

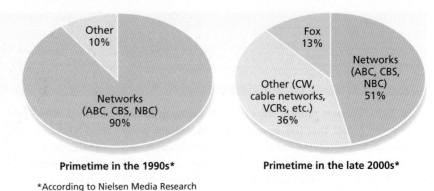

Figure 5.1 Eroding Audiences
Audience erosion had most notably affected the prime-time ratings of the "Big Three" networks—ABC, CBS, and NBC—as this figure shows.

Audience Segmentation

audience segmentation the process by which production and distribution are targeted to reach different types of people with messages tailored for them

The term **audience segmentation** means that producers and distributors try to reach different types of people with messages tailored specifically for them. No individual media materials can attract all of the approximately 300 million individuals in the United States. Instead, these materials reach segments, or parts, of society. These segments vary greatly in terms of the number of people involved and the time it takes for most of them to receive the material. *Grey's Anatomy* is an example of a television program that reaches tens of millions of viewers virtually instantaneously. The unexpected death of pop icon Michael Jackson in 2009 showed how huge audiences can build over a period of time. Although many heard the "breaking news" on television, many more learned about it in news programs, newspapers, and Web reports that appeared after it happened.

Then there are cases in which the number of people reached by particular mass media materials is relatively small. We all know that this happens when a TV show, movie, or musical recording fails to attract the large audience its producers intended. Increasingly, though, the pursuit of relatively small audiences by firms involved in the production, distribution, and exhibition of messages is purposeful and profitable.

targeting the process by which a mass media organization sets its sights on having as its audience one or more of the social segments it has identified in the population

When a mass media organization sets its sights on having as its audience one or more of the social segments it has identified in the population, that behavior is called **targeting**. Consider, for example, a magazine company that, for decades, has put out a periodical aimed at women in general. "Women" is, of course, an audience segment—quite a large one. Greater audience segmentation on the part of the publisher might involve deciding to go after specific types of women—say, women aged 18–35 who are mothers. Targeting would involve advertising to women who fit that profile in the hope that they will subscribe to the magazine.

target segments the desired segments that a media organization is trying to reach

Some **target segments** may be quite large—in the millions. Others might comprise only hundreds or tens of thousands of individuals. The targeted media typically portray the place of the members of these segments in the larger society—their problems, triumphs, and futures. A magazine for African-American women, for example, might explore the challenges that its readers face when they try to find mentors in their workplace. A magazine for golfers might rate the best restaurants near golf courses. A gardening magazine might assess the future of gardening societies in the United States.

Why would a media company want to reduce its audience by segmenting and targeting in that way? The answer is that segmentation and targeting are based on business considerations. Why and how executives engage in segmentation and targeting differs according to whether or not their media outlet is supported primarily by advertising funds. Recall from Chapter 2 that some media companies rely mostly on advertising for their revenues. Other companies get support from a balanced combination of advertising and subscription. Still others get most of their support from individual purchases or **subscriptions**.

Let's take a look at how segmentation works both when outlets are not advertiser-supported and when they are.

Segmentation When Outlets are not Advertiser-Supported

Why would a media outlet not be supported by advertising? So much media in the United States is ad-supported that it may seem odd when a particular medium isn't. Take books. Although you may have seen some ad inserts (for cigarettes, for example) in paperbacks, we're not used to thinking of books as featuring advertising, except maybe advertising for other books. The same is true for physical music albums. Instead of being supported by advertising, customers pay for them outright.

When a media outlet is not advertiser-supported, it must target segments of the population that are large enough or wealthy enough to cover the costs of the media product. Consider a low-budget horror movie that also has strong romantic elements. If the movie costs "only" $10 million or $15 million to make, a relatively small audience can support it. Nevertheless, because there is so much competition, studio executives will not give such a movie the green light unless they are convinced that a segment of the movie-going audience is likely to find the particular film interesting.

Producers make that determination by conducting or drawing on previous **market research**. Market research is different from the social research we discussed in Chapter 4, because its focus is on selling products. However, market researchers often use the same techniques that social researchers use. They carry out surveys, for example, and may even conduct experiments. So, based on a national survey by a commercial research firm, the producers may be able to show that "teenagers who like horror films" and "women aged 18–35 who like gothic romances" are two categories that are large yet specific enough to be expected audiences for such a film.

You might think that very expensive films, such as one of the *Transformers* or *Harry Potter* films, would have to go after just about everybody in order to justify their more than $150 million budgets. Certainly, energizing huge numbers of potential movie viewers is good; mega-hits such as *Avatar* make so much money that they warm the hearts of most movie executives. Still, the producers of even an expensive film have an audience segment in mind. The marketers of Quentin Tarantino's World War II drama *Inglourious Basterds* targeted most of their initial advertising at "men"; they specifically targeted African-American men by using the well-known black actor Samuel L. Jackson for radio commercials on African-American radio stations.[1] Producers of *Harry Potter* films also seem to have had particular, or core, audience segments in mind: children and their parents who will see the film several times and buy the many toys and clothes related to it (see Table 5.1).

Media organizations often set their sights on a target audience and tailor their products according to the audience segment they are pursuing. The women's magazines shown here each go after specific types of women—for example women aged from 18 to 35 years.

subscriptions purchases for a series of products that are paid for in advance

market research research that has, as its end goal, the gathering of information that will help an organization sell more products

Segmentation When Outlets are Advertiser-Supported

When a media outlet is advertiser-supported, production, distribution, and exhibition executives must identify population segments that sponsors will want to reach at prices that will pay for the media materials. Take a look at *Advertising Age* or similar magazines/websites that discuss the advertising industry. You will see that media and advertising practitioners continually pay for market research that breaks society into an enormous number of segments. This sort of research is often not very different from the market research we discussed earlier. The idea is to observe or survey samples of the population and then draw conclusions about how certain parts of the sample are different from other parts.

The more marketers find a group attractive, the more they are prone to take that group apart to look for subgroups that have uniquely attractive features. For example, women of childbearing age interest marketers because they purchase most of the goods for their homes. But marketers often don't stop there. They distinguish among single, married, and divorced women; between women with children and those without; between women in upscale and downscale households; and between women who work outside the home and those who work at home.[2]

Recall from Chapter 2 the terms "psychographics" and "demographics." These terms refer, respectively, to personality characteristics (optimist, ambitious) and social categories (teenager, Asian-American) that researchers use to distinguish among consumers. Marketers also separate people by their lifestyles—the kinds of activities they tend to engage in.

Consider Claritas, a market research subsidiary of research firm Nielsen that uses lifestyles and demographics to create descriptions of U.S. neighborhoods. Claritas starts with the premise that "birds of a feather flock together." That is, it assumes that neighborhoods can be defined in terms of clusters of similar demographic information and behaviors of the households in them. Companies that buy its research often use this information to decide where and on what media to place advertising money.

The Alltel telephone company, for example, found that middle-class clusters that Claritas labels "Mobility Blues," "Starter Families," and "Mid-City Mix," plus higher-income clusters labeled "Executive Suites" and "Winner's Circle," were good prospects for phone services that combined local, long distance, and cellular. These

Marketers for Quentin Tarantino's World War II drama *Inglorious Basterds* targeted much of their initial advertising at men. Teaser posters showed bloody bats, knives, and Nazi helmets.

Table 5.1 Targeting an Audience Segment: Two Ends of the Spectrum

Action Film (R rating)	Children's Film (G rating)
Show promotional trailers in theaters that exhibit other action films. Include some of the film's romance in the trailer so that women will not mind seeing the movie with men	Show promotional trailers in theaters that exhibit other children's films. Include scenes that imply to adults that they will like the film too
Commercials during wrestling, football, baseball	Commercials on Saturday morning TV, Nickelodeon, Friday night TV
Sweepstakes in connection with a beer company	Give out movie-related toys at Burger King or (if it is a Disney film) McDonald's
Radio commercials on hard rock stations	Contests on cereal boxes

households spent more than $50 a month on local phone service plus $45–65 on cellular service. The company targeted its marketing efforts at communities that are home to lots of these clusters, and saw bundled wireline sales in one market (Jacksonville, FL) go from 0 percent to 5 percent in ten months.[3]

As an example of how firms use psychographic research, consider the following comments about *Fortune* magazine by the vice president of marketing at the BMW North America car company. *Fortune* is "superb at capturing our psychographic: a 30- to 40-year-old person who works hard, plays hard." In fact, the vice president went on to say, studies of *Fortune* also show that its readers actually read the ads that advertisers place there. Phil Sawyer, director of advertising research for market research firm Roper Starch, noted that "In our *Read Most* scores—which measure how many readers read half or more of the ad copy—*Fortune* readers score 16 percent vs. 13 percent for newsweeklies on two-page spreads, for example." *Fortune*, he concluded, "brings you a quality customer."[4]

Distribution of Products Across Media Boundaries

Traditionally, understanding mass media has meant seeing the newspaper, book, broadcast, radio, recording, internet, and other mass media industries as separate worlds. A couple of decades ago, this approach was reasonably accurate. The difficulty with it today is that the boundaries between various mass media industries are blurring tremendously (see Figure 5.2).

Executives routinely create products for use in a number of mass media. Newspaper companies, for example, are increasingly moving their reporters' work—and even their reporters—to cable TV, broadcast TV, computer software, and the internet. Movie companies support their creations when they cross media boundaries with their materials by propelling them far beyond theaters through deals with broadcast TV, cable TV, home video, satellite TV, toy, book, and recording industries, among others.

What does it mean when a company crosses media boundaries with its

www.adage.com, the website of *Advertising Age* magazine

materials? It means creating content that can be used and appreciated in different media. As an example, consider the movie *The Princess and the Frog*. The Walt Disney Company, which provided the money for the film and distributed it, released it to U.S. movie theaters during December 2009. But Disney had no intention of limiting the showing of the movie to theaters. Instead, Disney saw the theatrical release of the motion picture as the first step in a marketing effort to place the film in a variety of media. These included pay-per-view television (as in hotels), DVDs, VHS tapes, pay cable television (for example HBO), and regular broadcast TV (on Disney-owned ABC, no doubt).

As this example shows, crossing media boundaries sometimes simply means transferring the exact same content to other media. Other times, though, it involves transforming the content so that it will fit the medium or the audience for that medium. An audio CD of the *Princess and the Frog*'s songs is an example. So is a book (actually, several versions), a video game, and a website based on the movie.

The need to cross media boundaries is related to two major goals. The first is to cover the costs of production and extend the revenue possibilities. The second is to make a substantial proportion of the target audiences in a variety of media locations aware of the material's existence. Marketing executives call that achieving a good share of mind. Let's take a look at each goal separately.

Crossing Media Boundaries to Cover Costs

In the past, media companies could cover all their business costs by concentrating on one medium. Book companies that aim at the general public could put out the works of popular novelists and hope to make a worthwhile profit from the hardback version. Even major movie companies, which have always spent a lot of money on their productions, assumed that they would make back their costs during the theatrical release of their motion pictures in the United States. Money from anywhere else—outside the United States, television—was easy profit.

Figure 5.2 The Blurring of Media Boundaries
In the past, a newspaper was just that—a stand-alone newspaper, delivering content through printed images and words. Today, and likely even more so in years to come, a newspaper is so much more, with content moving across media boundaries—from the traditional print piece to the paper's website, to the paper's own cable news network, to a downloadable version of the paper's top stories on your PDA device . . . and beyond!

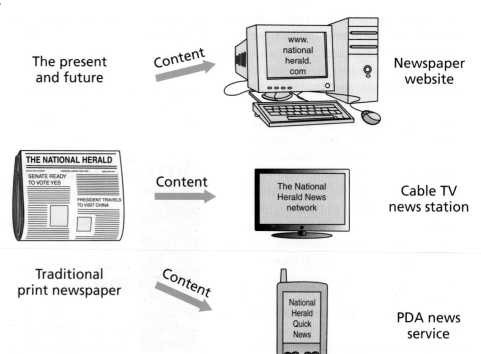

The past

Stand-alone traditional print newspaper

The present and future

Traditional print newspaper

Content — Newspaper website (www.nationalherald.com)

Content — Cable TV news station (The National Herald News network)

Content — PDA news service (National Herald Quick News)

CULTURE TODAY
ADVERTAINMENT

Advertainment refers to content that blurs the line between advertisement and entertainment. It has become an increasingly important tactic in a world so saturated by commercial content that marketers need to be innovative for their product to stand out. YouTube, the popular online video site, is becoming an increasingly important site for this strategy.

Some of the most popular YouTube ads are entertaining videos in which the product is incidental or in which the viewer is surprised at the end by the sponsorship. As one marketing director noted, the value of YouTube as an advertising platform is that the ads are free to display and the opportunity exists for the ads to go viral and become an online sensation. There is also the option for other sites to link to the ad.

After releasing the first iPad commercial during the Oscars, Apple put the video on its YouTube site where it quickly became one of the top-viewed online ads. A number of corporations have YouTube channels, including Porsche, Sony, and Doritos. Once a commercial is made, there is little financial cost to the company to post the ad on their online site.

There is substantial risk that goes along with posting advertisements on YouTube. Viewers can comment on ads and often make negative statements about the video itself or the company. YouTube also has the right to post about the company brand or its service. Moreover, the benefits of an ad going viral also come with costs. The ad may become part of a mash-up or decontextualized for the sake of anti-commercial statements. Many companies, however, are willing to take this risk. They see it as part of the cost of doing business in an era where many consumers are quite active in widely sharing their opinions, positive and negative, about products.

Sources: Rich Kirchen, "YouTube Becoming New Advertising Medium: Online Site has Advantages, Risks for Businesses Trying to Draw Customers," *The Business Journal of Milwaukee*, January 12, 2009. http://milwaukee.bizjournals.com/milwaukee/stories/2009/01/12/story12.html (accessed August 2, 2010); Stuart Elliot, "Old and New Media Coexisting Nicely, Thank You," *The New York Times*, March 18, 2010. http://www.nytimes.com/2010/03/19/business/media/19adco.html (accessed August 2, 2010).

The expectation of making a profit by releasing content in one medium is no longer realistic for many mass media firms; their costs have simply risen too much. In the book industry, for example, well-known authors often get advance payments in the millions of dollars by pitting book publishers against one another in bidding wars for their manuscripts. In the movie business, salaries of stars and directors that can soar above $20 million and the enormous cost of marketing a film make it highly unlikely that the tickets that U.S. audiences buy will lead to a profit.

One popular solution to the problem of profitability has been to try to increase revenues by moving the content across media. Different media industries have tended to address this challenge in different ways. Let's take a look at two particular approaches—those of the TV and film industries, and those of the print media industries.

COVERING COSTS IN TV AND FILM   In the television and film businesses, where production costs are quite high, the challenge of covering costs has forced production organizations to design their output with an eye toward moving it across mass media boundaries.

Consider broadcast television, for example. The major networks—ABC, CBS, Fox, and NBC—commission the most-viewed programs, those in prime time. But the production costs for these programs are often much higher than the amount of money that advertisers are willing to pay, and the executives can't cover the high cost of producing these shows with the revenues from advertisers alone. To address this situation, the network executives will often refuse to pay the full cost of episodes of a new series that they intend to air only a few times. In this way, the network executives force the production firm that is producing the series to make up the financial difference by finding cable, airline, hotel, video, or other outlets that want to air repeats of the programs after they show up on the networks. So, for example, reruns of *Law & Order: SVU* show up on the U.S. cable network. Spots from network news division shows such as *60 Minutes* and *Dateline NBC* show up on airplanes.

As this last example suggests, network executives sometimes try to keep control over their costs and potential earnings through *vertical integration*, a term that we first discussed in Chapter 2. **Vertical integration** means having control of all phases of a media product, from production through distribution to exhibition. In our cross-media case, it means that by getting one of its own production units to create the products it distributes the network can control distribution and even exhibition in the cable, home video, airline, and other industries—and all the revenues that come with it. So, for example, the ABC-TV network (which is owned by The Walt Disney Company) may pay Walt Disney Productions to create a TV movie that will be shown on ABC as part of its Sunday evening schedule. After two showings on ABC-TV, Disney might distribute the film to another exhibition outlet it owns—the Disney Channel, the Lifetime cable channel, ABC.com., or Hulu.com (which it partly owns). Some months later, Disney Home Video may sell the film to department stores and video outlets such as Blockbusters, Netflix, and Redbox to get further revenues from it. By controlling the distribution and sometimes even the exhibition of its own product, Disney can make a lot of money from it—money that it would not see if the movie aired on ABC-TV alone.

Network-owned production firms do not create all the programs that appear on the networks. However, when network executives do accept programs from unrelated production firms, they often require the production firm to bring the network in as a partner. Such partnering means giving the network a share in the ownership of the program. The production firm Atlantis Alliance, for example, shares ownership in the primetime drama *CSI* with CBS Productions; the program airs on CBS. That way, when the Atlantis Alliance makes money on the show in cable, syndication, or other places, CBS will receive part of those revenues.

Naturally, many production executives see partnering as a kind of extortion—the network demanding a piece of the action in return for a time slot. Network executives justify this demand by arguing that the network deserves a reward for helping to promote the program so that it can succeed after its network run. They add that, when production firms have a network as a partner, they can use the first broadcast run as a launching pad for revenue-making runs in other places.

The traditional way to make money from programs with a long network run has been to rent them to local stations; an activity called **syndication**. In recent years, syndication has taken on a much broader meaning. Some production firms license their programs first to local stations and then to cable networks. *Seinfeld* fits this description; so do virtually all the series on the TV Land cable network. Others go directly to cable with their shows. Increasingly, too, producers have even turned episodes into home video titles; notable examples are the adventure serial *24* (for those who want to watch a season's worth of episodes in just a few sittings) and TV classics such as *M*A*S*H*. Executives use the term **windows** to describe the series of exhibition points for audiovisual products through which revenues are generated. Our ABC-TV example suggests how this can work in television. When companies make theatrical films, their series of windows is typically quite a bit more varied than that of TV producers. You can see that if you compare the number of windows mentioned in the ABC television case with the number mentioned in our earlier discussion of *The Princess and the Frog.*

The reason for this is that for many years movie producers have realized that the number of tickets sold at U.S. theaters has been flat, even though both the cost of movies and the American population have grown substantially. Instead of watching

---

vertical integration an organization's control over a media product from production through distribution to exhibition

syndication licensing or renting to local stations or cable networks the right to air programs with a long network run (generally at least one hundred episodes)

windows the series of exhibition points for audiovisual products through which revenues are generated

newly released movies in the theaters, many people now watch films as they move through the gamut of windows spread over a few years—from pay-per-view cable at home, to pay cable (for example HBO or Starz!) to VHS tapes or DVDs, to digital satellite devices such as DirecTV, to network TV, to syndication. And that's just the domestic (U.S.-based) set of windows. Add to that list of windows the similar international exhibition gamut from which producers and distributors pull in money.

Two other activities that film producers and even some TV producers often engage in to make money from their creations are product placement and the sale of creative rights. A **product placement** involves a manufacturer paying— often tens of thousands of dollars and sometimes far more—a production company for the opportunity to have its product displayed in a movie or TV show. Remember Reese's Pieces in *E.T.*? Kellogg's cereals on *Seinfeld*? Apple Computers in *Independence Day*? Coke on *American Idol*? American Airlines in *Up in the Air*? Doritos, Mountain Dew, Reebok, and Target Stores on *Survivor*? All these are examples of product placements.

Sometimes products get into TV shows and movies because the producers need a product and ask the manufacturer if it wants to participate. That's how FedEx got into *Cast Away*. Increasingly, a production firm looking for extra money will make a deal with a product placement company that is looking to reach specific audiences for one or more of its clients. The contractual agreement that results often specifies the length of time the product will appear on screen.

The sale of creative rights involves encouraging other companies to hype the film or TV show through their products. When it sells **creative rights**, a producer allows companies that make or sell clothing, food, toys, or other goods the right to use characters or scenes from the film or TV show to attract customers. Some products based on creative rights can last for years (think of *Harry Potter* or *The Simpsons* toys); some last only for a few months (think of *Transformers* cereal or *Dora the Explorer* vitamins). But with certain event films or children's films, the sale of creative rights can bring the production company (and, depending on the deal, the distributor) a bonanza.

This cash flow from distributing products across media boundaries has proved particularly significant for revenues in the film industry. In the 1960s, the major film distributors raked in close to 90 percent of their revenues from domestic theatrical rentals (your basic U.S. movie theaters); in the late 1990s, domestic rentals accounted for only 13 percent of the incoming cash (see Figure 5.3). This low percentage should not be taken to mean that the release of films into U.S. theaters is unimportant. On

product placement the process by which a manufacturer pays—often tens of thousands of dollars and sometimes far more—a production company for the opportunity to have its product displayed in a movie or TV show

creative rights allowing companies that make or sell clothing, food, toys, or other goods the right to use characters or scenes from the film or TV show to attract customers

Writers Will Ferrell and Adam McKay poked fun at product placement in films and corporate sponsorship of NASCAR racing in the film *Talladega Nights: The Ballad of Ricky Bobby*. Because products such as Wonder Bread and Perrier were written into the script, none of the brands paid product placement fees to appear in the movie.

the contrary, a strong domestic theatrical release is the platform upon which the profit from all the other windows stands. That's because most consumers who pay to see films in the nontheatrical windows take their cues from what succeeded at the box office. Consequently, a film that bombs at the U.S. box office will simply not be that attractive to executives who purchase films for other outlets. Table 5.2 summarizes the various tactics used by the electronic media.

COVERING COSTS IN PRINT MEDIA   The amount of money it takes for an established magazine or newspaper firm to publish a new issue is typically far less than the amount of money needed to produce a new movie or TV series. Nevertheless, the operating costs of print media firms can be substantial, and print media companies are increasingly looking for ways to use, reuse, and repurpose the content they have. Their logic is not that different from the logic of movie and TV executives: the more windows of opportunity to eke more revenues from this material, the better.

Consider the New York Times Company as an example. You may think of it as just the newspaper that bears its name, but the $2.8 billion company (in 2008 revenues) actually extends far beyond this: it owns eighteen newspapers and more than fifty websites, including NYtimes.com, Boston.com, and About.com. Because news creation is such an expensive, labor-intensive business, the Times Company works hard to take fruits of its journalistic labors for its own papers and sell them to other papers, to use them for its websites, and to repurpose them for databases. In addition to using the news in its own papers, the firm runs news and feature **syndicates**. These are firms that, for a subscription fee, continually provide hard and soft news, respectively, to newspapers around the world. The *New York Times* also uses its daily news stories on its internet properties. When the news stories, photos, and illustrations are not "new" anymore, the conglomerate approaches them differently (or repurposes them). It incorporates them into news, photo, and graphics archives that sell stories, photos, and charts to companies and individuals that need such material. The Times Company also leases all the articles in its papers to database firms such as LexisNexis, which pays it money when people use the databases to read Times-owned articles.

Magazine and book publishing firms similarly look for ways to distribute their products. Consider the deal that Golden Books Family Entertainment made with Sony Wonder, the video subsidiary of the Sony Corporation. Golden Books Family

syndicates firms that, for a subscription fee, continually provide hard and soft news to newspapers around the world

Figure 5.3 The Increased Value of Other Windows to the Hollywood Majors
The six major U.S. movie distributors (Paramount, Walt Disney, Sony Pictures, Twentieth Century Fox, Universal, and Warner Brothers) are making far more money now than in the past from circulating movies through different windows—to hotel and airline viewings, in-home pay-per-view, home video sales and rentals, various types of television outlets, and more. Source: Hy Holinger, "MPA Study," *Hollywood Reporter*, June 15, 2007. http://www.hollywoodreporter.com/hr/ content_display/news/e3ic5575a8c4f61aadd68a0d344f476d5da (accessed March 7, 2008).

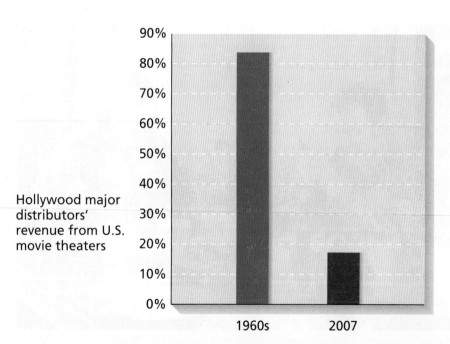

Hollywood major distributors' revenue from U.S. movie theaters

Table 5.2 Covering Costs: A Recap of the Tactics Used in the TV and Movie Industries

Strategy	Television Example	Movie Example
Distribution to a variety of windows	Beginning with network TV and moving to home cable, hotels, and airlines	Beginning with theaters and moving to hotels and airlines, then home video, pay-per-view cable at home
Vertical integration	ABC network buying movie from Walt Disney Productions	Viacom-owned Nickelodeon cable releasing movie through Viacom-owned Paramount Pictures
Partnering	Atlantis Alliance with CBS on the series *CSI*	Warner Brothers (WB) sells local stations the right to air a group of WB theatrical films after their appearance in other windows
Product placement	Ford vehicles on the series *24*	Apple PowerBook G4 used by Carrie Bradshaw in *Sex and the City*
Sale of creative rights	*Flintstones* vitamins	Toy figure based on Buzz Lightyear from the movie *Toy Story*

Entertainment calls itself the leading children's book publisher in North America. As a result of its book publishing operation, the company owns one of the world's largest libraries of family entertainment copyrights, including *The Lone Ranger*, *Lassie*, *Underdog*, and *Shari Lewis*. One way in which the company uses its copyrights beyond the printed page is through joint ventures that turn material from Golden Books and other sources into videos that are sold in book and department stores.

Crossing Media Boundaries to Achieve a Good Share of Mind

A media product will be successful only if the product's target audience learns about it and thinks about it. Marketers refer to getting a substantial percentage of their target audience to think about their product as achieving a good share of mind. Think about what happens when a company moves a mass media product across media outlets: more people get to notice the product's existence—and get to notice it more often—than if it just stayed in one medium. That exposure can help business. The idea is a basic one: if you see that a film is playing in many theaters, even if you don't pay to see it in the theater, you might pay to see it when it hits another window—the home video release, or the pay-per-view showing.

But **achieving a good share of mind**—making a substantial proportion of the target audiences in a variety of media locations aware of the material's existence—requires a lot more than simply getting people to notice a product as it moves in its entirety through a number of windows. In the highly fragmented and competitive media environment, executives have concluded that they must chase target audience segments across as many exhibition outlets as possible in order to convince them to see a movie, watch a TV show, or read a book or magazine. That is why, for example, you see movie stars appearing on morning talk shows, evening celebrity shows, and late-night talk shows just before their latest films appear in theaters. These stars are also on the covers of magazines that cater to the films' target audiences. Pick just about any major movie that has just come out and you will see the pattern repeated.

When we look at the chapters on advertising (Chapter 15) and public relations (Chapter 16), we will see that moving people and ideas across different media outlets

achieving a good share of mind making a substantial proportion of the target audiences in a variety of media locations aware of the material's existence is basic to what executives in those industries do. In recent decades, mass media executives have learned that they must use a wide variety of media for advertising and public relations activities to make their target audiences aware of their products. Some of this activity involves standard advertising and public relations activities—putting a commercial on TV, or trying to get your movie discussed on *Entertainment Tonight*. But many mass media production and distribution executives go further. They use the licensing of creative rights as a way to publicize their mass media products while making extra money on the product.

Examples include *Harry Potter* toys, *Hannah Montana* sweatshirts, and *Transformers* lunchboxes. Media executives view such paraphernalia as more than just a fun thing for people to buy. These items remind consumers of their interest in the movie and provide them with a continuing reason to pay for *Twilight* movies, books, home videos, and cable showings. Media executives use the term "brand" to describe products such as *South Park*, *American Idol*, and *60 Minutes*. By **brand** they mean a clearly identifiable image that attracts target audiences over and over again. Executives believe that they can extend the life of a powerful brand over many years by achieving the right kind of publicity and combining new products with reissues of old ones. That strategy amplifies the ability of the product to contribute to the company's bottom line.

brand a name and image associated with a particular product

Media executives use the word "brand" to refer to media outlets as well as individual products. The owners of media outlets such as *Cosmopolitan*, MTV, and Paramount stress to advertisers and consumers that these names do not just stand for a magazine (in the case of *Cosmopolitan*), a cable channel (in the case of MTV), or a film company (in the case of Paramount). Instead, the owners of these outlets say, each of these names stands for a certain personality, a certain kind of content, and a certain type of audience, no matter where the name appears. So *Cosmopolitan* will be recognized as the *Cosmopolitan* brand whether it appears on a magazine, on a book, or on cable TV, and MTV's image crosses media from cable to clothes to books to music. Executives believe that such cross-media branding is increasingly necessary to keep existing advertisers and audiences and to get new ones as sponsors and consumers scatter to different channels.

Globalization

In the face of media fragmentation, audience erosion, and the need to move materials to more outlets in order to increase revenues, U.S. production and distribution executives are looking to markets beyond those in America—to the global marketplace—as a way to solve their revenue problems.

It's not as if U.S. mass media firms have been ignoring the rest of the world until now. On the contrary, the movie, recording, radio, television, book, and magazine industries have all—to some extent—been distributing their products internationally for a long time. However, during the first three-quarters of the twentieth century, "going global" meant taking materials that had already generated profits in the United States and adding to those profits by selling them elsewhere.

Today, a new mindset about the world outside America's borders has emerged. Its logic is as follows: media fragmentation and audience erosion make it difficult for mass media distributors to reach the huge audiences they would like in the United States. When producers use audience segmentation to attract advertisers or cultivate consumer loyalty, they inevitably lower the number of American consumers who will view those products. Global consumers are a way to make the audience larger. In this way, media executives are viewing countries around the world as part of the initial marketplace for these mass media materials. The potential market thereby becomes huge, even in the face of audience erosion. Moreover, the world's population potentially provides producers and distributors with larger audiences than ever for targeted, niche materials.

In fact, the world market has become so strong that during the past twenty-five years many major mass media firms based in foreign countries have bought important U.S. media holdings. As illustrated in Figure 5.4, the Sony Corporation, headquartered in Japan, owns Columbia Pictures and Sony Music. Rockstar, a major video game company (the *Grand Theft Auto* series is one of their achievements), is based in the United Kingdom. The German firm Bertelsmann owns the Random House and Doubleday book publishing companies.

Miley Cyrus, star of Disney Channel's series *Hannah Montana*, makes an appearance at the International Licensing Expo in 2007. Disney Consumer Products launched a full collection of Hannah Montana apparel, accessories, home décor, and real electric guitars targeted at the increasingly powerful tween market.

For media critics, there are two questions about this global approach that particularly stand out. First, they ask, "Who's to say that there are audience segments outside the United States that have tastes similar to those of Americans?" Second, they ask, "Don't those parts of the world that have strong and growing consumer economies—Europe, Asia, and Latin America—have their own mass media firms that create materials aimed at their own consumers?" Let's explore each of these questions in turn.

Worldwide Media Tastes vs. American Media Tastes

Consider the first question, which raises the problem of finding audience segments that have tastes similar to those of Americans. Recording companies have decided that they can't, in fact, take it for granted that people throughout the world share American tastes. Tastes in music are often vastly different within each country, let alone worldwide. But the costs of producing a CD or selling digital copies through iTunes are so low relatively that it is often quite profitable to pursue audience segments within a country. Consequently, even the biggest firms have split themselves into different subsidiaries that concentrate on different parts of the world and funnel the profits back to the home office. At the same time, executives in these subsidiaries are on the lookout for musicians or acts that have the potential to be worldwide successes.

Consider the example of MTV Networks International, a subsidiary of Viacom. MTV may have started as a cable music channel, but its description on Viacom's website projects a far more widespread picture that emphasizes various distribution platforms and a commitment to locally targeted and produced programming. The MTV Networks International page says that "for cutting-edge entertainment, we speak your language." It boasts that,

> Multimedia brands like MTV, VH1, Nickelodeon, TMF (The Music Factory), VIVA, Flux, Paramount Comedy, Comedy Central, Game One, Neopets, GameTrailers, Shockwave, Addicting Games, Atom Films and Xfire give audiences around the

Figure 5.4 The Global Nature of U.S. Mass Media Ownership
Bertelsmann (of Germany) and Sony (of Japan) each have significant U.S. media holdings under their corporate umbrellas, as this figure shows. They have created a joint venture, Sony BMG, to manage their music holdings.

Bertelsmann

(Germany)

Books: Selected U.S. Holdings
- Random House
- Doubleday
- Bantam Dell
- Ballantine
- Crown Publishing Group
- Fodor's
- Knopf

Magazines: Selected U.S. Holdings
- *American Homestyle*
- *Family Circle*
- *Fast Company*
- *Inc.*
- *McCall's*
- *Parents*
- *YM*

Music: Selected U.S. Holdings
- Arista Records
- RCA Records
- BMG Music
- Bad Boy Records
- LaFace Records
- Windham Hill Group

Multimedia: Selected U.S. Holdings
- Barnes&Noble.com
- Cdnow.com
- Lycos
- BMG Direct
- Tripod

SONY

(Japan)

TV and Film: Selected U.S. Holdings
- Sony Pictures Entertainment
- Sony Pictures Classics
- Columbia Pictures
- TriStar Pictures
- Columbia TriStar
- Columbia TriStar Home Entertainment
- The Game Show Network
- Jim Henson Productions
- Mandalay Entertainment

Music: Selected U.S. Holdings
- Columbia Records
- Epic Records Group
- Sony Classical
- Legacy
- Nashville
- Sony Wonder
- Sony Music Video (SMV)
- Word Entertainment
- Columbia House

Multimedia: Selected U.S. Holdings
- Sony Online
- Sony PlayStation
- The Station@sony.com
- Columbia TriStar Interactive

world access to their favorite entertainment via 172 locally programmed and operated TV channels and more than 400 digital media properties.

Moreover,

globally the company has partnerships with approximately 80 digital carriers and is the largest wireless provider of video on the handset worldwide. Broadband services such as MTV Overdrive and TurboNick are available to growing audiences around the world, while cross-platform brands like Flux in Japan and QOOB in Italy, provide original, locally produced entertainment, clips from MTVN's global library and user-generated content. In Korea, audiences can experience a robust digital community on MTV Boombox, featuring local and international MTV programming on-demand, through podcasts and video blogs. In Latin America, bands and music fans can create their own virtual space on Lazona.com, reaching more than 45,000 registered music lovers, including 16,000 Latin American bands. MTV Revolution also offers Latin American viewers online access to locally produced shows and clips from global MTV hits.[5]

Traditionally, the U.S.-based movie industry has taken a very different approach. Rather than making different films for different parts of the world, the major producer–distributors (often just called "the majors") actively look for themes, plots, and actors that will play well around the world. Movie industry executives have concluded that this often means action films with huge special-effects budgets, internationally popular stars (like Arnold Schwarzenegger or Jackie Chan), and little important dialogue so that people don't have to know English, or even read subtitles, to understand the action. The advertising industry runs the gamut from global to regional to local planning of ads. In television, program producer–distributors typically try to sell U.S.-made shows to other countries. Often that makes up the difference between the money U.S. television networks pay them to air the shows and the money it costs to make individual episodes. In 2006, for example, a new U.S. series cost an average of $2.75 million an episode, and the U.S. networks paid the production firms about $1.5 million per episode; foreign returns helped fill in the rest.[6] Smaller production firms, especially those working in cable, have tried to get sufficient funding for their work by lining up cable, satellite, and broadcast outlets, some American and some not, that will pay at the start for the right to show it. For their part, U.S. cable network executives who want to extend their brands to other countries have been adjusting their programming (and its language) depending on the countries they want to reach.

Global Media Organizations vs. Local Media Organizations

At the same time that they are distributing their American products to countries around the world, major U.S. media organizations are acutely aware that their international presence angers local media production organizations in other countries. These organizations worry that locally made films will be swept aside at the box office by the Hollywood behemoths.

For their part, executives from the U.S. media organizations worry that this anger will result in laws restricting U.S.-made films or prohibiting the majors from building multiplex theaters in other countries. But they also see a plus side to international politics. The tax laws of some countries allow movies to be produced much more cheaply than in the United States. U.S. firms can get some of those tax benefits if they take on production partners from those countries and make movies there.

Because of these concerns and opportunities, major U.S.-based movie production firms such as Warner Brothers and Columbia Pictures have begun to fund and produce some films specific to particular areas of the world—France and India, for example—that seem to have a good chance at making a profit in those countries but might have relatively little interest for Americans. In addition, the major U.S. film producers have been getting more involved than ever in international coproductions. A **coproduction** is a deal between two firms for the funding of media material. So, for example, Warner Brothers may collaborate with Roadshow Pictures of Australia in the financing of a movie. The two companies would split the costs and perhaps the distribution duties. They would also split the profits between them.

To mass media executives, the goal of their global activities is to lower their risk of failure by controlling as many distribution and exhibition routes as possible to the largest audiences. This is the goal of their activities within the United States, as well. But this goal creates a key issue for production firms: what happens if competitors who have control of distribution and exhibition routes in the United States or around the world refuse to pick up their products? Fear of this nasty predicament is what has led to the next trend, conglomeration.

Conglomeration

A **conglomerate** is a company that owns a number of different companies in different industries. A **mass media conglomerate** is a company that holds several mass

coproduction a deal between two firms for the funding of media material

conglomerate a company that owns a number of different companies in different industries

mass media conglomerate a company that holds several mass media firms in different media industries under its corporate umbrella

media firms in different media industries under its corporate umbrella. Mass media conglomerates are not new. What is relatively new is the approach to them that their corporate leaders are taking.

Until the 1980s, the executives who ran media conglomerates typically did not require the different parts of their firm to work with one another. To them, the value of owning magazines, TV stations, music labels, and the like lay in the ability of each business to generate profits separately for the parent firm. But even then there were exceptions to this rule. As early as the 1950s, Walt Disney used his theatrical movies in his TV and theme park subsidiaries. The animated film *Snow White and the Seven Dwarfs* appeared both in movie theaters and in segments on TV's *Disneyland* series. The name of the series promoted the Disneyland amusement park, which, in turn, promoted the film *Snow White* and other Disney films and characters in many manifestations—dolls, posters, and other merchandise. But Disney's elaborate cross-subsidiary activities had few imitators for decades.

Things began to change in the 1980s for a number of reasons. One was simply that top media executives and financiers got caught up in the greedy merger-and-acquisition mania that swept through corporate America during that decade. An even more intense period of combinations took place during the mid-1990s, with multibillion-dollar linkages between such companies as Time and Warner and then between AOL and Time and Warner, Twentieth Century Fox and News Corporation, Sony and Columbia, Disney and ABC, and CBS and Viacom.

To justify the high costs of these mergers, the chief executives of these companies contended that they saw the media world evolving in a way that required them to

WORLD VIEW
VIACOM'S JOINT VENURE IN INDIA

The entertainment conglomerate Viacom has been most visible in India through a subsidiary called MTV Networks in India. It owns Indian versions of the youth-oriented music networks MTV and VH1 as well as the children's channel Nickelodeon. A Viacom press release called MTV Networks in India "the industry's most engaging multi-platform entertainment brands." Nevertheless, the conglomerate's executives clearly felt that they needed help in trying to reach wider segments of the world's second most populous nation with products from their movie and television businesses.

In 2007, Viacom therefore formed a joint venture with the Television Eighteen Group (TV18), a media company rooted in TV but with ambitions to spread far beyond it. In 2007, the two firms announced the creation of a 50/50 joint venture Indian operation, Viacom-18. What they said they were trying to accomplish makes a great case study of this chapter's discussion of cross-media activities, with the added international dimension. According to Viacom's president, Phillipe Dauman, "India is one of Viacom's priority markets for expansion internationally." He added that TV18 represents a guide into the Indian audience and media in a much deeper way than Viacom could do alone. The alliance will meld television, film, and online materials from both

firms into a variety of television and internet vehicles. Dauman said that the partnership "will transform and significantly enlarge our business . . . across platforms, and opportunities for advertisers to reach the full spectrum of demographics." Viacom and TV18 also intend to create a new motion picture partnership, The Indian Film Company, which will release Indian-made films as well as Viacom products. Viacom's stated reason fits right into this chapter's discussion: "The film operation of Viacom-18 will provide strong synergies with the TV and digital media business, as well as complement our Paramount and Dreamworks studios."

For TV18, an ambitious, growing, but relatively small Indian company, the joint venture with the American behemoth represents a great opportunity to leap forward in presence on the national scene. "We are confident," said the firm's managing director, "that Viacom-18 will entertain India's burgeoning film and television audiences. Viacom-18 will also propel the TV18 Group into the league of a truly diversified and broad-based media conglomerate."

Source: *PR Newswire* (U.S.), "Viacom and the TV18 Group Announce the Creation of New Joint Venture in India," May 22, 2007.

have holdings in several mass media industries if their companies were to remain major players in the next century. Their argument went something like this:

> Audience erosion is inevitable in established media as the fragmentation of old and new media channels takes hold. At the same time, the rising costs of producing content for these media require an ability to take the money back across a variety of sponsored and unsponsored windows in different media industries. Crossing a variety of media outlets is also necessary for getting the proper share of mind for the content and demands publicity that will lead the target audience to the theaters, videos, TV shows, books, magazines, websites, and theme parks that recycle the material in one way or another.

> The danger for a media firm is that its competitors will prevent it from accessing the distribution and exhibition outlets that it needs if it is to carry out its revenue-generating mission. True, we can make agreements with other firms that allow us to use outlets owned by them on the condition that they can use our outlets. Ultimately, though, a company's destiny in the new media world will be determined by its ability to own, alone or with others, the distribution and exhibition outlets that it needs in order to reach its audiences. Perhaps ten or fifteen companies from around the world will achieve this power. We want to be one of them.

As this imaginary speech suggests, top executives for mass media conglomerates argue that they have to take bold steps if they are to be major players in the next century. They have to move beyond encouraging the subsidiaries of their conglomerates to seek profits independently.

Recall that we have used the term "vertical integration" to describe an organization's control of a media product from the production of content through its distribution and exhibition. Vertical integration is now legal in the TV industry and, to a certain extent, in the theatrical motion picture industry. In circumstances in which vertical integration hasn't been legalized (as was the case in the movie and broadcast TV industries until recently), companies have tried to grab control of two of the three stages—production and/or distribution and/or exhibition—to keep their industry clout.

What the leaders of media conglomerates urge today is horizontal integration in addition to as much vertical integration as possible. **Horizontal integration** has two aspects. First, it involves the ownership of production facilities, distribution channels, and/or exhibition outlets in different, even potentially competing, companies across a number of media industries. Second, it involves bringing those parts together (integrating them) so that each can profit from the expertise of the others.

horizontal integration the ownership of production facilities, distribution channels, and/or exhibition outlets in a number of media industries and the integration of those elements so that each can profit from the expertise of the others

Synergy

A term that is similar to horizontal integration and that became a buzzword among media executives is *synergy*. **Synergy** describes a situation in which the whole is greater than the sum of its parts. When Time Warner's DC Comics provides the characters for Time Warner's Warner Brothers movies, which in turn provide the inspiration for *Batman* clothing, and when all of these elements get publicity through its TNT and TBS cable networks, that is synergy at work.

The goal of synergy underscores that at the turn of the century executives of mass media conglomerates were defining market power in a sweeping way. They saw it as the ability to channel products into a wide variety of mass media on a global scale

synergy a situation in which the whole is greater than the sum of its parts; the ability of mass media organizations to channel content into a wide variety of mass media on a global scale through control over production, distribution, and exhibition in as many of those media as possible

through control over production, distribution, and exhibition in as many of those media as possible. They considered the best content for these cross-media activities to be genres that are likely to cross geographic borders, reach audiences that are attractive to advertisers, and not raise the political hackles of certain governments. These executives believed that children's programs, sports, variety shows, action adventures, direct marketing, headline news, and certain kinds of music were the genres that travel best globally across media.

How can an American company get away with having that much clout across so many media, you may ask. Aren't there laws against the accumulation of this kind of capability, just as there are against vertical integration? The answer is no, since no one claims that any company that has such cross-media capabilities controls a large portion of the distribution channels and exhibition outlets in particular industries. Another reason for the U.S. government's laxity regarding horizontal integration by huge media firms is a concern about foreign media powers. Mass media products are this nation's second largest export, after airplanes. Government officials fear that if they restrict the capabilities of U.S.-based media firms, it will give their rivals in countries without such restrictions the power to surpass them. If there are to be media behemoths in this world, American politicians want the giants to be American.

In fact, according to a 2009 list of the "top thirty global media owners" prepared by the ad-buying company ZenithOptimedia, U.S. media companies do dominate the global media scene. Using 2009 data of the revenues companies make from activities supported by advertising, ZenithOptimedia found that sixteen of the top thirty are U.S.-based, five are French, three each are from Japan and the United Kingdom, two are from Germany, and one is from Italy. In its list, the biggest media firm is U.S.-based Time Warner, with $32.2 billion in revenues (see Table 5.3). A far number two is News Corporation, also based in the United States, though with roots in Australia. It brought in $20.6 billion in revenues. By ZenithOptimedia's counting, seventh-place Bertelsmann, a German company with $10.6 billion in revenues, is the largest media firm outside the United States.[7]

But no tally of such companies can be definitive because there are many ways to define a "media company." Some lists of top media firms (such as ZenithOptimedia's) don't include Sony Corporation, for example, because the rankings are based primarily on revenues from activities that support advertising. Companies that receive cash principally from consumers through admission tickets or product sales aren't included. That probably explains why Sony Corporation didn't make ZenithOptimedia's list. But with Sony's worldwide activities in movies, television, video games, and music, it would be foolish not to see it as a powerhouse mass media firm. Besides, those who created the list ignored the fact that the movies and video games distributed by Sony and other firms are increasingly presenting paid-for commercial messages in one form or another—whether directly in traditional advertising or through product mentions within the ongoing action.

Every list of powerful global media firms will have its critics, and Table 5.3 is no exception. Yet the aim of the table is not to create another set of rankings based on revenues but to place companies into rough groupings based on their movement of materials across media and across the world. Many companies on this list will be mentioned in this book, if they haven't been already. Those in tier 1 surely have the ability to create, distribute, and exhibit multiple product genres across a variety of media on a highly sustained, visible, and global basis through their own holdings. These are the companies that stand astride the most powerful lines of worldwide mass communication. The firms in tier 2 also have a global or cross-media capability, but not the reach of the tier 1 firms. As for the companies in tier 3, they typically are powerful in one or two industries (typically broadcasting and cable) within a particular country and have few, if any, worldwide media brands. They need help from other firms in order to compete globally across media boundaries. To get that help, they can join up with larger firms or turn to one or more of the thousands of smaller firms that are eager to extend their niches in the global media environment. Called **joint ventures**, these alliances involve companies agreeing to work together or to share investments. The television network Animal Planet, for example, is a joint venture between Discovery Communications and the BBC in all parts of the world except the United Kingdom and Italy, where Discovery controls it.

Note, though, that joint ventures are not limited to third-tier or second-tier firms. Time Warner's 2008 annual report contains several examples of how the company is extending its reach internationally with the help of local "partners." These are firms that know the territories, the government officials, and the interests of audiences. As we noted in our discussion of trends in globalization, this knowledge of audience is becoming increasingly important. Media firms realize that they can most easily attract audiences in different countries by customizing their programming to fit these countries' different languages and cultures.

Time Warner's Turner cable networks, for example, are familiar to U.S. viewers and those around the world through such brands as CNN and the Cartoon Network. While Time Warner owns those services in some parts of the world, in a number of regions Turner has launched local-language versions of its channels through joint ventures with local partners. These include CNN+, a Spanish language twenty-four-hour news network distributed in Spain and Andorra; CNN Turk, a Turkish language twenty-four-hour news network available in Turkey and the Netherlands; and CNN-IBN, a co-branded twenty-four-hour English-language general news and current affairs channel in India. Cartoon Network Japan and Cartoon Network Korea are both joint-venture local-language twenty-four-hour channels for kids. Turner also has joint-venture interests in services in China.

The distribution of materials across media boundaries globally and nationally has become so much a part of what media firms do that we all take this activity for granted. You probably aren't surprised when you see a CNN weather report in a hotel elevator, on your friend's home computer, on an airport monitor, or maybe even on your mobile phone. It seems so natural to see content discussed or displayed in many different places that we may believe that it was always that way. As we will see in the history chapters coming up, it wasn't. In today's world, the movement of much content across media is becoming more common at least partly because it is technologically easier. The reason for this involves the next trend we will discuss, digital convergence.

> **joint ventures** alliances formed between a large media firm and one or more of the thousands of smaller firms that are eager to extend their niches in the global media environment; the companies either work together or share investments

Digital Convergence

Convergence means coming together. **Digital convergence** refers to the use of computer technologies to allow different media to share the same or similar materials. Digital convergence is a remarkable development that is changing the way in which media firms do business and the way in which audiences use media. It is also encouraging and accelerating the blurring of media boundaries and the development of conglomerates that move materials across those boundaries. In the process, it is creating public controversies and forcing both government officials and companies to rethink their models of media in society.

> **convergence** coming together
>
> **digital convergence** the coming together of computer technologies as the basis for production, distribution, and even exhibition in many media industries

Table 5.3 Top 30 Global Media Owners

	Media Owner	Media Revenue 2006 US$ Million	Media Revenue 2005 US$ Million	Percentage Change 2006/2005
1	Time Warner	32,217	29,834	8.0
2	News Corporation	20,574	17,816	15.5
3	General Electric	16,188	14,689	10.2
4	The DirecTV Group	14,755	12,958	13.9
5	Walt Disney Company	14,638	13,207	10.8
6	CBS Corporation	13,550	13,389	1.2
7	Bertelsmann	10,573	9,622	9.9
8	Google	10,493	6,065	73.0
9	Cox Enterprises	10,358	9,452	9.6
10	Advance Publications*	7,700	7,536	2.2
11	Gannett	7,532	7,162	5.2
12	BSkyB	7,337	6,871	6.8
13	Clear Channel Communications	6,464	6,078	6.4
14	Yahoo!	6,426	5,258	22.2
15	Tribune Company	5,260	5,339	–1.5
16	Vivendi	4,554	4,331	5.2
17	Mediaset	4,260	4,317	–1.3
18	Viacom	4,217	3,963	6.4
19	Yomiuri Shimbun Holdings*	3,846	3,970	–3.1
20	Hearst Corporation*	3,525	3,276	7.6
21	Fuji Television Group	3,261	3,338	–2.3
22	ITV plc	3,225	3,387	–4.8
23	Grupo Televisa	3,126	2,746	13.9
24	Asahi Shimbun Company*	3,093	3,401	–9.1
25	DMGT	3,086	3,078	0.3
26	Lagardère	3,059	3,090	–1.0
27	New York Times Company	3,044	3,152	–3.4
28	TF1	3,016	3,358	–10.2
29	Axel Springer	2,821	2,796	0.9
30	NTV	2,304	2,522	–8.6

*Estimate.

Source: ZenithOptimedia, which defines *media* as services and content supported by advertising. See the text for further explanation.

The Development of Digital

When people use the word "digital," it is a quick way of referring to the use of computers. Computers use digits—1s and 0s—to carry out their functions. Of course, people who program computers have learned to manipulate these digits to produce an astonishing array of possibilities. During the past two decades, virtually every media industry has found it efficient to use computers in the production of its products. Book, magazine, and newspaper publishers use computers for the creation of text, the creation of formats, and the printing of the final product. Computers are used in movie and television production for title production, editing, and special effects. Although much of the photography for prime-time television and theatrical movies is still film-based, directors and cinematographers are steadily moving toward the use of digital movie cameras. Digital still photography has certainly become an important part of the outdoor advertising (that is, billboard) industry, which uses computers to create wall-size posters and bus-wraps.

Just as significantly, the use of computers is also critical to the distribution and exhibition of traditional mass media products. The *New York Times* and the *Wall Street Journal* both send digital copies of their papers to printing plants in different parts of the country so that the papers can be printed and circulated there. Public relations firms send emails and post videos on websites to communicate with members of the press and other media. Music companies release digital recordings of their latest artists to exhibition outlets such as iTunes, Rhapsody, and Napster. The major movie distributors have experimented with the satellite delivery of computerized versions of movies that can then be projected on the screen through special digital projectors.

We will discuss each of these developments in more detail when we get to the chapters on the book, newspaper, magazine, recording, movie, advertising, and public relations industries. The point here is to demonstrate more broadly that the digitization of production, distribution, and exhibition is changing the media system as a whole.

Because of digital convergence, media are converging like never before. The reason is quite basic: once mass media materials are converted to digits, they can be transformed into almost any form imaginable. Words that were intended for the printed page can also be used for a website, a database, or a CD-ROM; they can even be used in a voice recognition system that can read the words. Movies intended for the big screen can (given fast computers, enough data compression, and the proper memory chips) be shown over the Web or transferred easily to DVDs. Parts of films can also be used in the creation of digital video games. The music from digital movies can also be used in such games, and it can be moved from the soundtrack onto CDs or onto the Web.

Encouraging Cross-Media Distribution

Many of these activities are relatively new. They have, however, become so common that you probably consider them a natural part of everyday life. That is because companies have adopted them quickly as part of their attempts to increase their revenues through cross-media distribution. The digitization of content actually encourages cross-media distribution because it turns the material into **cross-platform data**. That means that the material has been converted to digits that can easily be used as resources for the creation of material in other media.

The clearest example of this activity is the use of content by newspapers for websites and databases. Hundreds of U.S. newspapers have websites, and many of them license their articles to database companies such as LexisNexis and Dow Jones Interactive. This **repurposing**—the industry term simply means the reuse of content for different aims—could never take place if computers were not involved in the creation of the papers in the first place. It would simply be too expensive to scan or retype all the articles and photos so that they could be accessed by computers.

The use of computers in printing is also making electronic books much more economical than they would otherwise be. As we will see when we discuss the book industry, books in electronic form are an emerging medium for members of the

cross-platform data digitized material that can easily be used as resources for the creation of material in other media

repurposing the reuse of content for different aims

general public as well as in schools. The transformation of text into voice is currently a developing technology that nevertheless presents many cross-platform possibilities for book, magazine, and newspaper publishers. Presently, print-to-voice technologies still don't have the diction and inflection to make many people comfortable listening to them for long periods. Consequently, audio "books" are still created by having real people read the text. This is quite likely to change in the not too distant future. Once technologists create software that causes the computer to read text in ways that really sound human, yet another set of realistic cross-platform possibilities will open for publishers. People will not necessarily read the news on commuter trains and in cars. For not much more than the print versions, they might download their favorite papers in their favorite voices into tiny recorders and listen to them on the way to work or while jogging in the morning.

Exactly this sort of listening already takes place with music, of course. Although typical CDs that you purchase in stores are not in a digital format that allows you to move them automatically across digital devices, many people have software that enables them to "rip" these CDs into a digital format called MP3 that creates cross-platform digital versions. Using an MP3 player, they can listen to the songs on their computer or carry them anywhere in an MP3 player. Using their computers, they can also create their own disks, which they can then use on computers and other digital players.

As yet another example of the power of digital convergence, consider Moviefone. A subsidiary of Time Warner, it provides the public with information about where and when films are playing in many major cities. Moviefone started as a telephone service with a website, but now is exclusively web-based at http://www.moviefone.com. Funded by advertising from production firms and extra charges from the tickets it sells, Moviefone allows you to type in your ZIP code and up will come a list of theaters in your area with the movies they are playing and their showtimes. For many of the theaters, you can purchase a ticket directly from the Moviefone site so that you won't have to stand in line at the box office. (Some theaters have signed up with a competing service, Fandango.) Just click the time you want, state the number of tickets, and pay the total by punching in your credit card number. (Moviefone assures you that its site is secure.) You print out the confirmation, and when you arrive at the theater you insert your credit card into a special reader that is linked to Moviefone's Web computer. If you've done everything correctly (and we're sure you have), your tickets should be printed right then and there.

Note that this activity very much fits our definition of mass communication even though it takes place through a vehicle—a website—that has not traditionally been considered mass media. Moviefone is an example of the industrialized production and multiple distribution in mass communication. When we think of the work of media industries, too often we consider the creation of the products but leave out the work it takes to get them to the people the companies intend to reach. Yet distribution is at least as important to the success of a firm as production. Moviefone's success is not primarily based on its list of which theaters are playing which films and when; that information can be found in almost any daily newspaper. It was figuring out a way to distribute that list in an efficient, customer-friendly, and advertiser-friendly way that made the difference for the company.

Encouraging Controversy

One of the most important features of MP3 technology is that people can send copies of the MP3 files to their friends via email, and those friends can then listen to that music on their computers and portable devices. That sounds useful and fun (as you may know); however, this aspect of digital convergence has shaken up media industries and caused broad social and legal controversy.

At the turn of the twenty-first century, Napster was the most popular early version of what came to be called **peer-to-peer computing (P2P)**—a process in which people share the resources of their computers with computers owned by other people. Napster served as a facilitator, or go-between, in this process. The ability to do this excited millions of people. They realized that they could build their own libraries of exactly the music "singles" they wanted without having to go to a store and buy albums made up mostly of songs that didn't interest them.

Moviefone started as a telephone service, but it is now exclusively Web based at http://www.moviefone.com.

peer-to-peer computing (P2P) a process in which people share the resources of their computers with computers owned by other people

At its core, this development raises critical questions for all sorts of media firms. In an era in which all of content is in digits, how can we keep control over it? Place yourself in the position of an executive of a media conglomerate who found out that all the latest hit songs in his music company's catalog were being traded on Napster. You would probably feel that this trading means that your firm is losing a great deal of money as people download singles rather than buy them or the albums connected to them. More important, you might see Napster as a sign of greater menaces to come.

"Who says it will stop with music?" you might say. "In the near future, our company's books, magazines and even movies may be swapped freely by people who have no right to do so. In fact, these products have already been traded. The movie *Pirates of the Caribbean* was available for download not long after it appeared in theaters. Napster and activities like it threaten our control over our copyrights. Control over our copyrights is the lifeblood of our company, the fuel that allows us to create products for a variety of media industries. If we can't keep control over our products, we can't make money, and we ultimately can't exist."

In the chapter on the recording industry, we will see how firms reacted to the challenge of piracy as well as the opportunities that digital media bring. We will see, too, that movie and book executives are busy trying to figure out ways to circulate their products in various forms while at the same time making money off them and keeping control over them throughout the world.

Media Literacy: Taking a Critical View of Blurring Media Boundaries

We have seen that the continual flow of new digital technologies poses major opportunities and challenges for global, cross-media giants such as Viacom, News Corporation, and Time Warner. The enormous changes that we have sketched in this chapter also challenge us as citizens to ask what they mean for society.

Many people worry that media conglomerates have accumulated enough assets to allow them to dominate the major channels of mass communication. They argue that these giant corporations use internal synergies and joint ventures to spread their content efficiently across as many media as possible. They point out that in addition to using well-recognized mass media such as broadcast TV, cable TV, home video, theatrical movies, comic books, newspapers, magazines, radio, and books, these firms are turning to the World Wide Web, theme parks, toys, clothes, and a huge variety of other outlets to spread the word about a firm's new creation.

Overall, investment experts who follow media companies agree that we are now rapidly moving toward a time when no more than ten to fifteen companies will control the most prominent channels of production, distribution, and exhibition of content in the world. This consolidation does not mean that the media giants will have exclusive access to the public; they will undoubtedly make deals with other companies to distribute and exhibit those companies' material as well.

The presence of websites such as YouTube, Facebook, and blog sites means that individuals and small companies will still have the ability to post textual and audio-visual materials on the Web for virtually anyone to notice. The conglomerates will, however, become the major gatekeepers to the public across a wide swath of media. In order to reach either huge, mass-market audiences or relatively small, targeted audiences in the surest, most efficient ways possible, one will have to utilize the services of Time Warner, News Corporation, Comcast, Viacom, CBS, Disney, or one of a few other huge firms.

We are not far from such a situation today. Journalism scholar Ben Bagdikian argues that the number of firms dominating U.S. media has already dwindled to six. It's rare to see a theatrical movie do well if it isn't distributed by one of the majors or their subsidiaries (such as Disney's Miramax). Most bestsellers in the book industry come from a handful of publishers (such as Random House's publication of John Grisham or Danielle Steele novels). Just a few companies own the cable and broadcast channels that reach the vast majority of people. The same is true in the magazine, home video, internet, and recorded music industries. Moreover, Comcast, Time Warner, Disney, News Corporation, Viacom, Sony, and Bertelsmann are each top firms in a number of these industries. Through alliances, Microsoft, Google, CBS, and a few other firms have also been able to command huge global audiences in several media domains.

CORPORATE SPONSORSHIP COMES TO HURRICANES

THE VERIZON WIRELESS HURRICANE KANDEE®

THE AOL TIME WARNER HURRICANE LAMAR®

THE BRISTOL-MYERS SQUIBB HURRICANE MIDGE®

Three Common Criticisms of the Growth of Conglomerates

What's the problem with this situation? Certainly, the companies' stockholders—thousands of people around the world who have invested in these companies—are happy when these firms bring in global profits. Why not let them count their money while we enjoy the latest news on Time Warner's CNN cable network, read the latest news from Time Warner's *Time* magazine, get lost in a bestseller from Warner Books, go to the movies to see the latest action film from Time Warner's Warner Brothers or New Line Entertainment, stop at Wal-Mart to buy a recent movie distributed by Warner Home Video, watch *Gossip Girl*, a series co-produced by Warner for the partly Warner-owned CW TV network, and then play a video game from Warner Brothers and Electronic Arts based on the Warner Brothers movie *Dark Knight*? After all, it's all very enjoyable.

That's missing the point, say scholars and activists who are concerned about the growth of huge media conglomerates. Here, briefly, are three of their major arguments.

- When a small number of firms exercise power over production, distribution, and exhibition, they narrow the mainstream agenda of society.
- When a small number of huge firms exercise power over production, distribution, and exhibition on a global basis, they accelerate the homogenization of world society in the interest of commercialism.
- When a small number of huge firms exercise power over production, distribution, and exhibition, the democratic political process is jeopardized.

Let's look at these criticisms one at a time.

NARROWING SOCIETY'S MAINSTREAM AGENDA   When a small number of firms exercise power over production, distribution, and exhibition, they narrow the mainstream agenda of society. This criticism recalls our discussion of agenda setting in Chapter 4. An **agenda**, in this context, is the list of items that people in a society talk about. The argument here is that, when a handful of companies have so much control over the content that most people receive, the diversity of news and entertainment they can get is limited.

agenda the list of items that people in a society talk about

Critics of media consolidation such as Ben Bagdikian and Robert McChesney are concerned about making sure a multiplicity of voices will be heard across media industries. One way to encourage diversity, they contend, is through ownership of mainstream media by diverse segments of the population. These critics point out that the federal government's emphasis on deregulation has led to a sharp decline in the ownership of electronic media channels by members of historically disadvantaged groups such as women and ethnic and racial minorities. In 1995 and 1996, for example, the number of TV station owners who were members of minority groups declined by 10 percent, according to Commerce Department figures. There weren't many of these owners to begin with. The most recent U.S. government data on this topic date back to 2000. The study found that members of minority groups and women owned less than 3 percent of broadcast properties in the United States.[8]

Media conglomerates, these critics point out, have grabbed so many of the powerful broadcast and cable outlets that minorities and the viewpoints that they might share with the rest of society are often locked out. The critics argue that having members of historically disadvantaged minority groups owning electronic media properties means that people with sensitivity to minority views have power to choose these properties' programming—increasing the chances that programming reflective of these groups' perspectives will make it to the air and thus to the public agenda.

Another aspect of conglomerates that narrows society's agenda, according to critics, is the cross-media mindset of their executives. As we noted earlier, capturing a large part of the audience's share of mind is critical to the leaders of major media firms. When they spend huge amounts of money to produce a new film, when they have a slate of new shows for the TV season, or when they have a new rock group on tour, they must have maximum publicity in front of the target audience if they hope to make a profit. In response to this need, conglomerates and their joint-venture partners turn their own media outlets and those of partners into formidable publicity machines.

Earlier in this chapter, we mentioned *Harry Potter* as an illustration of cross-media branding by Warner Brothers in search of good share of mind. Critics point out that, although these tactics help the companies, they make it more difficult for voices not supported by the conglomerates to make it into the target audience's consciousness.

social media sites that allow people to create networks of acquaintances and friends and to share their writings and audiovisual materials with them

It's hard to outshout Fox or Time Warner. That is the case, say the critics, even on the hugely popular **social media** sites MySpace, YouTube, and FaceBook. The term "social media" has come to mean sites that allow people to create networks of acquaintances and friends and to share their writings and audiovisual materials with them. The critics charge, though, that MySpace, YouTube, FaceBook, and similar sites are becoming major places for large media firms to spread their songs, movie trailers, television shows, and commercials. Often the sites receive payment from firms that want to "seed" the sites with these materials in the hope that people who like them will point them out to those on their networks. Marketers have learned they can gain attention by sponsoring contests that encourage people to create commercials for the marketers' products, with the winners having the commercials shown on TV. The use of social media sites for commercial cross-media aims shouldn't be surprising, say the critics. After all, they are moneymaking operations; in fact, the biggest ones, MySpace and YouTube, are owned by two major mass-media conglomerates, News Corporation and Google, respectively.

Critics also raise broader concerns about the agenda-grabbing power of huge media conglomerates. What happens, the critics ask, when information is released by the Justice Department or some other organization that reflects critically upon part of the conglomerate? Will a news organization that is owned by the conglomerate rush to do an investigative story on the subject? Will it do a story at all?

Robert McChesney, Joseph Turow, and others have written that journalists seem to be losing their ability to address the role and nature of corporate power in the U.S. media because the organizations they work for are part of that powerful establishment. Although research on this issue is too scant to give a definitive answer, journalists are often wary about reporting on the activities of their own companies. This problem is serious enough when their companies are separate entities that are not attached to entertainment giants. When cross-media conglomerates are involved, though, the issue of reporting becomes even more problematic.

How will ABC News cover a corporate problem at Disney? Should we believe *Time* magazine's version of what is going on inside Time Warner? What are we to make of articles about the New York newspaper business on Fox News, given that News Corporation owns the *New York Post*? The topic gets more complex still when we realize that most people probably don't know what firm owns the *New York Post*; nor do they have any idea when they read reviews of a *Harry Potter* film in *Entertainment Weekly* that Time Warner produces and distributes both. Do media outlets have an ethical responsibility to make people aware of ownership patterns?

People who work for conglomerates play down the importance of these questions. They argue that there are enough news firms to ensure that even if a company doesn't report on itself another will report on it. Media critics aren't so sure that such coverage will be widespread, as the conglomerates that control mainstream distribution have an interest in not making waves about ownership patterns.

THE THREAT OF COMMERCIALISM AND HOMOGENIZATION   When a small number of huge firms exercise power over production, distribution, and exhibition on a global basis, they accelerate the homogenization of world society in the interest of commercialism.

Just about everywhere you go, critics point out, you can get MTV, CNN, NBC News, and Hollywood movies. Through these and other media channels, people all over the world are increasingly sharing the same media materials. Right now, the programs are shared only by the wealthiest people. Over time, though, that will change, and billions of people will tune to Sony, Time Warner, and News Corporation for entertainment and news.

Critics such as Dan Schiller and Vincent Mosco worry that the power of global media conglomerates to distribute materials worldwide will lead the local media industries of many countries to join the conglomerates in producing and distributing U.S.-style fare. As a result, the prominence of indigenous cultures will decline in the media of many countries.

A related concern raised by media critics such as Sut Jhally is that, when companies around the world import or produce materials with U.S. partners, these companies are often communicating subtle and not-so-subtle messages that individual wealth and consumption of goods are what count in society. Although some populations around the world share this view, many do not. When these messages are heard over and over, though, they may persuade some impressionable people, especially younger ones, that commercialism is valuable. Western media materials therefore become the advance guard for Western companies that want to sell people in those countries the kinds of products that are shown in the movies, in magazines, and on TV.

Defenders of the large media firms vigorously disagree. First of all, they say, in most countries local media materials are still the most popular ones. The defenders add that, when media firms go global, many of them increasingly adapt their programming to the societies that they serve. MTV, a case in point, is programmed differently in Germany, in Russia, in Latin America, in India, and elsewhere. Besides, say the defenders, even when people do see the same programs, they will interpret them differently because they come from different cultures. So, even if local cultures do change as a result of such media fare, they will not become part of a single global culture. Cultures will still remain different because of the way in which people understand the programming

Whereas critics see the sameness created by cross-media materials, the defenders of these movements actually celebrate what they see as the creativity on the part of companies in bringing material to consumers. In his book *Convergence Culture*, for example, Henry Jenkins argues that a new type of media consumer is developing, who revels in a "convergence culture" and who actually influences media firms in their creating. These consumers, he claims, have a strong influence on what we see in media "in part because advertisers and media producers are so eager to attract and hold their attention."[9]

Defenders of global media conglomerates are often not embarrassed to stand up for commercialism. With the fall of Soviet communism, they argue, the world is moving toward a capitalist, commercial model. The transformation of the television systems of many countries so that they accept advertising is evidence of this movement. The popularity of Western media materials, with their capitalist values, should not be a surprise. They simply reflect what people around the world want.

The critics of global media conglomerates respond that the popularity of Western media reflects not so much the values that people want as their attraction to

Table 5.4 Contrasting Views on the Social Pros and Cons of Media Trends

Trend/Issue	The Pros	The Cons	Questions for Media Literates to Ask
Media fragmentation	Provides more media channels and outlets for people to use	Makes it difficult for "society" to talk to itself because people are spread across so many different outlets	What do you and others mean by words such as "diversity" and "society"?
	Provides more opportunity than before for a diversity of media voices	The media are not as diverse as one might think because the outlets reflect formulas of media conglomerates	How much "diversity" of media genres do the many media channels really present?
			Is media fragmentation merely encouraging huge conglomerates to own many more outlets than before?
			How important is it for different groups in society to share their ideas and argue in media used by many people who do not belong to their groups?
Audience segmentation	Shows that media firms recognize many segments of the population	Audience segmentation sometimes encourages social divisions by emphasizing differences between people, not their similarities	Which segments in society may benefit from advertiser and media interest and which may not?
	Encourages a diversity of media content because media firms and marketers want to attract the various segments	Audience segments are based on categories designed to sell to people and do not encourage them to be good citizens	To what extent do individuals who belong to audience segments (say, "tweens") accept the views media personnel have about them?
			How does audience segmentation shape the media content that you and others get?
			How does that affect the way you personally look at the world?
Distribution of products across media boundaries	Allows businesses to make money back on products that otherwise wouldn't be worth producing	Makes much of mass media into promotional vehicles for other mass media	Can reading trade media magazines alert you to understanding how particular cross-media activities are orchestrated by marketers?
	Increases the audience for media materials in an age of media segmentation and audience segmentation		Do cross-media activities increase a media product's "share" of your mind?
			When talking with your friends, which products are you more likely to discuss: those that are distributed across media boundaries or those that stay in one medium?

Table 5.4 Contrasting Views on the Social Pros and Cons of Media Trends

Trend/Issue	The Pros	The Cons	Questions for Media Literates to Ask
Digital convergence	Once information is digitized, the cost of moving useful material from one medium to another is low	Digital convergence makes it possible to surround narrowly defined customer groups with tailored content across several media in ways that make it difficult for different segments to share each other's views	To what extent is this creation of "electronic gates" of information, entertainment, and advertising between groups taking place?
	Makes it easy to move information from one medium to another, which is useful to people in both work and recreation		To what extent is digital convergence encouraging people to create their own audiovisual materials that question the mainstream media?
	Allows ordinary people to use media images for their own purposes and exhibit them on MySpace and similar sites		What areas of society benefit most from digital convergence, and what areas benefit least?
Globalization	Gives people from different countries a shared mirror on certain parts of the world	Often perpetuates cultural colonialism	Is there a diversity of countries from which media firms are getting the materials they send around the world?
	Encourages the use of media technology, which can help some countries' economic development	Drowns out much nation-specific entertainment	What is the nature of the debates about globalization in various countries?
		Perpetuates and extends a marketing view of the world	
Conglomeration	Large media conglomerates can afford to take risks on content that smaller companies wouldn't take	Media conglomerates often drown out distinctive social voices	What "risks" are conglomerates taking, and what kinds of distinctive social voices do they appear to be drowning out?
	Large media conglomerates can spend money on technological innovations that smaller companies cannot afford	Media conglomerates have the resources to exert enormous pressures on government to pass laws that benefit them and not smaller media firms	How active are media conglomerates in lobbying government, on what subjects, and how successful have they been?
		Media conglomerates often include major journalism firms, and that makes it hard for journalists to report on the activities and implications of conglomeration	To what extent and in what way do the news companies of media conglomerates cover their own firm?

stunningly produced images of sex, violence, and action. In the end, though, the values do get sold, especially to the young.

At heart, the argument is about whether global media firms reflect or create changes in world culture. Some critics agree that they do a bit of both. In any event, they say, the ultimate concern lies in the next argument.

HARM TO THE DEMOCRATIC PROCESS   When a small number of huge firms exercise power over production, distribution, and exhibition, the democratic political process is jeopardized.

Critics such as Edward Herman and Noam Chomsky argue that politicians are so worried about getting favorable treatment from the press during an election campaign that they cooperate with large media firms, fearing that they will not get enough coverage during the election campaign if they don't. These critics also say that the news divisions of conglomerates may not report much on bills in which they collectively have a vested interest. This failure, critics argue, allows politicians to proceed with less attention to the public interest than they would if they had to worry about intense news coverage.

Defenders of media bigness insist that such lapses of journalistic responsibility do not happen, but critics insist that they do and will. In fact, the large media conglomerates' potential power over the political process may even be greater outside the United States, in countries where democracies are fragile. Such power, say the media critics, seriously threatens to undermine the rule of law.

Determining Your Point of View as a Critical Consumer of Media

The issues regarding media conglomerates are clearly complex. So are those related to media fragmentation, audience segmentation, the distribution of products across media boundaries, digital convergence, and globalization. In the interest of media literacy, it's important that you see these developments as social phenomena that ought to be looked at critically. You might end up deciding that what is happening is fine, or you might decide that important changes should be made.

Table 5.4 outlines some views that people who are for or against the six developments might offer, and it suggests some questions that media-literate individuals might want to ask in order to extend their knowledge and decide which perspectives to support. At the heart of the debate that is reflected in the table is an idea we discussed in Chapter 1: how the mass media reflect portraits of society to society. The belief here is that mass media ought to help people in a society to understand their society and the various groups that make it up. Do the six developments help or hinder the achievement of this goal? The table offers differing views.

The "pro" views suggest that the movement toward media and audience splintering and corporate bigness is not necessarily a problem. In fact, the views suggest that fragmentation allows for the recognition of audience needs that hadn't before been recognized. They suggest that cross-media activities and digitization can encourage minority-oriented media, making it realistically possible to pay for their content by releasing it in several versions. And they argue that globalization and huge media conglomerates have a positive social role to play in introducing countries around the world to new technologies and new perspectives.

The "con" view sees these developments quite differently. It critiques media fragmentation as being contrary to the interests of having people of a society come together to share ideas and arguments with one other. It sees audience segmentation as a marketing tool that can needlessly emphasize people's differences rather than their similarities. A related problem is that the broad marketing approach that comes with this segmentation is used for the purpose of selling to people, not encouraging them toward civic commitments. That is also a difficulty with cross-media activities, especially when carried out by media conglomerates. In fact, according to this view, media globalization and conglomerates take the problems that media and audience fragmentation bring and spread them internationally. Media conglomeration also creates circumstances that make it difficult for journalists to cover the activities of these huge corporations, since the journalists often work for one or another of them.

As these developments take hold, they will affect all our lives profoundly. Think about where you stand on these issues when you read the next chapter, where we go in detail into the corporate strategies of some of the largest media firms. Think about them, too, when you tackle individual industries in the rest of the book. Remember that today every mass media industry is part of the big, cross-media picture.

Chapter Review

For an interactive chapter recap and study guide, visit the companion website for *Media Today* at http://www.routledge.com/textbooks/mediatoday4e.

Questions for Discussion and Critical Thinking

1 How is media fragmentation related to audience segmentation?

2 Over the years, the major television networks have tried to stop audience erosion, without much success. What are some of the ways in which they have tried to do that?

3 "The more marketers find a group attractive, the more they are prone to take that group apart to look for subgroups that have special features that attract them." Explain this statement and give an example that is not mentioned in the chapter.

4 What does it mean for media companies to achieve "good share of mind"? Give an example, and explain why crossing media boundaries can help firms achieve good share of mind.

5 Using news as an example, explain the three criticisms of mass media conglomerates. Also, show how the criticisms are related to one another.

Internet Resources

Center for Digital Democracy (http://www.democraticmedia.org/)
According to its mission statement, the Center for Digital Democracy is "committed to preserving the openness and diversity of the internet in the broadband era, and to realizing the full potential of digital communications through the development and encouragement of noncommercial, public interest programming."

Websites of media conglomerates
To get a good idea of the cross-media and global activities of first-, second- and third-tier media conglomerates, check out their "corporate websites"—the websites they have set up for investors—and take a look at the companies they

own and the media products they release. Getting to these websites is not at all intuitive. Some sites have obvious Web addresses—for example http://www.timewarner.com. http://www.newscorp.com is a bit of an unusual twist on News Corporation. But the New York Times Company's corporate site is quite unintuitive: http://www.nytco.com. The best way to find the corporate website of a media firm is to use a search engine such as Google, type the name of the company in quotation marks, and add the word "corporate." So, for example, to get to the Sony Corporation's corporate website, go to http://www.google.com or http://www.yahoo.com and type "Sony Corporation" into the search box.

FreePress.net (http://www.freepress.net/docs/talk_radio.pdf)

Free Press is a national, nonpartisan organization working to reform the media. Through education, organizing, and advocacy, it promotes diverse and independent media ownership, strong public media, and universal access to communications.

Media Access Project (http://www.mediaaccess.org)

Founded in the early 1970s, the Media Access Project is a "public interest media and telecommunications law firm which promotes the public's First Amendment right to hear and be heard on the electronic media of today and tomorrow."

Key Terms

You can find the definitions to these key terms in the marginal glossary throughout this chapter. Test your knowledge of these terms with interactive flash cards on the *Media Today* companion website.

achieving a good share of mind 169	mass media conglomerate 173
agenda 183	media fragmentation 158
audience erosion 158	peer-to-peer computing (P2P) 181
audience segmentation 160	product placement 167
brand 170	repurposing 179
conglomerate 173	social media 184
convergence 177	subscriptions 161
coproduction 173	syndicates 168
creative rights 167	syndication 166
cross-platform data 179	synergy 175
digital convergence 177	targeting 160
horizontal integration 175	target segments 160
joint ventures 177	vertical integration 166
market research 161	windows 166

Constructing Media Literacy

1 In your opinion, which of the six trends described in this chapter is having the most impact on media today?

2 Can you think of methods that the major television networks could have used in their attempts to stop audience erosion?

3 Some business observers doubt that synergy is as helpful to a mass media conglomerate as its supporters believe. Argue for or against this view, bringing evidence to support your argument.

4 How much of the news, information, and entertainment that you receive from mass media on a daily basis does not come from mass media conglomerates.

Companion Website
Video Clips
. . . .

Rich Media, Poor Democracy—Who is Sumner Redstone and Why Should We Care?

This clip from the Media Education Foundation documentary *Rich Media, Poor Democracy* looks at the effects of conglomerate ownership of the media on journalism in America. Credit: Media Education Foundation.

The Mean World Syndrome—A Tidal Wave of Violence

This clip from the Media Education Foundation documentary *The Mean World Syndrome* is based on the late George Gerbner's groundbreaking analysis of media influence and media violence. Credit: Media Education Foundation.

Case Study
. . . .

CROSS-MEDIA MARKETING OF MOVIES

The idea To get a sense of the cross-media power of major movie companies and the conglomerates to which they belong, track the cross-media marketing activities that are being used, and the windows in which the film will appear.

The method Pick a movie that a major studio—Warner Brothers, Columbia, Disney, Paramount, Twentieth Century Fox, or Universal—has released as a major summer or Christmas film. *Avatar, Sherlock Holmes* with Robert Downey Jr., the *Harry Potter* films, and the *Pirates of the Caribbean* movies are examples. Then use a newspaper and magazine database such as Factiva or NexisLexis to investigate the coverage the film received in the month before it was released. Check out (1) the various types of press articles about the movie; (2) toys and other licensed products (such as T-shirts and masks) that the studio may have licensed with the film's release; and (3) the publicity the movie has gotten through tie-ins with other product marketers, such as food companies, stores, and phone companies.

Write a report of what you learned, including who the target audience in the United States was for the movie and how the movie company tried to reach it. In view of what you have learned about cross-media activities, address the following questions: If you were a member of the target audience, would you have heard about the movie before its release? What notions about the film and its stars would you have heard (that is, what agenda about the movie did the publicity create)? And through what media would you have heard that?

6 Understanding the Strategies of Media Giants

After studying this chapter, you will be able to:

1 Evaluate the core businesses of two contemporary media conglomerates—The Walt Disney Company and News Corporation—as well as the core business of Google, a large web-based corporation that is on the way to becoming a cross-media conglomerate

2 Examine and evaluate other large media firms to better understand their scope and power

3 Recognize and understand the three main operating strategies of News Corporation

4 Recognize and understand the three main operating strategies of The Walt Disney Company

5 Recognize and understand the three main operating strategies of Google

6 Harness your media literacy skills in order to develop your own critical view of cross-media activities and their impact on society and on individuals

MEDIA TODAY

Have you ever considered how often and how much you live in "Disney World"? You may be thinking that you've been to the place only once or twice, or even that you've never been there at all. But whether or not you have ever gone to the physical place we call Walt Disney World Resort is not really the point of the question. In fact, you can live in Disney World even if you've never been to a Disney-owned theme park. That is because so much of the media world is shaped by The Walt Disney Company that you may be immersed in its products for many hours of your week, whether or not you know it.

- Do you get your news from ABC television? ABC is owned by Disney. How about the TV shows you watch—are any of those on ABC?
- On cable TV, if you're an ESPN fan, a Lifetime fan, an A&E or SOAPnet fan, a Marvel Comics fan, you're in Disney territory.
- What about your radio listening—is one of the sports stations you listen to part of ESPN Radio?
- What about going to the movies? Obviously, if you see a Disney film, you're in Disney World, but did you know that Touchstone Pictures, Pixar, and Miramax Films also fall under the Disney umbrella?
- Magazines, books, recordings, and toys, anyone? Hyperion is a Disney book company. *ESPN Magazine* is a Disney periodical. And if you or a toddler you know is into the *Little Einstein* series

on the cable TV Disney Channel, you might know that there are toys and books based on it, too.

In fact, Disney's presence extends even further to include music recordings, home video, the Web, video games, and much more. If you knew how many of the media products you use come from The Walt Disney Company—alone or in combination with partners—you might be surprised at how much time you spend in its world each week. The same can be said about other huge media firms such as Time Warner, Viacom, NBC Universal (majority owned by Comcast Corporation), News Corporation, Bertelsmann, and Google. Together, these companies create mass media worlds that we visit more often (and for a longer time) than we often realize.

In Chapter 5, we discussed the most important activities of mass media firms at the beginning of the twenty-first century—media fragmentation, audience segmentation, distribution of products across media boundaries, digital convergence, globalization, and conglomeration. Whereas that chapter mapped the considerations that drive cross-media activities, this chapter explores the way in which two conglomerates—The Walt Disney Company and News Corporation—are deeply involved in those activities in the real world. We'll also take a close look at Google, a large web-based corporation that is on the way to becoming a cross-media conglomerate.

Three Contemporary Media Giants

conglomerate a company that owns a number of companies in different industries

strategies overall, broad plans to accomplish set goals

Three definitions will be useful at the start of our journey. As we saw in Chapter 5, a conglomerate is a company that owns a number of companies in different industries. A mass media **conglomerate**, then, is a company that holds several mass media firms in different media industries under its corporate umbrella. Even when media executives think they have sound **strategies**—or overall, broad plans to accomplish their goals—to guide their firms, they regularly re-examine their approaches to make sure they are moving in the best possible direction. That kind of continual rethinking takes place in small and midsized mass media companies as well as at all levels of major conglomerates such as News Corporation (News Corp) and Disney. The reason for this has to do with the far-flung cross-media activities of these two firms. For its part, Google really doesn't yet fit our definition of a conglomerate. Its business is primarily located on the Web and involves serving advertisements to people based on what it knows about. As we will see, however, Google's strategies for expansion beyond the Web may soon place it among the ranks of key media conglomerates.

We will examine these three companies because their activities have such a large impact on the output of many media. In addition, they often affect what smaller firms can do—whether they can go it alone or whether they must find merger partners or enter into joint ventures with the conglomerates, and even whether they can survive.

We could easily have chosen other firms to make these points. Disney, News Corporation, and Google are the specific subjects of our analysis here for three reasons:

- All three exert enormous influence on the media world.
- Each firm has different ways of facing up to the challenges of the new media environment. Each, for example, has different ways of approaching media fragmentation, audience segmentation, distribution of products across media boundaries, digital convergence, and globalization.
- All three engage in activities that you may recognize but may not have considered from the perspective of a critical consumer.

MEDIA RESEARCH
HOW TO FIND AN ANNUAL REPORT

Annual reports are important informational tools when you are carrying out research on a specific company. Although annual reports are typically aimed at shareholders and contain a fair bit of information regarding financial performance, they also may lay out the company's vision going forward including information about product branding and target audiences. Even the images on the cover of a company's annual report can provide important clues about where the executives believe the firm's most important activities lie.

You can find the annual report of just about every public media firm on the Web. The quickest way is to go to the company's website and click on the link to investor relations. There you will find the annual reports or a category called SEC (that is, Securities and Exchange Commission) filings. Another name for the annual report is Form 10-K.

Having trouble? Make sure that you are on the company's corporate website. Many companies (particularly media firms) have a commercial site and a corporate site. For example, if you wanted to read today's *New York Times* you would go to http://www.nytimes.com/. However, if you wanted to find the New York Times Company's annual report, you would visit their corporate site at http://www.nytco.com/.

The Walt Disney Company

One look at the investor section of The Walt Disney Company's corporate website (http://corporate.disney.go.com/investors/index.html) and it's clear: Disney is aware and proud that it reaches people around the world in many ways. The company's mission statement emphasizes the global aim of its activities:

> The Walt Disney Company's objective is to be one of the world's leading producers and providers of entertainment and information, using its portfolio of brands to differentiate its content, services and consumer products. The company's primary financial goals are to maximize earnings and cash flow, and to allocate capital profitability toward growth initiatives that will drive long-term shareholder value.

Let's unpack the corporate strategies reflected in this statement. To do this, we'll use a useful tool—the company's annual report. Consider the cover of Disney's 2008 annual report, which can be found online at http://corporate.disney.go.com/investors/annual_reports/2008. It shows a Caucasian girl around the age of ten. She is dressed in a gray tank top, striped yellow skirt, and white tennis shoes and is running across a bridge. The wind is in front of her—her hair is flying back—and she is pulling a wind-pushed bouquet of blue, red, yellow, and pink balloons that are shaped like Mickey Mouse's head. Behind her is Cinderella Castle, a centerpiece in the Magic Kingdom at Walt Disney World Resort in Florida as well as in Tokyo Disneyland. The castle is slightly blurred and bathed in sunlight.

This image makes a number of points about the way Disney sees itself. The company is reflecting on its strong roots and powerful ability to move its products across media and across the world. At a time of major economic challenges (which the chairman discusses in his letter to shareholders), recalling Mickey Mouse, animated-film, and theme-park foundations upon which the company was built and continues to grow presents an optimistic view of the future. *Cinderella* was a highly successful animated film when it was released in 1950, and its endearing quality led the company to use the castle in that movie for the centerpiece in two of its parks, while the Sleeping Beauty Castle is the icon for two others (including Disneyland in California). *Cinderella* also embodies the cross-media impulse that has kept the company going strong. Over the decades it has appeared on different technologies—on television, video, and DVD. The movie led to two sequels made specifically for home video, and spinoffs relating to the character have succeeded as books, records, video games, costumes in Disney Stores, and ice-skating shows. Disney has even licensed a Cinderella wedding dress as part of a Disney Fairy Tale Weddings line.

The selection of a young girl for the 2008 annual report's cover may relate partly to the decision to profile a boy (from the animated film *Toy Story*) on the 2006 cover and a group of male and female teens (from the Disney Channel's *High School Musical*) on the 2007 cover. The 2008 cover nods to the importance of girls to Disney's economic well being—a theme that is carried through the rest of the annual report. Although the products and photos do depict men and boys as Disney audience members, they emphasize the importance of girls and young women to Disney's presence and future. Such female support is critical to much of the firm's home video line, with its emphasis on fairy tales such as *Cinderella, Sleeping Beauty*, and *The Little Mermaid*. Girl interest also lies at the core of success for the Disney Consumer Products Line, the world's largest licensor of images and brands for products. Disney Princess and Disney Fairies products, for example, aim at young girls, while Disney Channel's

CULTURE TODAY
DOES MICKEY MOUSE HAVE A PERSONALITY?

Psychologists have long grappled with the question of whether an individual's personality is formed during childhood or whether it continues to take shape over the course of one's life. Although you might argue that Mickey Mouse is not an individual per se, people in and out of the Disney empire have worried about his personality—in fact, about whether he really has one.

The story of Mickey Mouse's creation is perhaps as legendary as the cartoon himself. He was developed by Walt Disney in the late 1920s, a period that Disney later described as "when the business fortunes of my brother Roy and myself were at lowest ebb, and disaster seemed right around the corner." During a cross-country train ride, Disney came up with the idea for a cartoon mouse named Mortimer; at his wife's suggestion, he changed the name to Mickey.

Mickey debuted in the 1928 cartoon Steamboat Willie, and by the end of the 1930s he had appeared in more than 100 films. Yet as Mickey was becoming the central figure behind The Walt Disney Company, his personality became what one writer described as "less edgy, duller, and less subversive." As Disney archives director David Smith explained, "You didn't want to do naughty things with your corporate logo. He suddenly became sacrosanct."

Mickey's personality was briefly revived during the 1950s with the broadcast of the Mickey Mouse Club program. But as the Disney Company produced more and more films, his personality became eclipsed by the more dynamic characters of Donald Duck, Goofy, and others. In fact, Mickey has appeared in only two cartoons since 1960.

By the time Mickey Mouse celebrated his seventy-fifth birthday in 2003, many claimed that his personality had all but disappeared. Describing him as boring, neglected, and irrelevant, among others, they blamed Mickey's lackluster persona on Disney's globalization efforts. "The years have dulled Mickey's personality," notes reporter Mike Schneider, "a result of him

Mickey Mouse, Minnie Mouse, and Mortimer, c. 1930.

becoming the corporate face of a multibillion dollar entertainment empire." Some have even speculated that Disney is planning to remake the character.

While Mickey's personality in the twenty-first century remains to be seen, the early life of Mickey Mouse remains an important part of cartoon history. Animation artist David Johnson notes that the debut of Mickey Mouse brought something extraordinary to the world of animated characters. "[This] ungainly rodent with a falsetto voice squeaked his way not only into his own newly created niche but soon had an entire world waiting to cheer on each new exploit. This unprecedented phenomenon, whose impact and popularity continues to this day, defies any simple solution."

Sources: Mike Schneider, "Disney Icon Mickey Mouse Turns 75," *Newsday*, November 18, 2003. http://www.newsday.com (accessed August 2, 2010); David Johnson, "Personality of the Early Cartoon," *Animation Artist Magazine*, 2000. http://www.animationartist.com/InsideAnimation/DavidJohnson/Personality.html (accessed March 7, 2007); Jesse Green, "Building a Better Mouse," *The New York Times*, April 18, 2004.

High School Musical, Hannah Montana, and *Camp Rock* merchandise counts on the tween-girl consumer. By extension, much hit Disney programming for ABC TV— *Desperate Housewives, Grey's Anatomy, Private Practice, Brothers and Sisters*—targets a female audience. Photos in the annual report even overwhelmingly showed women in the Disney English learning center for kids aged 2–10 in Shanghai, China. Industry observers, in fact, have noted that Disney products' strong tilt toward females may have led the firm to buy the male-oriented Marvel Entertainment Company in 2009. But at the end of 2008, the annual report was quietly celebrating the Disney girl as a character and in the audience as a key to the company's strength even in difficult times.

In the annual report's "Letter to Shareholders," Disney president and CEO Robert Iger didn't mention girls or women as bulwarks of the Disney bottom line. Instead, nodding to the firm's general mission statement, he noted that, in the face of uncertain economic times, Disney was determined to follow a path it had identified in better times:

> Strategically, we continue to adhere to priorities established a few years ago. A commitment to high-quality creative work, a persistent focus on mastering new technology and selective investment in promising international marketers are strategies that have worked for us, and we believe they will continue to position us well for the long term.

Three Main Strategies

Disney's mission statement and the comment in Iger's "Letter to Shareholders" both hint at where Disney sees its strengths in its competitive environment. Using these and other tools such as the rest of the annual report, other recent Disney annual reports, and the approach that Disney has taken toward its holdings, we can see three major strategies that management believes will help Disney grow. They are:

- Exploit as much synergy as possible among subsidiaries
- Emphasize the global movement of content
- Adopt new distribution technologies.

Let's consider what the strategies mean, how they relate to one another, and how they relate to the company's overall mission.

EXPLOIT AS MUCH SYNERGY AS POSSIBLE AMONG SUBSIDIARIES   As we discussed in Chapter 5, **synergy** describes a situation in which the whole is greater than the sum of its parts. To implement this strategy, Disney looks for ways for the company's subsidiaries to profit from the distribution of new and old material in a wide array of media industries. It turns movies into DVDs and uses their plots for books and video games, for example. Another part of the strategy is to get the subsidiaries to work with one another to find new ways to profit from the creation, distribution, and exhibition of materials. For example, the Disney theme parks and cruise line work with the Disney movie division to bring popular film characters and plot ideas into the parks and cruises. The lucrative ESPN sports cable channel relates to the magazine, the radio network, and the website. (For a list of the companies Disney owns, see Table 6.1.)

Historically, Disney has used the content of many of its animated films—from *Snow White and the Seven Dwarfs* to *Beauty and the Beast*—for theme parks, books, stores, magazines, Broadway musicals, and the licensing of creative rights. As we saw in Chapter 5, **licensing** involves a firm granting other companies (usually manufacturers) permission to profit from the use of the firm's trademarked or copyrighted material in return for payment. The aim of licensing is the same as the aim of all uses of the content: both to draw attention to the material (in this case the animated film) and to profit from it in as many ways as possible. In recent years, Disney has not only continued this synergy strategy, but has extended it quite regularly to live-action movies and TV shows. Disney succeeded with a live-action *Hannah Montana*

synergy a situation in which the whole is greater than the sum of its parts; the ability of mass media organizations to channel content into a wide variety of mass media on a global scale through control over production, distribution, and exhibition in as many of those media as possible

licensing a firm granting other companies (usually manufacturers) permission to profit from the use of the firm's trademarked or copyrighted material in return for payment, with the aim of drawing attention to the material and profiting from it in as many ways as possible

Table 6.1 The Walt Disney Company Holdings, 2009

Film

Walt Disney Pictures

Touchstone Pictures

Hollywood Pictures

Miramax Films

Pixar

**General Television Production
and Distribution**

ABC Studios

ABC Media Productions

ABC Family Productions

Disney-ABC Domestic Television

Disney-ABC-ESPN Television
International

Broadcast television

ABC Network

Owned and Operated Television
Stations

    WLS – Chicago

    WJRT Flint

    KFSN Fresno

    KTRK Houston

    KABC Los Angeles

    WABC New York City

    WPVI Philadelphia

    WTVD Raleigh–Durham

    KGO San Francisco

    WTVG Toledo

Cable television

ESPN (80%)

ESPN2 (80%)

ESPN Classic (80%)

ESPNU (80%)

ESPNEWS (80%)

ESPN Deportes (80%)

ESPNU (80%)

ABC Family

Disney Channel

Disney Channels Worldwide

Toon Disney

SOAPnet

Lifetime Network (42%)

Lifetime Movie Network (42%)

Lifetime Real Women (42%)

A&E (42%)

History Channel

Playhouse Disney

Disney Cinemagic

Hungama

Disney HD

Radio

ESPN Radio Network

Owned Stations in
    New York, NY
    Los Angeles, CA
    Chicago, IL
    Dallas-Fort Worth, TX
    Pittsburgh, PA

Music

Walt Disney Records

Hollywood Records

Lyric Street Records

Buena Vista Concerts

Disney Music Publishing

Publishing

Disney Global Book Group

Global Children's Magazines

FamilyFun Group

Disney English

Book Publishing Imprints

    Hyperion

    Miramax Books

    ESPN Books

    Theia

    ABC Daytime Press

    Hyperion ebooks

    Hyperion East

    Disney Publishing Worldwide

    Cal Publishing Inc.

    CrossGen

    Hyperion Books for Children

    Jump at the Sun

    Volo

    Michael di Caupa Books

Magazine

Automotive Industries

Biography (with GE and Hearst)

Discover

Disney Adventures

ECN News

ESPN Magazine (distributed by
Hearst)

Family Fun

Institutional Investor

JCK

Kodin

Top Famille (French family
magazine)

US Weekly (50%)

Video Business

Quality: Wondertime Magazine

Parks and Resorts

Walt Disney Imagineering

Disneyland Resort

Walt Disney World Resort

Tokyo Disney Resort

Disneyland Resort Paris

Hong Kong Disneyland

Disney Vacation Club

Disney Cruise Line

Other

Disney Theatrical Productions

Disney Live Family Entertainment

Disney on Ice

The Disney Store

Club Penguins

ESPN Zone

Disney Toys

Disney Apparel, Accessories and
Footwear

Disney Food, Health and Beauty

Disney Home Furnishings and
Decor

Disney Stationery

Disney Consumer Economics

The Baby Einstein Company

Muppets Holding Company

Disney Interactive Studios

Walt Disney Internet Group

Sources: "Who Owns What," *Columbia Journalism Review*. Updated July 30, 2008. http://www.cjr.org/resources (accessed August 2, 2010); Disney Company, "Fiscal Year 2009 Annual Financial Report and Shareholder Letter." http://amedia.disney.go.com/investorrelations/annual_reports/WDC-10kwrap-2009.pdf (accessed August 2, 2010).

television series and concert movie that led to many other products. The company hit a synergy-and-licensing home run with its *Pirates of the Caribbean* movies, which took inspiration from a Disney theme-park amusement.

However, not all of Disney's live-action films fit this pattern. Disney has released many movies (such as *Scary Movie* and *The Queen*) under the Miramax banner that have little, if any, connection with the rest of Disney. Nevertheless, although these films sometimes bring the company strong revenues, there is a conviction at Disney that the company will usually derive greater profit over the long term from movies that carry the Disney name and are aimed at families with young children, movies such as *The Lion King, Beauty and the Beast, Toy Story, Pirates of the Caribbean*, and *National Treasure*. Such Disney movies have become key "franchises" to be mined by the conglomerate. In show business, a **franchise** is a media property that has a life beyond its original appearance as a film, TV series, or book series; often that life extends across media. Here is how Robert Iger's considers its importance in the annual report:

franchise a brand that is highly profitable across time as well as across media

> Thanks to our Imagineers, at our parks in California and Florida we opened Toy Story Mania!, an engaging attraction that combines the wonder and lovability of the *Toy Story* characters with breakthrough technology. The result is yet another theme park experience that distinguishes our Company and causes people to say: "What will they think of next?" or, "Only Disney can do that." Beyond these individual achievements, we continued to create and support several key franchises. These are stories and characters that can be leveraged across many of our businesses, on many technological platforms, in many territories, and over long periods of time.

> While we continue to break new creative ground, our substantial investment in such great Disney franchises as *Cars, Toy Story, Princesses, Pirates, Mickey Mouse, Winnie the Pooh, High School Musical* and *Fairies* continues to drive strong returns, differentiates us from our competitors and builds long-term shareholder value.

> Not only do we possess a significant number of such franchises, but our ability to make the most of their success is unrivalled. This comes from a collection of great assets and a commitment to manage them as a whole that is worth far more than the sum of its parts. This defines Disney and, as we have been saying, creates the Disney Difference.

Disney executives are well aware that particular areas, or **nodes**, of their conglomerate are more likely than others to generate cross-media hits. The 2008 annual report particularly singles out the company's cable channels:

nodes particular areas of a conglomerate

> The Cable Networks Group provides a strong foundation for franchise building across the Company as well as unique opportunities for exploiting international expansion and digital media opportunities. The Group includes the Disney Channels Worldwide portfolio of kids channels, ABC Family, SOAPnet and Jetix, as well as the Company's equity stake in Lifetime Entertainment Services and A&E Television Networks. Combined, these assets reach the full spectrum of audiences from preschoolers to adults.

When it comes to Disney, it's not very hard at all to see how children's attraction to Disney Channel characters such as *Cars, Hannah Montana*, and *Winnie the Pooh* especially drives successful corporate synergies across a variety of media. Kids and their parents grow up with Disney creations in activities that are cross-generational. Parents (and grandparents) remember Disney as a happy part of their childhood, and so they tend to pass on the "tradition." One can move from Mickey Mouse teething rings (a licensed product) to Disney plush toys for babies (also licensed) to early childhood toys (more licensed stuff) and videos from Baby Einstein (a Disney subsidiary). As toddlers grow into kindergarteners, videos based on Disney movies

IS IT ETHICAL?
DISNEY'S BABY EINSTEIN CONTROVERSY

In October 2009, the Walt Disney Company announced that they would be offering refunds on all their Baby Einstein videos. Baby Einstein, released by Disney in 1997, is a series of DVDs and other products that are designed to enhance the cognitive abilities of children. The products target children ranging in age from 0 to 18 months. The videos—which include videos dedicated to Baby Shakespeare and Baby Mozart among others—are wildly popular in the United States. A 2003 study suggests that one-third of children aged from 6 months to 2 years have at least one Baby Einstein video.

Susan Linn, director of the Campaign for a Commercial-Free Childhood, has complained to the Federal Trade Commission about the educational claims made on the Baby Einstein products. She and others have also threatened Disney with a class action lawsuit citing "unfair and deceptive practices." Linn notes that her organization sees the refund "as an acknowledgment by the leading baby video company that baby videos are not educational, and we hope other baby media companies will follow suit by offering refunds."

Although Disney is giving refunds and no longer states directly that Baby Einstein products will improve babies' thinking abilities, it still suggests the videos have educational benefits for children under the age of 2 years. Its ads now include words such as "introduces" and "reinforces" awareness of worlds around them when discussing the possible help the videos give very young children. One might suspect that educational claims help parents to feel that by allowing their babies to watch the videos they are doing something good for their child's development, even as they take a break. However, the American Academy of Pediatricians has suggested that children under 2 years of age should have very limited exposure to audiovisual materials.

What do you think? Are the Baby Einstein claims ethical? How might you pitch the products to parents—or should they be sold at all?

Source: T. Lewin, "No Einstein in Your Crib? Get a Refund," *The New York Times*, October 23, 2009, p. A1.

and cartoons become "age-appropriate," as do Disney broadcast TV programs and the Disney (cable) Channel. Visiting a Disney theme park reinforces the purchase of a wide range of products, from sweatshirts to watches. So does taking a vacation on the Disney Cruise Line, which conveniently makes Walt Disney World Resort a prominent stop. If you really want to be part of the Disney world, you can purchase a home in Celebration, Florida, a Disney-built housing development not too far from the theme park that incorporates the company's philosophy of living into the architecture.[1]

EMPHASIZE THE GLOBAL MOVEMENT OF CONTENT   As we have seen in the mission statement, a critical part of Disney's strategic activities is to be a leader in producing and distributing its products, not just in the United States but around the globe. As recently as a decade ago, Disney executives acknowledged that they did not take global distribution seriously enough and that they did not make much of an attempt to achieve the global exploitation of the kinds of synergies that made Disney brands highly profitable in the United States. In the 1999 annual report, then-chairman Michael Eisner wrote,

> Disney is in the ironic position of being one of the best-known brands on the planet, but with too little of its income being generated outside the United States. The United States contains only 5 percent of the world's population, but it accounts for 80 percent of our company's revenues.[2]

In 1999, Disney created a subsidiary company called Walt Disney International in order to boost revenues outside the United States. Since then, the company has moved aggressively to generate income in many countries. To make sure that all its activities and distribution platforms are as interrelated as possible, in 2007 Disney announced the formation of an "integrated global television distribution division with responsibility for the international distribution and sales of the far-reaching portfolio of entertainment and news content produced by The Walt Disney Company." One of Disney's executives was assigned to oversee the distribution of Disney's audiovisual products, including "all feature films, television series, kids' programming, made-for-TV movies, miniseries, news documentaries, TV animation and direct-to-video content—and their distribution to all platforms, including the burgeoning video-on-demand [that is, ability to watch a TV show when you want to] and broadband [that is, high-speed internet] markets."

Highlighting all sorts of Disney content for people around the world also seems to be a major aim of three theme parks outside the United States—Disneyland Resort Paris, Tokyo Disney Resort, and the part-owned Hong Kong Disneyland. Disney executives have acknowledged that the parks have not performed well financially, but they characterize them as crucial statements of the company's commitment to engaging consumers far beyond North America. One Disney executive noted that the parks boost sales of Disney-branded products and movies. "There is," she said, "good synergy between other Disney products and our parks."[3]

But Disney also recognizes that the way to attract populations around the world is to provide content that resonates with their worlds. The 2008 annual report states that "Today, Disney Channels Worldwide is a global powerhouse in kids entertainment." Disney Channel content reaches hundreds of millions of homes around the world. This access makes Disney Channel a daily touchstone for the Disney brand in more than 100 countries. While it is placing its traditional parade of characters (often

A woman prepares a media event in Beijing to introduce *The Magic Gourd*, an animated Chinese language film co-produced by Disney.

in translation) in different platforms around the world, the company is also increasingly creating materials for particular markets. In Latin America, for example, it created local versions of its U.S. television series such as *Desperate Housewives*. In 2007, it increased its non-U.S. activities by teaming up with an Indian studio to collaborate on movies there. In addition, Disney embarked on co-producing an animated Chinese-language film in China called *The Magic Gourd*, released in 2008; 2009 marked the release of a second China-made film, *Touch of a Panda*. Thomas Staggs, Disney's chief finance officer, said that the release of *The Magic Gourd* marked the beginning of a clear commitment to TV shows and feature films not made in the United States in developed and developing countries. He stressed that the locally made productions will nevertheless have all the classic storytelling elements. That way, the Disney brand would come through and so help the sale of all Disney products, whether they are films, toys, or theme parks. "That ability to drive our different businesses under a common umbrella sets us aside from our peers," he contended.[4]

ADOPT NEW DISTRIBUTION TECHNOLOGIES   In addition to Disney's newly energized global approach to its business, the company has been aggressive in using new forms of digital distribution to get its image and products out to its various target audiences. As early as 1999, CEO Michael Eisner suggested in Disney's annual report that the internet would be another place for the exploitation of synergy between divisions to further the Disney mission. He declared that:

> There can be little question that the Internet is the next major development in the realm of information and entertainment. During the coming years, broadband transmission will make it possible for the Internet to become a true entertainment medium. This is where our library, news and sports assets will be put to good use. So will our expertise in creating filmed entertainment.[5]

In the early years of digital technologies, Disney was reluctant to dive into them, since it feared that perfect digital copies of its valuable programming would be pirated. Since then, however, it has changed its corporate mind. The company has sold TV shows and movies on Apple's iTunes Web downloading site; it has experimented with a mobile phone service that delivered ESPN sports news and highlights; and it has invested in Hulu, a website through which people can stream network television programs (with commercials) when not watching them through traditional means. In 2008, to organize its approach to digital products, Disney created the Disney Interactive Media Group, which operates two "global content creation units": Disney Interactive Studios (DIS) and Disney Online. DIS creates and distributes "a broad portfolio of video games and interactive entertainment, distributed globally, for handheld, mobile and console platforms." As you might imagine, virtually all of these products tie into TV programs, movies, or other Disney properties. Disney Online produces and manages the company's websites, including "the No. 1 kids entertainment and family community Web site, Disney.com" and a variety of "age appropriate" virtual worlds. The goal is consistent with that of every other medium in which the company works: "build massive audiences around core Disney brands, characters and stories."

News Corporation

Take a look at News Corporation's 2008 annual report and you'll see both differences from as well as similarities to Disney's strategic vision. (You can view it online at http://www.newscorp.com/Report2008/AR2008.pdf.) The similarities are basic, since most media executives—including those at News Corporation and Disney—share common understandings of the changes riling their businesses. As such, News Corporation CEO Rupert Murdoch emphasizes the need for synergies among subsidiaries, global activities, and new technologies in his "Letter to Shareholders." And, in fact, News Corp's mission statement on its website is similar to Disney's desire to be "one of the world's leading producers and providers of entertainment and information." But News Corporation is a different company from Disney, with a different background and a very different leadership. As a result, the company places different priorities on these needs, and it interprets them quite differently from Disney.

Take the issue of globalization. News Corporation executives would probably sniff (or sneer) at Disney CEO Iger's note about the importance of spreading globally—in their view, News Corporation has globalization in its genes. A globe of the world is the company's logo. Moreover, the firm's ties to the world at large are made prominently on the cover of every annual report since at least 1997. (Check out http://www.news-corp.com/investor/annual_reports.html to see past covers of the company's annual reports.) Sometimes versions of the globe or maps of the world make up the dominant image. Other times the cover is built around images of the company's holdings in different countries. In 2008, it featured two nearly overlapping circular lines, and text that reads "Across the Globe, A Billion Times a Day We Capture Imaginations and Open Minds." In News Corp's 2009 annual report (Disney's hadn't been released as of this writing), the global images were in the shape of round lights from a television studio with images of continents on flat-panel monitors.

News Corporation's insistence on a global identity has strong roots in the firm's past. News Corporation Ltd is an American company with origins in Australia. Its CEO and majority stockholder is Rupert Murdoch, a man well known for his tenacity in achieving his goals. One small example: during the late 1980s, when he was building the Fox television network in the United States, Murdoch purchased Metromedia's chain of television stations. In the process, he came up against a federal law prohibiting non-U.S. citizens from owning more than a small percentage of a U.S. broadcast station. The Federal Communications Commission (FCC) had long interpreted this law as barring non-U.S. companies from indirectly owning or controlling more than 25 percent of a television station. Because he could not convince Congress to change the law, Murdoch took the next logical step: he abandoned his Australian citizenship and with great fanfare became an American citizen so that he could purchase U.S. television stations and build his TV empire.

Before the 1980s, News Corporation's financial strength came from its collection of powerful newspapers in Australia and the United Kingdom. By the mid-1990s, Murdoch had transformed the print-oriented Australian company into a multimedia firm with worldwide clout. Murdoch's major goal for the conglomerate, as stated in both the company's 2000 and 2006 annual reports, is "transformation"—to continue reshaping the firm so that it has a leadership position in the new global cross-media economy. In 2008, he used the term a bit differently, pointing to the "revolutionary changes" that, he said, "have shaped our world and transformed our company." News Corporation's activities respond directly to the trends toward media fragmentation and digital convergence that we discussed in Chapter 5. News Corporation also follows the trends regarding audience segmentation, globalization, conglomeration, and the distribution of products across media boundaries.

Murdoch is quite aware of the increased number of audiovisual channels that are competing to stand out in the marketplace, the fragmented audiences that result from giving people so many channel choices, and the increasingly global and computer-based nature of the media business. "Advances in technology are changing the means of delivering content and the very character of content itself," he asserts in the "Chief Executive's Review" in the 2008 annual report. "[I]ncreased speeds of

Table 6.2 News Corporation Holdings, 2009

Filmed Entertainment

United States

Fox Filmed Entertainment

- Twentieth Century Fox Film Corporation
- Fox 2000 Pictures
- Fox Searchlight Pictures
- Fox Music
- Twentieth Century Fox Home Entertainment
- Twentieth Century Fox Licensing and Merchandising
- Blue Sky Studios
- Twentieth Century Fox Television
- Fox Television Studios
- Twentieth Television

Latin America

Canal Fox

Television

United States

Fox Broadcasting Company

MyNetworkTV

Fox Television Stations

- WNYW New York City
- WWOR New York City
- KTTV Los Angeles
- KCOP Los Angeles
- WFLD Chicago
- WPWR Chicago
- WTXF Philadelphia
- KDFW Dallas
- KDFI Dallas
- WFXT Boston
- WAGA Atlanta
- WTTG Washington DC
- WDCA Washington DC
- WJBK Detroit
- KRIV Houston
- KTXH Houston

- KSAZ Phoenix
- KUTP Phoenix
- WTVT Tampa Bay
- KMSP Minneapolis
- WFTC Minneapolis
- WRBW Orlando
- WOFL Orlando
- WUTB Baltimore
- WHBQ Memphis
- KTBC Austin
- WOGX Gainesville

Asia

STAR

StarPlus

STAR One

STAR Chinese Channel

STAR World

STAR Utsav

Vijay

Xing Kong

STAR Chinese Movies

STAR Movies

STAR Gold

STAR News 26%

STAR Ananda 26%

STAR Majha 26%

Channel [V]

Channel [V] Thailand 49%

ESPN STAR Sports 50%

STAR Jupiter 81%

Phoenix Satellite Television 18%

Australia and New Zealand

Premium Movie Partnership 20%

Cable Network Programming

United States

Fox News Channel

FOX Business Network

Fox Cable Networks

- FX

Fox Movie Channel

Fox Regional Sports Networks

Fox Soccer Channel

SPEED

FUEL TV

FSN

Fox Reality Channel

Fox College Sports

Fox International Channels

Big Ten Network 49%

Fox Pan American Sports 33%

National Geographic Channel—Domestic 67%

National Geographic Channel—Latin America 52%

National Geographic Channel—Europe 52%

STATS 50%

Australia

Premier Media Group 50%

Latin America

LAPTV 55%

Telecine 13%

Fox Telecolombia 51%

Direct Broadcast

Satellite Television

Europe

SKY Italia

- Sky Sport
- Sky Calcio
- Sky Cinema
- Sky TG24

British Sky Broadcasting 39%

- Artsworld
- Sky News
- Sky Sports
- Sky Travel
- Sky One
- Sky Movies

Sky Deustchland 38%

Asia

TATA SKY 20%

Hathway Cable and Datacom 22%

Australia and New Zealand

FOXTEL 25%

Sky Network Television Limited 44%

Newspapers and Information Services

United States

The Wall Street Journal

Dow Jones Newswires

Dow Jones Indexes

Factiva

Barron's

MarketWatch

Dow Jones Financial Information Services

Dow Jones Client Solutions

Dow Jones Local Media Group

SmartMoney 50%

New York Post

Community Newspaper Group

Europe

The Times

The Sunday Times

The Sun

News of the World

thelondonpaper

The Wall Street Journal (Europe)

STOXX 33%

eFinancialNews

The Times Literary Supplement

Australia

The Australian

The Weekend Australian

The Daily Telegraph

The Sunday Telegraph

Herald Sun

Table 6.2 Continued

Sunday Herald Sun	**Papua New Guinea**	Other	**Europe**
The Courier-Mail	*Post Courier* 63%	**United States**	NDS 49%
Sunday Mail (Brisbane)	**Magazines and Inserts**	Fox Interactive Media	London Property News 58%
The Advertiser	**United States and Canada**	MySpace	Globrix 50%
Sunday Mail (Adelaide)	News America Marketing Group	IGN Entertainment	BrandAlley UK 49%
The Mercury	In-Store	Fox Audience Network	News Outdoor Group
mX	*FSI* (SmartSource Magazine)	RottenTomatoes	News Corporation Stations Europe
Sunday Tasmanian	SmartSource iGroup	AskMen	Multimedia Holdings 50%
The Sunday Times	News Marketing Canada	FoxSports.com	milkround.com
Northern Territory News	**Books**	Scout	**Australia and New Zealand**
Sunday Territorian	United States, Canada, Europe, New Zealand, and Australia	WhatIfSports	National Rugby League 50%
Asia	HarperCollins Publishers	kSolo	News Digital Media
The Wall Street Journal Asia	**Asia**	Flektor	Rugby Union
The Far Eastern Economic Review	HarperCollins India 40%	Photobucket	realestate.com.au 58%
Fiji		Fox Mobile Entertainment	**Asia**
The Fiji Times		hulu 32%	STAR DEN 50%
Sunday Times		Slingshot Labs	

Source: New Corporation 2009 Annual Report.

delivery have meant, for example, the popularization of video on the internet and a fundamental shift in the role of the mobile phone. These changes are providing remarkable opportunities for our Company around the world." The 2009 review was more somber, reflecting that during the year News Corp had to deal with both the cyclical impact of a terrible economy and the structural impact of a digital environment with low advertising rates (because of high competition among many sites) and fragmenting audiences that resist paying for online news and entertainment. In Murdoch's words, 2009 "was among the most challenging in our Company's 56-year history. The entire media industry is not only coping with the global recession but, at the same time, learning to navigate some of the most profound shifts to our business models in decades." Turning optimistic, he wrote, "I see a great opportunity to grow the business over the next few years by sticking to our core principle: News Corporation is a creative media company that attracts and retains customers by giving them the news and entertainment that they value."

A list of some of the conglomerate's holdings suggests the extent and manner in which News Corporation is moving toward that goal internationally. The company owns part or all of the subsidiaries listed in Table 6.2. In terms of media power, they range from the quite local (a television station in Philadelphia) to the national (the U.K.'s *Sunday Times*) to the international (Twentieth Century Fox).

Three Main Strategies

News Corporation's holdings will undoubtedly have changed by the time you're reading this. Even in tough economic times, media conglomerates continually add to their holdings when companies that match their strategic plans come on the market, and they sell firms that are not performing well or that no longer match the executives' vision for the company.

The point here is not to be absolutely precise about what the company owns. Rather, it is to identify the key strategies that News Corporation's management is using in its bid to establish media platforms through which to distribute its content globally. Three strategies, in particular, stand out:

- Continue to build strength in the internet and other new digital realms
- Nurture diverse global channels of distribution
- Emphasize entertainment, news, and sports in ways that will encourage paying audiences

Let's look at these strategies one at a time.

CONTINUE TO BUILD STRENGTH IN THE INTERNET AND OTHER NEW DIGITAL REALMS   The centerpiece of Murdoch's message in News Corporation's 2008 annual report is what he calls "our core strategy" that is "both global and digital." News Corp has been building the digital part of the strategy since its 2005 purchase of MySpace.com and other internet properties (for example the IGN gaming site) and folding them together with Fox Sports Interactive into a division called Fox Interactive Media (FIM). The 2008 annual report noted proudly that FIM "has a portfolio that contains many of the internet's most popular websites and reached 186 million unique visitors in June 2008—the largest global audience of any major media company." Those numbers have since changed. FIM has had its "uniques" eclipsed by Google sites (including YouTube) as well as by Facebook, and MySpace has been struggling to redefine itself as a go-to music site. Nevertheless, Murdoch's statement indicates the importance he places on leadership in this digital domain. A way News Corp is investing in its future, he states,

> is by using the revenues from our established enterprises to feed the growth of new enterprises. Fox Interactive Media is a good example of this evolution. In less than three years, it has become nearly a billion dollar business. Clearly, we're still in the early stages of figuring out the best ways to translate its huge potential into advertising revenue, but we are encouraged by what we see.

In addition, the company's 2008 annual report presents two other aims for its involvement in the digital realm. One is to extend News Corporation's operations beyond the Web to cellphones and other digital devices. As we noted in Chapter 5, the term "digital" extends far beyond the internet. It refers to any media that carry messages in the language of bits that computers speak. When materials are transmitted digitally, or can be translated into digital format, they can be made compatible with the Web and with a range of other mobile and stationary technologies. Stationary technologies include electronic boards in stores, malls, and on streets; think of electronic signs in places such as Times Square. Mobile examples include cellphones, personal digital assistants (PDAs), cellphones that include PDAs (these are often called smartphones), and handheld multimedia players such as the iPod. News Corporation understands these changes, Murdoch contends, and the company is acting to move its content across them. So, for example, it is making investments that allow readers to get the firm's *Wall Street Journal* wherever they need it—"whether in print, on the web, through a mobile phone, or a new device." Similarly, the annual report mentions that News Corp's Harper Collins trade book subsidiary "launched a 'browse inside' feature for Apple's popular iPhone, giving mobile readers a chance to preview many of our most popular titles." And it boasts that FIM "launched ad-supported mobile (WAP) sites for each of its core brands, signing mobile distribution deals with every major carrier in the world last year."

The 2009 annual report is not as celebratory about the firm's digital properties, but it nevertheless reinforces the principle that News Corporation must move its creative products into the new technological world. "We believe there are no forms of media too old to thrive or too young to take off," Murdoch writes. He adds:

> The teenager in Shanghai watching his favorite show on his mobile device and the 50-year-old investment banker in Los Angeles using hers to look for market updates have one thing in common: they want the news and entertainment that reflects their particular interests . . . they want it when they want it . . . and they want it delivered on the platforms most convenient for their individual lifestyles.

NURTURE DIVERSE GLOBAL CHANNELS OF DISTRIBUTION   As the above quote suggests, Murdoch believes that power in the digital space places a new twist on the importance of distribution. Being able to attract large audiences on the Web and elsewhere in the digital environment will truly give News Corporation the possibility of the global audience's eyes that it has always sought. The 2008 report reflects confidently that,

> Across the globe, a billion times a day, we capture imaginations and open minds to new ideas and new outlooks, new ways of perceiving the world around us in more than 100 countries and 30 languages across six continents through film, television, cable, satellite, newspapers, magazines, books and digital media.

The 2009 report, less boastful, underscores the importance of international activities to News Corporation's future. Murdoch notes the hiring of former AOL head Jonathan Miller in the new position of chief digital officer with the responsibility for the company's "global digital portfolio . . . leading a company-wide effort to establish a new economic model to transition all of our print properties to a profitable digital future." He underscores that this activity is indeed global:

News Corporation's Rupert Murdoch, left, and Disney's Robert Iger talk during an annual media conference in Sun Valley, Idaho.

> In developing nations such as India and China, hundreds of millions of people are entering the middle class and becoming consumers of news and entertainment. Around the world, people constantly and rightly demand more and better—whether it be high-definition video recorders to watch their favorite movies at home, news delivered to their mobile devices, a television channel devoted to the particular team or sport they follow, or the new 3-D film technologies that will find their way eventually to television. This new digital world is an enormous opportunity, and we continue to change News Corporation to take advantage of it.

Apart from a highly optimistic vision of News Corp's future power because of digital technology, Murdoch's words reflect the primary ability that his company has always sought: clout over distribution. The central images on the front page of the firm's corporate website during winter 2009, for example, were logos of the company's global properties—Twentieth Century Fox movie studio, Sky TV satellite platform, *The Times*, and the Australian newspapers and many more. Murdoch places great emphasis on the power of his company's worldwide distribution capabilities—even greater than the emphasis that Disney's Robert Iger places on his company's distribution channels. Although distribution is certainly important to Iger, his message seems to be that Disney content is so good that every distributor will want to carry it. From Murdoch's point of view, controlling the satellite platforms and TV networks to make sure News Corp content gets a chance to be seen or heard around the world is critical, no matter how good the content. The perspective is quite different from the one we saw in Iger's letter about Disney, in which attention to content outweighed attention to distribution. The different emphases reflect different historical and contemporary strengths of the two conglomerates.

EMPHASIZE ENTERTAINMENT, NEWS, AND SPORTS IN WAYS THAT WILL ENCOURAGE PAYING AUDIENCES   Still, Rupert Murdoch is well aware that it is the content that material firms distribute that helps News Corporation remain competitive and grow. That explains the conglomerate's third strategy: identifying popular entertainment, news, and sports content, and pumping them through those distribution channels. Although Disney notes the same three types of content on its website and in Iger's letter, its main corporate focus is clearly on family entertainment. News Corporation doesn't emphasize one genre over the other. The website and annual report remind the reader that News Corporation does have some mighty

Fox Sports is an important component of Rupert Murdoch's strategy to remain competitive.

popular brands of content in each area, from *American Idol,* to *Wolverine,* to Fox News, to collaborations with *National Geographic*.

Murdoch's 2009 "Letter" does address an issue that lies at the heart of his firm's struggle with content in the digital age. He also knows that his stockholders worry that the company's extensive newspaper holdings are particularly vulnerable to the long-term drop in U.S. readership, the difficulty of demanding high advertising rates for online news because of competition, and the skepticism that audiences will pay for news online because they have so many free choices. In the 2009 annual report, he confronts this issue directly. He trumpets the strong circulations of the firm's newspapers in Australia and the United Kingdom. At the same time, he acknowledges that the new economic realities of the digital age mean that newspapers can no longer rely on advertising to pay "all the bills." He adds that, "In addition to carrying advertising successful newspapers of the future will charge for their content . . . . Within the industry, people have come to recognize that when you give your hard-earned copyright away for free, you are undermining your ability to produce good journalism." He points out that his company's *Wall Street Journal* has been successfully charging for online access to most of its material and he says he would like to use that as a model for the firm's other less specialized news properties. He does not say precisely how he will do it; it's an issue that also bedevils his counterparts in many newspaper firms. He does note, though, "In the future, we see subscribers paying modest fees to get the news they want delivered in a way that is most convenient for their lifestyles—and we believe the more specialized the news, the less modest the fees." And he says that "Our pay-TV business in Europe is a good example of what we need to do in other parts of the Company: provide consumers with premium products and advanced technology they cannot get elsewhere for a subscription."

Google

During 2009, Rupert Murdoch and other news publishers spoke out loudly against Google. "Why?" you might ask. Isn't Google's search engine the vehicle through which people actually find information on the websites of News Corporation and other firms? It is probably the case that News Corporation has found what other large companies that own websites have seen: a substantial proportion of internet users do not come to their websites by directly typing in the Web address (for example http://www.newyorkpost.com). Rather, they do it by going to a Web search engine's site, typing in the topics they want to find, and sometimes ending up at a News Corporation site such as the *New York Post*. "How can that be a problem for News Corporation?" you might ask. The answer lies in the great power not just over search but over information aggregation and advertising that Google has amassed in just over a decade of its existence. Let's explain by exploring the basics of Google's business.

It starts with the search engine. A **Web search engine** is an information retrieval system designed to help find information on the World Wide Web. You undoubtedly use a Web search engine every day. So how would you use it to find the names of the people in TV's animated *Simpsons* family on Fox television? One way is to go to a search engine and type "Simpsons Fox Television" into the search box. Do it on Google (at http://www.google.com) and several links will appear that send you to online places with the information. The first three links, it turns out, lead to News Corporation sites (www.thesimpsons.com, http://www.fox.com, and http://www.fox.com/schedule).

If you ask most people to conduct a Web search, the chances are that they will use Google. Even though there are many other Web search engines—Yahoo, AltaVista,

Web search engine an information retrieval system designed to help find information on the World Wide Web

http://www.google.com

Lycos, Dogpile are just a few—Google is by all accounts the dominant one. The comScore Web analysis company estimated that in late 2009 Google attracted over 64 percent of all search requests in the United States; some estimates say the percentage is even higher and that Google is even stronger in other countries.[6] (In China, Google fell to a far number two and then left the country in 2010 because of a controversy it said related to Chinese censorship and government-instigated hacking; see World View box.) Google doesn't charge users for searching. But because it brings so many people worldwide to the advertising it shows them, Google has been raking in money. Its revenue in 2009 was about $22 billion, and its stock market value (the number of shares multiplied by the shares' value) in early 2010 was around $191 billion—about 8.7 times revenues.[7]

Contrasted with firms at the very top of the media food chain, Google's take was substantial but not dominating. News Corp's 2009 revenues, for example, were $25 billion. Yet News Corp's early 2009 market value of about $36.46 billion was only 1.5 times its annual revenues. That Google's was so much higher indicates that Wall Street clearly felt that the company has much more growth in it than does News Corporation. And many marveled that a company founded in 1998 took just a few years to become, in the words of one writer, "a tech and media titan."[8]

Three Main Strategies

But although Google is a household name in many places around the world, it is quite likely that many people don't really understand how the company makes its money and sees its strategies for growth. The aim of the next several paragraphs is to help you begin to understand that. The reason for the exploration is to help make you more literate about the important influence that Google is exerting on the direction of the media system, as well as on society. As with News Corp and Disney, you can get a sense of that influence by reading the company's annual reports and its website. The following three strategies are suggested by those sources as well as information from a wide-ranging tracking of Google and its activities over its short life:

■ Continue to improve the global attractiveness of the search engine
■ Expand Google's advertising activities to as many media as possible
■ Create non-search products that will keep users coming back despite competition

Let's take them one at a time.

CONTINUE TO IMPROVE THE GLOBAL ATTRACTIVENESS OF THE SEARCH ENGINE Google's 2008 "Letter from the Founders" says it quite concisely: "Search remains at the very core of what we do at Google, just as it has been from our earliest days." The desire for a better Web search is what got Larry Page and Sergey Brin energized to start the company in 1998; today it is Web users' preference for Google that allows the company to serve billions of ads to them and make billions of dollars. Brin and Page's central insight when they created Google involved the ranking of website results after the search. They reasoned that, when it came to a search term, the best sites were those that used the term and were linked by other sites. According to this view, the best sites are ones nominated by other sites. The more link nominations a site with the term received, the more that site deserved to be ranked highly.

Now, this approach to ranking websites certainly has its shortcomings. For one thing, it privileges sites that have been around long enough to have developed a lot of link nominations. Fascinating but newer sites relevant to the search term would not show up as highly. Another drawback is that it implies that popularity means credibility and accuracy, which may or may not be the case. A third difficulty is that people can try to rig rankings by trying to make sure that their sites link to a particular site they want to see high up on ratings when a particular word is entered into the search engine. Despite these drawbacks and others that we'll discuss in the chapter on the internet, Google works very well for most people. The company continues to hire additional computer programmers to improve its operation. Brin and Page noted in their 2008 letter that,

> In the past year alone we have made 359 changes to our web search—nearly one per day. Some are not easy to spot, such as changes in ranking based on personalization (launched broadly in 2005) but they are important in getting the most relevant search results. Others are very easy to see and improve search efficiency in a very clear way, such as spelling correction, annotations, and suggestions.

WORLD VIEW
GOOGLE IN CHINA

In light of Google's decision to censor search results in China, some are questioning just how closely the company adheres to its motto: Don't Be Evil. Faced with what amounted to a choice between omitting objectionable material and pulling out of the Chinese search engine race entirely, Mountain View, a California-based company, made what Google officials described as an excruciating decision to stay online at the expense of providing free access to content.

Initially, searches on Google.cn, the official Google China site, were slowed or blocked because the company didn't provide adequate barriers to information the communist government deemed inappropriate. Consequently, in an attempt to tap into the market of several hundred million Chinese Web users, Google agreed to restrict access to such subjects as Taiwan's independence and the 1989 Tiananmen Square massacre. As a result, when a user attempts to access blocked subject matter, he is alerted that the information he is seeking has been removed. The search engine hopes that, in spite of these restrictions, Google.cn will become the most popular search engine in the world's largest country.

Many outside observers, however, are extremely concerned by the precedent, "This is a real shame," said Julien Pain, head of Reporters Without Borders' internet desk. "When a search engine collaborates with the government like this, it makes it much easier for the Chinese government to control what is being said on the Internet." Google wasn't the only internet company Reporters Without Borders took issue with, as the media watchdog contended that similarly problematic decisions were made by Yahoo and MSN.com when they entered the Chinese market.

Even so, China isn't the only country that mandates some restrictions to internet access. In France and Germany, for example, Google agreed to censor references to Nazi paraphernalia, as is required by French and German law. In both those countries, however, internet users have access to Google mail. That service is not provided to Google users in China, out of concern that the Chinese government would order the search engine to turn over personal information. This fear is warranted; in 2005, Yahoo turned over the private email account information of a Chinese journalist to the communist government, a decision that was widely criticized as it ultimately led to the journalist being jailed.

Source: *Associated Press*, "Google Spells Censorship in China," *Wired*, January 24, 2006.

MEDIA PROFILE
GOOGLE FOUNDERS SERGEY BRIN AND LARRY PAGE

Google founders Sergey Brin (left) and Larry Page (right).

The rise of internet search behemoth Google is in many ways a classic Cinderella story: it was developed in the college dormitory of Stanford students Sergey Brin and Larry Page and launched from their friend's basement. Within a few years, the brainchild of these middle-class suburbanites had grown to become the world's most popular search engine.

Page, the son of a computer science professor and a computer programming teacher, claims to have fallen in love with computers at the age of six. Not surprisingly, then, he earned his Bachelor's degree from the University of Michigan with a concentration on computer engineering. Brin also seems to have inherited his scientific skill set: his father was a mathematician economist. As a child, he emigrated with his family from Moscow and went on to earn a Bachelor's degree in mathematics and computer science from the University of Maryland at College Park.

Page and Brin met in 1995 at Stanford University, where each was pursuing a computer science doctorate.

Working from their dorm rooms, they developed a new type of search system that listed results based on popularity. In 1998, they ended up putting their doctorates on hold so that they could launch their system commercially. They decided to name it Google after the mathematical term "Googol," which describes a one followed by a hundred zeros.

Now, more than a decade later, Google has achieved unprecedented growth as a search provider and is a recognized leader in the software, technology, and advertising service industries. Its string of recent acquisitions includes online video streaming site YouTube and internet ad service provider DoubleClick.

Google Inc. employs more than 10,000 people worldwide and has been ranked by Fortune magazine as the number one best company to work for. Particularly well known is the company headquarters—known as the Googleplex—which features a gym, two swimming pools, several cafeterias, and a lobby decorated with a piano and lava lamps.

Both Page and Brin remain deeply involved with the company as president of products and president of technology, respectively. And despite their company's unabashed success, they like to show that their daily lives invoke Google's more humble beginnings. Until recently, Page and Brin each owned a Toyota Prius; and, in 2007, Brin admitted that he continues to shop at Costco.

Sources: Will Smale, "Profile: The Google Founders," *BBC News*, April 30, 2004. http://news.bbc.co.uk (accessed August 2, 2010); Google Company website, http://www.google.com (accessed August 2, 2010).

A key point Brin and Page make is that "One of the most striking changes that has happened in the past few years is that search results are no longer just web pages." They note their the company is hard at work trying to maximize search results for people who want to know what's in videos (it owns the video site YouTube), for people who want to chart and learn about local geographies and businesses (through Google Earth, for example), and for mobile devices (where one can search both on a mobile-optimized Google page or through voice by phoning 1800-GOOG411). Because of its potential worldwide reach via the internet and a belief that everybody who uses the Web needs to have a way to search it, Google sees itself as a global firm. The Google website says, "We strive to provide our services to everyone in the world."

And, in fact, the Google interface is available in 120 languages. Google News provides an automated collection of frequently updated news stories in twenty-four languages aimed at sixty-four international audiences. The company also offers automatic translation of content between various languages and provides localized versions of Google in many developing countries. Employees outside the United States now make up around one-third of the company, based in such cities as Beijing, Dublin, Trondheim, Istanbul, Tel Aviv, Copenhagen, Vienna, Taipei, Warsaw, Haifa, Moscow, St Petersburg, Sydney, Mumbai, Cairo, and Delhi. International sources constituted 51 percent of Google's revenues in 2008.

EXPAND GOOGLE'S ADVERTISING ACTIVITIES TO AS MANY MEDIA AS POSSIBLE   About 97 percent of Google's revenues come from advertising. That is an enormous percentage—far higher than the proportion of money Disney and Fox make from ads compared with sources such as subscriptions and ticket purchases. The revenue source underscores what a lot of people do not understand about Google: the company is fundamentally in the business of serving advertisements to people based upon evidence it collects about who they are, what they care about, and what they might do. Its primary business involves serving those ads to people in two types of Web locations. The first location is its search engine. Businesses bid to have Google place their text ads next to Google's search findings on particular words. Say you sell binoculars, and you want to advertise it to Google users. You may bid a certain amount of money for a text ad linked to your binoculars website to appear (that is, to be served) when a person types the word "binoculars" into Google's search engine box. If Google accepts your bid, you must agree to pay each time a person clicks on your ad. Google calls this activity its AdWords program. Quite different is Google's AdSense advertising program. That involves thousands of websites not owned by Google who agree to allow Google to place ("serve") advertisements on their sites' pages in return for sharing the revenues. As with AdWords, Google accepts bids on words from advertisers who want to advertise on sites that are relevant to those words. Google's computers scan the many pages on the thousands of websites and, based on special formulas, determine what pages on what sites are most relevant to those words. That is where the text ads for those words show up. As with AdWords, advertisers pay based on the number of clicks on Google's ads. We'll discuss this further in the chapter on advertising.

This process may sound complex, and it is—by design. The reason: Google is constantly trying to perfect its understanding of the conditions under which people who enter particular search words or who go to particular sites are likely to click on text ads. That has led the company to record and analyze the activities of tens of millions of users without their knowing they are being tracked. Often, Google has personal information about them (for example, if they registered for Gmail) and sometimes it does not. These analytical procedures have two purposes. One is that they help Google to refine its search strategy. The company can learn, for example, how people with certain interests search compared with people with other interests. Just as important, Google's analyses of its users' activities can help the firm to refine its advertising serving model. Google is quite secretive about its activities in this area. It seems clear from various close observers of the company that its statisticians are continually trying to associate user activities and backgrounds to their clicking on ads and even completing transactions (such as buying things). Using special tracking files called cookies and other technologies, the company seems to be constructing enormous databases about its users. It has personal information about many of them through their registration with Google products such as Gmail and iGoogle, which gives users personalized search results in turn for allowing Google to store their web-surfing histories. But even those who are anonymous to Google still contribute enormously to its knowledge about how they act in searching and toward text ads on websites. Google's goal seems to be predicting whether a particular individual from a particular region with particular characteristics and search history would be more responsive to one type of ad for one type of product over another type of ad for another type of product.

The company's business, then, involves not just serving advertising. It involves serving advertising in ways that are guided by databases about the users. Until fairly recently, both the AdWords and AdSense programs involved text-only announcements, with links to the advertiser's website or mobile application. That is changing; Google now allows pictorial and video ads in AdSense and is experimenting with that in AdWords. The company's YouTube subsidiary carries video commercials as well. These changes parallel Google's 2007 purchase of DoubleClick, a leader in helping companies serve nontext advertisements (called "display ads") across the Web. Although Google has competitors in this database-driven ad-serving business— Yahoo and Microsoft are two—Google is by far the dominant player in the large and lucrative area of search advertising on the Web. But the company's executives don't want to stop there. As they see it, the company should be able to take the database-guided ad-serving approaches it uses with the Web and apply them to serve ads to other media. Google is already serving ads to mobile phones and video games as well as to a number of cable networks owned by NBC Universal. Attempts to carry this activity into the radio and newspaper industries were not successful. Perhaps the company will try again. In their 2006 "Letter from the Founders," Brin and Page wrote that "Our goal is to create a single and complete advertising system," and the company's activities on so many different areas suggest they are serious.

Google's collection of data about its users in order to make decisions about serving ads makes many privacy advocates nervous. One worry is that the personal data Google has collected about the interests of millions of people might be used to give some people more rewards (better discount coupons, free access to websites others pay for) than others because of the way Google has interpreted its data about them. Another concern is that the information may get into the wrong hands and be interpreted in a way that could harm individuals. For example, leaked information about the diseases a particular person searches for on the websites about psychological problems that a person frequents might lead health advertisers or malicious spammers to bother the person. Certain leaked information about someone's click and search behavior may even make it difficult for the person to get health insurance coverage. The company argues that it abides by all laws about handling people's information wherever it operates, but that still hasn't stopped critics from worrying that its databases may cause individuals harm. We will deal with the issue of database privacy in some detail in Chapter 14's discussion of the internet and related digital media.

CREATE PRODUCTS THAT WILL KEEP USERS COMING BACK DESPITE COMPETITION   All the material about AdWords, AdSense, DoubleClick ad-serving, and databases is not quite what Google executives want their users to hear. The public rhetoric of the company centers on the usefulness of its search engine and its related mission to "organize the world's information."[9] When Google does discuss its advertising business, it is as a secondary activity and in a way that makes it sound almost like a public service, explaining that its "relevant" advertising "makes the advertising useful to you as well as to the advertiser placing it."[10] Of course, a really big question must have occurred to Google's leadership: What would happen to Google's advertising if another company discovered a better way to search for information and the number of people using Google (or the number of times they came to Google) began to decrease? It's a critical question, because advertisers expect websites or Web networks to deliver huge numbers of people so that even the narrow segments of the audience they want to reach (for example, pregnant women who live in London) will contain very many individuals. A progressive slide in audience may lead advertisers to move on to sites that have more "scale" (that is, larger populations) and seem to be on the upswing in popularity.

One way that Google tries to avoid such a doomsday scenario (for a firm so heavily dependent on ads) is to pour enormous amounts of money to support talented people and cutting edge technologies that continually improve the chances that individuals get exactly the materials they would want to see and hear when they search. Eric Schmidt, Google's CEO, told the *Financial Times* in 2007 that the goal is to maximize the personal information it holds about its users so that they will feel comfortable asking the search engine "What should I do tomorrow?" and "What job should I take?"[11] Another way to keep the huge scale of its user population is to create technologies and services that may be hard for competitors to duplicate and that would encourage people to keep coming back even after they considered that a different search engine could give them better results. Google, for example, is reputed to be using its enormous revenue to build a network of computer servers that is bigger than that of any other company. Positioned around the world, their purpose is to make sure users always think of Google when they want lightning-fast results.

Making sure that users will always be able to reach out to Google has led the company to take a number of technological and policy steps relating to mobile phones that may have seemed out of step with the firm's typical business. Google's leaders realized that search, website, and social-media activities, as well as the advertising that relates to them, will become huge businesses in the mobile phone arena as more and more people buy "smartphones" that give them the ability to connect to the internet while on the move. The problem for Google is that carriers such as Verizon and AT&T exert enormous control over the mobile phone environment, even to the extent of determining what kinds of software by what firms to place on the handsets and what services people can receive. Google didn't want to be in the position of being held back by those firms, and so it took a number of policy and technology initiatives.

▦ For example, in the policy area, it supported an initiative to use "white spaces"—the unused frequencies between television channels—for wireless broadband, and it offered to help administer a database technology that would move the initiative forward. Although Google couched its activities in a "general belief in the potential for this spectrum to revolutionize wireless broadband," the company clearly sees the spectrum as a way to get around the phone companies that now control the mobile spectrum.[12] Larry Page even proposed that "spectrum could be auctioned off by the government on a real-time basis (similar to Google's ad auction), allowing devices and consumers to use spectrum as they need it."[13] Google is betting that, under these circumstances, many users would go to Google as their starting point for navigating the mobile environment.

▦ In the technology area, Google bought the Android mobile operating system and with a consortium of forty-seven hardware, software, and telecommunication companies announced that Android's standards for mobile devices would be "open"—that is, companies could learn the source code and, after applying for a free license, create applications for it without getting permission from phone companies or anyone else. That helped Google, as handset firms started turning out Android phones with software that featured Google's search engine and other tools quite prominently.

▦ Also in the technology area, Google released the Nexus One, a smartphone that uses the Android operating system. The handset is available unlocked to let users choose from among wireless providers. Selling a phone unlocked has not been common in the United States, and, although Nexus One could really work with only two U.S. carriers (it was not compatible with AT&T, for example), it did move forward Google's philosophy that carriers should not control the mobile environment. Google also said at the U.S. press launch that it was selling the phone through the Web to make it simpler for consumers to buy an Android phone. Clearly, though, the company's goal was to get mobile users to work with Google software, and the ads that come along with it. As the Google executive responsible for Android noted, the company expected to make "some margins on retail sales, but our primary business is still advertising."[14]

When Google released Nexus One, some commentators contended that Google was in danger of losing a sense of what it was, or spreading itself too thin, or looking for new businesses out of a fear that companies might best it in search. Others, however, made the point that we're making here: that Google's activities in other lines of business were not a way to get away from their search roots. As a consultant put it, "Quite the contrary, I see their other products as a way for them to capture more user eyes and time, which furthers their position as the dominant web advertising company."[15] The programs that aim to capture those eyes and time (and which

CRITICAL CONSUMER
THE POWER OF SOCIAL SEARCH

Social search refers to a feature that allows a person to conduct a basic internet search in which the results are prioritized based on the interactions that person has with other internet users. For example, if you were thinking about taking white water kayaking lessons, you would use a search engine to find prospective courses or teachers. At the same time, the search engine would check your friends' blogs, social networking profiles, and favorite Web pages to find out if any of your friends had a similar interest. The same logic would work for restaurant recommendations, book reviews, and travel information. Though there has been some experimentation with social search, no site has really perfected the logic.

In 2010, Google added the Buzz feature to all active Gmail accounts in an attempt to introduce a social component to its capabilities. Google, however, experienced backlash from users and commentators concerned about the privacy implications of automatically giving the people in one's address book access to their activities around the Web. Google had assumed that the people you email on a regular basis are the same people you would want to have access to your information updates, pictures, and blog posts. Turns out, Google got it wrong.

Although Google is the master of internet search, the incident with Buzz suggests that the internet giant has

not gotten its head around the logic of online social networking. Facebook, by contrast, is the most popular social networking site in a number of countries including the United States and Canada. Although many people use Facebook to communicate with friends, make social arrangements, and connect with old and new acquaintances, Facebook is not a widely used site for information searches.

But what if these two popular sites teamed up? Imagine that, when you searched for hotels in New York City, you were presented with a list of standard search results followed by information about your friends who live, work, or vacation in NYC. Imagine that this information also included pictures that friends had taken of NYC and a number of restaurant recommendations. Google has the search power to make this happen. Facebook has the data. By teaming up, Google and Facebook could revolutionize online searches by making them social.

Do think that would be a good thing?

Source: E. Schonfeld, "The Future of Social Search (Or Why Google Should Buy Facebook)," *TechCrunch*, December 28, 2008. http://techcrunch.com/2008/12/28/the-future-of-social-search-or-why-google-should-buy-facebook/ (accessed August 2, 2010).

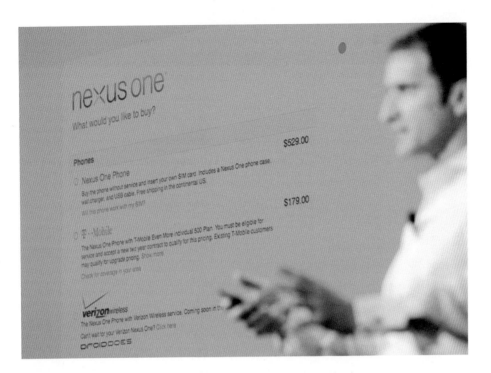

Mario Queiroz, vice president of product management for Google Inc., holds up the Nexus One touch-screen mobile phone during a news conference in 2010. The Nexus One uses the Android operating system and allows users to choose from among wireless providers.

not-so-incidentally allow Google to learn about people's habits) are numerous. The standouts include Gmail email service, the Google Voice phone service, the Chrome search engine, Google Docs and Spreadsheets (that allow someone to create, store, and share documents on the Web), and Google Books. Google Books is perhaps the most ambitious and controversial of these. It involves literally scanning millions of books in a number of major university libraries. The idea is not to release digital versions of the entire book onto the Web. Rather, Google intends to show users a few lines of the book that contain their search terms. In many cases, they would then get the book from the library or purchase it. Despite the small amount of the text that is revealed, some publisher and author groups believe that Google's act of scanning and storing the books infringes on their copyrights. Libraries worried that Google would maintain control over the price of "orphan" books that have no clear copyright owners, and retailers worried that Google would keep a stranglehold over the sales of such books. Eventually, though, Google hammered out agreements acceptable to most of those parties. The company undoubtedly realizes that this enormous project that involves so many resources and which risked a major lawsuit is an undertaking that will be unique in its scope. Consequently, it will be yet another facet of the firm that keeps people coming back even in the face of enormous competition.

After our discussion of Google's far-reaching businesses centered around search and serving ads, it becomes possible to understand why its activities get media executives such as Rupert Murdoch quite angry. They see Google fundamentally as an aggregator—a business that brings together links to content that News Corporation and others have spent loads of money producing. Google, they say, makes money off their firms' hard work simply by putting ads around links to their sources. Sometimes, the headlines or short abstracts that accompany the links (as with Google News) are enough so that readers don't even need to link. And even when people do click on the links, the executives argue, the amount of money the sites make by putting up ads to show those people is quite small—in large part because competition for advertising by Google and other aggregators (that is, search engines and sites that emphasize links to major media sites) has driven down the price. As you might imagine, Google executives deny that their work fundamentally involves poaching

Table 6.3 Google Inc. Acquisitions, 2001–2010

Year	Company/Product	Business Area
2001	Deja	Usenet
	Outride	Web search engine
2003	Pyra Labs	Weblog software
	Neotonic Software	Customer relationship management
	Applied Semantics	Online advertising
	Kaltix	Web search engine
	Sprinks	Online advertising
	Genius Labs	Blogging
2004	Ignite Logic	HTML editor
	BaiduA	Chinese language search engine
	Picasa	Image organizer
	ZipDash	Traffic analysis
	Where2	Map analysis
	Keyhole, Inc	Map analysis
2005	Urchin Software Corporation	Web analytics
	Dodgeball	Social networking service
	Reqwireless	Mobile browser
	Current Communications Group	Broadband internet access
	Android	Mobile software
	Skia	Graphics software
	Akwan Information Technologies	Search engines
	AOLB	Broadband internet access
	Phatbits	Widget engine
	allPAY GmbH	Mobile software
	bruNET GmbH	Mobile software
2006	dMarc Broadcasting	Advertising
	Measure Map	Weblog software
	Upstartle	Word processor
	@Last Software	3-D modeling software
	Orion	Web search engine
	2Web Technologies	Online spreadsheets
	Neven Vision	Computer vision
	YouTube	Video sharing
	JotSpot	Web application
	Endoxon	Mapping
2007	Xunlei	File sharing
	Adscape	In-game advertising
	Trendalyzer	Statistical software
	Tonic Systems	Presentation program

Table 6.3 Continued

	Marratech	Videoconferencing
	DoubleClick	Online advertising
	GreenBorder	Computer security
	Panoramio	Photo sharing
	FeedBurner	Web feed
	PeakStream	Parallel processing
	Zenter	Presentation program
	GrandCentral	Voice over internet protocol (VoIP)
	Image America	Aerial photography
	Postini	Communications security
	Zingku	Social network service
	Jaiku	Microblogging
2008	Omnisio	Online video
	TNC (Tatter and Company)	Weblog software
2009	On2	Video compression
	reCAPTCHA	Security
	AdMob	Mobile advertising
	Gizmo5	VoIP
	Teracent	Online advertising
	AppJet (EtherPad)	Collaborative real-time editor
2010	Aardvark	Social search
	reMail	Email search
	Picnik	Photo editing
	DocVerse	Microsoft Office files sharing site

Source: Wikipedia. http://en.wikipedia.org/wiki/List_of_acquisitions_by_Google (accessed March 26, 2010).

from production firms. In fact, they argue, Google organizes the Web for people so that they can find the sites that News Corporation and others put up. Google's leaders say that any media companies that do not want their sites listed by Google can simply tell the firm not to do it. So far, no one has taken them up on the offer. Still, the tension simmers, particular when it comes to newspaper sites that are having a tough time charging enough money for their ads to pay for the news work. The argument shows that big media firms often have clashing beliefs about where their best interests lie.

Media Literacy and Corporate Strategies

At this point in its short life, Google is only beginning to be and act like a conglomerate. It has made many acquisitions (see Table 6.3), but it has integrated almost all of them into the core of the company to help it increase its abilities with respect to searching and advertising. Moreover, virtually all of its revenues come from the Web.

Still, the company has begun to expand into other media through small subsidiaries that depart from the fixation on the Web. In not too many years, Google executives foresee their ability to serve ads across a variety of media. They may even help media firms decide what kinds of noncommercial content should be served to what people, based on those individuals' characteristics. These cross-media activities will likely be quite different from those of Disney and News Corporation, but Google's influence on the ads and even the content people see is nevertheless likely to be profound.

As we have seen in this chapter, media conglomerates are increasingly trying to find profits in the movement of products and ideas across media boundaries. More and more, executives are moving their targeted brands across media boundaries to pursue their customers in a highly competitive environment. The executives' mandate is to follow the consumers with their brand, expose the brand to new target consumers, and by doing so allow advertisers to reach certain types of consumers in as many places as possible. Even when media executives think they have good strategies for carrying out this and other mandates, they constantly re-examine their approaches to make sure they are moving in the best direction possible. That kind of continual rethinking takes place in small and midsized mass media companies, but it is especially common at all levels of major corporations such as News Corporation, Disney, and Google.

Cross-media strategies have become a major engine that drives the contemporary media system. Critics of media conglomerates argue that these activities are dangerous to society because they allow a small number of huge firms to dictate what society will see across its most important media channels. From a critical perspective, a blunt way to express what we have seen in this chapter is to say that many media channels today have become "retread" machines. Media firms see different mass media channels simply as new places to display their wares.

Consider the kind of database-guided personalization that we see particularly in Google, although—as we will see in forthcoming chapters—all companies and their advertisers are building audience databases and pursuing personalization technologies. We therefore ought to pay attention to these activities and try to think through how they might affect the media materials that we confront on a daily basis. It would seem that the more channels a company uses to send us news, information, and advertising, the more likely we are to notice that material. Similarly, the more materials we receive that reflect our individual interests, the more we are likely to pay attention. Critics further argue that the benefits of personalization across media channels are often outweighed by the problems of privacy that they bring.

How would you feel if you knew that the relevant material that you receive also means that you don't get offers and commercials and even programs that other people, with different data profiles, receive? As yet, this doesn't happen very often—though it does happen, as later chapters will show. In an era of so many cross-media activities and a fixation on a personalized media future, try to imagine the benefits of the opposite: a world in which different media were seen as unique, fresh ways to look at the world that surprised people because they offered views so different from what they would expect. Of course, as we have seen, the structure of media costs and opportunities makes the disentangling of these channels highly unlikely. As a media-literate person, however, you should consider alternatives and your opinion of them even if they do not presently seem realistic. You should realize, too, that you can't prove that media channels would be wildly different if cross-media activities ceased. Nevertheless, this sort of mind game does keep you asking the kinds of critical questions that can help you to understand better what does and doesn't exist in the mass media.

Cross-media activities and personalization activities are only two of the issues that we could tease out in thinking about media giants and their power. To keep your critical edge, it is important to consider what individuals and societies may not be receiving as a result of corporate power. Because we are so surrounded by the products of mass media industries, we may forget that very different alternatives can, and often do, exist. One goal of media literacy may be to think about alternatives, identify them, and then encourage media companies to pursue them. Trying to encourage change in the media is a tough challenge, but understanding the considerations that guide media firms in what they do is a crucial way to start.

Chapter Review

For an interactive chapter recap and study guide, visit the companion website for *Media Today* at http://www.routledge.com/textbooks/mediatoday4e.

Questions for Discussion and Critical Thinking

. . . .

1 In what ways are the News Corporation and Disney corporate strategies similar? In what ways are they different?
2 How is Google different from these media conglomerates?
3 Why are conglomerates increasingly concerned with moving their products globally as well as within their home countries?
4 Why are some social critics upset with media conglomerates?

Internet Resources

. . . .

The annual reports of media conglomerates online

The best way to find the corporate website of a media firm is to use a search engine such as Google, type the name of the company in parentheses, and add the word "corporate." So, for example, to get to the Sony Corporation's corporate website, go to Google or Yahoo and type "Sony corporate" into the search box. Once on the corporate site and directed to investor services, look for annual reports. You may need to click on the term "SEC filings" to get to them.

FreePress.net (http://www.freepress.net/docs/talk_radio.pdf)

The website states that "Free Press is a national, nonpartisan organization working to reform the media. Through education, organizing and advocacy, we promote diverse and independent media ownership, strong public media, and universal access to communications." Founded by professor and media activist Robert McChesney, it often presents strong critiques of the activities of media conglomerates.

Key Terms

. . . .

You can find the definitions to these key terms in the marginal glossary throughout this chapter. Test your knowledge of these terms with interactive flash cards on the *Media Today* companion website.

conglomerate 194	strategies 194
franchise 199	synergy 197
licensing 197	Web search engine 209
nodes 199	

Constructing Media Literacy

. . . .

1 How would you respond to the remark, "Google's business is search"?

2 How much of your media time in a typical day do you spend with material produced by Time Warner, Disney, Viacom, CBS, News Corporation, Sony, and Comcast? Try to keep track of what media you use and what companies own them. It isn't easy keeping track, and you may find it difficult to figure out the ownership of certain media—cable networks, for example. But the extent to which you rely on them might surprise you.

3 The next time you go to the movies, keep track of the number of product placements you see. To what extent do you think the placements give you a clue about the producer's intended audience?

4 If you were a school supplies advertiser, would you be concerned about using MySpace for reaching tweens and teens? Why or why not?

Companion Website Video Clips

. . . .

Mickey Mouse Monopoly—Disney's Media Dominance
This clip from the Media Education Foundation documentary *Mickey Mouse Monopoly* examines the stories about race, gender, and class that are propagated by Disney films. Credit: Media Education Foundation.

Consuming Kids—By Any Means Necessary
This clip from the Media Education Foundation documentary *Consuming Kids* considers the practices of a multi-billion dollar marketing aimed at children and their parents raising questions about the ethics of children's marketing and its impact on the health and well-being of kids. Credit: Media Education Foundation.

Media Ownership and Consolidation (audio)
This audio clip from the Internet Archive discusses the impact of media consolidation and the FCC's ownership rules. Credit: Internet Archive/Open Source Audio.

Case Study
. . . .

ANALYZING THE CEO'S STATEMENT IN AN ANNUAL REPORT

The idea The chief executive's (CEO's) statement in a media firm's annual report is often a useful way to present a vision of its strategies to investors and to justify the vision and the way it is being accomplished. Understanding that will help you understand many of the actions of the company that affect consumers.

The method Choose a large media corporation and go to its most recent two annual reports online. Read the CEO's statement in each. Also, take a look at the covers of the annual reports and the other matter created for investors, such as photos of the company's products and stars. (Don't worry about the financial numbers in the back; one has to be quite specialized to understand these.) In addition, read five articles in trade magazines (through a database such as Nexis or Factiva) that discuss the company's activities in the past year. Using this chapter's analyses of Disney, News Corporation, and Google as examples, write a report that answers the following questions: (1) What is the CEO's vision for the company—the idea of what the company's mission is and why? (2) How do the CEO and others in the company see the competitive environment that the firm is facing? (3) What strategies (broad ways to think of what to do) and what specific activities do they present for overcoming these and other obstacles? (4) How are these strategies and activities affecting the kinds of materials consumers receive from that company? In your report, also comment on what you think the media critics mentioned in this chapter would say about the company's activities.

Part Three

The Print Media

Traditionally, when we think of print industries, we think of reading materials manufactured from ink and paper. The largest of these print media industries—the book, newspaper, and magazine industries—are the focus of this section.

In Chapters 7 through 9, you'll learn about the history of the industries and their work today. We'll explore social and ethical concerns regarding the ways the industries carry out their work. We'll also investigate a change that ties in with what we discussed in Part Two: the transformation of newspapers, magazines, and books into forms that have nothing to do with paper and ink.

THE CHAPTERS

7 The Book Industry

After studying this chapter, you will be able to:

1. Consider today's books in terms of the development of books over the centuries

2. Differentiate among the different types of books within the book publishing industry

3. Analyze ethical pitfalls that are present in the book publishing industry

4. Explain the roles of production, distribution, and exhibition as they pertain to the book publishing industry

5. Realize and evaluate the effects of new digital technologies on the book publishing industry

> "If I rely on just the bookstore sales, I won't make a living. Putting [my book] online does not put my livelihood at risk; you make a living finding new ways to do business."
>
> – CORY DOCTOROW, SCIENCE FICTION WRITER AND BLOGGER

MEDIA TODAY

Do you still read books printed on paper? If so, you're not alone. Even so, the audience for reading on electronic screens called **e-readers**—though still small—is growing. According to the Association of American Publishers, **e-book** sales in the first half of 2009 were $81.5 million, up substantially from the $29.8 million of sales during the first six months of 2008. The leap in interest is due to Amazon's Kindle, an e-reader with a six-inch screen that allows its users to order books, and newspapers and magazines, wirelessly. The U.S. Kindle Store carried more than 350,000 titles at the start of 2010, and the company said it was selling forty-eight Kindle copies for every 100 physical copies of books offered in both formats. In 2009 Amazon began Kindle download sites for other parts of the world.

"This is going to be a big industry," Amazon's chief executive said in 2009. "There's room for multiple winners." And, in fact, competition around electronic books started heating up into 2010, as Sony, IRex Technologies, and Plastic Logic moved aggressively into the marketplace, and as the bookstore chains Borders and Barnes & Noble began offering books wirelessly. Meanwhile, Google had digitized more than one million books that could be read on laptops and smartphones as well as e-readers. Some people believed that the book world was poised on the edge of a revolution in the ways people access and read that classic print product, a book.

Most discussions of the Kindle and its competition center on people's reading of best-sellers—books by such writers as J. K. Rowling (the *Harry Potter* series), Dan Brown (*The Lost Symbol*), and Stephanie Meyer (the *Twilight Saga*). Yet many book-industry executives are concerned by the impact of electronic readers, websites, smartphones, and other digital technology on the reading of books that are far off the best-seller lists. That is because titles such as the *Harry Potter* series that aim at the general public do gather billions of dollars—$23.07 billion in 2008. Yet they represent only a small slice of a huge business that includes books for elementary schools, high schools, colleges, graduate schools, professional training centers, and more.

The book you are reading now is a product of one area of the book industry: the college textbook segment. *Media Today* is available via the Kindle. Moreover, if you think of the "extra" materials that come with the print version of the book—the website and the terms you can download to your mobile device, for example—you will realize that in this area, too, book publishers in the new media environment are going beyond the printed page in various ways. Their biggest long-term concerns involve figuring out how to compete in a digital environment, in which paper is one way to deliver the information in books. The challenge, as they see it, is to keep the essential features of a book that have drawn readers over the centuries, while giving those features wondrous new digital spins that will keep the book healthy for centuries to come.

For one of the oldest communication media—books are older than newspapers—and for an industry that has typically been pretty set in its ways, that is a tall order. It's by no means an impossible one, though, as we will see. If you were involved in the task, probably the first thing you would have to do is ask two basic questions: What *are* the essential features of a book that have drawn readers over the centuries? And what are the essential elements of today's book industry that would encourage or discourage bold new movements into the digital age?

e-reader a portable electronic device designed mainly for reading digital books and magazines

e-book an electronic version of a printed book that can be read on a computer or hand-held digital device

The History of the Book

Although the history of the book as we know it can be traced back only about 500 years, the idea of the book is much older. Scholars consider the papyrus roll in Egypt around 3,000 BC to be an early ancestor of the modern book. Papyrus was made from a reed-like plant in the Nile Valley, and it resembled paper. Scribes laid out sheets of papyrus, copied a text on the side on one side of the sheets, and then rolled up the finished manuscript. The Greeks adopted the papyrus roll from the Egyptians. They stored their rolls in great libraries. In fact, the Greeks considered the book so important that they began to use it, rather than the memory of speeches (what is called the oral tradition) as the main way to make ideas "public"—or available to large numbers of people. Greek writers of the era refer to a market in books and to prices paid for them. Large libraries maintained **scriptoria** where many books were copied by hand. Unfortunately, relatively little of this material has survived.

scriptoria areas located in ancient Greek libraries where books were copied by hand

The Romans picked up the idea of papyrus rolls from the Greeks. Apart from libraries, a fairly large number of upper class Romans owned manuscripts. The interest in these works led to a small-scale Roman industry of papyrus rolls. "Publishing" entrepreneurs used slave labor to create multiple copies at relatively low prices. One writer asserts that,

> In many ways these enterprises were prototypes for modern publishing houses. Roman publishers selected the manuscripts to be reproduced; advanced money to authors for rights to the manuscripts, thus assuming the risks of publication; chose the format, size, and price of each edition; and developed profitable markets for their merchandise.

But it was a long way from the slave-driving papyrus scroll businesses to Random House. Part of the difference had to do with the look of the book (its **format**) and the technology to make it. Manuscripts began to take on the look of a book around 100 AD, when religious Christians invented the **codex**—a document in which papyrus pages faced one another and were bound together, instead of rolled up. This form made it easier to find a particular passage quickly—the reader didn't have to unravel a large roll—and it enabled writers to write on both sides of the pages. The codex was followed by innovations in the material used for the manuscripts—animal skins (vellum and parchment) and then, by the fifteenth century, paper.

format the look of a book

codex the first manuscripts that began to take on the look of a book: papyrus leaves faced one another and were bound together, instead of rolled up; this form made it easier to find a particular passage quickly

If you were transported to the Europe of that period, you would recognize books. They were pages bound together and collected under hard covers. They were different from today's books in one important way, however—they were written by hand. Like the Greek scriptoria workers, fifteenth-century monks patiently copied manuscripts that they considered holy or otherwise important. They sometimes also added beautiful drawings to illustrate what was written. As you might imagine, it took a long time to produce these books, so relatively few were produced. Scholars have estimated that in all of Europe of the early 1400s, the total number of books was only in the thousands.

Gutenberg and the Advent of Movable Type

When the printing press was invented by Johannes Guttenberg around this time, a revolution took place in printing. As a result, only a hundred years later the number of books in Europe was about 9 million.

A fifteenth-century scholar working on a manuscript in a scriptorium.

Gutenberg, who lived in what is today Germany, didn't create his new machine totally from scratch. The Chinese had independently developed the art of manuscript production around the time of the Christian era. Lampblack ink was introduced in China in 400 AD and printing from wooden blocks in the sixth century. Europeans became familiar with both these innovations before the 1400s.

What made Gutenberg's approach unique was his creation of **movable type**— individual letters of the alphabet made out of wood or metal that can be rearranged in any number of combinations to make different words. Unlike a woodblock, which could be used only for one message, movable type could be used over and over because it could be constantly rearranged (see Figure 7.1). Gutenberg made a frame to hold the arranged type in place. He covered the type with ink, placed paper on top of the inked bed of type, and then applied pressure to the paper with a corkscrew device that was adapted from a wine press. The process enabled anyone who was strong enough to work the press to create multiple, identical copies of text that were as good-looking as those written by the most careful scribes of the day. Gutenberg's most famous creations, his forty-two-line Bibles, are quite beautiful even by today's printing standards. Once it became available on more than a limited basis, printing with movable type was immediately recognized as a truly extraordinary technological advance over woodblock printing. Gutenberg's idea caught on quickly. By 1500, printing presses had been established in 242 cities across various countries.

movable type individual letters of the alphabet made out of wood or metal that can be rearranged in any number of combinations to make different words; invented by Johannes Gutenberg

The Impact of the Book on Society

During the 1400s and early 1500s, most books were print versions of what monks had previously made by hand: works such as the Bible, books of hour (prayer books), and religious calendars. Beginning in the 1500s, book printers began to produce books that challenged the dominant (Catholic) church and that circulated non-religious (secular) ideas. This growth of anti-Catholicism and secularism in books both reflected and influenced the rise of new ideas about the world. As more and more people learned to read, the books helped foster important changes in European

Figure 7.1 Woodblocks Versus Moveable Type
Once it became available on more than a limited basis, printing with "movable type" was immediately recognized as a truly extraordinary technological advance over woodblock printing.

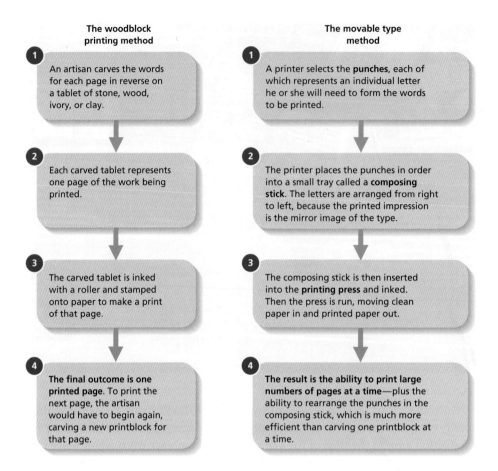

The woodblock printing method

1. An artisan carves the words for each page in reverse on a tablet of stone, wood, ivory, or clay.

2. Each carved tablet represents one page of the work being printed.

3. The carved tablet is inked with a roller and stamped onto paper to make a print of that page.

4. **The final outcome is one printed page.** To print the next page, the artisan would have to begin again, carving a new printblock for that page.

The movable type method

1. A printer selects the **punches**, each of which represents an individual letter he or she will need to form the words to be printed.

2. The printer places the punches in order into a small tray called a **composing stick**. The letters are arranged from right to left, because the printed impression is the mirror image of the type.

3. The composing stick is then inserted into the **printing press** and inked. Then the press is run, moving clean paper in and printed paper out.

4. **The result is the ability to print large numbers of pages at a time**—plus the ability to rearrange the punches in the composing stick, which is much more efficient than carving one printblock at a time.

understandings. In the sixteenth through eighteenth centuries, these changes helped encourage the Protestant Reformation, the Renaissance, the growth of science, and ideas about democracy.

Book printing helped to usher in remarkable changes that helped shape civilization as we know it. In the wake of these changes across Europe, printers, booksellers, authors, publishers, and rulers argued about what could be published and by whom. We'll concentrate on England, because its experience most influenced the development of printing in what would become the United States.

The Book in England

For centuries after the first printing shop opened in 1487, British printers were controlled by the government. The British Crown feared dissent and worried that printing presses in the wrong hands could lead to uprisings. As a result, British rulers kept close control over all printers and printing. For example, in 1509 King Henry VIII put out a list of prohibited books and established a **licensing system**, under which only people with written authority from the Crown could use a printing press. Queen Mary Tudor, Henry's daughter, extended those controls through the establishment of the Loyal Stationer's Company—an organization that regularly searched printing houses to report on the nature of the work in progress and the identities of customers. As a result of such measures, the books printed in England from the late 1400s through the 1600s reflected the religious and political convictions of the ruling monarchy.

In 1637, licensing procedures became even more stringent, reducing the total number of printers to twenty-three, and assigning severe penalties for violators. It was this act that prompted John Milton to write and publish a pamphlet called

licensing system in the history of print media, a system put in place by King Henry VIII in 1509 under which only people with written authority from the Crown could use a printing press

John Milton's
Areopagitica

Areopagitica, in which he pleaded for freedom of the press and argued passionately against censorship. Milton claimed that a free exchange of ideas would create a **marketplace of ideas** in which different opinions would compete for public approval. Milton felt that truth would always win out in such a contest. This notion became the rallying cry for those in England and America who wanted press freedom. It led to an English law passed in the 1680s that guaranteed free expression for Members of Parliament. In Britain's American colonies, this belief encouraged some printers to argue that the press should be free to attack the government.

The demand for a free press marked only part of the changes that were taking place in British book publishing. In the sixteenth and seventeenth centuries, booksellers often acted as publishers, paying for the making of the book so they could sell it. Printers were paid little for making the books, and the booksellers claimed total ownership over the material, meaning they could print it elsewhere at will. As a result, the author had no control over the work. By the eighteenth century, however, the figure of a publisher separate from the bookseller began to develop. This created a new three-way relationship—between the author (who wrote the work), the publisher (who supported the author in the creation of a book and paid for its printing with the belief it would be saleable to the public), and the bookseller (who sold the book to consumers).

The desire to encourage authors to create, and publishers to support them, led to the Copyright Act of 1709, the first of its kind in any country. It protected printed works for set periods of time, and also set forth penalties for those who stole other people's copyrights.

marketplace of ideas the belief, asserted by John Milton in *Areopagitica*, that in a free-flowing media system individuals will be able to make their own decisions about what is true and what is false, because media competition will allow different opinions to emerge and struggle for public approval (as in a market), and, in the end, the true opinion will win

The Book in the British Colonies

The idea of copyright and of books that were free from government control migrated to the British colonies that later became the United States. The first press in the British colonies was brought to Cambridge, Massachusetts, in 1639, and focused on religious publications. Soon after, however, more printers came to Massachusetts and other colonies, turning out a wide variety of materials. Works of theology formed the leading category of books. Almanacs, primers, and law books were the staples of book production.

The process of printing these materials was labor intensive, and not all that different from what it was in Gutenberg's time. The methods of getting the books to the reading public were also quite different from today. There *were* booksellers; often these were the printers themselves. Rich people might buy leather-bound books by subscription—giving the printer money in advance to turn out handsome volumes. And many who bought books, particularly unbound cheap paper books, got them from street vendors—hawkers they were called—who walked through cities and towns calling out about their printed wares.

hawkers—street vendors who sold unbound cheap paper books

As late as 1810, books were typically published by small printing companies, often family-run businesses. The presses these companies used were still not much different from Gutenberg's. Printing took root in the biggest cities on the East Coast, but it also spread west with the general national expansion. By wagons, by barges, and by whatever other means came to hand, printers dragged their presses and type across the new nation. Once they had settled in a place, these printer-entrepreneurs turned out pamphlets, local laws, commercial announcements, bills, legal forms, newspapers, and books.

U.S. Book Publishing Becomes an Industry

Then came a technological change that transformed the American book industry. The change was the invention of the steam-powered printing press. By the 1830s, developments in society and in technology came together to encourage a new approach to printing—including the steam-powered cylinder press. The paper was fed into the press' flatbed type by one or sometimes two cylinders. The machine had been invented by Frederick Koenig in Saxony (today a part of Germany), had been improved in England, and had reached new levels of efficiency with the work of R. Hoe and Company in the United States.

Frederick Koenig—inventor of steam-powered cylinder press

In 1830, a Hoe steam-powered cylinder press could produce 4,000 double impressions on paper in an hour—four times faster than earlier German and British versions, and twenty times faster than the colonial flatbed press. The potential for turning out huge numbers of copies quickly encouraged the development of cheaper methods for making paper. The speed of the Hoe press and the new low cost of paper meant that, for the first time, it was technologically possible to create huge numbers of printed pages for about a penny a copy, a price low enough that even working people could afford them. Around the same time as the steam-powered cylinder press and low-cost paper came developments such as mechanical typesetting, new methods of reproducing illustrations, and inexpensive cloth bindings.

To these technological developments add crucial cultural developments: the increase in literacy and the huge influx of immigrants into the United States. The growth of canals and railways during the nineteenth century meant that publishers could transport books to the inner parts of the American continent. These long trips also led people to buy books to read on the journeys.

Between 1825 and 1875, the book business developed into an industry. Large companies with departments specializing in different types of books aimed at different markets began to emerge. The tremendous social changes during this period also affected book publishing and made the sale of large numbers of copies realistic. With transportation and communication becoming easier, a publisher could expect to sell copies over a wider territory than was previously possible. In addition, the market was growing because literacy continued to rise. Education grew rapidly so that by the 1840s the United States had a huge reading public by that era's standards

By 1855, the United States surpassed England in book sales. That in itself probably would not have bothered British publishers, who might have sold to the United States as well as to the United Kingdom and the English-speaking parts of its empire. But the British publishers lost out because the American competitors published popular British novels in the United States without paying royalties to the authors or publishers. The problem from the British standpoint was that the federal government refused to recognize the legitimacy of copyrights taken out on books in foreign countries. Consequently, titles by highly popular British authors such as Walter Scott and Charles Dickens could be reproduced and sold by U.S. publishers with impunity. It was not until 1891, when foreigners began copying American works without paying, that the United States joined the International Copyright Convention at the insistence of U.S. publishers who were losing revenues because of it.

Despite the lure of cheap British titles for publishers in the nineteenth century, books by American authors also brought in a good deal of revenue. Dictionaries and books on law, medicine, and theology that were produced in the United States were selling well. By 1860, textbooks made up the largest part of U.S. book production, as they do today. There were successful U.S. fiction authors, too. Harriet Beecher Stowe's *Uncle Tom's Cabin*, published in 1852, had racked up 500,000 sales by 1857, and continued to sell a thousand copies per week. Around that same time, Washington Irving's works were posting 800,000 sales, a writer named T. S. Arthur was selling more than a million copies of his books, and James Fenimore Cooper's publisher was selling 40,000 copies of Cooper's books each year.

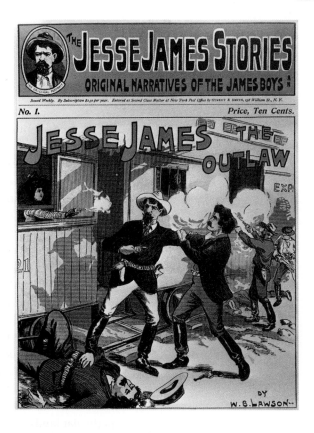

A 1938 dime novel about "Jesse James the Outlaw."

The Advent of Dime Novels and Domestic Novels

While works of fiction by individual authors continued to be popular, a new sort of fiction appeared in the early 1860s. Published in paperback, these books reflected the increasing industrialization of the publishing industry. Called **dime novels** because of their price of 10 cents a copy, these books were less important for their content than for the factory-like system in which they were created and distributed. The emphasis was on inexpensive publishing of predictable successes. Authors were given fees, not royalties, and their payment depended on the length of the novel, the type of novel, and the writer's reputation. The writers were expected to work according to pre-established adventure, western, and detective formulas that were aimed mostly at men and boys. The books were marketed by mail subscription in a series and in a variety of retail outlets.

In the 1870s, more traditional publishers began to turn out their own versions of predictable sellers. These **domestic novels**, aimed at women, were tearjerker stories about heroines who sin in their personal lives, suffer the consequences, and then repent. They were the predecessors of TV's soap operas and the publishing industry's Harlequin romances. The book publishing industry as a whole also began to copy the marketing tactics of the dime-novel producers. By the end of the century, all publishers were trying to sell inexpensive books individually and in series—for example, a series of Shakespeare's plays or Dickens' books. And like the dime-novel producers, more traditional publishers were trying to broaden the distribution and exhibition

dime novel a type of paperback book published in the early 1860s, so called because their price was 10 cents per copy

domestic novel a type of paperback book published in the 1870s, mostly aimed at women

233

of their products. High-quality books increasingly could be bought not only in bookstores and through the mail but also in department stores and discount outlets.

Conglomerates Enter The Book Industry

By the mid-twentieth century, book publishing in the United States was a highly segmented business. More than 22,000 publishing houses issued 49,000 new titles or editions every year, producing a total of nearly 2 billion books per year. Exceptions to this segmentation were the several large companies dominating the high-profile consumer fiction and nonfiction areas. The rest of book publishing began to follow in this direction in the 1960s, when large corporations began to see gold in the growing textbook market. In the ensuing decades, major corporations such as Time Warner, CBS, and Advance Publications bought up companies in the book business. In addition, European book companies bought American book publishing companies beginning in the 1980s. For example, Bertelsmann of Germany added Doubleday, Bantam, Dell, and Random House to its worldwide publishing empire; the Holtzbrinck Group of Germany bought Holt, Rinehart & Winston (renaming it Henry Holt); and Britain's Penguin Publishing Company added New American Library and E. P. Dutton to its roster of firms.

Owning several firms that targeted different types of readers became a common strategy. Bertelsmann's Random House, for example, had several firms under its umbrella in 1998, and some of those firms had departments that specialized in particular kinds of books (foreign reprints, for example), particular types of subject

---

CRITICAL CONSUMER
THE ADVENT OF THE SERIAL

The first highly popular paperback novels in the United States were not really books at all; nor were they written by primarily American writers. Instead, they were publications that looked very much like newspapers, and they contained mostly British novels in serial form, meaning that they appeared over several weeks.

The first such "story paper" was developed in 1839 by New York journalists Park Benjamin and Rufus Griswold. They named their weekly publication *Brother Jonathan*, which was an early national symbol for an American and was later replaced with Uncle Sam.

Benjamin and Griswold designed their publication to look like a newspaper to take advantage of the lower postage rates reserved for that medium. At that time, the federal government refused to recognize the legitimacy of copyrights taken out for books in foreign countries. Thus, by using British novels, Benjamin and Griswold could keep costs down by not paying royalties. As a result, they were able to maintain a successful publication while only charging 25 cents a copy, a low price for a book.

Although *Brother Jonathan* ceased publication in 1843, it spawned many imitators. Known as the "Mammoth Weeklies," this was a new generation of story paper. Firms would mail entire volumes in the now-familiar book format, but without covers, to those who paid for them, supposedly as "supplements" to the story papers.

More conventional U.S. book publishers tried to compete by drastically lowering their prices for books by British authors. In the end, the publishers managed to win their struggle with the paperback printers when the U.S. Postal Service declared that the supplements would no longer be carried at newspaper rates, but had to go at the higher book rates.

Although the ruling pushed the supplement publishers out of business, they left a legacy. They had shown that, after centuries of being available only to a comparatively small elite, books could reach large numbers of people. Cheap books, paperbound or not, were firmly established, never to disappear.

Source: Michael Davitt Bell, "Beginnings of Professionalism," *Culture, Genre, and Literary Vocation: Selected Essays on American Literature* (Chicago: University of Chicago Press, 2001), pp. 67–133.

matter (high-class novels, romances, quality nonfiction), and particular readers (children, members of ethnic groups). People who remembered consumer publishing before the 1960s also claimed that it had lost a genteel quality. Previously, they said, editors and publishers were in the business to generate truly good literature and great nonfiction. With the merging of book publishing into the big business of big media, they claimed, the politeness gave way to dog-eat-dog competition and mercenary calculation of a book's value that smacked more of Hollywood than the book business of old.

Let's take a look at the publishing world of today and then peer into its future.

The Book Industry Today

Book publishing is a big and generally healthy business with sales totaling $35.2 billion in 2008. The people who work in it make a variety of distinctions among types of books. The most general distinction is between professional and educational books on the one hand, and consumer books on the other. **Audio books**, however, are a type that can include professional and educational as well as consumer books. Let's get a bird's eye view of each category.

audio book a recording in which someone reads a printed book or a version of it

Educational and Professional Books

Educational and professional books focus on training. Most professional and educational books are marked by their use of **pedagogy** (or learning materials), which includes features such as learning objectives, chapter recaps, questions for discussion, and the like. Although a good deal of what professional and educational publishers turn out look like traditional books, the publishers are the first to acknowledge that a growing proportion of what flows from their firms doesn't look like the standard book. An example is **standardized tests**, which brought in almost $3 billion dollars to the U.S. book industry in 2008. They point to math workbooks, corporate training manuals, college course packs, online versions of textbooks, and text-related videos. Because some of the materials are not standard books (or even books at all, as we understand the term), some writers on the topic have come to refer to this area broadly as "educational and training media." Experts consider the area as part of book publishing, because the nonbook products are often closely connected to traditional books in the learning environment. People who work in the industry recognize three types of educational and training books:

pedagogy the use of features such as learning objectives, chapter recaps, and questions for discussion; this is characteristic of educational books

standardized test an examination that is administered and graded in the same way for everyone who takes it

El-Hi books and materials textbooks created for elementary and high school students

- **El-Hi books and materials**—created for students in kindergarten through the twelfth grade
- **Higher education books and materials**—focus on teaching students in college and post-college learning
- **Professional books**—titles that help to keep people who are working up to date in their areas as well as bring them to the next level of knowledge

higher education books and materials products that focus on teaching students in college and post-college learning

professional books titles that help to keep people who are working up to date in their areas as well as bring them to the next level of knowledge

Consumer Books

Unlike the publishers of professional and educational books, publishers of **consumer books** are aiming their products at the general public. They target readers in their private lives, outside their roles as students and highly trained workers.

consumer books books that are aimed at the general public

WORLD VIEW
THE SCARCITY OF TEXTBOOKS

Reading this textbook probably does not seem odd to you. After all, you have been reading textbooks your entire life, and college classes often require at least one expensive textbook, sometimes several. A textbook is as natural to you as a desk or a chalkboard. However, for many students in the world, a textbook is a precious and scarce item, or perhaps only a dream. For example, in rural areas of sub-Saharan Africa, there is one textbook for every thirty children. Many parents cannot afford the fees that schools with limited funding must charge.

Worldwide, more than 125 million children are not in school. Lack of schooling has led to the illiteracy of more than 1 billion members of the earth's population. Efforts to increase school funding and enrollment are underway, but poor countries are struggling under the weight of debt, and industrialized nations have not made good on promises to provide the funding necessary to support schooling.

Foreign-owned debt continues to devastate the budgets of Third World nations, leaving them strapped for funds that are desperately needed in other areas, such as for textbooks. Educational deficiencies mean that these nations are further hindered in their efforts to compete in the globalized economy, which they fear will widen the existing gross gap between rich and poor nations.

The problem has not gone unnoticed, as many have called for debt relief so that poorer nations can use their funds in areas where they are badly needed. Humanitarian aid has also helped in some areas. For more than two decades the Sabre Foundation of Massachusetts has helped to "support the educational infrastructure vital to countries in either conflict, or in transition, or countries that are already on the road to development." Particularly successful has been its book donation program, which by the end of 2006 had sent 2.3 million new books and CD-ROMs to Africa.

Sources: Justin Forsyth, "Globalization: Education Makes Moral and Economic Sense," *The Independent*, December 12, 2000, Features, p. 11; Rumman Farugi, "A New Approach to Debt Relief," *International Herald Tribune*, Opinion, p. 4; The Sabre Foundation website, "Book Donation Philosophy." http://www.sabre.org/about/Book_Donation_Philosophy.php (accessed August 5, 2007).

Informal teaching is certainly a significant part of consumer publishing, in areas as varied as religion (the Bible), science (*A Brief History of Time*), history (*Guns, Germs and Steel*), cooking (*Rachel Ray Express Lane Meals*), and ethics (*The Book of Virtues*). Noneducational genres are also a major part of consumer book publishing; these include everything from romance novels to joke books to travel books. Publishing personnel use these subject classifications and many more when they create titles.

When it comes to defining the major categories of the consumer book publishing business, though, publishers identify them quite differently. Using terms originated by the Association of American Publishers (AAP), people involved in publishing talk about the following categories:

- Trade
- Mass market paperback
- Religious
- Book club
- Mail order
- University press
- Subscription reference

Rather than describing the subject matter of books, all the AAP categories (with the exception of religion) refer to the way in which books are distributed or produced. Let's explore each of these categories one at a time. Table 7.1 shows the amount of money consumers spent for each of these categories in 2008.

TRADE BOOKS   **Trade books**—general-interest titles, including both fiction and nonfiction books—are typically sold to consumers through retail bookstores (both traditional and Web-based) and to libraries.

Publishing personnel further distinguish between adult and juvenile trade books. In 2008, they shipped about 489 million of the former and 408.5 million of the latter to retailers. Employees also distinguish between trade books that are *hardcover* (175 million copies of juvenile units and 219.5 million copies of adult units shipped in 2008) and those that are *paperbound* (a combined total of $503 million shipped).[1]

MASS MARKET PAPERBACKS   **Trade paperbacks** are standard-size books that have flexible covers. Smaller, pocket-size paperback books are called **mass market paperbacks**. They are designed to be sold primarily in so-called **mass market outlets**—newsstands, drugstores, discount stores, and supermarkets. Many types of books come in this format, but romance novels and science fiction tales are among the most common.

RELIGIOUS BOOKS   **Religious books** are essentially trade books that contain specifically religious content. They are sold in general bookstores as well as in special religious bookshops. The success of this category seems to vary with the level of interest in the topic. In the late 2000s, the sale figures have hovered above $3 billion,[2] dipping to $2.04 billion during the particularly tough economy of 2008. That figure includes sales of the Bible, the bestselling book of all time. It also includes Rick Warren's *The Purpose of Christmas*, which sold 1.8 million copies in 2008 and was the bestselling religious book of the year.[3]

BOOK CLUBS AND MAIL ORDER   This industry category is used for books distributed through **book clubs**, organizations through which individuals who have joined can select books from the club's catalog and purchase them through the mail or via the club's website, often at a discounted price. There are general-interest clubs, such as Book-of-the-Month Club, and special-interest clubs that aim at people with specific enthusiasms—cooking, the outdoors, history, the military, and many other topics. When you join a club, you get a certain number of books for a small amount of money, and then the company sends you a catalog every month with new choices that you can purchase.

In a nation with so many bookstores and the internet to find books, though, the allure of book clubs is not huge. The entire sales of this publishing segment amounted to $1.32 billion, a small fraction of consumer trade book sales.

trade books general interest titles, including both fiction and nonfiction books, which are typically sold to consumers through retail bookstores and to libraries

trade paperbacks standard-sized books that have flexible covers

mass market paperbacks smaller, pocket-sized paperback books

mass market outlets venues where mass market paperbacks are generally sold, including newsstands, drugstores, discount stores, and supermarkets

religious books trade books that contain specifically religious content

book clubs organizations through which individuals who have joined can select books from the club's catalog and purchase them through the mail or via the club's website, often at a discounted price

Table 7.1 Consumer Spending on Trade Books, 2008	
Type of Book	Amount (in millions of $)
Adult trade	9,710
Juvenile trade	3,380
Mass market paperbacks	2,725
Religious	2,920
Book clubs	1,280
Mail order	330
University press	585
Total	20,930

mail-order books books that are advertised on TV or in promotional mailings that can be ordered directly from the publisher and are shipped to the consumer's home

An even smaller business nowadays is **mail-order books**. You've undoubtedly seen TV ads or received promotional mailings for books on home repair, the Civil War, or gardening. You call an 800 number and give the operator your credit card number, and within several days the book shows up on your doorstep. Both book clubs and mail-order businesses ship titles directly to the consumer. The principal difference between the two is that the mail-order publisher actually originates new titles—creates new, original books—whereas the book club sells existing titles. Although mail-order sales made up 10.5 percent of the U.S. consumer book industry in 1982, the number had dropped to under 1 percent in 2008. Of course, people still buy many books through the mail—for example, after ordering online from http://www.amazon.com—but this bookselling business does not fit the definition of mail order.

university press books scholarly titles published by not-for-profit divisions of universities, colleges, museums, or research institutions

UNIVERSITY PRESS BOOKS   The nature of the publisher, not the distribution method, is what defines this AAP category. In truth, **university press books** could fit several of the categories previously named, as they are essentially trade books that end up in libraries and bookstores. Some of their titles are sold primarily through the mail to scholars who are interested in particular topics.

University presses are typically not-for-profit divisions of universities, colleges, museums, or research institutions, and they publish mostly scholarly materials—that is, books that are read by professors and graduate students. Even when they publish titles that have broad popular interest and end up in bookstores, the AAP and industry convention is not to lump those titles into the "trade" categories, but to still consider them university press books. These are not the best of times for university presses. Their main outlets are libraries, and their book-buying budgets are shrinking because of the rising costs of electronic databases and journals. The situation has forced many university presses to reduce output.

subscription reference books titles such as "great books" series, dictionaries, atlases, and sets of encyclopedias that are marketed by their publishers to consumers on a door-to-door or direct-mail basis; the distribution typically involves one large package deal—several volumes at a time—with a deferred payment schedule

SUBSCRIPTION REFERENCE BOOKS   The term **subscription reference books** refers to "great books" series, dictionaries, atlases, and sets of encyclopedias that are marketed by their publishers to consumers on a door-to-door or direct-mail basis. It is a separate category from mail order because the distribution typically involves one large package deal—several volumes at a time—with a deferred payment schedule.

Consumers receive the encyclopedia or set of "great books" right away, but they pay for the material by subscription, over a number of months. Perhaps your parents bought the *World Book Encyclopedia* or *Encyclopedia Britannica* in this way; millions of people have done so. During the past two decades, this category has been affected negatively by the rise of internet references; the *Britannica* and *World Book* are themselves available online. Their sales have remained a tiny 0.1 percent (that's one-tenth of one percent) of book industry sales.

Variety and Specialization in Book Publishing

No matter how obscure a subject is, there is probably a book about it. In fact, there may even be a publisher specializing in the topic. Take a virtual stroll through many of these titles via your nearest university library's catalog or through the "subject" section in *Books in Print*, a reference volume that you can find in print or online in any library or bookstore. Even though you've been dealing with books all your life, a close examination of the breadth of titles available is likely to surprise you.

Are you interested in maritime issues? *Literary Marketplace*, a standard reference volume on book publishing, lists sixty-one imprints in the United States that deal with the subject. Among the other specialties noted, fifty-two firms mention Hindu religion, forty-seven note real estate, thirty-seven list wine and spirits, and twenty-two claim veterinary science. Many of the publishers involved are quite small. *Literary Marketplace* devotes more than ten pages to listing "small presses," which it considers to be firms that publish fewer than three books per year.

Financing Book Publishing

These examples only begin to suggest the immensity of the book publishing business in the United States. More than 75,000 publishing houses issued more than 275,000 new titles and editions in 2008.[4]

Part of the reason for this huge number is that publishing a basic book really doesn't cost that much, although some titles (such as this textbook) can be very expensive to put together. For a few thousand dollars, a person can put out a handsome product. The low entry costs allow zealous entrepreneurs or people who are committed to disseminating certain ideas to get in on the activity. Moreover, new printing technologies allow publishers to make a profit turning out copies of books in small numbers or even "on demand"—that is, only when someone pays for it. (In the past, the nature of printing efficiencies meant that a publisher had to go through the expense of producing and storing lots of copies of a title so that any one of the copies could be priced competitively.)

Although many small publishers are founded every year, a handful of companies still dominate the most lucrative areas of the book publishing business. For example, three titles—Merriam Webster, Random House, and American Heritage—regularly dominate the field of English-language dictionaries, with a combined 90 percent or greater share. Moreover, under various imprints, only five publishers accounted for 79 percent of hardcover and 75 percent of paperback consumer trade books on the U.S. bestseller lists in 2008. The publishers are Random House, Simon & Schuster, Penguin USA, Hachette Book Group USA, and HarperCollins.[5]

These figures raise a logical question: If producing a book is often so relatively inexpensive, how is it that only a few companies dominate parts of the industry? The answer is that some parts of book publishing can be extremely expensive, and the greatest expenses are typically related to aspects other than the physical creation of the book.

The overwhelming majority of publishers do not own the basic machinery of bookmaking—a printing press and a machine that places bindings on finished pages. Typically, publishers contract out these services to firms that specialize in these activities. Publishers also contract out **composition** services, the work involved in inserting into a manuscript the codes and conventions that tell the page-making program or the printing press how the material should look on the page.

Color photographs and special layouts can be expensive. To sell the book at a reasonable price, the publisher has to sell many thousands of copies simply to make back the manufacturing costs. Still, the ability to contract out such services at reasonable costs is what makes the mere entry into book publishing so easy.

At its heart, though, book publishing is not really about writing or editing or printing. It is about finding, preparing, marketing, distributing, and exhibiting titles in ways that will get particular audiences to notice them and buy them. This process takes place in different ways in different sectors of the industry. Much more money is required in some sectors than in others to compete at the top level. As a result, in these sectors, the wealthiest companies can take the lead and keep it. To give you a sense of what book publishing means, we'll focus on comparing adult hardcover

composition the work involved in inserting into a manuscript the codes and conventions that tell the page-making program or the printing press how the material should look on the page

trade publishing and university press publishing from the standpoint of production, distribution, and exhibition.

Production in the Book Publishing Industry

As we've noted, the production of books involves finding them and preparing them for the marketplace. The same basic activities take place at every kind of book publisher.

Production in Trade Publishing

acquisitions editor a person who recruits and signs new authors and titles for the company's list of books

An **acquisitions editor** recruits and signs new authors and titles for the company's list of books. In major firms, because of the cost of running the company, acquisitions editors must find and produce a certain number of new titles that have a certain sales potential. The titles can come as completed manuscripts or as proposals for manuscripts. A contract is drawn up that promises payments to the author. Sometimes the payments are in the form of a flat fee for producing the work. Often the payments are in the form of **royalties**—shares of the sales income, usually based on the number of copies sold. After the acquisitions editor receives a completed manuscript, permission to go ahead with publication must typically be granted by an executive committee (sometimes called a publication board) of the firm. Once the go-ahead is received, the manuscript goes to a developmental editor. That person reads and edits the work carefully to make sure that it is clear and internally consistent. After the author addresses the developmental editor's suggestions, the manuscript is transmitted from the developmental editor to a production editor in the production department. The production editor then arranges all of the technical aspects of the book—from design to pagination to copy-editing—until the book is in final page-proof form (see Figure 7.2).

royalties shares of a book's sales income which are paid to an author, usually based upon the number of copies sold

This process sounds straightforward, but it can be quite complex. Probably the hardest step is the first, and it belongs to the acquisitions editor—identifying the "right" manuscript. You might not think that finding manuscripts would be a big deal; we all know people who are eager to get their ideas into print. Yet acquisitions editors have to deal with two major considerations when they sift through proposals. They have to find topics that match the personality of their imprint, and they have to find authors who can write about those topics and whose books can make profits for the firm. Getting the topic and the author together is the really hard part, the editors will tell you. Not surprisingly, acquisitions editors have developed strategies to overcome this challenge and reduce their risk of failure. These strategies require the editor to be familiar with the sales goals of the firm, with the intended audience, and with the way in which books are marketed to that audience.

literary agent a person who, on behalf of a client, markets the client's manuscripts to editors, publishers, and other buyers, based upon knowledge of the target market and the specific content of the manuscript

Adult hardcover trade acquisitions editors rarely read unsolicited manuscripts or proposals for manuscripts unless these are brought to them by known literary agents. **Literary agents** are people who, on behalf of a client, market the client's manuscripts to editors, publishers, and other buyers, based upon knowledge of the target market and the specific content of the manuscript. Agents understand the personalities of different imprints, and they make their pitches to the ones best suited to particular authors. This system saves editors enormous amounts of work, although some authors undoubtedly fall through the cracks because of it. If an agent succeeds in placing a work, the agent receives a commission, typically 10 percent of all income related to the book that is received by the author.

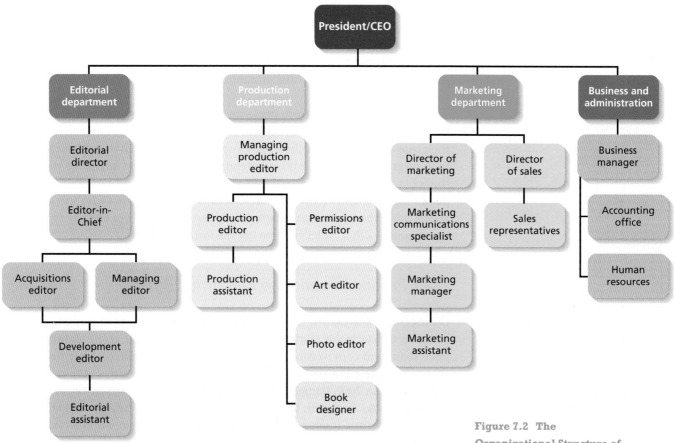

Figure 7.2 The Organizational Structure of a Typical Book Publishing House

Trade presses usually sell their titles through bookstores. Consumers find out about them by browsing through the shelves, reading reviews in newspapers and magazines, or noting discussions with the author in print or on TV.

In hardcover trade publishing, achieving success with a book means selling at least 50,000 copies. Achieving **bestseller** status means selling more than 75,000 hardcover copies or 100,000 paperback copies. And beyond the bestseller looms the realm of the **blockbuster**, which is a book that sells well over 100,000 hardcover copies—constituting an immense success. Major trade presses spend enormous amounts of money on marketing and publicity departments that have the expertise and resources to take books that have the potential to be bestsellers or blockbusters and help them to sell the requisite number of copies. The acquisitions editor's job is to find books with that potential.

bestseller a title that has sold more than 75,000 hardcover copies or more than 100,000 paperback copies

blockbuster a title that has sold well over 100,000 hardcover copies

Production at a University Press

Publishing at a university press is very different from adult hardcover trade publishing in this respect. In university press publishing, a "hit" realistically means selling several thousand copies. A title reaches hit status if it commands respect from professors, who then tell their students and university libraries to buy it.

Scholarly and trade publishers take different approaches to recruiting and acquiring authors whose books may or may not be hits. To reduce the risk that academics will not like their books, editors at scholarly presses will try to get manuscripts by well-known professors from well-known universities. Because acquiring books only from these professors would not yield enough titles for their lists, the editors go after the next best thing: young professors on their way up the academic ladder. To find them, the editors turn to consultants: well-known academics who have a reputation for being able to spot innovative new work in their field that their colleagues are likely to appreciate. Sometimes these academics get paid for their services. In addition to the help of consultants, many academic editors will read unsolicited manuscripts sent to them by professors from around the country in the hope of finding something good.

In contrast to the way trade books are sold, university presses usually publicize their books at academic conferences and by mail. Academic associations rent space at their conventions to booksellers. Salespeople set out titles that they think the professors and graduate students who are attending the convention might like and discuss the books with interested passersby. In addition, the marketing departments of these publishing companies send brochures specifically to academics who specialize in a book's topic; the brochures contain descriptions of the author and the topic along with blurbs by other professors who like the work.

Book Production and the Electronic Age

During the past few years, the biggest book publishers have been active in creating books for the electronic market—placing titles for sale online at the same or a lower price than hard-copy versions. Some observers have wondered what the rush is about, since there is actually rather little money being made from the sale of electronic books. In 2007, Daniel O'Brien, an book analyst for Forrester Research, called electronic books a solution in search of a problem. "Our research with consumers indicates very little interest in reading on a screen," he told *The New York Times*. "Maybe someday, but not in a five-year time frame. Books are pretty elegant."[6] But Jack Romanos, president of Simon & Schuster, one of the first traditional publishers to begin selling electronic books, argues that "the logic of electronic books is pretty hard to refute—we see it as an incremental increase in sales as a new form of books for adults and especially for the next generation of readers."

It turns out that Romano was more correct. With the hype around the Kindle, Sony Reader, iPhone, and other portable screens, spending on e-books soared 69 percent in 2008 over 2007. The amount was still tiny compared with the overall book industry—$113 million. But many of the country's largest publishers reported that sales of the format more than doubled for them between 2007 and 2008. The result is that in the early years of the twenty-first century, major book publishers, technology companies, online booksellers, and new electronic book middlemen are experimenting with digital books. One area outside of consumer books that seems to have clearly had some success is the sale of textbooks in digital form. A number of school districts around the United States have experimented with giving their students laptops loaded with their textbooks instead of giving hard copies of the books. By doing that the districts can more cheaply get updates of the books every year; the kids can use the laptops for their work at school and at home; and the children's backs aren't strained terribly by the weight of heavy textbooks that they must lug home every day.

Another area that has drawn the interest of academic publishers is the release of books online and offline at the same time. Yochai Benkler's 2006 book *The Wealth of Networks*, about the social and economic implications of the internet, is an example. Yale University Press allowed Benkler to post it on the Web at the same time that the company sold it through traditional channels. The logic was that most of the people who got a taste of the nearly 500-page book online would be enticed to purchase the physical book. But Yale, MIT Press, the University of Michigan Press, and other academic presses are trying to push beyond the boundaries of traditional publishing in

TECH & INFRASTRUCTURE
AN ONLINE MARKET FOR E-BOOKS?

For the struggling book industry, the introduction of e-book readers appeared to be an opportunity for recovery. Quickly after their introduction, e-books showed initial signs of success. However, the very logic that makes e-books profitable—the ease with which they can be downloaded—may by their downfall.

Some commentators contend it is only a matter of time before e-books fall victim to the black market of illegal downloading. The publishing industry is in a position similar to where the music industry was after the release of portable MP3 players. Illegal music downloads took a few years to catch on. Once the industry reached a tipping point where a critical mass of people had home computers and MP3 players, file sharing became a practical way to find and access music.

The question is, when will the e-book industry reach that critical mass? Some accounts suggest that it might already be there. In September 2009, Dan Brown's novel *The Lost Symbol* hit the shelves—in stores and online. Amazon.com reported that more of the books were sold for the Kindle e-reader than traditional hardcover books. However, less than a day after the book's release, copies could be found on file sharing sites. A few days later, pirated copies had been downloaded for free more than 100,000 times.

Some authors are so concerned about the potential for pirating and illegal downloads that they have not agreed to make digital copies of their books available. J. K. Rowling is one author who has not licensed her books for digital sales. Rowling has not explained the basis for her decision, but some commentators suspect that she is concerned about the potential for illegal downloads.

Industry experts have suggested that the publishing industry may be able to avoid the problems that plagued the music industry by keeping the quality of legally purchased e-books high and prices low—a model that is similar to the iTunes model for music and videos. What do you think?

Sources: Jack Shafer, "Does the Book Industry Want To Get Napstered?: If the Publishers Force Amazon to Raise Prices on E-Books, that's What Will Happen," *Slate*, July 15, 2009. http://www.slate.com/id/2222941/ (August 2, 2010); Matt Frisch, "Digital Piracy Hits the E-Book Industry," *CNN*, January 1, 2010. http://www.cnn.com/2010/TECH/01/01/ebook.piracy/index.html (August 2, 2010).

their online activities. Sometimes authors invite comments about the book online in order to encourage serious discussion of the topic. In some cases, the author uses the discussion to create an updated, corrected, or extended edition of the book, which may eventually be published in traditional as well as digital form. Will all of this pay for itself? Is there truly a reasonable business model here? The leaders of major university presses aren't sure, but they believe it is in their interest and in the interest of scholarship to find out.

In the long run, it may well be that electronic book publishing is, to quote the editor-in-chief of *Publishers Weekly*, "the next major thing after Gutenberg."[7] Still, don't hold your breath waiting for the disappearance of the book. Even the just-quoted editor was adamant that books won't go away. What seems certain is that book industry executives will respond to competitive pressures from electronic and other currents around them.

Ethical Pitfalls in Book Production

The process of finding and developing ideas and authors for books is filled with ethical pitfalls for authors, agents, and publishers. One of the biggest issues is that of stealing ideas. **Plagiarism**—using parts of another person's work without citing or otherwise crediting the original author—unfortunately seems to be much more common than many in publishing would like to believe. Sometimes such an act is clearly illegal, as when an author lifts sentences or paragraphs from copyrighted

plagiarism using parts of another person's work without citing or otherwise crediting the original author material. Plagiarism is not illegal when the author uses material that has not been protected by copyright; however, it remains a serious breach of ethics.

ETHICAL ISSUES FOR AUTHORS   Literary scholars and critics have concluded that many writers have been guilty of plagiarism, although the issue rarely makes the front pages. You might remember the case of Harvard student, Kaavya Viswanathan. In 2006 Little Brown publishing company released her first novel, *How Opal Mehta Got Kissed, Got Wild, and Got a Life*. Soon afterwards, her publisher asked bookstores to remove the book from their shelves after it confirmed accusations that she used paragraphs from two other novels without citing them. One of the most prominent authors to be accused of plagiarism in recent years was Alex Haley, the author of *Roots*, the bestselling book that became one of the most-viewed television miniseries of all time. In 1978, Harold Courlander sued Haley for extensively lifting material for *Roots* from his book *The African*. That book itself did quite well when it appeared in 1967: it sold 300,000 copies and was translated into several languages.

Haley eventually agreed to settle. Courlander received $650,000 just before the judge issued a ruling. Yet until Haley's death, he continued to claim that the numerous similarities between the books were unintentional and minor, even though a lot of evidence introduced in court indicated that he had used *The African* substantially in writing *Roots*. Courlander himself felt that the basic issue of copying never really made it onto the public agenda. He noted that, although he had felt vindicated at the time of the court settlement, public interest in the incident quickly disappeared. Haley, he added, "was a very persuasive public speaker" who dismissed questions about the settlement. "Nobody really raised the issue of literary ethics, and he continued to receive honorary degrees—it didn't slow him up. This troubled me."[8]

ETHICAL ISSUES FOR EDITORS AND LITERARY AGENTS   Editors and literary agents, as well as authors, also confront major ethical issues. Let's say you're an editor and you get a manuscript chapter out of the blue from an unknown author. She proposes a nonfiction book about how mothers who travel frequently on business balance home and work. You don't know the writer and you don't intend to use her. You do, however, like the topic, and you can think of at least two authors who

In 1978, Harold Courlander sued Alex Haley, author of the book *Roots*, for lifting extensive material from Courlander's book *The African*. Haley agreed to an out-of-court settlement.

have written for you who would do a great job with such a book. What do you do? Should you go ahead with it? Is it ethical to take one person's ideas for a book and pay someone else to write it?

Or let's say you are a literary agent just starting out on your own. You already represent a few authors, but you need to bring in more money. You know that among literary agents the rule is that you charge a percentage of an author's earnings, but you do not demand a fee for simply representing an author. The reason is that agents who accept fees have been known to represent authors simply to get their money, not because the agents really thought the authors would succeed in finding a publisher. You also know, however, that there are many aspiring writers out there who would love to have your input, even for a fee. You tell yourself you can be honest with them. Should you do it?

Reducing the Risks of Failure During the Production Process

These sorts of questions come up all the time as authors, agents, and editors struggle to make books and, in turn, see those books make money. Book publishers use a number of strategies to reduce the risk of failure. Among them are:

- Conducting prepublication research
- Making use of authors with positive track records
- Offering authors advances on royalties

Let's look at each of these strategies individually.

CONDUCTING PREPUBLICATION RESEARCH   You might wonder whether companies involved in publishing university press and trade books conduct **prepublication research** to gauge a title's chances of success with their likely audiences. In fact, they do, but they do it in a rather informal way. Editors may meet with people who are representative of their audience and ask them questions about the book being developed. In scholarly publishing, editors often pay a few professors to read the manuscript and comment on its prospects for success. Going a lot further in research—testing each title with large numbers of likely consumers to gauge their reactions—might raise the expense of publishing the book so much that if it was to make a profit it would have to be priced at an unrealistically high level. About the only systematic research that publishing executives carry out regularly is seeing how previous books on a topic sold. That information gives them an indication of whether going ahead with the book is worth the company's money.

prepublication research research conducted in order to gauge a title's chances of success with its likely audience

MAKING USE OF TRACK RECORDS   Of course, some authors have already proved their worth: they have **track records**, or histories of successes, in the book marketplace. Editors naturally like to sign these authors because doing so lowers the risk of failure. The authors' names are so well known in their area of publishing that their new titles almost sell themselves.

In academic publishing, prestige tends to be the best tool for successfully snagging an author with a substantial track record. Typically, the acquisitions editor who wants to snag such authors must work for one of the most prestigious scholarly presses—Harvard, Yale, Cambridge, Oxford, MIT, Chicago, and a few others. Of course, the

track record the previous successes or failures of a product, person, or organization

IS IT ETHICAL?
A MILLION LITTLE PIECES

Publishers know that when Oprah Winfrey's "Book Club" chooses titles, sales skyrocket.

The "Oprah's Book Club" sticker is one of the best endorsements a books can receive in the publishing industry. Volumes tagged by Oprah as must-reads—both new releases and venerable classics—often experience a dramatic increase in sales. This is precisely what happened to James Frey's book *A Million Little Pieces*. After Oprah discussed the book on her show and gave it the Oprah seal of approval, *A Million Little Pieces* shot to number one in *The New York Times* non-fiction bestseller list and stayed there for fifteen weeks. However, the attention Oprah paid to the book may have contributed to its eventual downfall.

The book was presented as a memoir written by James Frey, a drug- and alcohol-addicted criminal whose life was a compilation of drug-fuelled fights, drunk driving, and dramatic arrests. Eventually, Frey entered a rehab facility where he went through the painful process of sobering up and was eventually released back into society where he managed to remain sober. The book features graphic retellings of many of the incidents in Frey's life—including his experience of having multiple root-canal procedures performed without anesthetic because of concerns that the drug may cause him to relapse.

The book received mixed reviews, including suggestions by some that events it related to did not ring true. Despite these criticisms, Frey appeared on Oprah to discuss the events in the book and vouched for its veracity. As a result of that show, *The Smoking Gun*, a website dedicated to publicizing legal documents, dug into Frey's background. Early in 2006, they released an article that called into question many of the central claims in *Pieces*, as well as in *My Friend Leonard*, Frey's second novel about a member of the mafia Frey befriended in rehab.

Controversy regarding the book's claim to be a memoir mounted. Eventually, Oprah asked Frey and his Doubleday publisher Nan Talese back to the show. The host pressed the author on many of the book's events and Frey relented, admitting that he had taken artistic license and embellished a number of the stories to help maintain the book's flow. He also noted that he had attempted to publish the book as a work of fiction, but had been rejected by a number of publishers. On TV, Nan Talese justified her company's decision to publish the book. Later, however, Doubleday eventually recanted, offering refunds to consumers who had purchased the book under the assumption that it was a memoir and adding a publisher's note and an author's note to new editions explaining the alteration and embellishment of certain events.

Do you think Doubleday should have attempted to verify the details of Frey's life before selling the book as a memoir? Should a publisher be expected to check the honesty of its authors?

Sources: "A Million Little Lies," *The Smoking Gun*, January 8, 2006. http://www.thesmokinggun.com/ jamesfrey/010406ljamesfrey1.html (August 2, 2010); "James Frey and the *A Million Little Pieces* Controversy," *The Oprah Show*, January 26, 2006. http://www.oprah.com/showinfo/ James-Frey-and-the-A-Million-Little-Pieces-Controversy (August 2, 2010).

most prestigious presses continue to collect the most prestigious academic authors, and thus to dominate the scholarly sector.

In adult trade publishing, almost anything goes with regard to authors with positive track records or authors who for other reasons are expected to have high sales. The authors who garner large advances and are successful in sales are often those who are:

- Previously hugely successful (John Grisham, Stephen King, Patricia Cornwell)
- Controversial (former U.S. senator and then-presidential candidate Hillary Clinton, then-Alaskan governor and former presidential candidate Sarah Palin)
- Well known outside of book publishing (Madonna, Larry King)

OFFERING ADVANCES ON ROYALTIES   Offering authors an **advance on royalties**—a payment of money before the book is published that the publisher anticipates the author's earning through royalties on the book—to sign a contract is not as common in academic as in trade publishing, possibly because academic titles do not sell that many copies and possibly because the firms can lure academic writers without advances, as they are called. The amount of money that trade publishers offer in order to lure star authors can be impressive. For example, Simon & Schuster offered Houston televangelist Joel Osteen $10 million in 2006 for the right to publish his 2007 book, *Become a Better You*. The reason? His book *Your Best Life Now: 7 Steps to Living at Your Potential*, published by small publisher FaithWords, had sold millions of copies since its release in 2004. Probably at least as important was that its audience bought audio books, calendars, and other spinoffs that seemed to suggest the pastor's writing career has legs. He also has television and radio gigs that continually keep him in the eye of the people who would buy his books.

Those who are involved with such deals clearly believe that they are worth it. In addition to considering whether the book will sell enough in hardcover to justify the advance, the publishing firm considers the title's future attraction to paperback and foreign publishers. The reason is that, in return for the advance, the hardback publisher typically gets the opportunity to sell the paperback and foreign rights to other publishers. In the case of an attractive title, the hardback publisher might make back a substantial portion of the advance through the sale of these rights. As the advance

advance on royalties a payment before the book is published of money that the publisher anticipates the author earning through royalties on the book

CRITICAL CONSUMER
TARGETING IN THE BOOK INDUSTRY

We live in a highly segmented media world where TV programs, radio stations, magazine titles, and websites are targeted to specific groups of people in a society. It is perhaps not surprising, then, that the book industry is becoming increasingly segmented.

One noteworthy change in the industry has been the explosive growth of niche imprints tailored to reach such groups as women, Christians, and conservatives. Many publishing houses have also launched imprints to cater to racial minorities including Random House's One World Books, which emphasizes African authors, and Rayo, HarperCollins' Latino imprint.

Another site of increased segmentation in the book industry is on the exhibition front. Many bookstores segment literature by race, including Borders, which has for decades featured a separate African-American authors section.

To some, the rise of minority imprints and separate bookstore sections makes it easy for people to find books that they can relate to. This, in turn, helps certain groups to maintain a distinct cultural identity.

Yet others wonder whether organizing books by categories such as race makes it difficult for authors to secure a mainstream audience. On a larger level, these practices may reify group divisions. Commenting on the segregation by bookstores of African-American authors, longtime publisher Bennett J. Johnson says it "reinforces the notion that the United States remains a nation of 'two separate societies'."

Wall Street Journal reporter Jeffrey A. Trachtenberg describes these two arguments as a "debate between assimilation and maintaining a distinct identity." Which side of the debate do you fall on and why?

Sources: "Emerging Majorities Influence Publishers, Retailers to Develop Targeted Imprints and Books," *Marketing to the Emerging Majorities* 19, 7 (July 1, 2007), Factiva database; Jeffrey A. Trachtenberg, "Why Book Industry Sees the World Split Still by Race," *The Wall Street Journal*, December 6, 2006, p. A1.

to Osteen suggests, the largest advances typically go to authors whose involvement in other media can help them sell copies. A title based on a popular movie or one that is written by a popular sports figure will similarly have the instant recognition among certain audiences that will help it move off the shelves.

Of course, not all titles succeed, no matter what strategies the publishers might have taken to reduce the risk of failure. *Publishers Weekly* (PW) lists standard reasons why books with hopes for great sales ended in disappointment: "one too many sequels, a book where a magazine article would do, a celebrity whose day has come and gone." When a string of similar books sells strongly at the outset but ends with disappointing sales, acquisitions editors generalize about what people appear not to want to buy anymore, at least for a while. It also works the other way. When one or two books on a topic take off, editors begin to think a trend is at work and they look for books that relate to the same or similar topics. The large number of Sudoku puzzle books pouring into stores is one example. Another, perhaps stranger and more tentative, is a seeming mini-trend of books that try to promote atheism. *Publishers Weekly* pointed out in 2007 that at the same time that religious books were selling well, three titles against religion had also been garnering large numbers of readers: Christopher Hitchens' *God Is Not Great: How Religion Poisons Everything* (published by Twelve), Richard Dawkins' *The God Delusion* (Houghton Mifflin), and Sam Harris's *Letter to a Christian Nation* (Knopf). A *PW* reporter noted that "These brainy, skeptical takes on God and religion have quickly ascended to the top of national bestseller lists" and in interviewing editors found that they saw the topic as a reaction to fundamentalism among substantial segments of U.S. society. To them, that meant room for more, and a chance for substantial sales. As a Houghton Mifflin editor said, "If another great book came along tomorrow that I felt really advanced the issue, I'd snap it up."[9]

Distribution in the Book Industry

Ideas that are not well conceived or well executed and trends that have passed their peak can explain the failure of titles in every sector of book publishing, from juvenile hardback to mail order. Similarly, acquisitions editors and other executives in all areas of the industry realize that distribution can play an important part in making or breaking a title. In mail-order and book-club publishing, effective distribution means making sure that the right customers get the right book catalogs and that their orders get filled on time. In the other publishing sectors, effective distribution means getting the right number of copies of a title to the stores, schools, and libraries that order them.

The Role of Wholesalers in the Distribution Process

The biggest trade publishers—Random House, Simon & Schuster, HarperCollins—distribute books themselves to the largest bookstore chains (Barnes & Noble, Borders, and Books-A-Million) and a few others, such as the online bookseller Amazon. Otherwise, these publishers and others rely on three huge wholesalers—Baker & Taylor, Ingram, and Brodart—to distribute their books to bookstores and

Preacher Joel Osteen, whose internationally televised services at Lakewood Church in Texas reach millions of viewers each week, reportedly received a more than $10 million advance from Simon & Schuster to publish his 2007 book, *Become a Better You*. The advance was based on the success of his 2004 book *Your Best Life Now*, which sold millions of copies for its publisher, FaithWords.

libraries. These wholesalers stock huge numbers of titles from a great number of publishers in massive warehouses. This system allows librarians and book dealers to obtain a variety of books more quickly than if they had to order from individual presses.

The process works this way. A wholesaler purchases copies of a book from a publisher at a discount and then resells them to a retailer (the exhibitor) at a somewhat lower discount. Both the wholesaler and the publisher share the risks in their relationship. When a wholesaler purchases a certain number of copies of a title, it is committing itself to devoting valuable warehouse space to that title and to fulfilling orders for the book. The publisher, though, is not off the hook when the wholesaler receives the title. In the book industry, copies of the book that don't sell can ordinarily be returned to the publisher for credit toward other titles (see Figure 7.3). As a result of this returns policy, publishing executives must be realistic regarding the **print run**, or the number of copies that are printed.

Assessing a Title's Popularity

Throughout the distribution process, wholesalers keep a careful eye on indicators that help them to gauge how popular a book will be.

THE #1 *NEW YORK TIMES* BESTSELLER

god

is not

Great

How Religion Poisons Everything

Christopher Hitchens

POPULARITY INDICATOR 1: THE SIZE OF THE PRINT RUN   The size of the print run signals to wholesalers how popular a publisher expects a book to be. That indication helps the wholesalers decide how many copies of the title to stock. Looking at the publishing imprint also helps. Wholesalers associate certain imprints with certain levels of marketing power as well as with certain types of books. Imprints, therefore, telegraph expected sales. A distributor is more likely to stock up on a title with the Random House imprint than to take a large quantity of a title from Pantheon or Schocken, even though Random House owns those imprints.

POPULARITY INDICATOR 2: THE CONTENT OF REVIEWS   Review media are also vehicles for estimating the popularity of a forthcoming title. Review media are periodicals such as *Kirkus* and *Choice* that receive early versions of books from their publishers. Review magazine staff members read the books and predict their popularity among different audiences.

POPULARITY INDICATOR 3: THE SCOPE OF THE MARKETING PLAN   Finally, the publisher's marketing plan serves as a hint to wholesalers about a title's future. The marketing plan describes the specific ways in which the publisher will get the word out about the title to its target audience. Although the marketing plan of a small university press will probably be limited to a few mailings to appropriate libraries and academics, a trade publisher with high expectations for a title will typically do much more. The firm's publicity department might inform distributors that it will advertise the title in magazines and newspapers that deliver an audience similar to the book's.

In addition, publicists may promise to send the author on a book tour that will draw a lot of attention to the title. A **book tour** is a series of appearances that an

When books on a particular topic begin to sell well, publishers take notice of the trend and look to publish similar books to capitalize on demand. Christopher Hitchens' *God Is Not Great* was one of three skeptical books on religion to top bestseller lists in 2007.

print run the number of copies that are printed

book tour a series of appearances that an author makes in various cities in order to promote a title and stimulate sales

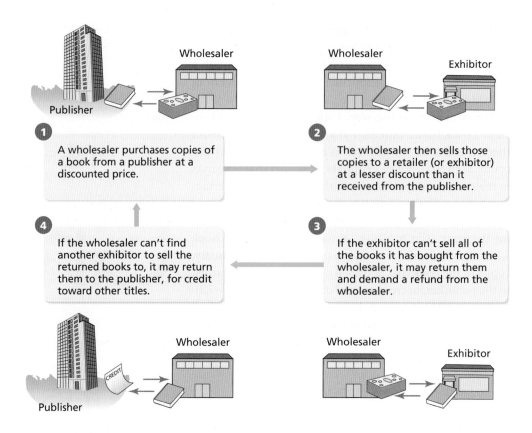

Figure 7.3 The Role of the Wholesaler

The wholesaler plays a crucial role in the book publishing process.

1 A wholesaler purchases copies of a book from a publisher at a discounted price.

2 The wholesaler then sells those copies to a retailer (or exhibitor) at a lesser discount than it received from the publisher.

4 If the wholesaler can't find another exhibitor to sell the returned books to, it may return them to the publisher, for credit toward other titles.

3 If the exhibitor can't sell all of the books it has bought from the wholesaler, it may return them and demand a refund from the wholesaler.

author makes in various cities to promote a title and stimulate sales. The publicist tries to make sure that in each city the author will discuss the book with TV personalities, radio talk show hosts, and newspaper columnists. In addition, publicists might arrange for the author to appear in bookstores to talk about the book and sign copies for customers. The belief in book publishing is that a vigorous and well-put-together book tour can spike the sales of a title substantially.

Exhibition in Book Publishing

The concern that trade publishers and distributors feel about printing and circulating the appropriate number of copies is shared by the stores that exhibit and sell the books to the public. However, this sort of tension is not the norm in publishing for the simple reason that a large percentage of the titles that publishers produce every year do not end up in bookstores. Juvenile books and Bibles are sold in stores, but most university press products end up in libraries. The mail-order, subscription, and book club sectors of the industry distribute titles from their warehouses directly to customers. Publishers in those businesses advertise for new customers through television and magazine ads and by phoning prospects whose names they have gotten from companies that rent lists of likely consumers to marketers. In addition to drawing new purchasers, mail-order, subscription, and book club publishers face the challenge of maintaining an inventory that piques the buying interests of their customers and keeps them coming back.

Exhibition in Textbook Publishing

Textbooks are yet a different story. The "exhibition" area for El-Hi texts is not primarily the schools; it is special evaluation boards that inspect various titles to determine their appropriateness for children in their area. In many states, this evaluation takes place at the state level. California and Texas are the largest states with centralized selection, and board decisions can influence whether a textbook publisher has a chance of selling thousands upon thousands of copies. As you might imagine, textbook company executives pay a lot of attention to the likes and dislikes of members of the selection boards in these states. The executives often instruct their authors to make sure they write in ways that will appeal to the selection boards of California and Texas.

This activity, in turn, has bred resentment among teachers and parents in states that buy fewer books. They have expressed anger that the attitudes of a few people should have so much influence over what American children learn. You may not have known it when you were in grades K through 12, but El-Hi textbooks are controversial commodities.

At the college level, the instructors choose the titles they want to use and ask students to buy them (sound familiar?). Presumably, if the students don't like the text, their feedback will encourage their teachers to look for a replacement. College textbook publishers regularly send professors free copies of new textbooks in the hope that they will like what they see better than they like whatever they are currently using and will order the book for their classes. Acquisitions editors must be alert for new trends in teaching that would suggest new text ideas, even while they encourage authors of current books to update their titles with new editions.

New editions of texts have two purposes. Most obviously, a new edition includes new facts or ideas that have come to light or have been incorporated into the course as it is usually taught since the earlier edition went to press. But there is also a strong marketing motive for new editions. Textbook publishers know that many students sell their texts after they use them and that the books then go on sale in the used-book market. The result is that publishing revenues from an edition plummet after the first year because students purchase used copies. The production of a new edition every three years or so is an attempt to derail this process, since students cannot get the updated version from used-book vendors. Revised versions of popular titles keep textbook publishers in business.

College students often complain about the high price of textbooks. During the last several years, a number of advocacy groups and politicians have taken up their cause, asserting that they are indeed paying too much and that publishers are encouraging professors to order too many extra materials—workbooks and online materials, for example—with the texts. Publishers reply that their costs are high, that the used book market means that many students pay far less than the original price, and that the extra (or "bundled") materials are useful to instructors and students. Nevertheless, during the past several years a number of states have taken action. In 2006, Connecticut passed a law requiring publishers to disclose textbook prices to college faculty, presumably so they would consider that in their decisions. In 2005, Virginia passed a law discouraging faculty from asking students to buy new editions that are minimally different from older ones that can be bought on the used-book market. That same year Washington state passed legislation that gives students the option of buying texts without buying CD-ROMS or other bundled materials. In the end, even in these states, the teachers of these college courses do make the final choices.

Exhibition via Bookstores

Most of us purchase the individual books that we read from bookstores. Think about where you went the last time you bought a hardback title for yourself or a friend. Did you purchase it from a physical bookstore with real doors and shelves (sometimes

Founded in 1953 by poet
Lawrence Ferlinghetti and
Peter D. Martin, San Francisco's
City Lights Bookstore is
one of the few truly great
independent bookstores still
running in the United States.

brick-and-mortar stores

stores that have a physical
presence in the offline world

called **brick-and-mortar stores**) or from an online bookseller? If you bought it from a bookstore, do you remember if it was a chain bookstore or an independent bookseller? An independent bookseller is a company that is based in a particular area and has at most a few locations (often only one). A chain bookstore is part of a large company that has outlets around the United States. Borders, Barnes & Noble, and Books-A-Million are the largest bookstore chains. Traditionally, the independent bookstore was the place where Americans went to buy hardback trade books. In the mid-1990s, bookstore chains overtook them, and many independents are now struggling to survive.

The brick-and-mortar bookstore chains, meanwhile, are themselves struggling to compete with a company that hardly existed in the 1990s: the online bookseller Amazon. The rapid spread of home computers and the internet has already brought about a wealth of changes in the book industry. By 2008, Amazon topped all outlets, accounting for 14 percent of book sales, ahead of Barnes & Noble, which held a 12.5 percent share of the market. In fact, the internet overall accounted for 23 percent of units sold, just beating out the major physical sides of the bookstore chains, which had a 22 percent market share. (When physical independent and religion bookstores are added to the chains, brick-and-mortar bookstores did beat the Web, accounting for 30 percent of book purchases that year.[10]) A report released in 2009 underscored the importance of the internet to the book industry beyond even exhibition. It noted that the internet is not only selling more books than ever, it is also playing an increasing role in making consumers aware of books. One out of five book buyers said they became aware of a book through an online promotion or ad rather than through the many offline opportunities they might have had to learn about titles.[11]

Media Literacy and the Book Industry

We have seen digital convergence in developments such as the Amazon Reader and the emergence of publishing on the Web. These activities also reflect the blurring of media boundaries, of course. We have also noted other types of boundary blurring, especially when it comes to trade books. Publishers promote trade book titles across a variety of media, from television shows, to magazines, to newspapers, to the Web.

Huge chain bookstores like this one owned by Barnes and Noble Booksellers are the most popular places for buying books in the United States.

As Chapters 1 and 5 noted, mass media executives today increasingly believe that, to reach their target audiences, they must pursue these audiences across media boundaries. We should therefore expect not only more multimedia promotion of books but more books that are *presold*. A **presold title** is one that publishers expect will sell well to specific audiences because it ties into material that is popular with those audiences across other media. So, for example, a book by Oprah Winfrey or

presold title a book that publishers expect will sell well to specific audiences because it ties into material that is popular with those audiences across other media

MEDIA PROFILE
STEPHANIE MEYER

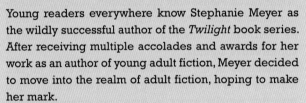

Young readers everywhere know Stephanie Meyer as the wildly successful author of the *Twilight* book series. After receiving multiple accolades and awards for her work as an author of young adult fiction, Meyer decided to move into the realm of adult fiction, hoping to make her mark.

Meyer burst onto the literary scene in 2005 with *Twilight*, the first book in a vampire romance series. Meyer later added *New Moon* (2006), *Eclipse* (2007), and *Breaking Dawn* (2008) to the series, which has sold over 100 million copies worldwide. The books are also the basis for a movie series of the same name. To the disappointment of her many teenage fans, *Breaking Dawn* marked the end of the Twilight series and the start of Meyer's foray into adult fiction.

The Host, Meyer's first book for adults, was released in May 2008. Tapped as "science fiction for people who don't like science fiction," *The Host* is a story about the invasion of earth by an invisible enemy who use human bodies as hosts. The story follows a young woman named Melanie as she and her invader negotiate romantic interests for the man the invader had been

tasked to kill. The book was wildly popular, spending twenty-six weeks in the number one spot on *The New York Times* bestsellers list. However, reviews of the book were mixed with one writer stating, "When it's good, the novel works well, and will appeal to fans of the author's hugely bestselling *Twilight* series, but it is little more than a half-decent doorstep-sized chunk of light entertainment." The book has also been tagged for a movie deal.

Meyer's most recent work, a novella called *The Short Second Life Of Bree Tanner*, was released in June 2010. Meyer also posted the short book on her website, making it free to all her "supportive fans." She noted that she never expected to publish the story and wanted to thank her fans for buying so many of her previous books by offering this one free of charge.

Sources: Keith Brooke, "The Host by Stephenie Meyer," *Guardian*. August 1, 2008. http://www.guardian.co.uk/books/2009/aug/01/host-stephenie-meyer-review (August 2, 2010); The official website of Stephanie Meyer. http://www.stepheniemeyer.com/index.html (August 2, 2010).

"We have a calendar based on the book, stationery based on the book, an audiotape of the book, and a videotape of the movie based on the book, but we don't have the book."

highlighted on her show is presold to fans of her TV show and magazine.

Many book lovers are anxious about this fixation on presold books and books that can be easily publicized across media boundaries. They worry that the books with the highest profile in bookstores and in the media are those that are reflections of popular characters or plot lines from other media—television, radio, magazines, the movies, or the Web. In an age in which the most powerful media conglomerates own the largest book companies, these cross-media relationships are not likely to change. In fact, for reasons we suggested in Chapters 5 and 6, cross-media activities may accelerate in the name of synergy. As a media-literate person, you might want to ask the following questions as you move through the book world:

CRITICAL CONSUMER
TEXAS AND THE TEXTBOOK INDUSTRY

State governors from around the country came together in March of 2010 to sign a bill that would allow for the adoption of a national education curriculum, replacing the state-by-state curriculum that had existed previously. Texas was one state that did not sign on. Its educational leaders cited concerns over the liberal bias found in textbooks and school curriculum.

Members of the Texas Board of Education argued that high school curriculum contained a bias towards the political left that did not match the state's point of view. They argued that Jefferson, whose notion of "separation of church and state" was critical to the evolution of the American political system, should be removed from a list of influential thinkers. They also added language to the social science curriculum suggesting that the actions of Senator Joseph McCarthy, who ran trials to uncover and punish Soviet and communist sympathizers in the 1950s, were justified.

Curricular decisions made by the Texas Board of Education have consequences beyond the confines of the states. Because of the large quantity of textbooks ordered by the Texas Board, publishers often cater to the states' curricular interests when designing, publishing, and distributing high school textbooks. Critics worry that the largely conservative ideals of the Texas Board could influence curriculum for high schools across the

United States. The Board tried (but failed) to remove mentions of Thurgood Marshall and César Chávez. An opinion piece in the *San Francisco Chronicle* was titled, "Dear Texas: Please shut up. Sincerely, History," reflecting national concerns that key pieces of history could be rewritten or removed from textbooks to further a conservative agenda.

Members of the Texas Board of Education argued that they were only correcting the overwhelming liberal bias that usually exists in American education. They suggest that this bias is so pervasive, many liberals do not even recognize it.

What do you think? Should each state write a curriculum that reflects its leaders' political and social ideals? Or are there other ways to have history written for American students?

Sources: Sam Tanehaus, "In Texas Curriculum Fight, Identity Politics Leans Right," *The New York Times*, March 19, 2010. http://www.nytimes.com/2010/03/21/weekinreview/21tanenhaus.html?pagewanted=print (accessed August 2, 2010); "Are America's Textbooks Too Liberal?" *ABC News*, March 11, 2010. http://blogs.abcnews.com/nightlinedailyline/2010/03/are-americas-textbooks-too-liberal.html (accessed August 2, 2010).

■ To what extent are the books that are getting most of the media attention today generated as a result of an author's or a character's popularity in another medium?

■ Are we seeing an increase in cooperative activities between movie companies and book publishers owned by the same conglomerate? That is, are movie companies mostly using the publishers to sell books that publicize the movies, and are book companies trying to come up with titles that can become films?

An optimist would answer "surely not." She or he would point out that there are many publishers who publish trade books that have no connection to TV or movies and who have no interest in making a TV show or movie of these books. A pessimist would concede this point but would emphasize that increasingly the titles that get the most publicity both in and out of the bookstore are those that fit the cross-media, conglomerate profile. As this chapter has shown, the history of the book is a long and complex one. Books have changed through the ages, with the currents of culture and interests of those who have the power to produce them. This long view is useful to take when you think about the future of the book.

Chapter Review

For an interactive chapter recap and study guide, visit the companion website for *Media Today* at http://www.routledge.com/textbooks/mediatoday4e.

Questions for Critical Thinking and Discussion

1 What were the initial reasons for a copyright law in England? *p. 231*
2 How do nonfiction consumer books differ from college texts?
3 What are some of the strategies that publishers use to try to reduce the risk of *p. 245* failure? *conducting prepublication research • Offering authors advances making use of authors with positive track records on royalties*
4 What are the major differences between large bookstore chains and the independents? *Independents has at most a few places while large bookstore chains are located around the nation*

Internet Resources

Literacy Marketplace (http://www.LiteraryMarketplace.com)

This site is a useful place to search if you want to learn about large or small publishers on particular topics. You can identify publishers by state, by size, or by more than 170 subject terms, or create a customized term through the keyword search. Although the site charges for use of certain areas, much of it is free with registration.

Publishers Weekly (http://www.PublishersWeekly.com)

This is the website of the major trade magazine of the book publishing industry. You need not pay a subscription to use much of it, and it is a good way to learn about fads and fashions in the business of books.

The Institute for the Future of the Book (http://www.futureofthebook.org)

According to its mission statement, "The printed page is giving way to the networked screen. The Institute for the Future of the Book seeks to chronicle this shift, and impact its development in a positive direction." The website describes an innovative approach that the Brooklyn-based institute is taking toward digital publishing, carries essays by its leaders and fellows, and has commentary threads by those interested in the institute and its work.

Book History Online (http://www.kb.nl/bho/)

A project of the National Library of the Netherlands, this is a database in English on the history of the printed book and libraries. It contains titles of books and articles on the history of the printed book worldwide. You can search for materials about the history of books in any country and any century through a simple but powerful search engine.

Key Terms

. . . .

You can find the definitions to these key terms in the marginal glossary throughout this chapter. Test your knowledge of these terms with interactive flash cards on the *Media Today* companion website.

Constructing
Media Literacy
· · · · · · · · · · · · · · · · ·

1 What are the threats to variety and diversity in the book industry? Do you think people who worry about such threats exaggerate the problem? Why or why not?

2 What segments of the book industry will gain, and which ones will lose, if a large number of people start using digital book readers? (Hint: Consider the suppliers of paper.)

3 What ethical issues relating to book publishing concern you the most? Why?

4 In what ways is the book publishing industry contributing to the digital media environment?

5 If you worked in book publishing, what career would you choose? Why?

Companion Website
Video Clips
· · · · · · · · · · · · · · · ·

Printing
This occupational film produced in 1947 discusses printing occupations and technologies before the computer age. Credit: Internet Archive/Prelinger Archives.

Learning to Set Type
This occupational film from 1959 demonstrates how to set type manually without the aid of computer technology. Credit: Internet Archive/Prelinger Archives.

Case Study
· · · · · · · · · · · · · · · · · · · ·

INDEPENDENT VERSUS CHAIN BOOKSTORES

The idea The number of independent bookstores has diminished over the past few decades as big chains and online bookselling have made it difficult for them to compete. Many independents have folded, and others have adapted so they can compete successfully. How are independents faring in your community?

The method Using electronic databases such as Nexis or Factiva, find statistics and discussions about the national trends regarding independent bookstores. What is happening and why? Is the death of independents accelerating, decelerating, or remaining the same? Why?

Then identify independent bookstores in your community. If they don't exist now, when did they cease business, and what took their place? If they do exist, what do they seem to be doing to compete with the chains in your area? Interview the owners or managers of the bookstores to get their perspectives. Write a report of your findings in which you lay out what you have found and suggest whether or not you believe the balance of independents and chains in your community is a good one.

8 The Newspaper Industry

After studying this chapter, you will be able to:

1. Describe key developments in U.S. newspaper history

2. Explain the production, distribution, and exhibition processes of various types of newspapers

3. Recognize and discuss the challenges faced by the newspaper industry today and some approaches to dealing with them

4. Describe the ways that newspapers have begun to reach out to audiences through digital technologies, on the internet and elsewhere

5. Apply your media literacy skills to evaluate the newspaper industry and its impact on your everyday life

MEDIA TODAY

In 1945, communication researcher Bernard Berelson decided to make the best of a newspaper strike that had shut down eight major papers in New York City. To Berelson, the strike offered a great opportunity to find out what missing a daily paper meant to people. In his interviews with regular readers, Berelson learned that what people really cared about was not so much the front page headlines—they could get those from other media sources. Rather, they missed reading the parts of the paper that had direct connections with their personal interests—the comics, crossword puzzles, advice columns, sports sections, even the classified advertisements.

Berelson's study underscores two important points about newspapers. One is that they are filled with much more than what people in mass media industries describe as *news*. In fact, the content of newspapers runs the gamut of the media genres described in Chapter 1. They carry entertainment (the puzzles, the comics), information (stock listings, for example), education (historical discussions, some columns for children), and, of course, advertisements.

The second point emphasized by the study is that—in the minds of readers—newspapers do not compete only with other newspapers. When Professor Berelson conducted his study, he and others saw radio and magazines as the only substantial competitors to the daily newspaper (television was only a very new technology at that time). Today, many companies are taking slivers of what newspapers have been presenting for a century—the puzzles, classified ads, the stock listings, the national and international news—and finding ways to profit from them in other media. Broadcast television, cable and satellite-delivered television, magazines, the internet, and more are drawing revenues from activities that used to be confined to newspapers. In particular, newspaper executives see the internet as the place that most of their readers go to find out what is happening, and they are trying mightily to remake themselves on the Web and elsewhere so as to remain relevant and profitable. How is this reinvention taking place? What considerations are shaping it? In the face of these changes, what are the prospects for the newspaper? For people who work in the newspaper industry, or who want to work in it, these are critical questions.

We will tackle these questions before this chapter is over. First, though, it is important to put these challenges in perspective by sketching the story of newspapers' development in the United States.

The Development of the Newspaper

newspapers printed products created on a regular (weekly or daily) basis and released in multiple copies

Newspapers are printed products created on a regular (weekly or daily) basis and released in multiple copies. By this definition, newspapers did not exist before Johannes Gutenberg invented the printing press in the middle 1400s (see Chapter 7). And although Gutenberg's printing press made it possible for newspapers to be produced, having the technical means to do so did not immediately result in an explosion of newspaper publishing.

In England, regular newspapers weren't even produced during most of the 1600s. England's ruling monarchs feared newspapers and greatly restricted their production. These rulers felt that, if newspapers were to report on happenings in the land, it might provoke political discussions that could lead to revolution. Newspapers published in Europe tended to mix political news with business news. Merchants were the main audience because they needed to know what was going on politically and economically throughout Europe and in the "New World" that was being colonized by European nations. In the late 1600s, England's ruling monarchs were forced to yield power to a feisty Parliament and the nation began to flex its naval and trading muscles—and newspapers become a regular feature in the country.

The Rise of the Adversarial Press

The idea of a press free of government control developed slowly through the 1700s. In the early years of the British colonies, newspaper publishers tended to be either postmasters appointed by the local governor, or printers who had won government printing contracts. As a result, they were unlikely to circulate ideas that were politically suspect. Over time, though, renegades such as James Franklin—printer and publisher of the *New England Courant*—challenged the authorities. The brother of the more famous Ben Franklin, James wrote that "to anathemize [that is, ostracize] a printer for publishing the different opinions of men is as injudicious as it is wicked."[1]

Others voiced similar opinions, like Andrew Hamilton, a Philadelphia lawyer representing John Peter Zenger, a New York printer, in 1735. Zenger was charged with "seditious libel" for printing facts in his newspaper that reflected badly on the royal governor. Even though a guilty verdict was the proper outcome under British law, Hamilton persuaded the jury that his client was innocent. The reason, he stated, was that "Nature and the Laws of our country have given us a Right—the Liberty—both of exposing and opposing arbitrary Power . . . by speaking and writing Truth."[2]

adversarial press a press that has the ability to argue with government

This belief in an **adversarial press**—a press that had the ability to argue with government—was taking hold among the intellectuals in the British-American colonies. It was strengthened when Britain attempted to impose taxes on paper to pay for its expensive war with France during the 1760s and 1770s. Lawyers and printers were hurt most by the rules. They banded together to publish strong denunciations of the British colonial policy of taxation without representation. The anger rose to a pitch that resulted in the outbreak of the American Revolutionary War.

Newspapers in Post-Revolutionary America

Newspapers were deeply involved in the political debates of the post-revolutionary period, including the push to add the First Amendment to the Constitution—stating that "Congress shall make no law . . . abridging the freedom of speech, or of the press." As late as 1815, newspapers were typically published by small printing companies, often family-run businesses. Nevertheless, newspapers achieved a dominant social and political position relative to books and magazines by the beginning of the 1800s. In 1820, the United States was home to 512 newspapers; 24 of them were published daily, 66 two or three times a week, and 422 once a week. The dailies tended to be in the cities with the largest populations. (*Largest* has to be understood in terms of the era. Philadelphia, the city with the most people in 1800, was quite small by today's reckoning: it had 70,000 residents. Today its population is well over 1.5 million.)

Many of the newspapers were allied with political parties, and much of the news that appeared took the form of fierce political argument against an opposing viewpoint. Some newspapers were even supported by party officials, who helped arrange valuable government printing contracts for the editors. Readers knew that the *Minerva*, edited by Noah Webster, was a Federalist newspaper, and they understood that the *National Intelligencer* supported Thomas Jefferson and his Antifederalist philosophy.

Even though newspapers were widely available, the great majority of Americans did not read them. Part of the reason for this was illiteracy, but, even for those who could read, the cost of purchasing a newspaper was often too high to afford. The printing process was a totally handicraft operation. The presses these companies used were not terribly different from Gutenberg's. Paper was either handmade from rag by the printer, or shipped from England. The labor-intensive nature of the process meant that, in the early 1800s, publishers had to charge from $6 to $10 a year, in advance, for a newspaper subscription. That was more than most skilled workers earned in a week. Because of the cost, **circulation**—the number of newspapers people paid for or received free in one publishing cycle—was rather small, even relative to the population size. A circulation of 1,500 was common in all but the largest cities.

circulation the number of newspapers people paid for or received free in one publishing cycle

Newspapers Become Mass Media

By the 1830s, developments in society and technology came together to encourage a new approach to the newspaper. Together, the steam-powered cylinder press created

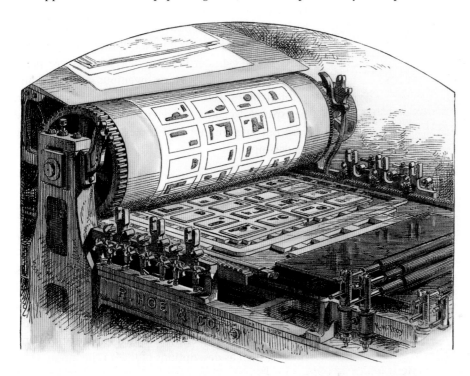

This engraving from 1865 shows an advanced Hoe rotary press.

by Hoe and Company and the development of low-cost paper (see Chapter 7) made it possible to create huge numbers of newspapers for about a penny a copy, a price low enough that even common working people could afford.

But could the common working people read? Would they read? Hoe introduced the steam-powered press at just the time when entrepreneurs were willing to take risks to find out the answer. If they had any chance to overturn the established press order, this was the time to do it. The 1820s and 1830s were a period in which American leaders began to emphasize the power of the "common man."

Andrew Jackson's election to the presidency in 1829 on a platform that celebrated the rough-hewn side of America reinforced the idea that the working class had assumed much greater political importance than in the past. Literacy among the working class continued to increase, and large numbers of workers began to take an interest in reading affordable newspapers. The brief popularity of union-supported newspapers during the 1820s was evidence of this interest. When the unions declined after that decade, their papers declined as well. A number of entrepreneurs took note, however, that there might be an untapped audience for daily newspapers. A few tried to create a paper that sold for a low price—some for only a penny a copy—but they failed.

penny papers newspapers produced in the early 1830s that were sold on the street at a penny per copy

Then, in 1833, a struggling printer named Benjamin Day started the *New York Sun* and sold it for a penny on a per issue basis. The slogan on the *Sun's* masthead was "It Shines for All." This slogan was not just a pun on the newspaper's name; it reflected Day's desire to entice great numbers of people, not just those with money, to read its material. Day got his wish. Within six months, the paper's circulation reached about 8,000, almost twice that of its nearest rival. Within the next few years, successful imitators of the *Sun* appeared in New York, Philadelphia, and Baltimore. The idea became so popular, in fact, that there were often a number of **penny papers** competing for readers in the same area.

"It Shines for All"—The banner of Benjamin Day's *New York Sun*, the first of the penny papers.

Newspaper circulation figures skyrocketed into the tens of thousands within a decade, and newspaper publishers found that even the best steam-powered flatbed presses, which produced a few thousand pages an hour, were inadequate for the job. That was when Hoe's rotary (or "type revolving") press entered the picture on a widespread basis. Instead of placing the type on the flatbed, Hoe put it on a cylinder, with different parts of the cylinder holding type for different pages of the paper. By 1855, Hoe's ingenious machine could print 20,000 sheets per hour. With this sort of power, newspaper executives were confident that they could turn out huge numbers of copies for an ever-growing readership.

Changing Approaches to News

To the typical newspaper reader of the early 1800s, the *Sun* and its imitators must have appeared shockingly different from their predecessors. Unlike the other papers of the day, these papers didn't print partisan political commentaries; instead, they were filled with stories of crime and love, humor and human interest. In the earliest years, they frequently included exaggerations and hoaxes, such as descriptions of life on the moon. Over the next few decades, though, the *Sun* and other penny papers developed the basic approaches to financing the paper, defining news, and organizing the news process that we still see in U.S. journalism today.

Financing the Paper

From the start, Benjamin Day's slogan, "It Shines for All," reflected his philosophy regarding the way to make money from the paper as well as reflecting his approach to its content. He believed that a publication that was affordable by the working class could make its profits one issue at a time. The paper was sold on the streets by ambitious **hawkers**—often young boys—who made about 37 cents for every hundred copies they sold. This form of distribution encouraged publishers to search for presses that could print drawings across the front page to lure readers' attention as competing hawkers screamed through the streets. When special events—a murder trial, a natural disaster—took place after a paper was printed, publishers hyped circulation by releasing special issues that covered the incident. These "extra" editions were possible because new presses offered faster, larger, and cheaper print runs than their predecessors had. As a result, increased circulation meant increased profits for the publisher.

Profits also grew because of an increase in the amount of newspaper space sold to advertisers. As circulation figures grew into the thousands and tens of thousands, companies that hadn't advertised in newspapers before began to see the penny press as a way to reach large numbers of people. Publishers quickly realized that the most ad money went to the papers that had the most readers. Because having the latest news seemed to be what drew readers to a particular newspaper when penny papers competed, publishers began to put revenues into improving news coverage. The hope was to raise both circulation and ad revenues at the same time.

Defining News

In this competition over news, publishers developed a new consensus about how to think of news, one that moved ever closer to the *news* genre that we discussed in Chapter 2. The development spanned several decades—from the 1840s through the Civil War in the 1860s. Compared with the papers of the early 1800s, the change was drastic. Those dailies tended to relay information that came from somewhere else. They printed such things as discussions of trends that had appeared in other newspapers, letters from readers expressing political opinions, government reports, speeches by political leaders that the editors admired, and shipping reports. The penny papers, in contrast, defined their primary role not as relayers of information but as aggressive searchers for events and developments that their readers would find compelling. That vision meant hiring people—reporters—to actually "gather" stories.

As the penny press developed, its publishers tried to attract more and more readers by adding new sections

hawkers young boys who sold newspapers on the streets, and who made about 37 cents for every hundred copies they sold

In the mid-1800s, it was common to see and hear newsboys like this one hawking papers on the street corners of most large American cities.

ONE OF THE NEWS-BHOYS.
SKETCHES OF N.YORK, Nº 18.

that reported on a variety of possible interests, including those of the wealthier classes of society. James Gordon Bennett's *New York Herald* was especially innovative in appealing to different segments of the population within the same issue. By the late 1840s, Bennett's paper had a sports section, a critical review column, society news, and a strong financial section.

With special sections as well as general news coverage, a large part of the competition among papers involved the claim that the paper's reporter was first with a story. As a result, reporting events quickly became a hallmark of the news process. Reporters tried just about every quick mode of transportation they could think of to speed their words along, from the carrier pigeon to the pony express to the railroad. The invention of the telegraph in 1844 was particularly important to what became known as **news gathering**.

news gathering the process by which reporters and editors gather and organize the news they include in their publication

Elements of today's news jargon began to develop around this time. The **byline** (which tells who wrote the story) emerged, as did the **dateline** (which tells where and when the reporter wrote it). So did different sizes of **headlines**, which informed readers of the content and the relative importance of a particular story.

byline a statement identifying who wrote the story

During the Civil War, a new element was added. Because reporters on both sides of the war feared that the telegraph wires would be cut, they began to summarize their major facts quickly at the beginning of their dispatches. Only after this summary did they elaborate on the incident or battle they were describing. This style of factual reporting is called the *inverted pyramid* style (see Figure 2.5 on page 48). It is the style used for most hard news stories today.

dateline a statement identifying where and when the reporter wrote the story

headline an identifying tag appearing at the top of a news story, cueing readers in on the content and relative importance of the story

Organizing the News Process

One consequence of the new financial and news considerations was that newspapers became complex organizations. The newspaper of the early 1800s tended to be created by a single printer–publisher–editor–reporter, with apprentices who were sometimes family members. That was possible when the work involved simply relaying information. It would not do, however, when creating a newspaper meant quickly finding and preparing material that would entice huge numbers of readers on a daily basis. Newspaper companies soon became large organizations, with different departments to take care of financing, creating, printing, distributing, and marketing their product.

In addition to becoming more complex internally, newspaper companies began to interact with other organizations that helped them to get news to their readers quickly and efficiently. The Western Union telegraph company was one such organization; it helped reporters relay news quickly. Another was the Associated Press. It was established in 1849 by seven New York City newspapers as a cooperative news-gathering organization. Newspapers in other cities were invited to join the service, which charged a membership fee in return for sending its stories to the paper over the telegraph wires.

objectivity presenting a fair, balanced, and impartial representation of the events that took place by recording a news event based on the facts and without interpretation, so that anyone else who witnessed the news would agree with the journalists' recounting of it; the way in which news ought to be researched, organized, and presented

The newspaper business was evolving into an industry. Publishers were using ever faster printing presses and other communication technologies to pursue larger and larger audiences. Still, it would be wrong to get the idea that the major urban newspapers of 1850 or 1860 could be mistaken for those of today. One major difference was the absence of photographs in the press of the mid-1800s; the technology for printing photographs in newspapers hadn't been invented yet. A bigger difference was the tone used by that era's major dailies compared with ours.

The notion of *objectivity* as it is used by today's journalists in hard news had not yet been developed. Today, once news workers have decided that something is hard news, they must decide how to present it. They use the word **objectivity** to summarize the way in which news ought to be researched, organized, and presented. It is possible, they believe, to recount a news event based on the facts and without interpretation, so that anyone else who witnessed the news event would agree with the journalists' recounting of it. The goal of a hard news reporter, then, is to summarize an event in an *objective* manner—that is, to present a fair and impartial representation of what happened (see Chapter 2 for a more detailed discussion of objectivity).

But this approach didn't yet exist in the mid-1800s. Publishers such as James Gordon Bennett (of the *New York Herald*) and Horace Greeley (of the *New York Tribune*) had no qualms about lacing their editions with long articles that included spirited attacks on political or philosophical rivals that would appear strange in daily newspapers today. Greeley in particular used his paper as a forum for wide-ranging discussions of new schemes to improve society. In the 1850s, for example, the *Tribune* devoted many pages to explaining socialism, and Greeley himself plunged into long debates with famous opponents of socialism on the desirability of a socialist society.

A Revolution in Newspaper Publishing

The technological and organizational developments in newspaper publishing from the 1830s through the 1860s paved the way for a big leap forward. The era of mass circulation in the 1880s, when newspapers with truly huge audiences emerged, had arrived. Two profound changes took place in the ways in which newspaper owners thought of their products. The first had to do with readership—the newspaper's new goal to attract hundreds of thousands, even millions, of customers. The second had to do with the financial support of the product. In earlier decades, readers' subscriptions had covered a large percentage of the publisher's costs, but advertisements soon began to provide most of the revenues.

A Readership Revolution

In the years following the Civil War, the United States went through an unprecedented period of industrialization. Factories, located in cities, were turning out an enormous number of products. They were hiring huge numbers of foreign workers as well as American-born farmers who were attracted to a new way of life. As the nation got wealthier, educational services increased. More children than ever before went to public schools, and literacy was on the rise. These changes meant that there were far more potential readers for newspapers than ever before. The growth of U.S. cities meant that large numbers of people were living in densely populated areas. Large-scale newspaper distribution was suddenly much easier than it had been in previous decades. What made the potential for newspapers particularly great was the existence of merchants and other businesses that became interested in using newspapers to reach huge audiences.

An Advertising Revolution

That meant advertising. The key to attracting customers, the manufacturers reasoned, was to take advantage of the crowded city. Signs throughout neighborhoods, on walls and on streetcars and trucks, were a popular way to trumpet the virtues of branded products and the stores that sold them. But manufacturers saw a high-circulation daily newspaper as a particularly valuable way to advertise consumer goods. Publishers new and old were eager to oblige. They aimed their content at the large, diverse populations that major manufacturers and department stores eagerly sought. The number of English-language general-circulation dailies increased from 489 in 1870 to 1,967 in 1900. Foreign-language newspapers also grew steeply in number and readership.

Inventors and newspaper owners worked together to make the newspaper attractive to huge audiences. They developed efficient techniques for printing wide headlines and advertisements. Speed became ever more important—not just in gathering news, but also in turning it out. By the early 1890s, the finest Hoe press could turn out 48,000 twelve-page newspapers in an hour. Owners of large papers were installing several presses to keep up with their quickly rising circulation. Full-color presses, first used in Paris, were adapted in the United States and used especially for Sunday comics. In 1897, high-quality reproductions of photographs made their first appearance, in the *New York Tribune.*

Newspaper firms kept the price of their dailies at around a nickel even as the cost of printing technology and paper rose. A new business philosophy was developing. Newspapers were relying mostly on advertising instead of circulation revenues for their profits. The percentage of newspaper revenue coming from advertising rose from 50 percent in 1880 to 64 percent in 1910.

Print Journalism in the Early Twentieth Century

In this competitive environment, the daily newspaper changed dramatically, taking on a form close to that of the kind of paper we are used to today. With color comics, syndicated columnists, hefty sports sections, photograph-filled Sunday magazines, and more, the newspaper became a mosaic of features designed to attract as many different types of people as possible. The complex product gave rise to a complex corporate structure, with advertising and circulation departments that were often as large and as important as the news departments themselves.

Major cities in every region of the nation had one or more newspapers that used the new approach. The *Atlanta Constitution* and the *Louisville Courier-Journal* were stars of the South. In the Midwest, the *Cleveland Press* and the *Detroit News* emerged as powerful evening papers. The West saw the *Los Angeles Times* and, in San Francisco, the *Examiner* and the *Chronicle*. Publishing entrepreneurs such as E. W. Scripps, William Randolph Hearst, and William Patterson built fortunes through their ability to sell ads by building circulation through well-liked features, fast-breaking news stories, coverage of sensational events, human interest tales, and civic campaigns that brought community goodwill.

The Era of Yellow Journalism

These developments reached their height in New York City, where Joseph Pulitzer and William Randolph Hearst competed for circulation and advertising leadership. The highly publicized fight between Pulitzer and Hearst over a Sunday comic character called "The Yellow Kid" seemed to symbolize the ferocity of the competition among papers in many cities. To this day, the newspapers of the1890s are said to be part of **yellow journalism**. The term is used for a newspaper characterized by irresponsible, unethical, and sensational news gathering and exhibition. The publishers of these papers used sensational stories of sex and murder and huge publicity gimmicks to lure each other's readers. Hearst brazenly used any story that would boost circulation. When the U.S. battleship *Maine* blew up in Havana harbor, Hearst offered a $50,000 reward to the person who could prove who did it. And when the United

yellow journalism a term used to refer to the newspaper products of the 1890s, which were characterized by irresponsible, unethical, and sensational news gathering and exhibition

HOGAN'S ALLEY FOLK HAVE A TROLLEY PARTY IN BROOKLYN.

In addition to standing for a certain type of newspaper competition, The Yellow Kid represented a technical advance in color printing. Richard F. Outcault's drawing of an urchin wearing a yellow nightshirt in New York's slums was selected to test the use of color in Joseph Pulitzer's *New York World* on February 16, 1896.

States went to war with Spain over the incident, both the *World* and the *Journal* covered the conflict in jingoistic, highly emotional tones.

At the turn of the century, the excesses of yellow journalism began to alarm people both inside and outside the newspaper business. Self-regulation became a by-word, and universities established schools and departments of journalism, often with the help of wealthy newspaper publishers; their goal was to turn journalism into a respected craft, with its own clear set of procedures and norms. The first university journalism school was at the University of Missouri; Pulitzer's estate funded the Graduate School of Journalism at Columbia University.

The Newspaper Industry Consolidates

newspaper chains companies that own a number of newspapers around the nation

Between 1910 and 1930, the number of U.S. dailies fell from 2,200 to 1,942. More significantly, the number of cities with competing daily papers fell from 689 to 288 during this same period. Part of the reason was competition: The high cost of equipment combined with circulation wars killed many papers. Another part of the reason, though, was the desire of the largest newspaper owners to reduce competition in the various cities in which they operated. These owners tried to ensure that they would attract most of the daily circulation, and therefore most of the advertising money, by buying and killing off other newspapers in places where they owned papers. The result was the creation of powerful **newspaper chains**, companies that owned a number of papers around the nation. By 1933, the six most powerful chains—Hearst, Scripps-Howard, Patterson-McCormick, Block, Ridder, and Gannett—controlled about one-quarter of all daily circulation in the United States. Hearst alone controlled almost 14 percent of daily and 24 percent of Sunday circulation in 1935.

The Rise of the Tabloids

tabloid form a printing format that uses pages that are about half the size of a traditional newspaper page

The 1920s saw the rise of papers that were printed in a **tabloid form**—that is, on a page that was about half the size of a traditional newspaper page. They became popular because they included a number of photographs, they were easy to handle on public transportation, and they featured sensational coverage of crimes and movie stars. The most popular of this sort of newspaper was the *New York Daily News,* which dubbed itself "New York's Picture Newspaper." Like its imitators, in its earliest years the *Daily News* seemed to reflect the idea of a newspaper that had been stripped of the real news that the new journalism schools were trying to promote. What the reader got instead was large doses of the entertainment part of the traditional paper: gossip, comic strips, horoscopes, advice columns, sports, and news about movie stars. Though there are still some echoes of this "jazz journalism" in today's *Daily News,* this particularly sensationalist style doesn't characterize it anymore. You can see more of this type of journalism in such weekly entertainment papers as the *National Enquirer* and perhaps even in headline-mongering dailies such as the *New York Post.*

Newspaper Industry Woes

The high-flying years that newspaper firms saw in the early 1900s ended with the Great Depression of the 1930s. During that decade, unemployment, low wages, and a more restrained society led consumers to buy one traditional paper instead of a traditional paper and a tabloid. Some people who had once purchased several papers on a daily basis found that they could not afford even one.

Between 1937 and 1939, the situation was so bad that one-third of salaried employees in the newspaper industry lost their jobs. The dominant reason for newspaper failures was a drastic decrease in spending by advertisers. Although loss of business was one factor that discouraged advertisers from buying space in papers, another was that they were shifting a substantial portion of their advertising funds to radio, which was just beginning to grow as an advertising medium.

DECLINING DAILIES   Radio was the newspaper industry's first substantial daily competitor for advertising. In the late 1940s, television arrived, adding to newspaper executives' worries. Still, in the years immediately following World War II their circulation figures rose and profits were strong. Yet by the year 2007, the number of dailies had decreased, ownership concentration had increased, and the number of cities with competing dailies was reduced to a handful (see Table 8.1). Then came 2008, a particularly rough year. Four newspaper companies—Journal Register, Philadelphia Newspapers, Sun Times Media Group, and the owners of the Minneapolis *Star Tribune*—filed for bankruptcy protection under Chapter 11 of the U.S. Bankruptcy Code. During the same year, the Seattle *Post Intelligencer* went to an online-only format. Advance Newspapers also announced it would offer its *Ann Arbor News* only online and added it would cut print publication of *The Flint Journal*, *Saginaw News*, and *Bay City Times* to three days. Throughout the country, newspapers were cutting jobs and cutting pay.

What can account for these long-term trends and more recent difficulties in the newspaper industry? Among several factors across the decades were a strong and steady increase in the price of newsprint, rising wages and salaries, and the loss of advertising to television as well as to radio. Labor strikes in several cities also hurt. Many of these strikes were sparked by craft-union anger over executives' desire to replace the typesetting machine operators with computers. Together with the other difficulties that weakened the papers, the disputes resulted in suspensions or mergers, especially in large metropolitan areas. In 1947, 181 of the nation's cities had competing papers, whereas only 38 cities had them in 2006.

DECLINING READERSHIP   Exacerbating all these changes was the fact that the percentage of the U.S. population reading daily papers declined between the 1930s and the 1990s. About 40 million copies were sold each day in 1930, when the population was 122 million; in 2000, when the population was about 250 million, only 60 million copies were sold. The number of newspapers for each household decreased from 1.32 in 1930 to 0.68 in 1990 and to 0.43 in 1994.

COMPETITION FROM THE WEB   At the end of the 1900s, newspaper companies generally remained quite profitable, as local advertisers still used them to reach large numbers of people. But as the industry moved into the twenty-first century, many newspapers began to not only suffer larger annual losses in readership than in earlier years, but also see signs that their growth in advertising money was also decreasing. As you might guess, a primary concern for those in the industry is competition over audiences and advertisers from the Web. By 2008 that competition had begun to reach a fever pitch. The migration of younger consumers to Web-based news sources such as blogs and news collection (or aggregation) sites such as Google News speeded up circulation declines. Many advertisers followed those people to the Web, and newspapers consequently lost money from them, as well.

Table 8.1 The Decline of US Daily Newspapers

Year	Total Papers	Total Circulation
1940	1,878	41,132
1945	1,749	48,384
1946	1,763	50,928
1947	1,769	51,673
1948	1,781	52,285
1949	1,780	52,846
1950	1,772	53,829
1960	1,763	58,882
1970	1,748	62,108
1980	1,745	62,202
1985	1,676	62,766
1990	1,611	62,328
1991	1,586	60,687
1992	1,570	60,164
1993	1,556	59,812
1994	1,548	59,305
1995	1,533	58,193
1996	1,520	56,983
1997	1,509	56,728
1998	1,489	56,182
1999	1,483	55,979
2000	1,480	55,773
2001	1,468	55,578
2002	1,457	55,186
2003	1,456	55,185
2004	1,457	54,626
2005	1,452	53,345
2006	1,437	52,329
2007	1,422	50,958
2008	1,408	48,820

Sources: *Editor & Publisher International Yearbook 2007* (New York: Editor & Publisher, 2007); Veronis Suhler Stevenson, *Communication Industry Forecast 2009–2013* (New York: VSS, 2009), part 12, p. 11.

THE RECESSION OF THE LATE 2000S The competition that newspapers felt from the Web worsened because of the severe economic downturn that began in 2008 and continued through 2009 and beyond. Circulation of printed papers continued to drop as readers switched to the internet to save money. Particularly startling declines came in newspaper advertising, as companies tried desperately to survive. Newspaper-industry experts therefore attributed the major decreases in total newspaper revenues during 2008 and 2009—3 percent and about 16 percent, respectively—largely to the economic environment.

CRITICAL CONSUMER
SHOULD THE GOVERNMENT
SUBSIDIZE NEWSPAPERS?

The past decade has seen newspaper industries in sharp decline. Several local dailies, such as Denver's *Rocky Mountain News* and the *Baltimore Examiner* have shut down, and the *Chicago Tribune* and the *Los Angeles Times* are among the handful of others that have gone bankrupt and are desperately reorganizing their finances. Vanguards of American journalism, such as *The Washington Post* and *The New York Times*, have been forced to cut newsroom jobs to stay afloat. Though both the current economic crisis and the proliferation of freely available content via the internet are frequently blamed for this decline, they likely only accelerated a pre-existing trend.

Following from the principle that a free society is contingent upon the existence of a free press, Robert McChesney, a professor at the University of Illinois, and John Nichols, a longtime journalist, propose in articles and a book that the government should provide a subsidy for the journalism industry—one to the tune of $30 billion a year. Though the idea may sound radical, McChesney and Nichols assert that it merely follows precedent set by previous government subsidization of America's post-colonial press, wherein subsidies were provided for both printing and postal service. Without these subsidies, journalism would never have survived, say McChesney and Nichols. The figure of $30 billion

is their approximation of what would correlate in contemporary dollars to media subsidies provided in the nineteenth century.

In the face of criticisms that media subject to government subsidy risk becoming tools of the government, McChesney and Nichols contend that government intervention does not equal government control. A proper comparison, they say, would be with government investment in the military or public education. An informed public, they say, is as vital to the health of a society as a protected or educated public.

Regardless of whether McChesney and Nichols' propositions are either practical or adopted in some form, they have further fueled discussions on the state of American journalism in the new decade and provoked debate on the role the government should have in regards to journalism. What do you think—should government subsidize the journalistic industry? Why or why not?

Sources: Robert W. McChesney and John Nichols, "The Death and Life of Great American Newspapers," *The Nation*, March 18, 2009; Robert W. McChesney and John Nichols, "Yes, Journalists Deserve Subsidies Too," *The Washington Post*, October 30, 2010; Robert W. McChesney and John Nichols, *The Death and Life of American Journalism* (New York: Nation Books, 2010).

The experts also note, however, that newspapers should not expect companies to return to the same level of prerecession print advertising when the economy improves. They suggest that much of the cash they have shifted online may not go to newspaper-owned sites because advertisers have found other outlets that provide the same or comparable audiences. They also suggest that a structural—that is, permanent and long-term—change may affect some types of newspapers more dramatically than others. To fully grasp the ways in which the Web is changing newspapers' production, distribution, and exhibition activities, it is important to understand the types of papers that exist, the companies that run them, and the support they receive from advertisers. This will also make it clear that the newspaper industry today is quite varied, and it is important to get a sense of that variety before making generalizations about "the newspaper's" future.

An Overview of the Modern Newspaper Industry

Perhaps the broadest way to think about newspapers in the United States is to divide them into **dailies** (newspapers that are published on newsprint every day, sometimes with the exception of Sunday) and **weeklies** (newspapers that are published on newsprint once or twice a week). According to the newspaper trade magazine

dailies newspapers that are published on newsprint every day, sometimes with the exception of Sunday

weeklies newspapers that are published on newsprint once or twice a week

CRITICAL CONSUMER
SELLING THE FRONT PAGE

Competition from other media and a bad economy has hurt newspapers' ability to maintain and build advertising, traditionally the backbone of the industry's economic model. In the four years from 2006 to 2009, total newspaper ad revenues declined by 44.1 percent, or just under $22 billion.

Looking for ways to sell advertising, the venerable *Los Angeles Times* sold its entire front page as advertising space to Walt Disney for its movie *Alice in Wonderland*. The ad, which included a picture of Johnny Depp as the Mad Hatter, was shown over articles that were reprinted without their titles and bylines. The word "advertisement" appeared in small letters under the masthead. Reports were that Disney had paid $700,000 for the space.

Though the *Times* defended their decision to sell the space, which a spokesperson described as their "most valuable real estate," critics were less enthralled with the choice. Referring to the $700,000 price tag, Roy Peter Clark, a senior scholar at the Poynter Institute for Media Studies, noted "That's a low price to sell your soul." Clark's concern was over the increasing blurriness between a newspapers' editorial voice and its bottom line. The Tribune Company, owners of the *LA Times*, filed for bankruptcy protection in late 2008.

Although Clark is sympathetic to the plight of newspapers in the digital age, he suggests that the selling of front page space for advertisements is a slippery slope. He states, "I want the Los Angeles Times to make a lot of money, and I want them to use that money to do some of the best journalism they've ever done. But I think that this strategy is deceptive, and that my old school ulcer is starting to burn a little a bit."

Do you think that newspapers should be selling their front pages for advertising revenue?

Sources: Eric Sass, "Analysts: Slight Uptick In Radio, Newspapers Slide," *Media Daily News*, March 26, 2010. http://www.mediapost.com/publications/?fa=Articles.showArticle&art_aid=125071 (accessed August 4, 2010); Steve Gorman, "*L.A. Times* Sells Disney Front Page for Movie Ad," Reuters, March 5, 2010. http://www.reuters.com/article/idUS-TRE6250BL20100306 (accessed August 4, 2010).

Editor & Publisher, in 2008 there were 1,408 dailies and 7,319 weeklies. Of the dailies, morning papers outnumbered evening papers 872 to 546. Of the newspapers mentioned, 902 had Sunday editions. That was a substantial rise from 1970, when there were only 586 Sunday editions (see Table 8.2).[3]

Daily Newspapers

Daily newspaper circulation has moved downward over the past quarter century, even though the nation's adult population has grown by more than a third. In 2008, it hovered at about 49 million, about 8 million fewer than in 2003 (see Table 8.3). The three dailies distributed across the country—the *Wall Street Journal*, *The New York Times*, and *USA Today*—have seen different fortunes. The *Journal* has held fairly steady in circulation, the *Times* has dropped a bit, and *USA Today* has dropped sharply, particularly in 2009. Large city newspapers have almost uniformly seen relatively large drops. For example, in 2005 dailies in the top fifty markets lost an average 4.1 percent in circulation, whereas the average across the country was a loss of 3.1 percent. By contrast, circulation in small cities such as Brockton, Massachusetts, or in rural areas such as Pike County, Kentucky, was often fairly stable. Newspapers in smaller markets, though, tend to place more emphasis on local news, and that is harder to find on the Web. Consequently, their hard-copy circulation isn't as negatively affected.[4]

One cause of the circulation drop of a few big-city papers is free newspapers, in particular a daily called *Metro*. A modern example of a tabloid, it claims a reach of 22.8 million readers daily, in fast-food and mass-transit locations.[5] A more generally important source may be the internet—in particular, the ability to access newspapers and other news sources from around the world largely for free.

Some big-city drops were startling. In Web-savvy San Francisco, for example, the *San Francisco Chronicle* lost 17 percent of its circulation in 2005; circulation kept going down toward the decade's end. The drops there underscored that it is not only the poor state of the economy that's threatening the business of big-city newspapers. Rather it's the availability of so many sources, particularly electronic. *The Economist* magazine suggested in 2009 that San Francisco could become the first major American city without a daily newspaper. Reflecting on how much physical newspapers had become devalued by certain groups, the magazine quoted the city's major as

Table 8.2 Number of U.S. Daily Newspapers, 1950–2008

Year	Morning (M)	Evening (E)	Total M&E*	Sunday
1950	322	1,450	1,772	549
1955	316	1,454	1,760	541
1960	312	1,459	1,763	563
1965	320	1,444	1,751	562
1970	334	1,429	1,748	586
1975	339	1,436	1,756	639
1980	387	1,388	1,745	735
1985	482	1,220	1,676	798
1990	559	1,084	1,611	863
1991	571	1,042	1,586	874
1992	596	995	1,570	891
1993	623	954	1,556	884
1994	635	935	1,548	886
1995	656	891	1,533	888
1996	686	846	1,520	890
1997	705	816	1,509	903
1998	721	781	1,489	897
1999	736	760	1,483	905
2000	766	727	1,480	917
2001	776	704	1,468	913
2002	777	692	1,457	913
2003	787	680	1,456	917
2004	814	653	1,457	915
2005	817	645	1,452	914
2006	833	614	1,437	907
2007	867	565	1,422	907
2008	872	546	1,408	902

* "All-day" newspapers publish several editions throughout the day. They are listed in both morning (M) and evening (E) columns but only once in the total.

Source: Newspaper Association of America. http://naa.org/thesource/14.asp#number (accessed February 19, 2007).

Table 8.3 U.S. Daily Newspaper Circulation, 2000–2008				
Year	Morning (M)	Evening (E)	Total M&E	Sunday
2000	46,772,497	9,000,350	55,772,847	59,420,999
2001	46,821,480	8,756,566	55,578,046	59,090,364
2002	46,617,163	8,568,994	55,186,157	58,780,299
2003	46,930,215	8,255,136	55,185,351	58,494,695
2004	46,887,490	7,738,648	54,626,138	57,753,013
2005	46,122,614	7,222,429	53,345,043	55,270,381
2006	45,441,446	6,887,784	52,329,230	53,175,299
2007	44,548,000	6,194,000	50,742,000	51,246,000
2008	42,757,000	5,840,000	48,597,000	49,115,000

Source: Newspaper Association of America. http://naa.org/thesource/14.asp#number (accessed February 19, 2007).

saying, "People under 30 won't even notice."[6] Table 8.4 lists the top twenty U.S. daily newspapers by circulation.

DAILY NEWSPAPER CHAINS It's important to note that, with the exception of the free papers that they often own alone or with the *Metro*, daily newspapers tend not to have competition from other dailies. Moreover, most of the dailies in the U.S. are controlled by a few large firms. In 2000, for example, newspaper chains (or groups) controlled about 1,083 dailies; only about 400 were independent. More recent data are not available, but observations of mergers and acquisitions in the industry suggest that the number of independent dailies has certainly not grown. The logic of chain ownership has traditionally been quite strong. A daily newspaper that was the only one in its area could pretty well dictate prices to local advertisers—car dealers, department stores, movie theaters—that wanted to reach high percentages of the population on a regular basis. Historically, daily newspapers' margins of profit were quite high, far higher than most other industries.[7]

In recent years, newspaper executives and their investors have begun to worry that this logic no longer holds. Losses in readership and increased competition for local advertising by the internet, free newspapers, and other local media have led investors to downgrade the monetary value of some of the biggest newspaper companies. In 2008 and 2009, a national mortgage crisis that left many people without homes, a weak job market, and reduced consumer spending drove many of the large newspaper firms into a tailspin, as advertising plummeted and circulation went down. A number of newspaper chains that had borrowed lots of money now found it hard to pay their debts. With online competition growing every day, analysts began to wonder whether the newspaper industry could rebound. The result was that many newspaper companies were struggling to stay afloat and publicly traded newspaper companies experienced sharp drops—as much as 90 percent—in their stock value. They and privately held

"I'm doing super, but Clark Kent can't find a newspaper that's hiring."

Table 8.4 Top Twenty U.S. Daily Newspapers by Average Circulation, March 2010

Newspaper	Circulation
USA Today	2,281,831
Wall Street Journal	2,070,498
New York Times	1,121,623
Los Angeles Times	907,997
Washington Post	740,947
New York Daily News	708,773
Chicago Tribune	643,086
New York Post	565,679
Long Island Newsday	527,744
Houston Chronicle	477,493
San Francisco Chronicle	468,739
New York Newsday	459,305
Arizona Republic	452,016
Chicago Sun-Times	432,230
Boston Globe	429,552
Atlanta Journal-Constitution	396,888
New Jersey Star-Ledger	382,055
Minneapolis Star Tribune	378,316
Detroit Free Press	370,875
Philadelphia Inquirer	364,974

Source: http://www.newspapers.com/top100.html (accessed March 28, 2010).

firms laid off reporters and closed bureaus in state and national capitals. For example, McClatchy Company, parent company of *The Miami Herald* and *Kansas City Star*, among many other papers, cut its work force by 4,000, or one-third of its previous full-time workers.[8] In 2008 alone, the newspaper industry dropped about 325,000 jobs overall, including 5,900 positions of reporters and editors.[9]

Weekly Newspapers

Weekly newspapers have been somewhat less buffeted by the enormous challenges that daily newspapers have been experiencing (see Table 8.5). In 2008, the total circulation of weeklies—that is, the number of papers people paid for or received free in one publishing cycle—hit about 45 million. Many weeklies have succeeded in carving out topic or audience areas that (so far) daily newspapers have not been able to cover easily. Four coverage topics stand out. Three are geographic—coverage of neighborhoods within cities, of suburbs, and of rural areas. The fourth area of coverage focuses on certain types of people—particular ethnic, racial, occupational, or interest communities. Often those communities cannot support a daily paper, and so a weekly takes hold. A hot type of city paper has been the **alternative weekly**. It is a paper written for a young, urban audience with an eye on political and cultural commentary. **Shoppers** are another popular form of weekly newspaper that bears

alternative weeklies a paper written for a young, urban audience with an eye on political and cultural commentary

shoppers free, nondaily newspapers, typically aimed at people in particular neighborhoods, that are designed primarily to deliver advertisements, but which may also carry some news and feature content

Table 8.5 Circulation for U.S. Weekly Newspapers (Millions)						
	2003	2004	2005	2006	2007	2008
Paid	21.2	20.9	21.4	20.6	20.6	20.3
Free	28.2	28.9	28.1	27.0	26.3	25.2
Total	49.4	49.8	49.5	47.6	46.9	45.5

Source: Veronis Suhler Stevenson, *Communication Industry Forecast 2009–2013* (New York: VSS, 2009), part 12, p. 13.

noting. These are typically aimed at people in particular neighborhoods who might shop at local merchants, are designed primarily to deliver coupons and advertisements, but may also carry some news or feature content.

Newspaper Niches

As the newspaper categories just mentioned suggest, the variety that exists among daily and weekly papers is fascinating. When was the last time you read the *Arctic Sentry*, a weekly North Pole paper that claims a circulation of about 4,000? Are you a lawyer in Philadelphia? If so, you might know that the five-times-a-week *Legal Intelligencer* in Philadelphia counts 5,000 subscribers. If you're a resident of New Orleans, perhaps you will be interested in the *Gambit Weekly* of New Orleans, a self-described locally owned "alternative weekly" that distributes 50,000 copies to 400 locations throughout the area. Did you say you're a college student? You're probably aware that virtually every campus has a newspaper, most of which are free to students and supported by advertising. The largest college paper is the University of Minnesota's *Minnesota Daily*. Actually, it's a daily during the normal school season and a weekly during the summer. And it's a printed daily Monday through Thursday during the normal school season, with an online-only version appearing Fridays.

The African-American press includes about 200 newspapers. With the exception of a few papers such as *The Philadelphia Tribune*, which is published four days a week, almost all appear weekly. Among foreign-language newspapers, Spanish is the most common. Latino papers range from the seven-days-a-week *El Diario* of New York City (circulation 50,000) to the weekly La Jara, Colorado *Conejos County Citizen* to the twice-monthly *El Veterano* published in Vineland, New Jersey. Spanish, though, is only the tip of an iceberg of foreign-language newspapers in the United States. Daily or non-daily newspapers target speakers of Mandarin, Vietnamese, Russian, Yiddish, and Ukrainian, among many other languages.

Financing the Newspaper Business

No matter what their size, topic, or language, newspapers need to make money. They can generate revenues in two ways: from *advertising* or from *circulation*. Advertising is by far the dominant source of money. Historically, printed daily newspapers have received about 75–80 percent of their revenues, and weekly newspapers about 90 percent of their revenues, in this way. Individual papers may have higher or lower percentages, depending on the ad environment. Larger newspapers and weeklies that charge for their copies receive a higher share of their revenues from circulation than do smaller papers and free weeklies.

CULTURE TODAY
ETHNIC NEWSPAPERS

Today, while many newspapers across the nation are struggling with declining circulations, ethnic papers have over the past decade increased in both size and readership. In fact, a poll conducted in 2005 by New California Media (now New American Media) found that 29 million ethnic adults, or 13 percent of the U.S. adult population, consider themselves "primary consumers" of ethnic media.

As such, ethnic papers have become a mainstay in regions with large immigrant populations, including in California, Texas, New York, and Washington, DC. The DC metropolitan area alone distributes about a dozen Spanish-language papers and three Korean-language dailies, among many others, reports *The Washington Post*. Elected State Representative Ana Sol Gutierrez says that minority-language newspapers act as "a lifeline to the community." She continues, "The main media simply [do] not address the issues or provide the information that various ethnic groups need to have."

One such ethnic group is the growing population of Vietnamese-Americans. As Vietnamese immigration to the United States only began in the wake of the Vietnam War, most are first- or second-generation Americans. As such, many Vietnamese-Americans rely on the ethnic press to remain connected to their country of origin while also keeping them informed about issues in their community. Today, Vietnamese immigrants have dozens of dailies and weeklies to choose from, and roughly 80 percent read ethnic papers regularly. The publishers of many of these papers are committed to fulfilling their social responsibility role by getting readers the type of information they are not likely to come across in the mainstream media or in their daily lives.

For example, *Mach Song*, a Vietnamese monthly that publishes in twenty cities across the United States, printed an article encouraging battered women to get help. The article prompted several domestically abused women to contact a social service agency. Other Vietnamese newspapers have also done stories on such sensitive issues as gambling, addiction, and abortion. According to Nguyen Dinh Thang, publisher of *Mach Song*, "We would like to break the silence on critical issues on the community . . . If you choose to ignore it, they don't go away. We have to transmit the information."

Sources: "Ethnic Media in America: The Giant Hidden in Plain Sight," report from California New Media, June 7, 2005. http://www.ncmonline.com/polls/full_em_poll.pdf (accessed February 18, 2007); Phuong Ly, "Ethnic Papers Seeking to Make Voices Heard; Publications Eye Larger Role," *Washington Post*, January 2, 2003, Factiva database.

Advertising

In 2008, physical daily and weekly newspapers together brought in about $40.5 billion in advertising.[10] That sounds like a lot of money, and it is. But consider that in 2005 the amount was $53.1 billion, and it decreased every year afterwards. To understand what's going on, you need to know that the term "advertising" as it applies to newspapers really refers to four different areas: retail advertising from companies with local outlets, classified ads, national ads, and inserts.

RETAIL ADVERTISING   Retail advertising is carried out by establishments located in the same geographic area as the newspaper in which the ad is placed. Think of ads from computer electronics stores, department stores, hospitals, car dealerships, restaurants, realtors, and movie theaters. Some of these advertisers may be parts of national chains, but the purpose of the ads is to persuade people to shop in the local outlets. Retail advertising is the most important of the four main areas of newspaper advertising. It currently makes up about 54 percent of the total in daily papers and an even higher percentage in weeklies.

CLASSIFIED ADVERTISING   The second most lucrative type of newspaper advertisement is the classified ad. A **classified ad** is a short announcement for a product or service that is typically grouped with announcements for other products

classified ad a short announcement for a product or service that is typically grouped with announcements for other products or services of the same kind

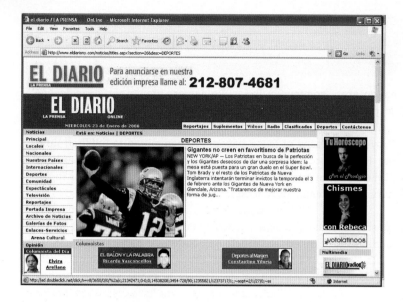

El Diario/La Presna is the oldest Spanish-language newspaper in the United States. Its Sunday edition has a full week-in-review of Latin American news, an arts and culture calendar, and highlights of Latino sports leagues.

national ads advertisements placed by large national and multinational firms that have branch stores and other operations that do business within the newspaper's geographic area

co-op advertising advertising in which the manufacturers or distributors of products provide money to exhibitors in order to help the exhibitor with the cost of promoting a particular product

freestanding insert (FSI) preprinted sheets that advertise particular products, services, or retailers, most often accompanying the Sunday edition of a newspaper; FSIs are not printed as a part of the paper itself, but are inserted into the paper after the printing process has been completed

or services of the same kind. Newspapers typically sell classified ad space by the line to people who want to offer everything from houses to beds to bikes. In recent years, the amount of money daily print newspapers has generated through classified ads has plummeted—from about $15.8 billion and 35 percent of daily newspaper advertising in 2003 to $9.9 billion and 28 percent in 2008. The drop has a lot to do with the rise of online real estate, auto, and general classified sites, especially free (or very cheap) ones such as Craigslist. They provide users with continually updated information, interactivity, and immediate responsiveness that papers cannot possibly match.

NATIONAL ADVERTISING   **National ads** are advertisements placed by large national and multinational firms that do business in a newspaper's geographic area. They represent about 17 percent of daily newspaper advertising. Airline and cruise line ads are often national purchases. Political advertisements and movie ads also often fit the "national" tag. The distinction between retail and national ads may not always be clear. Sometimes what appear to be retail ads are actually national ads. The reason is that national marketers often provide **co-op advertising** money to retailers that carry their products. In co-op advertising, manufacturers or distributors of products provide money to exhibitors in order to help the exhibitor with the cost of promoting a particular product. A soup manufacturer, for example, might provide a local supermarket chain with an allowance to purchase ads that highlight the manufacturer's soups. The money may be used to buy time on local radio and TV, as well as ads in local newspapers.

FREESTANDING INSERTS   Retail and national advertising can show up in newspapers next to the actual stories (the most common way) or as inserts, often called **freestanding inserts (FSIs)**. These are preprinted sheets that advertise particular products, services, or retailers. FSIs are not printed as part of the paper itself, but are inserted into the paper after the printing process has been completed. Typically, an FSI is sent to the newspaper firm, which charges the advertiser for placing it in the newspaper and distributing it. FSIs are most numerous in Sunday papers and can be devoted to one or multiple advertisers. Both types often carry discount coupons, which provide incentives for people to buy a product by giving them a certain amount off the retail price. The FSIs that carry products of more than one advertiser typically are created by an FSI company. News America Marketing, a subsidiary of News Corporation, is a major firm involved in this work. This insert company makes deals with advertisers to carry their messages in FSIs in specific areas around the country at specific times. The advertisers pay the FSI firm; that firm generates the sheets, pays the newspapers to carry the sheets, and pockets the profits.

When advertisers buy space in newspapers, a major way they evaluate it is by looking at the **cost per thousand readers** (often abbreviated **CPM**, for **cost per mil**). This is the basic measurement of advertising efficiency in all media; it is used by advertisers to evaluate how much space they will buy in a given newspaper or other medium and what price they will pay. If a full-page ad in a particular newspaper that reaches a thousand people costs $10,000, the CPM is $10. Because advertisers often compare media in terms of CPM, even firms that have the only daily newspapers in their cities worry about coming up with ad prices that can compete with radio, TV, or even local ads inserted into national magazines.

Advertising Challenges Facing Newspapers

As we have discussed, the Web is the greatest source of printed newspapers' long-term competition over advertising. In response, most newspapers have established websites with which they try to capture the retail, national, and classified funds that have gone online. Sometimes it means making a deal with classified advertisers to place both print and online ads for a package price. That is something the *Atlanta Journal-Constitution* has tried, for example. Another approach that newspaper firms have used to capture advertising that goes to the Web is to create non-newspaper sites that copy their competitors. Examples are cars.com, a car buying and selling site; apartments.com, where people can find places to rent in specific cities; and careerbuilder.com, a help-wanted site. These new businesses often involve joint ventures on the part of several firms. For example, Gannett, McClatchy, and Tribune Company own Careerbuilder, which has become a major job-hunting site. In 2007, the CEO of the Newspaper Association of America said that, during this time of "transition" in the business, newspaper companies "have to continue to work together closely and productively and with a shared sense of commitment."[11]

It is important to note that the advertising money that newspapers collect from activities online, though growing, represents a small percentage of the ad revenues they bring in. In 2005, for example, daily newspaper companies made about $3.1 billion from online advertisers. That sounds like a lot until you recognize that they draw $41 billion worth of ads to their printed pages.[12] You might think that there is really no problem here—as advertisers move their ads to the internet, the $40 billion that they now invested in the newspaper's printed page will simply move over to its electronic one. But it doesn't work that way. Advertisers have been leaving newspapers to put money on the Web, but they have often been doing it in places other than in those newspapers. Often they desert the papers because the other places are cheaper or because they can reach younger people than the ones who read the papers' sites. As for the advertisers who do come to the newspapers' sites, they insist on paying far less per thousand readers than they would pay in the print addition. They can do that because the competition for ads online among websites is so fierce that it has driven down prices drastically. The upshot is that, even when newspapers attract more people online than they do offline, the amount of money they make advertising to them is far lower.

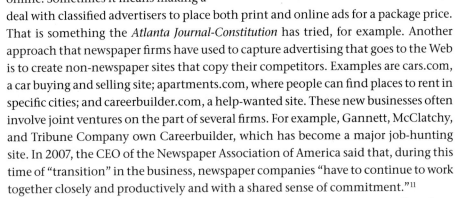

Free-standing inserts (or FSIs) like the ones shown here are used to get maximum impact at a minimal cost, pinpoint a target market, and target customers in their home.

cost per thousand readers or cost per mil (CPM) the basic measurement of advertising efficiency in all media; it is used by advertisers to evaluate how much space they will buy in a given newspaper or other medium, and what price they will pay

Circulation Challenges Facing Newspapers

As if the problem of advertising were not enough, circulation presents another major revenue challenge for newspapers. We have already noted that the circulation for

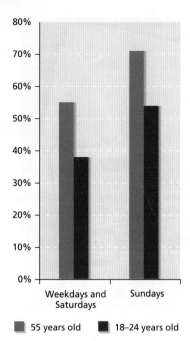

weeklies (especially free weeklies) has been steady, whereas a downturn in readership of the dailies has caused alarm among newspaper executives. Although newspaper income from circulation is far less than that from advertising, it is still critical because advertisers typically buy space in newspapers because of their circulation. Two particular circulation issues concern many daily newspaper executives. One is whether young people will stop reading printed papers because they are so heavily involved in electronic media. The other is whether young people or anyone else will pay for digital newspapers in amounts that will allow newspapers to survive as the printed version decreases in importance and the amount of advertising they receive online is not enough to support staffs of professional journalists.

Executives consider the question about young people critical. They believe that newspaper publishers' inability to attract new young readers is a major factor in the circulation declines. As Figure 8.1 shows, whereas in 1988 55 percent of those aged 18–24 reported being a daily newspaper reader, only 33 percent said that in 2008. Similarly, whereas in 1988 69 percent of those aged 35–54 said they read daily newspapers, the proportion dropped to 48 percent in 2008. One analysis of these data concluded that a generational sea change was occurring and that younger adults were leaving the printed page to go elsewhere for news. "The decline in overall readership can be attributed to the migration of readers to other media offering around-the-clock news coverage, including cable news networks and internet news sources, such as news areas on the leading search engines and blogs, RSS, social networking sites, Twitter, and widget feeds."[13]

If you don't know the meaning of some of these terms, don't worry—we'll cover them later in this chapter or in the one about the internet. Here we'll note that the movement of those under age 55 years to all these electronic places to get news raises two major challenges for publishers and editors. One is to try to stop people from leaving print by making it attractive to all groups. The other is to encourage visitors to their websites while figuring out how to make money from those sites. Newspaper executives are trying to deal with these concerns using both print and digital strategies. Print strategies involve trying to create products that are both attractive to readers and profitable. Digital strategies involve trying to rethink the presentation and delivery of news as well as who should pay for it. Both strategies affect the agendas of news that newspaper firms are offering their audiences. Let's look at both through our familiar categories of production, distribution, and exhibition.

Figure 8.1 Who Reads Newspapers?

This graph, based on research conducted in 2005, shows that Americans over fifty-five years old read the daily newspaper in much greater numbers than Americans aged from 18 to 24 years. Newspaper executives are trying to secure younger adult readership by using both print and digital strategies.

Production and the Newspaper Industry

In discussing the production of newspapers, we will focus on two general areas. One involves the creation of the content that goes into the papers, and the other involves the actual technical process of putting together a newspaper.

Creating Newspaper Content

The creation of a newspaper's content differs between dailies and weeklies, and between newspapers with large circulations and those with small ones. We can, however, generalize about the basic approach to

"I'd like to see you do this online."

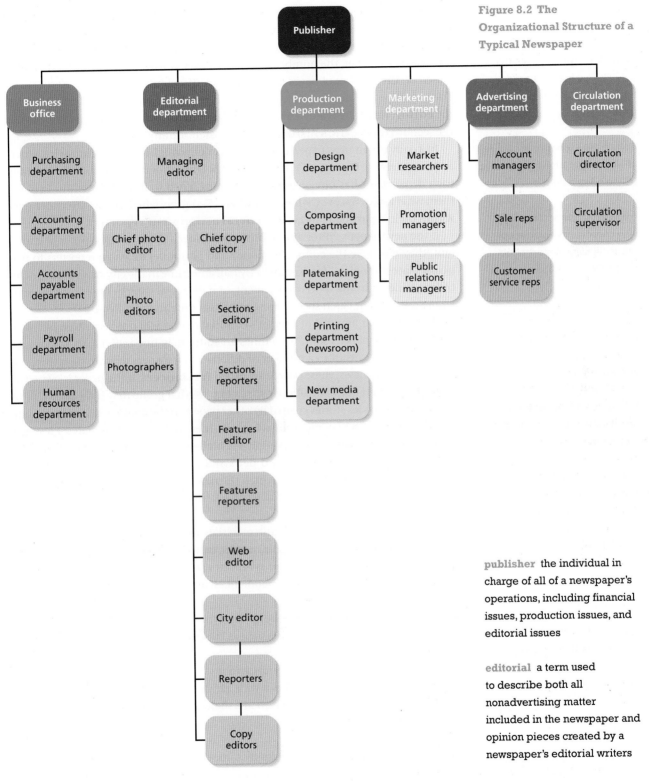

Figure 8.2 The Organizational Structure of a Typical Newspaper

publisher the individual in charge of all of a newspaper's operations, including financial issues, production issues, and editorial issues

editorial a term used to describe both all nonadvertising matter included in the newspaper and opinion pieces created by a newspaper's editorial writers

creating content (see Figure 8.2). The newspaper's **publisher** is in charge of the entire company's operation, which includes financial issues (getting advertising, increasing circulation), production issues, and editorial issues. **Editorial** in this case has two meanings. In a narrow sense, it means the creation of opinion pieces by the firm's editorial writers. More broadly, it means all non-advertising matter in the paper.

The publisher sets an **advertising–editorial ratio**, which determines the balance between the amount of space available for advertisements and the amount of

advertising–editorial ratio set by the publisher, this ratio determines the balance between the amount of space available for advertisements and the amount of space available for editorial matter in one issue of a newspaper

news hole the number of pages left over and available for editorial matter, based upon the number of pages needed to run advertisements

editor the executive in charge of all the operations required to fill the news hole

managing editor individual who coordinates the work of the sections or departments within the newspaper

general assignment reporters newspaper reporters who cover a variety of topics within their department

beat a specific, long-term assignment that covers a single topic area

freelancer a worker who makes a living by accepting and completing creative assignments from a number of different newspapers—sometimes several at one time

wire service an organization that, for a fee, supplies newspapers with a continual stream of hard news and feature stories about international, national, and even state topics via high-speed telephone and/or cable connections

syndicate a company that sells soft news editorial matter, cartoons, and photographs to newspapers for use

deadline the time when the final version of an assignment has to be in

space available for editorial matter in one issue of a newspaper. A typical daily newspaper carries 60 percent advertising and 40 percent editorial content. Weeklies have a higher percentage of advertising; some are virtually all advertising. For any particular issue of the paper, the number of pages left over and available for editorial matter (based on the number of pages needed for advertisements) is called the **news hole**. The executive in charge of all the operations required to fill the news hole is called the **editor**. He or she is aided by a **managing editor**, who coordinates the work of the sections (or departments) of the paper if there are any.

In a daily urban newspaper, typical departments might be sports, lifestyles, entertainment/leisure, business, TV, city news, a "neighborhoods" section, and real estate. Each department has one or more reporters assigned to it, and the editor may tell them what topics to cover, when, and where. Reporters who cover a variety of topics within their department are called **general assignment reporters**.

If the newspaper's editor and publisher consider a department especially important, they may give the editor the money and personnel to assign reporters to particular places or topics—for example, city hall and crime in the city news department, college athletics in the sports department, or movie reviewing in the entertainment/leisure department. Such specific long-term assignments are called **beats**.

However, a fair amount of a paper's editorial matter will not be written by members of the newspaper's staff. Sometimes an editor may hire individuals who accept creative assignments from a number of different newspapers to write such things as music or book reviews; these people are called **freelancers**. If the paper is owned by a group—Gannett or Knight-Ridder, for example—that group may have its own news service that provides stories created by other papers in the chain. A substantial number of stories also will come from **wire services** such as the Associated Press and Reuters. These services, for a fee, supply via high-speed telephone and/or cable connections a continual stream of hard news and feature stories about international, national, and even state topics for which the newspaper may have no reporters. Special wire editors and others continually check the stream of stories that "come over the wires" for likely material.

Syndicates also provide important materials for newspapers. A **syndicate** is a company that sells soft news editorial matter, cartoons, and photographs to newspapers for use. There are hundreds of syndicates that supply a variety of content for different departments and different audiences, including:

- The Washington Post Writers Group, the syndication arm of *The Washington Post*, circulates the work of columnists such as Ellen Goodman, George Will, and David Broder
- Copley News Service sells editorial cartoons
- Universal Press Syndicate offers a wide range of choices, from "Dear Abby" and Jeane Dixon's "Your Horoscope" to Marshall Leob's "Your Money" column to the "Doonesbury" comic strip

As you might imagine, syndicates supply some of the most popular parts of a paper.

For every issue, editors from all departments draw on all these sources to make up the paper. Under the watchful eye of editors, reporters on beats and those assigned to particular stories carry out their assignments. When it comes to the print version, everyone knows the paper's **deadline**—the time when the final version of their work has to be in. The news staff enter the stories into computers, which are linked to the managing editor and copyeditors, as well as to others on the paper. **Copyeditors** read the stories the reporters write and edit them for length, accuracy, style, and grammar. Headlines are written, and photographs and design work to accompany

CULTURE TODAY
PROPUBLICA

Managing Editor Stephen Engelberg, left, and Editor of Online Development Scott Klein, seated right, join with staff members of ProPublica in an editorial meeting in New York.

When people think of investigative journalism, they often mention classic 1970s examples—Woodward and Bernstein's reporting on Watergate for *The Washington Post* or Seymour Hersh's descriptions of the My Lai Massacre in *The New York Times*. There is, however, a long tradition of newspaper investigations to unearth corruption and abuses of power. But with the industry in grave shape and news outlets cutting staff, many publishers do not want to dedicate resources to the time-consuming, expensive process of investigative journalism. How can the public be ensured this valuable good in the wake of such losses?

Herbert and Marion Sandler's answer to that question is the independent, nonprofit news outlet ProPublica. Sensing a decline in investigative journalism nationwide as newspaper industries cut costs to stay afloat,

the Sandlers—former chief executives of the Golden West Financial Corporation—founded ProPublica in 2007 to fill that vacuum. They pledged $10 million annually to run the organization and hired a former managing editor of the *Wall Street Journal*, Paul Steiger, to helm the operation as the editor-in-chief.

With a staff of roughly thirty full-time journalists working out of an office in Lower Manhattan, ProPublica works to produce articles about the "abuse of power and failure to uphold the public interest." Work has included stories titled "New Orleans: Chaos in the Streets & in the Police Ranks, Too," "Buried Secrets: Gas Drilling's Environmental Threat," and "When Caregivers Harm: Unwatched Nurses." The organization offers its output to news partners such as USA Today for distribution. The stories are then made available for republishing under a "creative commons" contract.

The work of ProPublica has encouraged news observers to call for the creation of investigative journalism endowments in America's premier news outlets. "Endowments would enhance newspapers' autonomy while shielding them from the economic forces that are now tearing them down," wrote David Swensen and Michael Schmidt of *The New York Times*. "Enlightened philanthropists must act now or watch a vital component of American democracy fade into irrelevance."

Sources: Joseph Brean, "Journalism, at your Service," *National Post*, March 6, 2010, p. A6; Jaimy Lee, "Q&A—Paul Steiger, ProPublica," *PR Week*, December 9, 2009, p. 20; Hamilton Nolan, "ProPublica Set to Revive Investigative Journalism," *PR Week*, October 22, 2007, p. 3; David Swensen and Michael Schmidt, "News You Can Endow," *The New York Times*, January 28, 2009, Section A, p. 31.

---

the stories are selected. Computer-ready syndicated material is chosen and added to the mix. The newspaper is ready to be printed.

Until around 2005, that was it: the work cycle of a newspaper centered on the time at which one or more editions had to be printed. When newspaper organizations began putting their material online, they followed this approach. To a large extent what readers saw on the Web was a reproduction of the printed product. Updates rarely happened, and editors were hesitant to put a story online that would reveal happenings that would override or contradict the printed product. That reluctance changed rather quickly, as newspaper executives realized that they were now competing with local and national television sites, including all-news channels, that continually were updating stories and presenting new ones. Newspaper executives decided they had to do that as well, and so many sites have become

copyeditors the individuals who edit stories written by reporters; they edit for length, accuracy, style, and grammar, and write headlines to accompany the stories

24/7 around-the-clock news operations that continually update stories and present new ones

blog a sort of online diary or journal that often invites reader responses

users the audience of newspaper websites

round-the-clock—or **24/7**—operations. Today, stories are just as likely to premiere online as in the printed edition.

Moreover, the difference between the online and offline reportorial staff is blurring. For certain topics not covered in the printed version—say, technology or certain local neighborhoods—the website might hire special staff. In general, though, the expectation today is that reporters will create for both the print and online products. That often means that they have to learn new skills that go beyond straightforward reportage. "Creating" for the online "paper" often means preparing a photographic or videographic version of the written material. In many cases, it also means writing a Web log, or **blog**. That is a sort of diary or journal that may describe the events surrounding the coverage and that invites reader responses.

As you might imagine, this is a lot of work, and reporters have complained that the need to produce ever more materials for analog and digital forms does more than get them tired. Piling on the new reportorial tasks, they say, makes them focus so much on getting out the product in different ways that they have little time to conduct time-consuming legwork and thinking that will help them get below the surface of stories. Publishers and editors, though perhaps sympathetic, state that an expectation of intense cross-media activity is the direction in which the news world is moving.

If you've been to an online newspaper, you have probably noticed that the contents do not stop with the staff's takes on the day's news. Increasingly, newspaper websites aim to encourage their audiences—called **users** on the Web—to engage with the site in numerous ways. On many sites, for example, you can email a reporter

CRITICAL CONSUMER
SHOULD NEWSPAPERS DELETE OBJECTIONABLE MATERIAL?

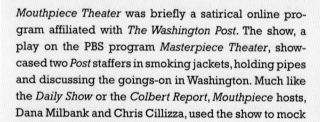

Mouthpiece Theater was briefly a satirical online program affiliated with *The Washington Post*. The show, a play on the PBS program *Masterpiece Theater*, showcased two *Post* staffers in smoking jackets, holding pipes and discussing the goings-on in Washington. Much like the *Daily Show* or the *Colbert Report*, *Mouthpiece* hosts, Dana Milbank and Chris Cillizza, used the show to mock the present state of political punditry.

However, in a segment that aired in late July 2009, Milbank and Cillizza suggested that the Secretary of State, Hillary Clinton, drinks "Mad Bitch Beer." The episode set off a series of angry post as bloggers and tweeters branded the comment sexist, inappropriate, offensive, and unfunny. The *Post* quickly pulled the segment from its website, but the backlash continued as people, directed to the episode through alternative websites, were able to find the segment and comment for themselves.

The Washington Post's decision to pull the segment without any notification on their website raised many eyebrows as critics berated the *Post* for the lack of transparency in the removal of the episode and for their failure to take responsibility for the comments made by their staffers and posted within their website.

On August 6, a full week after the episode was originally posted, *The Washington Post* published an article announcing that the newspaper was canceling *Mouthpiece Theater*, citing it as a failed journalistic experiment. Milbank and Cillizza took responsibilities for the comment and the termination of the show. Both staffers were retained by the *Post* in their original positions.

As many traditional newspapers move online, this event raises some important questions about the responsibility of journalists and editors in a digital environment. Do editors have the same responsibility for content that appears online as they do on their website? Should they? Further, when a decision is made to remove offensive material from a paper's website, is there an obligation to alert readers to this decision? Just because online material can be added and removed (if imperfectly) from a website, should it be?

Sources: Greg Marx, "*Post* Pulls Milbank's 'Mad Bitch' Video," *Columbia Journalism Review*. http://www.cjr.org (accessed September 11, 2009); Howard Kurtz, "*Post* Video 'Theater' Ends its Run," *The Washington Post*, August 6, 2009.

whose story you have read; join a "community" of readers to discuss particular news topics; create a blog around any topic you like; search the week's news by using key words of your choosing; browse an archive of newspaper issues that may go back decades and beyond; watch video reviews, product demonstrations, or news stories from the paper's staff or one of the wire services; click on an article so that the computer will read it to you; and (of course, and importantly for the sites) click on ads.

The Technology of Publishing the Paper

Despite this seeming cornucopia of material in the digital version of the daily or weekly newspaper, many people still do read the printed version or both. Creating a website for them to read on a 24/7 schedule is a challenging and expensive activity. It requires information technology professionals who tie the journalists into a world involving the creation of sites with many layers and the storage of huge amounts of material. Interestingly, much of the printed product starts out digital, too. Computers and related digital technologies are the mainstays of contemporary newspapers. Reporters now can go anywhere with portable computers and, if there is a telephone connection, send stories to the home department in a form that can be immediately read and printed. Even when local phone service isn't available, some reporters have telephones that beam messages to satellites so that they can "phone in" their stories. Similar portable transmitters allow photographers to beam images to the newspaper from the place of action. Digital cameras, which translate the world directly into computer code, allow images to be instantly entered into the computers.

Key to the activity is a process called **pagination**—the ability to compose and display completed pages, with pictures and graphics, on screen. In large daily and weekly newspapers, the technology enables the editors to transmit these images to the plates of the company's printing presses. See Figure 8.3 to see how *USA Today* uses electronic pagination in its production process.

Smaller papers use similar, though much less expensive, approaches. With personal computers, editors can use desktop publishing software to create the paper's layout. They can then take the results to a local printing shop, where the material can be printed relatively inexpensively. The costs of the operation are low enough that classified notices and ads from local merchants can support these small papers. The result has been the rise of free weekly papers that focus on sports, shows, politics, or neighborhood events in sections of large urban areas. Typically, the staff is quite small and the advertising–editorial ratio is quite high. Nevertheless, some observers see these smaller local newspapers as providing a wider range of information to their audiences than the dailies provided when they had monopolies.

pagination the process by which newspaper pages are composed and displayed as completed pages, with pictures and graphics

Distribution and the Newspaper Industry

Newspaper distribution means bringing the finished issue to the point of exhibition. For a newspaper, that might be a person's house, a newsstand, a supermarket, or a vending machine—or to a computer or mobile device. Distributing a website on a 24/7 schedule is at least as challenging as creating it. The company's information technology professionals must coordinate the serving of stories to users whose computers or mobile devices (typically "smart" cellphones) come to the sites, the serving of ads to those users (often with the help of separate ad-serving companies), and attempts to learn about users (in part to help sell ads) by getting them to register and by tracking their activities on the sites. Because these activities make the newspaper

newspaper distribution bringing the finished newspaper issue to the point of exhibition

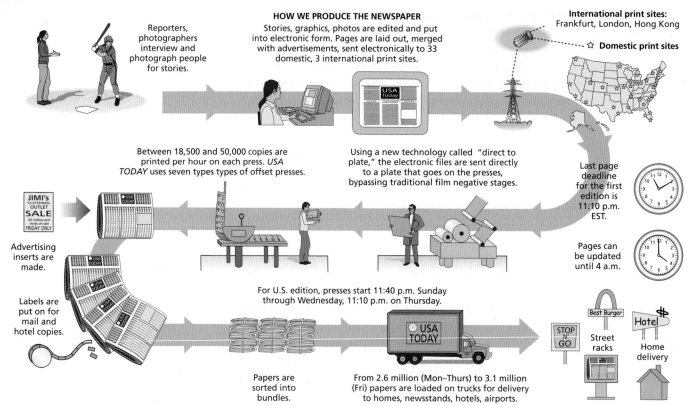

HOW WE PRODUCE THE NEWSPAPER

Reporters, photographers interview and photograph people for stories.

Stories, graphics, photos are edited and put into electronic form. Pages are laid out, merged with advertisements, sent electronically to 33 domestic, 3 international print sites.

International print sites: Frankfurt, London, Hong Kong

☆ **Domestic print sites**

Between 18,500 and 50,000 copies are printed per hour on each press. *USA TODAY* uses seven types types of offset presses.

Using a new technology called "direct to plate," the electronic files are sent directly to a plate that goes on the presses, bypassing traditional film negative stages.

Last page deadline for the first edition is 11:10 p.m. EST.

JIMI's CLOTHING OUTLET SALE All clothes and shoes on sale FRIDAY ONLY

Advertising inserts are made.

Labels are put on for mail and hotel copies.

Pages can be updated until 4 a.m.

For U.S. edition, presses start 11:40 p.m. Sunday through Wednesday, 11:10 p.m. on Thursday.

Best Burger   Hotel $

STOP N' GO

Street racks   Home delivery

Papers are sorted into bundles.

From 2.6 million (Mon–Thurs) to 3.1 million (Fri) papers are loaded on trucks for delivery to homes, newsstands, hotels, airports.

Figure 8.3 How *USA Today* is Produced

USA Today is the United States, only national daily general-interest newspaper. It is printed every Monday through Friday at thirty-three locations across the country. Source: Copyright © 2000, *USA Today*. Reprinted with permission.

firms part of the larger internet industry (along with news sites that have no relation to newspapers), we will discuss these topics in Chapter 14.

Distributing physical newspapers is enormously challenging as well. Newspaper firms, especially dailies, typically distribute their own products. The task is carried out by the circulation department's personnel, under the authority of the business manager and publisher.

Determining Where to Market the Newspaper

The most basic question the circulation department must confront has to do with the geographic area in which it will market the paper. Many considerations go into making the decision. Among them are:

- The location of consumers that major advertisers would like to reach
- The location of present and future printing plants
- Competing papers
- The loyalty to the paper, if any, that people in different areas seem to have

Any or all of these considerations can change, of course. New major advertisers may be found, new printing plants can be built in certain places and not others, and marketing can try to encourage loyalty to the paper and beat the competition. The newspaper's businesspeople, however, must examine the costs and benefits of every decision. The solutions they arrive at must necessarily vary with the newspaper's circumstances.

Executives at *The New York Times*, for example, have decided that their audience is an upper-income, educated class of readers that reaches far beyond the borders of New York City. As a result, they distribute a digital version of the paper by satellite to printing plants throughout the United States every day. The *Times* contracts with local companies to distribute the paper in those areas.

Most daily newspapers do not have such lofty circulation goals, but their executives do have to decide on the limits of their marketing territory. In deciding on those limits, they may be losing out on some ads from chain stores that have branches in the outlying areas that they have excluded. On the other hand, the paper won't incur the substantial costs of marketing and delivering papers beyond its primary territory.

ALTERNATIVE DISTRIBUTION AND MARKETING TACTICS   In recent years, some newspaper groups have been having their cake and eating it too when it comes to winning chain store ads and not incurring the high costs of "fringe" circulation. Their tactic has been to buy dailies that serve adjacent communities. The groups then offer advertisers, particularly national and regional retailers, a single buy for the larger geographic area. The newspaper groups also save substantial amounts of money by combining their existing production facilities and staff. At the same time, each individual paper keeps its traditional coverage area and the loyalty of the readers in that area.

One example of a group using this tactic is Media General Newspapers, a group that owns, among other media holdings, three daily papers along U.S. Highway 29, an important business and residential corridor from Danville, Virginia, to the outskirts of Washington, DC. A shopper company that takes this approach is Newport Media, which owns weekly *pennysavers* across New York City, Long Island, and New Jersey. The firm boasts that it can offer advertisers "near 100% saturation advertising."

Exhibition in the Newspaper Industry

An online newspaper has a distribution site; see *The Washington Post*'s Washingtonpost.com, for example. Like other online news outlets, it is distributed through exhibitors—typically cable and telephone companies—to computers, smartphones and other devices wherever users can and want to pick it up. In the physical world, the exhibition point of a newspaper is more specific and depends upon its type. Free weeklies are often placed in special boxes in stores or on streets, with placards inviting people to take a copy. Weeklies and dailies that cost money can, of course, also be found in stores and in coin-operated boxes on streets as well as on newsstands.

However, circulation executives for paid weeklies and dailies prefer the exhibition point for their papers to be their readers' homes or places of work, as opposed to a newsstand. The reason is that delivery to a home or office implies a subscription to the paper, a paid-in-advance commitment to receive the product. Such commitments help the paper's businesspeople sell advertising to the paper by enabling them to guarantee that advertisers can reach a fixed number of consumers in particular locations.

Achieving Total Market Coverage

Historically, paid-subscription daily or weekly newspapers could guarantee to advertisers that their ads would reach virtually every home in a newspaper's coverage area. However, because of the nationwide decrease in the percentage of homes receiving newspapers, the major dailies or weeklies in a region can no longer automatically provide advertisers with what people in the industry call **total market coverage (TMC)**. This problem, though, means opportunities for others. One direct

total market coverage (TMC) reaching nearly all households in its market area

direct mail firms advertising firms that mail advertisements directly to consumers' homes

marriage mail outlets advertising firms that specialize in delivering circular advertisements that might otherwise be inserted as FSIs in newspapers; these firms produce preprinted sheets and brochures from a number of advertisers, bundle them together, and send them directly to consumers' homes

competitor is a "shopper" firm, like Newport Media, which was mentioned earlier. Its marketing literature boasts that its free papers can offer "customized home distribution programs" that will result in "near 100% saturation" of the audiences that advertisers desire.

Other competitors offering TMC to advertisers are **direct mail firms**, which mail ads directly to homes. Companies that specialize in delivering circulars that might otherwise be newspaper inserts are called **marriage mail outfits**; they produce sheets and brochures from several advertisers that are bundled together (hence the term "marriage") and sent via the post office to every address in a particular area. With this approach, names are not nearly as important as reaching every house or apartment. In fact, the required postal cards accompanying the ads are often addressed simply to "current resident." There is little, if any, nonadvertising matter in the package. Some would say that what we have here is quintessential junk mail.

Retailers have found that marriage mail and shoppers are efficient ways to get their FSIs out to entire neighborhoods when local newspapers cannot offer that kind of service or when they are more expensive. As you can imagine, marriage mail firms and shoppers have siphoned away newspapers' coveted supermarket advertising and FSIs. But the newspapers are fighting back. One way is to compete directly. Some newspapers have started their own shoppers and marriage mail operations or have bought their competitors. Other papers have supplemented their regular paid circulation to certain key areas with a weekly TMC circulation. They accomplish that goal by delivering a special version of the newspaper (usually a compilation of stories or a sports section) to every nonsubscribing home in an area. Ads and FSIs are included with the package.

A Key Industry Issue: Building Readership

Despite such tactics for reaching large proportions of their target areas, publishers and editors are extremely concerned with the recent downturn in newspaper readership trends. They know that physical newspapers charge more per thousand readers for advertising than their websites do and bring in far more advertising revenue than their Web versions. In the foreseeable future, their organizations could not survive without a healthy print edition. As a result, then, many newspapers are pursuing two types of approaches to building readership. One group of approaches might be called analog strategies, which involve the physical paper. The other might be termed digital strategies, which involve the website and other internet-related ways that the paper can intersect with the lives of its readers. We will look at each group separately.

Building Print Readership

One question is basic, "What does a physical newspaper have to look like to attract more people, now and in the future?" Newspaper executives have been working hard to develop answers. Here are a number of approaches that they have tried, together and separately.

MORE ATTRACTIVE AND COLORFUL LAYOUTS   Most papers have switched to color presses and embarked on major redesigns aimed at stopping readers in their tracks and getting them to want to read every issue. Other features designed to be reader-friendly include fewer stories on the front page, more liberal use of white space, quick news summaries and notes about "what's inside," and more use of charts and pictures to convey information. Individual stories, too, have gotten shorter. The aim is to create a quick and not too taxing read.

SECTIONS DESIGNED TO ATTRACT CRUCIAL AUDIENCES   Newspapers aim to create a collection of articles that are relevant to the audiences that newspaper companies care about. For many papers, that means the people aged twenty-something to forty-something (and hopefully relatively well off) that most major national and local advertisers covet. To find out what those target audiences want, publishers employ research firms to conduct surveys and focus groups. The idea is to concentrate on news that people can "use"—that is, news that is clearly relevant to their lives.

EMPHASIZING LOCALISM   Many newspaper executives have come to the conclusion that it is reporting on the communities in which their readers live that give them a leg up on competition from other media firms, especially online news sources. Newspaper consultant George Hayes put it bluntly: "One should never underestimate the importance of being local! Newspapers own that."[14] Being local can mean many things. It may mean publishing news about local school events, photos of county fair winners, and letters to the editor that discuss community affairs. It may mean polling readers through surveys or focus groups to find out what they think are the most important issues in local, state, or national election campaigns. It may mean covering problems in the area and editorializing with vigor about ways to solve them. Newspapers are using these and other techniques to encourage people in their areas to see them as related to their lives on a regular basis.

Even papers in the biggest U.S. cities, which have tended to emphasize national and international coverage more than the goings-on in neighborhoods, have begun to increase their attention to local news. In some places, it means increasing the attention that city and regional stories get on the front page. That has been happening at the *Philadelphia Inquirer*. In many papers it means expanding or adding sections that relate to the goings-on in neighborhoods. Those sections are typically distributed once a week to the places that they cover. That specificity allows advertisers to target segments of the newspaper's market without buying the entire distribution of the paper. As newspapers increase their stress on localism, the number of sections is likely to grow, as is their frequency. The *Washington Post* may be a pacesetter in this regard. In 2007 it experimented with creating a twice-a-week section for a particularly wealthy DC suburb that its advertisers wanted to reach.

Related to this desire to reach out to various segments of readership are some major newspaper publishers' investments in, or outright purchase of, weekly and smaller daily papers in the markets that surround them. Some of these papers are useful to have because they represent direct competition for advertising. Other properties executives consider useful include free commuter dailies, ethnic publications, and alternative weeklies. These fill a different but still important niche: they attract with lower rates smaller advertisers who would not advertise in the larger daily.

Building Digital Newspapers

To make and keep their sites attractive to readers, newspapers have been continually updating the print and audiovisual materials mentioned earlier. Many offer users the ability to download audio stories automatically to their MP3 players; this activity is called **podcasting**. Another offering is the **RSS feed**. That is a flow of stories on topics the reader has chosen that the newspaper sends to the individual's computer

podcasting audio recordings that can be downloaded to MP3 players

RSS feed a flow of stories on topics the reader has chosen that the newspaper sends to the individual's computer (via a special reader or a website such as MyYahoo) so that the user does not have to go to the paper's website to see it

mobile feed stories specifically formatted for the user's cellphone, "smart" device, or personal digital assistant

(via a special reader or a website such as http://myyahoo.com) so that the user does not have to go to the paper's website to see it. Another service is the **mobile feed**— stories specifically formatted for the user's cellphone, "smart" device, or personal digital assistant. Also common on newspaper sites are blogs created by reporters who work for the newspaper. They write on a regular basis about the subject they cover in ways that shed light on both the topic and the journalism process; comment sections invite responses from readers. The overall aim of the blogs, comment sections, podcasts, RSS feeds, and mobile feeds is to encourage users to pull toward them parts of the newspaper that they like. Each of the feeds comes with advertising, and newspapers have been busy trying to figure out how to efficiently serve ads to people based on both their registration material and their activities online (for example their interest in the automotive section or the style section). The hope is that advertisers looking for people with those interests and backgrounds will pay a premium to reach them.

The interest in targeting users for advertisers parallels a belief by newspaper publishers that a key way for them to distinguish themselves from other news sites their users can visit is to emphasize the local. This is the digital version of the "own the local" strategy that newspapers are pursuing with their print versions. Because the digital world allows for so much more content than in a physical paper, some publishers have begun to say they are following a "hyper-local" strategy online. That is, that they want to reach out to many more geographic and demographic segments of the newspaper's area than the physical paper ever could—and garner advertisers who want to reach those very local segments. For a big-city paper, being hyper-local means covering school meetings across many neighborhoods, continually listing restaurants and entertainment activities in different parts of the city, reporting on many school and amateur sporting events, hosting the discussions of neighborhood clubs—in short, trying to become the go-to place for information about what is going on in the area. Carrying out this goal can be costly, and newspaper executives must balance their level of localism with the advertising that it brings in. In many cases, they can rely on volunteers to populate some of the local pages; in others, they hire special Web reporters whose job it is to work out of their cars, sending digital reports to the paper as they move from community event to community event.

The *New York Times* announced that, starting in January 2011, unlimited access to NYTimes.com will require either a paper subscription or payment of a flat fee.

In search of digital advertising, some large newspaper companies have been buying media properties that enlarge their audiences. The *New York Times* owns the encyclopedia-like site http://www.about.com, for example, and *The Washington Post* owns the opinion/feature articles site http://www.slate.com. By selling these visitors as well as the newspaper site users, the firms can attract more advertisers than their individual papers would. This approach certainly applies to the *Wall Street Journal*, owned by News Corporation. News Corp can package the sale of ads in the online *Journal* with ads for its other online sites based on what it knows about the demographics of the readers and their digital activities.

TECH & INFRASTRUCTURE
OHMYNEWS

OhmyNews editor and founder Oh Yeon-ho works at his office in Seoul.

Launched in 2000 as a journalistic experiment, the South Korean online newspaper *OhmyNews* began amidst a flurry of excitement and optimism. Operating under the axiom "Every citizen is a reporter," *OhmyNews* founder Oh Yeon-ho sought to revolutionize journalism by empowering the public through participatory citizen journalism.

Unlike any other newspaper at the time, the bulk of articles published by the newspaper were written by some 70,000 citizen contributors—averaging about 200 articles daily. A full-time staff of fewer than seventy journalists wrote the remainder of the articles, with a handful of editors revising and fact-checking submissions.

OhmyNews garnered international attention for seemingly tipping the 2002 South Korean presidential election in favor of its supported candidate, Roh Moo Hyun. With Roh behind in the polls, the newspaper prompted readers to text message friends and family, encouraging them to vote for Roh. The site's international communications director, Jean K. Min, described Roh's win as "Korea's Obama Moment."

Following the election, OhmyNews has begun hosting annual journalism conferences and has even founded its own school for citizen journalism. With international buzz and readership levels consistently high enough to place *OhmyNews* amongst South Korea's thirty most trafficked websites, the newspaper by all accounts seemed to be a success.

However, this hasn't amounted to financial viability for *OhmyNews*, which hasn't seen a profit since 2008. As of 2009, the newspaper reported that it was 700 million won—or over $600,000—in the red, and that it would have to hold back on plans for international expansion. The advertisers the newspaper has relied on for three-quarters of its revenue have been dwindling since the international financial crisis struck, and future prospects for *OhmyNews* look grim.

In an effort to survive, *OhmyNews* has turned to its readers for help, asking them to donate $8 a month, but the sustainability of the plan has been called into question. "It's unrealistic to expect people to pay for online content that is freely available," said Yoon Youngchul, dean of Yonsei University's Graduate School of Journalism in Seoul.

Regardless of its longevity, however, the *OhmyNews* experiment has introduced journalistic innovations that Min and fellow staffers see in its "partners in citizen journalism," such as the *Huffington Post*, *Daily Kos* and digg.com. Through outlets like these, they say, the legacy of *OhmyNews* will live on.

Sources: OhmyNews, "What Does OhmyNews Mean to You?" July 9, 2007. http://english.ohmynews.com/ArticleView/article_view.asp?menu=A11100&no=385441&rel_no=1&back_url= (accessed March 30, 2010); Moon Ihlwan, "Korea's OhmyNews Seeks a Fresh Business Model," *Business Week*, July 14, 2009. http://www.businessweek.com/globalbiz/content/jul2009/gb20090714_537389.htm (accessed March 30, 2010); Elizabeth Woyke, "The Struggles of OhmyNews," Forbes.com, March 11, 2009. http://www.forbes.com/forbes/2009/0330/050-oh-my-revenues.html (accessed March 30, 2010); Elizabeth Woyke, "OhmyNews Chooses Influence Over Income," Forbes.com, April 3, 2009. http://www.forbes.com/2009/04/02/internet-media-video-technology-korea-09-media.html (accessed March 30, 2010); Cynthia Yoo, "Giants of Citizen Media Meet Up," The Tyee, October 24, 2007. http://thetyee.ca/Mediacheck/2007/10/24/WikiVOhMyNews/ (accessed March 30, 2010).

Media Literacy and the Newspaper Industry

The *Wall Street Journal* is an unusual case because, in addition to serving ads as other U.S. newspaper sites do, it charges an annual subscription to get into the site. The U.K.'s *Financial Times* (which has a U.S. edition) also charges for viewing its stories after allowing a number to be viewed for free. Apart from these and a few other exceptions, though, U.S. online newspapers are open to users without charge. Many observers of the newspaper business see free online access as a big problem. Recall what we learned earlier about the difficulty—some would say impossibility—of profitably running a major national or big-city newspaper based on online advertising alone because the huge competition for advertising drives the ad prices papers can charge way down. You might wonder how this business model will allow the newspaper to survive in a future in which the printed edition is read by relatively few and the online version will have to carry the organization.

That ability to make money is at the heart of the concerns that knowledgeable observers have about the newspaper's future. Some of them believe that the print version is doomed to disappear and that the digital versions of most will not be able to make enough advertising money to support the staff that is required to put out an acceptable product. One controversial writer, the media consultant Henry Blodget, wrote bluntly on his blog in 2007 that "Newspapers are Screwed." More sober, but still pessimistic, was the 2007 assessment by the famously savvy investor Warren Buffett. Buffett, who owns a portion of *The Washington Post* and has a long connection with the business, wrote that "fundamentals are definitely eroding in the newspaper industry, [and] the skid will almost certainly continue." He went on to state that "The economic potential of a newspaper Internet site—given the many alternative sources of information and entertainment that are free and only a click away, is at best a small fraction of that existing in the past for a print newspaper facing no competition."[15]

Buffet and Blodget made their pronouncements before the economic downturn. The recession that began in 2008 underscored the dilemma, as physical newspaper advertising went south and the growth of online newspaper advertising slowed considerably. Rupert Murdoch, whose company News Corporation owns the *Wall Street Journal* and many other newspapers, has insisted that his newspapers would begin charging for their product online. Although other publishers have agreed with him that making visitors pay is key to newspapers' long-term survival, many have a general fear of putting their content behind a pay wall. The reason is basic—they worry that people will not want to shell out money and will go to other free sites for their news. Rather than increase revenues, they fear that the result will be a loss of advertising as readers desert papers that charge for sites that don't.

Regardless of those fears, a number of major newspaper firms apart from Murdoch's have announced that they are exploring the possibility of charging for at least some content, either by subscription or in micropayments—a few cents an article. Newspaper publishers have also fulminated against sites such as Google News and the *Huffington Post* that draw audiences by summarizing and linking to articles from newspapers, receiving the benefit of enormous resources that had gone into creating the material. Those sites should pay for that privilege, the newspaper leaders argue.

Now and in the foreseeable future, then, what you will see when you look at the newspaper industry and its products is a search for business models that will ensure the industry's viability. Many newspapers would like members of the public to believe that the health of journalism, and of democratic ideals, rests with the survival of the newspaper organizations we know today. Cheerleaders for this venture argue that without it American society will suffer greatly. Where, they ask, will the great investigative reports come from? Where will the great editorials about local issues appear? Certainly, they argue, neither bloggers nor volunteer reporters can play the role that newspapers have taken on for 200 years in keeping people in touch with their society, communities, and democracy.

Such arguments involving the future of democracy might well induce enough guilt to make some Americans shell out money to support their digital big-city newspapers, however begrudgingly. That is a proposition you should examine critically, because there is another perspective. The newspaper that Jefferson extolled was a fundamentally different product—it looked different and depicted news differently—from the big-city newspaper of today. Many of the changes were, in fact, good. As we learned in Chapter 2, the profession of journalism is not tied to the newspaper. There may be ways to encourage professional journalism that do not come from traditional newspaper companies. Some newspaper companies may still turn out to have the most persuasive solutions for keeping you and me abreast of what we need to know of the world. If so, we should pay for it. As for those that cannot survive, we should see their predicaments as an encouragement to rethink as a society what professional journalism means, why we should care about it, and how it should be supported.

Chapter Review

For an interactive chapter recap and study guide, visit the companion website for *Media Today* at http://www.routledge.com/textbooks/mediatoday4e.

Questions for Discussion and Critical Thinking

1 Why is the penny press important to the development of the contemporary U.S. newspaper? *more people were able to afford it*

2 What are some similarities and differences between daily and weekly newspapers? *diff: daily is everyday, weekly once/twice a week*

3 What effects can advertising have on the production, distribution, and exhibition of a newspaper?

4 When might a newspaper want total market coverage, and when might it want to carry out segmentation?

5 What are the arguments of people who believe that printed papers are doomed to disappear, and those who disagree with them?

Internet Resources

Chronicling America: Historic American Newspapers (http://www.loc.gov/chroniclingamerica)

Chronicling America, a project of the Library of Congress and National Endowment for the Humanities, represents a "long-term effort to develop an Internet-based, searchable database of U.S. newspapers with descriptive information and select digitization of historic pages." The site allows you to find out what libraries hold what newspapers and in what form—original or microfilm. You can also see digitized versions of front pages of newspapers—for example, *The New York Sun*—going back more than a hundred years.

Newspaper Association of America (http://www.naa.org)

On its website, the NAA calls itself "a nonprofit organization representing the $55 billion newspaper industry." "NAA members account for nearly 90 percent of the daily circulation in the United States and a wide range of nondaily U.S. newspapers." This site, then, is a good portal into the mainstream U.S. newspaper business. Various areas cover advertising, circulation, electronic publishing, diversity, and other aspects of the newspaper business.

Association of Alternative Newsweeklies (http://aan.org)

The Association of Alternative Newsweeklies (AAN) calls itself "a diverse group of 130 alt-weekly news organizations that cover every major metropolitan area in North America." This website reflects the breadth of its membership through a directory of its member publications, an ability to receive email newsletters on various topics of the business, an archive of articles about alternative weeklies, and more.

International Newspaper Marketing Association (http://www.inma.org)

This organization focuses on the marketing aspects of the newspaper business, with perspectives reflecting its diverse membership representing seventy countries. Its website contains useful papers and conference reports reflecting changes in the ways newspapers are trying to increase circulation and advertising.

Key Terms
. . . .

You can find the definitions to these key terms in the marginal glossary throughout this chapter. Test your knowledge of these terms with interactive flash cards on the *Media Today* companion website.

Constructing Media Literacy

. . . .

1 What relevance does the history of newspapers have to understanding the current situation of the newspaper?

2 From what you have read and seen around you, how pessimistic or optimistic are you about the newspaper's future. Why?

3 If you or some friends do not read a newspaper or visit a newspaper site, what would it take to encourage you (or them) to do that? Are the steps the industry is taking persuasive?

4 Do you agree with those who argue that localism—even hyper-localism—is the way for newspapers to remain relevant and profitable in an age of so many information sources? Why or why not?

Companion Website Video Clips

. . . .

Journalism

This 1940 film looks at writing and editing positions for newspapers and magazines before the computer age. Credit: Internet Archive/Prelinger Archives.

Newspaper Story

This film from 1950 examines how a newspaper comes together from when a story is reported to the actual publication. Credit: Internet Archive/Prelinger Archives.

Case Study

. . . .

ANALYZING A NEWSPAPER'S ATTEMPT TO ENGAGE ITS AUDIENCE

The idea As the chapter notes, many newspaper websites today are attempting to attract audiences by creating a variety of ways to receive the sites' content as well as encouraging them to interact around, and even contribute to, the websites' content. Examples are blogs, conversation areas, RSS feeds, and mobile capabilities. The purpose of this assignment is to encourage you to explore the techniques that your local paper is using and to carry out a hands-on examination of them.

The method Examine your local newspaper's website for ways that it is trying to interact with audiences and to encourage audiences to interact with each other around its content. Spend a week using these tools yourself. Then write a report of about four pages about your experience. In your paper, answer the following questions: To what extent did it allow you to get closer to news you want? To what extent did it extend your understanding of various sorts of news? Did the blogs or chat areas make you want to come back to the site more than you would if you hadn't connected with them? In general, how successful were these techniques in creating bonds between you and the newspaper?

9 The Magazine Industry

After studying this chapter, you will be able to:

1 Sketch a history of magazines and understand its importance

2 Describe the physical and digital production, distribution, and exhibition of different types of magazines

3 Explain the view that magazines are brands that need to follow their readers

4 List the risks and barriers involved in launching a new magazine

5 Analyze critics' concerns regarding the influence of industry ownership and advertising

MEDIA TODAY

Attendees at a breakfast arranged by the Magazine Publishers of America must have been surprised when Ann S. Moore, the top executive at Time, Inc., the largest magazine publisher in the United States, talked about the anxiety her job had brought her. It was May 2007, and Moore had gone through months of layoffs, and the sale or shutdown of several magazines under the Time umbrella. With her staff, she had also been immersed in trying to remake her magazine division of Time Warner into a powerful force that could attract large and desirable audiences and advertisers—not just in print but on the Web and in other areas of the digital environment. According to the trade magazine *Advertising Age*, Moore said that the goal—transforming her company from a firm focused on paper into a multimedia player—had been wrenching, professionally and personally.

"Steering an organization through change is hard," she said, knowing that many of the magazine-publishing executives in her audience were feeling the same pressures. But she also pointed to successes that had come out of her work—for example, growing revenue at *Sports Illustrated* and *People Magazine*, partly because of their popular websites. Her advice to her peers: "You know, everybody stay calm," she suggested. "This is a great business we're in."[1]

As Ann Moore suggests, the industry is changing dramatically in order to fit into the new media world. Magazine companies are killing magazines, rethinking magazines, trying out new magazines, and going online in their bid to succeed in the face of the changing demands of their marketplace. Critics say that not all of these changes have served readers well. They charge that the huge conglomerates that own the most popular magazines have been turning them into cross-media brands that are in danger of losing their editorial independence from advertisers.

How are we to understand and evaluate this concern? What forces are shaping the future of magazines, and what might that mean for the news and fashions that circulate through our society? To begin answering these questions, we first have to get a grasp on the industry itself. This chapter introduces the magazine business through the by now familiar categories of history, production, distribution, and exhibition. We start with history to show how we got to where we are now, and to demonstrate that our era is not the first in which the magazine industry has had to grapple with major change.

The Development of Magazines

The word "magazine" is French; it means storehouse. **Magazines** are collections of materials (stories, ads, poems, and other items) that their editors believe will interest their audience.

By the 1700s, magazines were being published regularly in England, as the growing power of Parliament allowed for more public arguments about governing. Political magazines and literary magazines made their debuts. Some, such as the famous *Tatler* and *The Spectator*, served up both politics and literature by famous writers of the day. Of course, these magazines were read by England's wealthy elite. Not only were most people of the time illiterate, they also couldn't afford to buy the magazines.

The same was true in colonial America. Like newspapers, magazines aimed to attract relatively wealthy people such as merchants or plantation owners who had literary and/or political inclinations. The first magazines appeared in 1741 in Philadelphia (Benjamin Franklin was one of the first periodical publishers), and printers in Boston and New York soon followed. It is estimated that around 100 magazines appeared and disappeared by the time of the Revolutionary War.

After the establishment of the United States, magazines seemed to fail as fast as they were introduced. One reason (aside from illiteracy and the expensive production technique) was the cost of transportation. Magazines were heavy, and the increased load led some postal workers to refuse to carry them.[2] By 1825, fewer than 100 magazines were being published in the United States. At that time, magazines were often more hobbies or extensions of book company activities than serious moneymaking enterprises. They reached only a small community of readers, and were dull-looking, with few pictures.

The Transformation of Magazines into Mass Media

By 1830, magazine entrepreneurs—like their counterparts in the newspaper and book industries—began to take advantage of the rise in education, the new steam-powered presses, and postal loopholes to expand the market. Between 1825 and 1850, the number, the nature, and the business of magazines changed dramatically; during that time, between 4,000 and 5,000 new magazines were introduced in the United States. Most of them died quickly, but the launch of new magazines meant that business people were beginning to see a large market emerging—numbering in the tens and hundreds of thousands—for magazines.

The magazines that survived were still more expensive than newspapers, and they assumed a higher intellectual level. Even so, they began to exert increasing influence on the nation's cultural life. Two outstanding periodicals launched around that time that are still in circulation today are *Harper's Monthly* (founded in 1850) and *Scientific American* (founded in 1845).

The Rise of Women's Magazines

An especially important development of the magazine age was the rise of magazines aimed at women. The most important one was the monthly *Godey's Lady's Book*, launched in 1830. By 1850, it had the highest circulation of any magazine in the United States, reaching more than 150,000 readers. It included hand-colored engravings of fashions, along with articles and fiction stories. Louis A. Godey was the first in a string of famous male editors of periodicals for females. He was helped

NUMB. 1

The SPECTATOR.

*Non fumum ex fulgore, fed ex fumo dare lucem
Cogitat; ut fpeciofa dehinc miracula promat.* Hor.

To be Continued every Day.

Thurfday, March 1. 1711.

I Have obferved, that a Reader feldom perufes a Book with Pleafure 'till he knows whether the Writer of it be a black or a fair Man, of a mild or cholerick Difpofition, Married or a Batchelor, with other Particulars of the like nature, that conduce very much to the right Underftanding of an Author. To gratify this Curiofity, which is fo natural to a Reader, I defign this Paper, and my next, as Prefatory Difcourfes to my following Writings, and fhall give fome Account in them of the feveral Perfons that are engaged in this Work. As the chief Trouble of Compiling, Digefting and Correcting will fall to my Share, I muft do my felf the Juftice to open the Work with my own Hiftory.

I was born to a fmall Hereditary Eftate, which I find, by the Writings of the Family, was bounded by the fame Hedges and Ditches in *William* the Conqueror's Time that it is at prefent, and has been delivered down from Father to Son whole and entire, without the Lofs or Acquifition of a fingle Field or Meadow, during the Space of fix hundred Years. There goes a Story in the Family, that when my Mother was gone with Child of me about three Months, fhe dreamt that fhe was brought to Bed of a Judge: Whether this might proceed from a Law-Suit which was then depending in the Family, or my Father's being a Juftice of the Peace, I cannot determine; for I am not fo vain as to think it prefaged any Dignity that I fhould arrive at in my future Life, though that was the Interpretation which the Neighbourhood put upon it. The Gravity of my Behaviour at my very firft Appearance in the World, and all the Time that I fucked, feemed to favour my Mother's Dream: For, as fhe has often told me, I threw away my Rattle before I was two Months old, and would not make ufe of my Coral 'till they had taken away the Bells from it.

As for the reft of my Infancy, there being nothing in it remarkable, I fhall pafs it over in Silence. I find, that, during my Nonage, I had the Reputation of a very fullen Youth, but was always a Favourite of my School-Mafter, who ufed to fay, that my Parts were folid and would wear well. I had not been long at the Univerfity, before I diftinguifhed my felf by a moft profound Silence: For, during the Space of eight Years, excepting in the publick Exercifes of the College, I fcarce uttered the Quantity of an hundred Words; and indeed do not remember that I ever fpoke three Sentences together in my whole Life. Whilft I was in this Learned Body I applied my felf with fo much Diligence to my Studies, that there are very few celebrated Books, either in the Learned or the Modern Tongues, which I am not acquainted with.

Upon the Death of my Father I was refolved to travel into Foreign Countries, and therefore left the Univerfity, with the Character of an odd unaccountable Fellow, that had a great deal of Learning, if I would but fhow it. An infatiable Thirft after Knowledge carried me into all the Countries of *Europe*, where there was any thing new or ftrange to be feen; nay, to fuch a Degree was my Curiofity raifed, that having read the Controverfies of fome great Men concerning the Antiquities of *Egypt*, I made a Voyage to *Grand Cairo*, on purpofe to take the Meafure of a Pyramid; and as foon as I had fet my felf right in that Particular, returned to my Native Country with great Satisfaction.

I have paffed my latter Years in this City, where I am frequently feen in moft publick Places, tho' there are not above half a dozen of my felect Friends that know me; of whom my next Paper fhall give a more particular Account. There is no Place of publick Refort, wherein I do not often make my Appearance; fometimes I am feen thrufting my Head into a Round of Politicians at *Will's*, and liftning with great Attention to the Narratives that are made in thofe little Circular Audiences. Sometimes I fmoak a Pipe at *Child's*; and whilft I feem attentive to nothing but the *Poft-Man*, over-hear the Converfation of every Table in the Room. I appear on *Sunday* Nights at St. *James's* Coffee-Houfe, and fometimes join the little Committee of Politicks in the Inner-Room, as one who comes there to hear and improve. My Face is likewife very well known at the *Grecian*, the *Cocoa-Tree*, and in the Theaters both of *Drury-Lane*, and the *Hay-Market*. I have been taken for a Merchant upon

The Spectator, an extremely influential early British magazine founded by Joseph Addison and Richard Steele in 1711, aimed to prepare its readers for intelligent conversation in polite society. It was the first daily periodical to cover literary and cultural matters, from philosophy to etiquette, rather than focusing strictly on news.

WORLD VIEW
MAGAZINES IN CHINA COME OF AGE

It's no secret that the publishing industry has fallen on hard times, with many newspapers and magazines struggling just to stay afloat. In China, however, the magazine industry has not only been able to buck this trend, it has also experienced a period of rapid growth. "Welcome to the World's Most Exciting Magazine Market," headlined a recent article in *Magazine World* that discussed China's booming publishing industry.

Indeed, the number of magazines in China has grown roughly tenfold in the last few decades. Lifestyle magazines have proven to be especially popular amongst the urban Chinese. These thick and stylized magazines, which are typically targeted toward wealthy consumers and packed with glossy fashion spreads, have been credited with boosting the magazine market in China. Marketers flock to lifestyle magazines as the readership typically has a high degree of disposable income, with luxury companies in particular advertising in them. "You have to feel and touch luxury," said Anne Lim-Chaplain, director of Prestige Hong Kong. "Our magazines are oversize, filled with beautiful pictures, beautiful people. It shouts luxury."

In contrast to the American magazine industry, nearly all of the Chinese magazine revenue has traditionally come from newsstand sales. However, publishers are already beginning to rethink their revenue model as magazine advertising in China continues to increase. In fact, with general advertising expenditures climbing over the last several years, China is projected to become the world's fourth largest global advertising market in 2010. The shift to an advertising-sales approach is also being driven by the large number of global publishers. Annie Yuan, an advertising research director, notes that "With the fast development of the Chinese economy and the emergence of a sizable group of middle-incomers with high disposable income, major international publications have been setting up in China." The result has been a boom for China's magazine advertising industry.

Sources: Zhang Bohai, "Welcome to the World's Most Exciting Magazine Market," *Magazine World*, 52, April 2007, pp. 16–17; Erica Ng, "China's Ad Spending Hits $120 Bil.," *Adweek*, February 11, 2010; Alexandra A. Seno, "The Glamour and the Gloss," *Newsweek*, 151, 21, May 26, 2008; Jamila Trindle, "China Steps Out: TV/Print," *The Guardian*, September 29, 2008, p. 3; Lu Xiang, "China, The Story So Far," *International Federation of the Periodical Press*, February 28, 2006. http://www.fipp.com (accessed September 2010); Annie Yuan, "China Magazines—Attractive Propositions," *Media and Marketing Europe*, November 30, 2006, Factiva database.

tremendously in his work by his female assistant editor, Sarah Josepha Hale, who joined him in 1837. Hale was a determined champion of education for women at a time when many didn't see the point of it. (She also gained a type of immortality by writing "Mary Had a Little Lamb" and persuading President Lincoln to declare Thanksgiving a national holiday.)

Fundamental Changes in Magazine Publishing

The expansion in magazines beginning in the 1830s changed the structure of the business. Magazines began to rely on the services of freelance writers—people who make their living by selling their works to different periodicals. They included notable freelancers such as Lydia Sigourney, Edgar Allan Poe, Margaret Fuller, and Henry Wadsworth Longfellow. The magazine editor—who was now paid a decent wage—also took on a new role, working with freelance writers rather than doing the writing alone.

Beyond these staffing changes, magazine publishers found themselves responding to faster printing technologies, new ways to reproduce pictures and even photographs, huge population growth, an increase in literacy—some of the same changes faced by the newspaper industry (as we discussed in Chapter 8). Whereas newspapers focused on reaching people in the local areas in which they were published, many magazines began to work to attract national audiences of sizes that no U.S. media had previously reached. The huge expansion of the railroad in the second half of the nineteenth century helped them do that. The expansion of the postal service to rural areas also meant that most of the nation could receive periodicals easily. Moreover, the Postal Act of 1879 substantially lowered the cost of mailing magazines.

In the wake of these advancements, publishers soon realized that advertisers were suddenly interested in using magazines to reach huge national audiences. As more and more factories sprang up across the United States, the large number of items being produced increased the competition between manufacturers of similar goods. One result was the creation of **brands**—products with distinctive names and identities that make them stand out from their competitors. But to make money on a particular brand of soap or any other mass-produced item, a manufacturer had to make sure that hordes of people recognized the brand and bought it.

In earlier decades, readers' subscriptions covered a large percentage of the publishers's costs. However, magazine owner Frank Munsey showed how advertising could pay most of the costs of producing the magazine. His low subscription prices for *Munsey's* magazine attracted a large number of readers, which in turn attracted advertisers who wanted to reach those readers. Munsey charged the advertisers for reaching his audience, and he proved quite successful. It wasn't long before Munsey's approach caught on industry-wide. For the first time, magazine publishers aimed to attract hundreds of thousands, even millions, of customers in order to deliver them to advertisers. On the strength of this approach, in 1901 the *Ladies' Home Journal* became the first magazine to pass 1 million in circulation. Two years later the readership of *The Saturday Evening Post* was an unprecedented 2 million. The *Post* brought in advertising revenues of $25 million that year.

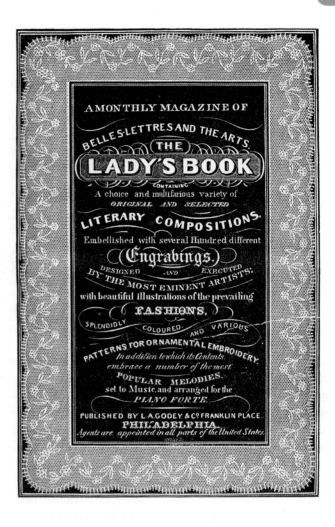

Godey's Lady's Book, launched by Louis A. Godey in 1830, led the wave of new periodicals aimed at women. It had the highest circulation of any magazine in the mid-nineteenth century in the United States.

brand a name and image associated with a particular product

New Roles for Mass-Circulation Magazines

The most popular magazines at the turn of the twentieth century provided their readers with an exciting mixture of sensational news about problems in their society and entertaining stories and helpful advice.

Sensational News: The Work of the Muckrakers

From 1900 to 1912, the *Ladies' Home Journal, Collier's, Everybody's, McClure's, Munsey's, The Saturday Evening Post,* and other magazines joined with great enthusiasm in crusades against big business, against corruption, and for social justice. A group of American journalists, novelists, and critics known as muckrakers attempted to expose the abuses of business and the corruption in politics.

A NAUSEATING JOB, BUT IT MUST BE DONE

The term "muckraker" was coined by President Theodore Roosevelt, depicted in this 1906 editorial cartoon cleaning up corruption in the meat packing industry.

muckrakers American journalists, novelists, and critics who, in the early 1900s, attempted to expose the abuses of business and the corruption in politics

The term **muckraker** was coined by President Theodore Roosevelt in a speech in 1906 in which he agreed with many of the muckrakers' charges, but asserted that some of their methods were sensational and irresponsible. He compared them to a character in John Bunyan's book *Pilgrim's Progress* who had a muckrake in his hands; he could look no way but downward and was interested only in raking the filth. Since the 1870s, there had been recurrent efforts at reform in government, politics, and business, but it was not until the advent of the national mass-circulation magazines that the muckrakers had sufficient funds for their investigations and a large enough audience to arouse nationwide concern. The writers were mostly newspaper reporters who liked both the extra money and the national exposure that such magazines offered. Their work sometimes had enormous impact.

The most famous muckrakers were Lincoln Steffens, Ida Tarbell, David Graham Phillips, Ray Stannard Baker, Samuel Hopkins Adams, and Upton Sinclair. In the early 1900s, magazine articles that attacked trusts—including those of Charles E. Russell on the beef trust, Thomas Lawson on Amalgamated Copper, and Burton J. Hendrick on life insurance companies—created public demand for regulation of these great corporations. Probably the most far-reaching of these stories were those in *McClure's* and the *Ladies' Home Journal* about the dangers of food and medicine. These articles helped encourage the passage of the first Pure Food and Drugs Act in 1906.

The muckraking movement lost support around 1912. However, historians agree that, had it not been for the revelations of the muckrakers, the Progressive movement would not have received the popular support needed for effective reform.

Entertainment Roles: The Ladies' Home Journal *and* The Saturday Evening Post

The focus of magazines in the first two decades of the twentieth century was more on entertainment—storytelling, humor, and information—than on sensational news. Colorful covers were combined with stories by famous writers and articles about famous people. The advertisements were also standouts: some were full page, in color, and entertaining in their own right. Because of their ads, mass-circulation magazines were often quite hefty. The *Ladies' Home Journal* stood out in this respect.

It sometimes carried more than $1 million of ads in a single issue, and an issue often ran to more than 200 pages.

The *Ladies' Home Journal* and *The Saturday Evening Post*—both published by the Curtis Publishing Company—were undoubtedly the most important periodicals of their era. Publisher Cyrus Curtis was an advertising, marketing, and distribution genius who helped shape the close relationship between advertisers and magazines. *The Saturday Evening Post's* editor, George Horace Lorimer, aimed to appeal to all the adults in the United States. Under Lorimer's direction, *The Saturday Evening Post* attained its greatest success, partly because of his astute judgment of popular U.S. tastes in literature. Lorimer published works by some of the best U.S. writers of the time: Stephen Crane, Frank Norris, Theodore Dreiser, Jack London, Willa Cather, Ring Lardner, F. Scott Fitzgerald, and Sinclair Lewis. In addition, he brought such European authors as Joseph Conrad and John Galsworthy to U.S. readers. Lorimer held conservative views, and this was reflected in the articles he published in the magazine. Upton Sinclair wrote that the material in *The Saturday Evening Post* was as "standardized as soda crackers; originality is taboo, new ideas are treason, social sympathy a crime, and the one virtue of man is to produce larger and larger quantities of material things." However, Lorimer also employed the radical David Graham Phillips, who wrote more than fifty articles criticizing the rich and powerful. By December 1908, Lorimer was able to announce in *The Saturday Evening Post* that for the first time the journal was selling more than a million copies a week. Circulation continued to increase under Lorimer's stewardship, and by the end of 1913 it had reached 2 million.

Edward Bok, editor of the *Ladies' Home Journal*, edited his periodical as if he were writing for all the nation's women. Bok, a Dutch immigrant, was one of the most powerful magazine editors in U.S. history. By 1900, the *Ladies' Home Journal* was the bestselling magazine in the United States. In addition to using his magazine to promote ideas on interior decorating and the appearance of cities, Bok campaigned for women's suffrage, pacifism, conservation of the environment, improved local government, and sex education—regardless of the effect on subscriptions. In campaigning for sex education, for example, Bok lost thousands of subscribers by running an article about syphilis. The topic shocked readers; it was, in fact, the first time that even the word "syphilis" had been used in a popular magazine. He also instituted a self-regulation measure known as the Curtis advertising code that banned financial, tobacco, playing card, and liquor advertising in the magazine.

From 1899 to 1969, millions of Americans saw themselves each Tuesday in the cover art of *The Saturday Evening Post*, the most popular magazine in the country.

THE EYES OF ASIA—By Rudyard Kipling. 'TWIXT THE BLUFF AND THE SOUND—By Irvin S. Cobb. TUBAL CAIN—By Joseph Hergesheimer

The *Ladies' Home Journal*, *The Saturday Evening Post*, and many other mass-circulation magazines thrived during the first four decades of the 1900s. During the 1920s, more specialized magazines made successful debuts. One type focused on the idea of distilling information for busy people. *Reader's Digest*, a compendium of "must read" articles, and *Time*, a weekly news summary, first appeared in 1922 and 1923, respectively. Both had predecessors in magazine history, and both had their imitators. The second type of magazine reflected an elite, knowing cynicism and humor that seemed to be the mark of the 1920s—the so-called "Jazz Age." The *New Yorker* was the most successful of these magazines.

Magazines Later in the Twentieth Century

During the 1960s and 1970s, the magazine industry again found itself in an environment that demanded fundamental change, thanks to the new medium of television. By the late 1950s, most U.S. homes (86 percent) had at least one television set; that number had jumped to 93 percent by 1965. The huge popularity of the television began to hurt mass-circulation magazines such as *The Saturday Evening Post*. Large advertisers abandoned magazines for TV because it could help them reach even larger portions of the U.S. population than mass-circulation magazines at a comparable cost. Not only that, television allowed for dynamic ads with moving pictures and sound, features that print media couldn't offer.

The shift of advertisers to television marked the beginning of the end of America's mass-circulation magazines, despite their large readerships. For example, even though popular magazine *Coronet* had a circulation of 3.1 million, it went out of publication in 1963. Around that time *The Saturday Evening Post* and several other magazines like it also died.

It took the magazine industry a few years to adjust to these stunning reversals, but by the early 1970s executives had developed a new approach to their business. Although there were already magazines that were tailored to particular ethnic, religious, occupational, and hobby groups, new magazines tried to go beyond those categories and tap into the newer, narrower interests and lifestyles of the relatively affluent in U.S. society—target audiences that advertisers especially wanted. Small, targeted audiences became especially profitable for magazines as computer-driven technology developed in the 1970s and 1980s—allowing companies to make substantial profits with magazines that reached hundreds of thousands, or even tens of thousands, of people instead of millions.

This potential for great profits drew giant firms who soon dominated the magazine industry by the early part of the twenty-first century. Time Warner's Time Inc. magazine company is the advertising and circulation leader. Other leading consumer magazine groups are Hearst Magazines, Advance Publications, and Meredith Publishing Company. But if the 1990s were a time of strong revenues and confidence, the 2000s and beyond are, as noted earlier, a time of worry and sober concern with the future. Let's look at the current profile of the industry.

An Overview of the Modern Magazine Industry

American newsstands regularly display over 2,000 magazine titles. Many others can be seen in the periodicals section of large university or city libraries. Magazines differ widely in both circulation and topic. As a mind-boggling example, consider that the 20,000 magazines that the Magazine Publishers of America refers to include *AARP: The Magazine* (circulation 24.6 million), *Inc.* (circulation 711,000), *American Woodworker* (circulation 191,000), and *Gun Dog* (circulation 41,000)—all in the same list!

Five Major Types of Magazines

People who work in the magazine industry categorize magazines in several ways, but there seems to be general agreement that, if a periodical fits into one of the following five categories, it is to be considered a magazine:

- Business or trade magazines
- Consumer magazines
- Literary reviews and academic journals
- Newsletters
- Comic books

Let's see what each of these categories includes.

Business-to-Business Magazines/Trade Magazines

A **business-to-business (b-to-b) magazine**, also called a **trade magazine**, focuses on topics related to a particular occupation, profession, or industry. Published by a private firm or by a business association, it is written to reach people who are involved with that occupation, profession, or industry.

Standard Rate and Data Service (SRDS), a firm that collects information about magazine audiences and ad rates and sells it to advertisers and ad agencies, devotes an entire reference directory to business magazines. The directory divides business specializations into over 200 categories. Examples are advertising and marketing, automotive, banking, building, ceramics, computers, engineering and construction, healthcare, and hotels, motels, clubs, and resorts.

business-to-business (b-to-b) magazine or trade magazine a magazine that focuses on topics related to a particular occupation, profession, or industry

Consumer Magazines

Consumer magazines are aimed at people in their private, nonbusiness lives. They are sold by subscription and on newsstands and magazine racks in stores. They are called **consumer magazines** because their readers buy and consume products and services that are sold through retail outlets and that may be advertised in those magazines. Think of a magazine that you or your friends read for fun—for example, *Men's Health, Time, People, Essence, Cosmopolitan, Vanity Fair, Details, Spin, Wired,* or *Maxim.* It's likely to be considered a consumer magazine.

consumer magazines magazines aimed at the general public

Literary Reviews and Academic Journals

literary reviews small-circulation periodicals about literature and related topics; usually funded by scholarly associations, universities, or foundations

This category includes hundreds of publications with small circulation figures. **Literary reviews** (periodicals about literature and related topics) and **academic journals** (periodicals about scholarly topics, with articles typically edited and written by professors and/or other university-affiliated researchers) are generally nonprofit; funded by scholarly associations, universities, or foundations, and sold by subscription through the mail. Examples are the *Journal of Communication* (a scholarly journal from the International Communication Association), *The Gettysburg Review* (a literary review of short fiction, poetry, essays, and art), *Foreign Affairs* (a journal of opinion from the Council on Foreign Relations), and *Harvard Lampoon* (the oldest humor magazine in America).

academic journals small-circulation periodicals that cover scholarly topics, with articles typically edited and written by professors and/or other university-affiliated researchers

Newsletters

newsletter a small-circulation periodical, typically four to eight pages long, that is composed and printed in a simple style

A **newsletter** is a small-circulation periodical (typically four to eight pages long) that is composed and printed in a simple style. The rather plain look of a newsletter often matches not only its need to suppress costs (due to its usually small circulation), but also its editorial purpose: to convey needed information in a straightforward way.

When we hear the term "newsletter," many of us may think of the information bulletin of a church or school. We are less likely to know about the large number of newsletters that are used in business. They often center on specific areas of an

CULTURE TODAY
ACADEMIC JOURNALS AND OPEN ACCESS

Chances are, your university library houses a collection of academic journals that is eclectic, impressive—and expensive. A subscription to the brain sciences journal *Brain Research* costs more than $20,000; many others are upwards of $10,000. In fact, subscription rates for academic journals have risen on average 226 percent from 1986 to 2000.

Despite the high price, university librarians feel under tremendous pressure to continue their subscriptions. "Librarians have long felt voiceless in negotiations with publishers," explains *Chronicle of Higher Education*'s Lila Guterman. "Since every journal's contents are unique, university libraries feel compelled to subscribe to journals that their faculty members need, almost regardless of cost."

A potential solution to this issue is the notion of "open access." Spearheaded by former head of the National Institutes of Health Harold E. Varmus, the open access model makes journals available to scholars at no cost. Instead, authors pay a small fee to get their work published. Not only does this reduce the direct costs

to universities, but it also helps authors get cited since their work is more freely available.

Although the open access movement is not without its skeptics, a number of publishers have already adopted this model. In 2007, Marquette Books announced that it would make eight of its communication journals available free of charge, making it the first private publisher to provide open access. According to Marquette's publisher, "At a time when most for-profit publishers are increasing the costs of their journals, we decided to go the opposite route and offer all of our journals free of charge." He added, "We want the scholarship in our journals to be read by as many people as possible."

As a student and researcher, where do you fall on the issue of open access?

Sources: Lila Guterman, "The Promise and Peril of 'Open Access'," *The Chronicle for Higher Education*, January 30, 2004. http://www.chronicle.com (accessed August 4, 2010); Marquette Journals, "Marquette Books Goes 'Open Access' With Communication Journals," press release, August 21, 2007. http://www.marquettejournals.org (accessed August 4, 2010).

industry, and they are published frequently—usually weekly or biweekly. They address decision-makers and provide statistical trends and news about a targeted area of business. Executives pay a lot of money for those newsletters, from a few hundred to a few thousand dollars per subscription.

Comic Books

A **comic book** is a periodical that tells a story through pictures as well as words. Comic books were developed in the 1930s as publishers of cheap ("pulp") magazines that presented detective, romance, action, and supernatural science stories tried to take advantage of the popularity of newspaper comic strips to boost sagging sales. They put their material into comic-strip form and sold it in a complete story unit as a comic book.

Today, comic books run a wide gamut. Archie Comics publishes traditional titles, aiming at girls and boys aged from 6 to 11 years—*Archie, Betty and Veronica, Sabrina the Teenage Witch*, and the like. IDW Publishing targets teens and young adults with heroic adventure and science fiction tales such as *The Transformers, 30 Days of Night*, and *Fallen Angel*. Verotik publishes titles that are aimed at adults only—such as *Jaguar God, IGrat*, and *G.O.T.H*—presenting fantasy tales with often violent and sexually charged situations.

By far the largest firms in terms of overall circulation are Marvel Comics Group and DC Comics. Marvel's titles alone reach about 5.7 million people a month, and target a number of demographics. For example, *Fantastic Four* aims at youngsters, whereas *The Punisher* and *Namor the Sub-Mariner* go after teens and adults. The company is a subsidiary of Marvel Entertainment, which merged with the Disney Company in 2010.

comic book a periodical that tells a story through pictures as well as words

Marvel Comics, one of the largest firms in comic book circulation, honored Spider Man collector President Barack Obama with an issue entitled "Spidey Meets the President!"

Financing Magazine Publishing

In 2008, advertisers spent $2.728 billion on space in trade magazines and $23.72 billion on space in consumer magazines.[3] Consumer magazines receive between 50 and 60 percent of their money from ads, whereas trade magazines rely on advertisers for an even higher proportion of their funds—between 70 and 80 percent. Table 9.1 lists the periodicals that draw the most ad money, and Table 9.2 lists the advertisers who spend the most money on magazine advertisements. According to the Magazine Publishers Association, the top fifty advertisers in magazine spending—about $7.7 billion—equaled 33 percent of all the revenue that magazines brought in.

Controlled Circulation Magazines

Beyond money from advertising, magazines bring money from readers. Readers pay more for consumer magazines than they do for trade magazines. In fact, nearly two-thirds of trade magazine readers receive trade periodicals for free. Advertisers are so interested in paying to reach people who work in certain industries

Table 9.1 Top Ten Magazines by Advertising Revenue During the First Nine Months of 2009

Rank	Magazine	Total Gross Ad Revenue, Jan–Sept 2009 (in millions of $)
1	*People*	647.2
2	*Better Homes and Gardens*	557.5
3	*Parade*	431.0
4	*Good Housekeeping*	344.7
5	*Sports Illustrated*	399.7
6	*Family Circle*	310.1
7	*USA Weekend*	288.9
8	*Woman's Day*	274.5
9	*Time*	263.1
10	*Cosmopolitan*	248.2

Source: Advertising Age DataCenter. http://adadge.com/datacenter (accessed August 4, 2010).

controlled circulation magazine a magazine whose production and mailing is supported not by charging readers, but (typically) through advertising revenues; the publisher, rather than the reader, decides who gets the magazine

custom magazine a controlled circulation magazine that is typically created for a company with the goal of reaching out to a specific audience that the company wants to impress

that trade publishers can support the production and distribution of these magazines at no cost to the reader. This type of magazine is called a **controlled circulation magazine**. Consider, for example, *Medical Economics*, a magazine for doctors about the business of medicine. Its circulation is "controlled" in the sense that the publisher—rather than the reader—decides who gets it. *Medical Economics* creates a list of doctors whom advertisers would likely consider useful targets and mails issues to those people only. Postal rules require publishers to ask readers annually if they want to continue receiving the material.

One type of consumer magazine that often has controlled circulation is the **custom magazine**. It is typically created for a company with the goal of reaching out to the company's customers or other people (such as government officials) that it wants to impress. One major custom publisher, Hachette Filipacchi, puts the goal this way: "Through a precise understanding of our client's strategic marketing and communication objectives, coupled with our proven ability to motivate consumers through meaningful and relevant content, we create one-to-one communications that foster a long-term relationship with a client and its customers."[4]

Advertisers have bought the idea. According to the Custom Publishing Council, custom publishers distribute billions of copies a year. *American Way*, given out on American Airlines flights, is one example of a custom magazine. Kraft Foods sends *Food & Family* free to 12 million homes, according to Redwood Custom Communications, which produces it for Kraft.[5]

Paid Circulation Magazines

paid circulation magazine a magazine that supports its production and mailing by charging readers money, either for a subscription or for a single copy

The overwhelming majority of consumer magazines are **paid circulation magazines**—in which the readers of a magazine purchase either a subscription or a single copy. Competition for advertising among consumer magazines is intense—as such, a magazine can't raise its ad rates enough to cover its production and distribution costs. As a result, consumer magazines must rely on a dual revenue stream—from both advertisers and readers.

Advertisers who are considering buying space in business or consumer magazines carry out research on the magazine's readers before they put down their money. The

Rank	Company	Total Ad Dollars Spent, 2008 (in millions)
1	Procter & Gamble Co	899.7
2	General Motors	433.0
3	Kraft Foods Inc	389.6
4	Johnson & Johnson	364.1
5	L'Oreal SA	312.7
6	Unilever	199.5
7	Time Warner	195.1
8	GlaxoSmithKline	187.9
9	LVMH Moet	184.5
10	Pfizer	172.8

Table 9.2 Top Ten Magazine Advertisers by Total Ad Dollars Spent

Source: Magazine Publishers of America, *Magazines: The Medium of Action*, p. 26. http://www.magazine.org/advertising/handbook/Magazine_Handbook.aspx (accessed August 6, 2010)

most basic information is **circulation**—the number of units of the magazine sold or distributed free to individuals in one publishing cycle. Publishers can hire a company such as the Audit Bureau of Circulation (ABC) or the Business Publications Audit of Circulation (BPA) to inspect ("audit") their shipments on a regular basis and certify that the number of copies they claim to circulate is, in fact, the number they do circulate. Small publications often can't pay for these audits and they may use a "sworn circulation" number that they hope potential advertisers will take seriously. For example, the circulation of *Medical Economics* (about 169,000) is audited by BPA, whereas the circulation of *Pharmaceutical Representative* magazine (about 72,000) is sworn.

> **circulation** the number of units of a magazine/newspaper sold or distributed free to individuals in one publishing cycle

Beyond offering an attractive and accurate circulation figure, in order to survive a magazine firm must prove to potential advertisers that its readers are of the kind that the advertisers want. Often, that means paying research companies to obtain information about readers that might lure sponsors. Publishers invest money in their own databases about readers as well as in custom and syndicated research. Magazine firms include this research to produce and circulate **media kits** to entice advertisers. Often these kits boast about why their readers are better buys than other magazines' readers. For example, in *Seventeen*'s 2009 online media kit, the magazine used data from the MRI research firm to make the claims that *Seventeen* "delivers more than twice the audience of *Teen Vogue*," "delivers the largest, richest, most diverse teen audience," and also "is a true bridge book, with two-thirds of readers age 18 and older." The kit also boasts that *Seventeen*'s articles influence readers' understanding of makeup, hair, beauty, and health in ways that will benefit the advertisers that surround those articles.

> **media kit** a database compiled by a magazine that tells potential advertisers attractive key facts about its readers

Market Segmentation

Seventeen's media kit also notes that the magazine can target ads to certain regions of the country. In fact, many consumer and trade magazines offer advertisers the possibility of paying for certain **segments** of the readership. During the printing process, certain ads (and even special articles) are bound into copies that go to certain

> **segments** portions of a magazine's readership that an advertiser wants to reach

TECH & INFRASTRUCTURE
SPORTS ILLUSTRATED EVERYWHERE

There are a few sure signs of spring. The birds start chirping, flowers start blooming, and *Sports Illustrated* releases its yearly swimsuit edition. In spring 2010, *SI* decided to use its most famous issue of the year to tap into the growing number of people who do their magazine reading online or on their mobile device.

Early in the 2010 swimsuit season, SI.com had already doubled its swimsuit video streams from 2009. The company redesigned its home page to move ad-supported videos to the SI.com mainstream site and planned to release additional clips each day. Allegedly in response to research on viewer preferences, the videos are about two minutes each. The release of the swimsuit videos represents a considerable contribution to SI.com's online video strategy. Although the website shows some sports highlights, the main focus will be the development of sports commentary and hot topics shows. *SI* hopes that the videos associated with the swimsuit edition will be the hook that will get people interested in its video offerings.

However, SI.com is not stopping with online videos. The company has also created an ad-supported *Sports Illustrated Swimsuit 2010* app that operates on a "freemium" business model. Freemium models offer a limited number of services or products for free while charging for more advanced features. SI.com charges $1.99 for the app upgrade, which gives users access to about fifty more videos, exclusive footage, and more magazine coverage. The campaign showed modest success in its early stages.

SI hopes that the swimsuit campaign will bring more users to the website and encourage people to download the mobile app. Perhaps it will even encourage some people to subscribe to the old-fashioned paper and ink copy of the magazine.

---

segments of people, and other ads and articles are printed in copies that go to other segments of people. Printing different ads based on audience characteristics is expensive, and small-circulation titles are usually unable to offer it. But publishers of small titles probably don't need to bear the costs of segmentation anyway, because they are already niche-oriented. Large-circulation magazines, however, do have a particular incentive to break their readership into segments: to allow advertisers to zero in on readers by geography or demographic type.

Consider *Reader's Digest*, which has an audited circulation of 8 million. To reach every subscriber, a marketer would place a **run-of-book ad**. That is an advertisement that goes to every person receiving the same issue of a magazine. Apart from a national run-of-book ad, the magazine sells advertisers the ability to appear in one or more of ten "regional editions." The New England edition reaches 348,000 readers; the Great Lakes edition reaches 952,000 readers; and the Pacific edition reaches 829,000 readers. *Reader's Digest* also offers advertisers the ability to segment their ads into ten "major markets," including "families" (4 million adults aged 18–54 and/or children in household) and "boomers" (3.5 million adults that fit that age bracket). For advertisers who find these segments useful, the savings can be substantial. Whereas *Reader's Digest* sells a full-page, full-color ad in its national edition at $171,000, the same ad reaching about 262,000 readers in New England costs $21,760. Of course, the number of people reached is substantially smaller with these editions, but for geographically or demographically focused advertisers who want to be associated with *Reader's Digest* in the minds of readers it might be a good deal.

Despite the diversity and the large numbers of magazines, to remain competitive these publications increasingly need to be produced with a clear sense of the audience they want to reach, the topics they want to cover, and the personality they want to present. Publishers are quite aware of the need for this approach. Let's look at how they go about it.

run-of-book ad an advertisement that goes to every person receiving the same issue of a magazine

Production and the Magazine Industry

In the magazine industry, the term "publisher" refers not to the company making the magazine, but to a person who works there. A **magazine publisher** is the chief executive of a magazine and is in charge of its financial health. Under the publisher are the business departments (in charge of advertising and circulation), the technical production department, and the editorial department. The magazine's editor-in-chief works for the publisher; several editors may, in turn, work for the editor-in-chief (see Figure 9.1).

Magazine publishers work with their editors to build their magazines around distinct topics that will attract segments of readers. In turn, the publishers expect that their magazines will pull in advertisers who need to reach those population segments with the best medium possible.

magazine publisher the chief executive of a magazine, who is in charge of its financial health

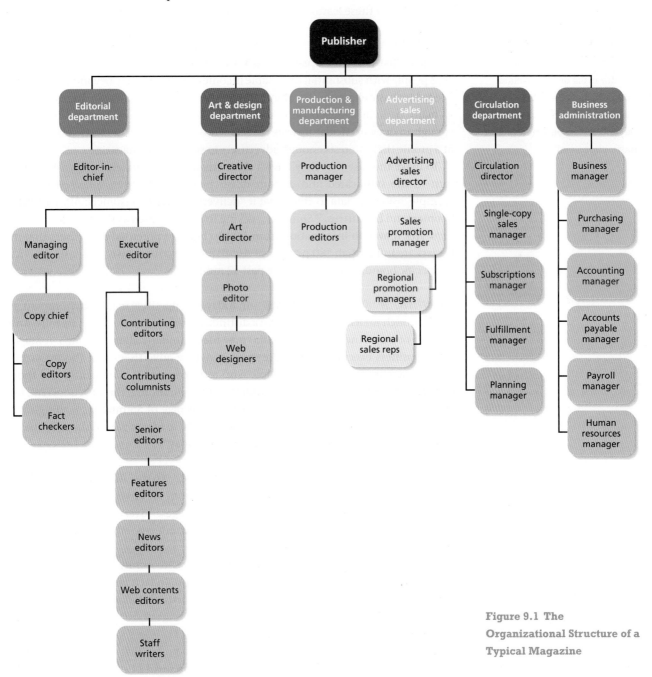

Figure 9.1 The Organizational Structure of a Typical Magazine

Magazine Production Goals

What makes a magazine the best medium possible for an advertiser? To both advertisers and publishers, the answer is a magazine that:

■ Draws an attractive audience
■ Draws an audience that is loyal to the content and personality of the magazine—its "brand"
■ Provides an environment conducive to the sale of the advertisers' products
■ Provides this audience and environment at an efficient price
■ Provides a way for advertisers to associate with the magazine's brand and audience beyond the magazine's pages

Let's look at these features one at a time.

upscale readers upper-middle-class or upper-class people with substantial disposable income (money beyond the amount needed for basic expenses)

DRAWING AN ATTRACTIVE AUDIENCE   Typically, magazine publishers want to reach what they call **upscale readers**. These are upper-middle-class or upper-class people with substantial disposable income—that is, money beyond the amount needed for basic expenses that they can spend on special or expensive items. Because so many periodicals reach these sorts of people, a magazine has to be distinctive enough to draw particular upscale readers whose social characteristics and lifestyles fit a profile that interests enough advertisers to support the magazine.

To make the case that they have a distinctly attractive audience, magazine firms turn to the syndicated and custom research described earlier. *Smart Money*, for example, uses MRI data to argue that it "delivers the right consumers: Affluent Baby Boomers and Executives."[6] Similarly, seeking to position itself as the place for car ads, *AutoWeek* draws on information from MRI to boast to potential advertisers that its readers are influential: "80 percent of *AutoWeek* subscribers gave purchasing advice on specific brands of vehicles in the past 12 months."

DRAWING A LOYAL AUDIENCE   In today's competitive media environment, it is not enough for a magazine to have a distinctly attractive audience on its rolls. Any number of magazines (or other media) may make similarly alluring claims. A magazine's business executives therefore must convince advertisers that the magazine is edited so effectively that the people who receive it read it consistently and thoroughly—presumably so thoroughly that they pay attention to the ads. *AutoWeek*, for example, asserts that its subscribers "spend an average of 55 minutes reading each Issue; 95 percent of them read 4 out of 4 issues." *Parade* magazine states it "has a conversation with 73 million Americans every Sunday"

CREATING A CONDUCIVE ENVIRONMENT   As the *AutoWeek* and *Parade* statements suggest, publishers understand that from an advertiser's standpoint a magazine is above all a platform for persuasive messages. Advertisers particularly like magazines with articles and photos that create a conducive environment for their products or services.

It is no accident that in *Ladies' Home Journal* and other women's service magazines you're likely to find ads for foods in the recipe section. In fact, publishers and editors often develop new magazine sections to attract advertisers that would find these sections appealing.

cost per thousand or cost per mil (CPM) the basic measurement of advertising efficiency; used to evaluate how much space an advertiser will buy in a given newspaper, and what price they will pay

SETTING AN EFFICIENT PRICE   Publishers know that they must present advertisers with a competitively low **cost per thousand** or **cost per mil (CPM)**

CULTURE TODAY
PRINT MAGAZINE ADS AND WEB TRAFFIC

Magazine firms worry that they are losing advertisers who are increasingly drawn to reaching audiences on the Web. As a consequence, magazine executives are working hard not only with arguments to convince sponsors that magazine ads help move merchandise; they are making the case that magazines also encourage people to interact with advertisers online.

The more traditional argument found in a magazine industry study suggests that magazine advertisements are the most effective vehicles to promote purchase intent. The publishers argue that, when it comes to driving brand favorability, magazine advertisements are twice as effective as television and four times as effective as online content. Magazine executives also claim their research shows that magazine ads are better at driving personal recommendations than either television or online content.

But the contemporary selling of magazines goes further. Publishers now argue that magazine advertisements are important for gaining exposure online. One industry study found that posting a URL (a Web address) in a magazine increased Web traffic by 40 percent. Further, executives claim that magazine ads are the number one drivers in Web searches among those aged from 18 to 44 years—an important marketing demographic.

Magazine companies' focus on the Web includes creating attractive websites supported by ads and encouraging readers to go there. But *Vanity Fair* is one magazine that has raised critics' ire by interrupting articles in the print edition and telling readers they must go online to finish it. Assessing the value of this type of media synergy, one analyst argues: "[P]rint and Web integration are, of course, all the rage these days, but while it's fantastic to, for instance, have additional content on the Web site—especially elements, like video, that don't work in print—stopping the reader short, mid-story, and asking him or her to jump to the Web site is counter-intuitive, to say the least."

Sources: Jack Loechner, "URLs Boost Magazine Ad Response," Media Post Blogs. http://www.mediapost.com (accessed September 11, 2009); "Magazine Ads Increase Web Traffic by More Than 40%," For Rent.com. http://blog.forrent.com (accessed September 20, 2009); David Weir, "The Dirty Truths About Web Traffic," bNet.com. http://industry.bnet.com (accessed September 20, 2009); Catharine P. Taylor, "Note to 'Vanity Fair': This Isn't How to Integrate Print and the Web," bNet.com. http://industry.bnet.com (accessed September 20, 2009).

readers if they want to get or keep business. Of course, a CPM is truly low only if the consumers that the magazine reaches are the consumers that the advertiser is targeting.

Say, for example, that you represent an advertiser that wants to use *Time* to reach upper-class executives who are interested in world affairs. If you advertise in the general edition of *Time* magazine, you might get a relatively low CPM (say $15) when all the readers are taken into account. When you consider only upper-class executives who read the magazine, however, your CPM may actually be much higher, because you are paying to reach so many people that you do not want. It is more efficient, you may have realized, to use one of the special *Time* editions that target highly paid executives. In fact, *Time*'s printing technology is set up so that your ad can target people based on their executive status and their geography—executives living in the northeast, for example. The CPM may be higher than the CPM for *Time*'s general audience, but you will get the specific audience you want.

Producing the Magazine as a Brand

An increasingly important way that a major magazine company tries to keep advertisers and get new ones is to position every title not just as paper-bound reading material but as a personality—a brand—with which readers want to engage in many areas of

In 2003 Conde Nast unveiled *Teen Vogue*, which used the established brand name of Anna Wintours *Vogue* to capture an established audience at a younger age.

their lives. In doing this, magazines have become central actors in the movement of materials across media boundaries that we discussed in Chapter 2. One major way in which they interact with their audience is through digital media. Another is by expanding into other media and staging events. In both, the magazines invite strong advertising participation.

DIGITAL MAGAZINES   Many magazine firms—both trade and consumer—are using the Web to extend relationships with their readers beyond the printed page. Even though the Web still contributes only a very small portion of magazine revenues (around 3 percent with consumer magazines, 14 percent with business-to-business), executives see it as key to their future. Consumer magazines have not been as aggressive as trade magazines in reaching out to their audiences online and drawing advertisers, but that is beginning to change. Many consumer magazines—especially the larger ones—feature sites that involve their users with podcasts, music, videos, blogs, and opportunities to interact with one another as part of the magazine's community. Some magazines, such as *Time*, place virtually all of the material in their hard-copy editions online in the belief that people will still purchase the hard copies. Others, such as *Maxim*, provide lots of material online but make it clear that to get the articles in the latest issue of the magazine you have to get the magazine. Still others, such as *Variety*, allow visitors into parts of their sites for free but charge for admission to other areas.

The Web has become a big selling point with advertisers. In its efforts to attract advertisers, *Parade* magazine flaunts its Web presence: *"Parade* has a conversation with 73 million Americans every Sunday through 510 newspapers and every day at Parade.com." These days, publishers must emphasize an advertiser's ability to buy space both in print and online in order to engage the reader deeply.

Increasingly, too, magazines are trying to engage readers on their mobile phones. That means encouraging them to download ringtones and photos, to enter contests via the text message, to read articles, and to interact with the magazine while they are on the move. For example, *Smart Money* features a website tailored to smartphone users, who can access magazine content without the heavy photo-loading time of its full website. Increasingly, too, magazines are offering applications (apps) for advanced mobile phones such as the iPhone and the Droid phones that allow a user to easily access relevant magazine materials and features. *Style* magazine offers an app that shows mobile videos from fashion shows. Such apps allow a magazine (and its advertisers) to reach out to readers who share the magazine's personality, and to encourage them to reach out to the magazine—wherever they are.

EXPANDING INTO OTHER MEDIA AND EVENTS   Some magazines go even further than expanding beyond the page to the Web and mobile devices. *Forbes*, a business-oriented consumer magazine, boasts what it refers to as "The Forbes Brand" and tells potential advertisers that it projects its personality as a "capitalist tool" to its audience "in ways that suit our audience's needs—at any given time of day, week or year—through our portfolio of brand properties." Those properties include the main magazine; several international editions; a separate *Forbes Asia* magazine; a magazine mailed to over 300,000 female readers of *Forbes*; a travel website aimed at upper-level executives; Forbes Events in which "Forbes editors and other business and lifestyle experts" offer "business leaders and affluent consumers . . . insights and information critical to their success";[7] *Forbes on Fox*, a weekly thirty-minute program on the Fox News channel; and Forbes Properties—yachts, art galleries in New York and Silicon Valley, and a number of estates that create environments in which advertisers can "foster relationships with current and potential prospects in unique and memorable settings."[8]

IS IT ETHICAL?
HOW SHOULD WEB MAGAZINES FIX ERRORS?

One of the biggest differences between digital publishing and traditional publishing in print is the potential for articles to change as writers discover new facts, or mistakes, relating to their stories. Journalistic print tradition holds that periodicals should inform readers of any mistakes in articles. But what if mistakes and old versions can simply be erased from the online world and corrected by the push of a button? Should readers be notified that changes have occurred since the initial version?

Editors from the *Columbia Journalism Review (CJR)* believe that the need for journalistic openness with readers requires that all changes in articles be acknowledged. In view of the speed required to keep websites current and the desire to save money on editorial activities, they wanted to know whether online magazines are following that approach. They also wanted to see whether traditional print-magazine emphasis on the importance of checking facts and careful editing is carried out in the online environment.

Their systematic study found that magazine executives were less concerned with copy-editing when it came to online editions of their magazines. While 48 percent of the magazines in the study were less rigorous

when editing online content, 11 percent said they did not copy-edit online articles at all. They also found that fact checking is less rigorous for online than for print copy.

The study also found that the vast majority of magazine websites—87 percent—corrected minor errors, including spelling mistakes, without acknowledging the change to readers. Further, although some magazines used editors' notes to cite changes made to factual information, a greater number routinely corrected factual errors without acknowledging the initial mistake to readers. Although magazines that had higher website traffic were more likely to correct mistakes, the study found that there was inconsistency, even among the more popular sites, over how changes were recorded.

Do you think it is ethical for websites to change typos and spelling errors without alerting readers to the change? Is it ethical to do the same for factual errors?

Sources: Stephanie Clifford, "Survey Finds Slack Editing on Magazine Web Sites," *New York Times*, February 28, 2010; Victor Navasky with Evan Lerner, "Magazines and Their Web Sites: A *Columbia Journalism Review* Survey and Report". http://www.cjr.org (accessed March 14, 2010)

Magazine events are by no means confined to this elite level. Look at any magazine's media kit and you'll see how executives try to help their advertisers reach their readers beyond the page and website. For example, *Seventeen* offers its advertisers the ability to associate themselves with mall events that it stages across the country. In 2009, *Seventeen* sponsored "Rock the Runway"—a fashion, beauty, and music show—together with MTV in major malls around the United States. Or consider the Martha Stewart Collection of upscale merchandise at Macy's. This venture is in addition to the image of pleasing domesticity that celebrity Martha Stewart projects not just in her magazines, but through satellite radio and various forms of TV as well. As the Sirius satellite radio website declares, "The Stars of Food and Design All Come to Martha Stewart Living Radio." The company designs its projects to reinforce one another.

Distribution and the Magazine Industry

magazine distribution the channel through which a magazine reaches its exhibition point

Magazine distribution refers to the channel through which the magazine reaches its exhibition point, the place where the reader sees it. When it comes to websites and other digital activities, distribution means sending content through website providers (cable or phone companies, for example) and through mobile providers (for example, AT&T, Verizon, or Sprint), which act as exhibitors. In the case of mobile services, getting to people's phones sometimes means making deals with the providers to share revenue from products such as ringtones and games. When it comes to print materials, trade magazines and newsletters are typically sent to subscribers

Forbes magazine has aggressively expanded beyond its flagship publication with international editions, travel websites, and a weekly thirty-minute television program called *Forbes on Fox.*

through the mail. Comic book companies distribute their products by themselves or through wholesalers to special stores that stock them.

Distribution for consumer magazines takes place in two ways. First, consumer magazines are distributed through the mail to readers who have a **subscription**—a long-term order for a magazine that is paid for in advance, for a predetermined period of time or number of issues. Second, independent distribution companies deliver consumer magazines to retail outlets where **single-copy sales**, or the sale of copies one issue at a time, take place (see Figure 9.2). Each of these avenues has its benefits and obstacles. From the standpoint of a small publisher, the mail is a useful distribution channel because the U.S. Postal Service (USPS) must accept all comers; therefore, a magazine from a major firm will not have precedence over a magazine from a minor firm. But small publishers are also angered that the USPS has raised rates for magazines that send out relatively few copies, but not for magazines that send out large numbers of copies that are bundled by ZIP codes. This approach privileges big mailers over small ones, and makes it difficult for magazine publishers with small circulations to stay profitable.

To create, build, and maintain circulation, small magazine firms may have to rely on rented lists to contact new potential readers. They may also turn to a direct-mail subscription firm such as Publishers Clearinghouse that advertises many magazines to consumers. However, subscription firms charge about 90 percent of the price the subscriber pays, meaning the magazine only benefits from the reader as a target for its advertisers. Recently however, subscription firms have generated far fewer subscriptions than they used to. In the past, they used the chance of winning a sweepstake as a lure to attract readers. But the Federal Trade Commission stepped in, forcing them to redesign their mailings to make it clear that not only has the recipient not actually won the sweepstake, but also that they don't have to buy periodicals to have a chance of winning.

Large magazine companies (although they too sometimes take the sweepstakes route) can do much more. With their own expensively produced databases of potential readers, they can mail highly targeted ads that entice desirable readers to subscribe; that way they get to keep the subscription money for themselves. Large magazine firms are also able to put a lot of money and effort into one of the most difficult aspects of their business—getting readers to renew their subscriptions—a process that can take several mailings and a lot of money.

subscription a long-term order, paid in advance, for the receipt of a magazine for a predetermined period of time or number of issues

single-copy sales the number of copies of a magazine sold not by subscription, but one issue at a time

Figure 9.2 Sources of
Magazine Revenue 2007
As this figure shows,
magazines typically earn more
revenue from advertising
than from subscription and
single-issue sales combined.
Source: Data from Magazine
Publishers of America,
*The Magazine Handbook,
2007/08*, p. 18. http://www.
magazine.org/content/Files/
magHandbook07_08.pdf
(accessed 27 July, 2010).

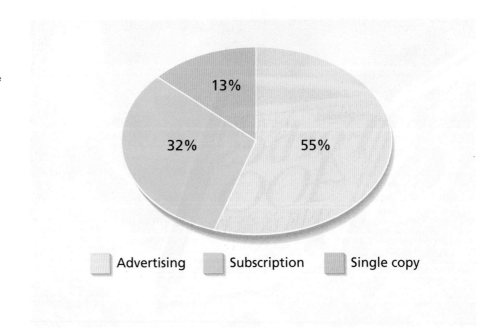

Advertising   Subscription   Single copy

Although creating, building, and maintaining a magazine's circulation by mail is difficult, doing it through magazine distributors is even harder. These national distribution firms reach a few hundred regional wholesalers, who, in turn, service well over 100,000 local retailers—typically supermarkets, drugstores, convenience stores, and newsstands. At retail, the field is complex and highly competitive, with the largest magazine racks carrying only about 200 titles. For this and other reasons, only a small number of magazines (notably *Woman's World*, *First For Women*, and *US Weekly*) use single-copy sales as their main strategy. At the same time, single-copy sales can bring in more per-copy revenues than subscriptions, which are often sold at substantial discounts off the cover price. Display on the newsstand and in the supermarket is an important way to introduce the magazine to new readers, who might use cards inside the periodical to become subscribers.

The distributor, the wholesaler, and the retailer are able to make money because they pay a discount off the cover price when they purchase the magazine. The total discount that a publisher typically gives up is about 50 percent; that is, if an issue's cover price is $1, the distributor, wholesaler, and retailer together make 50 cents on each issue. But, as in the book publishing industry, the publisher typically takes responsibility for unsold copies. If a wholesaler gets too many copies and returns proof of the unsold ones, the publisher refunds the money to the national distributor (which credits the wholesaler and retailer) and absorbs the loss.

Exhibition and the Magazine Industry

The challenge from the magazine publisher's standpoint is not just providing the wholesaler with only a few more copies than the retailers will sell. It is also to make sure that the wholesaler is placing the title in the retail outlets in which it will sell best, and in places in those outlets where it will best be seen. Walk over to a magazine stand or a supermarket checkout area and you will see the great number of magazines vying for your attention. In view of the large number of magazines that wholesalers have to stock, they may not pay much attention to new magazines from small companies unless the magazines are heavily advertised. In fact, it may be difficult for small companies to get retailers to accept their periodicals, and when they do get picked up they may not get prominent positions on the rack.

Securing display positions for magazines in retail spaces such as B. Dalton's DC's Union Station store (seen here) can be very costly. Therefore, few magazines use single-copy newsstand sales as their primary means to reach readers.

The largest magazine firms have an additional advantage at the newsstand. Companies such as Time Inc., Condé Nast, and Hearst own their own national distribution firms. They therefore have more influence with wholesalers concerning where and how their magazines should be placed with retailers. The large companies also have the cash to pay retailers **slotting fees**, or payments that ensure that their products will be placed prominently at the front of magazine racks or at the checkout counters of supermarkets. Smaller firms can't get this kind of treatment. In fact, during the past several years, major distributors have been buying up small firms because they simply couldn't compete effectively.

slotting fees payments that ensure that certain products will be placed prominently at the front of magazine racks or at the checkout counters of supermarkets

In general, single-copy sales are not moving in a direction that consumer magazine publishers like. From 2000 to 2008, the share of single-copy circulation declined from 15.9 percent of all consumer magazine copies distributed to 11.8 percent of the copies distributed (see Figure 9.3).[9] That is a particular problem for magazines that rely on single copies to recruit new subscriptions. They have to find new ways to get potential readers to see the value of a long-term relationship with their magazines.

Media Literacy and the Magazine Industry

Now that we have a good grasp of the way the magazine business works, let's step back as citizens and understand some of the complaints that social critics have lodged against the industry. Two of the major objections that critics have noted are conglomeration and the influence of advertisers. Let's take a look at each.

Conglomeration

Car and Driver and *InStyle* are very different magazines with different target audiences. Despite their differences in content, the periodicals share one crucial element: a powerful corporation backing them. *InStyle* is owned by the magazine powerhouse Time Magazines. Hachette Filipacchi, the major magazine firm that owns *Car and Driver*, is owned by the major French media conglomerate LeGardere. Making it big in the consumer magazine industry today requires more than just a good idea and a cross-media perspective. It requires the muscle of a big firm. In fact, as we've already

Figure 9.3 Single Copy or Subscription?
In 2008, 88 percent of total circulation in the consumer magazine industry was from subscriptions, while single-copy sales made up only 12 percent. Source: Magazine Publishers of America, *Magazines: The Medium of Action*, p. 14. http://www.magazine.org/advertising/handbook/Magazine_Handbook.aspx (accessed August 6, 2010).

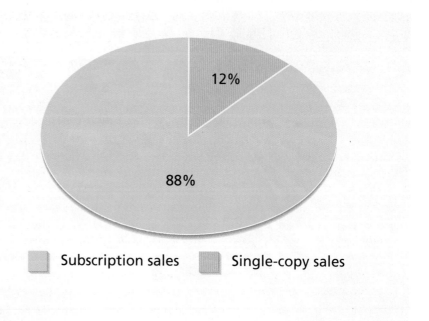

noted, the current magazine environment benefits big, rich firms. Publishers need to have huge amounts of cash and clout if they are to be noticed at the production, distribution, and exhibition levels.

Critics complain that this is the kind of influence that only the largest conglomerates can exert. As such, individuals and small firms have a far smaller chance of launching successful consumer periodicals than do major corporations. The unequal competition is not just connected to the print edition. Rich websites that have become the norm of media properties are expensive to create and keep up. In general, small firms find it nearly impossible to put together the kind of cross-media packages that today's advertisers demand. That makes their chances of staying in business over the long haul even dimmer than in earlier years, when putting out a magazine meant just working on a hard-copy periodical.

Advertiser Influence on Content

A great deal of what we have said about the U.S. magazine industry throughout this chapter comes down to attempts to attract advertisers. This fact raises another concern of media critics: the influence of advertisers on magazine content.

As the executives of consumer and business magazines feel increasing competition from other media and other periodicals, the possibility of direct and routine advertiser influence on editorial matter looms large. Some publishers and editors may not consider this a problem. After all, they will point out, advertisers have always had a profound influence on the magazine industry because they pay most of the costs. As a result, the very basic decisions about target readers—whom to attract and whom to ignore—are typically made with commercial sponsors in mind. Similarly, as we have noted, decisions about what types of sections to place in a new periodical, or to add to a mature one, are made with an eye toward potential advertisers. Recipe columns draw food ads. Travel columns draw travel ads. The list can go on.

Magazine publishers and editors have consistently recognized that this kind of sponsor influence is the unavoidable price of doing business in a commercial world. On the other end of the spectrum, one long-standing principle of magazine editing is that ads must be clearly separated and differentiated from other content—by using a different layout and a different font, for example. U.S. postal regulations require that ads that don't clearly look different from editorial matter be labeled "Advertisement."

CRITICAL CONSUMER
AN ELECTRONIC FUTURE FOR MAGAZINES?

The news for magazine publishers at the beginning of the twenty-first century has not been good. The economic downturn has made it difficult to sell advertising. Competition for readers and advertisers from free online publications has added to the traditional magazine publishers' woes. Magazines lost **58,340** ad pages in 2009 according to the Publishers Information Bureau. Condé Nast, a high-class titan of the periodicals world, lost more than 8,000 ad pages in 2009. The loss contributed to its decision to cease publication of its elite food magazine *Gourmet*, and focus instead on the more middle-class *Bon Appétit*. Condé Nast also shut down production of *Cookie*, *Elegant Bride*, and *Modern Bride*.

Looking for a long-term solution, traditional magazine firms such as Time Inc and Hearst have turned to the idea of a lightweight electronic tablet. Existing e-readers, such as Amazon's Kindle, don't support color. Magazine publishers believe that color is essential in order to carry forth the look and richness of editorial and articles in their print products. The iPad, Apple's answer to existing e-readers, does support color, and magazine publishers designed a number of iPad applications with magazines in mind. The intention was to create an application that would replicate the look of traditional paper magazines including opportunities for split screens and multi-column formats. Beyond the iPad, Time, Hearst, Condé Nast, Meredith, and News Corp have announced that they will work together to create and provide print publications for wireless devices including the iPhone and e-readers. The collaboration will enable customers to purchase magazines from a variety of publishers. Hearst, in collaboration with Sprint, has developed a prototype for the "Skiff"—an e-reader that features a color E-Ink display. Unlike the Amazon Kindle, the Skiff's color display and touch screen are specifically designed for use with newspapers and magazine subscriptions.

Though this may not save the magazine industry as it traditionally exists, these alternative formats may provide opportunities for the industry to transform itself.

Sources: Magazine Death Pool website. http://www.magazinedeathpool.com/ (accessed September 2010); Clifford, S., "Condé Nast Closes Gourmet and 3 Other Magazines," *The New York Times*, October 5, 2009; Andrews, R., "iPad's Killer App: It Looks A Bit Like A Magazine," February 14, 2010. paidContent.org.

Situations in which advertisers are mentioned or shown as part of the editorial content of the magazine are more difficult. Some companies, such as Time Magazines, have had explicit policies separating the business and advertising activities of the magazine from its editorial activities. The separation is supposed to ensure that editors do not worry about offending advertisers, since they do not deal at all with people from the ad department. Nevertheless, for obvious reasons, most magazine editors do not go out of their way to antagonize regular sponsors, and this can sometimes lead to ethical problems. Should, for example, a women's magazine run articles about the dangers of smoking if its major advertisers are cigarette firms?

Research on the relationship between smoking ads and the lack of articles about smoking in women's magazines suggests that cigarettes have quietly "bought" protection from bad publicity by paying for ad space. Publishers counter that, because cigarettes are legal, they have a right to carry these ads. Besides, publishers say, cigarette companies often purchase expensive space, such as the back cover, that is difficult to sell on a regular basis.

Publishers and their editors often face other difficult decisions relating to advertisers. For example, say you are running a controlled circulation magazine and a potentially large advertiser agrees to purchase space on condition that the advertiser's activities are also regularly mentioned in the editorial matter of the periodical. What do you do? If your magazine needs (or covets) the money, would you say to yourself that the advertiser would probably be mentioned in the magazine anyway, so it would be fine to agree? The American Business Press code of ethics states that such activities are prohibited. Trading ads for editorial coverage certainly occurs in the business press, but because this practice is rarely admitted no one really knows how often it takes place.

CRITICAL CONSUMER
THE PRESIDENT'S NEW CLOTHES

Media have historically both helped and hurt the images of U.S. presidents. Examples on the plus side are startling. Members of the press agreed, for example, not to photograph Franklin D. Roosevelt in his wheelchair to avoid portrayal of the president as weak. Ronald Reagan once appeared on the cover of a magazine in a picture in which his head had been imposed onto the torso of a body builder. The picture was an obvious forgery, but it did help promote an image of the president as a strong and vibrant leader.

Since Barack Obama's arrival on the national political scene, many media outlets have focused on the portrayal of the politician as young and active—photographing him playing basketball, at the gym, and even on a beach in his swim shorts. When *Washingtonian* magazine ran a picture of President Obama in his swim trunks, concerns were raised. Concern was not over the paparazzi photo of the president without a shirt, but over

the apparent alteration of the photograph. President's Obama's trunks, which were black in reality, were red on the magazine.

Spokespeople for the *Washingtonian* argue that they were trying to "get across a concept" and that the slight alteration did not cause any harm. Media critique Howard Kurtz, however, says the alterations are problematic. "While the alterations of this picture might seem to some people to be kind of minor, it is absolutely unethical," he said. "It is dishonest. It is not journalism. You cannot present a news photo, particularly of a president, but of anybody, and alter it through digital technology without being honest about it with readers." Do you think such alterations are unethical?

Source: CNN Politics, "Magazine Takes Heat for Doctoring Obama Pic." http://politicalticker.blogs.cnn.com (accessed September 20, 2009).

What about consumer magazines? How vulnerable are they to mixing advertising and editorial matter and to making themselves merely the instruments of the highest bidders? Magazine specialists J. William Click and Russell Baird quote a former editor of *Good Housekeeping* as contending that although "to set out deliberately to antagonize advertisers would be senseless . . . when there was reason to investigate and expose, there was no hesitation." But Click and Baird also note that "editorial integrity is much easier to maintain if the [magazine] is in solid financial condition and does not desperately need to woo advertisers." The problem is that, as magazines compete for narrower audiences than ever before and as publishers worry about losing advertisers to a bad economy and other media, worries about their financial stability increase.

An article about breaking into the magazine industry quoted the advertising production manager of *Entrepreneur* as encouraging editorial people to cooperate with the advertising staff. Speaking to aspiring publishers he said, "You'll want to work hard to develop a strong relationship between your advertising and editorial production departments. One of the reasons we're so successful is that we've always worked well with our editorial team to develop the give and take that's necessary to make both sides of the business happy and successful."[10]

Many people in the magazine industry would cringe at these sorts of relationships. But with even the largest magazines struggling, signs are emerging that the lines between the business and editorial departments are beginning to blur in some magazines, that the publishers of some magazines are actively encouraging "partnerships" with advertisers that they feel reflect their audiences' lifestyles. The practice of seeing magazines as brands that set up events and internet sites sometimes encourages dimmed lines between the editorial department and advertisers. An example is when a fashion magazine mounts a show of the latest dresses and the bulk of the clothes going down the runway are by the companies that are sponsoring the event. Or consider Hachette's *Car and Driver* website's decision to develop "virtual test drives" based on car reviews from the magazine. The videos are sponsored by car companies as part of advertising packages that include the print magazine, the website, and perhaps other associations with the *Car and Driver* brand. Although the magazine's writers have no hesitation in giving a negative review to a car they evaluate, Hachette's marketing director of men's titles acknowledged that the videos about the car would likely eliminate the negative aspects of the review to make sponsors (likely the car company) comfortable. "If the editorial staff has said that the vehicle is overweight, we'll never say it's light," he said. Instead, "We'll focus on other aspects of the vehicle on behalf of the consumer."[11]

The extent of widespread editorial sensitivity and collaboration will become one of the most basic questions that we can ask about the changing magazine industry. In the interest of your media literacy, it will be useful to follow this trend through industry trade magazines such as *Advertising Age* and *Folio*. In the long run, the integrity of the U.S. media system is at stake in the outcome.

The magazine industry is an enormously varied business that runs the gamut from widely read consumer periodicals to narrowly read newsletters. There are huge differences in types of readership and sources of financial support. Perhaps the one major similarity among magazine practitioners is that all are being buffeted by the changes taking place in the broad media environment. New electronic media present both challenges and opportunities. Competition for readers, always intense, is becoming more intense. In decades past, such challenges have led to profound changes in several parts of the industry. There are signs that advertisers are having a growing influence on content in some areas of consumer magazines. It will be interesting to see how the magazine industry adapts to the twenty-first-century media world—and how that affects what we get from magazines and how we get it.

Chapter Review

For an interactive chapter recap and study guide, visit the companion website for *Media Today* at http://www.routledge.com/textbooks/mediatoday4e.

Questions for Discussion and Critical Thinking

. . . .

1 Why did President Theodore Roosevelt use the term "muckrakers" to describe the investigative magazine writers of his day? By using the term, did he mean to compliment or disparage them?

2 Why did magazines such as *Coronet* and *The Saturday Evening Post* stop publishing in the 1950s and 1960s despite high circulation numbers?

3 Describe the benefits and drawbacks of controlled circulation and paid circulation magazines.

4 "Magazines increasingly need to be specialized with a clear sense of audience they want to reach, the topics they want to cover, and the personality (that is, attitude and viewpoints) they want to present if they are to remain competitive in their industry." Why?

5 What does it mean to say that publishers believe they need to treat their magazines as brands?

6 Why is conflict between "church" and "state" more pronounced in major magazine companies today than in the past?

Internet Resources

· · · · · · · · · · · · · · · · · · · ·

Folio magazine (http://www.foliomag.com/)

> *Folio* is the major trade magazine of the magazine publishing industry. On the website you can read articles from the magazine and a newsletter, learn about industry events, and browse through a directory of companies, from list brokers to publishing technology firms, that supply the industry with the wherewithal to carry out its tasks.

Magazine Publishers of America (http://www.magazine.org)

> Established in 1919, the Magazine Publishers of America (MPA) calls itself the industry association for consumer magazines. It is a strong advocate for magazines to advertisers and the government. The website reflects these roles in addition to having sections about magazine careers, magazine retailing, and other aspects of the industry. The site also hosts the American Association of Magazine Editors.

International Regional Magazine Association (http://www.regionalmagazines.org)

> This is a group of companies that produce magazines aimed at particular geographic areas—for example *Vermont Life* and *Oklahoma Magazine*. The site includes a reference area with links to useful sites that are relevant to all sorts of magazines.

Custom Publishing Council (http://www.custompublishingcouncil.com)

> The Council "is focused on promoting the growth and vitality of this dynamic marketing discipline." Its website includes an explanation of custom publishing, profiles of custom publishers, and research, case studies, and how-to articles that explain and promote this type of magazine publishing.

Key Terms

· · · · · · · · · · · · · ·

You can find the definitions to these key terms in the marginal glossary throughout this chapter. Test your knowledge of these terms with interactive flash cards on the *Media Today* companion website.

Constructing Media Literacy

1 Make a case for the argument that comic books are not magazines.

2 Based upon your own use of print magazines and internet resources, in what ways does the internet present a significant threat to the print magazine industry at this time? How might you see this changing in the future?

3 You are the editor of a women's magazine, which is having a hard time selling ads. Cigarette companies are offering to buy full-page ROB sponsorships. Should you accept the ads? Should you run articles about the dangers of smoking if you know your major sponsors might leave? What would you do? Why?

Companion Website Video Clips

Killing Us Softly 4—Introduction

This clip from the Media Education Foundation documentary *Killing Us Softly 4* explores the portrayal of women in advertising and how this affects women's views of themselves and others. Credit: Media Education Foundation.

Case Study

EXPLORING MAGAZINE MEDIA KITS ONLINE

The idea Many magazines post their media kits online for prospective advertisers to consider. The kits can provide interesting insight into the different ways that magazines try to position themselves among the competition and promote their ability to reach certain audience segments.

The method Choose two magazines that you believe aim at similar audiences—for example, two women's magazines or two consumer automotive magazines. In Google, type the name of the magazine in quotation marks and the words "media kit" in quotation marks. For example, type "car and driver" "media kit."

Explore each media kit along the following lines: the magazine's description of its goals or mission; the way it talks about its editorial material; the ways it describes its circulation; the ways it talks about its audience and audience segments; the various ad formats and offers for reaching its audience and audience segments; and the media activities in which it engages beyond the magazine pages. Then write a five-page report that explains similarities and differences among the ways the magazines argue their place and advantage within their industry.

Part Four

The Electronic Media

The industries engaged in electronic media are a part of a broad landscape that's changing rapidly, in which the boundaries among businesses are blurring. Will radio, recordings, movies, television, and electronic games merge into one vast electronic network we call the Web? If the answer is no, what forces are stopping this from taking place? If the answer is yes, who will control the Web and with what consequences?

This section will help you to answer these questions. Chapters 10 through 14 examine the recording, radio, movie, television, and internet and video game industries. We'll investigate social controversies related to each of the industries and focus a critical eye on the impact and influence of the most powerful firms.

THE CHAPTERS

10 The Recording Industry

After studying this chapter, you will be able to:

1 Sketch the history of the recording industry

2 Explain how a recording is developed—from the time an artist creates a song to the time the recording ends up in your CD collection

3 Explain the ways in which artists and labels turn profits

4 Recognize the promotional techniques used by record labels to push sales

5 Decide where you stand on the major controversies facing the recording industry today

MEDIA TODAY

How many people do you know (including yourself) who have downloaded music from internet sites without paying for it? If you answered "everyone" or "too many to count," you're like many people who are taking advantage of digital technologies to share perfect copies of songs without reimbursing the copyright holders. Though illegal, the activity is widespread. The Recording Industry Association of America (RIAA), the major association that represents the recording industry, doesn't put a particular number on digital piracy. According to its website, "One credible analysis by the Institute for Policy Innovation concludes that global music piracy causes $12.5 billion of economic losses every year." Until recently, the RIAA filed lawsuits against individuals, including college students, who it believed were sharing illegal music. It stopped doing that partly because of the bad public relations it created, partly because universities and internet providers agreed to put safeguards in place to prevent illegal downloading, and partly because the increased availability of relatively cheap or free digital music (think iTunes and Pandora) have stopped the growth of illegal downloads and brought recording companies new revenues through individual purchases and advertiser support. In fact, as the RIAA points out, the digital market in recorded music has been surging, accounting for over 30 percent of the recording industry's revenues in 2008.

One point is clear: the rise of digital technologies in music represents the most profound change in a century regarding all aspects of the recording industry, from production to distribution to exhibition. Not everyone is suffering because of the transformation. Some companies and artists have learned to adapt to the new realities, and others are working hard to figure out how to adapt.

Who is winning, who is losing, and why? How are their actions affecting the kind of recorded music that is circulated in the United States and the rest of the world? The aim of this chapter is to help you address these questions and think about how they affect you. To understand where the industry is now and why it is so nervous in its response to digital challenges, it is useful to take a quick look at where it came from. As you'll see, over the past hundred years or so, a handful of recording companies developed the power to control much of the music that Americans heard. In the early twenty-first century they fear they are losing that control, and they are fighting hard to reclaim it.

Before the rise of recorded sound in the late nineteenth century, most American families entertained themselves at home by singing and playing musical instruments. Pianos were especially popular in middle-class homes.

minstrel show a touring show popular in the mid-nineteenth century, in which performers dressed up in special "blackface" makeup, made jokes, and sang songs that, though supposedly drawn from "black songfests," actually had little to do with the African-American lifestyles and rhythms they claimed to mimic

The Rise of Records

As late as 1880 or 1890, people growing up in a middle-class U.S. household had no recorded music in their homes in the sense that we understand it today. That's not to say that homes didn't have music. For one thing, family members often played musical instruments. Pianos were especially popular in middle-class homes. Many family members learned to play, and there was a vigorous and growing industry that published sheet music and sold it in music stores around the country.

How did people know which of the latest sheet-music compositions to buy? Sometimes the salesperson at the store would play the piece so the customer could hear it. Other times, people heard the songs they wanted to buy from attending the concerts of musicians and singers. If audience members at these concerts liked a particular piece, they might purchase a copy from the sheet-music proprietor. Two particularly important touring sources for popular new songs were the minstrel show, which was popular around the mid-nineteenth century, and the vaudeville show, which was popular from the late nineteenth century through the 1920s.

Minstrel Shows

The **minstrel show** is said to be derived from a black songfest. Performers (usually white, but sometimes black) dressed up in special "blackface" makeup and made jokes and sang songs that actually had little to do with the African-American lifestyles and rhythms that they claimed to present.

Minstrel shows first appeared in the early 1840s. At the height of their popularity, dozens of minstrel show companies toured the United States; some even played theaters in England. By 1910, the genre was nearly obsolete. Though the minstrel show had all but vanished, some variety performers and motion picture actors, notably Al Jolson, adopted the minstrel's blackface makeup in the 1920s and 1930s.

Vaudeville Shows

Vaudeville shows had some things in common with minstrel shows (including some blackface singers) but drew from a broader range of social experiences. Within one show, vaudeville presented comedy acts, acrobats, animal acts, and even famous people simply talking to the audience about their lives. Much of vaudeville involved music, and an entire popular music publishing industry grew up around it. It was nicknamed **Tin Pan Alley**—after a street in Manhattan—and it, in turn, used vaudeville to publicize its music.

The competition among song publishers to promote their songs around the country was strong. It was common knowledge in vaudeville that "song pluggers" often paid popular vaudeville performers a lot of money to sing a particular publisher's tunes on stage. Sometimes an image of the performer's face even appeared on the sheet music as a way to hype the song.

Listening to Music at Home

People who couldn't play sheet music could enjoy other forms of music in their homes, even before the advent of records. Wind-up music boxes were a popular way of providing in-home music. Inside these music boxes were metal rolls with specially arranged pegs on them. As the rolls turned, the pegs struck steel combs. When the combs were struck, they played notes, and so the music box played a song. By around 1890, people were buying much larger music boxes that used interchangeable disks to hit the metal bars, so that one music box could play many songs.

Another popular "music machine" was the player piano, which used a perforated roll of paper and a pneumatic mechanism to get the keys to hit the strings. Some player pianos reproduced not only the notes recorded on the paper roll, but also other characteristics of the original performance, such as the pressure applied to individual keys and the loudness of notes.

The Advent of the Record Player

Despite the popularity of such mechanical players, there were systematic attempts in the nineteenth century to reproduce the actual sound vibrations of a performance. The first device that could record and play back sound was invented by Thomas Alva Edison in 1877. The **phonograph**, as Edison called it, recorded sound on tin foil with spiral grooves on it that was wrapped around a metal cylinder (see Figure 10.1). To record, a person would use a crank to turn the cylinder while speaking into a tube with a vibrating diaphragm. Air pressure from the diaphragm caused a needle to vibrate against the foil so that grooves of different depths and lengths were created. To play back the recording, the person would connect the needle to a hollow horn, place the stylus on the cylinder, and turn the crank.

Edison's first recorded statement was the poem "Mary Had a Little Lamb." His company's publicity department extolled the invention highly and sold it as a business recording device, but the foil was hard to use properly; by 1880, a disappointed Edison described his invention as a "toy, which has no commercial value." The machine's fortunes changed in 1885, however, when Chichester Bell and Charles

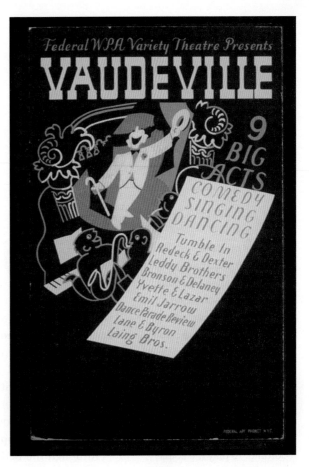

Federal WPA Variety Theatre Presents
VAUDEVILLE
9 BIG ACTS
COMEDY SINGING DANCING

Tumble In
Redeck & Dexter
Leddy Brothers
Bronson & Delaney
Yvette & Lazar
Emil Jarrow
Dance Parade Review
Lane & Byron
Laing Bros.

For more than 150 years, vaudeville was America's most popular form of entertainment. People who sit glued to their TV sets today would have been flocking to their local auditoriums to see programs like the one advertised here.

vaudeville show a touring show comprising several types of acts that were popular in the United States from the late nineteenth century through the 1920s

Tin Pan Alley term describing the popular music publishing industry of the early twentieth century

phonograph invented by Thomas Alva Edison in 1877, this device recorded and played back sound on tin foil wrapped around a metal cylinder with spiral grooves on it

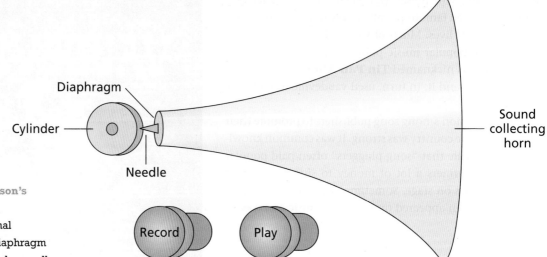

Cylinder

Diaphragm

Needle

Record

Play

Sound collecting horn

Figure 10.1 Edison's Phonograph

In Edison's original phonograph, a diaphragm directly controlled a needle, and the needle scratched an analog signal onto a tin foil cylinder. You spoke into Edison's device while rotating the cylinder and, as the diaphragm vibrated, so did the needle. Those vibrations impressed themselves onto the cylinder, thus making a recording. To play the sound back, the needle moved over the groove scratched during recording, causing the needle and the diaphragm to vibrate and play the recorded sounds.

graphophone Chichester Bell and Charles Tainter's 1885 modification of Edison's phonograph, which featured a wax cylinder rather than a tin foil cylinder for recording and playback

gramophone Emile Berliner's 1887 modification of both the phonograph and the graphophone, which featured wax disks for recording and playback, rather than a cylinder

Tainter introduced wax rather than foil as the recording medium; they called the device a **graphophone**.

In 1887, Emile Berliner modified the invention still more by abandoning Edison's cylinder model and using zinc disks for recording. To record, Berliner covered the surface of the disk with a wax substance that could be recorded upon. After the sound waves had been recorded on the wax coating, the disk was immersed in acid, which ate through the grooves in the wax and cut into the zinc (see Figure 10.2). He called the device a **gramophone**.

Although the Berliner system was very loud, the quality of playback was not as good as that of Edison's cylinder. The real weak point was the playback machine. This machine had a small crank that was connected to a belt that moved the turntable. You needed to hold the machine while you were cranking and at the same time lower the needle onto the record, which was turning (you hoped) at 70 revolutions per minute (rpm). You also had to continue cranking for as long as you wanted to listen. Hardly anyone could keep the turntable moving at the right speed, and, even if they could, someone else had to hold the machine so that the cranking wouldn't jolt the needle and disrupt playback. Despite these problems, Berliner had made an important discovery: he could use the zinc disks to make molds that would press out copies of the records on hard rubber. The molds could be used to make copies in almost unlimited numbers.

Unfortunately for Berliner, there was little demand for his records as a result of the manual machine that had to be used to play them. (Some people compared operating the machine to using an eggbeater.) Still, he did find some success owing to the gramophone's low price. At a time when the average worker was earning only $6 a week, Edison's North American Phonograph Company was selling its machines for $150, targeted at businesses. Berliner's modest success awakened Edison to the moneymaking possibilities of his invention. His company tried to maintain control over Berliner's device by claiming that it retained the patent rights to all cylinder versions of the machine.

In the end, however, it was Emile Berliner's machine (and eventually an easier one to use) that won out—thanks to some shrewd marketing. He and a partner had established the Victor Talking Machine Company. Its trademark was a dog named Nipper looking into the speaker of the gramophone (hearing "His Master's Voice"). In 1906 the firm marketed their machine as a Victrola, the first talking machine that was also a piece of furniture. Consumers preferred Berliner's flat disks over Edison's cylinders

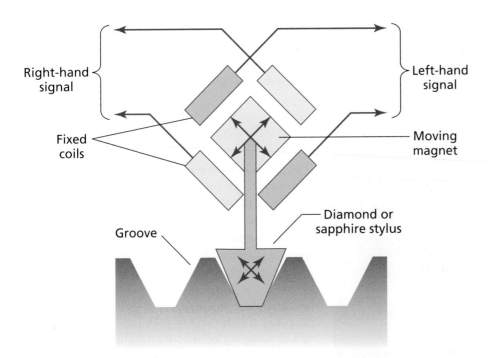

Right-hand signal

Left-hand signal

Fixed coils

Moving magnet

Groove

Diamond or sapphire stylus

Figure 10.2 Berliner's Gramophone
The gramophone's major improvement over Edison's phonograph was the use of flat wax records with a spiral groove (instead of a tin foil cylinder), making mass production of records easy.

because they sounded better and were easier to store without breaking. In 1912, even Edison's company realized that Victor had won and began producing disks.

By that time, Americans' interest in recorded music had grown tremendously. The annual production of phonographs (both cylinder and disk players) grew from 150,000 in 1899 to 500,000 in 1914. In 1910, at least 20 million records were sold. By 1921, the number of records sold reached 140 million. The popularity of recordings encouraged AT&T to perfect the "electrical recording" process in 1924, amplifying the voices of musicians and singers for the first time. All-electric record players, which allowed much better reproduction of sound, soon became available. Records had become part of American life.

THE EFFECT OF RECORDS AND THE RECORD PLAYER ON THE EARLY MUSIC INDUSTRY   Records changed the music industry in profound ways. One effect was to make the sheet-music business much less important. Think about it: the phonograph made music available to everyone. If you had no piano (or if you couldn't play it), for a small amount of money you could still listen to recorded versions of the latest music, expertly performed. To get people to buy sheet music, publishers had to lower their prices for songs drastically—from 40 cents per copy in 1902 to 10 cents in 1916. Music publishers found themselves making more money from the sale of recordings of their music (royalties) than from the sale of sheet music.

The effect of records on popular songs was even more extraordinary. Before the phonograph, Tin Pan Alley's songwriters had created tunes that could be played and sung by amateurs at home. Now they could write more complicated works, since people could buy them on disks and did not have to play them on their own instruments. Musical arrangements could be more intricate, with harmonies and ranges suited to better-trained musicians. For example, compare "A Bicycle Built for Two" (1892)—with its simple melody and easily managed lyrics—with "Stardust" (1920), a hard-to-play melody that didn't even have lyrics initially. (This book can't sing, but maybe you can find recordings elsewhere.)

One more point about the effects of records: because their playing time was set by the manufacturers at about three minutes, songwriters and arrangers had to work with about two choruses of songs. This lyric format became the standard unit for decades until the arrival of long-playing records, and it had enormous consequences

Record companies worried that radio might discourage the purchase of recorded music, but sales remained brisk for types of music that radio stations wouldn't play, such as jazz and blues. Records of "torch" singer Bessie Smith are said to have helped keep Columbia afloat.

label a division of a recording firm that releases a certain type of music and reflects a certain personality

for the nature of the popular song. The sixteen-bar narrative song, which had been popular for nineteenth-century sing-alongs, did not fit this format and fell by the wayside. Lyrics had to be short and direct.

Records and the Rise of Radio

The 1920s marked a decade in which the recording industry confronted another industry that would be critical to its existence over the next eighty years: commercial radio. A large part of the development of commercial radio in the 1920s involved playing music over the airwaves. Initially, that created problems for the record industry. Record companies worried that radio might discourage the purchase of recorded music. In fact, the presence of popular music on the airwaves—often "live" rather than recorded—created severe problems for the phonograph industry during the mid-1920s, as people listened to radio instead of buying disks. Worried about the future of its business, the Victor Talking Machine Company merged with RCA. The Columbia Phonograph Company, also fearful that its business was trickling away, tried to profit from broadcasting by financing a radio network to be called the Columbia Broadcasting System. The project lost money, Columbia pulled out, and what became known as CBS proceeded on its own. (Years later, in 1938, CBS purchased Columbia Records.)

There were, however, some types of music that radio stations wouldn't play: jazz, blues, hillbilly music, ethnic songs, and other compositions that executives did not consider refined enough to broadcast. That practice created opportunities for record producers. African-Americans were particularly avid record buyers; records of the black "torch" singer Bessie Smith are said to have kept Columbia afloat. Soon Victor and Columbia expanded their "race" catalog and even issued jazz under their more general-market **labels**. In addition, many small record companies appeared (for example Brunswick, Vocalion, Okeh, Cameo) that recorded materials a person wasn't likely to hear on the radio. As one media historian notes, "radio, putting pressure on records, was edging them firmly into a new world."[1]

The variety of music available on radio expanded in the 1930s. That sounds good, but, partly because people could get music without paying for it, the economic depression of the early 1930s hit the recording industry harder than many others. Record sales fell to one-tenth of 1929 levels, and some companies went bankrupt. By 1935, only Victor (now part of RCA) and Columbia-Brunswick remained significant.

Just as things were looking terribly bleak for the industry, though, sales increased again. Singing stars from radio and movies, such as Bing Crosby, along with newly popular "swing bands," such as those of Benny Goodman and Artie Shaw, encouraged millions of youngsters and young adults to buy records. Two new companies emerged as important in American and international music: Decca (a U.S.–British firm) and EMI (a British firm).

Music publishers and composers were beginning to think of radio as a new source of stable income. They also saw it as a better platform for publicizing songs and encouraging record sales than the now-dying vaudeville. They began to get substantial royalties from radio through the American Society of Composers, Authors, and Publishers (ASCAP), which charged stations and the networks an annual license fee for broadcasting music. By using the lists of music played on some stations and paying people to audit the songs of other stations, ASCAP decided how much of the money each of its individual members should receive. Broadcasters, angry at what they contended were ASCAP's excessive fees, started their own licensing organization, Broadcast Music Incorporated (BMI). The competition lowered music costs for broadcasters and showed how important radio had become to the musical recording world.

Rethinking Radio and Recordings, 1950–1980

Major changes that occurred in American society after the end of World War II in 1945 deeply affected the radio and, as a result, the record industry. Two of the most important developments were the rise of television and the emergence of the baby boom generation.

The Development of Formats

Television, a new medium during the late 1940s, rapidly began to draw audiences and advertisers away from radio. The national radio networks found that they could not afford to mount the expensive programs and support live orchestras that had made up so much of their broadcasts throughout the previous two decades. They gave back a lot of their time to local stations, which found it more profitable to play records rather than bring in performers for live shows. To draw advertisers, radio executives decided to go after specific local audience segments by devoting most of their airtime to broadcasting music that those segments would tune in to hear. Playing records was inexpensive compared with creating drama or comedy or adventure series. Often record companies would send records to the radio stations for free, in the hope that the stations would play them and their listeners would buy them. As a result, stations around the country developed different **formats**. A radio format is the personality of a station organized around the kind of music it plays (country, rock, hiphop) and the radio personnel (called disk jockeys or DJs) who are hired to introduce the recordings and advertisements.

That's how baby boomers entered radio's universe. In the mid-1950s, the creators of radio formats realized that the generation of youngsters born in the early and mid-1940s was becoming the richest generation in history. These people had money to spend and time to spend it, and they

format the personality of a station organized around the kind of music it plays, and the radio personalities who are hired to introduce the recordings and advertisements

DJ Murray Kaufman with rock 'n' roll rhythm and blues singer Frankie Lymon

wanted to listen to their own music. A few enterprising disk jockeys (including Alan Freed and Murray "the K" Kaufman) developed quick-moving "rock 'n' roll" formats that included new music that borrowed heavily from African-American rhythm and blues. On the air, the DJs introduced songs with lingo and sounds that they felt teenagers could identify with. The idea caught on throughout local radio and it reshaped record executives' ideas about what music to record.

From the standpoint of the record industry, the increasingly specific formats of radio stations enabled record promoters to target their intended audiences much more carefully than before. College radio stations, for example, became useful vehicles for introducing "alternative" music, which most commercial stations would not touch until it had sold well in stores. Recording executives hated the fact that they had to rely on the interests of radio programmers to get their music out to potential customers. The pressure to get "airplay" encouraged bribes with money, drugs, and other gifts, and produced a number of scandals.

New Developments in Technology

The explosion of music formats in radio was a great benefit to the recording industry. It came at a time when the technology of recording and playback was changing. First, Columbia and RCA introduced records that played at slower speeds ($33\frac{1}{3}$ and 45 rpm instead of the previous 78), which permitted longer recordings. Second, the sound quality of records was enhanced by the introduction of high-fidelity and stereophonic record players. Third, almost unbreakable vinyl replaced highly breakable shellac as the material for making records. These developments encouraged consumers to purchase recorded music. Recording executives noted that radio—and especially teen-oriented rock 'n' roll radio—was driving a high percentage of the purchases. When a song was played over and over again on the air, it stood a good chance of selling a lot of copies.

Aiding this growth were the long-playing record, FM radio, the transistor radio, and the tape player. Long-playing records allowed rock musicians to try out ideas that were much longer and more conceptual than the traditional three-minute song that had been standard since the start of records. The Beatles' *Sgt. Pepper's Lonely Hearts Club Band* (1967) was a milestone of this development. Although the entire **album** would not typically be played on standard rock 'n' roll radio, portions—known as **cuts**—of it were.

album a collection of a dozen or more individual musical recordings

cuts individual portions of a recorded album

Listening to albums outside the home became much easier with the developments of the transistor radio and the tape player. The transistor, invented at Bell Laboratories in the 1940s, quickly became a replacement for the vacuum tube in radio devices. Transistors were much lighter, less fragile, less bulky, and more energy efficient than tubes—allowing for lightweight radios with small batteries that could be carried virtually anywhere. And while the transistor radio allowed people to access stations on the go, the tape recorder did that and more. The idea of recording and playing sound on tape originated in Germany in the years leading up to World War II; German tape recorders were discovered by Allied soldiers toward the end of the war. By the 1960s, tape recording was allowing musicians more freedom in the way they created and edited their works, changing the way in which records (and music) were created. By the same token, tape players powered by transistors and light batteries were changing the way audiences listened to music. Now the albums of their choice were portable: for the first time, people could take them to the park or the beach and even play them in their cars.

Toward a New Digital World: The 1980s and 1990s

The spread of cable television in the 1980s provided an opportunity for recording companies to reach target audiences beyond radio. At the forefront of cable music were MTV and VH1, two cable networks owned by the same firm (Viacom) that played nonstop music videos supplied by music companies. MTV pioneered the twenty-four-hour music video approach in the early 1980s. Other music video programs, on broadcast television as well as on cable networks such as Black Entertainment Television (BET), also seemed to influence music purchases.

The compact disk (CD) was the record industry's newest attempt to entice people to recordings. It was brought to the market in 1983 by a number of Japanese firms. CD technology abandoned Thomas Edison's analog method of reproducing sound in favor of a digital approach. That is, instead of creating grooves that held sound analogous to the original sound, the recording process laid down digital codes that could tell a computer chip how to reproduce the sound. In playback, a laser beam read the codes and sent them to the chip, which in turn sent them through the amplifier to the speakers. The recording industry promoted the CD as an alternative to the standard vinyl record; it argued that CDs had superior sound, were more durable, and would never wear out. Although there were skeptics (and there still are), recorded music sales surged as people rebuilt their collections of records and tapes with CDs. By the late 1990s, though, this rebuilding had run its course, and the growth rate of recorded music sales slowed a bit. The digital nature of the CD, however, made it straightforward to create copies of albums in the home computers that spread through the United States and the rest of the world during the 1990s. Although people had long been making copies of records through their tape recorders, the analog duplication method degraded the sound quality. CD copying worried executives because the digital reproductions are identical to the originals.

As CD piracy became rampant in the United States and around the world, the recording industry was hit by another stream of copying. The spread of the internet in the late 1990s marked the start of uploaded music (often from CDs) for all to share. So, although recording firms still saw radio as the major promotional medium for their business, they worried that the new technologies would reduce the sales that might result from their promotional work because people could get the music off pirated CDs and the Web and pay little or nothing at all. The concern raised important issues for the industry: What would the rise of these and other Web technologies do to the music industry? To what extent, and how, would it transform the production, distribution, and exhibition of music in the twenty-first century? Would the traditional role of radio for the recording industry change as a result of all this?

Answers to these questions—and to the related ones we asked at the start of this chapter—are beginning to emerge. Let's look at how the recording industry is arranged today, including the ways it is changing in response to the digital challenges that face it.

An Overview of the Modern Recording Industry

A broad look at the recording industry in the United States makes three things about the industry very clear:

- Its ownership is international
- Its production is fragmented
- Its distribution is highly concentrated

Let's look at each of these statements individually.

International Ownership

To get an idea of the international nature of the recording business, consider that only one of the four largest recording companies—Universal Music Group, Sony Music Entertainment, Warner Music Group, and EMI—is even partly based in the United States. EMI is a British firm. Sony BMG Music Entertainment is a global joint venture equally owned by German Bertelsmann AG and the U.S. subsidiary of Sony of Japan. Universal is owned by Vivendi, a French conglomerate. Warner is owned by a Canadian group led by Canadian Edgar Bronfman. The country of origin of each of these firms, however, does not typically dictate the kind of music it tries to circulate in the United States.

"Think globally; act locally" is a phrase that is very apt for executives in the recording industry. Fifteen or twenty years ago, however, their perspective was quite different. Then the major firms concentrated on taking American and British hits and making them into worldwide mega-hits. Now, although many top American and, to a lesser extent, British artists still sell well globally, the real action and money seem to be in finding top local and regional talent.

Fragmented Production

This realization leads us to the second statement about the recording industry: that it is fragmented at the production end. In this context, fragmentation means that there are literally thousands of companies turning out recordings that they would like to sell. These recording firms are called independents because they are not owned by the major companies mentioned above, which are also the major distributors in the industry. Although the United States has always had many small firms producing recordings, the number of independents has soared in the past decade. In fact, independent record distributors as a group have become the third largest distributor

Figure 10.3 Music Distributors by Percentage of Total Albums Sold, 2007
Source: Nielsen SoundScan press release, January 3, 2008.

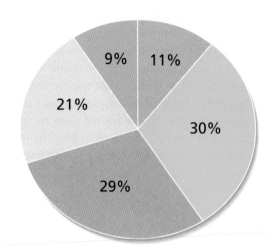

of recorded music in the United States, after Sony.

One reason for the rise of independent firms is that newly affordable powerful personal digital recording technology has enabled small companies to produce compact disks. The availability of this technology has led to a flood of independent recordings. Many small production firms circulate their products to stores or sell them directly on the Web or at concerts instead of hooking up with the major distributors. Some independents are actually quite large operations. An example is Rounder Records, which specializes in bluegrass and other "American roots" music.

http://www.universalmusic.com, website of Universal Music Group, the largest group of music labels in the recording business

Concentration of Distribution

Still, the four major recording companies are the distributors of choice because of the immense power they bring to the marketplace (see Figure 10.3). Because they represent many popular artists, they have access to stores and radio stations for the promotion of new acts that small distributors might not have. Being large organizations, they are able to spend a lot of money to push artists that their executives believe have promise. In fact, these distributors insist that their size and their strong international presence give them a stature and credibility that make them the distributors of choice. The Universal Music Group's website proudly stated in 2009 that "The company discovers, develops, markets and distributes recorded music through a network of subsidiaries, joint ventures and licensees in 77 countries, representing 98 percent of the music market. UMG also sells and distributes music video and DVD products, and licenses recordings, encouraging the legal distribution of music online and over cellular, cable and satellite networks."[2]

Unique Features of the Recording Industry

U.S. Sales and Audiences

In 2008, the industry sold about 1.9 billion recordings in various formats in the United States, representing sales of $8.5 billion.[3] That may sound like a lot of money, but it's a real come-down for an industry that just three years earlier was bringing in $12.2 billion. Most experts agree that piracy sucked away much of those revenues, but they add that a fair amount of the decline may relate to apathy about the music, the ability to listen to music free online through MySpace and other advertising-supported sites, and a turn toward buying video games rather than musical recordings. So who does buy all this music? From a gender standpoint, the split has long been around 50 percent male, 50 percent female. When it comes to age, the record industry targets its marketing to young people because traditionally they have bought more recordings than people in other age groups. According to the RIAA, people aged from 15 to 24 years accounted for 21 percent of the spending on recordings in the United States in

2008—more than their percentage in the population. People aged 45 years and older accounted for 33.7 percent of the spending—less than their presence in the population (see Table 10.1). It's interesting to note, though, that the percentage of older buyers has been creeping up, while the percentage of younger ones has been declining a bit. In 2000, people aged from 15 to 24 years bought 25.4 percent of recordings while the 45+ age group bought 23.8 percent. The older group's rise in 2008 reflects the large baby-boom generation's movement into this age group, and the decision by a substantial number of them to continue buying recordings.[4]

Singles vs. Albums

single a product that contains only one or two individual musical recordings

The recording industry releases its product in two lengths: singles and albums. An album is a collection of a dozen or more individual songs, whereas a **single** contains only one or two songs. Singles are the building blocks of radio formats, and the airplay of these singles is often how the public first learns about an artist. However, artists and labels make their money from album sales, and the recording companies often do not price physical singles so they are worthwhile purchases relative to the albums. As a result, in 2008 sales of physical singles were negligible compared with sales of albums; they comprised only 3.8 percent of sales.[5] By contrast, though, Web sales of singles through iTunes and other sites are often far less expensive than albums—$1.29, 89 cents, or even 69 cents compared with several dollars. In that space, buyers go after their favorite songs. According to Nielsen SoundScan, in 2008 U.S. consumers bought more than a billion digital single tracks, but only 65 million digital albums. Total album sales (including physical product) declined by 14 percent in 2008 over 2007.[6] Although the sale of singles is impressive, recording executives worry about the decline in album sales because their firms have a harder time maintaining profits when consumers buy single songs instead of albums.

Diverse Recording Media Formats

Whether the recording is a single or an album, commercially sold music can be placed on a number of media. Those that are best known today are:

Table 10.1 How Does Age Relate to Music Purchases?	
Age Group, Years	% of Music Purchases
10–14	7.3
15–19	10.9
20–24	10.1
25–29	8.3
30–34	8.9
35–39	9.8
40–44	11.0
45+	33.7

Source: Recording Industry Association of America, "2008 Consumer Profile." http://76.74.24.142/8EF388DA-8FD3-7A4E-C208-CDF1ADE8B179.pdf (accessed August 4, 2010).

■ Compact disks (CDs)
■ Cassettes
■ Videos
■ Vinyl records
■ Audio DVDs
■ Super audio CDs
■ Digital platforms

The first six media are physical; that is, a person can hold them in his or her hand. Among the physical media, about 91 percent of the units that recording companies ship are compact disks. CDs are, in fact, durable and have excellent sound quality.

Table 10.2 Top-Selling Recording Artists as of March 2010

Artist	Certified Units in Millions	Artist	Certified Units in Millions
Beatles, The	170	Madonna	64
Brooks, Garth	128	Springsteen, Bruce	64
Presley, Elvis	120	Carey, Mariah	63
Led Zeppelin	111.5	Metallica	59
Eagles	100	Van Halen	56.5
Joel, Billy	79.5	Houston, Whitney	55
Pink Floyd	74.5	U2	51.5
Streisand, Barbra	71.5	Rogers, Kenny	51
AC/DC	71	Dion, Celine	50
John, Elton	70	Diamond, Neil	48.5
Jackson, Michael	69.5	Fleetwood Mac	48.5
Strait, George	68.5	Kenny G	48
Aerosmith	66.5	Twain, Shania	48
Rolling Stones, The	66	Journey	47

Source: Recording Industry Association of America, "Top Selling Artists." http://www.RIAA.org (accessed March 1, 2010).

Table 10.3 Top Ten All-Time Bestselling Albums

Position	Album	Artist/Record Label, Year
1	Thriller	Michael Jackson/Epic, 1982
2	Eagles Their Greatest Hits	The Eagles/Elektra, 1976
3	Led Zeppelin IV	Led Zeppelin/Swan Song, 1971
4	The Wall	Pink Floyd/Columbia, 1979
5	Back in Black	AC/DC/Elektra, 1980
6	Double Live	Garth Brooks/Capitol Nashville, 1998
7	Greatest Hits Volume I & Volume II	Billy Joel/Columbia,1985
8	Come on Over	Shania Twain/Mercury Nashville, 1997
9	The Beatles	The Beatles/Apple, 1968
10	Rumours	Fleetwood Mac/Reprise, 1977

Source: Recording Industry Association of America, "Top 100 Albums." http://www.RIAA.org (accessed March 1, 2010).

Audio DVDs and super audio CDs are engineered to have even better sound, but they are new, expensive technologies that so far haven't caught on; they represent about 1 percent of shipments. Cassettes, which constitute less than 1 percent of recorded music shipments, have declined markedly because of the tremendous success of CDs in the 1990s and 2000s. As recently as 1995, cassettes made up a quarter of all shipments; in 1990, they constituted half of them. Portability and convenience made them popular despite their lower fidelity and fragile nature. The declining cost of portable CD equipment for pedestrian and car use has eroded cassette use, however.

The term **digital platforms** stands for the several ways that people can purchase music without holding a medium in their hands. All typically involve a form of **downloading**, which means that the company sends the song as a digital file to the buyer's computer or computer-like device (for example a mobile phone). In 2003, digital downloads represented just 1.3 percent of all music sales. In 2008, digital downloads comprised 13.5 percent of all sales. Some companies that sell digital music download the files in forms that can be played only on particular devices with the right hardware or software. Apple's iTunes site uses the AAC format that works only on iPods. That doesn't seem to bother many consumers, because iPods are so popular. Apple is by far the leading purveyor of music; it has sold billions of downloads (audio songs and music videos) from its site.

Although people's payment for owning songs is the most common way recording companies sell music via digital platforms, they do have two other major opportunities. One involves streaming and the other involves ringtones. **Ringtones** are bits of songs (or even new musical compositions) that people download to their mobile phones so that they play when someone calls them. **Streaming** takes place when a website sends an audio file to a computer-like device so that it can be heard while it is coming into the device and then disappears. Some sites such as Rhapsody sell subscriptions for streaming. You pay $75 a year and you can stream as many songs as you want, but you cannot keep them. (The sites do give you the opportunity to buy the song or an album, though.) Many sites also give users the opportunity to listen to

digital platform vehicle for receiving digital information; a computer, mobile phone, and iPad are three digital platforms for downloading music

download to transfer data or programs from a server or host computer to one's own computer or digital device

ringtones bits of songs (or even new musical compositions) that people download to their mobile phones so that they play when someone calls them

streaming an audio file delivered to a computer-like device from a website so that it can be heard while it is coming into the device but cannot be saved or stored

Table 10.4 Genres of Music Sold

Genre	Percentage
Rock	31.8
Country	11.9
Rap/hip-hop	10.7
R&B/urban	10.2
Pop	9.1
Religious	6.5
Children's	3.0
Classical	1.9
Jazz	1.1
Soundtracks	0.8
Oldies	0.7
New Age	0.6
Other	9.1

Source: Recording Industry Association of America, "2008 Consumer Profile." http://76.74.24.142/8EF388DA-8FD3-7A4E-C208-CDF1ADE8B179.pdf (accessed August 4, 2010).

pre-chosen music streams based around certain genres—for example jazz or classical—for free if they listen to commercials. Because it is much like a radio station, the activity has come to be known as **internet radio**.

Diverse Music Genres

The recording industry releases music in many genres, targeted to different slices of the music-buying public. According to the RIAA, in 2008 rock music remained the most popular genre of physical product; it accounted for one of every three recordings sold in the United States. As Table 10.4 shows, country held the second spot, with rap/hip-hop and R&B/urban music closely behind, followed by pop. You may (or may not) be surprised that classical music made up only 1.9 percent of the recordings, while "religious" music (which includes gospel, inspirational, and spiritual recordings) made up a higher 6.5 percent.

So we know what kindsof musical recordings have moved more quickly than others. But how do those products get to their audiences in the first place? What happens between the time someone gets an idea for a song and the moment the recording of that song is sold? To answer this basic, but difficult, question, we turn to issues of production, distribution, and exhibition.

Production and the Recording Industry

Chances are, you know someone who is in a band. Maybe the band plays at local college bars, and the members practice when they are not working at day jobs to pay the bills. Perhaps the band's members have even recorded a demonstration (or "demo") song at a local studio and given you a copy. They are working hard while they wait for their big break: a contract with a record label, which they know will bring them fortune and fame in Hollywood. Will they still take your phone calls when they become big stars?

Across the country, many aspiring recording artists are waiting for their big break. Most of these artists never record a professional album and eventually move on to other, more lucrative lines of work. The age-old advice to struggling artists—Don't quit your day job—is especially true in the record business.

Artists Looking for Labels; Labels Looking for Artists

Many struggling bands dream about recording for a label of one of the major record production and distribution companies. A label is a division of a recording firm that releases a certain type of music and reflects a certain personality. It is very much like an imprint in the book industry. For example, among Universal's many labels are Island Def Jam (for rap and hip-hop), Verve (for jazz and blues), MCA Nashville (for country), and Mercury Records (for classical). Realistically, artists know that they are much more likely to start their recording careers with small independent firms that are willing to take a chance on them. They hope to sign with one of the majors once they have proven themselves.

The point person in a recording company for signing new artists is the label's **A&R** person. A&R stands for **artist and repertoire**, a term that dates back to the time when record executives saw themselves as shaping artists by choosing the collection of songs (the repertoire) that an artist played or sang. Today, the function of the A&R person is to screen new acts for a firm and determine whether or not to sign

internet radio pre-chosen music streams based around certain genres—for example jazz or classical—provided free of charge to listeners and paid for by commercial advertisements, much like a radio station

A&R or artist and repertoire describes the function of screening new musical acts for a recording company and determining whether or not to sign these acts; the record executives consider it their duty to shape artists by choosing the collection of songs (their repertoire) to be played or sung by the artist

CULTURE TODAY
LATIN MUSIC

Until the early part of 2007, Latin music had been the most consistent genre in the U.S. record industry. Sales of Latin music records—those with at least 51 percent Spanish-language content—had increased since 2001, even posting all-time high marks in 2006, a monumentally difficult year for the rest of the record industry. In early 2007, however, sales of Latin music albums began a slide. *Rolling Stone* reported that Latin music sales declined 34.3 percent in 2009 after a significant decline in 2008.

This trend has been described as a delayed response to changes in digital music technology. Because Latin markets lag mainstream trends by a few months or years, music downloads, both legal and illegal, could be eating away at recent album sales. There are other theories for the seemingly sudden dip in Latin music sales. Some blame high gas prices. Some argue that the sharp decline was the result of circumstances specific to the Hispanic population, namely increased pressure on local authorities to deal with illegal immigration. Latin industry insiders have noted that immigrants are reluctant to shop at *bodegas* selling Latin music or attend concerts by Mexican artists for fear of being deported. Others see the problem as a consequence of the fact that most Latin albums are purchased not from independent retailers but from mass merchants such as Wal-Mart. As large stores generally carry only established artists, the diminished relevance of indie record stores can have a direct affect on the development of up-an-coming musicians.

Although several new types of Latin music have created stable niches in the Latin market—reggaetón and bachata, for example—none has been able to curb the decline seen in Latin record sales of late. After recognizing the falling record sales, the Latin music industry tried a number of techniques to increase sales. First, it has leveraged the capabilities of the internet by using music and video sites such as Batanga.com and Billboard en Español to promote Latin music and attract advertisers through the provision of a targeted audience. Second, it hopes that, as Hispanics in the United States increasingly have access to high-speed internet connections, online sales will increase. Distributors are using online resources such as iTunes and Pandora to help reach these target audiences. Finally, the industry has leveraged its stars to promote the genre of Latin music more generally. Whether it is the promotion of Shakira and Gloria Estefan or Microsoft's Zune promotion of Latin recording stars as a way to encourage music consumption and social networking among U.S. Hispanic consumers, the genres is attempting to make its music accessible.

Sources: Leila Cobo, "Sales Slow for Latin Music; Distributors Say Sales Have Been Dropping for Three Years," Billboard, July 8, 2007; Daniel Kreps, "2009 Wrap-Up: Music Purchases Up, Album Sales Down," *Rolling Stone*, January 7, 2010. http://www.rollingstone.com/rockdaily/index.php/2010/01/07/2009-wrap-up-music-purchases-up-album-sales-down/ (accessed March 16, 2010); "Latin Music Industry Retunes: A Special Report on the Latin Music Industry," *Hispanic Marketing Weekly*, November 10, 2008. http://www.hispanicmarketweekly.com/article.cms?id=10288 (accessed March 16, 2010).

those acts. Like baseball scouts looking for the next Cy Young Award winner, A&R people are constantly searching for new acts for their label (see Figure 10.4).

Suppose your friends, after years of paying their dues in nightclubs throughout the state, are approached by the A&R person for Universal's Interscope record label. (It distributes work by Lady Gaga, 50 Cent, and Eminem, among many others.) Somehow, the record company executive learned about the band—perhaps through hearing a demo record or attending a performance at a local bar—and wants to sign it to a record deal. At this point, certain relationships come into play. Negotiating the terms and conditions of these relationships is very important. Many struggling artists, unfamiliar with the business side of the artistic process and desperate to make it in the record industry, have entered into bad, one-sided agreements. Billy Joel, *NSYNC, Janet Jackson, and Tupac Shakur are only a few of the well-known musical acts who have fallen into this trap.

Many artists on their way up realize the necessity of hiring a competent manager to coordinate the development of the artist's career; help to arrange business opportunities for the artist; and handle the receipt, disbursement, and accounting of the

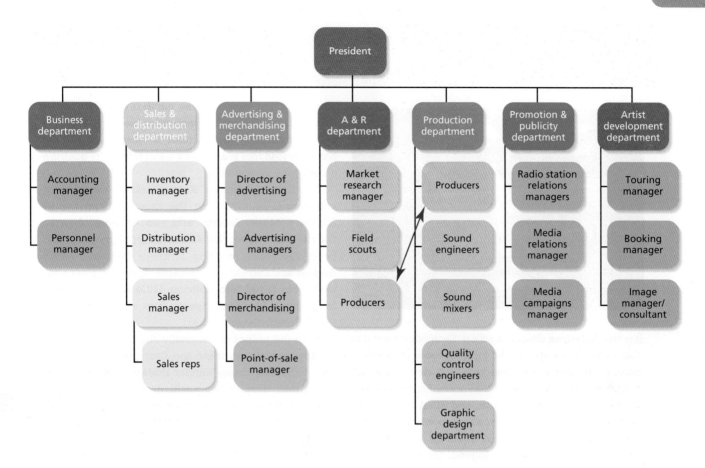

Figure 10.4 Organization of a Typical Recording Company

artist's revenues. In return for these services, the manager earns a percentage—typically 10–25 percent—of all the revenue the artist earns. Of course, artists try to hire a manager who will further their career, preferably one who knows the intricacies of the music business and most of the important people in the business. Despite artists' understandable wish for a manager who will act exclusively on their behalf, good managers often handle several artists at once.

Other business relationships for the band quickly follow. Most acts hire an attorney and an accountant to assist their manager in handling their often complex business affairs. Artists may also join a union such as the American Federation of Musicians (AFM) or the American Federation of Television and Radio Artists (AFTRA), which provides access to television and motion picture work, represents the artists' interests with various media industries, and offers benefits such as group health insurance. Joining a royalty-collecting association, such as ASCAP or BMI, is also important. But of all these contractual relationships, the most important one is the one the artist develops with a record label. Simply put, the music industry today revolves around the issuance of recorded music and the joint effort of the artist and the company to sell as many records as possible.

Finding Music to Record

Artists, of course, need music to perform. Many popular artists today perform music that they have written themselves. Yet at some point in their careers, virtually all artists record music that someone else wrote. There are several ways for an artist or group to find music. Music publishing companies maintain catalogs of songs, and many record stores sell printed copies of music, usually intended to be played on a guitar or piano. When an artist uses any song in these libraries commercially,

CRITICAL CONSUMER
AMERICAN IDOL AND THE TALENT HUNT

It is the American dream in action. Each contestant has a story as they step into the judging room to perform before the four individuals who will determine the course of their life. In 2010 they were Randy Jackson, Simon Cowell, Kara DioGuardi, and Ellen DeGeneres. The four *American Idol* judges are responsible for wading through the thousands of would-be superstars to find America's next singing legend. Once the judges have decided on their finalists, it's up to Americans to call in and vote for their favorite singers. The winner receives a record deal and a chance at stardom.

The amateur format itself is not new. Frank Sinatra got his start after singing on the *Major Bowes Amateur Hour*. Jimi Hendrix won an amateur talent contest at the famous Apollo Theater in New York City. Performers such as Justin Timberlake, Britney Spears, and Beyonce Knowles with Destiny's Child were all contestants and winners on *Star Search*—an amateur talent television show in the 1980s and 1990s. *American Idol*'s recent iteration of the star search format has been wildly

successful. The show was the number one show in the United States for five consecutive seasons and has spawned spin-offs in a number of other countries. But has *American Idol* really been successful in its goal: the search for a superstar?

The first *Idol* winner, Kelly Clarkson, did achieve commercial success after the show, winning twelve Billboard Music Awards and two Grammy Awards. Carrie Underwood, the Season Four winner, has also been successful, winning fourteen Billboard Music Awards and five Grammy Awards. However, other winners have faded into oblivion. Little has been heard from Ruben Studdard (Season Two winner) or David Cook (Season Seven winner).

Even the judges occasionally suggest that the public does not always make the best choice when they vote. In Season Three, Jennifer Hudson finished in seventh place, despite her position as a judge favorite. Although Fantasia Barrino went on to win that season, Hudson achieved more commercial success post-*Idol*, winning a Grammy and an Academy Award. In Season Five, Chris Daughtry finished in fourth place, losing to Taylor Hicks. The cast-off, however, formed a band simply called Daughtry, which has won six American Music Awards and four Billboard Music Awards.

There are many routes to being "discovered" in the music industry. Lady Gaga sang in nightclubs in New York City. Sheryl Crow worked as a music teacher and back-up singer until she found a producer and released her first album in the early 1990s. With all the various avenues to stardom, what role do amateur talent shows like *American Idol* play in the music industry? Do you think that *American Idol* has been successful in its goal of finding the next American superstar?

---

royalty the share of money paid to a songwriter or music composer out of the money that the production firm receives from the sale or exhibition of a work

songwriters and their publishing companies expect to be paid a share of the money the production firm receives; this payment is called a **royalty**.

Royalties

There are important legal steps that songwriters must take, such as filing their songs with the U.S. copyright authorities, in order to ensure that they make money from a song they have written even if they do not sing it themselves. But it is difficult for the owner of a song to keep track of where and how the song is performed. For example, songwriters are entitled to compensation whenever a radio station plays their songs, a band performs their work at a nightclub, or a record company releases their songs.

Agencies like ASCAP, BMI, and Harry Fox exist to make sure that publishers and songwriters are compensated for the use of their work. These agencies take over the daunting task of verifying compliance with the law on behalf of the rights holder. As we noted earlier, ASCAP is the largest of the performing-rights organizations and represents more than 370,000 songwriters, composers, and publishers. Though the airing of one covered song on a radio station may result in a royalty payment to ASCAP or its agents of only a fraction of a penny, these small amounts add up. According to its annual report, in 2008 ASCAP received more than $945.7 million on behalf of its member songwriters and publishers. After operating expenses, the organization distributed 87.5 percent of that money.[7] ASCAP uses formulas derived from surveys that rank the popularity of each songwriter's songs during the year to determine each member's share of the revenue after expenses and distributes that share to each member.

http://www.ascap.com, website of the American Society of Composers, Authors, and Publishers, which licenses performance rights and distributes royalties for hundreds of thousands of music creators worldwide.

Compensating Artists

Artists are compensated for their performance on recorded music in one of two ways. Artists who help to make an album, but are not central to it, are paid an hourly fee. In accordance with the rules of their union, these studio musicians or singers are paid at least the industry scale. The central artists on the recording, in contrast, typically are not paid by the hour. They receive royalties for their work. Many artists believe that they can hit the jackpot if their recordings sell well and so prefer royalties over flat fees. A typical recording industry contract will give an artist or group 10–15 percent of the retail price of an album. At the same time, many studio musicians and singers are quite comfortable with their more predictable payments. Artists who are in great demand as backup talent for albums receive far more than scale and can make a very good living.

Producing a Record

The firm that has signed a contract to record an artist's album will often line up a producer to oversee the recording of the album and its final sound. The producer, like the artist, is generally compensated on a royalty basis. A typical royalty percentage for a good producer is 2–4 percent of the total retail sales of the album.

The producer is responsible for obtaining copyright clearances, lining up session musicians if needed, staying on budget, and delivering a high-quality master tape to the record company. An important first task for a producer is to line up a good place to record. Studios with good equipment and good engineers can be found all over the world, and producers carefully select a studio where the artist will be comfortable and productive. It may come as no surprise to you that many major albums are produced in quiet, out-of-the-way places where the artists are unlikely to be disturbed.

A producer also works to keep the project on budget. Each extra day in the studio can cost thousands of dollars. Record companies can financially penalize the recording artist for cost overruns by taking the money out of the artist's royalties. After the recording sessions have been completed, the producer and artist finish mixing the

Guitarist Robert Fripp, (unknown), David Bowie, and Brian Eno at Hansa Studio by the Wall, recording the album "Heroes."

songs on the album. They pay special attention to making the songs fit the specific technical requirements of the label, such as the length of each song, and also to identifying any potential singles on the album.

First-time artists, however, often find themselves in a very weak position with their prospective label. They quickly learn that signing a recording contract does not mean becoming an instant millionaire. Most labels pay for manufacturing, distribution, and promotion, but they deduct recording costs from the artists' royalties. In major recording studios these costs typically run to as much as $50,000 for putting down the sound "tracks," mixing them, and preparing a master for reproduction. Moreover, for every $10 sale, the record label may pocket $5 on an initial contract. Therefore, an artist who spends $50,000 in the studio must sell 10,000 recordings at $10 a unit—just to break even!

Independent labels generally have even more restrictive artistic contracts than the majors do. Contracts with independent labels are for a longer period than those with the majors, provide lower royalty rates than those of the majors, require the artists to share the copyright on songs with the labels, and may even demand a share of the artists' merchandising monies. Independent-label executives claim that such contract stipulations are necessary, because the label incurs large financial risks when it subsidizes a new artist. Recording companies can spend hundreds of thousands of dollars breaking a new artist in, and many new artists, despite the best efforts of both sides, never contribute to the overall profitability of the record company. In addition, the executives argue, independent firms have to pay a percentage of their income to the firms that distribute their product.

The hope of making it truly big is always there for the artists, however. If they become superstars, their power relationship with the record label equalizes. For artists with proven market demand, their agents and lawyers can negotiate generous deals. At the height of his popularity, Michael Jackson reportedly received a royalty rate of 20 percent from a unit of Sony.

Self-Producing CDs for Sale

For the many struggling singers and musicians who don't have contracts with any recording firm, there is another route. Because of the difficulty of getting noticed even by independent companies, artists may decide to produce their own CDs for sale and sell them at performances, and maybe even in some stores. The good news is that affordable, professional-quality equipment has recently become available in recording studios. In many cases, studio rates have been halved in the past few years. Some artists don't even bother with studios. It is possible to make a perfectly acceptable recording in someone's basement, and people often do. Moreover, because of intense competition in the CD manufacturing business, the cost of making CDs has plummeted too.

Distribution in the Recording Industry

And who says you need a CD at the start? Many musicians load their work onto sites such as MySpace and YouTube with the hope they'll get noticed. MySpace is, of course, a distribution venue, but you don't have to pay anything to get on it. You can sell your music from it, and, although the site may take a cut of the sale, the amount is far less than a label takes. If a group called The Morning Light can produce its music in a basement and release its songs on MySpace just a click away from Justin Timberlake, why would any group choose to sign with a recording firm, whether an independent or a major?

It's a good question, particularly if you pay attention to stories such as Ingrid Michaelson's. Her experience makes the MySpace model of distribution seem extremely attractive. An aspiring singer/songwriter/pianist and part-time teacher of theater to kids, Michaelson was 24 when in 2005 she set up a page on MySpace with the aim of networking with musicians and potential fans. Within a year, her soft vocals and romantic piano attracted a management company that specializes in finding little-known acts for TV shows, advertisers, movie companies, and video games. The firm placed three of her songs on ABC's popular *Grey's Anatomy*, and the exposure sent one of her songs, "The Way I Am," to number 13 on the iTunes pop music chart. She had to pay 15–20 percent of her music royalties to the management company. But not having a label allowed her to keep most of what was left. As the *Wall Street Journal* pointed out, "Because Ms Michaelson doesn't have a record-label contract, she stands to make substantially more from online sales of her music. For each 99-cent sale on iTunes, Ms Michaelson grosses 63 cents, compared with perhaps 10 or 15 cents that typical major-label artists receive via their label."[8] By mid-2007, she had sold about 60,000 copies of her songs on iTunes and other digital stores. She used some of that money to press (and sell) her own CDs, arrange distribution for them, make T-shirts for concerts, and hire a marketing company to produce promotional podcasts.

What, then, does a label bring to an artist's career? The short answer is sustained cross-media exposure. Getting the ears of powerful concert promoters, radio program executives, and cable gatekeepers who select music for large, though targeted, audiences is a task that requires a strong organization with much experience. Don't ignore that even Michaelson didn't get her TV exposure on her own; a management company led the way. Record labels have the ability to push her further. Because she had no record label or distributor, her two CDs, "Slow the Rain" and "Girls and Boys," which she put out herself in 2004 and 2006, weren't carried by many traditional music stores, even in 2007.

The manager for several bands, including Death Cab for Cutie, adds that an unsigned artist risks losing momentum. "There's a lot more components to an artist's career than being featured prominently on a show, just as there's more to it than having one hit on the radio," he stated. Michaelson agreed. She told the *Wall Street Journal* in 2007 that she hopes to sign with a label eventually. But knowing the pitfalls

CULTURE TODAY
A TRANSFORMATION IN MUSIC DISTRIBUTION

In May 2009, fans of the punk rock band Green Day were anxiously awaiting the release of the band's newest album, *21st Century Breakdown*. However, on the day of the release, there were no lines outside record stores or barricades holding back excited fans. Days before the official release of the album in music stores, Green Day and its label, Reprise, allowed fans to stream the new songs from the band's website—for free.

The trend of providing free access to music is representative of a large shift in the distribution of recorded music. Another part of the shift is the movement of artists away from traditional labels. More and more often, recording artists are deciding not to sign with the major record labels—Sony Music, Warner Music, EMI, Universal Music, and their subsidiaries. Some artists are joining smaller labels, and a growing number—including Trent Reznor and the Barenaked Ladies—are charting their own paths through the creation of artist-run labels.

Artist-run labels allow the musicians to keep a larger share of the revenue they generate from CD sales, merchandise, and concerts. Backlash against the control that major labels have exercised over their artists and the direction of the music industry is not new. In 2004, Danger Mouse released the *Grey Album*, a mash-up, or remix, of songs from the Beatles' *White Album* and rapper Jay-Z's *Black Album*. EMI, the copyright holder of the Beatles songs, tried to prevent the album's distribution. To protest the control of the recording label over the distribution of music, Danger Mouse allowed the *Grey Album* to be downloaded free from his website for one day. This day of electronic civil disobedience came to be known among fans as "Grey Tuesday."

The recording industry has responded to this backlash by loosening its control over recording artists and their music. Some of the big labels are beginning to provide more flexible options for artists who are not interested in signing restrictive contracts but do want the publicity advantage afforded by a larger recording company. It is noteworthy, for example, that Green Day's label, Reprise, is owned by Warner Music.

Sources: Brad Stone, "Artists Find Backers As Labels Wane," *The New York Times*, July 21, 2009; John Shiga, "Copy-and-Persist: The Logic of Mash-Up Culture," *Critical Studies in Media Communication* 24, 2 (June 2007), pp. 93–114.

---

of the business, she is playing it smart. First, she says, she wants to build up her reputation and fan base. "I want to make my presence known before that happens, so I can have some clout," she said.[9]

All these comments emphasize the point that distribution holds the key to potential success in the recording industry. In recent years, in fact, the major labels have been exercising their clout even on MySpace. As recently as 2007, MySpace did not distinguish between the unknown and the well known in its publicity. It boasted that it had more than 8 million bands using the site. A press release stated that "MySpace music has allowed bands to share music and videos, announce tour dates and communicate with fans and others in the MySpace community, seamlessly integrating the Web into shared online and offline experiences."[10] In fact, some artists who started on MySpace went on to get contracts with recording companies and substantial radio airplay. Examples are Colby Caillat ("Bubbly") and Sara Bareilles ("Love Song").

You can still find plenty of unknown and hardly known acts on MySpace Music, but the stress isn't on them anymore. Go there now and you'll find that the main page has been taken over by high-profile artists typically represented by labels owned by the major recording companies. MySpace executives wanted to lure as many music fans as possible, and they decided they would do it with the help of known quantities. During a day in October 2009, for example, MySpace Music's landing page highlighted experienced performers with rosters of concert dates: Julian Casablacas (on Universal Records' RCA label), Gift of Gab (on the independent Quannum Projects label), Taylor Swift (Big Machine Records—an independent distributed by the Universal Music Group), and Tegan and Sara (Vapor/Sire/Superclose indie label). The "Popular Searches" tab on the landing page directed visitors to the MySpace pages of particularly hot artists with major-label connections—for example, Lil Wayne

(Universal Records), Eminem (Universal's Interscope Records), and Miley Cyrus (Walt Disney Records, distributed by Universal in the United States and EMI in the United Kingdom). Despite the potential for being seen on MySpace Music, the prime territory belongs to well-known artists, and especially those with connections to major labels.

As in other mass media industries, having good distribution avenues does not ensure that a recording will be a hit. Without the strong ability to place recordings in stores and other exhibition areas, however, the chances that a recording will be a hit diminish considerably. And having a hit with a major label builds on itself so that the label can make a deal for the kind of visibility on MySpace and other music sites that a band without a marketing power behind it would not have.

Distribution does not simply mean being able to send recordings to a store. Although major firms such as Universal send recordings to their biggest retail clients directly, many of their albums, singles, and videos end up in stores through huge wholesalers. The wholesalers work with all the majors as well as with independent distribution firms that handle some of the recordings produced by independent companies. The real distribution power of the Big Four and the other major producer-distributors lies in their ability to generate a buzz among an artist's potential fans that will induce retailers to carry his or her records and display them properly.

The task is an imposing one. The statistics must be frightening to anyone who is hoping to hit it big without the Big Four, who together control 75 percent of global music sales. Powerful distributors have the benefit of big promotional teams, liaisons with radio stations, and money for cooperative advertising. Let's take a look at these areas.

The Importance of Promotion

More than anything else, distributors contribute marketing expertise to building a recording artist's career. **Promotion** involves scheduling publicity for a recording artist, such as an appearance on the cover of *Spin* magazine and performing charity work that will make news. This includes liaisons with radio stations or setting up cooperative activities with radio stations in different cities that reach the people who are likely to buy an artist's albums. The deal may entail generating excitement on the air about a concert tour by the artist that will come through the station's area. In return for the on-air promotion of a group and its rock concert, for example, a radio station might receive free tickets to give away and exclusive radio interview rights when the artist hits town. Promotion may also include cooperative advertising, which means that the recording firm provides a retailer with a portion of the money the retailer needs in order to buy space in local newspapers or time on local radio and TV stations. All this may sound easy, but in the competitive media environment it is extremely difficult. Recording firms have particular difficulty motivating people to buy the albums of new groups because people need to hear music before they buy it. Attractive cover art is nice, but it is hard to visually "window shop" for a new album. You really have to hear the music.

promotion the process of scheduling publicity appearances for a recording artist, with the goal of generating excitement about the artist, and thereby sales of his or her album

The recording industry is therefore dependent on other media to inform its audiences about new products. Some retailers are trying to alleviate this problem by encouraging customers to sample new music before they buy it. A few stores allow you to try out any album, but most highlight a limited number of albums, chosen because recording firms have paid to promote them. Moreover, despite the incorporation of listening posts into music stores, research has shown over the decades that customers credit radio airplay for getting them interested in buying particular music.

THE RECORDING INDUSTRY AND THE RADIO INDUSTRY   Historically, as we have seen, music distributors have directed a lot of marketing attention to the radio industry. That is still the case. Recording-industry promotion executives focus particularly on radio program directors, because they are the ones who choose the particular pieces from albums (the cuts) that get airplay on the station. The relationship between the two groups is quite symbiotic; that is, each lives off the other. Both are in the business of targeting a large but fairly narrow audience with a particular genre of music. A hit recording keeps listeners tuned in to a radio station and helps the station in its battle to win ratings; and airplay on the radio station converts listeners to buyers, fulfilling the goals of the record company and its artists.

Still, the needs of recording-company promoters sometimes conflict with those of the programmers. Many radio stations are conservative about adding new music. Program directors give preference to existing artists because those artists have a track record of success and because listeners are familiar with their sound. New artists are very much an uncertainty, and gambling on new material from unknowns might hurt the station's ratings. Music promoters also face the problem of competition. In any given week, a station may add only one new song to its playlist, whereas the various record labels may have a dozen new songs that they believe fit the station's format.

Radio station programmers, faced with the daunting task of deciding which of the many new songs that come out each week to add to their playlists, supplement their own impressions of the quality of music with outside data. Several firms, such as Broadcast Data Services, now electronically monitor radio stations across the country, verify the identity of every song played on those stations, and report these data to subscribers. A second system, known as SoundScan, automatically records the sales of music at participating retail stores. Each week the SoundScan findings are used to compile lists of record sales across the country. Based on such data, various trade publications compile weekly lists of the top-selling or most-played songs.

Radio programming executives often look at these lists to help them make decisions about airplay. Station program directors also monitor their own station's request line to see whether typical listeners want to hear more of a new song. Some conduct phone surveys of listeners in which they play bits of songs and ask whether they would want to hear them on the station.

MUSIC PROMOTION TECHNIQUES Knowing that radio stations use various pieces of data to make decisions on airplay, record executives have to work hard to get the airplay in certain markets and on particular stations that will convince program directors on the largest stations to insert a song into a playlist rotation. There are many ethical ways of doing that. The enormous pressure to succeed in radio has also led to unethical tactics. There are reports, for example, that record company representatives have organized campaigns to flood stations with requests for a particular song. An even more unsavory activity aimed at placing songs on radio stations is **payola**—the payment of money by a promotion executive to a station program director to ensure that the program director includes certain music on the playlist. In the late 1950s, the federal government made payola illegal. In view of the millions of dollars at stake in the recording industry, though, you shouldn't be surprised that prosecutions for this kind of improper influence continue. Stories consistently circulate that newer versions of payola, in the form of drugs or other noncash favors, are given to radio executives or consultants in return for adding new songs to their stations' playlists.

payola an activity in which promotion personnel pay money to radio personnel to ensure that they will devote airtime to artists that their recording companies represent

Video, Internet, and Movie Promotions

Despite the importance of radio, music distributors do try to excite potential buyers about their music in other ways. TV is a critical medium for promoting many genres.

During the past two decades, music videos have played an important role in driving rock, pop, and rap sales. Recording companies often help artists produce these videos because of the proven ability of a sizzling video to lead consumers to stores. The MTV network has been the major focus of television's rise as a video outlet. Other sources of video exhibition include Country Music Television, the Nashville Network, VH1, and Black Entertainment Television (BET). BET plays a crucial role in presenting music to African-American viewers.

As Ingrid Michaelson's experience shows, television series have also become important venues for new music, particularly by new performers. For TV producers who want to reach young adults, introducing indie artists is less expensive than paying huge amounts for stars, and it may signal to the audience that the program is in tune with the newest sounds. Advertising agencies are beginning to imitate TV series' use of new songs in this way for commercials. Although these sorts of programs and commercials may not be a place for major labels to introduce big releases from hit acts, the venues may be good for relative newbies. Moreover, the indie acts that make it to the TV series are getting the kind of promotion that may well make the major labels take a look at them and decide that the publicity makes them ready to move to higher levels of popularity.

As we have seen, the Web is similarly a place where hugely popular artists and unknown ones are out there waiting for fans. Most record labels have websites where you can read about your favorite artists, download photos, hear snippets of new songs, and sometimes even listen to these songs in their entirety. More controversially, record executives have been known to pay teens to spread buzz in chat rooms and through emails about an artist the company is trying to promote.

Increasingly, companies allow consumers on a variety of sites to download several songs from a new album in the hope that they will ultimately buy the CD anyway. Going further, recording firms have collaborated with those Web powers to highlight and sell album releases from artists such as Gnarls Barkley, Panic! At the Disco, Lily Allen, Fall Out Boy, Timbaland, Modest Mouse, and The Used. The publicity seems to pay off. In 2007, exclusive album releases on MySpace by T-Pain, The Used, Timbaland, Modest Mouse, and The Shins coincided with those albums showing up that week in the number one or two positions on *Billboard* magazine's popularity chart.

Concert Tours

Presenting live concerts across the country is a time-honored way to promote an album. In fact, in a digital world where songs are often given away free as promotions, the way artists (and, increasingly, their labels) make money is through concert tours; the songs act as vehicles to publicize the tours. Performing is second nature for most groups; after all, many groups start out by playing local gigs in their hometown. A good manager tries to book a new group as the opening act in a tour by an established superstar, thus quickly introducing the new group to the established superstar's large audience. One often overlooked fact is that, although tours have the potential to generate lots of money, the expenses are often quite high. Experienced help has to be hired, and trucks and buses must be rented. Schedules have to be reasonable so as not to wear out the artist. Millions of dollars can be lost if a major artist comes down with pneumonia and has to cancel performances. One technique for reducing the financial uncertainty of a major tour is to find a national sponsor, such as a beverage company.

At each stop along the tour, the artist seeks to build support for his or her records. The artist may visit local radio stations in an attempt to influence their decisions on airplay and help generate a large crowd at the arena. T-shirts, sweatshirts, and other memorabilia are given away free by promoters and sold at the concerts; so are albums. The total take from concert paraphernalia can be surprisingly high. Recording artists often make a substantial percentage of their income from such sales.

A local promoter may help make some of the arrangements and also share in the risks and potential rewards of putting on a concert. Involving a local promoter ensures that the arena chosen is the right size and configuration for the nature of the act. The promoter carefully prices concert tickets so that the venue will be 60 percent full at the very least. After all, it costs virtually the same amount to perform for a small audience as to perform for a large audience, but empty seats generate no revenue.

Exhibition in the Recording Industry

After all the work of making the record and all the work of distributing it is completed, recordings are laid out for members of the public to choose. Recordings make it into the hands of the public through six major paths. They are:

- Digital downloads
- Internet stores
- Traditional record stores
- Other retail stores
- Record clubs
- Direct sales

Digital Downloads

It's useful to start with this exhibition mode because we've already described it during the discussion of various vehicles for recorded music. According to the RIAA, in 2008, of music purchased over the six paths, digital downloads represented 32 percent percent of sales.[11] The tag *digital download* actually can mean a variety of activities—downloading a single or album from the Web, doing that from a mall- or store-based computer setup called a **kiosk**, downloading a music video, downloading ringtones or other sounds to a mobile phone, or paying a subscription for streaming music via a site such as Rhapsody. These activities have grown quickly. Just a year earlier, in 2007, digital downloads represented 23 percent of total sales.

kiosk a freestanding device that houses a computer terminal for the purpose of specific activities, such as downloading music

Traditional Record Stores

For decades, the record store on the street or in the mall was probably the best-known place to buy music. There were hundreds of music stores across the country. Prominent chains were Sam Goody and Tower Records. But both chains went out of business, and the stores that still exist are struggling. Change came rapidly, for as recently as 1998 record stores accounted for 50.8 percent of the sales of recordings in the United States. By 2008, the percentage of sales linked to record stores had slid to 30 percent, and the trajectory over the years was pretty consistently southward. It seems that the decline can be blamed on two types of stores, other physical retail stores and internet stores.

Other Retail Stores

The phrase "other retail stores" refers to any legitimate emporium that sells records along with other items. Department stores do that, as do electronics, clothing, and truck stops. In 2008, this category represented 28.4 percent of all recorded music sales. Chains such as Best Buy, Barnes & Noble, Newbury Comics, and Gray Whale sell lots of CDs, with a fairly wide range of titles. At other retailers the range of recordings sold is very thin, customized to the store's image. You may have noticed, for example, that the Starbucks coffee chain sells CDs that reflect a cool, sophisticated take on life. But the biggest business of CD selling is taking place at very large retailers such as Wal-Mart, Target, and K-Mart. Wal-Mart, in fact, has become the largest single purveyor of musical records in the United States.

Many retail shops do not actually run their own record department. Instead, they farm out the section to an intermediary known in the business as a **rack jobber**. A rack jobber is actually a separate company that maintains a small retail space for recorded music within a store, following rules set by the retailer. Partnering with a rack jobber means that the merchant doesn't have to worry about keeping up with what is hot in the music industry, constantly ordering new products, and periodically adjusting the store's record displays. Typically, the revenue generated from sales of these products is split between the rack jobber and the owner of the retail store.

The biggest retailers often sell CDs through exclusive deals with record distributors that give the seller a reason to hype the albums and the artists. For example, in 2008 Sony Music arranged to release AC/DC's album *Black Ice* through Wal-Mart only for a certain number of weeks. The album sold more than 2 million copies, making it the fifth-ranked album of the year.

> **rack jobber** a company contracted by a department store to maintain its rack of records, tapes, CDs, and/or DVDs

Internet Stores

Internet stores are online sites that sell CDs and mail them to the buyer—think of http://www.amazon.com (the clear leader), http://www.lala.com, http://www.ebay.com, and many more. With their efficiency, low costs, and wide selection, these virtual places seem to be taking away business from physical retailers. Whereas in 2003 they constituted 5 percent of record sales, according to the RIAA, in 2008 the number had nearly tripled to 14.6 percent. By comparison, "other retail stores" made up 50.7 percent of the pie in 2003 and only 30 percent in 2006. It seems that the long-term direction is in favor of these sorts of merchants and the ones that sell digital downloads.

Record Clubs

Another major way to distribute recordings is through clubs such as Columbia House. RIAA data indicate that these clubs have gone up and down in recent years, from 4.1 percent in 2003 to 12.6 percent in 2006 and then down to 7.2 percent in 2008. It's hard to know if the economic recession was a factor in the most recent downturn. Record clubs do encourage long-term consistent purchases. Individuals are enticed into joining these clubs by newspaper or magazine ads offering low-cost introductory specials, such as seven CDs for 1 cent. Members also sometimes agree to buy a certain number of albums later at the regular price. Often artists receive a lower royalty on sales of recordings through these clubs.

Direct Sales

Direct sales account for just 1.8 percent of all revenues. Products sold through the "direct" channel frequently are compilations of old songs on such themes as Christmas hymns or the greatest disco hits. The popular *Now That's What I Call* series are sold via direct sales—directly to individuals through television ads. These ads may feature short selections of a song or its accompanying music video. The ads repeatedly urge you to call a toll-free number and use your credit card to place an order now.

Two Major Public Controversies

With all the changes riling the recording industry, you would think that the last thing record executives need is a public controversy that strikes directly at the core of their activities. It turns out that they have not one such controversy to worry about; they have two. One has to do with the lyrics in certain genres of popular music. The other has to do with the ways people are allowed to have access to songs on the internet. Both raise serious social questions that have no easy answers.

Concerns Over Lyrics

A large number of music consumers are also parents. In this role, many have been less concerned about the ethics of music downloads than about the lyrics of the songs their kids get off the Web and buy from the stores. This is not a new concern. For decades, recording companies, artists, and stores have been pelted with complaints from parents and teachers around the country that their children are purchasing music with lyrics unsuitable for the children's—and maybe some parents'—ears.

Many of their concerns came to a head during the 1980s when Tipper Gore, the wife of U.S. senator Al Gore, joined with other wives of influential Washington politicians and businessmen to form the Parents Music Resource Center (PMRC). The PMRC had a number of goals. It aimed to lobby the music industry to print lyrics on album covers. It wanted explicit album covers kept under the counter. It demanded a records ratings system similar to that used for films, and also a ratings system for concerts. The group also suggested that companies reassess the contracts of those performers who engage in violence and explicit sexual behavior on stage; and it proposed a media watch by citizens and record companies that would pressure broadcasters not to air songs that the group considered problematic.

The anger succeeded in leading major recording companies to put parental advisory labels on albums that warned parents about objectionable lyrics. The nation's leading retailer, Wal-Mart, has in fact refused to stock albums with controversial lyrics. As a result, some recording firms resorted to distributing two versions of an album: one with safer, censored lyrics and the original one that the musician intended to distribute.

The rise of gangsta rap in the late 1980s raised more concerns about violent or sexually explicit lyrics in censored and uncensored albums. Others objected to the depiction of women in many rap songs as well as in other musical genres. In the mid-1990s civil rights activist C. Delores Tucker launched a highly visible campaign to clean up rap music. She focused on Time Warner, whose subsidiary Interscope was home to hardcore rappers Snoop Dogg and Tupac Shakur. In 1995, Tucker and her allies succeeded in forcing Time Warner to get rid of Interscope. But Time Warner simply sold Interscope to Polygram (now Universal Music Group), and the label continued to turn out songs that Tucker and others reviled, through immensely popular artists such as 50 Cent and Eminem. A dozen years later, the battle reached another crescendo, with Al Sharpton and other public figures objecting particularly to racial epithets (particularly the N word) and sexual profanities (the omnipresent B word) in the music.

Some people have lauded these calls for reining in rappers and other songwriters who use what they considered immoral lyrics. They have argued that popular music speaks to an enormous number of impressionable young people and teaches them about romance and love and relationships. Bleeping out a word here and there on the radio or a censored album doesn't erase many of the objectionable words and ideas in the songs, they have argued.

Many of rap's defenders have responded that outsiders should not impose their values on an important field of artistic endeavor. Rappers, they have said, reflect views that many angry African-Americans have about their surroundings; such hard-edge views need to be heard and understood, they argue. During the past few years, though, even rap's defenders have acknowledged that sometimes the lyric writers aim for the obscene, the violent, and the derogatory, simply to stand out. In 2007, the filmmaker Byron Hurt released *Beyond Beats and Rhymes*, a documentary critical of rap that, in the words of a *Time* magazine writer, was notable "not just for its hard critique but for the fact that most of the people doing the criticizing were not dowdy church ladies but members of the hip-hop generation who deplore rap's recent fixation on the sensational."[12] Many rap artists disagreed strongly, and the arguments continued.

Concerns About Access to Music

Of course, many of the songs that some people find so objectionable can be downloaded from the Web. Some parents worry that their children have access to this material too easily, and so a small industry of advice-givers and software creators has arisen to help people control the access that their young people have to certain music. Record executives, for their part, have been embroiled in broader struggles with a variety of groups about access to their company's music. The struggles center on issues of piracy.

PIRACY **Piracy** is the unauthorized duplication of copyrighted music. People concerned about this activity add two special types, **counterfeiting** and **bootlegging**. Counterfeiting also involves unauthorized duplication, but it is more serious because the copy is packaged to look like an authentic copy so that it can be sold as authentic. Bootlegging is the unauthorized recording of a musical performance and the subsequent distribution of that performance. For example, if you go to a concert, secretly record the program, and then sell your recording to your friends, you are bootlegging.

The counterfeiting of CDs and the bootlegging of concerts take place on a huge scale around the world. Most experts consider China the center of counterfeiting, but the sale of illegally created CDs takes place everywhere. In the United States, many people seem to have no problem buying what they know are counterfeited products, including music CDs. A 2007 Gallup poll of Los Angeles residents found that one in four residents bought pirated goods.[13]

Although the counterfeiting of physical albums and the creation of bootlegged concert CDs remain a big problem, it is the illegal downloading of music around the world that has record executives particularly challenged. When a person grabs a song off the Web without the permission of the recording firm or copyright holder, it is

piracy the unauthorized duplication of copyrighted material for profit

counterfeiting the unauthorized duplication of copyrighted music and packaging, with the goal of making the copy appear authentic for sale

bootlegging the unauthorized recording of a music performance, and the subsequent distribution of that recording

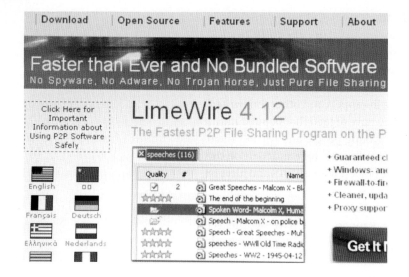

In 2006, a coalition of major recording companies sued the operators of LimeWire for copyright infringement, claiming the firm encourages users of the popular online file-sharing software to trade music without permission.

peer-to-peer computing (P2P) a process in which people share the resources of their computers with computers owned by other people

against the law. It's not hard to do. Individuals continually make songs available online in a compressed file form called MP3. These files can be circulated quickly to anyone who wants them via special **peer-to-peer** (or **P2P**) downloading sites such as LimeWire. P2P software relies on the cooperation of many computers to exchange files over the internet. Aside from being fast, P2P software makes it difficult for copyright owners to blame a website or company for the downloading. The MP3 recordings can be played on computers or on players, including iPods, that can be taken anywhere.

Paying for online music is rare in some countries. In 2007, almost 100 percent of music downloaded from the Web in Asia was illegal, according to Leong May See, Asia director for the International Federation of the Phonographic Industry. It's an industry group that includes Sony Music, Universal Music, and Warner Music.[14] In the United States illegal downloading is also rampant but it seems to be slowing. The RIAA stated on its website in 2009 that "since 2004, the percentage of Internet-connected households that have downloading music from P2P is essentially flat."[15] Executives and government officials who worry about this situation point out that much of the U.S. economy is based on intellectual property. When people in the United States and the rest of the world take songs without paying for them, that takes billions of dollars away from the economy and subtracts jobs that would otherwise exist. Exactly how much money and how many jobs this costs the U.S. economy is a matter of argument. Some people who argue that numbers relating to piracy may be inflated point out that a lot of songs may be downloaded without fee by people who would not otherwise have bought that music.

Still, most people agree that the record industry is losing lots of money on all sorts of piracy. The industry is moving against this problem on a number of fronts, including raids and legal actions against people suspected of pirating CDs. The industry has also enlisted the help of the U.S. government to influence governments around the world to clamp down on the pirating of American albums offline and online. Inside the United States, the RIAA has embarked on a highly controversial activity. It has initiated lawsuits against people who it determines—through analysis of Web files—have uploaded lots of music for others to share. In fact, from September 2003 through September 2007 it initiated more than 21,000 lawsuits. Many of these have been against college students, who have been involved in P2P activities using their schools' high-speed networks. Users who download music illegally face fines for each song, which can quickly add up to thousands of dollars.

The Electronic Freedom Foundation, which has railed against this approach, noted that overwhelmingly the people targeted are "children, grandparents, single mothers," rather than commercial copyright pirates. "The industry shows no signs of slowing its lawsuit campaign . . . filing hundreds of new lawsuits each month including, most recently, 400 per month targeted against college students," the report said. "Today downloading from P2P networks is more popular than ever . . . The lawsuit campaign has enriched only lawyers, rather than compensating artists for file sharing."[16] The RIAA justified its lawsuits as holding people accountable for their actions. Nevertheless, in 2008 the organization announced it would no longer begin lawsuits against individuals for illegal downloading—though it would continue existing lawsuits. It also reflected a new conciliatory attitude:

We're realistic. As an industry, we have lived with street piracy for years. Similarly, there will always be a degree of piracy on the Internet. It's not realistic to wipe it out entirely but instead to bring it to a level of manageable control so a legitimate marketplace can really flourish.[17]

Media Literacy and the Recording Industry

David Card, a New York-based senior analyst with Forrester Research, once said bluntly, "The thing is, nothing can stop piracy."[18] His larger point was that, although the record industry must be cautious about how it circulates its music, the best approach may be to give people what they consider the best music with the best price in the easiest way possible. Some people in the industry worry that it may not be enough. It's hard to compete with "free," they say, and too many people will download songs and other materials for free if they have the chance and know they won't get caught. The industry cannot afford to give away music, they say.

Putting aside for a moment the illegality of downloading music without permission, it is useful to think about many of the points we've discussed in this chapter about the recording industry from the standpoint of several parties involved. We already know the position of the RIAA and the established record companies about giving away music. They want to control when it happens, and they want to stop most of it. They say that their businesses are at stake. Let's look at other constituencies, struggling artists, artists with label contracts, and consumers.

Struggling recording artists and those who are still trying to find a label and make a name for themselves might well have a different viewpoint from established ones about some of these issues. For one thing, these players and singers are likely to resent the power that just a few large firms have over the music, and the musicians, that are heard in the United States and much of the rest of the world. They realize that, although music may be fragmented at the production end, it is highly concentrated at the distribution end, and it is likely to remain that way. Unlike the established artists, they may see the big recording companies not as allies but as enemies who are keeping them out of the distribution pipeline. To many aspiring artists, control of the music industry by Warner, Sony, Universal, and EMI is preventing them from achieving the success they deserve. And they may be gleeful at the prospect of the Web weakening these companies' power.

Moreover, artists who are just starting out may not be upset by the trading of their music on the Web. In fact, they may welcome it. Aspiring musicians can place their material on websites much more easily than they could place it on radio. For basement bands and garage bands, the Web has become a great vehicle for getting their sound out and hoping that people will hear it. Some artists on their way up—even those with label contracts—see the Web in the same way. They realize that the structure of their contracts with the recording companies mean that making lots of money through their albums is a long shot. They make most of their living through the concerts they give, and they may see the pirating of their albums as great publicity that will translate into the kind of popularity that will lead people to pay to hear them at concerts. So in effect they may be grateful that fans care enough about their music to steal it.

Many consumers care little about the problems that the recording companies and their stars have with piracy. In fact, millions of people act as if sharing copyrighted music with millions of other people on the Web is not a legal or ethical issue. The fact that a federal court has ruled that sharing music in this way is legally wrong hasn't stopped music lovers—especially teens and young adults—from scouring the Web

CULTURE TODAY
JUSTIN BIEBER AND YOUTUBE

Justin Bieber performs on the set of BET's 106 & Park at BET studios in New York City in March 2010.

It's hard to believe that Justin Bieber's climb to pop super-stardom began before he had even entered high school. When he was 12 years old, Bieber entered a local talent competition in his hometown of Stratford, Ontario, where he placed second by performing a rendition of Ne-Yo's R&B hit "So Sick." In order to allow Bieber's friends and family who couldn't make it to the show to see his performance, Bieber's mother uploaded a video of the performance to YouTube. The performance reached people beyond Bieber's friends and family, though, and fans began to form around Bieber's profile.

As Bieber's mother continued to upload videos of her son covering R&B songs, his fan base continued to expand, until it eventually included a former marketing executive for the hip-hop label So So Def—Scooter Braun. Braun was so impressed with Bieber's YouTube videos that he flew Bieber from his hometown in Canada

to Atlanta, where he was introduced to R&B singer/songwriter Usher and the CEO of Island Records. Shortly thereafter, Bieber was signed to the recording label and began his career as an R&B star. *My World*, his first album, quickly made it onto the Billboard Top 40 in the United States as well as the Billboard Worldwide Top 100 after its release in November 2009. Bieber even performed live for President Barack Obama during a Christmas celebration.

Bieber's rise to fame reads like a modern-day rags to riches, wherein a seemingly ordinary person is rescued from obscurity after being discovered by a high-up media executive and made into a star. Now, the vehicle for discovery is YouTube, or possibly MySpace or Facebook, or another site where people can upload their creative products. It must be noted that Bieber is far from an ordinary adolescent. Despite his humble beginnings, raised by a single mother in low-income housing, Bieber taught himself how to play the drums, piano, guitar, and trumpet—and all before he was even a teenager. The role of YouTube in facilitating his discovery is undeniable, however, as is its growing relevance as a tool for talent scouts.

Sources: Monica Herrera, "'Time' is Right for Teen Singer Justin Bieber," Reuters, July 19, 2009. http://www.reuters.com/article/idUSTRE56I2BM20090719 (accessed September 20, 2010); Jan Hoffman, "Justin Bieber Dream," *The New York Times*, January 3, 2010, Style section, p. 1; Archana, Ram, "Justin Bieber Joins Mary J. Blige and Others for 'Christmas in Washington'," *Entertainment Weekly: News Briefs*, December 2, 2009. http://news-briefs.ew.com/2009/12/02/justin-bieber-joins-mary-j-blige-and-others-for-christmas-in-washington/ (accessed September 20, 2010).

for MP3 cuts of their favorite new and old works. Research BigChampagne calculates that U.S. fans swipe 1 billion songs a month illegally off the Web.[19]

Is it just selfishness that leads to these wholesale copyright violations? Some commentators argue that consumers are ignoring the interests of the recording industry because for a long time the industry—and especially a handful of firms that are intent on controlling music across as many media as possible—has ignored their interests. The top record companies, they say, have continually taken advantage of the switch to new recording forms (such as tapes, minidisks, and CDs) to charge consumers far more than necessary for singles and albums. Moreover, they say, many consumers feel that albums are often rip-offs; that to buy two or three of a group's songs they must purchase an album that also includes eight or nine other songs that are not terribly good. Consumers therefore have developed no loyalty to or concern for the firms and have no qualms about picking the songs that they really want off the Web without paying for them. The industry, they say, ought to try to understand what consumers want and respond to their interests. Industry officials reply that this has begun to happen. They point to consumers' ability to buy many songs for 69 cents on iTunes and elsewhere. Moreover, there are so many sites—from YouTube to Revver to internet radio streams—where advertising supports listening to music for free.

In the end, of course, it is up to you to decide where you stand in relation to these issues. Arguments about piracy, and about the morality of certain songs underscore the fact that recordings play a huge role in people's lives. Our trip through the recording industry in this chapter sketched the ways in which this industry produces, distributes, and exhibits products in the United States. That is changing in momentous ways. New technologies promise new opportunities, as well as challenges to traditional distribution, exhibition, and promotion routes. It will be interesting to see how the recording industry responds, and how that response affects not only the recordings we can buy but also how we can buy them in years to come.

Chapter Review

For an interactive chapter recap and study guide, visit the companion website for *Media Today* at http://www.routledge.com/textbooks/mediatoday4e.

Questions for Discussion and Critical Thinking

1 How does the phrase "think globally; act locally" apply to the recording industry? To what extent does it apply to other media industries you have studied so far?
2 Who in the recording industry needs to know the personalities of particular labels? As a consumer, do you feel that it is important to look at the labels of recordings you buy? Why or why not?
3 Consider the following statement: "For a singer trying to establish herself, being signed by a major label is both a blessing and a curse." Explain why someone might make this claim.
4 Why is the U.S. government interested in helping the recording industry fight piracy outside the United States?
5 Why might a new artist, not yet signed by a major label, approve of the acts of piracy and bootlegging that others argue will ruin the industry?

Internet Resources

Recording Industry Association of America (http://www.riaa.org)

As its website says, "the RIAA works to protect intellectual property rights worldwide and the First Amendment rights of artists; conducts consumer, industry and technical research; and monitors and reviews state and federal laws, regulations and policies. The RIAA also certifies Gold, Platinum, Multi-Platinum, and Diamond sales awards, as well as Los Premios De Oro y Platino, an award celebrating Latin music sales." The website reflects these activities as well as presenting statistics about record industry revenues.

Sony Music (http://www.sonymusic.com)

An interesting site of one of the big four recording firms. It has information about its labels, artists, executives, and careers.

Rounder Records (http://www.rounder.com)

Rounder is now one of the biggest independent record labels in the United States, with several specialized subsidiary labels. It was founded in 1970 by three university students. The website is a showcase for its activities, which center on American roots music, such as bluegrass.

Bemuso (http://www.bemuso.com)

This site is aimed at DIY (do it yourself) music artists and independent labels. It is a primer about the recording business, with acerbic comments about the big record companies.

Key Terms

You can find the definitions to these key terms in the marginal glossary throughout this chapter. Test your knowledge of these terms with interactive flash cards on the *Media Today* companion website.

album **336**	minstrel show **330**
A&R or artist and repertoire **343**	payola **352**
bootlegging **357**	peer-to-peer computing (P2P) **358**
counterfeiting **357**	phonograph **331**
cuts **336**	piracy **357**
digital platform **342**	promotion **351**
download **342**	rack jobber **355**
format **335**	ringtones **342**
gramophone **332**	royalty **346**
graphophone **332**	single **340**
internet radio **343**	streaming **342**
kiosk **354**	Tin Pan Alley **331**
label **334**	vaudeville show **331**

Constructing Media Literacy

1 Where do you stand about the ethics of downloading copyrighted music off the Web without getting permission from the copyright holders? Explain your viewpoint.

2 Based on your experience and the experience of your friends, do you think that music CDs have a future? Why or why not?

3 If you were a member of an aspiring rock band, what vehicles might you use to get your band known? Would you want to work with a label? Why or why not?

4 Do you think Wal-Mart is right in refusing to stock albums with lyrics it considers potentially offensive to some of its customers? Explain your viewpoint.

5 You'll notice in Table 10.3, "Top Ten All-Time Bestselling Albums," that most of the albums were released many years ago. Can you think of three explanations for the finding that albums of the past decade did not sell as many copies as those of decades past?

Companion Website
Video Clips
· · · · · · · · · · · · · ·

Hip Hop: Beyond Beats and Rhymes—Manhood in a Bottle
This clip from the PBS documentary *Hip Hop: Beyond Beats and Rhymes* provided by the Media Education Foundation examines the rap music industry's portrayal of manhood and the stereotypes it perpetuates. Credit: Media Education Foundation.

Dreamworlds 3—Female Artists
This clip from the Media Education Foundation documentary looks at the portrayal of girls and women in music videos and how this affects people's attitudes about sexuality. Credit: Media Education Foundation.

Hindenburg Disaster Radio Broadcast
This clip depicts the Hindenburg's arrival in Lakehurst in May 1937 and its disastrous explosion. Credit: Internet Archive/Prelinger Archives.

Case Study
· · · · · · · · · · · · · · · · · · · ·

MYSPACE VERSUS AMAZON AS EXHIBITORS

The idea Owned by the conglomerate News Corporation, the social website MySpace has worked hard to become an important platform for aspiring and established artists. In return, the recording industry has been using MySpace (along with other sites) as a platform for promoting its products. Amazon.com has also become an important place for noting and listening to music. There are many differences between the two sites, not least of which is that you cannot buy music directly from MySpace whereas you can from Amazon. But it is not hard to imagine that MySpace will sell music, too. From that standpoint, it is interesting to consider which makes the best exhibitor of music.

The method Spend time exploring the MySpace Music site over a week. Study the main page and its links. Then focus on a music genre and the way its artists and their sites are laid out. Do the same regarding Amazon.com. Imagine that MySpace sells music on its site just as Amazon does. Write a report laying out your view on how the sites compare from the standpoint of (1) promoting aspiring and established artists; and (2) displaying songs and albums. Try to find out why MySpace does not sell music as yet, and about possible plans for doing so.

11 The Radio Industry

After studying this chapter, you will be able to:

1 Sketch the history of the radio industry

2 Explain the relationship between advertising and programming

3 Detail the role of market research in the radio industry

4 Critically examine the issues surrounding the consolidation of radio station ownership

5 Discuss ways in which new digital technologies are challenging traditional radio

MEDIA TODAY

Consider the enormous challenges that the radio industry faces. The home—the place where radio was once the dominant medium—has now been invaded by broadcast TV, cable and satellite TV, CDs and computer-based jukebox programs, VCRs and DVD players, computer game systems, digital music players, and internet music sites—all of which compete with radio for people's attention. How well can the radio industry possibly compete for audiences and advertisers?

Although the radio business started the twenty-first century healthy, its growth in both audience and advertising has stagnated in the face of its competition. At the same time, the radio industry is working to become an important part of the digital media revolution. This transformation will be substantial, because media powers have built the U.S. radio system to be powerful and to last. In fact, exploring radio today, you'd be hard-pressed to realize that it was once the central, most important medium in Americans' lives. Let's take a look.

The Rise of Radio

As we noted in Chapter 10, just as records were developing, a potential competitor was emerging. Its inventors called it radio broadcasting.

The Early Days of Radio

radiotelephony or radio the broadcast of speech and music through wireless transmission

broadcasting term referring to radio transmissions that can be widely received; originally an agricultural term meaning to scatter seed over a broad area rather than in particular places

The first radio transmitter was invented by Guglielmo Marconi in 1894, at the age of 20. Initially, he could transmit signals only over short distances, but a year later he finally succeeded in sending signals over longer distances.

Radio was not originally intended to be a medium for entertainment. After Samuel Morse developed the telegraph in 1842, scientists began to look to send messages over the air using electric waves or frequencies. In 1895, Italian Guglielmo Marconi succeeded in sending messages over long distances using the code of dots and dashes that Morse had developed.

Because the Italian government showed no interest in Marconi's find, he took it to England, where people quickly saw its value to the far-flung British Empire. The Marconi Company was formed to equip the commercial and military ships of England, the United States, and other countries with wireless telegraphy for communicating with one another and with shore points around the world.

Other inventors added to the value of the wireless radio. On Christmas Eve 1906, Reginald Fessenden gave wireless operators on ships in various parts of the Atlantic Ocean a scare by broadcasting not just dots and dashes, but a speech and music, played on a phonograph. This new twist on Marconi's device suggested both radiation (dissemination) through the air and the telephone, and it got the name **radiotelephony—radio** for short (see Figure 11.1).

U.S. inventor Lee De Forest took the invention even further. At first, radio transmissions could be heard only through earphones. DeForest's Audion vacuum tube, patented in 1907, made radio transmissions much clearer, and even made it possible for people to listen to the radio in groups through speakers. He envisioned stations sending out continuous music, news, and other material, and the idea came to be known as **broadcasting**—from an agricultural term meaning to scatter seed over a broad area rather than in particular places.

Determining the Use of Radio

In the United States, it took more than two decades to develop the radio system De Forest imagined—centering on the broadcasting of music, news, and other types of programming. This was partly owing to expensive and drawn-out fights that broke out between various radio inventors over the patent rights—derailing the business plans of Fessenden and others.

When the United States entered World War I in 1917, the U.S. Navy took control of domestic radio, got the government to declare a moratorium on patent suits, and developed radio in ways that would most benefit the military. After the war, the Navy sought congressional permission to retain control over radio for reasons of national security. Its argument was that,

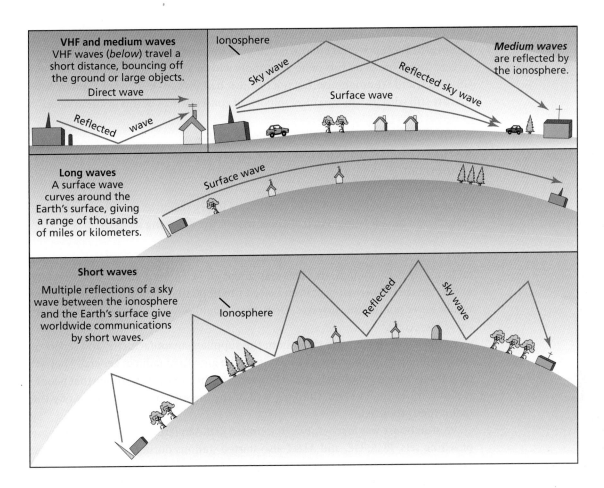

if enemies of the United States got control of radio stations, they could disseminate propaganda that could be damaging to the interests of the country.

However, American tradition dictates that mass media should not be under government control. Both business and government leaders believed that the best way to develop radio's great potential was to move it from the public to the private sector. A radio station could spread words further than an individual newspaper or magazine. Allowing the U.S. Navy to dictate its use would mean that a government agency could potentially control the ideas presented to large segments of the population—a controversial proposition.

Figure 11.1 Radio Waves
Radio waves are broadcast in several wave bands, often called long-wave, medium-wave, VHF (very high frequency), and short-wave bands. Each band contains a range of radio wavelengths, and each station has its own particular wavelength within a band.

The Creation of the RCA

As a result of this debate, Congress decreed in 1919 that broadcasting was to be a privately sponsored enterprise, available to any citizen who paid for a license. But radio's split from government had a catch: to ensure that dominant control of radio would remain in friendly hands, the government forced the British and Italian Marconi Company to sell its interests to General Electric (GE). The U.S. Navy then encouraged a number of American firms that owned major broadcast patents (notably American Telephone and Telegraph (AT&T), GE, and Westinghouse) to form a **patent trust**. That is, a company owned by a number of firms that is formed to share their patents in order to prevent other firms from entering their industry unless the trust allowed them to use the patents.

They called this trust the **Radio Corporation of America (RCA)**, and gave it the power to force anyone interested in setting up a radio station to pay for a radio

patent trust a company owned by a number of firms that is formed to share their patents in order to prevent other firms from entering their industry unless the trust allowed them to use the patents

RCA Radio Corporation of America

patent. RCA, in turn, imposed conditions for the use of the airwaves; the trust quickly became the most powerful force in developing the airwaves.

U.S. courts broke up this radio monopoly within a decade, separating RCA from GE, AT&T, and Westinghouse, but not before it had shaped the new medium in ways that are still with us. The two most important consequences of this decision were:

- The development of advertising to support radio
- The creation of networks to spread advertiser-sponsored programming around the country

These activities led RCA and other radio firms to beg the government to exert more control over broadcasting! We'll discover why in the following sections.

RADIO AND ADVERTISING   The idea of advertisements on radio seems natural to us. In 1919, though, this idea was not at all taken for granted. U.S. Secretary of Commerce Herbert Hoover even voiced the hope that the babble of advertising would never pollute the airwaves. How, then, could privately owned radio stations cover their costs?

In the 1920s, the answer came from the suppliers, manufacturers, and sellers of radio equipment, who wanted to encourage the growth of radio in general. They set up stations with regularly scheduled programs in the more specific hope that people would want to tune in and, thinking well of the manufacturers' activities, buy the radios they produced.

Westinghouse was first—in 1920 it founded KDKA in Pittsburgh with the purpose of selling sets. RCA, GE, and AT&T also started stations during the next few years. Stores also got in on the action, using in-store stations as publicity for the radios they sold; other organizations also began radio stations as signs of goodwill. Some of the stations' call letters were self-congratulatory. Sears, Roebuck, and Co. in Chicago started WLS (it stands for "world's largest store"), the Chicago Tribune Company, a newspaper firm, started WGN (for "world's greatest newspaper"), and WSM in Nashville was begun by the National Life Insurance Company ("we shelter millions").

However, such promotional stations didn't make sense in the long run. The cost of running a serious station with popular programming was climbing into the tens, or even hundreds, of thousands of dollars. Eventually, radio stations would turn to the sale of advertising—a practice that started in a strange way.

radio network a group of interconnected radio stations

O&O stations local radio stations that are commonly owned and operated by a network that often provides a regular schedule of programming materials for broadcast

network affiliates local radio stations that transmit network signals, but that are not owned by the network; in exchange for the transmission of their signals, the network agrees to compensate the affiliate with a portion of the revenues received from network advisers

AT&T executives in New York became convinced they could make money through radio by letting people pay to speak over the radio—in much the same way as they paid to speak over the phone. When it didn't look as if individuals were really prepared to ante up for a chance at the microphone, the company agreed in 1922 to allow the Queensboro Realty Company to pay $3,000 for five "talks" extolling properties it had for sale. The rest, as they say, is history. Other stations picked up AT&T's idea and rushed to sell time on their airwaves. To draw listeners, the advertisers often mixed entertainment with their commercial pitches.

THE CREATION OF RADIO NETWORKS   The creation of **radio networks**— groups of interconnected stations—was a logical extension of the desire to attract advertisers. In the mid-1920s, as radio advertising took off, executives at RCA realized that they could encourage large advertisers to buy time on the company's several stations by linking them (**O&O stations**, or those owned and operated by the networks) and other stations (**network affiliates**, or stations that transmit network signals, but are not owned by the network) around the country through AT&T's telephone lines. The advertisers' programs could be heard by many more people, and the cash received by RCA could be shared by the linked stations.

RCA's idea came together in 1926 in the establishment of the National Broadcasting Company (NBC). By that time, AT&T had sold its broadcast stations to RCA, so the company owned two stations in New York. It therefore started two NBC networks, the Red and the Blue, which carried different programs. That same year, another network, United Independent Broadcasters, was also formed. After stumbling badly, it was reorganized under new ownership in 1927 as the Columbia Broadcasting System (CBS). Though it struggled during its early months, CBS eventually stabilized and became a formidable competitor to NBC.

Government Regulation of Radio

The growth of advertising and the birth of NBC made it clear that radio was becoming a big business. For radio executives in the mid-1920s, though, radio's newfound popularity meant that a large number of small broadcasters were creating havoc on the airwaves, interfering with the ability of commercial stations to get their signals into homes reliably.

THE RADIO ACT OF 1912   In response to this problem, Congress passed the **Radio Act of 1912**. It empowered the Secretary of Commerce to issue licenses to people who wanted to broadcast, and to decide what frequencies should be used for what kinds of services (for example, maritime use, military use, police use, and public broadcast). Once the available public frequencies had been established, the Commerce Department allowed individuals and companies to pay a small fee for a license to start up their broadcast operations. The broadcasters could use any frequency they wanted, as long as the frequency they used was within the designated range of public frequencies.

From the standpoint of broadcasters wanting to turn radio into a big business, the result was chaos. In the 1920s, a large number of stations came on the air across the United States—many on the same frequencies. Because they interfered with one another, it was difficult for audiences to hear any of them consistently. More and more radio executives complained that the airwaves had to be put in order if advertisers were to get their money's worth and radio was to grow as an industry.

They appealed to the federal government to stop giving out licenses. However, in 1926, the U.S. attorney general ruled (and the courts concurred) that the 1912 law did not allow the Secretary of Commerce to refuse a license, assign broadcast hours, or assign specific frequencies. Undefeated, the radio executives then demanded a rewrite of the Radio Act of 1912 to include the right of stations to have exclusive frequencies. They wanted predictable places on the consumer's radio dial.

THE RADIO ACT OF 1927 AND THE ADVENT OF THE FEDERAL RADIO COMMISSION   In 1927, radio executives got that rewrite. The Radio Act of 1927 created a **Federal Radio Commission (FRC)** to issue radio licenses and bring order to the airwaves. The FRC kicked some stations off the air and told the remaining ones the maximum power at which they could broadcast. The stations that were the most powerful and had the best technology got the best frequencies with the maximum power allowances. These stations were generally commercial broadcasters, and often they were network affiliates. Educational and religious stations were consigned to inferior positions on the dial, if they stayed on the air at all.

However, even though a station received a dial position, it did not mean the station owned that position. Rather, the new Radio Act noted quite clearly that the airwaves belonged to the public and that the station was receiving its dial position through a license that would be renewed as long as it acted "in the public interest,

Radio Act of 1912 passed by Congress in 1912, this act gave the Secretary of Commerce the right to issue licenses to parties interested in radio broadcasting, and to decide which radio frequencies should be used for which types of services (that is, public broadcast, military use, police use, etc.)

Federal Radio Commission (FRC) created by the Radio Act of 1927, this commission's purpose was to issue radio licenses to those who applied for them, and to bring order to the nation's radio airwaves

convenience and necessity." Just what that phrase meant, no one was exactly sure. As the 1920s were a time when many people around the nation were nervous about the potential of mass media to carry content that might harm the morals of youngsters and cheapen the American culture, it's likely that this message was inserted into the law to induce broadcasters to keep their programming in good taste.

THE FEDERAL COMMUNICATIONS ACT OF 1934   It was a message that would become the pillar of the government's approach to all broadcasting: the ability of business interests to develop the public airwaves for commercial purposes would be protected, but only if their programming or other activities did not create public controversies. The message was repeated in the **Federal Communications Act of 1934**, which turned the Federal Radio Commission into a larger **Federal Communications Commission (FCC)** with responsibilities for regulating the telephone and telegraph industries as well as the radio broadcasting industry.

Radio in the 1920s, 1930s, and 1940s

Network radio executives and their sponsors indicated that they had gotten the message. Even as the new law was being considered, a number of high-minded series were already in place on NBC's two networks. Network executives noted that the networks distributed many unsponsored hours of farm programs, religious programs, talks, and music-appreciation concerts for schools. The money for these "public service" activities came from sponsored programs such as *The Maxwell House Hour*, *The Palmolive Hour*, *The General Motors Family Party*, *The Wrigley Review*, and *The Eveready Hour*, among others.

As their names suggest, each of these programs was entirely supported by an individual advertiser. When they sold time to advertisers, NBC and CBS simply gave a period of airtime to the advertisers and allowed them and their advertising agencies to produce both the programs and the commercials. The networks collected the advertisers' fees and distributed them to stations across the United States.

To find out how well a program was doing, the advertisers paid ratings companies to call listeners at different times or to give families diaries to find out what station they were listening to. People listened at home, often on radios powered by car batteries. By the 1930s they also listened in cars, since car makers had begun selling models that featured built-in radios.

Network Programming

In the 1920s, the programs that listeners could hear on NBC and CBS throughout the United States were mostly musical—often "live" rather than recorded. As Chapter 10 notes, this created problems for the phonograph industry during the mid-1920s, as people listened to radio instead of buying disks. The Victor Talking Machine Company merged with RCA over worries about the future of its business. The Columbia Phonograph Company, also fearful that its business was trickling away, financed a radio network to be called the Columbia Broadcasting System. The project lost money, Columbia pulled out, and what became known as CBS proceeded on its own. In 1938, however, CBS purchased Columbia Records.

But radio was much more than music. In the 1930s and 1940s, the medium's content was more like the television of today than the radio of today. National networks dominated radio—the NBC Red and Blue; CBS; and, beginning in 1934, the Mutual Broadcasting Company. There were also a few smaller networks of stations in

Federal Communications Act of 1934 the Congressional act that turned the Federal Radio Commission into a larger Federal Communications Commission, with responsibilities for regulating the telephone and telegraph industry as well as the radio broadcasting industry

Federal Communications Commission (FCC) a federal agency specifically mandated by Congress to govern interstate and international communication by television, radio, wire, satellite, and cable

some parts of the country, such as the West Coast-based Don Lee Network and the New England-based Colonial Network. The FCC became concerned that NBC's ownership of two networks gave it excessive power over radio, and it ordered NBC to sell one of them; the Supreme Court agreed. In 1943, the network sold off the weaker Blue, which became the American Broadcasting Company (ABC).

Radio listeners heard talk-and-variety programs (*The Breakfast Club, Arthur Godfrey*) in the morning, continuing dramas (*The Romance of Helen Trent, One Man's Family*) in the late morning and early afternoon, children's adventure programs (*The Shadow, Dick Tracy*) after school, and sports broadcasts during weekends. In the evening, in addition to musical variety programs, listeners could hear the same genres of shows that TV viewers see today: situation comedies (*The Charlie McCarthy Show, Burns and Allen, The Jack Benny Program, Allen's Alley, Blondie*), general drama (*The Lux Radio Theater, The Mercury Theater of the Air*), quiz and game shows (*Take It or Leave It, The $64,000 Question, Truth or Consequences*), police shows (*The FBI in Peace and War*), detective programs (*Philo Vance*), doctor shows (*Doctor Christian*), mysteries (*The Black Castle, The Shadow*), and more.

News slowly developed into an important part of radio. In the 1920s, newspaper executives saw radio as a major competitor for advertising dollars. They consequently pressed the wire services (AP and UPI) to severely restrict their services to broadcasters. Soon, however, the wire services saw that there was money to be made from radio, and the newspapers realized that they could increase their sales by printing what was on the air. The major networks created their own news divisions and beefed them up during the Spanish Civil War and the outbreak of World War II in Europe. President Franklin Roosevelt recognized the importance of radio for informing the nation and embarked on a series of radio talks to promote his administration's policies—popular broadcasts became known as "fireside chats."

The Shadow was an enormously popular radio mystery program of the 1930s and 1940s. The narrator's introduction remains a familiar part of American popular culture: "Who knows what evil lurks in the hearts of men? The Shadow knows!"

Rethinking Radio, 1950–1970

Major changes were taking place in American society after World War II ended in 1945, and they deeply affected the radio and recording industries. Two of the most important developments were:

- The rise of television
- The baby boom

Radio and the Rise of Television

When television entered the picture around 1948, executives from NBC, CBS, and ABC began to shift the profits of their radio networks into building television networks. They saw TV as the wave of the future because it combined the sound of radio with the pictures of movies. In fact, some of radio's biggest stars—Jack Benny,

Jack Benny began his career as a vaudeville performer, but came to national attention as host of *The Jack Benny Program*, which was one of the most highly rated radio shows from 1932 to 1955.

baby boom the huge spike in the population that was created during the late 1940s through the 1950s as soldiers who returned from World War II married and started families

transistor device for amplifying, controlling, and generating radio signals; a smaller replacement for the Audion vacuum tube, leading to the miniaturization of radio receivers

payola an activity in which promotion personnel pay money to radio personnel in order to ensure that they will devote airtime to artists that their recording companies represent

George Burns, Ed Wynne—moved their programs to TV, and a number of other entertainers—Milton Berle, Sid Caesar—became major celebrities as a result of the home tube. Advertisers followed them.

By 1960, more than 90 percent of homes had a television. Instead of listening to network radio, people tended to watch network television. With network audiences declining, nervous radio station owners began to drop their affiliations and look for other ways to make money. In total, 97 percent of all radio stations were affiliated with a network in 1947, but only 50 percent were network affiliates by 1955. Radio was undergoing a revolution.

To draw advertisers, radio executives decided that they would do what TV wasn't doing. They would devote most of their air time to broadcasting music that specific local audience segments would tune in to hear. As a result, stations around the country developed different music formats based on the kind of music they played (country, rhythm and blues, big band) and the radio personalities (called disc jockeys or DJs) who were hired to introduce the recordings.

The Baby Boom, Radio, and Recordings

This revolution in radio coincided with the **baby boom**. Because advertisers in the 1950s were interested in reaching members of this generation—known as "boomers"—many radio stations dedicated their air time to playing rock 'n' roll and featuring disc jockeys that spoke in the lingo of the day. Other stations targeted different age groups with different styles of music and DJs.

This new sort of station that focused on particular music preferences caught on because radio was now more portable than ever. The development in 1948 of the **transistor**, a much smaller replacement for the Audion vacuum tube, led to the miniaturization of radio receivers. Now radio became something that people could literally take with them throughout the day. Suddenly, the medium had a new life, and companies rushed to get new licenses. The number of stations jumped dramatically, from about 1,000 in 1946 to nearly 3,500 in the mid-1950s.

Ethics and Payola

The new station formats made local radio more important to music marketers than ever before. The music that DJs around the country decided to play grabbed listeners' attention, and that translated into record sales. Recording firms pressured their promotion personnel to persuade DJs to give "airplay" to the singers their company was pushing. The pressure was so great, and the influence of certain DJs on audiences was apparently so strong, that many promotion people started paying DJs to highlight their company's recordings—a process known as **payola**. The amounts of money delivered to one DJ could run into the tens of thousands of dollars.

In many cases, disc jockeys were being paid by their stations to choose songs that they genuinely thought their audience would like, not songs that companies bribed them to play. The DJs who were caught accepting bribes could argue that they took money only for songs that they would have played anyway; the cash was just a perk of their job. Song salespeople, in turn, noted that paying to publicize songs was nothing new. (Recall that back in the days of vaudeville, song pluggers greased the palms of performers to sing their publishing firm's songs.)

When newspaper articles exposed the payola to the public, many DJs were fired, Congress held hearings on the subject, and lawmakers amended the Federal Communications Act to make the practice illegal. Many radio stations took song selection away from individual disc jockeys and centralized the activity in the hands of the station's program director. Radio was so critical for the promotion of records, however, that the practice continued in one way or another—often with the program director as the focus of the activity. Expensive gifts, including sex and drugs, often took the place of money and payola remains an ethical issue even today.

FM Radio and the Fragmentation of Rock Music

Despite public controversies over payola and over the airing of rock 'n' roll music, the growth of radio formats continued, based on the targeting of certain age groups and musical tastes. One factor that encouraged the changing of radio to include longer songs and the expansion of the number of station choices was the development of **FM** radio—which stands for **frequency modulation**—an invention of Columbia University engineer Edwin Armstrong during the 1930s. From the start, leading radio executives realized that the static-free sound of FM was far superior to the sound produced by the **AM (amplitude modulation)** technology upon which existing radio transmitters and sets were based. But for technical reasons, the FM technology could not simply be used to improve AM radio. FM would have to either replace AM or co-exist with it. Broadcasters worried that their huge investment in AM would be threatened if they developed FM as a substitute. They also worried that the development of a whole new set of FM stations would reduce their profits by dividing both audiences and advertising money. For these reasons, radio executives tried hard to influence the FCC to derail the development of FM radio. At the same time, however, they protected their business interests by getting FM licenses and simply duplicating on FM stations what they were airing on AM—just in case FM caught on. The debate was so strong and so ugly that FM's inventor, Edwin Armstrong, became deeply depressed over what he saw as the radio industry's attempts to derail his invention, and committed suicide.

FM radio did emerge, though years later than its supporters wanted. By the 1960s, the FCC was not handing out new AM licenses, and the amount of money needed to buy an existing AM station was soaring. In the face of these developments, new business interests saw opportunities in FM radio and pressured the FCC to encourage the growth of FM by passing a nonduplication rule. The FCC passed this rule in 1965, stating that an owner of both an AM and an FM station could not play the same material on both stations more than 50 percent of the time. The rule had the effect the supporters of FM wanted. FM stations, looking for things to play and not having many commercials, developed formats that played long cuts or even entire albums,

Early rock 'n' roll artists such as Elvis Presley fueled an explosion of teen-oriented rock 'n' roll radio programming in the 1950s.

frequency modulation (FM) a means of radio broadcasting, utilizing the band between 88 and 108 megahertz; FM signals are marked by high levels of clarity, but rarely travel more than eighty miles from the site of their transmission

amplitude modulation (AM) a means of radio broadcasting, utilizing the band between 540 and 1,700 megahertz; AM signals are prone to frequent static interference, but their high-powered signals allow them to travel great distances, especially at night

an approach that AM stations resisted. Many listeners migrated to FM; they liked the music and the static-free sound. FM radio began an astounding rise in popularity. In 1972, FM had 28 percent of the radio audience in the top 40 radio markets, with AM taking 72 percent. By 1990, these figures were reversed.

Challenges of Fragmentation and Digitization, 1970 to the Present

Just as radio executives in the 1940s had feared, the popularity of the many new FM stations scattered audiences across more channels and made it harder for stations to draw advertisers. From the 1970s onward—and especially during the 1980s and 1990s—radio executives found that they had to position their stations toward very

TECH & INFRASTRUCTURE
HOW THE RADIO SPECTRUM WORKS

All your life you have heard about "AM radio" and "FM radio," "VHF" and "UHF" television, "citizens band radio," "short-wave radio," and so on. Have you ever wondered what all of those different names really mean?

A *radio wave* is an electromagnetic wave that is propagated by an antenna. Radio waves have different frequencies, and by tuning a radio receiver to a specific frequency you can pick up a specific signal. In the United States, the FCC (Federal Communications Commission) decides who is allowed to use what frequencies for what purposes, and it issues licenses to stations for specific frequencies.

When you listen to a radio station and the announcer says, "You are listening to 91.5 FM WRKX The Rock!" what the announcer means is that you are listening to a radio station with the FCC-assigned call letters WRKX that is broadcasting an FM (frequency-modulated) radio signal at a frequency of 91.5 megahertz (MHz). *Megahertz* means "millions of cycles per second," so saying that the frequency is 91.5 MHz means that the transmitter at the radio station is oscillating at a frequency of 91,500,000 cycles per second. Your FM radio can tune in to that specific frequency and give you clear reception of that station. All FM radio stations transmit in a band of frequencies between 88 and 108 MHz. This band of the radio spectrum is used for no other purpose but FM radio broadcasts.

In the same way, AM radio is confined to a band from 535 to 1,700 kilohertz (kHz) (kilo means "thousands," so this means from 535,000 to 1,700,000 cycles per second). So an AM radio station that says, "This is AM 680 WPTF!" means that the radio station has the

FCC-assigned call letters WPTF and is broadcasting an AM (amplitude-modulated) radio signal at 680 kHz.

Common frequency bands include the following:

- AM radio: 535 kHz to 1.7 MHz
- Short-wave radio: bands from 5.9 to 26.1 MHz
- Citizens band (CB) radio: 26.96–27.41 MHz
- Television stations: 54–88 MHz for channels 2–6
- FM radio: 88–108 MHz
- Television stations: 174–220 MHz for channels 7–13

Why is AM radio in a band from 535 to 1,700 kHz whereas FM radio is in a band from 88 to 108 MHz? It is all completely arbitrary, and a lot of it has to do with history. For example, AM radio has been around a lot longer than FM radio. The first radio broadcasts occurred in 1906 or so, and frequency allocation for AM radio took place during the 1920s. (The predecessor to the FCC was established by Congress in 1927.)

In the 1920s, radio and electronic capabilities were fairly limited, hence the relatively low frequencies for AM radio. Television stations were pretty much nonexistent until 1946 or so, when the FCC allocated commercial broadcast bands for TV. By 1949, a million people owned TV sets, and by 1951 there were 10 million TVs in America. FM radio was invented by a man named Edwin Armstrong in order to make high-fidelity (and static-free) broadcast of music possible. He built the first station in 1939, but FM did not become really popular until the 1960s.

Source: Adapted with permission from http://www.howstuffworks. com/radio-spectrum.htm (accessed February 20, 2007)

particular types of people with very particular lifestyles and listening tastes to attract sponsors. Industry consultants helped station executives relate particular social categories (age, race, gender, ethnicity) to particular formats (album-oriented rock, Top 40, middle of the road, country, and multiple variations of these) to signal to people scanning the airwaves whether or not a station was for them.

AM stations struggled to find niches for themselves in the new radio world. Many had a hard time staying afloat, and some even went out of business. The ones that remained tended to focus on nonmusic programming (all talk, all news, all business/financial, all sports), religious, and ethnic (often Spanish-language) formats. In the 1990s, talk stations hit a sort of a jackpot. The popularity of such on-air characters as Rush Limbaugh, G. Gordon Liddy, Laura Schlessinger, and Oliver North drew millions to those stations and boosted advertising sales.

Radio executives also redefined the idea of a network. The traditional notion of a network as a distributor of all sorts of programming to affiliates had faded with the rise of television. In its place emerged organizations that delivered material tailored to the new demands of segmented, targeted radio. The ABC radio network set the pattern for this approach in 1968, when it reorganized into four services—contemporary, informational, entertainment, and FM. It offered hourly news reports styled to mirror different formats. As the delivery of programming by satellite became possible in the 1970s, more and more network-like services arose to provide stations with everything from around-the-clock music formats to special music concerts that matched their formats. Cable television firms even began to offer their customers audio music services that could not be received over the air.

To distinguish themselves from services provided by new delivery technologies, executives in the traditional radio industry began to refer to their business as **terrestrial radio**. Terrestrial radio involves signals that are broadcast from transmission towers on the ground and picked up by radio sets. That is different from **cable radio**, where cable firms send music to customers through their wires, from **satellite radio**, which involves transmitting signals to satellites that retransmit them to radio sets, and from **internet radio**, where audio is distributed to digital devices that access the Web location. Apart from encouraging new networks, the fragmentation of terrestrial radio encouraged consolidation—the purchase of several radio stations in an area by one company. Before the late 1990s, the FCC did not allow broadcasters to own more than one FM and one AM station in a given area. However, the Telecommunications Act of 1996 did away with such restrictions, allowing broadcast companies to snatch up several AM and FM properties in the same market. That sparked the creation of large radio conglomerates, most notably Clear Channel Communications, which controlled large proportions of radio advertising in markets across the country.

The rise of the radio conglomerates has sparked the criticism that much of terrestrial radio is repetitive, not innovative, and clogged with commercials. This criticism is happening at a time when digital media such as satellite radio, internet-linked computers, iPods, MP3 players, mobile phones, and related technologies are opening up new ways for people to get audio programming that radio has long provided to them. Once again, radio executives stand between an old and new world. They have a lot invested in traditional broadcast radio, but their audiences are declining. So they are trying to understand how to adapt to, and compete with, the new technologies. Let's take a look at the established and emerging worlds of radio. We start with today's terrestrial radio world, then examine digital competition to the radio industry and the industry's response to it. As we will see, there certainly is a lot of music streaming out there.

terrestrial radio traditional broadcast radio, which involves signals that are broadcast from transmission towers on the ground and picked up by radio sets

cable radio a service in which cable firms send music to customers through their wires

satellite radio radio broadcast by transmitting signals to satellites that retransmit them to radio sets

internet radio a service in which streaming audio is distributed to digital devices that access the Web location

An Overview of the Terrestrial Radio Industry

It's certainly a world with a lot of stations. In 2008 there were 13,977 radio stations in the United States. At the same time, the ownership of the stations in big cities and their surroundings has become concentrated. As we have seen, the federal government has greatly relaxed its limitations on the number of stations one party can own. The Telecommunications Act of 1996 allowed the owners of station groups to hold up to eight stations in large markets and up to five stations in smaller markets—with no limit on the total number they can have. As a result, most large market stations are now part of station groups that are owned by companies such as Clear Channel, Cumulus, Citadel, and CBS.

MEDIA PROFILE
RUSH LIMBAUGH

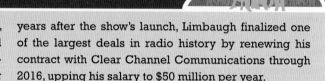

During the primaries of the 2008 presidential election, conservative talk show radio host Rush Limbaugh urged his primarily Republican listeners to temporarily register as Democrats and vote for Hilary Clinton. Under the assumption of an Obama nomination, the strategy—deemed "Operation Chaos"—aimed to prolong the primaries and divide the Democratic Party. "[Obama] needs to be bloodied up politically since McCain is not going to do it," said Limbaugh. "The only person that can do it is Hillary, and she can't do it if she's not in the race."

Whether or not Limbaugh was successful in tipping the vote in certain states is debatable, but Limbaugh was undeniably successful in stirring up controversy with his plan, and, as a result, publicity for his media platform, *The Rush Limbaugh Show*. For Limbaugh, controversy means ratings—a link he is well aware of. Limbaugh has frequently stood at the center of a storm of controversy and reaped the benefits—whether it involves accusing Michael J. Fox of exaggerating his symptoms of Parkinson's disease for a TV commercial, playing a parody of "Puff the Magic Dragon" entitled "Barack the Magic Negro," or stating that he hopes Obama fails as a president.

With his provocative polemics, bombastic bravado, and keen sense of showmanship, Limbaugh has crafted a highly profitable program. The show, airing weekdays on nearly 600 AM radio stations, consists of Limbaugh's monologues inspired by the daily news, call-ins from listeners, and comedy segments. Peaking at 20 million listeners, *The Rush Limbaugh Show* is by far the most widely listened to radio talk show in the United States, and has been since 1991. With MP3 players siphoning off radio listenership and advertising revenue drying up, media executives take note of successes like Limbaugh and conservative talk radio in general. In 2008, twenty

years after the show's launch, Limbaugh finalized one of the largest deals in radio history by renewing his contract with Clear Channel Communications through 2016, upping his salary to $50 million per year.

While Limbaugh's antagonistic conservatism may make for good ratings, it may not necessarily make for good politics. Limbaugh's success has made him a prominent figurehead for an increasingly fragmented Republican party, but his contentious style risks polarizing the electorate and alienating more moderate voters. "If you're a talk radio host and you have 5 million who listen and there are 50 million people who hate you, you can make a nice living," said former George W. Bush speechwriter David Frum. "[But] if you're a Republican Party, you're marginalized."

Frum illustrates the tensions Limbaugh faces as both an entertainer and a political advocate, as well as the ever more blurred boundaries between entertainment and politics. Through *The Rush Limbaugh Show*, we can see the complicated relationship between the two realms, able to simultaneously feed and undercut one another.

Sources: Perry Bacon, Jr., "GOP Seeks Balance with Conservative Icon Limbaugh," *The Washington Post*, March 4, 2009; Paul Farhi, "Rush Limbaugh Signs $400 Million Radio Deal, *The Washington Post*, July 3, 2008; "Michael J. Fox Fires Back at Critics," *ABC News*, October 29, 2006. http://abcnews.go.com/ThisWeek/story?id=2613377&page=1 (accessed September 20, 2010); Brian Stelter, "Times Topics: Rush Limbaugh," *The New York Times*, December 31, 2009. http://topics.nytimes.com/top/reference/timestopics/people/l/rush_limbaugh/index.html (accessed September 20, 2010); "US DJ Criticized over Obama Song," *BBC News*, May 10, 2007. http://news.bbc.co.uk/2/hi/americas/6642029.stm (accessed September 20, 2010).

Where and When People Listen to the Radio

Arbitron, a company that makes money supplying radio ratings to the industry and its advertisers, notes in a 2008 brochure that "the big picture for radio is its remarkable, enduring reach." We noted earlier that, since the 1950s, radio's strength in the face of competition from other media has to do with its portability—allowing people to use radio outside the home, where they have had less access to the medium's audiovisual competition. According to Arbitron, listening at home has been on a long-term decline. Whereas in 1986 53 percent of all radio listening (as measured in quarter hours) took place at home, by 2008 that percentage had dropped to 39 percent. Listening to terrestrial radio has become a predominantly "away-from-home" (in cars, at work, on the beach, in the park) activity.

In the brochure, Arbitron adds that "Far more than 90% of all consumers 12+ years old listen to radio each week—a higher penetration than television, magazines, newspapers or the internet."[1] But what Arbitron means by "listen" is tuning in at least once for a quarter hour during a week. A tougher gauge of attention to radio is time spent with it. The company acknowledges that the time spent listening (TSL) has gone down. The erosion is greatest overall with teens; in spring 2007, for example, teen boys and girls tuned in thirty and forty-five minutes fewer per week, respectively, compared with spring of 2006. For the entire population, TSL fell thirty minutes per week between spring 2006 and spring 2007.[2]

Moreover, the number of Americans aged twelve years and older tuning into terrestrial radio on average during a quarter hour has been declining steadily since 2003, with a marked drop in 2008, as Table 11.1 indicates. The decline has been taking place both in home and out of home, as other technologies that carry music—most prominently the internet, the iPod, the mobile phone, and other digital music players—take terrestrial radio's place. As we will see, this drop in audience has profoundly hurt the ability of radio stations to draw advertising revenues.

AM vs. FM Technology

You already know that terrestrial radio stations broadcast using one of two technologies, AM or FM. The two technologies operate on different ranges of frequencies (called bands) and utilize two different means of broadcasting their signal (see Figure 11.2). There are about 4,700 AM stations and 9,200 FM stations in the United States. Since the 1970s, listeners clearly have preferred FM. In 1981, AM stations attracted 41 percent of the listeners; in 2005, they managed to grab only 18.5 percent. To put it another way, AM's share of radio listeners fell by 55 percent between 1981 and 2000. At the same time, FM's share of listeners increased by 38 percent.

Table 11.1 Radio Listeners (Aged 12+ Years) in the Average Quarter Hour (in Millions)						
	2003	2004	2005	2006	2007	2008
All radio stations	27.8	27.6	27.6	27.2	27.1	25.8
At home	11.4	11.4	11.0	10.9	10.8	10.1
Out of home	16.4	16.2	16.4	16.3	16.3	15.7
AM stations	5.5	5.2	5.1	4.9	4.8	4.5
FM stations	22.4	22.3	22.4	22.3	22.4	21.3

Source: Veronis Suhler Stevenson, *Communications Industry Forecast 2009–2013* (New York: VSS, 2009), p. 10.

Figure 11.2 AM and FM Signals

Both AM and FM radio stations transmit a carrier wave that is somehow changed or "modulated" to carry audio signals such as music or voice. With AM (amplitude modulation) radio, the amplitude or strength of the carrier wave's vibration fluctuates with the sound. With FM (frequency modulation) radio, the strength of the carrier wave remains constant, and instead it is the frequency or number of vibrations within the wave that changes based on the sound.

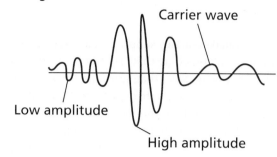

AM Signal

Carrier wave

Low amplitude

High amplitude

FM Signal

Carrier wave

Low frequency

High frequency

commercial station a radio station that supports itself financially by selling time on its airwaves to advertisers

noncommercial station a radio station that does not receive financial support from advertisers, but rather from donations from private foundations and listeners, or from commercial firms in return for mentioning the firm or its products at the start or end of programs airing on the station; most of these stations are located at the very left of the FM band (88–92 MhZ) because these frequencies have been reserved by the government exclusively for noncommercial use

billboards the mention of a sponsor's name or products at the start or end of an aired program in return for money

Commercial Radio Stations vs. Noncommercial Radio Stations

In addition to distinguishing radio stations by their positions in the AM or FM bands, we can also characterize them by the way they get the money they need in order to survive. In terms of funding, there are two types of radio stations:

- Commercial stations
- Noncommercial stations

The vast majority of stations in the United States—about 11,000—are **commercial stations**. As the name implies, these stations support themselves financially by selling time on their airwaves to advertisers. In 2008, advertisers spent about $17.6 billion on terrestrial radio.[3]

Noncommercial stations do not receive financial support from advertisers in the traditional sense of airing commercials. Most noncommercial stations are located at the very left of the FM band (between 88 and 92 MHz) because these frequencies have been reserved by the government exclusively for noncommercial use. If your college or university owns a station, it may very well broadcast here. Because the FCC does not permit these stations to sell products directly, the stations support themselves through donations from listeners, private foundations, and corporations—the latter in return for mentioning the firm or its products in announcements at the beginning and end of their programs. These announcements, called **billboards**, often sound suspiciously like the commercials these stations aren't allowed by law to run.

Radio Market Size

Radio stations can be grouped according to the size of the market they serve (see Table 11.2). Listeners in small cities like Laramie, Wyoming, or Kenai, Alaska, may have only a handful of stations available to them. In fact, despite the availability of frequencies, many rural towns cannot attract the advertising or noncommercial support to field even a single radio station. Contrast that situation with the one that exists in major markets like New York City or Los Angeles, where more than sixty stations compete for residents' ears. Moreover, despite the large number of stations fighting for listeners, a frequency in a large city can be worth hundreds of millions of dollars.

How can so many stations survive in a major urban environment? The answer lies in the second major reason radio has so far been able to compete in the new media world: segmentation—specifically, format segmentation and audience segmentation. To understand what these activities mean and how they guide the radio industry, let's turn to the categories of production, distribution, and exhibition.

Production in the Radio Industry

Research suggests that, despite the large number of signals they may be able to receive, people tend to be loyal to no more than two or three radio stations. Think about the stations that you listen to at different times during the day. Most likely you listen to a station that plays music. Perhaps you listen to a "talk station," where listeners can phone in and speak their mind, or to an all-news station or an all-sports station.

Table 11.2 Top Fifteen Radio Markets by Population, Spring 2010

2009 Rank	Market Location	Spring 2010 Population*
1	New York	15,669,500
2	Los Angeles	10,999,100
3	Chicago	7,862,200
4	San Francisco	6,145,800
5	Dallas—Ft. Worth	5,216,100
6	Houston—Galveston	4,815,700
7	Atlanta	4,413,800
8	Philadelphia	4,357,600
9	Washington, DC	4,279,900
10	Boston	3,977,400
11	Detroit	3,831,100
12	Miami—Ft. Lauderdale—Hollywood	3,580,000
13	Seattle—Tacoma	3,390,900
14	Puerto Rico	3,344,200
15	Phoenix	3,300,300

*Metropolitan area, 12-year-olds and older.

Source: Arbitron Radio Market Ratings, spring 2010. http://www.arbitron.com/home/ mm001050.asp (accessed September 10, 2010).

Let's focus on the music station for the moment. What does that station create or "produce"? Unless the station is broadcasting a special concert, it almost certainly does not produce the music. Today, virtually all radio stations rely on recordings for their musical repertoire. Those recordings were created elsewhere; typically they are CDs made by recording companies.

Radio Formats

format the personality of a station organized around the kind of music it plays and the radio personalities who are hired to introduce the recordings and advertisements

If you think about it, you'll realize that what music-oriented radio stations produce is an overall sound: a flow of songs punctuated by the comments of the DJs, the commercials, the station identification, the news, the weather, and sports. Radio industry practitioners call this flow of on-air sounds a format. A **format** is the personality of a radio station. As such, it attracts certain kinds of listeners and not others. In the highly competitive media environment, radio practitioners have found that the way to prosper is not to be all things to all people. In both commercial and noncommercial radio, profits come from breaking the audience into different groups (segments) and then attracting a lucrative segment. For commercial broadcasters, a lucrative segment is one that many advertisers want to reach. For noncommercial broadcasters, a lucrative segment is a population group that has the money to help support the station or that corporate donors want to impress.

The fragmentation of the radio spurred the creation of many different radio formats, as radio executives struggled for ways to reduce their risk of failure amid enormous competition. They hoped that the formats they created would help them hone in on audiences that would be large and desirable enough for local and national advertisers (or donors) to support. As Table 11.3 shows, the popular format with the largest number of stations is "Country music". It is carried on over 2,000 stations. According to Arbitron, it also garners the highest share of audience listening per average quarter hour (AQH) between 6 a.m. and midnight. For example, it lassoed 12.7 percent of the audience in spring 2007, whereas "News/Talk/Information," #2 in station numbers, was also #2 in audience share, with 10.7 percent per AQH. "Adult contemporary," "Contemporary hit radio," "Spanish," and "Urban" formats had lower shares of the national audience.

music style the aspect of a radio station's format that refers to the type of music the station plays

music time period the aspect of a radio station's format that refers to the release date of the music the station plays (that is, "contemporary," "oldies," etc.)

DETERMINING A STATION'S FORMAT   A radio station's music format is governed by four factors:

- Music style
- Music time period
- Music activity level
- Music sophistication

music activity level the aspect of a radio station's format that refers to the measure of the played music's dynamic impact (that is, "soft rock," "smooth jazz," etc.)

Music style refers strictly to the type of music a radio station plays, regardless of how the music is packaged for airplay. **Music time period** refers to the time of the music's release. "Current" music generally refers to music released within the last year, "contemporary" music generally refers to music released within the past ten or fifteen years, "oldies" generally refers to music released between the mid-1950s and the mid-1970s, and "nostalgia" generally refers to music released prior to the mid-1950s.

music sophistication the aspect of a radio station's format that refers to the simplicity or complexity of the musical structure and lyrical content of the music played

Music activity level is a measure of the music's dynamic impact, ranging from soft and mellow to loud and hard-driving. The names of some music styles include built-in descriptions of the music's activity level: "hard rock," "smooth jazz." **Music sophistication** is a reflection of the simplicity or complexity of the musical

Table 11.3 Radio Station Formats in the United States, January 2010

	Total Counts	Commercial	Noncommercial	Total AM	Total FM
Adult Contemporary	643	630	13	73	568
Adult Standards	339	323	16	281	52
Alternative Rock	365	102	263	8	342
Black Gospel	259	238	21	195	62
Classic Hits	610	600	10	60	547
Classic Rock	481	473	8	8	470
Classical	181	21	160	3	174
Contemporary Christian	929	162	767	50	838
Country	2,007	1,992	15	507	1,495
Easy Listening	28	19	9	4	22
Ethnic	145	127	18	105	36
Gospel	34	26	8	24	9
Hot Adult Contemporary	421	412	9	10	410
Jazz	126	44	82	10	108
Modern Adult Contemporary	19	18	1	0	18
Modern Rock	165	114	51	3	162
News/Talk	2,107	1,422	685	1299	770
Oldies	659	624	35	280	366
Pre-teen	52	52	0	49	3
R&B	150	124	26	6	132
R&B Adult/Oldies	50	46	4	21	25
Religion (Teaching, Variety)	1,397	323	1,074	364	662
Rhythmic Adult Contemporary	18	18	0	0	18
Rock	310	299	11	0	308
Soft Adult Contemporary	192	190	2	28	164
Southern Gospel	296	201	95	159	126
Spanish	937	799	138	474	430
Sports	642	641	1	537	105
Top 40	528	493	35	3	521
Urban AC	162	159	3	30	131
Variety	705	46	659	51	388
Format Not Available	25	22	3	9	15
Stations Off the Air	294	234	60	146	131
Construction Permits	1,365	360	1005	155	1,198

Source: Inside Radio, "Format Counts." ftp.media.radcity.net (accessed March 1, 2010).

structure and lyrical content of the music played. This factor often determines the composition of a station's audience, and it is also reflected in the presentation of the station's on-air staff.

Table 11.4 A Guide to Radio Station Formats in the United States

Symbol	Format Name	Description	Demographics
AC	Adult Contemporary	An adult-oriented pop/rock station with no hard rock; often a greater emphasis on noncurrent music	Women 25–54
AH	Hot AC or "Adult CHR"	A more up-tempo, contemporary hits format, with no hard rock and no rap	Adults 25–34
AP	Adult Alternative	Eclectic rock, often with wide variations in musical style	Adults 25–44
AR	Album Rock	Mainstream rock 'n' roll; can include guitar-oriented "heavy metal"	Men 25–44
AS	Adult Standards	Standards and older, nonrock popular music from the 1940s to the 1980s; often includes softer current popular music	Adults 35+
BG	Black Gospel	Current gospel songs and sermons	Adults 35+
CHR	Contemporary Hit Radio (Top 40)	Current popular music, often encompassing a variety of rock styles; CH-RB is dance CHR, CH-AR is rock-based CHR, and CH-NR is new rock or modern rock-based CHR	Teens and adults 20–24
CR	Classic Rock	Rock-oriented oldies, often mixed with hit oldies of the 1960s, 1970s, and 1980s	Men 25–44
CW	Country	Country music, including contemporary and traditional styles; CW-OL is country oldies	Adults 25+
CZ	Classic Hits	A rock-based oldies format, focusing on the 1970s	Adults 25–44
EZ	Easy Listening	Primarily instrumental cover versions of popular songs, with more up-tempo varieties of this format including soft rock originals; may be mixed with smooth jazz or adult standards	Adults 35+
ET	Ethnic	Programs primarily in languages other than English	Variety of ages
FA	Fine Arts—Classical	Fine arts classical music often includes opera, theater, and/or culture-oriented news and talk	Adults 35+
FX	Farm News and Talk	Farm news, weather, and information	Men 25+
JZ	Jazz	Mostly instrumental, often mixed with soft AC; includes both traditional jazz and smooth jazz or new AC	Adults 25+
MA	Modern AC	An adult-oriented modern rock format with less heavy guitar-oriented music than the younger new rock	Mostly women 25–44
MT	Financial Talk	All financial or money talk	Adults 25+
NR	New Rock—Modern Rock	Current rock, mainstream alternative, and heavier guitar-oriented hits	Teens and adults 20–35
NX	News	All news, either local or network in origin; stations may also have this description if a significant block of time is devoted to news	Adults 35+
OL	Oldies	Popular music, usually rock, with 80 percent or greater noncurrent music; CW-OL indicates country oldies and RB-OL indicates R&B oldies	Adults 25–55
PT	Pre-teen	Music, drama, or readings intended primarily for a pre-teen audience	Children 12 and under
RB	R&B—Urban	Covers a wide range of musical styles; can also be called urban contemporary	Teens and adult 20–24
RC	Religious—Contemporary	Modern and rock-based religious music	All ages
RG	Religious—Gospel	Traditional religious music; BG indicates black-oriented and SG indicates country-oriented southern gospel	Adults 25+
RL	Religion	Local or syndicated religious programming, sometimes mixed with music	Adults 20+

Table 11.4 Continued

Symbol	Format Name	Description	Demographics
SA	Soft Adult Contemporary	A cross between adult contemporary and easy listening, primarily noncurrent soft rock originals	Mostly women 25+
SB	Soft Urban Contemporary	Soft R&B sometimes mixed with smooth jazz; often heavy in oldies	Adults 35+
SG	Southern Gospel	Country-flavored gospel music; also includes the Christian country or positive country format	Adults 25+
SS	Spanish	Spanish-language programming, often paired with another type of programming; equivalents of English formats include SS-EZ (easy listening), SS-CH (contemporary hits), SS-AC (modern music), SS-NX-TK (news talk), SS-RA (ranchero music), SS-TP (salsa, tropical), SS-TJ (tejano), SS-MX (regional Mexican), or SS-VA (variety)	All ages
SX	Sports	Listed only if all or a substantial block of a broadcast day is devoted to play-by-play, sports news, interviews, or telephone talk	Men 25+
TK	Talk	Talk, either local or network in origin; can be telephone talk, interviews, information, or a mix	Adults 25+
VA	Variety	Incorporating four or more distinct formats, either block-programmed or airing simultaneously	All

Source: http://www.newsgeneration.com/radio_resources/formats.htm (accessed September 22, 2007). Copyright, News Generation, Inc., 2001.

TYPES OF FORMATS   Table 11.4 presents a guide to radio formats, giving the format's target demographic, and a brief description of the people in the format's target audience. This list of formats, although long, is not exhaustive. By some counts there are more than forty different formats, including "Hawaiian" and "farm," with every format having variations. Moreover, new formats are born each year.

SELECTING THE RIGHT FORMAT   Because the format is the basis for attracting a target audience, radio station executives spend a lot of time developing it—often hiring **format consultants** to analyze the competition and choose a format that will attract the most lucrative audience niche possible. Most of the formats are based on music, but to format consultants the bottom-line issue is a station's ability to gather a distinct audience for sponsors—not the aesthetics or diversity of its sound. People in the industry often use the term **narrowcasting** to describe the activity of going after specific slices of the radio audience that are especially attractive to advertisers. One well-known radio consultant explained that a radio station's need for distinct listeners was the reason behind narrowcasting. "As the [audience] pie gets thinner and thinner [because of the large number of competing stations], it's not so much whether you have ten thousand listeners at any given time . . . [but] what's the difference between [stations] A, B, C, and D."[4]

format consultant an individual hired by a radio station to analyze the competition and select a format that will attract the most lucrative audience niche possible

narrowcasting going after specific slices of the radio audience that are especially attractive to advertisers

Determining Listening Patterns

Listening patterns are the habits that describe people's use of radio. Radio industry executives suggest that the following five propositions about listening patterns help them effectively segment audiences:

listening patterns the habits that describe people's use of radio

- Individuals tend to listen to only three radio stations at any particular period in their lives, with the most "preferred" of those stations taking up 65–70 percent of their listening time
- In the United States, there tends to be a large and widening divide between the music preferences of black, white, and Hispanic people
- Men and women often have separate musical interests
- People who are ten years apart in age tend to belong to different "music generations" with different tastes
- These music preferences can be useful tools for identifying people with distinct styles of living and buying

Format consultants argue, for example, that they can construct formats that will divide the African-American audience by age and lifestyle. For example, several cities have urban/adult contemporary stations that combine the features of both adult contemporary and urban contemporary stations. They try to reach an older African-American audience by playing both current songs and the "soft" tunes that were popular in these listeners' youth. In a similar vein, the news/talk format can be further divided into distinct subformats such as all news, sports talk, motivational talk, and political talk.

Consultants point out that it is the combination of a radio station's cues—the kind of music or talk, the presence of announcers and their speech patterns, the presence or absence of jingles and other identifiers (interstitials)—crafted in particular ways, that keep listeners of particular genders, ages, races, and ethnicities coming back.

Working with Formats

Once station management chooses a target audience and a format for a local station with the help of consultants, the station's personnel are typically responsible for working with the format—producing it and making it attractive to the target audience on a daily basis (see Figure 11.3).

The general manager is in charge of the entire station operation. He or she represents the owners of the station and is responsible for its activities. The station's sound is controlled by the chief engineer, the news director, and the program director. The chief engineer makes sure that the station's sound goes over the air reliably and, with the help of the compliance manager, that the station's equipment complies with the technical rules of the Federal Communications Commission. The news director supervises news that is read over the air, perhaps assisted by reporters. In preparation for delivering the news over the air, these workers scan the news wires for relevant stories, and conduct brief interviews with local officials to supplement their stories.

The program director works to make sure that the station's programming is consistent with the format and popular with the target audience, and controls the station's on-air functions. Almost everything a listener hears over the air is the responsibility of the program director. The air personalities, or DJs, work for the program director. The program director is often assisted by a music director and a promotions manager. In many cases, these individuals also handle a shift on the air.

on-air talent term referring to radio workers whose voices and personalities are broadcast over the radio's airwaves

The average on-air personality (also known as **on-air talent**) works a four- or five-hour shift. Although this may sound like cushy work, it isn't. Running a format requires being able to handle many different, time-sensitive tasks simultaneously. During his or her hours on the air, a personality may play up to seventy-five records and an equal number of commercials. In addition, the personality will answer select listener phone calls, perhaps give away a few tickets to lucky listeners, and update the weather forecast or sports scores. Keeping all these format elements in order while

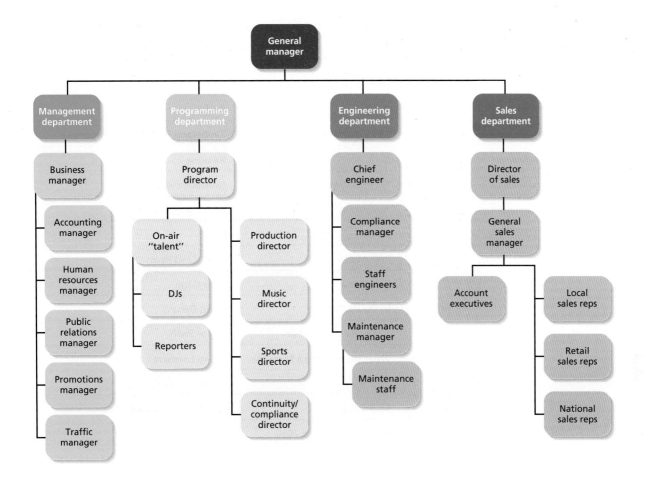

sounding upbeat on the air requires a fair amount of technical skill. Station employees carefully ensure that when a song ends a new one smoothly begins. Otherwise, the station will transmit **dead air**—that is, nothing. Silence is a big taboo in radio, because the mandate is to keep the target audience interested. Figuring out how to fill time attractively is a big challenge for a DJ. After their shift in the on-air studio, many disc jockeys move to a production studio, where they create items like commercials or comedy bits for later airing.

Figure 11.3 The Organizational Structure of a Typical Radio Station

dead air the silence on the airwaves that is produced when a radio station fails to transmit sound

Producing the Playlist

Let's assume you have been named the program director of a new Top 40 station. What do you play to attract your target audience of young people in their teens and twenties? Your DJs need a playlist to guide them. The **playlist** is the roster of songs the DJs can put on the air (see Figure 11.4). The first step in creating a playlist is to listen to new music. Sometimes an artist is so well known that his or her songs will be played automatically, or a new song just sounds so good that it is immediately added to the playlist. But more often than not, adding a song requires careful thought. After all, listeners are fickle and will tune out of a station if it plays a song they don't want to hear. When in doubt, programmers use research.

playlist the roster or line-up of songs that a radio can play on the air during a given period of time

Conducting Research to Compile the Playlist

Research can take many forms. Local stores may be polled to see what records are selling well. Stations using a similar format in other cities may be surveyed to see

KIIS FM playlist for 03.08.2010		
Rank	Title	Artist
1	Nothin On You	B.o.b.
2	Tik Tok	Kesha
3	Carry Out	Timbaland Feat. Justin Timberlake
4	Rude Boy	Rihanna
5	Tie Me Down	New Boyz/Ray J
6	Telephone	Lady Gaga/Beyonce
7	Solo	Iyaz
8	Imma Bee	Black Eyed Peas
9	Bad Romance	Lady Gaga
10	In My Head	Jason Derulo
11	Today Was A Fairytale	Taylor Swift
12	What Do You Want From Me	Adam Lambert
13	Bedrock	Young Money/Lloyd
14	Sexy Chick	David Guetta/Akon
15	We Are The World 2010	Various
16	According To You	Orianthi
17	Young Forever	Jay-z/Mr. Hudson
18	Blah Blah Blah	Kesha/3 Oh! 3
19	Lalala	Lmfao
20	Empire State Of Mind	Jay-z/Alicia Keys

Figure 11.4 A Sample Playlist

This excerpted playlist from KIIS 102.7—Los Angeles, California's number 1 hit radio station—represents some of the songs that KIIS can play for a certain period of time—in this case, on August 3, 2010.

call-outs periodic survey of representative listeners in which a station representative plays a snippet of a song and asks a listener to rate the song

focus group an assemblage of eight to ten carefully chosen people who are asked to discuss their habits and opinions about one or more topics

what they are playing. Executives check trade periodicals such as *Billboard*. They go on the internet to see what people are talking about and downloading, and they may even subscribe to a company that audits what songs people are downloading illegally. They may also survey listeners from time to time and ask them about their preferences. In these interviews, called **call-outs**, a station representative plays a snippet of a song and asks a listener to rate the song. Only songs that test well with the audience will receive substantial airplay.

Research can shape the overall direction of a station. Stations or a research firm they hire may conduct **focus groups**—gathering and interviewing a group of area residents (usually eight to ten) that fit the profile of the station's target audience. The individuals may be asked for their thoughts on various local radio stations, and what they like and dislike about a certain station personality. The sessions are designed to get the spontaneous reactions of the participants. Radio industry executives believe that focus group research gives them a feel for what their target audience really thinks about the station.

Maintaining the Format and Retaining the Target Audience

No matter what their format, programmers work hard to please the largest possible segment of the station's target audience. To hold the interest of those who fall within the target audience but rarely listen to a particular station—that is, **fringe listeners**—the programmer wants to play only the most appropriate songs. Otherwise, when these fringe listeners tune in, they will quickly tune out again because the station is playing something they do not know or like. But the **core audience**—listeners who spend a lot of time listening to a radio station—quickly tire of hearing the same songs over and over. A programmer must carefully balance the desires of the station's fringe listeners and its core audience.

To strike this balance, most radio stations create an hourly **format clock** (also called a **format wheel**). This circular chart divides one hour of the station's format into different, timed program elements (see Figure 11.5). The clock helps the programmer to maintain stability while making sure that key service elements show up at specific times. For example, a radio station may schedule its news at the top of the hour, followed by a hit song. To help listeners remember which station they are hearing, the clock instructs DJs to broadcast the station's call letters and frequency often. Stations may also use jingles to improve their listeners' retention of the station's identity. Perhaps most important from the station owner's viewpoint, the clock also dictates when air personalities play those vital commercials.

fringe listeners listeners who fall within the target audience but rarely listen to a particular station

core audience listeners who spend a lot of time listening to a radio station

format clock or format wheel a circular chart that divides one hour of a radio station's format into different, timed program elements

Figure 11.5 A Sample Format Clock

Radio programmers and disc jockeys use a format clock like this one to program what will be played in one hour's time on their station—from local and national advertisements, to news, to songs, to station jingles and promotions—all to keep the listener tuned in.

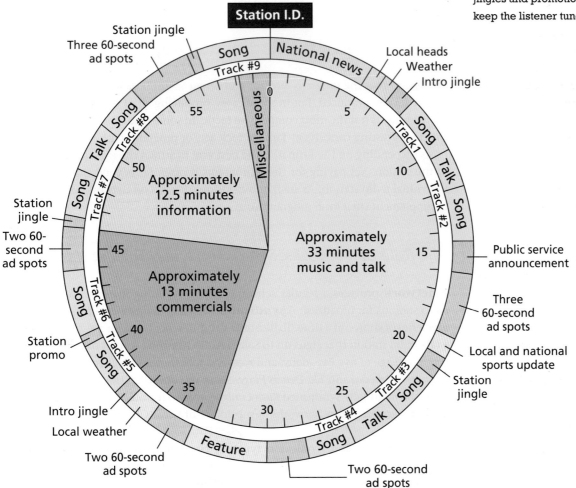

The clock also provides the framework for the scheduling and placement of music. Many stations use complex music-scheduling programs to make sure that individual songs are properly spaced and balanced. The clock guarantees that the most popular records are repeated more often while less popular records air less often.

The approach may vary somewhat during different times of the day. In radio, **drive time**—or the period when people are driving to and from work during early weekday mornings and late afternoons—is when radio stations expect to capture their largest audience. Given the large audience during drive time, advertising rates are also at their highest during these time slots. The morning shift is especially important for the station, and finding the right person or team to handle a station's early morning shift is often a great challenge. Funny morning personalities can command large salaries. It is well known in the radio business that a good morning personality will keep listeners tuned in to the station for the rest of the day.

Because so much listenership (and advertising money) rides on drive time, program directors cannot afford much risk in terms of what is aired. During times when there are fewer listeners—like late at night or on weekends—program directors can be more adventurous, using these hours of lower listenership to introduce new music. Through its request lines, a station can hear from members of its audience about whether they like a new song or not. That might affect whether the program director will slot it in drive time.

It is interesting to note that most air personalities have little input into what music they play. Program directors and their general managers believe that the stakes are too high and the risk too great to allow a single DJ to decide what music to play based on his or her mood. In contemporary radio, a carefully crafted format must be consistent throughout the broadcast day.

Distribution in the Radio Industry

The sound that the program director and on-air talent broadcast every day may be mostly locally produced. But in some cases, producing all of the station's programming locally is not the most competitive tactic. In some cases, for example, it may be that broadcasting concerts by famous rock acts or programs with famous talk show hosts (depending on the format) is the best way to attract the right kind of listeners to the station. Yet paying for these programs is often far beyond the means of an individual radio station. As such, most stations depend on networks or syndicators to supplement their local programming.

The Role of Networks, Syndicators, and Format Networks

A **network** provides a regular schedule of programming materials to its affiliate radio stations for broadcast. A **syndicator** typically makes a deal for one show (or one series of shows) at a time. To illustrate the difference between these two, consider a talk radio station that signs on to Salem Radio Network. As part of this network, it gets a package of five live, daily, and weekend talk shows—for example *Bill Bennett's Morning in America* and *The Dennis Prager Show*. By contrast, if the same station wants to air the nationally syndicated *Rush Limbaugh Show*, it would make a deal with syndicator Premiere Radio Networks (a subsidiary of Clear Channel) for that program alone.

Both networks and syndicators typically circulate their material to stations via satellite. Stations usually don't pay to receive programming from a network. In fact, the network may pay the station for the privilege of using its airwaves; the amount

---

drive time early weekday mornings and late afternoons, when people are driving to and from work; this is the time during which radio stations expect to capture their largest audiences

network a company that distributes programs simultaneously to radio stations that agree to carry a substantial amount of its material on an ongoing basis; typically, a network will provide a regular schedule of programming material to its affiliate stations for broadcast

syndicator a company that licenses programming to radio stations on a market-by-market basis

format network programming firm that provides a subscribing radio station with all the programming it needs to fill its airwaves twenty-four hours a day, seven days a week; often the stations needs only to insert local commercial spots into the programming

is highly negotiable. Syndicators usually do charge for their programs, although their fees are also negotiable. If a particular station reaches exactly the target audience a syndicator wants, the syndicator may charge that station very little for the show or even give it away for free.

The ultimate in network programming is the growing phenomenon of round-the-clock **format networks**. ABC Radio Networks (now a subsidiary of Citadel Broadcasting) provides nine round-the-clock formats, including "classic rock" (targeting the "lucrative 25–49-year-old demographic with the music they crave") and "today's best country" (which "attracts a broad demographic of 18–54-year-old listeners").[5] These format networks provide a subscribing station with all the programming it needs, and the station can insert local commercials and break into the programming with local news and weather when needed. A station that is affiliated with one of these networks no longer needs to have a fully staffed programming department, which means a saving of perhaps hundreds of thousands of dollars annually. The stations can still have a

Through Rush Limbaugh's three-hour daily political call-in show, he reaches approximately 20 million weekly listeners on nearly 600 stations across the United States.

CRITICAL CONSUMER
THE NEED FOR LOCAL RADIO

In 2002, a Canadian Pacific Railway train derailed just outside the town of Minot, North Dakota, spilling poisonous anhydrous ammonia. Clear Channel owned six of the town's radio stations and was running them essentially on autopilot. Emergency workers were unable to contact personnel at the radio station to have them alert listeners to the disaster and the need for evacuation. Because only one news broadcaster supported all six Clear Channel stations, there was no local voice to alert citizens to the present danger. Clear Channel argued that it was a technical glitch that prevented the information from reaching the public. This event sparked controversy over the lack of local coverage on Minot's radio stations. If residents were not alerted about a toxic spill in their community, people argued that it was unlikely that they were receiving local everyday news coverage.

A second concern over the power of Clear Channel was raised during the Iraq war. In 2002, the Dixie Chicks, a country band, had a song, "Travellin' Soldier," at the top of the country singles chart. While the song was flying high, being played by country radio stations across the United States, one of the band members made a disparaging comment about then-President George W. Bush. "Travellin' Soldier" began slipping down the charts. Clear Channel had its stations pull the song from its playlists. Despite the radio ban, the Dixie Chicks refused to apologize for their comments. In this case, the decision not to play the Dixie Chicks music was made centrally and forced on radio stations across the country, instead of having local radio stations decide what was in the best interests of their community.

In both the Minot case and the Dixie Chicks case, the concern is that local voices were not given the opportunity to be heard. Critics of Clear Channel and other radio conglomerates argue that these incidents, unusual though they are, reflect deep tensions between the needs of a local area and the concerns of a conglomerate. Clear Channel, CBS, and other firms that own multiple radio stations in cities respond that their ratings reflect that people want to listen to their output. Where do you stand in this debate?

Sources: http://www.wifp.org/FCCandMediaDemocracy.html; Eric Klinenberg, *Fighting for Air: The Battle to Control America's Media* (New York: Holt, 2008).

Ryan Seacrest counts down the hits on radio as host of *American Top 40*, which can be heard on more than 400 radio stations worldwide.

person who delivers local news and weather so as to give listeners a sense that they are linked to the community.

Networks, syndicators, and format networks make most of their money by selling time on their programs to advertisers that want to reach the listeners of certain types of radio stations around the United States. They may also give the local station some of the advertising time that is available during the programming. In Philadelphia, for example, the station that airs *The Dennis Prager Show* makes money during the first six minutes of the hour by running its own commercials during the news. During the fifty-four minutes of the *Prager Show*, there will be sixteen minutes of commercials. The Salem network will make money running commercials across its networks during five of those minutes. The remaining eleven minutes make up commercial time that the station can sell to local or national advertisers.

Even noncommercial stations use networks. The largest, National Public Radio (NPR), distributes cultural and informational programming to its member stations across the country. It is probably best known for its news programs such as *All Things Considered* and *Talk of the Nation*. The second-largest noncommercial network is Public Radio International (PRI), which distributes such well-known programs as *Marketplace* and *Prairie Home Companion*. Because noncommercial networks are prohibited from soliciting advertisements, these networks help defray their costs by getting foundations or companies to support a program in return for being mentioned on the air, as well as by charging a fee to their affiliated stations. Foundations and companies are attracted by the chance to parade their names in front of the typically well-educated, prosperous, and influential audience that NPR and PRI deliver.

Exhibition in the Radio Industry

From the standpoint of the radio station's owner, the purpose of producing a format and/or buying one from a distributor (a network) is to make money at the exhibition point—the moment at which the format is actually broadcast from the station.

Advertising's Role in Radio Exhibition

For the general manager and the program director, the success or failure of their product depends on whether the station's sales team can sell enough advertising to bring the station adequate profits. Two kinds of advertising come into radio stations:

- National spots
- Local advertising

In **national spot advertising**, airtime is purchased from a local station by major national advertisers or their representatives, such as Nabisco, Paramount Pictures, and Maybelline. The word "spot" distinguishes this kind of sponsorship from **network advertising**, in which sponsors (perhaps also Nabisco, Paramount, and Maybelline) purchase airtime not from the station, but from a network that serves the station. National advertisers use spots to target certain cities with particular ads. Buying network ads is often more efficient when the aim is to reach a particular radio audience across the country.

Of the $17.6 billion of advertising going into radio in 2008, about $16.5 billion went to radio stations as a result of national and spot commercial buys; the rest (about $1.1 billion) went to networks. Of the money that went to radio stations, **local advertising** accounted for about 82 percent of the total. A radio station's local market represents advertising dollars that the station can collect from businesses in the area. The station's sales manager and staff must convince local business and organizations to advertise on the station.

The sales manager works with the traffic manager to coordinate the placement of commercials. The traffic manager ensures that advertisements are scheduled and broadcast correctly. For example, it is considered bad practice to schedule commercials from directly competing companies, say Pepsi and Coca-Cola, right after each other.

Learning Who Listens

Advertisers need to be convinced that they will benefit from paying for time on a radio station. The most basic question they ask is: How many people are listening? Answering that question with certainty is nearly impossible. Newspaper and magazine companies can actually count the individual copies of the paper or magazine that are sold to people. In the electronic media, however, the product being delivered is by definition untouchable; it is sent out free over the air. As a result, the people who choose to listen to the product must be counted. Because it is nearly impossible to ask all the people in a community what radio station they listened to this morning, radio stations pay research firms to ask this question of a sample of the population that is designed to represent the entire community.

Conducting Market Research to Determine Station Ratings

The largest firm that conducts radio audience measurement is Arbitron. The area in which Arbitron surveys people about a station is called the station's market. Des Moines, Iowa; Los Angeles, California; and Madison, Wisconsin, are radio markets of different sizes. On a regular basis, Arbitron selects a sample of listeners in each radio market to participate in its survey. Arbitron then repeatedly tries to contact its selected sample. For example, say Arbitron reaches you at your home and asks you to participate. Given your interest in the mass media, you agree. The Arbitron representative asks you to fill out a diary listing all your radio listening for a week and then to return the diary electronically, via the internet. The company pays you a token fee—usually a dollar or two—for your cooperation.

The diary contains space for a week's worth of responses. You fill it out every time you listen to the radio. You promptly submit it through the company's website at the end of the week. The firm now has an accurate survey, right? Not so fast. This technique of audience measurement has some drawbacks. First, the research firm may

national spot advertising form of radio advertising in which airtime is purchased from a local radio station by national advertisers or their representatives

network advertising form of radio advertising in which national advertisers or their representatives purchase airtime not from local radio stations, but from the network that serves the radio station

local advertising advertising money that comes from companies within listening range of the radio station

have had difficulty getting a random sample of everyone in the area to participate. For example, people such as college students or seasonal workers move frequently or are hard to find, so they are often underrepresented in the survey sample. In addition, evidence suggests that people with busy lifestyles are less likely to participate than those who have more time on their hands. Therefore, the assumption that the sample is representative of the community is often invalid.

In addition, many of the people who do make it into the survey drop out or fail to fill out the diary completely. Though Arbitron designs the diary to be taken along throughout the day, many participants do not do so and then, at the end of a day or week, have to try to remember their station choices and to recreate their listening activity before they write it down in the diary. Even listeners who try to participate conscientiously may accidentally record incorrect information. If you are like many people, you sometimes jump between stations while you are in your car. Would you be able to record which ones you heard?

portable people meter (PPM) Auditron's electronic device for tracking radio listening, both at home and on the street

Recognizing these problems, Arbitron has rolled out a device called a **portable people meter (PPM)** for tracking radio listening, both at home and on the street. At this point, the company is using it in only a few markets—for example, New York, Philadelphia, and Houston—though it expects it to eventually replace the diary in all U.S. markets. The PPM is a mobile phone-sized device that consumers wear throughout the day. It works by detecting identification codes that can be embedded in the audio portion of any transmission. The PPM can determine what consumers listen to on the radio; what they watch on broadcast, cable, and satellite TV; what media they stream on the internet; and what they hear in stores and entertainment venues.

You've probably already noticed a flaw in this system: just because a person passes by a radio station's sound doesn't mean that he or she is really listening. It's certainly a problem, but executives believe the PPM is still superior to the diary method. Another controversy arose during the early use of the PPM. Executives at stations targeting African-American and Latino audiences complained that Arbitron did not include enough people with those characteristics in its PPM samples. The result, say the executives, is that ratings for their radio stations dropped drastically. In the face of angry protests, Arbitron executives agreed to make their panels more representative.

rating point one rating point equals 1 percent of the population in a market

Although no one believes Arbitron data come close to being flawless, most local stations and advertisers use the diary-based Arbitron rating results because they are the best data available. When ratings are reported to subscribing stations, employees await the news with trepidation. Ratings are to station employees what report cards are to students: rows of raw numbers that summarize many months of effort. One **rating point** equals 1 percent of the population in a market. Because typically there are dozens of stations broadcasting in major markets, the ratings for individual stations are often quite small. Stations are considered successful if they manage to garner only four or five rating points. Yet the raw number is often not the only thing of interest to a radio advertiser. The extent to which the advertiser's target audience—in demographic and lifestyle terms—is being reached with an efficient cost per thousand listeners is often more important. For example, a concert promoter may want to know which station in town attracts the greatest share of the young adult audience so that she can effectively buy advertising to attract a rock band's core audience.

Arbitron results give radio executives and advertisers information on such basic categories as listener gender, race, and age. These characteristics form the basis for discussions between a radio station's sales force and potential advertisers about the appropriateness of the station's target audience compared with those of other stations. To gather evidence about other audience characteristics that might also attract advertisers, many radio stations subscribe to Scarborough Research surveys. Scarborough conducts telephone surveys of a market's population and asks people questions about various aspects of their lives—from purchasing habits to hobbies to radio listening preferences. Radio stations' sales forces often link these data with Arbitron data. They then use the findings to try to convince certain local advertisers that their station can deliver the most appropriate audience.

This doesn't always work, however, because Scarborough studies and others like them have their own drawbacks. Sometimes advertisers purchase time on a radio station primarily because they believe that the format is suitable for their product or message and because the sales staff has arranged to tie them to a **promotion** (a contest or event in which prizes are given out) that will both highlight the advertiser and result in concrete responses from listeners toward the advertiser. Almost everyone knows of a radio station that has given away cash prizes, trips, or concert tickets. The prizes are geared to the demographic and lifestyle categories of the listening population that the station's management wants to attract.

A station whose ratings are up will often try to raise its advertising rates to reflect its increased popularity. Some station employees may directly benefit from the ratings report because their salaries are tied to ratings. But the celebration cannot last too long because a new ratings report card is always being prepared. Most large radio markets, such as Chicago, are surveyed year-round by Arbitron.

> **promotion** the process of scheduling publicity appearances for a recording artist, with the goal of generating excitement about the artist, and thereby sales of his or her album

When Stations Fare Poorly in the Ratings

When stations have fared poorly in the ratings, managers may institute immediate changes. Sometimes managers blame internal factors such as a poor choice of recorded music. They may also blame factors outside the station's control. For example, many music-intensive stations have poorer ratings during severe winters because listeners flock to competing news/talk stations for updates on school closings and icy roadways. In that case, a program director of a Top 40 station, for example, will recognize that the ratings fluctuation was due to unusual circumstances and may decide to make no changes in the hope that listeners will return to their normal habits with the approach of milder spring weather.

Often, however, poor ratings lead to personnel changes. A careful analysis of Arbitron data may indicate that a particular time slot is not performing as well as the program director and station manager expected. In this case, the on-air personality during that period is likely to be replaced. When stations have a history of poor ratings and revenue performance, station owners will frequently decide to try a new station format in an effort to grab a larger target audience and more advertisers. Overnight, a station that is known for playing classical music may start playing country tunes. With these wholesale makeovers, it is not unusual for all employees associated with the station's old format to lose their jobs.

"Starting Monday, this radio station will switch from classical music to hard-core rap."

Although management may consider it deadly to stick with an unprofitable format, instituting a new format on a radio station also has risks. Listeners to the old format are likely to feel abandoned and angry, and it may be tough to get the new target audience to find the station. Attempts to attract new listeners through publicity stunts and advertisements on billboards, on TV, and in newspapers can be quite expensive. And if the new format doesn't work, management may be in a worse situation than it was in before the change. Nevertheless, the formats of certain stations do change fairly frequently; their managers believe that the benefits of responding to the shifting interests of audiences and advertisers outweigh the costs and risks of change.

Radio and the New Digital World

Radio executives today find themselves in a world that goes far beyond problems with new format trends. The most obvious change is that, after decades of revenue growth, the financial strength of the terrestrial radio industry has plummeted. Whereas broadcast radio revenues were $20.2 billion in 2005, in 2007 they were $19.6 billion, and the number dropped to $17.7 billion in 2008 and $16 billion in 2009.[6] Part of the decline undoubtedly relates to the economic downturn of the late 2000s, in which key local companies substantially reduced their overall spending on media. But radio executives recognize that the drop in revenues also reflects the realization by advertisers that the time audiences—especially young audiences—spend with radio is decreasing. Recall from Table 11.1 that listeners to an average quarter hour of FM radio stations declined from 22.4 million in 2005 to 21.3 million people in 2008.

These people didn't disappear from the United States—they were simply lost to terrestrial radio. Some—a relative few—have switched to satellite radio. But many people have shifted toward listening to digital sources of music—downloading songs from certain internet sites, listening to streaming songs from others, and sharing their favorites with friends. Their laptops, iPods, MP3 devices, and smartphones are becoming their replacements for portable radio, as they decide what to play in what order. To traditional radio executives, these scenarios are truly scary. They realize the change in music-listening habits is only beginning, and they must find a way to join it rather than fight it.

Satellite radio has so far proven to be only a minor annoyance to the industry, but some industry insiders have great hopes for it. Most observers agree that internet developments threaten to cause the radio industry great damage in the long term if it doesn't adapt. Let's look at each.

Satellite Radio

Satellite radio is a technology through which a consumer can receive streaming channels of music and/or talk to a special receiver (see Figure 11.6). Even though it is connected to the word "radio," the activity has little to do with the technology of broadcasting as it developed over the past century. In 2008, the two competing players in the satellite-radio market, Sirius and XM, merged to become Sirius XM Radio. Sirius XM makes money from subscription (about $20 a month) as well as through advertising on some of the hundreds of channels it offers, with a wide variety of formats. The company produces the programs, sometimes in joint ventures with other firms (Oprah's Harpo Productions, for example, produces *Oprah and Friends* for the XM channel). The channels are uploaded to satellites and can be picked up in most places around the country by receivers that stores such as Best Buy sell. In addition,

Figure 11.6 How Satellite Radio Works

To Space and Back

1. Sirius and XM both produce live and taped programming, ranging broadly from Alanis Morissette to sports and news.

2. The programming is beamed to satellites from dishes operated by each company.

3. The satellites broadcast the signal back to Earth, where it's picked up directly by receiver units. The signal is also received and rebroadcast by repeater stations in metropolitan areas. XM uses two geostationary satellites (right) that remain constantly above the United States. Sirius uses three satellites, two of which are always over the country.

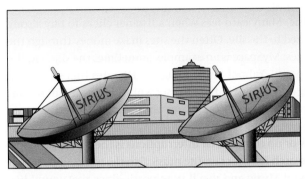

4. A receiver buffers the broadcast for a few seconds, so if it loses the satellite signal it can use one from a repeater station, helping ensure a continuous broadcast. Overpasses and tall building are particular problems.

Source: http://www.space.com/businesstechnology/technology/satcom_radio_operations_031112.html.

Sirius XM has made deals with major car companies to offer their receivers as original equipment. Some of the equipment is portable, making it possible to listen at home and while outdoors, not just in the car.

In the years leading up to the merger, observers worried that the combination could create a behemoth that would set prices and squeeze consumers. Yet by early 2008, Sirius XM had 19 million subscribers, not a small number but not the large proportion of the population some had predicted. Ominously for the firm, several years of high growth seemed to be slowing, and most new subscribers entered because of a free year of programming that came with a new car they bought. Even more problematic, the company had owed $3 billion to creditors by 2008, and only a last-minute investment by Liberty Media Corporation saved it from bankruptcy. Radio-industry analysts now believe that, although satellite radio may have an enduring role to play in the U.S. media system, it is not a fundamental threat to broadcast radio.

Internet Radio

audio streaming an audio file delivered to a computer-like device from a website so that it can be heard while it is coming into the device but cannot be saved or stored

Internet radio could more appropriately be called **audio streaming**, as it involves the flow of music or other audio signals from their originator to a computer via the packet switching technologies that are at the core of the internet. Unlike downloading a song from the Web, streaming music from a website is not designed to be saved by the computer through which it is playing, unless a special recording device captures it and translates it into a saveable format (MP3, for example). Thousands of websites offer streaming music. Many earn fees when a listener clicks to buy a song from a digital music store linked to the site. Often the sites make money through the advertising placed on their sites; MySpace is an example. Sometimes the sites require subscription fees; think Rhapsody. Yahoo! Music is among the sites that shows you ads before streaming the song and has ads in the browser while playing it. But the ads are nothing like the commercial barrage on many commercial terrestrial radio stations.

At least as attractive as few or no commercial interruptions is the diversity of possibilities. MySpace lets you "search for your favorite music," in the words of its search box. Go to Rhapsody or Yahoo! Music and you'll note possibilities that sound like radio station formats—including "rock," "today's big hits," "classic country," "oldies," "contemporary christian" and the like. But you'll also find niche channels that would never make it on traditional AM or FM stations—"Celtic," "India," "Klezmer," "naughty comedy," "modern broadway," "forgotten hits of the nineties," and more. The music site Pandora goes further. Its software identifies patterns in the musical compositions a person chooses to stream and then offers music that fits those genres or combinations of genres. Its challenge to traditional radio is explicit: "It's a new kind of radio—stations that play only music you like."[7]

But these activities are only the start of the way people can shape music streaming to their own interests. Most music sites have forums that allow fans to talk to each other and suggest tracks or albums. AH.FM is a streaming music site and forum for techno and dance music. Napster is among sites that allow people to share music with others. imeem, supported by advertising, highlights what others have played among a large number of different music categories. Rhapsody trumpets the ability of its subscribers to share the lists of streams they have created. Say, for example, you are interested in movie scores in Warner Brothers films. Clicking through Rhapsody you could create a set of list links to music that as a group would represent your understanding of Warner Brothers movie scores; it might be three hours long. You can then "publish" that on Rhapsody so that by clicking on a link any subscriber could hear all the pieces you've strung together.

http://www.pandora.com, website of the online radio station, Pandora

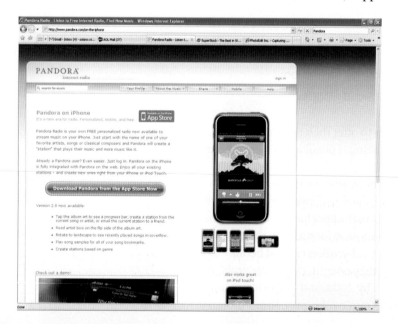

Traditional Radio's Responses to Digital Music

The internet's new music distribution and exhibition platforms perform many of the same functions that contemporary AM and FM stations do. They are available when people want them. And they help to guide listeners through the thicket of songs that they feel they should know about, or might want to learn about. In fact, internet radio sites often present a lot of information about the music they are playing, including biographies of the artists and discographies (lists of the records they have put out).

The one advantage that broadcast radio has retained is its presence in virtually all automobiles. Americans report that fully one-quarter of their music listening takes place in the car, and much of that is still captured by traditional radio stations. Even the relative lack of auto competition may represent short-term relief, however. With the increasing ability to connect to the internet outside the home via mobile phone handsets and other devices (see Chapter 14), it will not be long before many people will have the choice to stream sounds from the internet virtually anywhere.

The radio industry has responded to the challenges posed by satellite radio and the internet by addressing three major areas: commercial time, HD radio, and their own internet participation.

Commercial Time

Executives for major station groups admit that the amount of time that they have traditionally devoted to commercials and promotions—as many as twenty minutes per hour—has driven some listeners away. Some stations have tried to soften the blow by bunching commercials together into long strings; listeners are guaranteed twenty minutes or more of music before they hear any ads, for example. Although this approach may assuage some in the audience, it may get advertisers upset if they are stuck in the middle of the commercial break, worried that many listeners have long since changed the station, if only temporarily.

In late 2004, Clear Channel, the nation's largest broadcast radio station owner, tried to set a new example with an approach it called "Less is More." Clear Channel committed itself to reducing its available ad time to no more than fifteen minutes of ads per hour and no more than six ads in a row. The policy didn't stop audience loss and it lowered revenue. Consequently, Clear Channel has embarked on another strategy. Instead of emphasizing traditional thirty-second commercials, the firm is intent on dropping some commercial time in favor of integrating promotions for products into the fabric of the station—through the DJ's comments, contests, and other activities. They hope activities integrating commercial messages into the fabric of what listeners care about will allow the station to bring in ad revenues while not pushing listeners away.

HD Radio

HD or **hybrid digital/analog radio** is a system in which digital signals of AM and FM stations are sent along with the traditional analog station sounds on the same frequencies allocated to the analog stations. The technology was developed by the company iBiquity Digital in 1991 and approved for use by the FCC in 2002. HD stations simulcast programs digitally, providing listeners with better audio quality than traditional radio as well as data services and side channels that allow for additional

hybrid digital/analog radio (HD) a system in which digital signals of AM and FM stations are sent along with the traditional analog station sounds on the same frequencies allocated to the analog stations programming. HD radio programming is free, but people who want to listen must have a special receiver to get the signals. So far, only 12 percent of American adults say they have ever listened to HD radio, and the technology doesn't seem to be drawing nearly the interest that internet radio is generating.

Internet Participation

Broadcast radio executives are moving rapidly to work with internet radio. Just about every radio station management realizes that it has to have an internet site. The site streams what the radio station is playing but it goes beyond that to deepen and engage the user with the personality that the station aims to project. Consider the website of Power99FM, one of five Clear Channel radio stations in Philadelphia. This station focuses on "Bangin hip hop and R&B," to quote the site. It is filled with songs, music videos, and in-studio performances that reflect the radio station's theme and website's "music on demand" refrain. Surrounding all this music is a large promotional and advertising environment. Listeners can go to the site to find out about the station's contests and promotions. It also conducts its own contests to involve visitors. You can sign up for a VIP club to "enter exclusive online contests for concert tickets, hot prizes, movie passes, sporting event tickets, cash, trips, cars, you name it." All of this comes with advertising for local and national companies. In addition, the site connects to iheartradio.com, Clear Channel's platform for websites for its "350+ stations." The site also allows you to stream albums for free, create a personal playlist of music videos, and see various kinds of ads, some of which (for example movie trailers) are integrated into the site as if they are merely more Clear Channel content.

All these activities leverage the power of Clear Channel to create deals with recording companies and artists for the right to post material across Clear Channel's many websites. Like other internet music sites, visitors can purchase the albums online from the site, for which the company gets a transaction commission. In fact, with the idea of guiding consumers to the purchase of music online and through broadcast, Clear Channel reinforced the company's sense of itself as a part of the new digital environment. In 2007 it was among the radio groups cheerleading a new development in HD radio technology: users who "tag" a song on a special HD receiver have the option to purchase it or find more information about it when their iPod is synced with iTunes software.

http://www.power99.com, website of Power99 FM

The websites of stations owned by CBS Radio, Citadel, and other firms have many of the same features as the Clear Channel sites. CBS, in fact, owns LastFM, which "recommends music, videos and concerts based on what you listen to," while it also tries to facilitate discussions ("community") around the music. It involves streams of its radio station programming from its website or from a central site, with specially inserted commercials. These activities reflect a changing radio industry that senses it must define itself to its audiences and its advertisers as far broader than AM and FM radio.

Broadcast Radio and Social Controversy

Radio industry executives argue that the many formats and format variations that exist throughout the country indicate that the industry is diverse and in touch with its listeners. However, others argue that Americans should find some of the activities at the core of the radio industry troubling. In the interest of better understanding the environment of sound that surrounds us, let's note two related issues, radio consolidation and the radio industry's influence over copyright fees.

Radio Consolidation

Media watchdog groups such as the Media Access Project and consumer groups such as Consumers Union argue that the purchase of hundreds of stations by large companies is reducing the amount of diversity in American radio (see Table 11.5). Media critics say that such consolidation is narrowing the actual range of music broadcast. According to these critics, when the big radio firms buy up stations, they put in place cookie-cutter approaches to formats that have proved efficient in other markets. As a result, cities and towns around the country increasingly have the same line-up of formats with the same line-up of sounds—sometimes even played by twenty-four-hour format computers in places far away. As a result of consolidation, they argue, radio doesn't reflect different regional or local tastes; nor does it encourage live performances by local artists. They add that the growth of round-the-clock format networks that has resulted from consolidation has further homogenized radio despite the large number of stations.

THE RADIO INDUSTRY'S INFLUENCE OVER INTERNET ROYALTY FEES   Individuals who want to see music flourish on the internet worry that the large radio firms and the major recording companies could make it difficult for small websites to compete online. For example, if these large firms set royalty fees for the copyright holders of the music at levels that the big firms with a lot of ad revenues could afford but that small firms could not, the traditional industries could block

Table 11.5 Number of Stations Owned by Top Broadcasting Companies

Rank	Owner	Number of Stations
1	Clear Channel Communications	844
2	Cumulus Broadcasting Inc	303
3	Citadel Broadcasting Corp	205
4	CBS	130
5	Entercom	112
6	Sega Communications Corp	91
7	Univision Communications	71
8	Regent Communications	62
9	Radio One	52
10	NextMedia Group	34

Source: Pew Project for Excellence in Journalism, "Top Audio Companies (as of Spring 2009)." http://www.stateofthemedia.org/2010/media-ownership/sector_audio.php (accessed August 19, 2010).

new players. Critics argued that SoundExchange, the nonprofit organization that collects and distributes digital royalties on behalf of artists and labels, had pushed the government's Copyright Royalty Board toward a two-part fee that was unrealistic for small firms. One part was a high per-song charge, 17 cents. The other part was a $500 annual fee for each music channel run by a company. Independent sites such as Pandora argued that not only was the per-song charge tough to support without a lot of advertising, the annual fee would make it prohibitive for companies to stream a large variety of channels.

Such a royalty regime would, in the words of *The New York Times*, put internet radio on its "death bed."[8] But supporters of internet music resisted the Royalty Board and tried to convince SoundExchange that the record labels would gain a lot from the many sites that lower fees would encourage because they would be a useful way for millions to discover music. In 2009, they came up with a compromise that allows small sites with less than $1.25 million in revenue to pay 12 percent of revenues, going up to 14 percent by 2015, with no per-song fee. That approach will encourage even the smallest firms to have a variety of channels, even personalized channels, streaming together. Webcasters with higher revenues, like Pandora or Slacker, will pay the greater of 25 percent of revenue or a fee each time a listener hears a song, starting at 8 cents and going up to 14 cents in 2015. Internet music executives breathed a sigh of relief. "This is definitely the agreement that we've been waiting for," said Tim Westergren, the founder of Pandora, one of the most popular internet radio sites with 30 million registered users.[9]

Media Literacy and the Radio Industry

If you had to create an industry that streams music and talk formats to Americans, would the radio industry as it is now organized be what you would choose?

As we have seen, the U.S. radio industry developed over decades in response to a variety of forces relating to industry, technology, and society. Powerful organizations work hard to protect the industry's turf so that challenges to the ways radio firms approach the airwaves are difficult to mount. Yet challenges are taking place, mainly from companies and individuals with new digital technologies that ignore the traditional airwaves. To make sense of all these changes, their problems and possibilities, it may be useful to think of the radio industry not only as it currently exists. Rather, think of streaming audio, the industries that are involved in providing it, and the consequences they seem to be having on the variety and diversity of sounds and ideas that Americans can access.

Next time you take a long car trip, try to listen to as many radio stations as you can along the way. Pay attention to their formats and try to determine how much variety there is in the sounds you can hear in different parts of the country. Think, too, of this chapter's discussion of the way these formats are chosen, produced, and evaluated. Then consider what streaming audio in a car, or on a walk, or at work, or in the home might be like in a decade. Winds of change are certainly blowing from various directions. Relaxed federal ownership rules allow companies to own far more stations in a given market than ever before. Yet heightened competition from other media for audiences and advertising revenues poses new threats to traditional radio. How will these and other trends affect the landscape of streaming audio? Will the developments really introduce people to a greater variety of the music enjoyed by many communities in American society, or will they primarily allow individuals to fall into areas of comfortable sounds that are narrower than those found on contemporary radio? Are there ways to encourage a balance of both approaches? How would you like to see streaming audio develop? Why? Keep listening, and thinking.

Chapter Review

For an interactive chapter recap and study guide, visit the companion website for *Media Today* at http://www.routledge.com/textbooks/mediatoday4e.

Questions for Discussion and Critical Thinking

1 What methods do stations use to signal their formats to listeners?
2 How do radio stations know who their listeners are?
3 What are ways in which radio stations deal with poor ratings?
4 What impact does consolidation have, according to media critics?
5 Why hasn't internet radio taken more of traditional radio's audience?
6 What changes in technologies suggest that this situation might change?

Internet Resources

National Association of Broadcasters (http://www.nab.org)

The National Association of Broadcasters (NAB) is the trade association that represents radio and television stations and networks before government bodies.

United States Early Radio History (http://www.earlyradiohistory.us/)

This site explores the history of radio technology and stations (but not programming) from the mid-nineteenth century to the early 1950s. Aside from essays on various historical periods, it has links to many websites with documents that expand on its writings.

Radio Days (http://www.otr.com/index.shtml)

This website contains essays about and examples of network radio from the 1930s and 1940s. There are mystery programs, private eye shows, comedy programs, and science fiction series.

Opry.com (http://www.opry.com/MeetTheOpry/History.aspx)

The Grand Ole Opry in Nashville was a staple for country music fans on radio from the time WSM started carrying it in 1925. This website reviews the past and present of the Opry, including its radio history.

Radio & Records (http://www.radioandrecords.com/RRWebSite)

Radio & Records is a trade magazine of the radio and record industries. Its website offers useful information on station formats, ratings, and industry conventions.

Key Terms

· · · · · · · · · · · · · ·

You can find the definitions to these key terms in the marginal glossary throughout this chapter. Test your knowledge of these terms with interactive flash cards on the *Media Today* companion website.

amplitude modulation (AM)   373
audio streaming   396
baby boom   372
billboards   378
broadcasting   366
cable radio   375
call-outs   386
commercial station   378
core audience   387
dead air   385
drive time   388
Federal Communications
   Act of 1934   370
Federal Communications
   Commission (FCC)   370
Federal Radio Commission (FRC)   369
focus group   386
format clock or format wheel   387
format consultant   383
format network   388
format   380
frequency modulation (FM)   373
fringe listeners   387
hybrid digital/analog radio (HD)   397
internet radio   375
listening patterns   383
local advertising   391

music activity level   380
music sophistication   380
music style   380
music time period   380
narrowcasting   383
national spot advertising   391
network   388
network advertising   391
network affiliates   368
noncommercial station   378
on-air talent   384
O&O stations   368
patent trust   367
payola   372
playlist   385
portable people meter (PPM)   392
promotion   393
Radio Act of 1912   369
Radio Corporation of
   America (RCA)   367
radio network   368
radiotelephony or radio   366
rating point   392
satellite radio   375
syndicator   388
terrestrial radio   375
transistor   372

Constructing Media Literacy

· · · · · · · · · · · · · · · ·

1 In what ways do you think new technologies will affect traditional radio?
2 If you had the power to recreate the formats of radio stations in your area, how would you do it?
3 How important do you think "localism" should be in radio? How would you describe what it should mean?
4 Let's say more and more Americans started taking mass transit to and from work. How would that affect terrestrial radio, and what (if anything) could radio stations do about it?

Companion Website
Video Clips
· · · · · · · · · · · · · · ·

Money for Nothing—Gatekeepers: Radio
This clip from the Media Education Foundation documentary *Money for Nothing* examines the effects of corporate financial backing of certain artists on the recording and radio industries and on popular and independent music. Credit: Media Education Foundation.

"Mary Had a Little Lamb"
Hear Thomas Edison making the first recording on his tinfoil phonograph. Credit: Internet Archive/Open Source Audio.

"Over There"
This 1918 recording of Enrico Caruso singing the song "Over There" by George M. Cohan was popular with soldiers in both world wars. Credit: Internet Archive/Open Source Audio.

Case Study
· ·

RADIO'S PEOPLE METER RATINGS

The idea When Arbitron instituted portable people meter (PPM) ratings in Philadelphia and Houston in 2007, it changed the way advertisers and radio station owners thought of their audience. In Philadelphia, the first sets of ratings showed dramatic differences from the old diary method of keeping track of people's listening habits. Some stations even changed their formats because of the findings. The PPM is an example of how an audience measurement technology can change the nature of reality for a media industry about its audience. It caused a lot of controversy and deserves to be examined in more detail.

The method Using a periodical database, follow the discussions that radio and advertising executives have had over the past several years about problems with Arbitron's diary method and with the benefits and problems that the PPM technology would bring. If everyone understood the problems with the diary method, why were station owners loath to move over to the portable people meter? What were problems that Arbitron found when it tried to implement the new technology? How hard was it to roll out the technology in Philadelphia, in Houston, and beyond? Is it right to assume that the PPM gives the radio stations and their advertisers the correct read on what stations are most popular and when? Do you think it represents the last word on radio ratings?

Write a report of your findings that addresses these questions and this more sociological one: In what ways does the PPM experience show how an audience measurement technology can change the nature of reality for a media industry about its audience?

12 The Movie Industry

After studying this chapter, you will be able to:

1 Explain the history of movies in the United States and how it affects the industry today

2 Analyze the production, distribution, and exhibition processes for theatrical motion pictures in the United States and recognize the major players in each realm

3 Describe how movies are financed, and how they make money through various exhibition arrangements

4 Analyze the relationship between movie distributors and theaters

5 Explain the impact of new technologies and globalization on the movie industry

6 Consider the impact of the American movie culture on world culture

MEDIA TODAY

You get to the theater a bit late with your date on a Saturday night, hoping the movie you want to see isn't sold out. Just your luck—it is. You agree on one of the other movies that the theater is showing. Next question: Will you share buttered popcorn? Your date says no (too greasy); how about some Raisinettes? Where do you want to sit? This seemed like a good place, but the person in front is too tall. It might be best to move. Next issue: Where will you go when the movie ends? Ice cream? No, too fattening. Coffee?

Movies and dating seem linked, don't they? But although people on dates go to the movies more often than other people in the United States, movie theaters draw more than just the romantic crowd. Check out the Saturday and Sunday afternoon theater hordes around malls, and you'll see a lot of children and their parents. Married baby boomers with older kids attend movie theaters fairly often, and senior citizens frequent early evening ("twilight") shows.

As for the movies themselves, even if you don't actually see many of them, you're likely to learn about the most expensive ones that are coming out. The advertising and publicity surrounding such movies tell you about the basic plot and who the stars are—along with the enormous salaries those stars may be getting, why they choose to act in particular films, and how much

their screen characters relate to their real personalities. You may even learn how much money top films are taking in at theater box offices around the country.

This chapter goes beyond the glitz of movies to sketch what these reports rarely explain: how the motion picture industry actually works. What companies are involved in production, distribution, and exhibition? Where does the money come from to support these activities? To what extent are new media technologies changing the way motion picture executives do their jobs?

The motion picture industry is at the center of much popular culture production in the United States and throughout the world. Films that are made for the "big screen" influence a variety of other businesses—from home video to television, toys to clothing. Moreover, the ways in which the movie industry is changing in response to new technologies and the needs of media conglomerates raise important questions about the control of popular culture in the twenty-first century.

How and why did a handful of companies associated with a place called Hollywood become so influential in the creation of America's popular culture? To answer these questions, we have to go back in time to a period when moving pictures were associated with magic shows.

The Rise of Motion Pictures

Magicians were the master showmen of Europe and the United States in the 1800s. What most people in their audiences didn't know was how important projected images were in their acts. As early as the 1790s, magic performances used slides to project mystical pictures onto smoke rising from canisters in their darkened theaters. This "magic lantern" effect grew more sophisticated through the 1800s. It makes sense, then, that magicians were particularly interested in the experiments in creating, and even projecting, moving pictures that inventors in the latter part of the century were conducting.

In one way or another, these experiments took advantage of the phenomenon known as **persistence of vision**, in which the human eye continues to see an image for a fraction of a moment after the object is removed from sight. In the early 1800s, inventors created devices that took advantage of this phenomenon to fool the brain. All of these devices involved preparing a series of drawings of objects in which each drawing was slightly different from the one before it. When the drawings were made to move quickly (say, if they were pasted next to one another on the side of a revolving drum), it appeared to the viewer that the objects were moving.

Using Photographic Images to Simulate Motion

While some inventors were trying to make still drawings appear to move, others were developing the same idea using photographic images to simulate motion. One particularly important figure in this blending was Edward Muybridge, who emigrated to the United States from England. In 1878, Leland Stanford, a wealthy sportsman, recruited Muybridge to settle a $25,000 bet that he had made; he had bet that all four feet of a galloping horse were sometimes off the ground at the same time. Muybridge set up twenty-four cameras close to one another at a racetrack to take photos as a

persistence of vision natural phenomenon in which the human eye continues to see an image for a fraction of a moment after the object is removed from sight

Shown here are the photographs Edward Muybridge took to help Leland Stanford win his bet that a galloping horse sometimes has all four feet in the air at the same time. Can you see why a talented inventor like Thomas Edison would see the seeds of motion pictures in photos like these?

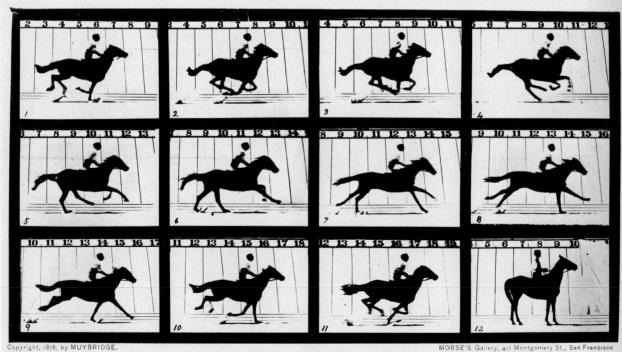

Copyright, 1878, by MUYBRIDGE.   MORSE'S Gallery, 417 Montgomery St., San Francisco

THE HORSE IN MOTION.

horse ran by. Stanford got his money (the photographs showed all four feet off the ground), and Muybridge's work got inventors to think that motion picture photography might be possible. The trick was to be able to take twenty-four photographs with one camera rather than with twenty-four different cameras.

It was Thomas Edison and his assistant, William Dickson, who figured out how to solve this problem in 1889. Dickson discovered that the key was to use the flexible photographic film that had recently been invented by George Eastman (the founder of the Kodak film and camera company). The photographer would turn a crank, moving the flexible film in front of the lens at a constant speed. The result would be several photographs, each slightly different from the previous one. When the strip of film was developed and passed quickly in front of the eye, it gave the illusion of a moving object.

Just as he had misunderstood the potential of his recording machine, however (see Chapter 10), Edison misjudged the value of his moving-picture device, which he called a **kinetoscope**. He insisted that the only way to make money from it was to place it in a box into which individuals would have to drop coins in order to watch movies.

kinetoscope a moving-picture device, invented by Thomas Edison and his associates in 1892, that allowed one person at a time to watch a motion picture by looking through the viewer

Two Frenchmen, Louis and Auguste Lumière, proved Edison wrong in 1894, demonstrating that popular interest could be whipped up and money could be made by projecting movies to large groups. The Lumières refused to sell their cameras or projectors. Instead, they trained people around the world to show their movies using their equipment. They focused on documenting "real life"—street scenes, parades, royalty. In contrast, Robert Paul, a competitor in England, sold moving-picture cameras and projectors to anyone who wanted them. Magicians were some of the first to recognize the power of this new technology and put it to use. They put it in their act as part of the whole business of illusion making.

When film projecting caught on in the United States and elsewhere, Edison rethought his movies-in-a-box approach. His agents quickly arranged to buy the rights to a projector invented by Thomas Armat and C. Francis Jenkins. Calling it the **Edison Vitascope**, the inventors arranged for its public debut on April 23, 1896, at Koster and Bial's Music Hall, a vaudeville site in New York City. (It's where Macy's 34th Street department store now stands.) When the Vitascope premiered, the sensation of the evening was a film entitled *Rough Sea at Dover*, made by Robert Paul. The view of waves crashing on Dover beach was so realistic that people in the front rows actually shrank back in their seats, fearful of getting wet.

Edison Vitascope a projector that made the showing of film on a large screen possible; invented by Thomas Armat and C. Francis Jenkins, and premiered in 1896

Edison's choice of location for the unveiling of his Vitascope film was significant. Unlike the Lumière brothers, who were interested in documenting real life, the films from Edison's company were typically silent "entertainment" performances. (An especially famous one, *The Kiss*, depicts a man's attempt to kiss a woman as they sit on a park bench.) In linking his moviemaking to entertainment, Edison was following the tradition of the many magicians who had used photographs, including moving ones. Although films documenting life were certainly to become an important area of filmmaking, the major thrust of commercial moviemaking focused on entertainment.

Films Become Mass Entertainment Media

Until 1903, a film typically was less than a minute long, consisted of a single shot, and was generally shown during breaks between vaudeville acts. Two filmmakers who helped to change that approach were Frenchman George Méliès and American Edwin S. Porter. Méliès was a magician and graphic artist who made fantasy films with elaborately painted scenery and skillful camera effects; his film *A Trip to the Moon*

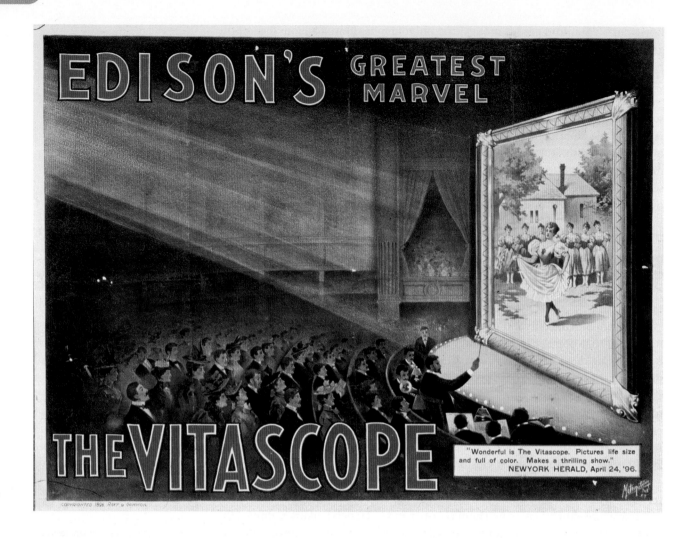

The Edison Vitascope, as advertised in 1896, was a modified "Phantascope," jointly designed by C. Francis Jenkins and Thomas Armat. Armat sold his rights to Edison, who then claimed the modified projector (which he dubbed the Vitascope) as his own invention. In later years, however, Edison acknowledged that the device was the work of Armat.

nickelodeon an early movie theater that charged an admission price of 5 cents per person

is particularly well known for introducing animation and science fiction narrative to the movie business. Porter experimented with more realistic genres (he made *The Life of an American Fireman* and *The Great Train Robbery*, among other films), showing that moviemakers could go beyond simply filming stage plays and create a new art form through the use of imaginative editing and camera work. Along with close-ups and other innovations, *The Great Train Robbery* has a startling ending: a cowboy points his gun directly at the audience and fires a shot.

With the development of the film narrative came larger and larger audiences. Theaters called **nickelodeons** (so named because they charged an admission price of a nickel per person) sprouted up throughout the United States. The immigrants who were streaming into the United States from eastern and southern Europe in the early 1900s were especially attracted to nickelodeons—not only because of their low cost, but because the medium was silent. Stories were told through mime, with title cards inserted into the films at special moments to tell viewers exactly what was going on. Because a filmmaker could change the language of the titles fairly simply to suit a particular audience, and because most viewers could usually follow the action even without the titles, the movies were popular with people who had just moved to the United States and didn't speak English.

THE MPPC AND THE FIGHT OVER PATENTS   By 1910, the demand for movies had become so great that small movie-production firms, many owned by immigrants, were churning out films. The biggest film companies—Edison, Biograph, and

MEDIA PROFILE
HATTIE MCDANIEL

Hattie McDaniel in *Song of the South*.

Back in the days when Hollywood allotted very few major roles to African-Americans, Hattie McDaniel appeared in more than 300 films. In 1940, she won the best supporting actress award for her role as Mammy in the film *Gone with the Wind*. This achievement made her the first African-American to win an Academy Award and helped her to earn the reputation as the most successful black movie actress of her time.

Unfortunately, most of McDaniel's accomplishments were criticized by progressives in the black community. In almost every film she appeared in, McDaniel played the role of a maid or cook, a fact that did not go unnoticed. It was in 1935 that McDaniel first drew criticism for her work in *The Little Colonel*. Many members of the black community felt that her role as the happy black servant reinforced stereotypes that black people had been content with slavery. Five years later the National Association for the Advancement of Colored People (NAACP) criticized McDaniel for her role as Mammy, even though many journalists in the black press viewed her work in *Gone with the Wind* positively.

In the late 1940s, Walter White, the executive secretary of the NAACP, began an intense crusade to diversify the roles played by black people in Hollywood movies. He openly attacked any role that "smacked of Uncle Tomism, or Mammyism" and singled out McDaniel in particular. She stood up to her opponents and responded, "Hell, I'd rather play a maid than be one," a quote that became forever linked to the actress.

McDaniel firmly believed that actors ought to be allowed to choose any role they wanted. Born to a family of entertainers in 1895, she dropped out of high school to become a minstrel performer. Before making her film debut in 1931, the actress also dabbled in radio, worked in a club, and took a variety of menial jobs to support herself during the Depression. Having lived through tough times, McDaniel had no intention of throwing it all away.

Toward the end of her life, Hattie McDaniel won the starring role in *The Beulah Show*. At the height of its success in 1950, this program attracted a multiracial audience of 20 million Americans each night. Although she was once again playing the role of a maid, McDaniel generally received approval from the NAACP and the Urban League for her comedic work as Beulah. Playing this character allowed McDaniel to prove that black people could perform comedic roles without degradation. McDaniel was so committed to this show that she continued to work on it following a heart attack she suffered in 1951. Sadly, she succumbed to breast cancer one year later, leaving behind a rich legacy in Hollywood.

Sources: [No author], *Contemporary Black Biography* (Detroit: Gale Research Inc., 1993); Al Young, "I'd Rather Play a Maid than Be One," *The New York Times*, October 15, 1989, Section 7, p. 13.

Vitagraph—all based in the New York City area, were alarmed at the competition and at the fact that the small filmmaking firms generally were not paying royalties on the patents for the camera and projection equipment that the big companies owned. In 1908, the ten largest companies banded together to form a trust called the **Motion Picture Patents Company (MPPC)**, also known as the Movie Trust, the Edison Trust, or simply the Trust. From 1908 to 1912, the MPCC attempted to gain complete control of the motion-picture industry in the United States, primarily through control of patents. The MPCC's intention was to sue any company making or projecting movies without first getting permission.

The MPPC entered into a contract with Eastman Kodak Company, the largest manufacturer of raw film stock, under which film would be supplied only to licensed

Motion Picture Patents Company (MPPC) also known as the Movie Trust, Edison Trust, or the Trust, this coalition, which lasted from 1908 to 1912, was organized by the ten largest movie companies, whose producers and distributors attempted to gain complete control of the motion-picture industry in the United States primarily through control of patents

members of the coalition. It even went so far as to dictate the form of the movies produced by its members and licensees. It decreed that movies should not be longer than ten minutes, because audiences would not tolerate longer films. The MPCC also refused to allow the names of actors to be listed on the screen, fearing that if actors became well known they would ask for raises.

Despite its efforts, the MPPC failed to stop its upstart competitors. Many of these new startup filmmakers were eastern European Jewish immigrants who were intent on making their fortunes in a trade that, unlike railroading, auto building, and other entrepreneurial businesses, had few startup costs. They broke the MPPC's filmmaking rules—by making longer films and revealing stars' names—and they succeeded. To escape from the demands of the MPPC, and to operate in a climate that would allow them to film year round, many of them moved their studios from New York to a suburb of Los Angeles, California, called Hollywood. The MPPC, for its part, was investigated by the federal government for antitrust violations and was dissolved by court order in 1917. (See Chapter 3 for a discussion of antitrust laws.) By 1920, the MPPC had disappeared altogether, along with the filmmaking companies that had once belonged to it.

The new immigrant-run studios, on the other hand, prospered; some eventually became the major film studios we know today—Columbia Pictures, Paramount, Warner Brothers, Universal, Twentieth Century Fox, and Metro-Goldwyn-Mayer (MGM). Not only were large audiences in the United States eager to see the movies these studios were making, but also markets in Europe and elsewhere were wide open to them as well. Part of the reason was that the young European film industry had been destroyed during World War I. The American companies saw an opportunity for worldwide distribution of their products. By 1918, U.S. movie firms controlled about 80 percent of the world market.

Vertical Integration and the Advent of the Studio System

Keeping control of that business was a high priority. The immigrant studio chiefs were quite aware that they had defeated the previous movie regime, and they didn't want the same thing to happen to them. To protect and extend their companies' power, they engaged in one or both of two key strategies: vertical integration and the studio system.

VERTICAL INTEGRATION   Recall from Chapter 2 that, in the mass media industries, **vertical integration** is control of all steps in the process from creator to audiences—production, distribution, and exhibition. Vertical integration dictated that a major film company should possess moviemaking facilities (the studio), a division that distributed its films to theaters (its distribution arm), and many theaters in the key areas. If a firm had all these activities under its control, competitors could not stop its movies from being shown to the public.

THE STUDIO SYSTEM   From the early 1920s to the 1950s, the **studio system** was the approach the movie companies used to turn out their products efficiently. One element of this process was the **star system**. This operation was designed to find and cultivate actors under long-term contracts, with the intention of developing those actors into famous "stars" who would enhance the profitability of the studio's films. Another element was the division of the studio into **A and B movie units**. **A films** were expensively made productions featuring glamorous, highly paid stars. **B films** were made more quickly, with much smaller budgets.

vertical integration an organization's control over a media product from production through distribution to exhibition

studio system the approach used by American film companies to turn out their products from the early 1920s to the 1950s

star system an operation designed to find and cultivate actors under long-term contracts, with the intention of developing those actors into famous "stars" who would enhance the profitability of the studio's films

A and B movie units an element of the studio system in which films were divided into two categories of production

A films expensively made productions featuring glamorous, high-paid movie stars

B films lower-budget films that were made quickly

Sometimes the studios produced **series pictures**—movies that featured the same characters (and actors and sets) across a number of films, thus lowering the costs and increasing profits. The A films were the prestige films; they were designed to get audiences excited, and to think highly of the companies that made them. The movie companies also used A films to force independent theaters (those that the film companies didn't own) to carry their films. Distribution executives simply said that if theater owners didn't carry a certain number of B films they would not get the A pictures. They called this practice **block booking**.

Alone or together, vertical integration and the studio system kept the seven immigrant-built firms—sometimes known as **the majors**—at the top of the movie industry during the 1920s, 1930s, and 1940s. Small companies emerged to create niche pictures (children's films, comedy shorts, documentaries, and the occasional big drama), but the majors ran the industry.

This is not to say that times were always healthy for all of these companies. During the 1920s, and especially during the Great Depression years of the 1930s, many firms had a hard time staying afloat. In fact, it was during the late 1920s that a struggling Warner Brothers decided to gamble on a technique for adding talking and singing to movies. After experimenting with short **talkies**, or films that featured sound as well as images, the company released *The Jazz Singer* in 1927 starring the vaudeville singing sensation Al Jolson. The film was a hit, and it sparked a worldwide conversion of movie theaters to handle sound. A new era had begun. By the early 1930s, the majors were only turning out movies with sound.

Self-Regulation and the Film Industry

It wasn't long before people around the country worried that the violence and sex in the movies Hollywood was turning out were poisoning youngsters' minds and debasing American culture. Film titles such as *Traffic in Souls* (about prostitution) and drug, sex, and murder scandals in the movie community linked Hollywood with sin as well as with glamour.

Complicating the situation for the studio heads was a 1919 Supreme Court ruling that movies were entertainment and were therefore not protected by the First Amendment's free-speech guarantees (see Chapter 3). As states and towns passed censorship laws, the studios feared that they would have to make different versions of movies for different areas of the country. Instead, in 1922 they formed a self-regulatory body called the **Motion Picture Producers and Distributors of America**. Headed by Will Hays, it created a code that defined movie morality and had the power to enforce it. The plan worked: with the advent of the Hays Office or Hays Code (as it was sometimes called) the majors managed to stave off government regulation and keep the studios in control of their product. It also set a precedent for self-regulation in other media industries, including radio, television, and even comic books.

New Challenges for the Film Industry

By the late 1940s, the major U.S. movie companies were riding high. The difficult Depression years of the 1930s were behind them: people were going to neighborhood movie theaters an average of twice a week or more, and the studio system was working like a well-oiled machine. Just then, though, things began to fall apart. Two developments took place that led to major changes.

---

series pictures movies that feature the same characters, storylines, and sets across a number of films

block booking a tactic under the studio system in which distribution executives ensured that theaters showed both their A films and their B films; if theater owners refused to carry a certain number of a studio's B films, they would not be allowed access to certain A films produced by that studio

the majors the immigrant-built motion picture studios at the top of the movie industry during the 1920s, 1930s, and 1940s—Columbia Pictures, Paramount, Warner Brothers, Universal, Twentieth Century Fox, and Metro-Goldwyn-Mayer (MGM). The majors in the early twenty-first century are Disney, Warner Brothers, Twentieth Century Fox, Universal, Paramount, and Sony (Columbia)

talkies films that featured sound (such as singing, talking, sound effects, etc.) as well as images

Motion Picture Producers and Distributors of America also known as the Hays Office, this self-regulatory body of the film industry created and enforced a code that defined movie morality, setting a precedent for self-regulation in other media industries

Star of stage, screen, radio, and vaudeville, Al Jolson has the monumental credit of being the first person to speak in a feature film (in *The Jazz Singer* as shown in this photo). Jolson often performed in what is known as "blackface"—where white men blackened their faces and performed songs and dances in the style of African-Americans—a controversial part of the earlier era of show business. Ironically, *The Jazz Singer* and the advent of sound led to the demise of blackface's popularity. With sound came a greater emphasis on realism, and it soon became impossible for the motion picture industry to maintain that white actors in blackface could realistically portray African-American characters.

ANTITRUST WOES   One was the 1948 settlement of an antitrust suit by the U.S. Justice Department against Paramount, Warner, MGM, and Fox—the majors that owned theaters. The suit claimed that these companies were preventing producers who were not affiliated with them from getting their movies exhibited. The settlement forced the firms to split off their production and distribution divisions from the theaters where the films were exhibited. Government officials hoped that these actions would weaken the studios and encourage competition.

THE ADVENT OF TELEVISION   As television made its way into the mainstream of American life, attendance at movie theaters dropped. Studio executives argued that the drop was the temporary by-product of the post-war baby boom, which was keeping parents with babies at home. They refused to help the new industry by allowing stations to telecast their movies. Yet by the mid-1950s, the movie studios realized that television was not going away. After Warner Brothers and the Walt Disney Company (one of the smaller movie firms) made deals to produce programs for the ABC TV network, the gates opened wide and all the studios rushed in. Hollywood was now in the TV business.

Movie executives soon realized that television was a place where their B pictures could be shown. The challenge now became what to do with their traditional exhibition arena—the theaters. During the 1950s, movie studio executives believed that they could entice people back to "the big screen" by emphasizing its bigness. They made movies with ultra-wide projection technologies such as Todd-AO, Cinemascope, and Cinerama (think of today's IMAX). They even tried 3-D pictures, for which members of the audience had to wear special glasses. Although individual films such as *The Ten Commandments* drew huge crowds, the executives began to realize that neither ultra-wide screens nor 3-D gimmicks were going to bring the U.S. population back to the twice-a-week moviegoing habit that had been common during the 1940s.

Increasingly, studio executives no longer saw theatrical movies as part of Americans' weekly habits (now that they had TV); rather, they saw movies as individual events that had to lure people into theaters. Because of this lack of audience predictability, the studios could no longer afford to support the star system. The studios got rid of it, preferring instead to let talent agents find and cultivate actors and actresses.

Under the new model of films as special events, movie executives began to release their most expensive films at times when most people were at leisure (for example, during summer vacation and around Thanksgiving and Christmas) and had the time to go to a movie. Executives also believed that people wanted to see stories in the movies that they could not see on television. TV executives, wary of the FCC's ability to withdraw licenses, had picked up their own code of good practices that was modeled after the ones used by network radio and the Hays Code. Now movie people began to question whether their code was too rigid.

Happily for movie executives, in 1952 the U.S. Supreme Court had overturned its 1919 ruling and stated that movies were entitled to First Amendment protection. The upshot was that, as the 1950s gave way to the 1960s, producers and directors increasingly ignored the Hays Code, turning out pictures with scenes of violence, sex, addiction, and other subjects. To replace the Hays Code, the industry began a very different self-regulatory activity: a **film ratings system** in which an independent panel of viewers assigned labels to movies that indicated their appropriateness for audiences of different ages (as discussed in Chapter 3). This meant that the film industry itself would no longer approve or disapprove a film's content. Instead, it would provide film consumers with advance warnings so that they could make their own decisions about which films to see and which films to avoid. (See Figure 12.1 for a snapshot of the percent of films with each rating classification.)

Changes in Technology

Between the 1960s and the 1990s came an unending stream of inventions that reshaped the distribution and exhibition of movies in the twenty-first century. The development of the home videocassette recorder (VCR) was initially opposed by Hollywood, until the studios developed a market in films to the home that eventually exceeded traditional theater revenues. The VCR gave way to the digital video disc (DVD)—yet another outlet for moviemakers to bring in profit. New cable and satellite technologies spawned hundreds of movie viewing options via licenses from the studios. The rise of the broadband internet in the mid-2000s provided yet another place where movies could be shown. Of course, there is a downside of these technologies for movie executives, too—they make it easy to create counterfeit versions of Hollywood films. The movie industry has been fighting bitterly against this activity in the United States and around the world.

An Overview of the Modern Motion Picture Industry

The most appropriate name for the enterprise that we're dealing with in this chapter is the theatrical motion picture industry, so called because the business is set up in such a way that much of its output (movies) initially goes to theaters. Virtually all **theatrical films** (sometimes called **feature films**) now made commercially in the United States appear in nontheatrical locations *after* they have completed their runs in movie theaters in the United States and abroad. These movies are typically turned

film ratings system the system by which a motion picture rating is assigned to a film by the Motion Picture Association of America (MPAA), with regard to the amount and degree of profanity, violence, and sex found in the film

theatrical film or feature film a film created to be shown first in traditional movie theaters; once these films have had their run at movie theaters, often they are redistributed as home videos and DVDs for rental or for sale, as pay-per-view films in hotels and in homes, as in-flight movies on airlines, and as featured films on cable, satellite, and broadcast television channels

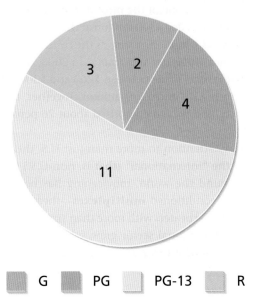

G   PG   PG-13   R

Figure 12.1 Ratings of Top Twenty Grossing Films During 2008

James Cameron is the writer, producer, and director of the top two grossing domestic films, *Avatar* and *Titanic*.

blockbuster a film that brings in more than $200 million at the box office

multiplex a modern, air-conditioned building that houses between eight and fifteen screens and has the capacity to exhibit a number of different films at the same time

megaplex a modern, air-conditioned building that houses sixteen or more screens and has the capacity to exhibit a number of different films at the same time

into videos for rental or sale; shown in hotels, airplanes, and homes on pay-per-view systems; shown on cable, satellite, and broadcast TV; downloaded from the internet to computers, TV sets, and mobile phones; and more. Still, "the movie industry" continues to mean the industry that produces films that will first be exhibited ("featured") in theaters.

In 2008, Americans purchased about 1.4 billion tickets to see theatrical films, spending $9.8 billion (the box office receipts, or the sum of money taken in for admission) at an average price of a little over $7.00 per ticket (see Tables 12.1 and 12.2). That $7.00 may seem low in view of what you pay to see a film, but keep in mind that this price includes discounts for senior citizens and children. Moreover, prices in some parts of the country are a good deal lower than those in other areas. In New York City, for example, moviegoers in Manhattan typically pay $12.50 per person or more to see a new movie. Across the river in some parts of Brooklyn, the price might be a couple of dollars lower.

Going to the movies continues to be most common among young people. Around 34 percent of all tickets for movies in the United States are purchased by people aged 12–24 years, even though these people make up only 19 percent of the nation's population. People aged from 25 to 39 years represent 23 percent of the ticket holders, which is very close to their percentage in the population, whereas Americans 60 years of age and older, who make up about 18 percent of the population, account for 10 percent of the admissions (see Figure 12.2).

During the 2000s, between 500 and 600 movies a year made it to around 40,000 U.S. movie screens. Industry executives tend to pay most attention to the movies that bring in more than $200 million at the U.S. box office; they call such films **blockbusters** (see Table 12.3). There aren't very many blockbusters each year, but they tend to bring in a high percentage of the money that theatrical films as a whole make at the box office. For instance, one of the most recent and one of the biggest blockbusters, released in 2008, exceeded $500 million at the box office. The movie was *The Dark Knight,* which, at $533.2 million, stands as the third highest ever theatrical revenue in initial release, next to *Avatar* and *Titanic.* In 2008, three movies made more than $300 million, three films made between $200 and $300 million, and thirteen films brought in between $110 and $200 million. Together, the top ten movies of 2008 brought in $2.5 billion, which comprised about 26 percent of total domestic box office spending.[1]

Movie executives pay attention to more than just U.S. theaters, however. What movie executives call the "international" (that is, non-U.S.) marketplace has been expanding rapidly. Around the world, moviegoing has been encouraged by the building of modern, air-conditioned **multiplexes**—theaters with eight to fifteen screens, and **megaplexes**—theaters with more than sixteen screens. As a result, box office receipts in the international sector grew substantially faster than U.S. box office revenues. In fact, from 2001 to 2008, the percentage of international receipts

Table 12.1 U.S./Canada Gross Box Office Receipts, 2000–2009

Year	Box Office Gross (US$ billions)
2000	7.5
2001	8.1
2002	9.1
2003	9.2
2004	9.3
2005	8.8
2006	9.2
2007	9.6
2008	9.6
2009	10.6

Source: MPAA. http://www.mpaa.org/MPAATheatricalMarketStatistics2009.pdf (accessed March 10, 2010).

Table 12.2 Average Annual Admission Price at U.S. Movie Theaters, 1988–2009

Year	Average Annual Admission Price (US$)
1998	4.69
1999	5.08
2000	5.39
2001	5.66
2002	5.81
2003	6.03
2004	6.21
2005	6.41
2006	6.55
2007	6.88
2008	7.18
2009	7.50

Source: National Association of Theater Owners (NATO). http://www.natoonline.org/statisticstickets.htm (accessed March 10, 2010).

from outside the United States moved consistently upward, from 50 percent in 2001 to 54 percent in 2003 to 65 percent in 2008.

The decisions and activities made in Hollywood radiate outward, influencing the films that people around the world see in their neighborhood theaters and on DVDs and TV sets. Consequently, a large part of the movie business focuses on getting films and people together in theaters. What does the "Hollywood" way of doing business look like? Let's start with production.

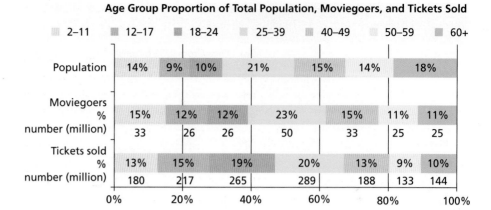

Figure 12.2 Admissions by Age Group

Production in the Motion Picture Industry

People tend to think that when they see the symbols for Twentieth Century Fox, Universal Pictures, Warner Brothers, and other famous Hollywood firms at the start of films this means that those companies produced the movies. In most cases, however, they didn't.

The Role of the Majors

The companies that people most associate with Hollywood are called the majors, and they are the most powerful companies in the movie business. The majors in the early twenty-first century are Disney, Warner Brothers, Twentieth Century Fox, Universal, Paramount, and Sony (Columbia). Despite their prominence and power, these firms create only a small fraction (often one-third or less) of the movies to which their names are attached. Their names appear on screen because of their role as distributors, but more often than not the films have been produced by other companies.

Table 12.3 All-Time Top Ten Grossing Domestic Films

Rank	Title	US Distributor, Release Date	Gross (US$ millions)
1	*Avatar*	Twentieth Century Fox, 2009	706.9
2	*Titanic*	Paramount, 1997	600.8
3	*Dark Knight*	Warner Brothers	533.2
4	*Star Wars: Episode IV—A New Hope*	Twentieth Century Fox, 1977 (re-released, 1997)	461.0
5	*Shrek 2*	DreamWorks, 2004	437.0
6	*E.T.—The Extra Terrestrial*	Universal, 1982	435.0
7	*Star Wars: Episode I—The Phantom Menace*	Twentieth Century Fox, 1999	431.0
8	*Pirates of the Caribbean: Dead Man's Chest*	Buena Vista, 2006	423.4
9	*Spider Man*	Sony, 2002	407.7
10	*Transformers: Revenge of the Fallen*	DreamWorks, 2009	402.1

Distinguishing Between Production and Distribution

The distinction between production and distribution in the movie industry is critical to understand. **Film production firms** are involved in coming up with story ideas, finding scriptwriters, hiring the personnel needed to make the movie, and making sure the work is carried out on time and on budget. **Film distribution firms**, in contrast, are responsible for finding theaters in which to show the movies around the world and for promoting the films to the public. Distribution firms often contribute money toward the production firms' costs of making the film.

The one generalization we can make is that when you see the phrase "a Warner Brothers release," for example, you should be aware that it does not necessarily mean that the company's studio arm has fully financed and produced the movie. Although the Warner studio does fully produce movies that its distribution division circulates to theaters, most of the films that it deals with as a distributor come from separate production firms such as Darker Entertainment. It was one of the companies behind the 2009 thriller *The Box* that Warner Brothers released. Warner typically kicks in a portion of the money, but the production firm takes on a lot of the risk itself.

The Role of Independent Producers

Why don't the majors produce all the movies that they distribute? The reason is straightforward: for a distribution firm to maintain a strong relationship with theaters, it has to provide a strong roster of films to help fill theater seats. If a distributor offers theaters fewer than fifteen or twenty movies a year, theaters will not take the distributor seriously and it will not be an influential force in the movie industry. Yet movies are both very expensive and very risky to make. They typically cost tens of millions of dollars each, and many of them lose money. A firm such as Universal cannot afford to risk the amount of cash that would be required to fully fund many films. Consequently, Universal's own studio generates five to ten films itself, and the company picks up the rest of its distribution roster from **independent producers**—that is, from production firms that are not owned by distributors.

Consider the 2007 movie *3:10 to Yuma*, which was released by the independent distributor Lionsgate. According to *Variety* it was mostly financed by its executive producer Ryan Kavanaugh and his company Relativity Media, with Lionsgate acting as a minority investor of $42.5 million on the $87.5 million-plus project.[2]

The Process of Making a Movie

The process by which a movie goes from an idea in someone's head to a film that the distributor can ship to theaters is time-consuming and torturous as well as expensive (see Figure 12.3). Production company executives will also say that overseeing the filming and editing of their movies is only a small part of what their company does. Other important steps involve getting the idea, getting the talent, and getting the money. Only after these steps have been performed can the activities involved in actually making the movie take place. Let's look briefly at each stage in this process.

film production firm involved in coming up with story ideas, finding scriptwriters, hiring the personnel needed to make the movie, and making sure the work is carried out on time and on budget

film distribution firm responsible for finding theaters in which to show movies around the world and for promoting films to the public

independent producer a production firm that is not owned by a distributor

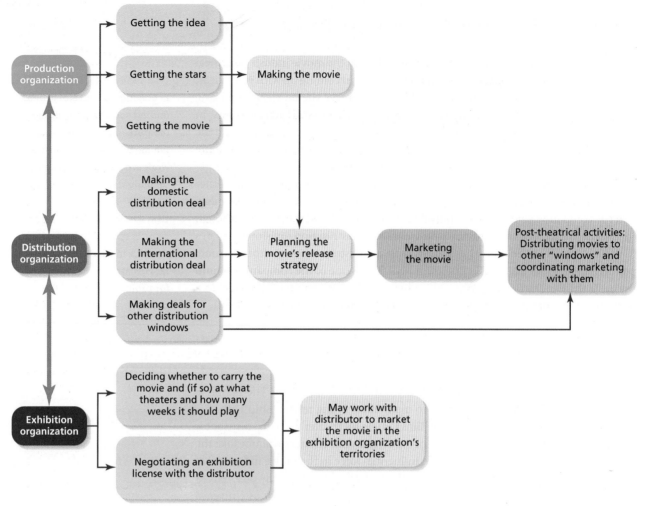

Figure 12.3 Producing a Movie and Releasing it to Theaters

scriptwriters individuals who create plays for the movies, with scenes and dialog

talent agent an individual who represents creative personnel (such as actors, directors, authors, and screenwriters) and aims to link them with production firms in exchange for a percentage of the creator's revenues from the finished product

treatment a detailed outline of an initial pitch to executives of a production or distribution firm; if the executives approve of the treatment, they will probably order a script to be written

GETTING THE IDEA   An idea for a movie can come from virtually anywhere. Producers have gotten ideas for movies from television shows, comic books, toys, short stories, and newspaper articles. Scriptwriters and books have traditionally been the most common sources, however.

Scriptwriters are individuals who create plays for the movies, with scenes and dialog. Plot ideas from them often come to production firms from the writers' **talent agents**, individuals who represent various creative personnel (such as actors, directors, authors, and screenwriters) and aim to link them with production firms in exchange for a percentage of the creators' revenues from the finished product. An agent's job is to gain a reputation around Hollywood for having good creative and business ideas so that, when he or she knocks on a producer's door with a suggestion, the producer will listen. Agents know what has been popular. They also know what kinds of films certain producers like to make.

An idea for a film from an established writer will sometimes be only a few lines that go to the heart of the plot. ("A small wooden box arrives on the doorstep of a troubled married couple, who open it and become instantly wealthy. Little do they realize that opening the box also kills someone they do not know.") If the producer likes the idea (this one actually came from an episode of the classic TV series, *Twilight Zone*), the writer might be paid to write a detailed outline, which is called a **treatment**. If the producer likes the treatment, the next step might be payment for a full script. Less-established writers may write an entire script without getting paid, which

WORLD VIEW
WORKING MORE, EARNING
LESS IN HOLLYWOOD

When most people think of television or film actors in Hollywood, they probably think of big salaries, award shows, and stardom. And although this is indeed the case for a lucky few, the majority of Hollywood actors are relatively unknown, even though they may appear daily on our TV screens.

Take Beth Broderick. She's an actor who has appeared in dozens of television shows and made-for-TV movies. Her best-known roles include Aunt Zelda in *Sabrina the Teenage Witch* and more recently Kate's mother on the popular drama *Lost*.

Broderick is an example of what National Public Radio (NPR) has called "Hollywood's Middle Class," and although she feels "blessed" to have a stable career as an actor, it is not as good a living as it used to be. Although she once earned a comfortable living as a guest star, earning between $25,000 and $30,000 for "an hour episode of television," the same role may now garner her only $6,000. Annually, this means a decrease in income from $300,000 or $500,000 to $70,000 a year.

Broderick thinks that this is due to several changing dynamics in the industry, which have led to a decrease in wages for "middle class" actors. For instance, she agrees with NPR that "there is less work because there's more reality and less scripted drama" being produced for television. Moreover, she suggests that "shows like *Cheers* that took a year and a half to catch on would never have made it on the air in today's climate." Lastly, many film actors are making the transition to television, which costs studios "quite a bit." To have a movie star on a television series means that "the people two, three, four, five, six and seven on that call sheet are not making what they would have made five years ago or seven years ago." The Writer's Guild strike of 2007 was also a significant factor in these diminishing roles and wages for actors used to making a living as guest stars.

Broderick points the finger at producers, directors, and headliners, suggesting that if they took $19 million, instead of a $20 million paycheck, they could "divvy the rest up between the next 10 people on the call sheet."

What this has come down to for actors like Broderick is that, as she says, "I'm on TV every day in every country in the world, and I don't make any money."

What do you think about Broderick's proposal? Should major Hollywood stars be paid so much in the first place? How do we put a price on celebrity status?

Source: "For Hollywood's Middle Class, 'Cut' Has New Meaning," National Public Radio (NPR), transcript, July 20, 2009.

---

is called writing a script **on spec**. The writer's agent will pass around a spec script to various production firms in the hope that they will bid for it. Attractive scripts can fetch hundreds of thousands of dollars or more.

The second traditional source for film ideas—books—became especially popular in the late 1990s. Producers had long looked for successful books with stories that fit the types and budgets of films that they expected to make; now they were furiously trying to beat one another to new books, or even books that had not yet been published, with stories that seemed to suggest a cinematic gold mine. *The Horse Whisperer* was an early example of the stampede. In 1994, while the book was still in manuscript, the writer's agent orchestrated an auction of film rights that netted the author $3 million. The amounts involved can go much higher than that. According to the trade magazine *Variety*, producer Dino de Laurentiis plunked down $10 million in 1999 for film rights to Thomas Harris's sequel to the successful book and movie *Silence of the Lambs* before the sequel hit the bookstores. It was a shrewd move. The movie that resulted from that investment, *Hannibal*, was a major hit of 2001. Books are still a healthy source of movie ideas. Think of the hit *Twilight* vampire series, which started as books; it's handled by an independent distributor, Summit Entertainment.

When top production executives approve the making of a movie, they give it the **green light**. A project will have the chance of being given a green light only if it fits a movie production firm's ideas about what will succeed in the marketplace.

on spec writing a script for a film without a contract to do so, with the hope that when the script is passed along to various production firms by the scriptwriter's agent it will be bid for and purchased

green light a term used to describe production and distribution executives' approval of the making of a particular film

Production company heads have ideas about segments of the market that are useful to target with particular types of films. Teens and young adults, for example, are thought to like horror films (*Halloween*). Women are thought to like romantic comedies (*He's Just Not That Into You*), while men are typed as adventure movie (*Transformers*) or gross-out comedy (*The Hangover*) oriented. People over forty-five years old are the targets of small films (sometimes British made) that have a subtle comedic or deeply dramatic sensibility. Think of *It's Complicated* or *Bright Star*. Of course, many women and men attend the movies together, so executives often try to leaven movies targeted to one type of audience with some material that another type would like. An adventure film will often have a strong romantic component, for example.

The rising importance of the non-U.S. market to Hollywood has meant that, when executives green light a film, they think about its potential around the world. Historically, most U.S.-made comedies do not "travel" well, so a budget for a comedy will typically have to be low enough to be profitable from U.S. revenues alone. Adventures do travel well, and some action stars—Jackie Chan and Sylvester Stallone are examples—do better outside than inside the United States. As a result, action movies tend to emphasize violence and hair-raising stunts and usually require little knowledge of English to understand. Some of these films have been made in the United States, many elsewhere. Others have been coproductions that blend the investment and production talents of a U.S.-based firm with those of a firm of another country, for example France and India.

Increasingly, U.S. firms are making movies for other parts of the world, with the notion that they may make money even if they don't do well in the United States. Universal Pictures was deeply involved in funding and distributing the latest installment of the British Mr. Bean comedy in 2007 (*Mr. Bean's Holiday*); the films traditionally do terrifically in the United Kingdom and very well in parts of Europe, but are weak in the United States.

GETTING THE TALENT   When a production firm purchases a script or book, its executives typically have certain actors and directors in mind. Sometimes a major actor may get control of a property with the idea of starring in a film based on it. The actor's agent may even go further in dealing with production firms that are interested in the project: the agent may take a number of people from his or her roster of clients—actors, a well-known director, a highly regarded cinematographer—and tell production firms that the deal comes in a package. To many observers of the film industry, the fact that a number of talent agencies have the power to organize such major film deals with production firms is evidence that talent agencies are among Hollywood's most powerful players.

The money to pay actors and other creative personnel must, of course, come from the overall budget. The salary requirements of the most popular stars (some make more than $20 million a picture) mean that only the major studios and a few other production companies that expect to make extremely expensive movies can afford to hire these stars. Sometimes a production firm will make a deal with a famous actor or director in which the actor or director takes a lower salary but gets a percentage of the money that the production firm receives from the distributor, known as a **back-end deal** or **percentage of the gross**. Stars often negotiate variations on such deals to help themselves and help movies get made. For the Warner Brothers' comedy *Yes Man*, for example, Jim Carrey gave up his upfront salary (usually $22 million) to become a one-third investor in the film. He also agreed to start receiving a back-end percentage until the studio recouped the $53 million Warner said the film cost. The deal paid off handsomely. *Yes Man* was expected to gross $200 million worldwide. Carrey stood to earn far more than his regular salary.[3]

back-end deal or percentage of the gross a deal in which a production firm convinces a major actor or director to take a lower salary in return for a percentage of the money that the production firm will later receive from the distributor

In November 2007, the Writers Guild of America, which represents more than 10,000 film and television writers, went on strike over a variety of issues in their negotiations with the Alliance of Motion Picture and Television Producers. Members of the Screen Actors Guild (SAG) supported the writers on the picket lines, including SAG president Alan Rosenberg, shown here (right) with Writers Guild of America president Patric Verrone.

Some industry insiders have suggested that the high salaries stars are demanding are leading producers to hold off on hiring established, experienced actors in secondary roles in favor of more-affordable relative newcomers. Rules about actors' minimum pay and working conditions have been established through deals between the Screen Actors Guild and the major production firms. Similar arrangements for screenwriters have been made by the Writer's Guild of America. These **guilds** are unions established by writers, directors, and/or actors to protect their mutual interests and maintain standards.

guild a union established by writers, directors, and/or actors to protect their mutual interests and maintain standards

The guilds provide the less highly paid workers with a collective voice. Sometimes that results in a strike, as in 2007 and 2008, when writers expressed their frustration when the major studios and the Writers Guild of America could not come to terms with the Alliance of Motion Picture and Television Producers about how much pay the writers should receive from the major studios for work that appears on the internet. The strike of over 10,000 Writers Guild members crippled Hollywood. It ended production on TV dramas and comedies, caused the Golden Globe Awards to be canceled, and delayed a number of movie productions.

GETTING THE MONEY   Getting a well-known actor to agree to play the lead in a movie can help a production firm get the cash it needs to make the film. Getting the money is what makes generating a motion picture so painful. The amount it costs to make a movie varies over a wide range, from way over $100 million dollars (*Avatar, Spider Man, Pirates of the Caribbean*) to between $50 and $100 million (*The Simpsons Movie* reportedly cost about $75 million) to less than $50 million (*Knocked Up* cost $40 million to produce). The word in Hollywood is that it is the most expensive movies that tend to become mega-hits. Still, a moderately inexpensive film can also reap great benefits for its production firm. *Once*, a 2007 musical romance from Ireland, cost about $150,000 to make. In the United States alone it brought in $7 million in box office returns.[4]

A film's budget isn't typically created based on the producer's calculations of what is necessary to tell the story. Instead, a story is often chosen and developed to fit the

genre film a movie that fits a classic storytelling formula (science fiction, horror, action) and is typically made relatively inexpensively

box office receipts the sum of money taken in for admission at movie theaters around the country

track record the previous successes or failures of a product, person, or organization

distribution rights the rights to circulate a particular movie to companies in different parts of the world (different territories)

budget that executives of a production firm can manage. Consequently, a production firm's heads decide what kinds of monetary risks they want to take (or can take). They then go about choosing a story, or tailoring it, to fit the budget they have. Take as an example Dimension Films, the company that produced the hit movies *Halloween* (2007) and *Halloween II* (2009). Dimension Films is a division of The Weinstein Company, an independent production and distribution firm. Dimension makes **genre films**—movies that fit classic storytelling formulas (science fiction, horror, action) and are typically relatively inexpensive to make. Movie industry executives believe that successful genre films can be made with relatively low budgets. If a movie soars beyond its niche, as *Halloween* did (and the *Saw* series before that), its success makes up for films that brought the production firm little return.

When millions and millions of dollars are hanging in the balance, giving a film the green light is not easy. Not only must executives believe in the script, the director, and the stars, they also must have the money to make the film and a company to distribute it. If the production firm is part of a major studio, the chief executive officer of the studio typically discusses the proposed film with the production and distribution chiefs. Once the film and its budget are approved, the studio as a whole (encompassing both the production and distribution divisions) provides the money. It is the distribution division, however, that works to make the money back, and more, through a percentage of the **box office receipts**.

Independent firms have a harder time getting the money to make a film. If the independent firm has had previous successes, it may be fortunate enough to have a multi-picture distribution deal with a major that includes some financing. However, the independent may still have to use its own funds, or funds borrowed from banks, to make up the rest of the film's budget. The banks, of course, are hoping that the movie will make back its costs for the production firm so that they can retrieve their money with interest.

The most consistently successful independent production outfits are so tightly linked to particular distributors that they are virtually extensions of the distribution firm's own studio output. When it was independent, the Pixar animation firm had a distribution deal with Disney. Pixar films became so important to Disney's slate that eventually Disney decided to buy the company. More recently, Morgan Creek Productions has a steady output deal with Universal.

Production companies that don't have long-term deals with distributors have to work a lot harder to find cash and a distributor. Sometimes wealthy investors will put up the money in the hope that they will get lucky and the film will be a hit. (Often these rich people also want to be close to the glamour of Hollywood.) Sometimes an independent production firm with a record of successes (a **track record**) will be able to convince a major bank to provide a revolving credit agreement for several pictures. When a production firm is seeking a loan for part of a film's budget, the loan will be easier to get if the production firm can show that an established star has been signed for the film, and that an established distribution firm has agreed to take it on and to advance it money.

A popular way for independent producers to get the money for film projects is to sell **distribution rights**: the rights to circulate a particular movie to companies in different parts of the world (different territories). For example, a production firm's executives might get $2 million from an Asian firm that wants the rights to distribute the film to theaters (and perhaps home video rights) in Southeast Asia. Another distributor may bid $2 million for distribution rights in Australia and New Zealand. A third distributor might buy North American theatrical and home video rights. By accumulating these territory deals, often before the film is fully made, the production firm can show banks that a substantial portion of the film's budget is already in hand. Go to http://www.imdb.com/title/tt1125849/companycredits and check out the many regional distributors involved in circulating (and financing) *The Wrestler*, a 2008 release produced by Wild Bunch, Protozoa Pictures, and Saturn Films. The film turned out to be a hit in many territories. That kind of financing is, however, a difficult puzzle to put together, and in the late 2000s the economic downturn and the popularity of local films in different regions of the world made it quite difficult for independent production firms to gather substantial parts of their budgets from international presales.[5]

GETTING TO THE ACTUAL MAKING OF THE MOVIE   As you can see, a lot of work has to be done on a movie project before the actual moviemaking even begins. The moviemaking process involves a large number of people with widely different talents. To get an idea of how many, first take a look at Figure 12.4. Then watch all the credits at the end of the next movie you attend. (Tell the people with you that it's a class assignment.) Alternately, look up any

U.S. actor Mickey Rourke attended the Moscow premiere of his movie *The Wrestler* in March 2009. Central Partnership distributed the movie in Russia.

movie on a site such as the Internet Movie Database (http://www.imdb.com) and look at the cast and crew listings. Pay particular attention to the different jobs that are involved. Experienced personnel scout locations for certain scenes in the movie and try to minimize problems that might occur while filming there; casting directors help the director choose many of the actors; set designers, costume designers, makeup experts, and computer graphics personnel help create the physical shape of the space in which the actors work; stand-ins and stunt people help actors with boring or dangerous parts of the work; the cinematographer and the film crew create the look of the film as it will appear on screen; recording engineers make sure the sounds of the movie are appropriate (much of the dialogue will have to be re-recorded in a studio for clarity); a wide variety of personnel handle the equipment, the sound stage work, the salaries, the food, and all the other duties connected with a large project; and the editor decides (usually with the director) which versions ("shots") of different scenes should end up in the final version of the film.

Because of the large number of resources involved, every extra day of filming can be an enormous drain on the production firm's budget. Keeping the production on schedule is the role of the director, who controls the pace of filming, along with a **line producer**, who makes sure the equipment and personnel are there when they are needed. Some lenders, worried about spiraling costs, require production firms to hire **completion bond companies**. These are insurance companies that, for a large fee, will pay any costs of a film that exceed an agreed-upon amount. When a completion bond company signs on to a movie, especially one that is in danger of going over budget, it often sends its own executives to the sites where filming is

line producer the individual responsible for making sure that the equipment and personnel necessary for a film's production are available when they are needed

completion bond company an insurance company that, for a large fee, will cover the costs of film production that exceed an agreed-upon amount

Understanding film and television credits

The reason film credits can be so long is that film-making draws on the efforts of numerous people over an extended period of time. The process of taking a film or television show from idea to audiences involves several key phases and a wide assortment of skills. Based on a typical live action film, following are a few examples of workers involved in a film. Many of these workers are involved on all or multiple phases of the production.

1. DEVELOPMENT
Coming up with an idea, writing a script and pitching it.

Agents	Business managers	Investors	Personal Assistants	Screenwriters
Assistants to the producers	Consultants	Lawyers	Producers	Studio executives
	Executive producers	Line producers	Publicists	

2. PREPRODUCTION
Developing, planning and visualizing the idea. Preparing a budget, hiring crew members, and making a schedule.

Art department assistants	Choreographers	Costume supervisors	Location assistants	Props masters
Art department coordinators	Concept artists	Costumers	Location managers	Set designers
Art directors	Construction coordinators	Dialogue coaches	Paint foremen	Set decorators
Artists	Construction electricians	Directors	Production assistants	Set dressers
Assistant directors	Construction first aid	Directors' assistants	Production designers	Set staff assistants
Carpenters	Construction foremen	Directors of photography	Production managers	Storyboard artists
Casting directors	Construction grips	Financial executives	Props builders	Stunt coordinators
	Construction workers	Illustrators		Tailors/seamstresses
	Costume designers			Wardrobe

3. PRODUCTION
Shooting scenes, working with cast, locations and reviewing footage.

Accounting clerks	Electricians	Payroll accountants	Property workers	Stills photographers
Actors	Extras	Picture car coordinators	Script supervisors	Stunt performers
Animal handlers	Extras casting coordinators	Picture car drivers	Set strike workers	Swing gang workers
Assistant accountants	First aid workers	Picture editors	Sound editors	Teachers/welfare workers
Assistant directors	Gaffers (lighting)	Production accountants	Sound technicians	Technical advisors
Boom operators	Grips (set operations)	Production coordinators	Special effects coordinators	Transportation coordinators
Camera loaders	Hair stylists	Production sound mixers	Special effects supervisors	Transportation captains
Camera operators	Makeup artists	Property masters	Special effects technicians	
Caterers	Office coordinators		Standby painters	
Cinematographers	On-set dressers			
Drivers				

4. POSTPRODUCTION
Editing the film, adding titles, music and special effects.

Audio recording engineers	Dubbing editors	Film and video editors	Musicians	Special effects technicians
Composers	Editing room assistants	Lab technicians	Projectionists	
			Sound designers	

5. DISTRIBUTION
Taking the finished product and bringing it to theaters, home video, television, online and other venues for audiences to see it.

Accountants	Distribution executives	Licensing executives	Partnership developers	Sales staff
Advertising executives	Financial managers	Marketers	Publicists	

Figure 12.4 Understanding Film and TV Credits

taking place. By contract, those executives have the right to take control of some of the film's activities to keep it on budget.

Theatrical Distribution in the Motion Picture Industry

When you're putting tens of millions of dollars into a movie, you want it to have a chance to reach the intended audience so your firm can make its money back and hopefully turn a profit. As we've seen, helping a movie get that chance is the job of the distribution company. The most powerful companies in the movie business have distribution arms that have the reputation of being able to place films in theaters in the United States and around the world. Their power to move films is enormous. The major distribution firms have offices around the world, and the mandate for their personnel is twofold: to get the films they distribute into theaters, and to market these films effectively to target audiences.

Finding Movies to Distribute

The first order of business for a distributor is to get movies to distribute. You might suspect that the major distributors would have it easy, as they are linked to studios that create their own films. Certainly, they have a simpler time of it than the independent distributors. Executives in those firms have to scour the world for the rights to films that will attract the audiences they know how to reach. But even the majors cannot afford to circulate only films that their studios make. They distribute several films from their own studio and get the rest from other places.

In recent years, the majors have collaborated on the cost and distribution of particularly expensive films to lower their risk of losing enormous amounts of money if those films fail. For example, Warner Brothers and Sony helped to fund the 2009 movie *Terminator: Salvation*, which cost $200 million plus marketing charges. The deal was that Warner would distribute the movie in the United States, while Sony would have international distribution rights.[6] Because the firms expected the film would earn more outside the United States, Sony put more money into the deal than Warner did.

Releasing Movies

Once a distributor has set its slate of motion pictures and these pictures are completed (or nearing completion), the challenge is to choose a release date and a release pattern. The **release date** is the day on which the film will open in theaters. In setting a film's release date and release pattern, executives take into consideration the kind of film it is, how popular its actors are, its target audience, and the other films in their slate. They also try to figure out when their competitors' movies will be released.

Typically, executives schedule the release of potential blockbusters in the United States during the summer or between Thanksgiving and Christmas. These are periods when students are off from school and when many adults spend extra time with their families. Because different societies may have different moviegoing habits, a film's release date may be different around the world. In recent years, though, movie distributors have tended to release blockbuster films at the same time in many different countries—a practice known as a **day-and-date release**. The reasons have to do

release date the day on which the film will open in theaters

day-and-date release a simultaneous release date for a movie in different countries

425

Fueled by an aggressive marketing campaign and buzz over Heath Ledger's last performance as the Joker, *The Dark Knight* grossed over $1 billion worldwide and is the second-highest grossing film in North America after *Titanic* with $533 million.

wide release opening a film in more than 2,000 theaters simultaneously, usually accompanied by a large publicity campaign to incite people to see the film; the most common release pattern in the United States

saturation release the initial release of a film in more than 2,000 theaters simultaneously

platform release the initial release of a film in a small number of theaters in a relatively small number of areas; executives use this approach when they believe a film has the potential for wide appeal but needs time for newspaper reviews and other media discussions of the film to emerge and encourage the film's target audience to go see it

exclusive releases the release of a film to only a handful of carefully selected theaters and target audiences throughout the country

with concerns with piracy, along with the technological ability to promote a movie efficiently across the world at the same time.

RELEASE PATTERNS   In addition to the release date, distribution executives must agree on the release pattern in which the movie will be released to theaters around the country. Three release patterns are common in the United States:

- A **wide release**, the most common pattern, typically involves opening a film in more than 2,000 theaters simultaneously. (At the higher end, wide releases are sometimes called **saturation releases**.) Putting a film in thousands of theaters beginning the same weekend is increasingly common as distributors hype potential blockbusters around the country (and the world) at the same time. In 2009, Disney's *A Christmas Carol*, Michael Jackson's *This is It*, *Couples' Retreat*, and *Saw VI* all opened with far more than 3,000 engagements.
- A **platform release** involves the initial release of the movie in far fewer theaters in a relatively small number of areas. Executives are likely to choose this approach for films that they feel have potentially wide appeal, but that need time for media reviews and other discussions of the film to emerge and ignite interest among the target audience. They hope to increase the number of theaters as the movie's popularity builds and thus encourage the snowballing of attendance.
- **Exclusive releases** are not set up with the intention of "going wide." These films go to only a handful of carefully selected theaters around the country. Films with this distribution pattern are typically specialty films, often foreign, that their distributors believe will do well with very specific audiences in particular places around the country.

Of course, the number of movie theaters available to show a film is also an important consideration in determining release dates and release patterns. Theater-chain executives have their own ideas about what pictures they want in what locations, and they negotiate with the distributors regarding what pictures they will take and for how long. By law, movie distributors are not allowed to force exhibitors to book blocks of their films—a practice known as block booking. Paramount, for example, is prohibited from telling the Regal theater chain that it can have a particular film only if it takes three other motion pictures. Over the decades, though, the major distributors and the major theater chains have developed ways to accommodate each other's needs.

Marketing Movies

One reason that theater chains like dealing with the major distributors is that the majors have sophisticated marketing operations. To help reduce the risk of failure, distributors often conduct two types of research before a film is released. **Title testing** involves conducting interviews with filmgoers in shopping malls and other public places to determine the most alluring name for an upcoming picture. **Previewing** is a type of concept testing that takes place after a film is completed but before it is formally released. Theatergoers see a preliminary (**rough cut**) version of a movie and answer survey questions about what they like or don't like about it. The reactions may be used to re-edit parts of the film. The original sad ending of *Fatal Attraction*, for example, was changed to make it happier after it received negative audience reactions during previews.

title testing conducting interviews with filmgoers in order to determine which of a number of titles (or names) for an upcoming film will draw people in the target audience to the theater to see the film

previewing a type of concept testing to evaluate newly completed films in order to determine what members of the film's target audience like and/or dislike about the film

rough cut a preliminary version of a film, shown before its final editing process and formal release

CULTURE TODAY
LIONSGATE AND KICK-ASS

For the April 2010 superhero movie *Kick-Ass*, film distributor Lionsgate launched an innovative marketing campaign across YouTube, Facebook, MySpace, and Twitter. On each site, consumers had access to the same brand content, including official Lionsgate updates, Facebook activity, YouTube comments, and Twitter streams. They were also able to upload and share content accessible through each site.

The campaign was in part an effort to capitalize on the so-called "Twitter Effect," the notion that Twitter buzz can help or hinder the box office performance of a newly released film. After the films *Julie & Julia* and *District 9* appeared to benefit from positive Twitter buzz—and *Brüno* to suffer from negative buzz—movie marketers have been hunting for a way to harness the potential powers of the social media platform to their advantage.

In a typical social media campaign, a brand sponsors pages on various sites, but the marketing for each site remains independent of one another. Lionsgate claimed to create the first campaign to sync up sponsored brand pages across different social media sites through a single platform (called Distributed Engagement Channel, DEC). This way, brand marketing and engagement is not partitioned off into unconnected sites. "For example, a user can sign in with their Facebook account on YouTube, pull from their existing Facebook photo albums to create a submission (in this case, their best "Kick-Ass" move), and then once it's posted, a MySpace user can view and comment on it because the channel is connected across these three sites," noted Ankarino Lara from ThisMoment, the company that sold Lionsgate the DEC platform. "At a basic level, you can think of DEC as a system that creates one connected community around a brand."

By allowing the campaign to be rooted to the brand itself instead of to different sites, Lionsgate's *Kick-Ass* campaign aimed to make it easy for movie fans to share material about the movie across social media. "The web overall is a social place, but I don't think fans and users see it in a siloed way," said Lionsgate's VP of new media and marketing, Danielle DePalma. "It's important to have all the buzz and great fan reaction in one place."

Sources: Andrew Hampp, "Forget Ebert: How Twitter Makes or Breaks Movie Marketing Today," *Advertising Age*, October 5, 2009. http://adage.com/madisonandvine/article?article_id=139444 (accessed August 4, 2010); Andrew Hampp, "How Lionsgate Plans to Take on 'Twitter Effect' for 'Kick-Ass'," *Advertising Age*, March 1, 2010. http://adage.com/madisonandvine/article?article_id=142350 (accessed August 4, 2010).

P&A or prints and advertising the expenses that distributors incur in making prints of their films for theaters and marketing the films to the public

publicity the process of creating and maintaining a favorable "buzz" about the film among its target audience

word of mouth the discussions that people who see the movie have about it with their friends

tracking studies research on the public's awareness of and interest in a film, beginning two weeks before the film's release and continuing through the film's first month of release

PRINTS AND ADVERTISING   The expenses that distributors incur in getting their films to theaters and marketing them to the public are part of what the movie industry calls **P&A**, or **prints and advertising**. The "prints" part means the cost of reproducing the original film negatives to circulate to theaters around the country and around the world. The "advertising" part means the money the distributor spends to publicize and advertise the film.

You're undoubtedly familiar with **publicity** and advertising for movies—from lavish parties for a film's cast on the day of the movie's premiere with the press in attendance, interviews with the film's actors on TV programs such as *The Late Show with David Letterman* and *Entertainment Tonight,* putting previews of the film on You-Tube and MySpace, posting comments about it on Twitter, and giving out free preview tickets to college students before a film formally opens. The aim of publicity is to get a favorable "buzz" going about the movie among its target audiences. The aim of advertising is to turn that buzz into actual moviegoing by telling people that the movie is playing near them and urging them to see it.

The flurry of publicity and advertising for a film is intense and short (a few weeks at most), and it takes place before and around the time the movie is released to the theaters. Although marketing can prepare moviegoers for a movie, after the first weekend of its release it is **word of mouth**—the discussions that people who see the movie have with their friends—that determines whether more people will go to see it. The life of a film in theaters is no more than a few months. The greatest proportion of the money received from a film comes in during the first few weeks; in fact, executives believe that they can predict the total amount of money a movie will make by looking at how it does during that short period of time.

TRACKING   Distribution executives often order **tracking studies**—research on the public's awareness of and interest in a film—beginning two weeks before the film's release and continuing through the film's first month of release. Three times during each of those weeks, a company called National Research Group surveys a random sample of Americans by phone. National's operators read a list of current or soon-to-be-released films to people who say they have recently seen theatrical movies. For every film on the list, the people are asked if they are aware of it and if they want to see it. The film's marketers may use the results, which are broken down by age

CULTURE TODAY
WHEN FANS "DEMAND IT"

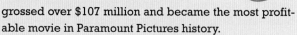

The low budget film *Paranormal Activity* was a horror thriller that had spent years in semi-obscurity except to a certain form of cult film enthusiasts. Recently, marketing executives at Paramount decided to use social media to promote the film through an online "Demand It" campaign. The messages encouraged users to demand that the movie be shown in their hometown. Paramount promised that if the film got 1 million demands, it would screen the movie in every town where a person had demanded it. It took less than a week for *Paranormal Activity* to reach 1 million demands. The result of the "Demand It" campaign was a nationwide rollout of what was once an underground cult film. The film, which never used a trailer or television ad and cost next to nothing to make,

grossed over $107 million and became the most profitable movie in Paramount Pictures history.

Paranormal Activity had already achieved cult status when Paramount picked it up. Do you think that the "Demand It" approach could be used to promote a new movie or is it a technique that should be reserved for movies with some credibility with fans already?

Sources: Andrew Hampp, "'Paranormal Activity' Wins by Listening to Fans' 'Demands': Most-Profitable Film in Paramount's History Uses Eventful, Twitter to Stoke Web Buzz," *Advertising Age*, October 12, 2009. http://adage.com/madisonandvine/article?article_id=139588 (accessed August 23, 2010).

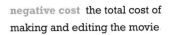

and gender categories, to determine whether revisions in their publicity, advertising, or even release plans are needed.

All this activity requires a lot of money. On major domestic releases in the early twenty-first century, P&A costs amounted to around half of the film's **negative cost**—the total cost of making and editing the movie. According to *Variety*, the negative cost of *3:10 to Yuma* came to roughly $60 million, to which distributor Lionsgate added $27.5 million for prints and advertising.[7] In rare instances, marketing a film costs even more than putting it together. *Scream*, a 1996 Miramax release that became a box office phenomenon, reportedly had a negative cost of about $15 million and more than $20 million of marketing expenses to send it into wide release. In this case, it payed off. Three weeks after its debut, the trade magazine *Variety* was predicting that the movie would bring in $70–80 million in theatrical receipts.

But not all the money made at the box office comes back to the distributor. Let's look at the exhibitor's side of the story.

negative cost the total cost of making and editing the movie

Theatrical Exhibition in the Motion Picture Industry

Just as about ten major distributors control over 90 percent of U.S. theatrical activity, so the largest 3 percent of movie chains control 60 percent of the screens on which the films are shown. Recall that in 1948 the federal government and the major studios signed a settlement that prohibited the major film distributors (several of which are still majors today) from owning theaters. As a result, from the 1950s onward, large chains developed that were outside the ownership orbits of Hollywood moviemakers. The chains with the largest numbers of screens are Regal, AMC, Cinemark, Carmike, Cineplex Entertainment, Keresotes, and National Amusements.

The Relationship Between Distributors and Theater Chains

Negotiations over what movies to choose and how much to pay have long been part of the relationship between exhibitors and distributors. Just as distributors have to set up a slate of films to show to the public, exhibitors must have pictures that will fill the seats of their theaters. Executives who book movies want popular films to come out on a schedule that allows the chains to maximize the use of their theaters on a year-round basis. This desire has created tensions with the major distributors, who have traditionally tried to release most of their films during the summer and during the Thanksgiving and Christmas vacation periods. Nevertheless, because distributors and exhibitors need each other, distributors try to adjust some of their release strategies to accommodate theaters' needs, and theaters try to help distributors get screens for hoped-for blockbusters during times of the year when every studio, it seems, wants to have a place in theaters.

The relationship typically works this way. A theater chain often has booking divisions in different areas of the United States, depending on where it concentrates its screens. AMC, for example, has three booking divisions—one handling the Northeast, one the South, and one the West. Each division has a number of bookers. Say you work as a booker for a chain of movie theaters in a particular region of the United States. Movie distributors inform you months in advance of what films they intend to release, and when. That information allows you to begin thinking about the kinds of movies you might have in your theaters at different times of the year. As a particular film's release date gets closer, the distributor sends you publicity material about the film, and you also have the opportunity to see uncompleted versions. These uncompleted versions of films (often without music) are called rough cuts. Based upon this information and what you know about the other movies that are coming out around the same time, you make an estimate of how well you believe the film will do at the box office compared with the others.

TECH & INFRASTRUCTURE
MOVIES STILL START WITH FILM

It is safe to argue that digitization has caused a revolution in moviemaking over the past decade. Entire films can now be shot and edited digitally, reducing costs and making anyone with skill and a good idea a potential moviemaker. For instance, box office hits such as *Star Wars: Episode II* and James Cameron's *Avatar* were shot entirely on digital cameras. But it isn't only big-budget films that embrace digital capturing. David Lynch's much-touted *Inland Empire* is an example of another type of film to take advantage of digital cameras. Moreover, entire film schools are going digital, thereby providing a cheaper alternative to film for students trying to make their final projects.

Digitization has also begun to replace the traditional methods when it comes to post-production. When a movie has finished being shot the negatives need to be treated to enhance and clean up colors. The traditional method is a photochemical process; however, this is quickly being replaced by a device called "digital intermediate," or DI. Although many industry observers are suggesting the medium of "film" is at an end, to be replaced by digital capturing, those who work with DI continue to argue for film's superiority to digital photography. Indeed, as trade magazine *Variety* notes, "DI has proved to be so effective at bringing out the subtleties of film that some feel it's extending the life of film as a capture medium."

Moreover, film continues to be an essential part of many companies that specialize in post-production, such as UK-based Deluxe Laboratories. And although Deluxe has been improving its digital offerings, "film remains a vital business" for the company, according to *Variety*. In fact, in 2003, when involved in post-production

with such films as *The Lord of the Rings: The Return of the King* and *Master and Commander*, "Deluxe saw its total film footage output grow by 3%."

The logic behind this has to do with information: 35mm film contains much more information than a digital image. Moreover, "film has a big advantage over digital in its ability to capture wide extremes, particularly the highlight extremes, which tend to be a downfall for a lot of digital cameras," says Ingrid Goodyear, general manager of Kodak's image capture business. As such, when it comes to color and texture manipulation, many post-production personnel still prefer movies shot on film and then digitally manipulated, rather than the all-digital route. According to *Variety*, most digital intermediate suite projects are rendered in 2K resolution, with the higher end movies done in 4K. But as John Baily, director of photography for such films as *Groundhog Day* and *He's Just Not That Into You*, notes, "a 35mm film negative can contain a resolved image equivalent to up to 8K . . . that's far superior to the best digital capture available today." Those behind the camera, such as Steven Spielberg and M. Night Shyamalan, also continue to espouse the virtues of shooting a movie using film.

The debate between digital and film will no doubt continue to rage on, with purists on both sides vying for supremacy.

Sources: Michael Behar, "Analog Meets Its Match in Red Digital Cinema's Ultrahigh-Res Camera," *Wired Magazine*, August 18, 2008. http://www.wired.com/entertainment/hollywood/magazine/ 16-09/ff_redcamera?currentPage=all (accessed August 23, 2010); David S. Cohen, "The Digital Divide," *Variety*, March 14–20, 2005, Section B, p. 1.

The distributor of the movie, for its part, has an interest in getting the movie into theaters that fit its sense of audience interest in the film. If the film will have a limited or exclusive release, the distributor will want to place it in locations where the target audience for the film lives. Executives may try to place a movie aimed at African-American moviegoers, for example, in areas where many African-Americans live. If distribution executives anticipate that a film will be a blockbuster, they will insist that an exhibitor that wants to carry the film place it in the largest theaters within its multiplexes. In areas where a couple of exhibition chains have competing theaters, the distributor may try to satisfy them all in order to keep its long-term business relationships solid. The distributor may offer the film exclusively to one chain in one area and to another in another part of the neighborhood. Or it may offer one potential hit to one company and another potential hit to the other company.

FINANCIAL AGREEMENTS BETWEEN DISTRIBUTORS AND THEATER CHAINS   Negotiations on the issues that are important to distributors and exhibitors may continue until just a few weeks before a movie's opening. Eventually, distribution and exhibition executives negotiate an **exhibition license** for each theater, specifying the date the distributor will make the picture available to the theater, the number of weeks the theater agrees to play the picture, and when and where competing theaters can show the same film. The exhibition license also sets the financial arrangements between the distributor and the theater chain. These arrangements take into consideration the distributor's huge expenditure on the film, on the one hand, and, on the other, the exhibitor's need to cover its costs and make a profit.

One common approach is for the distributor to take a certain percentage of the ticket revenues from the film, with the exhibitor keeping the rest. Another approach is the **percentage-above-the-nut approach**. It works this way. The executives of the theater chain and the distribution firm come together to agree on what it costs to operate each theater (the electricity, salaries, rent, maintenance, and the like). That break-even point is called the nut. For each picture, the theater chain negotiates what percentage of the amount "above the nut" it will pay to the distributor. Typically, an exhibitor will return around 90 percent of ticket revenues above the nut to the distributor. That percentage may get lower several weeks into the run of a film. "Discount" theaters, which may show movies a few months after they were first released, typically pay a substantially lower percentage above the nut to the distributor.

In the end, distributors typically get back about half the box office receipts. As a general rule, the 50 percent that exhibitors get covers their costs, plus about 10 percent. Although a 10 percent return isn't bad, theaters typically make a lot more money than their cut of the admission take through their concessions—popcorn, soft drinks, candy, and other food. Big theater chains, such as AMC, fully control their concession operations and do not have to share the profits of these operations with other firms. Selling food can be quite a lucrative proposition, particularly in view of the high prices the chains charge. (Remember the last time you bought a soft drink at a movie?) An increasing number of theaters now sell pizza and other noncandy foods.

Digital Theaters

Every year distributors spend huge amounts of money sending films to theaters. This may sound like a very basic activity: placing reels of movie film in a box and shipping them to the theaters that will use them. But although the activity is basic, it is a monetary and logistical nightmare. For every film that goes out in wide release, distributors must make more than 2,000 separate film prints. Every film must be

exhibition license an agreement between a distributor and an exhibition firm that specifies the date on which the distributor will make the film available to the exhibition firm's theaters, the number of weeks the theaters agree to run the film, and when and where competing theaters can show the same film; it also sets the financial arrangements between the distributor and the exhibition firm

percentage-above-the-nut an agreement drawn between a distributor and an exhibition firm in which the executives of the exhibition firm and the distribution firm agree on the costs of operating each theater (the electricity, salaries, rent, maintenance, and the like), a break-even point called the nut; then, film by film, the distributor and the exhibition firm negotiate what percentage of revenues "above the nut" the exhibition firm will pay to the distribution firm

CULTURE TODAY
MARTIN SCORSESE AND FILM PRESERVATION

At the 2010 Golden Globe awards, Martin Scorsese received the Cecil B. DeMille Award for Lifetime Achievement for his outstanding contributions to the entertainment field. Scorsese is the well-known director, screenwriter, producer, and actor. Some of his movies include *Taxi Driver*, *Raging Bull*, *The Color of Money*, *The Last Temptation of Christ*, *Goodfellas*, and *Gangs of New York*. Upon accepting his award, instead of focusing on his numerous directorial accomplishments, Scorsese took a minute to tell the crowd about an initiative that he is proud to be a part of: the Film Foundation.

Founded by ten filmmakers—including Woody Allen, Francis Ford Coppola, Steven Spielberg, and Scorsese—one of the Film Foundation's primary goals is the preservation of historic films. The members of the Foundation's board share "the common belief that a full understanding and respect for the history of film plays a decisive role in the advancement of the art form." Advancements in technology have opened up new opportunities to preserve movies in various conditions.

The method that has historically been used to create movies—the film reel—has not stood the test of time. Currently, 50 percent of American films made before 1950 have disintegrated and 90 percent of those made before 1929 have perished. The Film Foundation currently houses a substantial quantity of film waiting to be preserved.

Films build on their predecessors. Techniques are borrowed, storylines are adapted, and historical cultural references are buried in films awaiting discovery by avid film watchers. When Martin Scorsese founded the Film Foundation his goal was to ensure that this tradition continued. When films are lost, with them go the stories, culture, and traditions of the past. Scorsese's goal has been to ensure that, as much as possible, these memories are not lost for future generations.

Source: The Film Foundation website. http://www.film-foundation.org/who/content.cfm?TopicID=2&contentID=147 (accessed).<date of access??>

http://www.netflix.com, website of online DVD rental service Netflix, which offers more than 90,000 titles to more than 6.7 million subscribers

shipped to a theater and then shipped back to the distributor. Many of the prints can be used again overseas, but the distributor must still pay shipping costs. Moreover, international releases of many films have increasingly been taking place at around the same time as North American releases, in part to take advantage of global marketing activities. That practice means even greater expense for creating prints.

One way to get around this problem is to deliver films to theaters via satellite and then project them onto a screen, thus creating digital theaters. Much of the production of movies is already carried out using digital cameras—and the final product is later transferred to film. Even if film is used during shooting of the movie, the pictures are often transferred to computers for special effects and editing. Companies already make projectors that they claim have both the clarity and resolution to match those of traditional motion picture technology. In fact, more than 600 screens in the United States are already equipped to show digital movies. Distribution executives see a time in the not-too-distant future when much of the toil involved in circulating films will be eliminated. Instead of making prints and paying delivery services, distributors may connect to a satellite delivery service that allows them to circulate one master copy of their product to theaters around the world at virtually the same time. To foil piracy attempts, they envision sending the digital copy in a code that could be deciphered only by particular theaters.

The reason digital projection hasn't spread far and wide has less to do with the technology than with the expense. Each digital projector costs over $10,000 plus substantial installation costs.[8] Multiply that times the 39,000 screens in the United States alone and you can see that the cost of moving to digital exhibition will be enormous. The major movie distributors and the theater chains have been arguing about who will pay for digital projectors and how much. Despite the disagreements, observers within the industry suggest that the parties will eventually compromise and that we will see digital movie distribution as the standard within a decade or two.

A redbox automated DVD rental kiosk in Golden, Colorado. Already facing tough competition from Netflix's mail-order service, Blockbuster is closing a multitude of its stores. Now the brick-and-mortar company is struggling to reposition itself while fending off new competition from redbox, which rents films for $1 per night.

Nontheatrical Distribution and Exhibition in the Motion Picture Industry

Theatrical distribution is the pad that launches a film toward many other exhibition locations. As we have noted in earlier chapters, different types of exhibition points are known as **windows**. The importance of theaters as a movie's first window explains why distributors pay a lot of attention to marketing movies when they are first released to theaters, and why distribution executives must maintain good relationships with their counterparts in the theater business. When it comes to making money off the movies, though, a number of other windows are terribly important. They include video stores and television exhibition of different sorts.

Traditional and Online Video Stores

During the course of a single year, the money that movie distributors receive from the sale of home videocassettes (VHS) and DVDs of their movies exceeds the revenues they receive from theatrical showings. Videocassettes are actually a dying medium

windows the series of exhibition points for audiovisual products through which revenues are generated

CULTURE TODAY
AVATAR AND SMOKE-FREE MOVIES

James Cameron's recent blockbuster mega-hit, *Avatar*, has suffered from no shortage of media attention. The film was the highest-grossing film of all time in North America, raking in more than $2 billion at the box office. *Avatar* also received wide critical acclaim, garnering Academy Award nominations for Best Picture and Best Director, among others.

Not all reaction has been positive, however, as some critics have voiced concern over whether the film had anti-American, anti-capitalist, anti-monotheistic, or anti-military themes. Others have questioned the film's depiction of environmental, racial, and indigenous issues. The element of the film that perhaps generated the most controversy, however, was a seemingly throwaway line in the film, when Sigourney Weaver's Dr. Grace Augustine asks, "Where's my damn cigarette?"

The Smoke-Free Movies campaign condemned the line and the portrayal of Weaver's character as a smoker, stating that the line acted as nearly $50 million in free advertising for the tobacco industry. According to Smoke-Free Movies, the portrayal of Weaver's character as a smoker should warrant the film an R rating by the Motion Picture Association of America, as opposed to the PG-13 it received.

The attack is part of an overall push by Smoke-Free Movies to require almost all movies depicting smoking to garner at least an R rating. Though the MPAA currently takes into account use of tobacco and other drugs in determining a film's ratings—as well as sex, violence, and profanity—tobacco use does not automatically garner a film an R rating. Citing evidence suggesting that smoking among adolescents is greatly influenced by depictions in film, Smoke-Free Movies argues that the use of a drug responsible for the deaths of nearly half a million Americans a year should have more bearing on a film's ratings than the level of profanity, for instance.

Behind the debate lies the question of what role the MPAA should have in American society. In determining what distinguishes a PG-13 film from an R film, the MPAA is determining what adolescents should be shielded from. Although the dangers of smoking are undeniable, is an automatic R rating for movies portraying tobacco use the appropriate mode of recourse? *New York Times* columnist A. O. Scott asks, what's next? "What about guns? What about trans fats? What about beer and Styrofoam and high-fructose corn syrup?" What can be certain is that, as social norms evolve, the MPAA must be ready to evolve with them.

Sources: "'Avatar' Sinks 'Titanic' Record," *Newsday*, February 4, 2010; Michael Cieply, "Ads to Protest Smoking in 'Avatar'," *The New York Times*, January 11, 2010; Michael Cieply, "Oscar Race: More Films, a Few Surprises," *The New York Times*, February 3, 2010; Dave Itzkoff, "'Avatar' Has a Little Something for Everyone with an Axe to Grind," *The International Herald Tribune*, January 21, 2010; A. O. Scott, "This Article Is Not Yet Rated," *The New York Times*, January 24, 2010.

from the standpoint of commercial sales. Consider that in 2003 Americans spent about $4 billion on VHS rentals and $6.2 billion on VHS sales; in 2008 the amounts were $21 million and $45 million, respectively. DVDs are taking the place of VHS, with digital downloads of films beginning to pick up steam. In 2008, Americans spent $8.1 billion on DVD rentals and $15.8 billion on purchases.[9]

Generally, the movies that have done well in theaters are also the ones that do well in video and DVD. There are important exceptions, though. Children's films and some types of horror films may have lackluster theatrical distribution but bring in enough money in video and DVD to justify the production. Revenues from home video come from two sources: sell-through outlets and rental outlets.

sell-through outlets stores in which consumers buy the videos rather than just renting them

Sell-through outlets are stores in which consumers buy the videos rather than just renting them. Some stores such as Blockbuster, Target, and Wal-Mart sell videos in physical locations as well as online. Amazon (http://www.amazon.com) is an example of an online-only video store.

Rental outlets are companies that purchase releases from movie distributors and then rent them to individual customers on a pay-per-day basis. The traditional way to carry this out is to go to a physical ("brick-and-mortar") store such as one in the Blockbuster chain and pay to take out the film for a number of days; bringing it back late means paying for the extra days. In recent years, the rental business has seen the growth of subscription services, in which a person pays to be a member and then gets to take out a certain number of DVDs for any length of time. There are no late fees, but subscribers can only take out more DVDs if they return the ones they've currently checked out. In the model popularized by Netflix, a person signs up online and both receives and returns the DVDs by mail, with Netflix paying the postage. Seeing a competitive threat, Blockbuster went a step further. It allows subscription customers to return the DVDs either by mail or to its stores. An even newer model, threatening both Netflix and Blockbuster, has been pioneered by Rebox. That company has made deals with stores such as 7–Eleven, McDonald's, and Barnes & Noble to place vending machines in or near the stores so that you can rent a DVD directly from the machine using a credit card. If you are looking for a particular film, you can go online to find out which redbox machine in your area (if any) has it, and you can reserve it. After viewing, you can return the DVD to any redbox.

The growth of broadband internet in American homes led some online firms to offer downloadable or streaming movies for rent. (You get to keep movies you download; streaming movies disappear after viewing.) They do it with the permission of the distributors and with digital rights management (DRM) software to prevent wholesale copying. Sites that allow one form or another of downloading include biggies iTunes, Amazon, and Netflix, but also smaller players such as CinemaNow, Vongo, ifilm, Movielink, Movieflix, and AtomFilms. Those who pay for the films can watch them on computers, on TV sets that can be connected to the internet, or even on so-called smartphones such as the iPhone.

Exhibition of Movies on Television

Once a movie leaves the theater, and often even before it lands in home video, it begins an exhibition journey through a number of windows that typically starts a couple of months after the theatrical release with pay-per-view cable and satellite outlets in hotels. The movie might then be released on DVD and also show up on home cable or satellite pay-per-view and "on demand" systems, as well as on transatlantic or transcontinental airline flights. Later, it might appear on a subscription cable channel such as Showtime or HBO. Still later, the movie may run a number of times on a major broadcast or cable network. Eventually, a local television station might pick it up as part of a package of films it licenses for late-night or weekend airing. All this amounts to a lot of money. In fact, the post-theatrical windows can turn a hit film into a bonanza for the production and distribution firms. It can also turn a disappointment at the box office into a break-even or even mildly profitable film.

The Problem of Piracy

Profits in the motion picture industry are continually threatened in the United States and around the world because of **film piracy**—the unauthorized duplication of copyrighted films for profit. The activity is illegal under international copyright laws, but it is rampant around the world. You can see it pretty openly in many U.S. cities: vendors selling videos of films that are still in theaters. Sometimes pirated copies are

rental outlets companies that purchase releases from film distributors and then rent them on a pay-per-day basis to individual customers

film piracy the unauthorized duplication of copyrighted material for profit

produced by having someone take a video camera into a theater and shoot the movie. In more sophisticated cases, pirates smuggle a movie out of the theater, copy it as a video master, and then return the original. These illegal practices made it possible to purchase cheaply many major films on the streets of major cities on the days that the films debut theatrically. Stripping the copy-protection codes off DVDs and uploading movies to the internet means that many people can illegally download hit films for free.

Consider the ethical responsibility of the buyers of these DVDs as well as the behavior of the pirates. The U.S. movie industry estimates that such theft is costing the industry billions of dollars a year—money that it would have received if its companies had sold those DVDs or digital streams. Within the United States, federal and local law enforcement groups have been trying to combat piracy. On a global level, the U.S. government, aware of the importance of the film industry to U.S. exports, has been pressuring the governments of countries in which enforcement of copyright regulations is particularly problematic. In addition, the MPAA, the group that represents the major production and distribution companies, has hired detectives who roam the world trying to identify the pirates.

As for internet piracy, which the MPAA on its website calls "a global avalanche," the organization states that it has a "multi-pronged approach," including educating people about the consequences of piracy, taking legal action against internet thieves, working with law enforcement detecting piracy operations, and helping to advance technologies that will "allow the legal distribution of movies over the internet." Like the recording industry's RIAA (see Chapter 10), the MPAA has sued Americans for copyright infringement in the smallest of towns and the biggest of cities. Penalties can be severe. For example, by federal law a person caught illegally recording movies in theaters can get up to five years in prison and be fined up to $250,000.[10] Unfortunately for the industry, all sorts of piracy continue.

Media Literacy and the Motion Picture Industry

"I need an ensemble film. Take five star vehicles and smush them together."

Despite its expensive and risky nature, moviemaking in many ways lies at the center of American popular culture. Not only are movies shown, they are also discussed. Especially when movie companies first release films, huge waves of publicity blanket the mass media. It often becomes impossible to avoid hearing about certain movies. You'd almost have to be on another planet not to know something about the *Spider Man* and *Harry Potter* flicks. Moreover, movie stars and songs that come from movies are themselves major topics on television, in magazines, in newspapers, around the water cooler, and in the lunchroom.

It may be startling to realize how many of these performances and discussions across so many media in so many parts of the world are sparked by just a handful of corporations, the major movie distributors. Moreover, all the majors are tied to huge mass media conglomerates—Time Warner, Disney, Viacom (which owns Paramount), News Corporation (which owns Fox), Sony (which owns Columbia), and General Electric (which owns Universal). These conglomerates use their Hollywood assets as content for their holdings in different media industries around the world. Materials get packaged, sold, and hyped many times. In that way, even extremely expensive movies have a decent chance of making their money back, and blockbuster hits have a chance of making stratospheric sums.

Cultural Diversity and Cultural Colonialism

Some observers of popular culture look at these activities with dismay. They express two types of concern. One relates to the narrowing of cultural diversity. A second involves what they call cultural colonialism. Let's look at each of these.

THE NARROWING OF CULTURAL DIVERSITY   Critics of the mainstream movie industry argue that movie executives are sending a rather narrow range of stories into American theaters and homes. Many contemporary Hollywood movies, they argue, are made according to simplistic formulas that use sex and violence in ways designed to ignite the interest of the central moviegoing audience easily: 14- to 24-year-olds. Expensive films that can become blockbusters are the name of the game in Hollywood because they have the potential to travel across so many different media and make so much more for the majors than small films ever will. But the major studios will not take artistic risks on such films because the stakes are so high. As a result, films that push the envelope and challenge the audience to see the world differently are few and far between.

Exhibitors also work against cultural diversity, say the critics. By cultural diversity, they mean a reflection of the broad differences that exist in and across societies. Overwhelmingly, they book movies that fit the Hollywood profile. Few theaters in the United States show **art films**—movies created on small budgets that often do not fit into Hollywood stereotypes and standard genres. Even fewer theaters show foreign-language films, even dubbed or with subtitles. The theater chains justify their choices by saying that Americans simply won't go to see these movies in numbers that justify booking them. The critics respond that the movie industry worked for decades to keep such films out of the mainstream in order to protect the standard Hollywood product. It will take time, they say, for Americans to develop the habit of watching non-Hollywood-style films.

The critics add that by not encouraging Americans to see movies made in other countries, the U.S. movie industry is keeping Americans isolated from important aspects of world culture. We live in a time, they say, when business is global, and Americans—especially young people—need to be able to understand the viewpoints of other people. Watching other people's movies can help that understanding enormously. The U.S. movie industry's activities are counterproductive in this regard, they say.

CULTURAL COLONIALISM   Another strong criticism lodged against the movie industry is that it represents a leading edge of American cultural colonialism. As we noted in Chapter 4, cultural colonialism is the process by which the media content of a dominating society (in this case, the United States) surrounds people of another

art films movies created on small budgets that often do not fit into Hollywood stereotypes and standard genres

WORLD VIEW
BOLLYWOOD AND HOLLYWOOD

Indian actor Hrithik Roshan and Uruguayian-born actress and model Barbara Mori, stars of the film *Kites*.

Bollywood, India's Mumbai-based film industry, is the largest producer of films in the world, drawing in over 3 billion audience members a year worldwide. Although a large portion of audiences are Indian, Bollywood popularity reaches to countries as varied as Germany and South Korea. As the last decade drew to a close, Hindi cinema revenues were over $2 billion. Although less than a tenth of Hollywood revenues, Bollywood is growing at four times the rate of Hollywood, and is expected to have doubled in size by the year 2012.

Nonetheless, American audiences have historically been apathetic toward Hindi cinema. The enormous success of Danny Boyle's *Slumdog Millionaire*, however, indicated that things may be changing. Although the movie was produced by a U.K. company, it told the story of a young man from the slums of Mumbai and had several elements of Bollywood films. The film's acclaim and positive buzz left American moviegoers reconsidering

their stance on Bollywood cinema and industry execs intrigued by the possibility of a latent market for Indian films in the United States.

No one sees more potential in Bollywood–Hollywood relations than Indian media tycoon Anil Ambani. Ambani's India-based film company, Reliance Big Pictures, has produced some of India's biggest blockbusters and has become Bollywood's largest production company. Now Ambani's eyes have turned toward Hollywood. After gaining a controlling stake in director Steven Spielberg's DreamWorks studio and striking deals with the likes of George Clooney, Julia Roberts, and Brad Pitt to produce their films, now Ambani aims to take over Hollywood's famed Metro-Goldwyn-Mayer studio.

As boundaries between Bollywood and Hollywood begin to blur, a new genre of crossover cinema is open to emerge. Indian films are being created with American audiences in mind—and vice-versa. *Kites*, a Hindi film about mismatched lovers on the run in New Mexico, has been receiving one of the biggest pushes for crossover success. Re-edited to appeal to Americans, *Kites* is set for a global release in May of 2010. "For me it's about breaking barriers," said the film's Indian star, Hrithik Roshan. "The larger goal, the big dream, is to have an Indian film being watched by a world market."

Sources: Rhys Blakely, "When Holly Met Bolly," *The Times*, July 16, 2009, Business, p. 47; Anupama Chopra, "Bollywood Soars to Hollywood," *The New York Times*, March 7, 2010, Section AR, p. 18; Anand Giridharadas, "Hollywood Starts Making Bollywood Films in India," *The New York Times*, August 8, 2007, Section E, p. 1; Heather Timmons, "Bollywood goes to Hollywood, With Some Tinsel of Its Own," *The New York Times*, June 23, 2008, Section C, p. 1

society with values and beliefs that are not those of their own societies. Rather, the content's values and beliefs reflect and support the interests of the dominating society.

As you can see, this criticism is in some ways a mirror image of the first criticism. The concern over the lack of cultural diversity in movies argues that American society is being harmed. The concern about cultural colonialism, in contrast, argues that

American-based companies are harming other cultures. They are doing this, the argument goes, by drowning out the presentation of local cultural experiences in the media with Hollywood-based formulas.

The critics point out that this cultural colonialism helps American business by creating markets for consumer goods. Moviemaking in the United States is big business. (In fact, filmed entertainment of all sorts, for television and home video as well as the theaters, is one of America's top exports.) At the same time, critics say, it erodes local cultures because they can't compete with U.S. marketing glitz.

One result of the U.S. movie industry's focus on the international market in recent years has been the search by the majors for smaller, more literary movies—so-called art films—that might connect with relatively cultivated audiences around the world. The conglomerates have set up divisions such as Miramax, Fox Searchlight, and Sony Classics to handle these films. You might think that critics and producers in other countries would be happy about this development. The problem is that so far all but a few of the movies that these divisions and others have picked up have been English-language pictures, from either the United States, England, Australia, or New Zealand. Distribution executives point out in frustration that American audiences, still the largest moviegoing audiences, don't like to watch movies that have been dubbed or that have subtitles. As a result, even European film companies have been moving toward making films in English and then subtitling them for non-English-speaking lands. The Americans are colonizing even the art-film world, critics say.

The critics point to the majors' worldwide success as evidence that cultural colonialism is taking place. The international power of the majors, they say, has made U.S. films dominant in the box offices of many countries around the world. True, several of the conglomerates that own the studios are not American. The filmmaking activity, however, is very much based in the United States and presents the U.S. view of the world. Furthermore, they add, the popularity of U.S. movies is merely the tip of a huge iceberg. Under the guidance of powerful multimedia conglomerates, U.S. theatrical product blankets all sorts of print and electronic media. U.S. stars are favorites the world over. And the U.S. way of life that is shown in the movies—with its strong commercialism, lack of environmental sensitivity, and urge toward immediate gratification—becomes an attraction for young people throughout the world.

Not surprisingly, Hollywood's supporters reject this view of their role in global culture. They point out that Hollywood employs many Americans as a result of the movie industry's global reach. They add that many countries support local filmmakers and encourage them to make movies that reflect their own societies. It is not the U.S. movie industry's fault that people like Hollywood films more than those types of movies.

Hollywood's defenders also argue that people around the world like U.S. movies because they are good stories filmed in a high-quality way. They also say that it is patronizing to believe that people in other countries see the movies in the same way that American audiences see them. Rather, they accept or reject what they see in movies from the vantage point of their own cultures. They may even understand the stories differently because they are coming at them with different cultural "eyes."

This is not an argument that will go away. It may, in fact, become louder as media conglomerates increase their use of Hollywood moviemaking in their bids to create global content for the many channels they need to fill. Where do you stand on these issues, and why?

Chapter Review

For an interactive chapter recap and study guide, visit the companion website for *Media Today* at http://www.routledge.com/textbooks/mediatoday4e.

Questions for Discussion and Critical Thinking

1 Compare the ways that the earliest movie firms and the ones started by immigrants tried to keep control over the movie business.
2 Why can it be said that the B movie part of Hollywood migrated to television?
3 In what ways are movie theaters at risk of losing audiences as a result of the growth of video and DVD rentals and sales, pay-per-view and cable showings, video on demand, and other venues? How about through piracy?
4 If the major U.S. movie companies make more money distributing their product outside theaters than in them, why is theatrical distribution so important?
5 Imagine you are a major media executive looking to produce a hit film. What are the basic steps you would have to go through to begin production?

Internet Resources

Motion Picture Association of America (http://mpaa.org/)

According to its website, the MPAA "and its international counterpart, the Motion Picture Association (MPA) serve as the voice and advocate of the American motion picture, home video and television industries, domestically through the MPAA and internationally through the MPA." The site contains much interesting data about the performance of the industry in the United States and abroad. It also presents the association's positions on piracy, film ratings, and U.S. movies internationally.

Internet Movie Database (http://imdb.com/)

Owned (but seemingly not biased) by Time Warner, it is truly (in its own words) "the biggest, best, most award-winning movie and TV site on the planet."

The Greatest Films (http://www.filmsite.org/filmh.html)

Tim Dirks has put together a fascinating and useful website that moves across film history by decade. The site also includes "quotes," "genre," and "reference" sections.

Writers Guild of America, West (http://www.wga.org/), Directors Guild of America (http://www.dga.org), and Screen Actors Guild (http://www.sag.org)

They are the key labor unions for theatrical movies made in the United States. The websites present news about and for their members and insight into critical aspects of the movie business.

Variety (http://www.variety.com/)

This legendary show-business magazine provides deep coverage of the movie industry, including film reviews. Many aspects of the site are open to subscribers only, but visitors can get a flavor of the topics they cover.

Key Terms

· · · · · · · · · · · · · ·

You can find the definitions to these key terms in the marginal glossary throughout this chapter. Test your knowledge of these terms with interactive flash cards on the *Media Today* companion website.

Constructing
Media Literacy
· · · · · · · · · · · · · · · · ·

1 How big an impact do you think the movie industry has on American pop culture?
2 Do you agree that the export of Hollywood movies crowds out or taints foreign cultures? Why or why not?
3 Support or refute the following statement: Hollywood movie companies should take risks in producing a more stylistically diverse set of films, instead of producing films that simply use the formulas audiences want.
4 To what extent do you agree or disagree with the argument that Hollywood is a major instrument of American cultural colonialism?

Companion Website
Video Clips
· · · · · · · · · · · · · ·

Behind the Screens—Limiting Stories
This clip from the Media Education Foundation documentary *Behind the Screens* looks at how the advertising and movie industries are becoming increasingly intertwined. Credit: Media Education Foundation.

Reel Bad Arabs—Myths of Arabland
This clip from the Media Education Foundation documentary *Reel Bad Arabs* examines the negative portrayal of Arab characters throughout cinematic history. Credit: Media Education Foundation.

Fred Ott's Sneeze
This 1894 Thomas Edison film is the first film ever to be copyrighted. Credit: Thomas Edison Company/Internet Archive.

Annie Oakley
This 1894 Thomas Edison film depicts Annie Oakley, "Little Sure Shot," shooting a rifle. Credit: Thomas Edison Company/Internet Archive.

The Kiss
This 1896 Edison film is the first ever moving picture image of a kiss. Credit: Thomas Edison Company/Internet Archive.

Trapeze Disrobing Act
This 1901 Edison film showcases vaudeville trapeze artist Charmion in a suggestive performance considered very risqué in its day. Credit: Thomas Edison Company/ Internet Archive.

Let's Go to the Movies
This 1948 RKO film gives a brief history of movies and explains how they were made. Credit: Internet Archive/Prelinger Archives.

Flip the Frog – Fiddlesticks
This 1930 film is the first full-length sound cartoon in color, created by Ub Iwerks for Metro-Goldwyn-Mayer. Credit: Internet Archive/Ub Iwerks.

Case Study

. . . .

THE EXHIBITION OF INDEPENDENT AND NON-ENGLISH-LANGUAGE FILMS

The idea Critics of movie exhibition in the United States argue that most Americans have no chance to be familiar with films that are off the beaten track. They specifically point to movies distributed by firms not affiliated with the major studios—Fox, Disney, Sony, Universal, Paramount, and Warner Brothers. How true is this criticism in the area in which you live or attend school?

The method Chart the movie theaters within twenty miles of your house. If you can find historical data, track the movies that were exhibited in them over the past three months. If you cannot find such data, track the movies that are exhibited in each theater over the next month. For each film, note the name of the production studio, the distributor, country of origin, language, and (if you can find it) the countries in which the film's story takes place. Write a four-page report describing what you have found.

13 The Television Industry

MEDIA TODAY

"Did you watch television last night?" That used to be a simple question. You either turned on that electronic box in your home and viewed it or you didn't. Today, though, the question can hold different meanings for different people. For some, watching TV will always be associated with viewing the box, so if they downloaded and watched *CSI* on their laptop computer they would say they "didn't watch TV." Others might well say that they viewed "television" even when they saw *CSI* or another program on their computer (or phone!)—or as in-flight entertainment—rather than on their traditional television set.

You probably have your favorite television shows, and you may access them in different ways depending on where you are and what technologies you have. For most of us, television is a relaxing form of cheap, familiar entertainment. You may even feel that there is a comforting predictability about the medium. Your favorite shows always seem to be there, whether in new episodes or in reruns. Yet the business behind the box is anything but predictable these days. The whole idea of what television means is up for grabs as the traditional ways of creating, sponsoring, distributing, and exhibiting programming clash with new approaches and new technologies. This chapter explores the U.S. television industry at a time of enormous change. It presents the basic building blocks for understanding how things are done now, how they are changing, why they may be changing even more in the decades ahead, and how they relate to the trends toward conglomeration and globalization that we have mentioned in previous chapters.

The Rise of Television

To really understand the TV enterprise and the tensions involved in its current transformation, you have to understand how it started. Let's take a look.

Television in its Earliest Forms

Television was commercially introduced in the United States in 1946, right after World War II. Yet the idea of television had been around for some time before that. The word "television" was used as early as 1907 in the magazine *Scientific American*. Even earlier, in 1879, the British humor magazine *Punch* published a picture of a couple watching a remote tennis match via a screen above their fireplace. Three years later, a French artist drew a family of the future watching a war on a home screen. Pretty prophetic, huh?

television broadcasting the transmission of visual images, generally with accompanying sound, in the form of electromagnetic waves that when received can be reconverted into visual images

Although the idea of television was in the air, the reality of **television broadcasting**—scanning a visual image and transmitting it electrically, generally with accompanying sound, in the form of electromagnetic waves that when received could be reconverted into visual images—was harder to accomplish. Laboratory work started in Germany during the 1880s and continued in the United States, Scotland, Russia, and other countries throughout the next several decades.

Between 1935 and 1938, the Nazi government in Germany operated the world's first regular television service, sending propaganda broadcasts to specially equipped theaters. Engineers did not consider the technology used for these performances very acceptable, however. The whirring mechanical disk that was used to scan the broadcast images had too many drawbacks. During the 1930s, an RCA team brought together inventions that allowed electronic rather than mechanical scanning. RCA introduced the system at the 1939 World's Fair in New York; in introducing the new medium during formal ceremonies, President Franklin D. Roosevelt became the first U.S. president to appear on TV. Regular broadcasts began and TV sets went on sale, but television did not take off. World War II intervened, and resources were diverted to defense production.

very high frequency (VHF) a band of radio frequencies falling between 30 and 300 MHz; VHF signals are widely employed for television and radio transmissions. In the United States and Canada, television stations that broadcast on channels 2 through 13 use VHF frequencies, as do FM radio stations. Many amateur radio operators also transmit on frequencies within the VHF band

It was after the end of World War II—in 1946—that commercial television came into being in the United States. From the start, commercial television was tied to the companies that controlled radio—including NBC (owned by RCA), CBS, and ABC. Recognizing a direct threat to the radio business, executives from those firms poured their profits into developing television stations and networks. But between 1948 and 1952, the Federal Communications Commission (FCC) declared a freeze on new station licenses and new television manufacturing in order to review its standards for television. It decided to use the desirable **very high frequency (VHF)** band of frequencies—those between 30 and 300 MHz—for channels 2 through 13, and an **ultra high frequency (UHF)** band of frequencies—those between 300 and 3,000 MHz—for channels 14 through 83. All the best channels and network affiliates were on the VHF band; in fact, most televisions didn't even have a UHF dial during the first two decades of television.

ultra high frequency (UHF) a band of radio frequencies from 300 to 3,000 MHz; UHF signals are used extensively in television broadcasting, typically carrying television signals on channels 14 through 83

Television Gains Widespread Acceptance in the 1950s

When the freeze on new licenses ended, it was as if a national dam had broken. People poured into stores to buy televisions. People who couldn't afford them, or who wanted to wait until the televisions improved, stood outside TV stores during the day

watching the screens and went to bars in the evening to do the same thing. By 1955, almost two-thirds of all U.S. households—64.5 percent—owned TVs. By 1961, that number had grown to 88.8 percent. Today, 99 percent of all U.S. households—a total of about 115 million households—report owning at least one TV set.

Recall from our discussion in Chapter 12 that the rise of television hurt movie theaters, as Americans stayed home to watch the tube. As TV clearly gained a permanent hold on the population's interest in the early 1950s, movie studio executives refused to deal with broadcasting executives. As a result, most network television in its first commercial decade was broadcast from New York, not Hollywood, and it was **broadcast live**—that is, it was broadcast as it was actually being performed, rather than being taped, filmed, or recorded. Variety shows with vaudeville and radio stars, as well as dramas from aspiring theatrical ("Broadway") writers and actors, gave television an accessible, real-world feel that was missing from many Hollywood films. The 1950s, which historians have nicknamed the **golden age of television**, included powerful, original dramas such as *Marty*, *Judgment at Nuremberg*, and *Requiem for a Heavyweight*, and the standard-setting comedy performers that appeared, including Milton Berle, Sid Caesar, Imogene Coca, and Ernie Kovacs.

It was an age that ended quickly. The grittiness of TV's live dramas made some major advertisers nervous. Hollywood's version, a world that was more upscale and populated with beautiful people, seemed to fit better with the advertisers' commercials for automobiles and other symbols of the good life. And Hollywood was finally getting interested in television. Even in the early 1950s, West Coast film producers and actors outside Hollywood's studio system had begun to sell new-filmed series to television. The most important of these were Desi Arnaz and Lucille Ball, whose *I Love Lucy* was an enormous hit with audiences on CBS television. Movie and network executives were quick to recognize the advantages of having a hit on film—as opposed to broadcast live. Unlike the live performances of Berle or Caesar, an *I Love Lucy* episode could be aired over and over again, or **syndicated**. These "repeats" could even be leased to local television stations on a market-by-market basis, to be aired when the network was not operating.

broadcast live broadcast while actually being performed; not taped, filmed, or recorded

golden age of television the period of time from approximately 1949 to 1960, marked by the proliferation of original and classic dramas produced for live television

syndication the licensing of mass media material to outlets on a market-by-market basis

I Love Lucy was first broadcast in 1951 on CBS, and soon became a show so beloved (thanks to syndication) it actually runs more frequently today than it ran in the 1950s! *I Love Lucy* ran for six years of original episodes (180 in all) and stopped production in 1957, despite the fact that it was still the number one show on American television. But good planning kept *I Love Lucy* fresh for decades after the show's original run, as from the start Lucille Ball and Desi Arnaz insisted on filming the shows in front of a live studio audience. Three separate cameras were used, allowing the show to be edited into its final form. Not only did this become the later standard for all sitcoms, it also ensured that high-quality prints of *I Love Lucy* would be preserved for syndication for years to come.

television program ratings audits of people's viewing behaviors that gauge which shows households are viewing and how many are viewing them; they help network executives decide which shows should stay, which should be dropped from the line-up, and how much advertisers should pay to hawk their products during breaks in the program

Recognizing the huge potential of such activities, the studios began to deal with television on a regular basis. Warner Brothers was the first major studio to do so, with a production deal in 1954 to supply ABC with three westerns—*Cheyenne*, *Sugarfoot*, and *Maverick*. The floodgates were open, and within a few years live television was rare. The medium had gone Hollywood.

Television in the 1960s

Meanwhile, the broadcast television industry was rapidly moving ahead. Advertisers were rushing toward the new medium as it became clear that TV was the most efficient way to reach a high percentage of the U.S. population. By the early 1960s, the approach to selling advertising time on TV had changed. Instead of advertisers buying the time and producing the show themselves (as they had done in network radio and early television), network executives began to plan the schedule and order the shows. This allowed advertisers to buy time on various programs, thereby reaching people at different times and on different networks. The AC Nielsen company supplied **television program ratings**, or audits of people's viewing behavior. Nielsen's ratings gauged which shows households were viewing and how many households were viewing them. TV network executives could use the ratings to decide which shows should stay, which should be dropped from the line-up, and how much advertisers should pay to sell their products during breaks in the programs.

Television executives soon found themselves in the midst of political and social problems raised by their new medium. In the early 1960s, public anger over rigged quiz shows, over the large amount of violence on the home tube, and over what many influential individuals in society considered idiotic entertainment ("a vast wasteland," the FCC's head called it) led to congressional hearings. After the urban riots of the mid- and late 1960s, many politicians, educators, and others blamed television for the nation's violence. TV executives, taking a cue from their movie-industry predecessors, made the appropriate apologies, toned down the violence for a few years, and adjusted their self-regulatory mechanisms. Generally, though, they continued to air Hollywood-produced programs (and made-for-TV movies, a new form of entertainment in the 1960s) that they believed would appeal to the largest number of people in order to grab the highest ratings.

THE ADVENT OF FIN-SYN AND PRIME TIME ACCESS RULES   In fact, during the 1960s, the commercial success of ABC, NBC, and CBS and their affiliates was so great that production firms in the industry began to complain that the networks had too much power. Some producers argued that, because of the financial success of reruns, the networks were forcing producers to hand over a share in the ownership of a show in exchange for the network agreeing to air it. Other producers noted that the networks took up such a large part of evening programming that it was virtually impossible to sell new syndicated material to stations for airing. The consequence, critics argued, was that television was totally controlled by three companies that had an economic stranglehold on the industry and limited the diversity of voices that could be heard.

The Justice Department and the FCC agreed. In 1970, the FCC passed the **prime time access rule (PTAR)**, forcing the networks to stop supplying programming to local stations for a half hour of evening programming during prime time (the period chosen turned out to be from 7:30 to 8:00 EST) six days a week. This regulation was supposed to help new TV companies come up with new ideas for syndicated programming. In practice, however, the ruling helped large Hollywood firms get stations to buy their cheap quiz shows, game shows, and gossip programs. PTAR's results were far-reaching; in fact, they can be seen quite readily every day on the home tube. For its part, in 1970, the Justice Department established **financial interest and syndication rules**, or **fin-syn rules**. These rules prohibited ABC, NBC, and CBS from owning most of the entertainment programming they aired, and it also limited their involvement in producing shows for syndication.

Despite these drawbacks, ABC, NBC, and CBS were flying high in the 1970s. Government rulings were limiting their revenues only slightly, and the few UHF stations that existed hardly affected the earnings of the networks' own stations or their affiliates. But in a situation eerily similar to what had happened with movies in 1948, an emerging technology would soon begin to erode the dominance of broadcast TV. The technology was **coaxial cable**, a type of copper cable in which one physical conductor that carries the signal is surrounded by another concentric physical conductor. Coaxial cable is able to carry information for a great distance.

The Rise of Cable Television

Coaxial cable was invented in 1929 and was first used commercially in 1941 by AT&T, who had established its first cross-continental coaxial transmission system in 1940. By the 1940s, coaxial cable was recognized as a way to carry telephone, radio, and television signals across long distances. In the late 1940s, entrepreneurs realized that coaxial cable could be used to supply broadcast TV signals to communities that had no stations and couldn't use regular rooftop antennas to pick up signals from faraway cities.

Imagine living in a Pennsylvania town somewhere between Pittsburgh and Philadelphia. You are surrounded by hills, so you cannot receive signals from either city. Then some people come along with a bright idea: they place a huge antenna on the tallest hill, string cable from there to people's homes, and charge them for the service. All of a sudden you can get both Philadelphia and Pittsburgh stations for a small subscription fee—it's a great deal.

That's how cable television started, as a **community antenna television (CATV) service** for small towns and suburbs that needed better reception. In fact, this was the way most cable-industry executives saw their business until the late 1970s. In the 1950s and 1960s, broadcasters were quite happy to have cable companies relay their signals to out-of-the-way areas. Broadcasters recognized early, though, that if cable companies started laying wires in and around cities, they could dilute the value of the broadcasters' stations. Residents of a Chicago suburb could, for example, enjoy the sports programming of Cincinnati, New York, or Atlanta channels. These could be relayed to the cable operator by microwave transmission facilities and distributed to the operator's customers via the coaxial cable.

prime time access rule or PTAR a 1970 FCC rule that forced the networks to stop supplying programming to local stations for a half hour during prime time—from 8 to 11 p.m. (from 7 to 10 p.m. in the Central and Mountain Time Zones) six days a week

financial interest and syndication rules, or fin-syn rules rules established by the U.S. Justice Department prohibiting ABC, NBC, and CBS from owning most of the entertainment programming they aired, and limiting their involvement in producing shows for syndication

coaxial cable a type of copper cable used by cable TV companies between the community antenna and user homes and businesses; it is made up of one physical channel that carries the signal surrounded by another concentric physical channel and is able to carry information for a great distance

community antenna television (CATV) service an early name for cable television

Government Regulation of the Cable Television Industry in the 1960s and 1970s

During the 1960s, the FCC agreed with broadcasters' arguments that the government had to protect "free" broadcasting in metropolitan areas from cable operators who demanded payment for their signals. As a result, the agency formulated the Cable Television Rules that made it nearly impossible for cable firms to expand their operations to the center and the suburbs of major cities. But by the mid-1970s, the forces supporting cable television began to gain more political clout. Realizing that encouraging cable would expand the number of television options available to Americans, the FCC changed its rules to allow cable firms to expand into metropolitan areas (and to compete directly with traditional broadcasters).

free skies a policy instituted by the U.S. government that for the first time allowed satellites to be used freely for a wide variety of business purposes

Another federal policy that opened the TV world to competition between technologies was the **free skies** entrepreneurial approach to satellite use in the 1970s, which for the first time allowed satellites to be used freely for a wide variety of business purposes. This approach permitted two developments that pointed to cable TV's future impact on national advertising—the advent of Home Box Office (HBO) and Ted Turner's superstation.

HOME BOX OFFICE AND TED TURNER'S SUPERSTATION   In 1976, HBO, a subsidiary of Time Inc., began to deliver fairly recent films to cable systems around the United States via the Satcom 1 satellite. Cable systems that purchased a satellite dish could carry HBO, charge subscribers an additional fee, and share the proceeds with HBO. Instantly, HBO gave cable a national brand and a unique service: programming that home viewers could not get from over-the-air stations.

superstation term coined by Ted Turner to describe his cable station concept, which aired old movies, Atlanta Braves baseball, and Atlanta Hawks basketball that his station provided. Turner benefited financially in several ways—from the transmission fee charged to cable firms for picking up the signal, from the broad attention his teams would receive, and from the extended audience his advertisers would get

Close on HBO's heels was Atlanta broadcaster and sports financier Ted Turner. Early in 1976, he announced that he was going to make the programming of his Atlanta UHF-TV station available to cable systems via the same Satcom 1 satellite used by HBO. Coining the term **superstation** to describe his concept, Turner reasoned that cable system owners and viewers would appreciate the mix of old movies, Atlanta Braves baseball, and Atlanta Hawks basketball that his station provided. Turner would benefit financially in several ways—from the transmission fee charged to cable firms for picking up the signal, from the broad attention his teams would receive, and from the extended audience his advertisers would get. By the end of 1976, Turner's station was being carried by twenty cable systems in different parts of the country.

The movement to a new television world had begun. The early 1980s saw the launching of a raft of new satellite-delivered television channels—most prominently the Cable News Network (CNN), Nickelodeon, and Music Television (MTV)—that further enticed upscale viewers to subscribe to cable even if they could easily receive the broadcast networks.

cable networks program channels offered by a cable television system to its customers in addition to what is broadcast over the airwaves in their geographic area (now more appropriately called cable/satellite networks, as they can be delivered to the consumer through cable television systems or by satellite)

The **cable networks**, or program channels offered by a cable system beyond what is broadcast over the airwaves in their area, benefited from a dual revenue stream. Their most important source of support was the exhibitors—the cable television systems that carried their programs. Recognizing that original networks generated new subscribers, the cable companies paid a monthly fee (about 15 cents per subscriber) to the new networks. The second source of support was national advertisers, who saw cable's programming as a way to help them reach selected audiences in the same way that magazines did. Because homes with cable TV in the 1980s tended to be wealthier than those without it, advertising on MTV or CNN enabled a sponsor to reach upscale people with particular interests—an opportunity the broadcast networks rarely offered.

A Fragmented Television Era

As the number of cable networks grew, cable system operators added channels to their line-ups—giving cable subscribers more viewing choices. Many observers noted, however, that the sheer number of channels—150 in some areas in the early twenty-first century—should not be equated with diversity. A large proportion of cable programming was made up of reruns from broadcast TV.

In the late 1970s, the FCC, aiming to inject competition into the over-the-air business, started assigning a large number of new, mostly UHF, broadcast TV licenses. As a result, the number of **independent TV broadcasters** (those not affiliated with ABC, NBC, or CBS) soared, from fewer than 100 in 1979 to 339 in 1989. Airing mostly old TV shows, movies, and sports, these stations managed to garner high enough Nielsen ratings and find enough advertisers to sustain themselves.

independent TV broadcasters broadcasters not affiliated with ABC, NBC, or CBS

New Networks Emerge

By 1986, the number of independent TV broadcasters around the United States was great enough to convince media mogul Rupert Murdoch that he could accomplish a feat no one had been able to do since the 1950s: start a fourth network that could compete seriously with the Big Three. His Fox network started out shakily, but in the ensuing years, on the strength of a popular Saturday morning children's line-up and quirky, youth-oriented evening programs such as *The Simpsons, Married . . . with Children,* and *The X-Files*, it managed to draw advertisers and become a permanent TV fixture. Trying to imitate that success, in the mid-1990s Time Warner launched the WB network, and broadcast-station firm Chris Craft partnered with Viacom to launch UPN. By 2006, WB and UPN merged into one network, called the CW. Two Spanish-language networks, Univision and its less popular rival Telemundo, became mainstays of the quickly growing U.S. Hispanic population.

videocassette recorder (VCR) an electronic device for recording and playing back video images and sound on a videocassette tape

digital versatile disk (DVD) an optical disk technology with two layers on each of its two sides, holding up to seventeen gigabytes of video, audio, or other information; DVD-video is the usual name for the DVD format designed for full-length movies and played through a box that will work with your television set

New Technologies Mean New Opportunities and New Challenges

TV options were further enlarged by the spread of the **videocassette recorder (VCR)**, the **digital versatile** (or digital video) **disk (DVD)**, and **direct-to-home satellite services**. The last of these digital technologies, new in the 1990s, beamed up to 150 channels to a plate-sized receiver on a subscriber's house. Carrying mostly recent movies and cable networks, direct-to-home satellite firms like Dish Network and DirecTV initially served as substitutes for cable television in rural areas where cable wasn't available, or in communities where subscribers didn't like their local cable operator.

The merger of computer and television technologies led to the beginnings of digital television. Audiovisual choices were exploding, and regulators tried to keep up. The **Telecommunications Act of 1996** allowed anyone to enter any communications business and let any communications business compete in any market against any other business, and so allowed telephone and cable companies to compete with each other for the first time.

The result was that, more than ever, people were going to different places for their TV viewing. In one sense, family members were spending a lot of their viewing time separated from one another. Survey companies found that, by 1995, more than 66 percent of U.S. homes had multiple television sets—10 percent more than a decade

direct-to-home satellite service a digital technology that delivers up to 150 channels to a plate-sized receiver on a subscriber's house; these services include the DBS format in the United States and the DVB format in much of the rest of the world

Telecommunications Act of 1996 a law that allowed anyone to enter any communications business and let any communications business compete in any market against any other business

digital video recorder
(DVR) device that allows
people to record shows and
view them later

earlier. About 28 percent had three or more sets. By 2007, 84 percent owned a DVD player, and 86 percent received cable, satellite transmission, or phone transmission of TV signals. Moreover, almost one out of five households had a **digital video recorder (DVR)**, which allowed people to record shows and view them later. It also allowed viewers to race through the commercials. The increasing number of choices encouraged parents to watch separately from their children—and encouraged different children in the family to watch separately as well. TV executives worried that the growing DVR use meant fewer people were attending to commercials.

In another sense, people were also watching programs from new sources. Not only were they viewing cable and broadcast TV, they were going online to view videos from both amateur and professional sources. They were moving through audiovisual video game adventures online, on computers, or via game players. And in growing numbers they were even viewing videos on their mobile phones and other handheld digital devices such as iPods.

Consolidating Ownership

With these technological changes came changes in the ownership of the television business. Despite the fragmentation of television and the competition between channels, a few conglomerates had a substantial amount of power over this new audiovisual environment. Those conglomerates stood at the center of the Hollywood industry that fifty years earlier had hoped that TV would go away. Disney, News Corporation, Time Warner, Viacom, Sony, and General Electric (GE) (through NBC Universal) took command not just of theatrical moviemaking, but also of distribution in the home video (VCR and DVD) business, and still control a huge share of the market today.

Because the Telecommunications Act of 1996 eliminated the fin-syn rules, it became possible for the first time since the 1960s for a major movie studio to own a broadcast network. Disney, News Corp, Time Warner, and GE did just that. By the end of the twenty-first century's first decade, all of these conglomerates also owned lucrative cable networks that further extended their audiovisual distribution capabilities. And, in 2009, GE sold 51 percent of NBC Universal to the largest cable company (and media conglomerate), Comcast.

Increasingly, then, competition meant a battle among titans in television, as in other media. Small producers, distributors, and exhibitors had a difficult time surviving; they often could do so only by creating an alliance with one of the major firms. At the same time, a couple of new twenty-first-century titans also emerged to add new meaning to competition in "television." These were Google and Yahoo, internet firms that were posting videos online. So were smaller websites such as Joost and Revver. These developments raised the question of what exactly television meant in the twenty-first century, and they led the long-standing TV powers to begin to rethink what they were doing in the television industry. As a result, today's TV industry involves activities that are both traditional and experimental. Let's look at both.

An Overview of the Contemporary Television Industry

We'll start with the traditional, mainstay activities of the business, where most of the action and money still remain. It's useful to think of today's television world as divided into three domains:

- TV broadcasting
- Cable services
- Satellite services

Let's take a look at the three domains.

Television Broadcasting

Television broadcasting, or the broad, over-the-air transmission of audiovisual signals, has historically been the most popular of these three domains. Its signals are transmitted from towers owned by local stations on frequencies allocated to them by the Federal Communications Commission. People can receive the signals without charge by simply turning on a television set. More than 99 percent of American households can do that.

About 1,600 television stations existed in 2009. Each station is licensed by the Federal Communications Commission to send out signals in a particular area of the country. Until recently, the FCC gave out licenses to operate on frequencies in one of two bands of the electromagnetic spectrum: the VHF band and the UHF band. Because VHF could deliver clear pictures to more people than UHF could, VHF stations were considered more valuable. By FCC ruling, however, in 2009 all stations moved to a new part of the spectrum and broadcast using digital rather than analog technology. That part of the spectrum was auctioned by the government for use by other companies and public service organizations. Newer TV sets are able to receive the digital signals. But Americans with older analog sets in their homes had to purchase special equipment so their old TVs would be able to receive the new over-the-air digital signals. People who pay for cable and satellite television subscriptions can also bring in most of the over-the-air channels through set-top boxes, as we will see.

Most of the 1,600 stations are what people in the TV industry call commercial; the rest are noncommercial. **Commercial stations** make their money by selling time on their airwaves to advertisers. **Noncommercial stations** receive support in other ways, such as viewer donations and donations from private foundations and commercial firms in return for billboards. **Billboards** are mentions of a sponsor's name or products at the start or end of programs airing on the station. When a company pays to sponsor a program on a noncommercial station, that is called **underwriting**.

The television industry in the United States is divided into 210 broadcast television markets. New York City is the largest, followed by Los Angeles, and then Chicago.

commercial station a broadcast television station that supports itself financially by selling time on its airwaves to advertisers

noncommercial station a broadcast television station that does not receive financial support from advertisers, but rather supports itself through donations from listeners and private foundations, and from commercial firms in return for mentioning the firm or its products in announcements at the beginning and end of programs airing on the station

billboard the mention of a sponsor's name or products at the start or end of an aired program in return for money

underwriting when a company pays to sponsor a program on a noncommercial station

Table 13.1 Household Penetration Rates of Television Services in the United States, 2008	
Television Service	% of Households (total HH = 115.7)
Overall television households	98.9
Wired cable	55.1
Satellite TV	27.0
Teleco TV	4.5

HH, households.

Sources: *Veronis Suhler Stevenson, Communication Industry Forecast 2009–2013* (New York: VSS, 2009), Chapter 9, p. 30.

CRITICAL CONSUMER
CBS UNDERWEAR CONFLICT

If you were one of the nearly 107 million people who watched the 2010 Super Bowl on CBS, you may have noticed an uncharacteristically high degree of pantslessness during the commercial breaks. An ad for the online job site CareerBuilder featured workers taking casual Fridays to an absurd level, opting to attend work in only their underwear. Interestingly enough, the ad immediately following portrayed a parade of pantsless men chanting out, "I wear no pants!"

Dockers—the company behind the second ad—voiced disappointment over CBS's placement of its ad, with the concern being that the two commercials would have blurred together and the brand impression been lessened. In response, CBS granted Dockers three free ad spots during the NCAA men's basketball tournament as compensation.

It's not unusual for networks to comb through a broadcast's commercial line-up to check for unfavorable juxtapositions between commercials. Most commonly, commercials for competing brands are kept far apart from one another. For example, an ad for Burger King would not be placed next to an ad for McDonalds. However, it is much less common for networks to inspect a commercial line-up for recurring motifs

(pantslessness included). To do so may even prove unrealistic. It turns out that Dockers and CareerBuilder were not the only two brands running back to back with similar visuals. Both Dr. Pepper and TruTV ran ads featuring miniature versions of celebrities—specifically, members of the rock group KISS and football star Troy Polamalu, respectively.

Though networks carry an obligation to judiciously place advertisers' commercials, how cautious should they be about similar presentations? Do you think back-to-back advertisements with similar elements make a difference in viewers' memories of the brands? And what, if anything, does all this say about the nature of advertising creativity when expensive commercials in major venues use similar tactics?

Sources: Jeff Bercovici, "CBS Says Sorry to Dockers for Pantsless Déjà Vu During Ad Spots," *Daily Finance*, March 4, 2010. http://www.dailyfinance.com/story/media/cbs-says-sorry-to-dockers-for-pantsless-deja-vu-during-ad-spots/19384004/ (accessed August 4, 2010); Brian Steinberg, "CBS Offers Dockers Free Air Time After Underwear Imbroglio," *Advertising Age*, March 3, 2010. http://adage.com/mediaworks/article?article_id=142401 (accessed August 4, 2010).

television network an organization that distributes television programs, typically by satellite and microwave relay, to all its affiliated stations, or stations that agree to carry a substantial amount of the network's material on an ongoing basis, so that programs can be broadcast by all the stations at the same time

Big Four commercial networks the four largest television networks: ABC, CBS, Fox, and NBC

vertical integration an organization's control over a media product from production through distribution to exhibition

broadcast outlets organizations that transmit broadcasting signals

The New York City market boasts about 7.5 million homes. Glendive, Montana, the smallest market, has 4,000 (see Table 13.2).

More than 80 percent of local TV stations have linked up or affiliated with a television network for at least part of their broadcast day. A **television network** is an organization that distributes television programs, typically by satellite and microwave relay, to all its affiliated stations, or stations that agree to carry a substantial amount of the network's material on an ongoing basis, so that the programs can be broadcast by all the stations at the same time. ABC, CBS, Fox, and NBC are the broadcast networks that regularly reach the largest number of people. They are advertiser-supported, as are two smaller networks: the CW and ION. A number of commercial Spanish-speaking networks also exist. The biggest are Univision, TeleFutura (owned by Univision), and Telemundo, owned by NBC Universal. The Public Broadcasting Service (PBS) is the network for noncommercial stations.

The **Big Four commercial networks**—ABC, CBS, Fox, and NBC—are the giants of the broadcast television business, primarily because of their role in coordinating the distribution of shows to hundreds of local stations, which then transmit the shows to homes. But ABC, CBS, Fox, and NBC are more than just distributors. They are **vertically integrated** operations. Each company has divisions that produce news, sports, situation comedies, dramas, and other types of programs for use on the network. Each company also owns stations (sometimes called **broadcast outlets**) in the biggest cities; these outlets serve as exhibition anchors for their

Table 13.2 The Top Ten Broadcast Television Markets in the United States, 2009

Rank	Designated Market Area (DMA)	TV Households	% of U.S.
1	New York, NY	7,493,530	6.524
2	Los Angeles, CA	5,659,170	4.927
3	Chicago, IL	3,501,010	3.048
4	Philadelphia, PA	2,955,190	2.573
5	Dallas—Ft. Worth, TX	2,544,410	2.215
6	San Francisco—Oakland—San Jose, CA	2,503,400	2.179
7	Boston, MA (Manchester, NH)	2,410,180	2.098
8	Atlanta, GA	2,387,520	2.079
9	Washington, DC (Hagerstown, MD)	2,335,040	2.033
10	Houston, TX	2,123,460	1.849

Source: Television Bureau of Advertising. http://www.tvb.org/rcentral/markettrack/us_hh_by_dma.asp (accessed March 3, 2010).

respective networks. In the TV industry, these local stations are called **O&O**—short for **owned and operated**.

Local stations that are not owned by broadcast networks and yet transmit their signals and programs are called network affiliates. A **network affiliate** transmits the network's **program feed** (that is, the succession of shows) on a daily basis. In return, the network promises to compensate the affiliate with a portion of the revenues received from advertisers that have bought time on the network. Many affiliates are part of **station groups,** or collections of broadcast television stations owned by a single company. In the wealthiest station groups, such as Allbritton Communications, each station is an affiliate of one of the major networks. Stations in other groups hook up mainly with CW or ION.

According to the Federal Communications Commission, no group may own more than two television stations in any market. That dictum is based on the desire to limit the power of broadcast groups in any one area. The FCC has also ruled, however, that a company can own two networks as long as both are not among the Big Four networks. A station that is not affiliated with one of the Big Four networks is called an **independent broadcast station**. (Industry executives often consider CW and ION affiliates to be independents because they air relatively few hours of network programming per week.) Practically speaking, independents must find all (or almost all) of their programming themselves. Actually, even network affiliates and O&Os must look to sources other than ABC, CBS, Fox, and NBC for some of their programming. The reason is that the Big Four do not distribute twenty-four hours' worth of shows. As we will see later in this chapter, the broadcast industry has no shortage of companies trying to interest independents, affiliates, and O&Os in programming.

owned and operated or O&O stations broadcast television stations that are owned and operated by a network that often provides a regular schedule of programming materials for broadcast

network affiliates local broadcast television stations that are not owned by broadcast networks and yet transmit network signals and programs on a daily basis; in return, the network promises to compensate the affiliate with a portion of the revenues received from advertisers that have bought time on the network

program feed the succession of shows sent from a network to its network affiliates

station group a collection of broadcast television stations owned by a single company

independent broadcast station a broadcast television station that is not affiliated with one of the Big Four networks

http://www.pbs.org

http://www.ionline.tv, website of the Ion Television network

commercials short audiovisual advertisements that call attention to certain products or services

retransmission fees the money television networks and local stations charge cable and satellite firms for the right to carry their material

cable television the process of sending TV signals to subscribers through a wire (usually a coaxial cable, but increasingly via fiber optic lines)

cable a type of flexible tube or pipe through which programs are exhibited in the home

cable television system the cable television retailer that physically installs the cable and markets the program service to consumers in a particular geographic area

multiple system owner (MSO) a cable television firm that owns two or more cable television systems

With the help of advertising agencies (which Chapters 15 and 16 discuss in some detail), advertisers pay for time between programs and segments of programs. In return, broadcasters allow advertisers to use this time to air **commercials**—short audiovisual pieces that call attention to their products or services. In 2008, advertisers spent about $45 billion on television broadcast advertising.[1] Viewers of broadcast TV do not have to pay to receive the programming. Consequently, almost all the money that broadcast stations and networks receive has come from a single revenue stream—commercials. That is still the case, though the networks and local stations now make about half a billion dollars a year charging cable and satellite systems for the right to pick them off the air and retransmit them to subscribers; these are called **retransmission fees**. Stations and networks are also beginning to take advantage of digital media to develop sources of revenue other than broadcast commercials; in 2008 they brought in about $3.5 billion that way.[2]

Cable and Satellite Services

One way in which cable and satellite services differ from broadcasting is their strong reliance on two major revenue streams:

- Advertisers pay to have their commercials shown during programming
- Consumers pay to get the service in the first place

Both revenue streams are substantial, although the money received from subscriptions is far greater than advertisers' contributions. In 2008, American consumers paid around $59 billion to receive cable or satellite services. Advertisers paid $22 billion to advertise on these services.[3]

THE CABLE TELEVISION BUSINESS   **Cable television** refers to businesses that provide programming to subscribers via a wire (historically a coaxial cable, but increasingly a fiber optic line). The cable television business is by far the most developed in the cable and satellite area. Stripped to its basics, a **cable** is a type of flexible tube or pipe through which programs are exhibited in the home. The retailer that physically installs the cable and markets the program service to consumers in a particular geographic area is called a **cable television system** (see Table 13.3). A cable television firm that owns two or more cable systems is a **multiple system owner (MSO)** (see Table 13.4). Much like a store, every cable system has a certain amount of shelf space, which in this case is the channels it carries through its pipes. Each system offers consumers in its community an array of channels that includes special networks as well as independent local broadcast stations and network affiliates. Though they are called cable networks because they first appeared on cable, the nonbroadcast channels are more appropriately called **subscription networks** because people pay a monthly fee (a subscription) to receive them via cable or satellite. In 2008, Americans spent $66.9 billion on cable subscriptions.

Table 13.3 Top Ten Cable Systems, February 2009

Rank	System	Basic Subscribers (millions)
1	Cablevision of Greater New York	3.1
2	Comcast Freedom Region	2.5
3	Comcast California Region	2.4
4	Comcast Greater Chicago Region	2.2
5	Comcast Beltway Region	2.0
6	Comcast Greater Boston	1.8
7	Time Warner Cable Los Angeles	1.7
8	Comcast Mid-South Region	1.6
9	Comcast Michigan Region	1.3

Source: http://www.multichannel.com (accessed March 3, 2010).

Table 13.4 Top Ten Multiple Systems Owners, September 2009

Rank	MSO	Subscribers (millions)
1	Comcast Corporation	23.8
2	Time Warner Cable	13.0
3	Cox Communications, Inc	5.2
4	Charter Communications, Inc	4.9
5	Cablevision Systems Corp	3.1
6	Bright House Networks	2.3
7	Mediacom Communications Corp	1.3
8	Suddenlink Communications	1.3
9	Insight Communications	0.72
10	CableOne Inc	0.68

Source: http://www.ncta.com (accessed March 3, 2010).

subscription networks nonbroadcast program channels for which people pay a monthly subscription fee to receive them via cable or satellite

THE TELCO BUSINESS   Recently, traditional telephone service providers, notably AT&T and Verizon, have also begun to offer a multichannel television service in many parts of the country, competing with the cable TV firms. Although they wouldn't be called cable companies by people in the business, Verizon and AT&T do use wire technologies (as opposed to the unwired satellite approach) to reach people's homes. Some people in the business call them the **telcos** (short for telephone companies). Verizon and AT&T have different technical philosophies, but they share the idea of using advanced communication lines called fiber optics to send cable programming to TV sets. In years to come, the telcos, and especially Verizon, could pose a formidable threat to providers of television services. At this point in time, though, the threat posed by the telcos to traditional cable firms and to the satellite business is small because they are just beginning to roll out their services widely. In 2008, they brought in about $2.4 billion for their services.

telcos telephone companies that offer television and internet services

THE SATELLITE BUSINESS   **Satellite television** means programming that comes directly to the home from a satellite orbiting the earth. In 2008, 64 percent of U.S. households with a TV were hooked up to a cable service, 5 percent got TV

satellite television programming that comes directly to the home from a satellite orbiting the earth

WORLD VIEW
DISCOVERY TAKES TLC GLOBAL

In March of 2010, Discovery Communications' cable channel TLC began an international launch. Although initially starting only in Norway, Discovery expects TLC to be available in more than 100 million households in seventy-five countries in a little over a year after the launch.

TLC is Discovery's female-targeted channel. It includes the shows *LA Ink*, *Cake Boss*, *Say Yes to the Dress*, and the now defunct but widely discussed *Jon & Kate Plus 8*. In addition to TLC's traditional line-up, its global incarnation will also provide programming from other Discovery channels, of which there are thirteen in the United States. These include Animal Planet, Planet Green, and the crime and forensics channel Investigation Discovery.

TLC is not Discovery's first channel to reach an international scale. Discovery's Science Channel was similarly distributed globally, among others. Discovery's chief executive, David Zaslav, said that in order to complement the company's more male-oriented programming that dominates its international market, Discovery needs "one or two more women's networks around the world," and that TLC may fill that market. Some of this will be achieved by simply rebranding channels Discovery already owns

After coming on board at Discovery Communications, Zaslav introduced a global programming group to encourage collaboration across the corporation's numerous global branches. Discovery's international strategy has been paying off so far. In 2009, Discovery's stock market value doubled. Nearly a third of Discovery's total revenue in 2009 came from outside of the United States, and its international revenue has quadrupled over the previous three years. Media companies are now looking toward Discovery Communications for cues on how to succeed. "I think that Discovery has the best secular growth prospects in the industry," said media analyst Jessica Reif Cohen of Bank of America Merrill Lynch.

Industry experts note that Discovery's success is in part due to the company's ability to cheaply reproduce programming internationally, as the company produces and owns most of its fare. At Discovery, "They produce shows with a mind toward how they can use them around the world," said David C. Joyce, an analyst at Miller Tabak. Many other networks, however, get their programming from independent production companies, restricting their ability to distribute it internationally.

Sources: "Discovery Takes TLC Global," *Media Daily News: News Brief*, March 3, 2010. http://www.mediapost.com/publications/?fa=Articles.showArticle&art_aid=123580 (August 4, 2010); Brian Stelter, "Global Strategy Turns Discovery into Powerhouse," *The International Herald Tribune*, March 16, 2010, Finance, p. 15.

---

direct broadcast satellite (DBS) technology technology that allows a household to receive hundreds of channels that are delivered digitally to a small dish installed on the side of a house or apartment building; a set-top box converts the digital signals to analog signals that are accepted by the TV. The DBS satellites operate from orbits directly above the earth's equator and just over 22,000 miles up

through telco services, and about 31 percent subscribed to a satellite operation. You may have seen old-style satellite dishes, large structures that typically sat behind people's homes. The backyard satellite dish business was built in the 1980s on the proposition that a homeowner could cut out the cable system by installing a dish-shaped instrument in the backyard and getting programs directly from the satellite that sends them to the cable system. Unfortunately for the homeowners, though, most networks now encode their programs so that a person with a dish cannot view them free of charge. Most of the backyard receivers have been replaced by **direct broadcast satellite (DBS) technology**. Introduced in 1994, it allows a household to receive hundreds of channels. The signals are delivered digitally to a small dish installed on the side of a house or apartment building; a set-top box decodes digital signals so they appear on the TV set. The DBS satellites operate from orbits directly above the earth's equator and just over 22,000 miles up. DirecTV and Dish Network are currently the largest DBS companies in the United States.

For the foreseeable future, it seems clear that competition over television will be among broadcast, cable, and satellite providers. TV executives fear that audiences will continue to flee to the new channels and away from the Big Four; analysts speculated that Comcast bought NBC for its cable networks (Bravo, Syfi, USA, and others) rather than for the (then fourth-place) broadcast network. You might also have gathered that cable and satellite systems are themselves engaged in sometimes ferocious fights for consumers. To get an idea of how these providers are jockeying for viewers' eyeballs, we have to understand the basic elements of the evolving television industry. To do that, we turn to our familiar categories of production, distribution, and exhibition. Production takes up the lion's share of this discussion, simply because there are so many different ways to look at it.

Production in the Television Industry

Production is a tricky word when it comes to the television business. In the broadest sense, at least three forms of production are going on at different levels of the industry. To get a sense of what this means, think of your local cable television system. Chances are, your local cable system produces very few of its own programs. (Maybe it aids in the production of an access channel, where local officials and citizens can state their problems and parade their interests.) But making shows is not the only way a cable TV system can be involved in production. Your local system is very much involved in producing the number and nature of network channels that it offers potential subscribers; this menu of channels is called a **line-up**.

Each network is also engaged in a second sort of production. For example, the MTV network creates its **format**—the flow of series, news, and videos that defines MTV's overall personality and helps it stand apart from other networks in cable system line-ups. Of course, MTV personnel select the programs that are crucial building blocks of their network. However, these programs are often created by other firms that have very little input into decisions about the formats or line-ups in which they appear.

Trying to understand production in the television world, then, means getting a grip on the considerations that affect the line-up of channels, the formats of individual channels, and the elements of individual programs. Let's look at each of these categories as it relates to the subscription (cable/satellite/telco) and broadcast TV businesses.

line-up the menu of channels that a cable television system offers potential subscribers

format the collection of elements that constitutes a channel's recognizable personality, created through a set of rules that guide the way the elements are stitched together with a particular audience-attracting goal in mind

Producing Channel Line-ups

Creating a channel line-up is a high-priority job for cable and satellite exhibitors. Executives from these companies believe that the number and kinds of programming networks that they offer potential customers are major features that attract people to pay for their service. For instance, take MTV, Nickelodeon, VH1, E!, CNN, C-Span, TBS, AMC, ESPN, ESPN2, the Cartoon Network, HBO, or another network. For which of these networks would you consider subscribing to another service if your cable or satellite system didn't carry it?

With so much riding on customer satisfaction, you would think that cable and satellite executives would simply poll their customers and put on everything they want to see. The firms do, in fact, conduct surveys of consumers, and executives do look at ratings reports that indicate how many people watch different networks. Nevertheless, the choice of networks is based as much on three other considerations as on consumer feedback. These considerations are:

- The technological limitations of the system
- The amount of money a network demands from exhibitors
- Whether or not the exhibitor owns a piece of the network

High definition television (HDTV) channels use substantially more bandwidth than standard TV signals, a factor that has affected the number of HDTV channels cable and satellite firms have offered.

TECHNOLOGICAL LIMITATIONS   Technological limitations restrict the number of channels that a cable or satellite service can deliver. High definition TV (HDTV) signals use substantially more bandwidth than standard TV signals, a factor that has affected the number of HDTV channels that cable and satellite firms have offered. As a telecommunications analyst said in 2007, "HDTV takes an enormous amount of (transmission) capacity. They're going to be sticking 10 pounds of potatoes into a 5-pound bag. Something will have to give."[4] The increasing popularity of HDTV sets, and competition with Verizon's very high-capacity FIOS system, has been encouraging satellite and cable firms to add more HD channels. That is technologically easier for satellite firms than for cable companies, which have to implement major system upgrades across neighborhoods to add capacity. All the services, though, have to weigh the often huge cost of adding channels and other services against the additional subscribers they may bring.

COVERING COSTS   In addition to technological limitations and the costs of upgrades, the line-ups set by cable and satellite exhibitors depend on the amounts of money that particular networks charge exhibitors for carrying their networks. These costs are called **license fees**. The notion that a subscription video network should charge exhibitors for carrying it goes back to the early 1980s, when advertising support for cable networks such as CNN and A&E was meager and cable systems agreed to chip in to help the networks survive.

Cable and satellite systems typically pay between 15 and 25 cents per month for each subscriber for many of the networks they carry. ESPN, an exceedingly popular set of channels, demands over $4 per subscriber per month. With millions of subscribers out there, this can add up to money that the delivery service can use for technology upgrades. Consequently, when cable and satellite systems make decisions about their line-ups, the mix of channels that they choose is influenced by the amount they will have to pay to those channels. A channel that charges more than another with the same level of audience popularity will have less chance of getting on a system than one that demands lower license fees.

license fees the costs that particular networks charge exhibitors for carrying the networks' line-ups in the exhibitors' cable or satellite systems

Part of the way cable systems pay for many of these channels and make technological improvements is to make money from advertising on them. Advertising-supported channels such as CNN or Lifetime typically leave room for the companies that carry them to insert commercials from national or local companies interested in reaching people in particular areas served by the satellite, cable, or telco operation. Of course, another way that a cable or satellite system can bring in revenues is to charge subscribers more money. Still, the possibility of competition and a desire for consumer goodwill led firms to keep their most basic rates relatively low and to charge more for extra packages of programs. The relatively low rate often offers the customer all the broadcast channels available in the area, channels with local government and other "access" programming, and a relatively small number of subscription channels, such as TBS and TNT. To get more clusters of channels, the subscriber must pay more. This strategy of charging different amounts for different levels of programming is called **tiering**. (It's not spelled tearing, though some people might cry when they see their bills). The number and variety of tiers has gone up dramatically in recent years, especially among cable firms. They include packages of movie channels (HBO and Cinemax, for example), sports, Spanish-language channels, international channels, and more.

Another way to make money is through pay per view (PPV) or video on demand (VOD) or by renting digital video recorders. In **pay-per-view** programming, the cable or satellite company charges the customer for viewing an individual program, such as a boxing event, a live broadcast of a concert, or a newly released motion picture. The customer must wait for the specific time that the program airs to view it, or the customer can use the DVR he or she rents per month to capture the program at that time. With **video on demand**, a customer uses a remote control to navigate to a menu of programs and then click on the program he or she wants to watch. Unlike PPV, where the customer has to wait for the show to appear at a certain time, the program immediately appears for viewing. As this description suggests, VOD requires the customer to be able to communicate directly with the computer providing the programming. That is possible in most cable and telco television systems because the wire connected to the television carries a signal two ways—from the system's regional delivery location (called the **head end**) to the home set and back. Satellite companies, however, don't typically provide the ability of a home television remote to communicate instantly with the computers delivering the programming. Consequently, they cannot offer true video on demand. They try to make up for it by providing their customers with digital video recorders that download selections viewers might want to try, but the selections are more limited than the ones that cable firms provide. Seeing a competitive advantage, cable firms and telcos have been trumpeting their VOD offerings, many of which are free and some of which are in high definition.

THE EXHIBITORS' OWNERSHIP ROLE IN THE NETWORK   A third important consideration that influences the line-up of a cable system is whether or not the MSO or its parent company owns the network. It stands to reason that, if a company has a financial interest in the success of a channel, it would include it. So, for example, if you live in an area served by Comcast, you'll probably find that it carries SportsNet, E!, Style, The Golf Channel, and G4—all owned wholly or partly by Comcast. Time Warner Cable similarly carries networks that it owns. That doesn't mean that cable systems that do not own these channels will not carry them. It does mean, however, that if a major cable MSO decides to create a channel, it will put it on enough systems in favorable channel locations to give it a good chance of success. That kind of boost would not be so easily available to independent companies with interesting channel ideas.

tiering the strategy by which different levels of television programming are priced differently

pay per view (PPV) a transaction in which a cable provider, satellite company, or telco charges the customer for viewing an individual program, such as a boxing event, a live broadcast of a concert, or a newly released motion picture

video on demand (VOD) a television viewing technology whereby a customer uses the remote control to navigate to a menu of programs and then click on the program he or she wants to watch. Unlike pay per view, in which the customer has to wait for the show to appear at a certain time, the program immediately appears for viewing

head end a cable system's regional delivery location

Producing Broadcast Channel Line-ups

The method of creating line-ups in the subscription video industry is just beginning to happen in the broadcast industry. Since late 2009, broadcasters have been sending all their programs in the digital format. Under this new format, broadcasters now have the ability to send high definition signals, which they could not do under the old analog system—their bandwidth wouldn't allow it. The digital frequencies do allow it, but broadcasters have decided that they will not always use their new digital frequencies only for **high definition television (HDTV)**. Many figure that they may send out HDTV signals during the evening, when the large number of viewers available will justify beaming shows in expensive, spectrum-hogging HDTV. At other times, they reason, they can make more advertising money by doing what is called **channel multiplexing** or **multichannel broadcasting**—that is, splitting their new digital signals into two, three, or even four separately programmed channels and sending them in the form of a complex signal that is separated at the receiving end instead of broadcasting one channel of HDTV. So, rather than just broadcasting Channel 6, a network could broadcast on Channels 6a, 6b, 6c, and 6d.

That's where questions related to program line-ups enter the picture. Should each channel aim as broadly as possible, or should it focus on a particular topic (food or sports, for example), as many cable systems do? Should the stations target people at home, in school, in hospitals, in nursing homes, or at work? Should the channels be related to one another thematically—all of them programming news but programming different types of news, for example? How different should the channels be from the offerings of other stations? How involved should the network with which the local station is affiliated be in creating programming for the channels? What will advertisers think about all this?

These are among the questions TV broadcasters have begun to ask about their new digital world. They also face the challenge of trying to persuade—or get the government to require—local cable systems to carry their digital and HDTV signals. Although federal law requires cable systems to carry local stations, the cable firms are reluctant to carry the multiplexed channels of these stations. They argue that these channels would take up so much space on their systems that they would interfere with the systems' ability to carry the popular national networks that cable outlets typically exhibit.

Producing Individual Channels: Cable, Satellite, and Broadcast

The task of producing any channel itself is huge, whether it is carried out for a subscription TV network such as CNN or for a broadcast station. Programmers—the people in charge of operations as different as the Weather Channel and MTV on subscription video, and WWOR (Channel 9) in New York and KNBC (Channel 4) in Los Angeles on broadcast TV—have to fill twenty-four hours of airtime every day of the year.

DETERMINING THE CHANNEL'S INTENDED AUDIENCE   The most basic issue that confronts a local or network programmer relates to the intended audience: Whom should the programmer try to attract as viewers? This critical question is typically thrashed out by a number of top executives in the organization. The answer generally depends on four interrelated considerations:

high definition television (HDTV) a television display technology that provides picture quality similar to that of 35mm movies with sound quality similar to that of today's compact disks. Some television stations have begun transmitting HDTV broadcasts to users on a limited number of channels, generally using digital rather than analog signal transmission

channel multiplexing or multichannel broadcasting sending multiple signals or streams of information on a carrier at the same time in the form of a single complex signal, then recovering the separate signals at the receiving end

MEDIA RESEARCH
HGTV'S NATURALISTIC EXPERIMENT

http://www.hgtv.com, website of Home and Garden Television, a cable network

The Web represents a new frontier in television advertising. With millions of people going online to sites that mesh with the topics of particular television programs, online advertising would seem to be a natural tactic for encouraging people to view programs relevant to them. That's what executives of the home-fashion cable network Home and Garden Television (HGTV) thought, but they wanted proof that their money would be well spent.

That's where a research program—a naturalistic experiment—came into play. HGTV wanted to test the power of an online advertising campaign for its interior design competition show, *Design Star*. The cable network worked with Google's advertising network to place banner ads on websites that seemed relevant to the program's topic. To note whether people who saw the ads ended up viewing the show, HGTV worked with Nielsen, which tracks both the internet activities and TV viewing activities of a large panel of individuals. A third of the panel saw regular HGTV ads and a third were exposed to the *Design Star* banner campaign. The remaining third—the control group—saw unrelated ads.

The results suggested that exposure to the campaign increased viewership by more than half. Additionally, the campaign resulted in an increase in visits to the HGTV website and membership in the HGTV Facebook group. HGTV leveraged this success by using the Facebook group to help fans keep in touch with their favorite television personalities. New television advertisements reflected this emphasis by publicizing online conversations and fan posts. The success of this campaign suggests that the internet may well be a good place to encourage people to watch TV—at least HGTV.

Sources: Lisa Lacy, "Ad Network Buy Drives Tune-Ins for HGTV's 'Design Star'," *ClickZ*, March 2, 2010. http://www.clickz.com/clickz/news/1706599/ad-network-buy-drives-tune-ins-hgtvs-design-star (accessed August 8, 2010); HGTV website: http://www.hgtv.com (accessed August 8, 2010).

Jim Samples, president of HGTV, during a *Design Star* contest held in Greeley Square, New York.

- The competition
- The available pool of viewers
- The interests of sponsors
- The costs of relevant programming

competition the programming alternatives that already exist

ratings the audits of people's viewing behavior that help to determine where much of the money for programming and advertising should go

people meter a small box installed by Nielsen on television sets in about 5,000 homes that it has chosen as a representative sample of the U.S. population. The meter holds a preassigned code for every individual in the home, including visitors. Nielsen asks each viewer to enter his or her code at the start and end of a TV viewing session. Information from each viewing session is transmitted to Nielsen's computers through television lines and is the basis for the firm's conclusions about national viewing habits

audimeter a Nielsen device that measures whether a TV set is being viewed and notes the channel

Nielsen diaries a method used by Nielsen to determine television ratings information, which requires selected individuals to keep a written record or "diary" of their television use during a given time period

Competition means the programming alternatives that already exist. If a channel that emphasizes history is already succeeding, starting a similar channel may not be useful unless you are sure that you have a clearly more attractive way of doing it or that there are enough people who are interested in history to accommodate two somewhat different approaches to the subject. But even if there are enough history buffs around, executives who are thinking of starting a second history channel must ask whether there are enough advertisers that want to sponsor programs on such a channel. If the channel is in the cable/satellite domain (as it probably would be), the executives have to ask whether they could successfully place a second history channel on enough systems to interest advertisers. They also have to ask whether the costs of history programs are appropriate in view of the projected revenues that would be received from advertisers that wanted to reach the projected audience. If the programs are so expensive that the costs can't be recovered from advertisers and cable subscriptions, the channel won't succeed, regardless of how interesting it is.

Programmers for cable/satellite/telco channels often focus on rather specific topics to guide their choices of materials. They aim to reach people with particular lifestyle habits or interests—an available pool of viewers. Think of HGTV (Home and Garden Television) or the Golf Channel. In contrast, broadcast stations, because they are well known and accessible to virtually everyone in their area, do not differentiate themselves so narrowly. When they go after new audiences, they choose broad segments of the population that advertisers want to reach. In some large cities, for example, where the FCC added several stations and increased competition for audiences, a few stations have decided to pursue Spanish-speaking viewers, or non-English-speaking viewers generally, to maximize their profits.

Whether they are working for a network or a local station and whether they are programming in English or in another language, programmers want to keep audiences tuned to their channel. For commercial stations, the reason is simply that the more of the target audience that is watching, the more the channel can charge for its commercials and the more money it can bring in. Even noncommercial stations want to reach large numbers of their target audiences, however, because this tells supporters that the stations are accomplishing their aim. It also means that more people might contribute money to the stations.

RATINGS   In the television industry, the audits of people's television viewing behavior that help to determine where much of the money for programming and advertising should go are called **ratings**. Nielsen Media Research dominates this business. The stations, networks, and major advertisers foot most of the bill for the firm's reports. Nielsen uses meters and diaries to determine what people are watching and when.

For a snapshot of what America is watching, Nielsen uses an instrument called a **people meter**. The company installs this small box on all of the television sets in over 9,000 homes containing over 18,000 people that it has chosen as a representative sample of the U.S. population. The meter holds a preassigned code for every individual in the home, including visitors. The research firm asks each viewer to enter his or her code at the start and end of a TV viewing session. Information from each viewing session is transmitted to Nielsen's computers through television lines, and is the basis for the firm's conclusions about national viewing habits.[5]

However, meters in 9,000 homes scattered around the country can't tell stations in individual markets how many people are watching them and who these people are. To get these data, Nielsen uses two approaches. For nonstop research on the largest fifty-six markets, Nielsen installs what it calls an **audimeter** on every television in the homes of several hundred people in each market. This meter measures whether a TV set is being viewed and notes the channel (a specific over-the-air number, a specific cable number, the VCR, or a video game). Unlike the people meter (which it actually does use in four of the fifty-six markets), the audimeter notes only whether someone is watching, not who is watching. Its results therefore allow the company to generalize about TV use for the household, not for specific individuals.

Nielsen finds a way to generalize about the habits of individual viewers in these markets by comparing the data collected from the people meters with entries in **diaries** that are distributed six times a year to another sample of viewers in the same markets. Nielsen asks the family members to fill in the viewing experiences during the month for each member of the household. These diaries are also used to determine viewing habits during four months of the year—February, May, August, and November—in all 210 television markets. Broadcast industry workers call these months the **sweeps** because the ratings measurements during these periods are comparable to giant sweepstakes in which winners and losers are determined.

Nielsen's results are arrayed as ratings and shares. Ratings and shares, in turn, can be discussed in household and people terms. **Household ratings** represent the number of households in which the channel was turned on, compared with the number of households in the channel's universe (the local area, or the number of people who receive the cable network). **People ratings** refer to particular demographic categories of individuals within each household—for example, those aged from 18 to 49 years or those who are female. For a particular channel during a particular time, a **household share** represents the number of households in which the channel was turned on compared with the number of TV-owning households in the area where the channel can be viewed.

Because of their wide **reach**, or the percentage of the entire target audience to which they circulate, broadcast networks often answer to advertisers in terms of their **national rating points**. In 2010, every national household rating point represented 1,149,000 households (about 1 percent of U.S. homes with a TV). **National people ratings** are expressed in terms of the number of individuals in the United States who fit into a particular category. Each rating point in the 18- to 49-year-old category, for example, represented 1.24 million viewers (1 percent of the U.S. total for people in that age range in 2007).

For example, if the *Late Show with David Letterman*—which is distributed nationally on CBS—receives a 5.4 household rating and a 16 household share, what does that mean? The rating means that of the 111.16 million households in the United States that own a TV set, 5.4 percent (6 million households) had at least one TV tuned to Letterman. That may look like a very small percentage, but the program airs at 11:30 p.m. Eastern and Pacific times, when many people are asleep. The 16 household share means that, of the households in which people are viewing at that time of night, about one in six (about 16 percent) has a set tuned to Letterman. Of course, households often have people viewing different TV sets. Increasingly, then, networks and their advertisers prefer ratings and shares to be expressed not in terms of households but in terms of categories of individuals who are viewing. So, for example, you might read in the trade press that Letterman received a 19 share among the 18- to 49-year-olds in its audience.

Nielsen reports each program's rating and share for a particular night to its clients (typically advertising executives). In the 2000s, advertisers began to pressure Nielsen

sweeps the survey of TV viewing habits in markets across the United States, as performed by Nielsen four times per year—during the months of February, May, August, and November; competition among TV programmers is especially keen during these periods

household ratings ratings that represent the number of households in which the channel was turned on compared with the number of households in the channel's universe (the local area, or the number of people who receive the cable network)

people ratings particular demographic categories of individuals within each household—for example, those aged from 18 to 49 years or those who are female

household share the number of households in which a particular channel was turned on compared with the number of TV-owning households in the area where the channel can be viewed

reach the percentage of the entire target audience to which a media outlet will circulate

national rating points a measure of the percentage of TV sets in the United States that are tuned to a specific show. In 2001, each national rating point represented just over 1 million U.S. TV homes

national people ratings measurement of TV audience segments expressed in terms of the number of individuals in the United States who fit into a particular category

http://www.nielsenmedia.
com, website of Nielsen Media
Research, the leading provider
of television information
services in the United States
and Canada

**average commercial
minute** Nielsen's reporting
standard for determining
ratings and household
viewings during commercials.
This information gives
advertisers measurements
not just for each program
taken as a whole, but for the
commercials that run during
the programs

C3 standard Nielsen
technique of measuring the
average commercial minute of
a program by including in the
ratings people who recorded
commercials on DVRs and
viewed them within a three-day
period

schedule the pattern in
which television programs are
arranged

day part a segment of the day
as defined by programmers
and marketers (examples:
prime time, daytime, late night,
etc.)

to report ratings and shares not just for the average viewing of programs but in terms of the viewing of commercials within and around the shows. After all, for advertisers, the shows are there mainly to get the right people to watch the commercials. Nielsen determines ratings and household viewings during commercials and reports them in terms of the **average commercial minute**. That way, advertisers have measurements not just for each program taken as a whole but of the commercials that run during the programs. In addition, Nielsen determines the ratings for a program and its average commercial minutes not just by whether a person viewed it at the actual time it ran on broadcast or cable. The company includes in the ratings people who recorded it on a DVR and viewed it within a three-day period. The reason for this is that by mid-2009 about a third of U.S. households had a DVR-connected TV set; in the 18- to 49-year-old segment particularly desirable to advertisers, the number hit 36 percent.[6] The TV networks argue that advertisers should take viewing of DVRs into account as well as so-called live viewing. This approach—measuring the average commercial minute of a program within a three-day window—is called the **C3 standard** and is used for today's ratings reports.

Preliminary evidence suggests that the commercial ratings of some shows rise substantially when time-shifting via the DVR is added to the picture. However, it doesn't take into account ways beyond the DVR that people—especially young people—view television. For this reason, Nielsen is working on technologies that create ratings for the viewing of "TV" programs across a variety of platforms. These too may well suggest larger audiences than standard "live" ratings for certain programs.

PREPARING A SCHEDULE   The size of a program's audience helps determine the amount of money a station or network can charge an advertiser for time during that program. Consequently, ratings are always on the minds of the programmers who produce schedules for their stations or networks. Many programmers break down their work into creating discrete **schedules**, or patterns in which programs are arranged, for different **day parts**, or segments of the day as defined by programmers and marketers. The most prominent of these day parts is the period from 8 to 11 p.m. (from 7 to 10 p.m. in the Central and Mountain Time Zones), when the largest number of people are viewing. Called **prime time**, these are the hours in which the Big Four broadcast networks put on their most expensive programs and charge advertisers the most money for thirty seconds of commercial time. Prime time is the most prestigious day part, although not necessarily the most profitable. CBS, for example, makes more profits from its afternoon soap opera schedule (for which it pays relatively little) than from its pricier evening fare.

In prime time, as in all day parts, the different goals of different channels lead to different schedules. As noted earlier, household ratings are usually not as important as individual ratings to advertisers and programmers. Age, gender, and sometimes ethnicity are particular selling points. The Fox network, for example, wants to reach children on Saturday morning, whereas NBC is interested in "selling" adults to advertisers during much of Saturday morning. It's a no-brainer, then, that an animated comedy about kids is a more appropriate choice for Fox than for NBC.

When adults are the targets, most programmers start with the assumption that they must attract mostly people between 18 and 49 years old, because this is the market segment that most television advertisers want to reach. Although people older than 50 actually have more money than those who are younger, many advertisers believe that once people pass the age of 49 they are not as susceptible as younger adults to new product ideas. Advertisers are also aware that people who are 50 and older are less likely than younger adults to be taking care of children at home. More people in a household means more repeat purchases of goods such as soap, cereal, and frozen foods.

The building block of a television schedule is the **series**—a set of programs that revolve around the same ideas or characters. Series can be as varied as *Grey's Anatomy*, a weekly dramedy about physicians in a Seattle hospital; *Nightline*, a daily late-night news interview program; or *Are You Smarter than a 5th Grader?*, a game show that pits an adult's knowledge against knowledge held by kids. Series are useful to programmers because they lend predictability to a schedule. Programmers can schedule a series in a particular time slot with the hope that it will solve the problem of attracting viewers to that slot on a regular basis.

Programmers generally try to bring viewers to more than just one show on their station or network. Their goal is to attract certain types of people to an entire day part so that the ratings of that day part, and therefore its ad fees, will be high. Keeping people tuned to more than one series also means keeping them around for the commercials between the series. In TV industry lingo, the challenge is to maximize the **audience flow** across programs in the day part.

That's a tall order when so many viewers clutch that ultimate ratings spoiler, the remote control, securely in their hands for the duration of their viewing sessions. The idea of audience flow is particularly precarious when a substantial portion of households have digital video recorders that can capture one network's program while they watch a different channel. Still, Nielsen ratings do suggest that certain scheduling techniques can improve audience flow. One is the use of a strong lead-in to programs that follow. A **lead-in** is a program that comes before, and therefore leads into, another program. Ratings suggest that a strong lead-in tends to bring its audience to sample the program that comes after it. The chance for **sampling**, or trying a new series for the first time, is also increased if the **lead-out**—the program that follows the new series—is popular. Many people who are interested in seeing the first and third programs will stick through the second if they consider it at all good.

Say you're a programmer and have a new series that you want to give the maximum chance to succeed. By the logic of lead-ins and lead-outs, you should place the new series between two well-established shows that appeal to the same audience. This position, known as a **hammock**, gives the right viewers a huge opportunity to sample the show.

Sometimes what seems like a good program for a particular position in the schedule, or **time slot**, may be judged unacceptable because it is aimed at the same kinds of people (in terms of age, gender, ethnicity, or interests) who are flocking to a popular program on another channel at the same time. When programmers don't want to compete directly with a popular series, they turn to **counterprogramming**—placing a program that aims to attract a target audience different from that of other shows in a particular time slot. For example, in 2007 some local stations began to place game shows in the late afternoon (4 to 6 p.m.) time slot as counterprogramming to talk shows that their competitors were running at that time.[7]

prime time the hours in which the Big Four broadcast networks put on their most expensive programs and charge advertisers the most money for commercial time

series a set of programs that revolve around the same idea or characters

audience flow the movement of audience members from one program to another

lead-in a program that comes before, and therefore leads into, another program

sampling trying out a new series by watching it for the first time

lead-out the program that follows the program after the lead-in

hammocking the strategic placement of a program between two other programs; positioning a new series between two well-established shows that appeal to the same target audience often gives the right viewers an opportunity to sample the new series

time slot a particular position in the schedule

counterprogramming placing a program that aims to attract a target audience different from those of other shows in the same time slot; often done to avoid competing directly with a popular series

PRODUCING INDIVIDUAL PROGRAMS   To program producers, being successful doesn't just mean coming up with an idea that programmers like (as difficult as that may be). It also means coming up with an idea that programmers for local stations, broadcast networks, or cable/satellite networks need—at a cost they can afford.

Daily news programs tend to be the focus at the local broadcast level. Local programmers believe that morning, evening, and late-night news shows give viewers a sense of their station's commitment to the area. Early- and late-evening newscasts that draw good ratings also bring the station strong revenue. Apart from news, local broadcasters tend to produce little of their own material.

For many production companies, the biggest prize is for one of the broadcast networks to order a prime time series. That can be tough, because often network-owned production companies sometimes seem to have an inside track. Even apart from the competition with the networks' production divisions, however, the chances of getting such an order are not high. Network programming executives meet with many producers to hear brief summaries of program ideas. Creators may present several of these summaries, called **pitches**, at one sitting. Most of the time, the network people say that they are not interested. Sometimes they tell the creators that they will pay for a **treatment**, a multipage elaboration of the idea. The treatment describes the proposed show's setup and how it relates to previous popular series. It also discusses the collection of elements that will propel the series and give it a recognizable personality—the setting, the characters, typical plots, and the general layout, tone, and approach. This collection of elements, which often are created using a set of rules that guide the way the elements are stitched together with a particular audience-attracting goal in mind, is called the format of a show. (We have already seen how networks such as MTV can have formats.)

If network officials like the format and believe that it fits their programming strategy, they may commission research known as **concept testing** to try out this idea and the ideas of other producers with audiences. Concept testing involves reading one-paragraph descriptions of series formats to people who fit the profile of likely viewers. Sometimes these people are contacted by phone, and sometimes they are questioned in preview theaters where they have been invited to evaluate new shows. Researchers ask these viewers if they would watch the series based on the descriptions. If a producer's concept rates well with the appropriate audience, the interested network may contract for a sample script and a test program, called a **pilot**.

When the pilot is completed, the network tests it, too. Often the process involves showing the pilot to a group of target viewers, either on specially rented cable TV channels or in **preview theaters**. When cable TV is used, the individuals chosen are asked to view a movie or series pilot on the channel at a certain time. After the program, the viewers are asked questions over the telephone about what they saw. Viewers in preview theaters sometimes sit in chairs equipped with dials that they can use to indicate how much they like what they see on the screen. These responses, along with their written comments, help network executives decide whether or not to commission the series.

Let's assume that everything works out fine with a series' concept testing and pilot. The network executives then give the production company a contract for several episodes—typically thirteen. The contract is for permission—called a **license**—to air each episode a certain number of times. You might think that with such a deal in hand, production firm executives would be wildly ecstatic, sure that the show will enrich their firm. Not so fast. For one thing, the network may reduce the firm's potential profits by asking for co-ownership of the show as a way of paying for the risk the network is taking to fund and air it. Moreover, even with network backing, the show may not last long. Many prime time series receive bad ratings and are yanked by the networks even before their first thirteen episodes have aired.

---

pitch brief summary of a program idea

treatment a multipage elaboration of a television series producer's initial pitch to network programming executives; the document describes the proposed show's setup and the way in which it relates to previous popular series

concept testing research commissioned by network executives in order to determine whether the format of a proposed series appeals to members of the series' target audience; this often involves reading a one-paragraph description of series formats to people who fit the profile of likely viewers

pilot a single episode that is used to test the viability of a series

preview theater a venue to which members of a target audience are invited to engage in concept testing or to evaluate newly completed series pilots

license the contract between a production company and network executives that grants the network permission to air each episode a certain number of times; usually thirteen episodes of a series are ordered

Another item that makes production executives nervous is that network licensing agreements typically do not cover the full costs of each episode—even for shows from companies the networks own. If an hour drama is slated to cost the production firm $2.5 million per episode, the network may pay $1.5 million. The producers have to come up with $1 million per episode themselves. Over thirteen episodes, that will put them $13 million in a financial hole.

Why would any company do that? The answer is that production firms see network broadcast as only the first of a number of TV domains in which they can make money from their series. They can make money from local stations, from cable networks, from stores, from the internet, and from broadcasters outside the United States. And if a show succeeds on TV, these extra windows can become goldmines. But to learn more about how the money comes in, let's shift the discussion from production to distribution.

Distribution in the Television Industry

As we noted earlier, a broadcast television network is involved in both the production and distribution of material. When a network licenses programs from its own production divisions or from outside producers, it sends them to its affiliates, and they broadcast them (usually simultaneously) to homes. Not all TV programs are distributed in this way, however. One reason is that not all broadcast TV stations are affiliated with networks, and the independents need to get their programming from somewhere. Another reason is that even network stations do not broadcast the network feed all the time. Certain hours in the morning, in the afternoon, in the early evening, and after 1 a.m. belong to the stations. Therefore, they can take for themselves all the ad revenue they bring in during these periods, but first they must find programs that attract an audience at a reasonable price.

Syndication

Many nonnetwork distributors are willing to help local stations find attractive shows through syndication—licensing programs to individual outlets on a market-by-market basis (see Table 13.5, which presents ratings of the top twenty syndicated programs during a week in 2010). One way to attract audiences "off network" is with programs that are newly created for syndication. Examples are *The Oprah Winfrey Show*, the celebrity news program *Entertainment Tonight*, the cooking show *Rachael Ray*, and the game show *Wheel of Fortune*, which are made to be shown every weekday, and that is typical of new syndicated programming. This five-day-a-week placement is called **stripping** a show. Local programmers believe that, in certain day parts, putting the same show in the same time slot each weekday lends predictability to the schedule that their target audiences appreciate.

Stripping is also a popular tactic in **off-network syndication**—in which a distributor takes a program that has already been shown on network television and rents episodes of that program to TV stations for local airing. Consider *Law & Order: Criminal Intent*, a police and law drama produced by Wolf Films and NBC Universal, and shown on a first-run basis on NBC television and USA cable network. In 2007, NBC Universal Domestic Television Distribution syndicated it to local stations on a stripped basis. The distributor made deals with stations covering 95 percent of the country.[8]

Not all network programs make it into off-network syndication, though. The popularity of stripping means that a lot of episodes are required, and so shows with fewer than 100 episodes are unlikely candidates for syndication. Programs that the networks take off the air quickly because of bad ratings don't have a chance to go into reruns. Also, local stations are more likely to select situation comedies over dramas, as sitcoms get better ratings in reruns and tend to attract the audience profiles (young mothers and children) that local stations need after school and before the five and six o'clock news.

SUBSCRIPTION, OUT-OF-HOME, AND INTERNATIONAL DISTRIBUTION   If producers fail to place their reruns on local stations, there are other avenues that they can use. Cable and satellite networks have become voracious consumers of off-network programming, in part because these programs are less expensive than new shows and in part because they reliably attract certain categories of viewers. Nick at Night and TVLand are two subscription video networks that air television programs that people in their thirties and forties viewed when they were young. The Lifetime channel goes after programs that in their broadcast network lives were popular with women, and the Family Channel looks for material that few moms and dads would find objectionable.

Another venue for making extra money from television programs is what marketers call **out-of-home locations**; sometimes they are called **captive audience locations**. These include places such as airline waiting areas and store checkout lines where people congregate and would likely pay attention to TV clips and commercials. CNN distributes its news programming as the Airport Channel. NBC sends parts of its programs to a supermarket checkout TV network. CBS provides some of the news and entertainment programs it owns to airlines; it also owns a network that sends some of its programs (with commercials) to healthcare offices. ABC News provides material for a company that puts video screens on gas station pumps.

Foreign countries have also been a useful market for certain types of reruns. Broadcasters around the world purchase U.S.-made series as components of their schedules. The popularity of programs from the United States rises and falls, and in many cases homegrown programming gets better ratings than the U.S. material. Generally speaking, action dramas do better than sitcoms in this market, as American humor doesn't cross borders as easily as sex appeal (*Baywatch* was popular around the world) and violence (so was *Walker, Texas Ranger*). During the late 2000s, the increase in

stripping five-day-a-week placement of a television show; programmers believe that, in certain day parts, placing the same show in the same time slot each weekday lends a predictability to the schedule that their target audiences appreciate

off-network syndication a situation in which a distributor takes a program that has already been shown on network television and rents (licenses) episodes of that program to TV stations for local airing

out-of-home locations or captive audiences places such as airline waiting areas and store checkout lines where people congregate and would likely pay attention to TV clips and commercials

Table 13.5 Top Twenty Syndicated Shows for the Week ending February 21, 2010

Rank	Program	Network	Day	Duration (minutes)	HH Rating	Viewers (thousands)
1	Wheel of Fortune	CTD	MTWTF..	30	7.2	11,697
2	Jeopardy	CTD	MTWTF..	30	6.2	9,722
3	Two-Half Men-Syn (AT)	WB	MTWTF..	30	5.5	8,760
4	Judge Judy (AT)	CTD	MTWTF..	30	4.7	6,735
5	Entertainment Tonight (AT)	CTD	MTWTF..	30	4.4	6,473
6	The Oprah Winfrey Show	CTD	MTWTF..	60	4.6	6,249
7	Wheel of Fortune-WKND	CTD	......S	30	3.8	6,019
8	Family Guy-MF-Syn (AT)	2/T	MTWTF..	30	3.5	5,458
9	Office-Syn (AT)	NBC	MTWTF..	30	3.1	4,979
10	Law & Order: CI-WKL (AT)	NBC	......S	60	3.1	4,655
11	CSI New York-Syn (AT)	CTD	......S	60	3.2	4,578
12	Inside Edition (AT)	CTD	MTWTF..	30	3.2	4,477
13	Two-Half Men-WKND B (AT)	WB	......S	30	2.6	4,201
14	Seinfeld (AT)	SPT	MTWTF..	30	2.7	4,182
15	George Lopez (AT)	WB	MTWTF..	30	2.8	4,085
16	Evry Lvs Raymond-Syn (AT)	CTD	MTWTF..	30	2.7	3,906
17	Dr. Phil Show (AT)	CTD	MTWTF..	60	2.8	3,836
18	Millionaire (AT)	DAD	MTWTF..	30	2.7	3,789
19	Seinfeld-WKND (AT)	SPT	......S	30	2.5	3,743
20	King of the Hill-Syn (AT)	2/T	MTWTF..	30	2.4	3,591

For syndicated shows that air on multiple days, the viewership shown is the average of all telecasts. HH rating stands for household rating.

2/T, Twentieth Television; CTD, CBS Television Distribution; DAD, Disney ABC Domestic Television; NBC, NBC Universal; SPT, Sony Pictures Television; WB, Warner Brothers.

Source: "Syndicated: Judge Judy Tops Oprah." http://tvbythenumbers.com/2010/03/02/syndicated-judge-judy-tops-oprah-legend-of-the-seeker-sees-season-lows/43554 (accessed March 3, 2010). The article uses Nielsen TV ratings data. © 2010 The Nielsen Company. All Rights Reserved.

digital television channels in some countries led both new networks looking to raise their profiles and established networks wanting to stem audience losses to scramble for highly polished programs at reasonable prices. U.S. firms have been ready to fill the gap. In Spain, for example, the Telecinco network signed a deal with NBC Universal to show the new drama series *Trauma: Life in the ER* and the older *Parenthood* movies. "U.S. dramas bring prestige and work well for Spanish channels," said a Madrid-based research company executive.[9]

Note that a reverse flow of programs is also taking place. The increase in channels in the United States, combined with the need for less expensive programming, has led programmers to scour the world for series ideas. They may decide to copy an international series idea for use in the United States—even using the same basic scripts, but adapting the program to suit their idea of what their American audience wants. Examples include NBC's *The Office* and HBO's *In Treatment*, based on British and Israeli versions, respectively.

Challenges to Traditional TV Production and Distribution

The growth of digital media has presented many new challenges to the TV industry that are encouraging important new avenues for production and distribution. The internet has become a competitor to the traditional TV set for viewers' time, and so have video games and the DVD player. TV ratings are slipping as a result, and advertising rates are not rising as high as license fees in many cases. Producers and network executives are trying to find ways to profit from the programs that they make and circulate.

New Avenues for Network Distribution

The television networks have been especially active in pursuing ways to engage viewers with their programming across as many media as possible. The aim is not to replace the viewing of their programming on traditional channels, but to allow for ways for viewers to connect with shows they enjoy but didn't have time to view, or want to view again soon after they have aired. Both possibilities allow the networks to sell time to advertisers that want to reach those audiences. At this point, broadcast and subscription networks use four ways to make extra money from their programming:

- Insisting on DVR ratings
- Allowing cable firms to offer programs through video on demand
- Encouraging people to view programs with commercials on the internet
- Offering shortened or promotional versions of the programs for use on mobile handsets.

Let's elaborate a bit on each.

INSISTING ON DVR RATINGS   The main cable and broadcast networks have convinced advertisers that they should determine the ratings of a program not just by its viewing on a particular night and time. Rather, they argue, audiences increasingly use digital video recorders to postpone their viewing, and when they view those programs they should be counted. Such arguments lead to the adoption of the C3 ratings approach described earlier in this chapter.

OFFERING PROGRAMS THROUGH VIDEO ON DEMAND   Video on demand allows people to view programs at their leisure. The programs can be shown with commercials or without them, depending on the deal the network makes with the initial advertisers. At this point, Nielsen doesn't count VOD viewing in the ratings, but that could change.

ENCOURAGING VIEWERS TO VIEW PROGRAMS WITH COMMERCIALS ON THE INTERNET   An increasing number of homes have been paying for fast broadband connections to the internet. Such fast connections allow users to view audiovisual presentations with acceptable clarity, and as a result, just about every television network is posting much of its programming on the Web for people to view. The shows **stream**—that is, they start playing when you click on their links—and they are not designed to be saved on the user's computer. The program streams

stream the act of sending digital materials so they can be heard or viewed as they are sent, without having to be saved first

come with commercials that are much fewer in number and shorter in time than the ones people see on traditional TV. The catch, however, is that online a viewer cannot speed through ads.

Different networks have different philosophies about how much programming to put online and where. The biggest networks, though, have decided that putting shows only on their own sites is not enough. CBS, for example, has been making deals with many places on the Web, including TV.com (in which it has invested), to display links to its shows. Sites that bring viewers to CBS programs share in ad revenues. NBC Universal, Fox, and Disney, are among the firms investing in Hulu, which streams their programs and others.

Some observers contend the major networks are—or soon will be—cannibalizing their audiences by placing their first-run prime time programs for viewing on the Web. That is, they say people will watch the programs online (where there are fewer and less expensive commercials) and so make it difficult for the networks to profit from prime time showings. Network executives disagree, arguing that Web versions allow fans to view shows they miss occasionally, and they create new fans who end up watching the programs in their broadcast time slots. Either way, cable and satellite executives are annoyed that the programs can be found for free online. They note

CULTURE TODAY
SHOULD TV VIDEO BE FREE ON THE WEB?

From free peer-to-peer file-sharing groups to officially sanctioned sites such as Hulu and pay sites such as iTunes and Amazon, one doesn't have to canvass the internet far to find an episode of the latest hit television series that network and cable broadcasters have aired only days, if not hours, before. The most recent iteration of television on the internet has been a joint venture by Time Warner and Comcast called "TV Everywhere." This idea, which in 2009 was in the pilot project stage, would give only Comcast cable subscribers access to programming from Time Warner-owned stations such as TBS and TNT through the internet. Customers would also be able to access Time Warner on-demand programs through their cable boxes.

This project departs from the traditional notion of television on the internet, which has seen the major broadcasters (NBC, ABC, CBS, Fox, Disney, etc.) stream content online, either through their own websites or through industry-backed sites like Hulu. Not only is this service free, but it is also available without subscription to all Americans with access to the internet.

Two separate debates have emerged from opposite ends of the corporate–public spectrum surrounding the launch of "TV Everywhere." The first is from Disney, which believes that if content is to be streamed for subscribers, only those subscribers should have to pay a premium. "Our product is extremely valuable," Disney CEO Bob Iger says, "and if we are offering it on another platform or in another location for the consumer to

access it, I believe that's more value we are delivering [to a distributor or consumer] and we should get paid appropriately."

The other body of criticism stems not from rival corporations, but interest groups such as Public Knowledge. They contend that with "TV Everywhere," Comcast and Time Warner are "violat[ing] the open nature of the internet. By adding this additional toll lane, Comcast and Time Warner want to create their own 'managed channel' within the internet and turn the internet into their own private cable channel." On the flip side, Time Warner and Comcast argue that they are providing customers who have already paid for the programming through cable subscriptions another medium by which to view it. The debate becomes one of access and of corporate and copyright profits.

The success of "TV Everywhere" raises several interesting questions about access to programming and models of profitability in an era of converging media.

Sources: Staci D. Kramer, "Disney's Iger On Authentication: 'We Should Get Paid Appropriately'," paidContent.org, July 30, 2009. http://paidcontent.org/article/419-disneys-iger-on-authentication-we-should-get-paid-appropriately/ (accessed August 8, 2010); Eliot Van Buskirk, "Cable Departs from Hulu Model with 'TV Everywhere'," *Wired*, June 26, 2009. http://edition.cnn.com/2009/TECH/biztech/06/26/wired.tv.everywhere/ (accessed August 26, 2010).

that they pay money to carry those and other programming, and they worry that increasing numbers of households will drop their subscription TV contracts and simply view many entertainment and news programs online—and purchase some from digital retailers such as iTunes or Amazon. Comcast, Time Warner, and other cable firms have therefore suggested a program their executives call "TV Everywhere"—a password system for the Web so that you will not be able to watch a program on, say, Hulu, unless you pay for a subscription service.

OFFERING PROGRAMMING FOR USE ON MOBILE DEVICES   In addition to focusing on the internet, many media and advertising executives look to the mobile phone as the next great place for programming. A growing number of Americans have phones that can play videos. Mobile phone companies offer such programming and have made deals with firms such as MobiTV and MediaFLO to sell such services to their customers. Television and cable networks have been trying to figure out ways to create sponsored mobile offerings that people would want to watch on the go. Fox tried a mobile version of its cult hit, *24*. The other networks have been experimenting with promotional videos for programs in the belief that some viewers would find them interesting on the go.

New Avenues for Production Firms

The television networks have been more aggressive about taking advantage of the new media environment than TV production firms have been. The producers have, however, recognized the value of DVDs and have been selling boxed sets of popular TV series such as *Grey's Anatomy, 24, Entourage,* and *Mad Men*. One direction that producers have only begun to take is to make material specifically for the Web. With so many amateur videos showing up on YouTube and MySpace, the notion of distributing a professional TV series on the Web sounds intriguing. However, the producers would need to find places to show the material that would get attention and justify the large amounts of money such a series might cost.

High-profile Hollywood talent has been involved in working on Web-initiated programming. When the Budweiser beer company started Bud.TV in 2006, it turned for material to Kevin Spacey's Triggersteet Productions, Matt Damon's LivePlanet Productions, and the Warner Bros Television Group's Studio 2.0—an outfit created for less expensive Web-based projects. Consider, too, the path of Emmy award-winning writer/producer team Marshall Herskovitz and Edward Zwick (*My So-Called Life, Thirty-Something, Glory*). In 2007, they decided to take the pilot of an ad-sponsored program called *Quarterlife* that did not make it to traditional network television and to recreate it in smaller bits as an internet series. They enlisted the enormously popular site MySpace (owned by News Corporation) to distribute the series' thirty-six episodes, and did not count out showing it elsewhere on the Web as well. The endeavor wasn't wildly popular, but their move did point to a distribution platform for new professionally created television programming outside of the traditional channels. It's a new world for video professionals, and it stretches the term "television" far beyond what people would have thought a decade ago.

Exhibition in the Broadcast Industry

Local stations, cable systems, satellite delivery systems, and wired phone and wireless phone companies take on the role of exhibitor when they deliver material directly to viewers. Like theaters in the movie business and stores in the book publishing industry, the broadcast exhibitors are retailers. Their business is to attract the number and the kind of viewers who can help them make a profit for their shareholders.

The early twenty-first century finds the television exhibition system in the midst of a major upheaval. Local broadcasters—the bedrock of the medium since its commercial introduction in the late 1940s—are facing ever-escalating competition from the cable, satellite, internet, and even mobile phone businesses. Moreover, those other businesses have the potential for making money from both subscription fees and advertising, whereas local broadcasters make money only from advertising. To make matters even more difficult for local broadcasters, the increased number of channels that cable and satellite services bring into people's homes has meant that ratings for the network and local programming that broadcast stations deliver have been declining rather steadily. Local television stations still make money, but observers wonder whether this will still be true later in this century as hundreds of channels race into American homes.

Network affiliates are particularly worried about the declining ability of ABC, CBS, and NBC to grab the lion's share of the U.S. television audience. Local TV executives are also concerned about the networks' strong and increasing participation in the subscription video world. Disney-owned ABC controls cable/satellite networks ESPN, ESPN2, the Disney Channel, and Disney Family, among others. NBC-Universal controls MSNBC, CNBC, USA, Syfy, and Bravo. All the broadcast networks are placing hit programs on the Web, with the consequence that viewers don't have to watch local channels (and their commercials) to see prime time TV. Network executives reply that as their O&O properties are extremely important to them (as a group they often make more profits than the networks), they would not do anything that would fundamentally harm local service. They are also helping the local stations to beef up their websites, where they make money from advertising. These are among the places viewers can find network shows. Nevertheless, the tension between the two parties continues.

Another strain in exhibition involves the recent conversion to digital television. As we noted earlier in this chapter, this conversion essentially gave every network and broadcast station the capability of sending out either one high definition television signal or a number of regular definition channels. As a result of this conversion, local stations hope they will be able to exhibit their programming via a new type of mobile TV, such as MediaFLO and MobiTV—TV feeds you can get on certain mobile phones. In 2009, broadcast began on a separate standard for mobile television that uses the digital TV spectrum and doesn't interfere with phone calling. It allows local television stations to broadcast entertainment, emergency alerts, news, local tourism guides, and other materials to netbooks, portable DVD players, and in-car displays, as well as phones. At this point, the activities are still experimental, with tests by the public expected to begin in 2010. Will local broadcasters be able to profit from it? Stick around for a few years to find out the answer to this tension-filled question.

Tensions are also running high in the cable exhibition business. For decades cable systems were the only major exhibitors competing with local TV stations. Now cable operators worry that their power will be eroded substantially by DBS firms such as DirecTV and DISH, as well as by broadband services from Verizon and AT&T that will duplicate cable services.

Television and Media Literacy

Americans spend enormous amounts of time with television, companies spend billions of dollars feeding programming endlessly to the tube, and governments (particularly the federal government) spend many hours deciding how to regulate it. From the standpoint of media literacy, it will be useful to apply our knowledge of the industry from this chapter to concerns about three interrelated areas: audience, content, and control.

Audience Issues

As we have seen, audiences are critically important to the people who run the television industry. Go to any meeting of industry executives or turn to any trade magazine on the industry and you're likely to note intense discussions of the size of the audience and its nature. The term **tonnage** shows up frequently; the word describes a hefty number of viewers and indicates that, at least in network television, reaching large numbers of people for advertisers is still a key goal. Also showing up a lot, though, are phrases such as "18- to 49-year-olds," "18- to 34-year-olds," "bilingual Hispanics," "the African-American audience," and "high-spending teens." They indicate a strong and growing concern with targeting that parallels what we have seen in other media industries.

When you hear or read these terms, step back and think about what they really mean. You might remember our discussion in Chapter 2 about how mass media executives consider people primarily as consumers of media materials and other products. The audience research that media firms conduct and the ways in which

tonnage describes a hefty number of viewers and indicates that, at least in network television, reaching large numbers of people for advertisers is still a key goal

CULTURE TODAY
HISPANIC TELEVISION

Many of the nation's 40 million Hispanics tune in to Spanish-language television on a regular basis. It shouldn't surprise you to learn that Spanish-language television is set up a lot like English-language TV. Instead of CBS or ABC, Hispanics have two broadcast networks, Univision and Telemundo. Like their English-language counterparts, these networks utilize dozens of local affiliates across the country.

Univision claims the lion's share of the Spanish-language audience (75 percent). It is closely associated with Mexico's Televisa network, and its schedule mostly consists of imported shows from Mexico and other Latin American countries. Telenovelas (which are basically soap operas) are a key component of its prime time schedule. Sports programming, such as soccer and boxing, is a common weekend feature. The network has also become well known for its nightly U.S. programs. Jorge Ramos, one of Univision's anchors, is basically the Tom Brokaw of the Spanish-speaking community. Boosted by the popularity of its news programming, Univision's affiliates regularly earn higher ratings than the affiliates of some English-language networks in cities such as Miami and Los Angeles.

Telemundo, purchased by Sony in 1998 and then NBC in 2001, has always been a far second to Univision, reaching only 25 percent of the Spanish-language audience. Its first season under Sony proved disastrous,

resulting in free advertisements that cost the network more than $1 million in potential revenue. Telemundo turned to several strategies to recover including a partnership with TV Azteca and attempts to provide original programming that reflects the experiences of Latinos in the United States.

More recently, trends in television viewing among Hispanics have been changing owing to the increasing number of second- and third-generation Latinos. Of the Hispanics born within the United States, 75 percent watch English-language television; and only 26 percent of this group watch any Spanish-language programming. This has resulted in a rise in demand for English-based Hispanic-oriented programming. There has been an increase in courtroom shows featuring English-speaking judges of South American descent and English-language adaptations of popular telenovelas. Some analysts claim that it is this area where the greatest possibilities of growth lie for networks such as Telemundo.

Sources: Jeff Zbar, "Law and Disorder are Hot," *Advertising Age*, March 27, 2006; Jay Sherman, "Experts Say Net Missed Chances; Ratings Are Up, but Telemundo Still No Match for Univision," *Television Week*, April 10, 2006; "Know Cristina." http://www.cristinaonline.com/english/know_cristina/index.asp (accessed March 16, 2010)

they interpret that research are aimed at figuring out two things: what people who are attractive to certain types of advertisers are like, and how to get these people to be loyal consumers of certain media and advertised products.

These considerations of the audience take place in all media industries. A chapter on television is an interesting place to emphasize them because so many of us are so often part of TV's audience. But as we think about being part of that audience, we also ought to think of another point made in Chapter 2: mass media executives do not think about audience members in the same way that audience members think about themselves. A TV network may be interested in whether you are in the 18–49 age bracket, but you may consider age relatively unimportant in your life. Churchgoing or friendships, lifestyle categories that may have little significance to the media firms, may well be key to the way you see the world.

When you come across the audience labels that television companies and their advertisers promote, think about how they are created for commercial purposes. Realize that what the executives leave out in considering the audiences for their programming may be just as important as what they put in. Also, consider what it means to define so much of U.S. society through lenses created for commercial purposes. For many broadcast network TV executives, the optimal viewer is an 18- to 24-year-old with money to spend. As we have seen, these executives' dedication to reaching people in this demographic segment shapes much of the way programs are selected and schedules are crafted. From *CSI* to *Cougar Town* to *Nip/Tuck*, TV executives' way of looking at the world shapes the way we as viewers see it.

Critics of the medium—and of all advertiser-sponsored media—have a term for this approach to audiences. They call it the **commodification of audiences**. By commodification, they mean that everything in life, both private and public, is being shaped by the values of business and commercialism. In this logic, such categories as age, gender, and ethnicity and such ideas as friendship and knowledge are understood only in terms of their monetary value. People within certain age brackets are more important than people in other brackets because they bring in more money. People are described by characteristics that relate to what they buy, and when they buy things.

Because of the TV industry's commodification of audiences, people themselves are treated as products to be compared and sold to advertisers based on their value to those advertisers, critics say. By extension, the television programs that are created to attract audiences typically are not aimed at making people better citizens, smarter individuals, or more friendly neighbors. Rather, they are designed solely to get their attention so that they will watch the commercials. Critics further argue that a TV industry built around programming that demands attention for the purpose of commercial persuasion is not an industry that can hope to better society.

commodification of audiences the idea, held by critics of the advertiser-supported media's approach to audiences, that everything in life, both private and public, is being shaped by the values of business and commercialism

Content Issues

Many critics of the U.S. television industry believe that it is the industry's commercial motives, and the resulting commodification of its audience, that has led to what they consider programming that emphasizes violence, sex, and sensationalism at the expense of quality. They acknowledge that there are some good programs on TV—programs that compellingly challenge audiences to think about themselves or the world around them—but much programming, they insist, exists simply to get people's attention in the most basic ways possible so that they will watch the commercials. TV producers have learned that human beings are drawn instinctively and quickly to images of sex, violence, and other types of fast-paced "action." They

TECH & INFRASTRUCTURE
TV RATINGS AND KIDS

The Telecommunications Act of 1996 enabled parents to exercise greater control over the television content to which their children were exposed. In addition to requiring TV manufacturers to produce sets with a V-chip that allows parents to block objectionable programming, a rating system was enacted to alert viewers to the nature of program content. The ratings strategy was highly controversial because its categories were based on the age of the viewer, like those of the motion picture industry, and not on the program's content (for example violence, adult language, sex).

Joanne Cantor of the University of Wisconsin—Madison conducted several studies that showed that the age-based ratings system did not help parents make informed television content decisions for their families. Cantor and other researchers analyzed national surveys that showed parents' overwhelming preference for a content-based ratings system over one based on age appropriateness.

In addition, these researchers found that a TV ratings system akin to the movie industry's ratings was fairly uninformative and unpredictable. They coded more than 1,400 PG-rated movies to determine what elements contributed to the rating: adult language, violence, and/or sexual content. Of these movies, 26 percent were rated PG on the basis of language only and another quarter contained both violence and coarse language, but 18 percent had no sex, violence, or coarse language. Based on these findings, the odds were that an age-based TV rating system would not give parents the information they needed in order to assess whether a program's content might be harmful to kids.

Cantor also examined whether ratings and advisories produced a "forbidden fruit" effect, leading some children to want to watch programs that the system implied might be inappropriate. Blander ratings such as "viewer discretion advised" did not affect the attitudes toward viewing programs of kids in any age or gender group. However, ratings that could be seen as more restrictive, such as "parental discretion advised" or film ratings of PG-13 or R, did heighten the appeal of the programs for older kids, especially older boys.

Professor Cantor's research raises provocative questions about whom the ratings really benefit—the parents or the broadcasters.

V-chip a small computer device that allows parents to block programs automatically from a television set if the programs are transmitted with a code that will activate the chip; the codes are content ratings that reflect concerns about violence, sex, and "strong" language (the V in the V-chip stands for violence)

therefore exploit these images in the most efficient manner possible in order to gather the audiences they need.

There are many advocacy groups that don't emphasize the commodification argument, but that nevertheless have problems with sex, violence, and stereotyping on TV. Parent, teacher, religious, and other groups have expressed grave concerns about what they consider to be too much of these three depictions on TV, as well as a scarcity of programs that seriously try to educate as well as entertain children. Table 13.6 sketches some of their major concerns and the typical replies of industry executives.

Most of the time, the industry's replies have not persuaded the advocacy groups. Individuals and organizations have advocated a wide variety of solutions, ranging from boycotting the offending networks to boycotting their advertisers to passing laws that would require certain kinds of programming. Every so often, their ideas strike a responsive chord with society at large, possibly because of particularly offensive programs. Government regulators sometimes step in and put pressure on offending producers and networks. Nervous advertisers may also use their clout to tone down the obnoxious programming. Critics contend that these steps work for only a short while; the sex, violence, and stereotyping come back with a roar when public concern turns to other things.

Industry officials naturally say that they prefer self-regulation to government regulation. They especially prefer "rating" systems that alert parents and others to potentially objectionable aspects of shows while not taking away the ability of producers to create such shows. This approach has been in effect in the movie industry since the 1960s, as we noted in Chapter 12. In the late 1990s, a rise in public concern about television's portrayal of sex and violence and its use of vulgar language led

Table 13.6 Concerns and Replies Regarding Current TV Issues

Issue	Some Concerns	Some Industry Replies
Violence on television	TV violence is encouraging children and even adults to see physical force as the solution to problems, to see the world around them as more mean and dangerous than it really is, and to be less sensitive than they might otherwise be to real-world violence	Violence is a part of life, and television reflects life. Some of the greatest literature includes violence. Much of the violence on TV is unrealistic, and most viewers can distinguish between TV violence and reality
Sex on television	Television portrays sex and sexuality in a casual manner, not linked to love. Nudity (on cable) or semi-nudity (on broadcast) is seen too often. Sex is often not linked to issues of birth control or safe sex	Sex is part of life, and television reflects life. If programs with this sort of content were not popular, producers would not offer them
Stereotyping on television	On television, people who belong to certain groups, especially women, people who have physical handicaps, and members of minority ethnic groups, are portrayed in patterned ways that sometimes demean them. Fat people are often the object of humor, for example, and highly intelligent black men are few and far between. Such images extend and reinforce patterns of prejudice in the society at large	Stereotyping is part of life, and television certainly reflects that part, as well. Yet although it does still exist on TV, stereotyping is much less a part of programming today than it was years ago. As the United States becomes more and more a multiethnic society, television is increasingly reflecting that diversity

industry critics, members of Congress, and industry executives to agree on a similar system for broadcast TV. They added an interesting technological addition, however: beginning in 2000, all television sets sold in the United States must come with a so-called V-chip.

Invented in Canada, the **V-chip** is a small computer device that allows parents to block programs automatically from a television set if the programs are transmitted with a code that will activate the chip. The codes are content ratings that reflect concerns about violence, sex, and "strong" language. (The V in V-chip stands for violence.) Table 13.7 gives the ratings categories that most networks have agreed to present at the beginning of their programs and in codes that can be read by the chip. Advocacy groups, members of Congress, and the FCC chairman in the late 1990s saw the V-chip as a way to give harried parents power over what their children were watching even when they were not in the room with them. However, researchers found that most parents didn't understand how the chip works and didn't use it, and critics suggested that all it really did was let the TV industry off the hook for the programming it created.

Lawrence Lien, CEO of Parental Guide Inc., points out how the new "V-chip" can be used for blocking television programs containing violence, sex, and/or inappropriate language.

Industry Control Issues

More generally, critics have complained that the major companies in the television industry have become so powerful that it is difficult, if not impossible, for public groups to influence their activities. For one thing, critics say, the federal government's move to deregulate the industry to encourage competition and the

Table 13.7 TV Rating Categories

Rating	Meaning	Description
Children's categories		
TVY	All children	Animated or live action; shows' themes and elements are specifically designed for a very young audience, including children from ages 2 to 6 years. Program not expected to frighten younger children
TVY7	Directed at older children	Program designed for children aged 7 years and up. May be more appropriate for children who have acquired the developmental skills needed to distinguish between make-believe and reality. Themes and elements in this program may include mild physical or comedic violence and may frighten children under the age of 7
General categories		
TVG	General audience	Although this rating does not signify a program designed specifically for children, many parents may allow younger children to watch this program unattended. It contains little or no violence, no strong language, and little or no sexual dialogue or situations
TVPG	Parental guidance suggested	May contain some material that some parents would find unsuitable for younger children. The program may contain infrequent coarse language, limited violence, and some suggestive sexual dialogue and situations
TV14	Parents strongly cautioned	Program may contain some material that many parents would find unsuitable for children under 14 years of age. May contain sophisticated themes, sexual content, strong language, and more intense violence
TVM	Mature audience only	Specifically designed to be viewed by adults and therefore may be unsuitable for children under 17 years. May contain mature themes, profane language, graphic violence, and explicit sexual content

growth of new services has meant that executives feel increasingly confident that business can effectively sidestep government and public concerns when it comes to shaping television's future. For another, they add, although on some levels competition between the satellite, cable, broadcast, and telephone industries may be fierce, the number of major companies involved in the competition is getting smaller all the time. Moreover, these companies are the media conglomerates that we've discussed in previous chapters.

The names should be familiar by now—Time Warner, News Corporation, Disney, CBS, and Comcast. These and a few other firms have their hands across cable, satellite, and broadcast TV and the Web. In these media, they are involved in production, distribution, and/or exhibition. Clearly they play major roles in other media as well, from airlines to supermarkets to healthcare sites. Critics say that their influence throughout the TV industry cements the control that a small number of firms have over the dominant channels leading to Americans' minds. More optimistic observers point to the millions of video clips on the internet as evidence that the creation of television programming is not locked up by just a few firms. Those who disagree reply that, although these clips certainly exist on places such as Revver, MySpace, and YouTube, they have nowhere near the impact on the population that the major TV distributors have.

In addition to raising important points about social power, these arguments also highlight the point that began this chapter: the changing meaning of television. Once confined to a box in living rooms and bedrooms, television programs now swirl across media. It's both fascinating and important to note how the TV industry is adjusting to all these changes, and what spaces the changes—and the major industry players—are allowing for new and diverse audiovisual voices.

Chapter Review
For an interactive chapter recap and study guide, visit the companion website for *Media Today* at http://www.routledge.com/textbooks/mediatoday4e.

Questions for Discussion and Critical Thinking

1 What is meant by "the golden age" of television?
2 Think about ideas you might have for a new television series. What steps would you need to follow to get your series on the air?
3 How many types of television distribution now exist?
4 Describe the C3 TV ratings system.
5 What is the difference between how media executives conceive of audiences and how audiences conceive of themselves?
6 How might an advertiser consider the pros and cons of the variety of television viewing modes, such as viewing in real time, with the help of a DVR, in a captive audience situation, through the internet, or through a mobile device?
7 Think about all the TV shows you typically watch. How many media conglomerates can these shows be traced back to?

Internet Resources

Internet Movie Database (http://imdb.com)
A useful catalog of television programs that have appeared over the decades.

Variety (http://www.variety.com/)
This show business magazine specializes in coverage of television programming. The website requires subscription, but your college may have a password for students.

Broadcasting & Cable (http://www.broadcastingcable.com)
Broadcasting & Cable says it covers "the business of television," and that includes local and national broadcast and cable developments. The website also includes information about industry events and conferences.

Key Terms

You can find the definitions to these key terms in the marginal glossary throughout this chapter. Test your knowledge of these terms with interactive flash cards on the *Media Today* companion website.

Constructing
Media Literacy

. . . .

1   What program scheduling strategies can you note on yesterday evening's broadcast network television schedule?

2   "Audiences are not real things. They are constructed by media firms." What do you think this statement means? Do you agree with it? Why or why not?

3 Where do you stand with regard to critics of TV who say that violence, sex, and stereotypes are problems on the small screen?

Companion Website
Video Clips
· · · · · · · · · · · · · · ·

Further off the Straight and Narrow—Here and Queer

This clip from the Media Education Foundation documentary *Further off the Straight and Narrow* looks at the increased presence of gay, lesbian, bisexual, and transgender (GLBT) characters on television. Credit: Media Education Foundation.

Norman Lear Interview

In this clip from the Archive of American Television, show creator, writer, and director Normal Lear discusses what he considers to be television at its very best. Copyright Archive of American Television. http://Emmys.org/archive.

Class Dismissed—From the Margins to the Middle

This clip from the Media Education Foundation documentary *Class Dismissed* explores the way television shows depict African-Americans and how this affects cultural attitudes and public policies. Credit: Media Education Foundation.

The Story of Television

This film tells RCA's story about the development of television. Credit: Internet Archive/Prelinger Archives.

Kennedy on Telstar—Europe Sees News Conference (1962)

This newsreel footage shows President John F. Kennedy's press conference that marked the broadcast over the first communications satellite, Telstar. Credit: Internet Archive/Universal Newsreels.

Case Study
· · · · · · · · · · · · · · · · · · · ·

OUT-OF-HOME TELEVISION

The idea As noted in the chapter, television can now be seen in many places outside the home, and the major providers of broadcast and cable programming (CBS, NBC-U, ABC) are providing some of that material. How common is out-of-home television where you live, and who is providing it?

The method Use your postal ZIP code as the geographic territory and try to uncover the use of out-of-home television sets in stores, healthcare offices, travel depots, and other waiting and shopping areas. What is the programming like, and what is the format? Is the material repurposed—that is, taken from general broadcast or cable TV—or is it new material? Try to determine who the program producers and distributors are in each case. Write a report of your findings.

14 The Internet and Video Game Industries

After studying this chapter, you will be able to:

1 Sketch the development of the computer, the internet, the Web, and video games

2 Explain the workings of the internet industry

3 Discuss business models in the online world

4 Describe video game genres

5 Sketch the production, distribution, and exhibition of video games

6 Chart major social controversies surrounding the internet and video games

MEDIA TODAY

As recently as twenty years ago, college students were unlikely to have heard of the internet. Now, a large majority of undergraduates use the internet regularly—from various sites on campus and from home. In fact, around 80 percent of American homes are connected to the internet, most with high-speed connections. And increasing numbers of people are accessing the Web through smartphones. Not all of these developments are the work of mass media industries (that is, industries that focus on the industrialized production and multiple distribution of messages through technological devices). As we saw in Chapter 1, when you send a computer message (electronic mail, or email) to a friend, that action is mediated interpersonal communication, much like a telephone conversation. When an organization works methodically with other organizations to reach members of the public, however, that activity is mass communication.

A great deal of mass communication activities take place on the internet. Millions of people go to websites to watch television shows, read newspapers, download music, and do so many things that have traditionally been associated with separate noncomputer media industries. Yet the internet itself has an industrial aspect to it, with production, distribution, exhibition, and finance activities that are both different from and similar to traditional media industries. One aim of this chapter is to understand how the commercial Web is organized.

A second aim is to survey another business rooted in the digital technology: the video game industry. People play video games both on and off the Web—on their computers or on separate consoles connected to monitors. In fact, the total revenue of the U.S. video game industry exceeds $10 billion.

This chapter, then, examines two relatively new mass media industries that center on advances in computer technology: the commercial aspects of online services and the video game industry. You probably deal with these industries every day without thinking very much about how they work or how they relate to other media. Here's your chance to find out, and to think about the implications of these media for yourself, people close to you, and the society at large.

analog electronic transmission accomplished by adding signals of varying frequency or amplitude to carrier waves of a given frequency of alternating electromagnetic current. Broadcast and phone transmission have conventionally used analog technology

digital electronic technology that generates, stores, processes, and transmits data in the form of strings of 0s and 1s; each of these digits is referred to as a bit (and a string of bits that a computer can address individually as a group is a byte)

convergence the ability of different media to interact with each other easily because they all deal with information in the same digital form

This mechanical adding machine, built by French philosopher and mathematician Blaise Pascal in 1642, was the first digital calculator. His design may not have been commercially successful, but it did lay the groundwork for today's computer engineering.

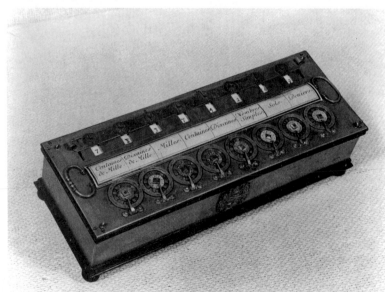

An Industry Background

The crucial difference between computer-centered mass media and other media technologies is that they are *digital* rather than *analog*. A simple way to understand the distinction between digital and analog is to think about what distinguishes an old-fashioned vinyl record from a CD. If you look at a record, you will see grooves. When the phonograph needle moves through the grooves, it picks up vibrations that were made by the sound coming from the singer's vocal cords. When the record was made, a machine cut grooves that reproduced these vibrations into the vinyl. The record grooves, then, hold a literal physical reproduction—an **analog**—of the singer's sound that can be reproduced with the right equipment.

The CD, by contrast, does not contain a physical reproduction of the sound. During the CD's recording process, computers transform the singer's voice patterns into a string of binary digits, or bits (0s and 1s). Each sequence, or string, of 0s and 1s represents a different sound. The strings serve as a code—a symbolic representation of the sound. This **digital** code is placed on the CD in an order that conforms to the sequence of sounds made by the singer. When you turn on your CD player, a laser beam reads the code and sends it to a computer chip in the player. The computer chip is programmed to recognize the code and to understand which strings of numbers represent which sounds. At the speed of light, the chip transforms the code into electrical impulses that, when sent through an amplifier and sound system, reproduce the singer's voice.

The basic idea applies, too, to digital music files that reside in your computer, digital music player, or mobile phone. In that case, you don't even have a piece of plastic that carries the tune into the device. Rather, you download a digital file in one of a number of formats (MP3, WAV, AAC, or others), and if your device has the ability to recognize and decode the file it transforms it into sounds that reproduce the original. If the file you are using is not copy-protected (and MP3 and WAV files are not) you can copy the music from your phone to one of your other players. Being able to move digital files (music or not) from one device to another is an example of the **convergence** of media technologies—the ability of different media to interact with one another easily in parallel digital formats. Convergence also means that different media can end up carrying out similar functions because they all accept digital information. So, for example, a computer can take on the functions of a DVD player, a CD player, and a cable television set.

Just as important, the application of computer codes to mass media materials allows audience members to manipulate the materials to suit their interests. Audience members who are connected to the producers of an audio or audiovisual program via a cable or telephone line can respond to those producers via the computer. The producers, in turn, can send out a new message that takes the response into consideration. This sort of manipulation and response—which is much easier in digital than in analog technology—is known as **interactivity**. We are leaving the analog age and entering the age of digital interactive media.

The Rise of Computers and the Internet

The roots of digital interactive media can be traced at least as far back as a primitive computing machine that French mathematician Blaise Pascal built in the 1600s. Around the same time, German mathematician Gottfried Leibnitz set out important theoretical principles for the use of **binary digits**, the zero-to-one system that is at the core of digital technology. Morse code—the dot–dash system devised by American inventor Samuel Morse when he created the telegraph in the 1840s—is another example of the use of a binary code to represent letters in the English alphabet. It wasn't until a hundred years later, though, that scientists figured out how to build a machine that could use binary digits to perform much more complex manipulations of mathematical data.

In 1940, at Harvard University, mathematician Howard Aikin constructed a computer that used the binary system to calculate; it used open and closed mechanical gates to represent binary digits. The machine was huge and noisy. A profound advance came in the mid-1940s when electrical engineers at the University of Pennsylvania replaced the mechanical gates with electronic "gates" in the form of vacuum tubes. These engineers constructed **ENIAC (Electric Numerical Integrator and Computer)**, as this machine was called, to help the U.S. military predict the trajectory of missiles in flight. Like the Harvard machine, ENIAC was very big. It took up a large room, weighed thirty tons, and used about 18,000 tubes.

What was brilliant about ENIAC, though, was its use of electronic rather than mechanical components as the basis of its operation. Building on the success of ENIAC, scientists at Bell Labs invented the **transistor** in the 1950s—featuring the same capabilities as the vacuum tube, but in a smaller package. Private firms began to turn out computers, and over the next few decades these computers got smaller, faster, and more powerful. By the 1970s, inventors had created the **microprocessor**, a miniaturized version of the central processing unit (the "brains") of a computer on a single chip. The microprocessor made it possible to build complex calculators and video games. As early as 1975, the Midway arcade company sold a Japanese home-arcade game cartridge called *Gunfight* that relied on a computer microprocessor for displaying its images.

interactivity the ability to track and respond to any actions triggered by the end user, in order to cultivate a rapport

binary digits the zero-to-one system that is at the core of digital technology

ENIAC or Electric Numerical Integrator and Computer the world's first operational electronic digital computer

transistor a device that amplifies current and regulates its flow, acting as a switch or gate for electronic signals

microprocessor a miniaturized version of the central processing unit (the "brains") of a computer processor on a single microchip (sometimes called a logic chip); designed to perform arithmetic and logic operations that make use of small number-holding areas called registers. Typical microprocessor operations include adding, subtracting, comparing two numbers, and fetching numbers from one area to another

The Electronic Numerical Integrator and Computer (ENIAC) was so big that it took up an entire room. The two women in this 1946 photograph are programming the computer by adjusting its wiring. These two women and four others—Kay McNulty, Betty Jennings, Betty Snyder, Marlyn Wescoff, Fran Bilas, and Ruth Lichterman—hired to run ENIAC, were the first computer programmers in history.

The Advent of the Personal Computer

The invention of the microprocessor also led to the creation of the personal computer (PC), a computer that could fit on a desk. The first people to use PCs were hobbyists who built PCs from kits. By the early 1980s, Apple Computer, Commodore Corporation, Tandy Corporation, Osborne, and IBM were building fully assembled PCs for home as well as business use. An entire industry developed to create programs that allowed personal computers to do useful things for people. Software companies marketed word processing programs that made the computer function like a super typewriter. Spreadsheet programs helped companies calculate projected expenditures and earnings. Educational programs helped kids do schoolwork. Computer games helped people have fun and persuaded them to buy computers in the first place. Just as surely as network television programs did, these computer programs involved mass communication. Over the next decade, in fact, executives in the television industry began to worry that the computer software industry was luring audiences away from their traditional TV sets.

Personal computers like the Apple II GS seen here began to find their way into homes and businesses in record numbers in the 1980s. *Time* magazine named the personal computer its "Person of the Year" for 1982. In 2006 *Time* would return to computers again for its "Person of the Year," this time honoring "You," the anonymous online contributors to blogs and sites such as Wikipedia and YouTube.

Online Capability

The typical 1980s-vintage personal computer that sat in a home office consisted of a video display, a keyboard, a microprocessing unit, and a storage device (a replaceable, or "floppy," disk drive and often a permanent, or "hard," drive). What the earliest home-based computers generally didn't have was a way to send messages to computers elsewhere in the world. Before too long, however, computers did come equipped with the ability to go online—to receive digital information from anywhere by telephone. The hardware that made online activity possible is the **modem**, a device attached to the computer that performs a digital-to-analog conversion of data and then transmits the data to another modem. That modem reverses the process, performing an analog-to-digital conversion that permits the computer to which it is attached to use the data (see Figure 14.1).

modem a device attached to the computer that performs a digital-to-analog conversion of data and then transmits the data to another modem, which reverses the process

An entire industry developed around the use of the modem. Commercial online networks, such as Prodigy and America Online, aggressively offered consumers the ability to play games with people across the nation, get help with homework through online encyclopedias, and chat with people about common interests. By the mid-1990s these firms came into competition with an enormous online network that threatened to push them aside: the internet.

internet a worldwide system of computer networks; a network of networks in which users at any one computer can, if they have permission, get information from any other computer (and sometimes talk directly to users at other computers)

The **internet** was developed by the National Science Foundation (NSF) from a project started by the U.S. Department of Defense. ARPANet, as it was first known, was conceived by the Advanced Research Projects Agency (ARPA) of the Department of Defense in 1969 to create a network that would allow users of a research computer at one university to "talk to" research computers at other universities. Because messages could be routed or rerouted in more than one direction, ARPANet could continue to function even if parts of it were destroyed in the event of a military attack or

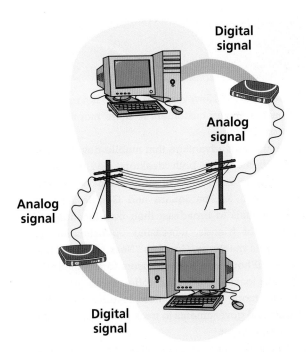

Figure 14.1 How a Modem Works
A voiceband modem—short for modulator–demodulator—allows computers to "talk" to one another over great distances by modulating, or converting, the digital computer signals into sounds that can be transmitted over telephone lines. A modem on the other end then demodulates the signal—that is, it converts the analog sounds back into digital information that can be understood by another computer. Today, cable and DSL modems are more commonly used as they provide faster connections between computers, and unlike voiceband modems they do not need to modulate or demodulate the digital signals that they transmit.

other disaster. At its core were three parts: a computer code (software) that allowed messages to be addressed and sent to particular individuals, a series of interconnecting computer networks that could coordinate the transmission of these messages around the nation and even around the world, and modem hardware that made it possible to use regular analog telephone lines to send digital computer messages.

Although the network was initially meant for scientific use, nonscientists within universities and executives from companies outside universities saw linking their computers to this network as a new and speedy way to communicate with others around the world. Universities and private firms spent huge sums of money to purchase computers and make sure that they could handle the rush of internet traffic. The research, education, and business benefits that accrued through the internet, though, would have cost much more if the work had been done in other ways—through travel or regular phone calls, for example.

hyperlinks highlighted words or pictures on the internet that, when clicked, will connect the user to a particular file, even to a specific relevant part of a document

The earliest form of the internet was developed in 1969 by the Advanced Research Projects Agency (ARPA) of the Department of Defense and it was first known as the ARPANet. As this map from 1973 shows, the network allowed users of research computers at distant locations to communicate with one another.

The Hyperlink and the World Wide Web

But some computer scientists had even more ambitious ideas. They didn't want the internet to be a vehicle for simply transferring messages or documents between individuals. Instead they wanted to create a way for large groups of people to access and work on the same files. And they wanted to be able to send people to those documents through **hyperlinks**—highlighted words or pictures that, when clicked, connect the user to a particular file, even to a specific relevant part of a document. Researchers at CERN, a nuclear research center in Geneva, Switzerland, made this possible in 1989. Tim Berners-Lee and Sam Walker from the United

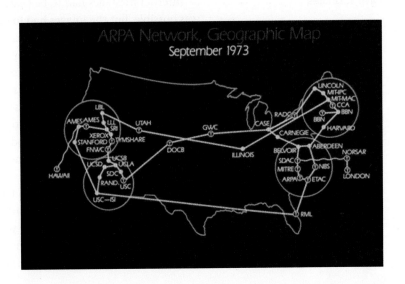

CRITICAL CONSUMER
IF MOBILE OUTPACES THE DESKTOP

Do you remember the first time you saw someone walking around talking on a Bluetooth or hands-free phone? Did you think they were crazy? Just a few years ago, only the truly technologically inclined were able to speak on a cellphone without the use of their hands. Now, the sight of a person speaking loudly, seemingly to his or herself, is commonplace. Technology has changed so much over the past decade that it's hard to imagine what the technological landscape will look like in even a few short years.

Gartner, a U.S.-based information and technology research firm, has made that speculation a little bit easier. By their predictions, personal computers will be eclipsed by mobile phones as the most common Web access device by 2013. Including smartphones and browser-equipped enhanced phones, Gartner expects that there will be 1.82 billion mobile Web units, and only 1.78 billion PCs, by 2013.

This change in the primary mode of access will cause major changes for Web companies that have yet to create sites compatible with the mobile Web. Already, many sites allow for easy access to shopping, banking, entertainment, news, and networking, all from a handheld device. However, sites that do not make the transition risk losing customers to more mobile Web-savvy organizations.

One important advantage that mobile devices have over traditional PCs—both desktops and laptops—is the ability to keep track of an individual's location. Programs such as FourSquare and Google Latitude allow individuals to broadcast their own location and keep track of friends, increasing opportunities for serendipitous meetings. Google's "Near Me Now" feature allows iPhone and Android users to automatically search their location for banks, coffee shops, bars, and a whole lot more. Of course, these features also allow marketers and governments to track people, often without their knowing it.

Do you think your cellphone will become more useful than your PC? How advantageous are the local features offered by mobile devices? What are the negatives of making a mobile device such a critical part of your life?

Source: Mark Walsh, "Gartner: Mobile To Outpace Desktop Web by 2013," *Online Media Daily*, January 14, 2010.

HTML (HyperText Markup Language) a computer language system that allowed people to access a system of interlinked documents through the internet. HTML is used to define the structure, content, and layout of a Web page by using what are called tags that have attributes

World Wide Web A system of documents linked by hypertext that can be accessed through the internet

browser software that interprets HyperText Markup Language (HTML) and displays it on a computer screen

cyberspace the online world of computer networks

Kingdom and Robert Cailliau from Belgium created **HTML (HyperText Markup Language)**—a computer language system that allowed people to access a system of interlinked documents through the internet. HTML is used to define the structure, content, and layout of a Web page by using what are called tags that have attributes. As the viewer of a Web page you don't see the HTML; it is hidden from your view. However, you do see the results. A key aspect of this system—what they called the **World Wide Web**—was that users could go to the materials by typing in a specific World Wide Web address or by clicking on a link in a document that contained the address, which would automatically "link" them to that place.

Internet messages had to be transmitted in text form. Sending graphical images was possible, but the images had to be decoded by the receiver before viewing. That situation changed in 1993, when computer scientists at the University of Illinois created the **browser**, a graphical way to access the World Wide Web. Using software like Apple's Safari, Microsoft Internet Explorer, or Mozilla Firefox, a computer user can easily view complex drawings or photographs. As computer experts devised increasingly sophisticated and easy-to-use browsers for finding information, students and their professors began to "surf" the Web. The idea that millions of well-educated people around the world could access pictures, sound, and even video intrigued marketers and media firms. They started websites and tried to entice potential customers to visit them.

By the mid-1990s, the internet had moved far beyond its original military and academic purpose to become a vast communication system. Much of the activity in **cyberspace** (that is, in the online world of computer networks) still involved mediated interpersonal communication—individuals interacting one-on-one with other individuals through written words, voice, and video. But a large and growing portion of the online world involved commercial attempts to reach out to various audiences. Companies sprang up to create sites on the Web or the commercial online networks, to determine who was coming to these sites, and to encourage advertising on them. The digital world of the internet, in short, had become a new mass medium.

The Rise of Video Games

The period from the 1940s through the 1990s is also roughly the period in which video games developed to become a mainstay in many American homes.[1] The birth of video games can be traced back to two separate developments that initially were unrelated to the computer. The first development was the advent of the **pinball machine**, a coin-operated game in which a player scores points by causing metal balls to move in certain directions (often using flippers) inside a glass-covered case. These games were made popular by David Gottlieb beginning in the early 1930s at **entertainment arcades**—commercial locations featuring coin-operated machines such as pinball machines, fortune tellers, and shooter games.

The bestselling arcade game of all time, *Pac-Man*, is widely considered one of the definitive classic video games of the 1980s. The remarkable popularity of the game upon its release in 1980 was dubbed "Pac-Man Fever," and the phenomenon launched countless toys and merchandise, an animated *Pac-Man* TV series on ABC, and even a pop music single that sold 2.5 million copies.

While the mechanical pinball game was a fixture of arcades, scientists working on video electronics and computers were amusing themselves with games that could be played on TV-like displays. In 1958, for example, scientists at the Brookhaven National Laboratory set up a video tennis game on an oscilloscope for play during its annual visitors' day. Similarly, computer students at MIT, Stanford, and other schools began to use their universities' computer systems to create games such as *Spacewar!* that were tied to their love of science fiction. Activities like these taking place at the University of Utah influenced Nolan Bushnell and Ted Dabney, in 1972, to start Atari—the first successful U.S. company to create video arcade games.

During the late 1970s and the early 1980s arcade video games became very popular with entertainment genre, such as shoot 'em ups (*Defender*), racing games, maze games (*Pac-Man*), and platform games that challenged players to navigate a series of levels through ladder-like structures while dodging obstacles (*Donkey Kong*). This arcade fever encouraged toy companies such as Mattel and electronics companies such as Magnavox to try to make video games for the home. Mattel released a hand-held game machine with a screen, but most of the games were placed on computer chips that were placed into cartridges that in turn were inserted into electronic boxes ("consoles") that were attached to TV sets. There were several failures among the console games, and for a time in the 1980s gaming attention shifted from consoles to a new invention, the personal computer. Companies sold disks that could be played on specific computers—for example the Commodore 64, the Apple II, and the IBM PC. Strategy video games and simulation video games—genres that had already been used for some consoles—caught on as particularly appropriate for computer play, including *Dune* (strategy) and *SimCity* (simulation).

When the internet began to be used by more and more academics in the 1980s, it too became a location for playing games. People even figured out how to use internet **bulletin boards**, in which many users could send text messages to one another, as a place where many people could share a game. Multi-player computer games that combined elements of chat rooms and fantasy role-playing games, such as *Dungeons & Dragons*, emerged as extremely popular in these environments and the games

pinball machine a coin-operated game in which a player scores points by causing metal balls to move in certain directions (often with flippers) inside a glass-covered case

entertainment arcade a commercial location for coin-operated machines such as pinball machines, fortune tellers, and shooter games

bulletin boards software that allows users to exchange messages with other users, read news, publish articles, and perform other activities such as play games

MUDs or multi-user dungeons fantasy role-playing games such as *Dungeons & Dragons*, they were the predecessors of today's online games, with hundreds of thousands of players

MMORPGs or multi-player online role-playing games computer games accessible via the internet in which a very large number of players who control certain characters interact with one another

became known as **multi-user dungeons (MUDs)**. They were the predecessors of today's massively popular **multi-player online role-playing games (MMORPGs)**, such as *World of Warcraft*, with millions of players worldwide.

By the time the early 1990s came around, then, the basic types of video game vehicles had been established. Although some had almost vanished during the previous years, the next decade would reveal that many different types of video game platforms—consoles, computers, handheld, and internet—could co-exist. At the end of the first decade of the twenty-first century, video games and the commercial internet are intertwined as places to distribute, play, and buy the many types of gaming products. So let's take a look at the commercial internet industry and then focus on the video game business. Our primary lenses for both explorations will be the by-now familiar categories of production, distribution, and exhibition.

An Overview of the Internet Industry

Reaching out from home or from work through the computer has become common for many people in the United States. In 2009, about 76 million U.S. households had internet access. That number represented about 67 percent of all U.S. households, and 95 percent of computer households. As Table 14.1 shows, in late 2009 the percentage of American men and women who said they use the internet or email (at home or out of home) was around the same at 74 percent. Internet use is more likely with younger than older adults, with higher education, with greater income, and with parents with children under the age of 18. Black people tend to say they use the internet less than white people, and both groups use it more than Hispanics. Data from 2006 suggest that Hispanics whose main language is Spanish are less likely than English speakers to use the internet; this difference may be related to income and education. Another interesting data point: in September 2009, 93 percent of Americans aged from 12 to 17 years reported using the internet.

The findings above come from the Pew Internet and American Life Project, which continually surveys the U.S. population regarding its internet use, knowledge, and habits. Table 14.2 reflects the answers that a representative national sample gave Pew regarding uses that people make of the Web. As you can see, there are generational differences in some activities—playing games, for example, goes down with age—but there are other areas such as using email and getting news for which large percentages of almost every age group find the internet valuable. Clearly, teens and young adults find social and entertainment uses on the Web—playing games, downloading music, sending instant messages, and social networking—that show that the internet is pretty well a central aspect of their world.

In the chapters about the individual media industries we have explored their online activities and strategies—noting that it is impossible for a media firm to remain separate from the internet in today's competitive environment. Our purpose here is not to repeat these points, but to examine features of the online world that affect all companies, explore some businesses that are unique to an internet environment, outline ways that companies make money online, and consider some of the social issues that are relevant to these activities.

Production and Distribution in the Internet Industry

When it comes to the commercial internet, it is useful to discuss production and distribution together. That is because these two activities are often very much intertwined. When a company (say, *The New York Times*) produces a website (or works with a specialized firm to create the site) and posts it online, it is engaging in

Table 14.1 U.S. Internet Use, 2009

Below is the percentage of each group who use the internet, according to our December 2009 survey. As an example, 74% of adult women use the internet.

	Internet Users (%)
Total adults	74
Men	74
Women	74
Race/ethnicity	
White, non-Hispanic	76
Black, non-Hispanic	70
Hispanic (English- and Spanish-speaking)	64
Age	
18–29	93
30–49	81
50–64	70
65+	38
Household income	
Less than $30,000/year	60
$30,000–$49,999	76
$50,000–$74,999	83
$75,000+	94
Educational attainment	
Less than high school	39
High school	63
Some college	87
College +	94
Community type	
Urban	74
Suburban	77
Rural	70

Source: The Pew Research Center's Internet & American Life Project, November 30 to December 27, 2009 Tracking Survey. N = 2,258 adults, 18 and older, including 565 cell phone interviews. Interviews were conducted in English and Spanish. Margin of error is ± 2%. http://pewinternet.org/Reports/2010/Internet-broadband-and-cell-phone-statistics.aspx, accessed March 5, 2010.

production and distribution of the site. Often, companies and individuals create content for sites that they don't control. Consider the example of a video production firm that creates a travel video for *The New York Times* website, or the videos, songs, and photos that individuals post on MySpace, YouTube, and Facebook. Creative products by the people who visit the sites are often called **user-generated content (UGC)**. Still, even in these situations, the commercial firm that is distributing these works also acts as a production firm because it creates the elements on the sites that organize where these materials go.

user-generated content (UGC) creative products, such as videos and music, generated by the people who visit websites such as MySpace, Heavy, and Facebook

Table 14.2 Generational Differences in Online Activities

	Online Teens[a] (12–17)	Gen Y (18–32)	Gen X (33–44)	Younger Boomers (45–54)	Older Boomers (55–53)	Silent Generation (64–72)	G.I. Generation (73+)	All Online Adults[b]
Go online	93%	87%	82%	79%	70%	56%	31%	74%
Teens and Gen Y are more likely to engage in the following activities compared with older users:								
Play games online	78	50	38	26	28	25	18	35
Watch videos online	57	72	57	49	30	24	14	52
Get info about a job	30[c]	64	55	43	36	11	10	47
Send instant messages	68	59	38	28	23	25	18	38
Use social networking sites	65	67	36	20	9	11	4	35
Download music	59	58	46	22	21	16	5	37
Create an SNS profile	55	60	29	16	9	5	4	29
Read blogs	49	43	34	27	25	23	15	32
Create a blog	28	20	10	6	7	6	6	11
Visit a virtual world	10	2	3	1	1	1	0	2
Activities where Gen X users or older generations dominate:								
Get health info	28	68	82	74	81	70	67	75
Buy something online	38	71	80	68	72	56	47	71
Bank online	*	57	65	53	49	45	24	55
Visit government sites	*	55	64	62	63	60	31	59
Get religious info	26[c]	31	38	42	30	30	26	35
And for some activities, the youngest and oldest cohorts may differ, but there is less variation overall:								
Use email	73	94	93	90	90	91	79	91
Use search engines	*	90	93	90	89	85	70	89
Research products	*	84	84	82	79	73	60	81
Get news	63	74	76	70	69	56	37	70
Make travel reservations	*	65	70	69	66	69	65	68
Research for job	*	51	59	57	48	33	9	51
Rate a person or product	*	37	35	29	30	25	16	32
Download videos	31[c]	38	31	21	16	13	13	27
Participate in an online auction	*	26	31	27	26	16	6	26
Download podcasts	19	25	21	19	12	10	10	19

a Surveys conducted Oct–Nov 2006 and Nov 2007–Feb 2008. Margin of error ± 4% and ± 3% respectively.

b Surveys conducted between Aug 2006 and Dec 2008. Margin of error ± 3% for these surveys.

c Most recent teen data comes from survey conducted Oct–Nov 2004. Margin of error ± 4%.

* No teen data for these activities.

Source: Pew Internet & American Life Project, http://pewinternet.org/Infographics/Generational-differences-in-online-activities.aspx#, accessed March 4, 2010.

MEDIA RESEARCH
THE PEW INTERNET AND
AMERICAN LIFE PROJECT

The rise of the internet has led to a host of questions regarding its impact on society. Although it is agreed that the internet affects the way people live and interact, it is an ongoing process to understand the nature(s) of this influence. The Pew Internet and American Life Project (http://www.pewinternet.org) produces reports that examine the impact of the internet on a variety of aspects of American life. The project covers the following eleven areas: demographics; E-Gov and E-Policy; education; family, friends and community; health; internet evolution; major news events; online activities and pursuits; public policy; technology and media use; and work. According to its mission statement, "The Project aims to be an authoritative source on the evolution of the internet through collection of data and analysis of real-world developments as they affect the virtual world."

Utilizing nationwide random telephone surveys and online surveys, the project collects both quantitative and qualitative data to aid research initiatives throughout the country and the world. Both individual and group use is tracked through the surveys, painting detailed portraits of the internet in its many forms and functions. The Pew Internet and American Life Project is a project

of the Pew Research Center, a nonpartisan "fact tank" that provides information on the issues, attitudes, and trends shaping America and the world. (http://www.pewresearch.org). Funding is provided by the Pew Charitable Trust, an independent nonprofit organization dedicated to improving public policy, informing the public, and stimulating civic life.

Source: http://www.pewtrusts.org.

FUNDING INTERNET CONTENT   Companies produce and distribute websites in order to make money, but the methods they use vary widely. Some companies see their sites as carrying out image-making activities. Others see their sites as selling products. Still others display content aimed at making money by attracting audiences through subscriptions or through advertising. Sometimes, firms approach sites with more than one of these goals. Let's take a look at each.

http://www.kraftfoods.com/jello/, the website for Jell-O, promotes a fun, friendly image for the product by posting music, videos, and other interactive features, as well as recipes.

Sites Involved in Image Making

The idea behind using a site for image-making activities is typically to encourage fans of a product or service to purchase the product or service offline. Kraft Food's Jell-O website (http://www.kraftfoods.com/jello/), for example, is a site that provides recipes based on various forms of the product. The site also allows people to watch Jell-O commercials and learn about Jell-O products. The site also urges people to use various forms of the product with other Kraft items (Cool Whip, for example). None of these activities directly makes any

CRITICAL CONSUMER
PLEASE ROB ME, FOURSQUARE, AND TWITTER

With the logo of a masked burglar carrying a sack of money, the site PleaseRobMe (pleaserobme.com) made its debut in February 2010. True to its name, the site allowed users to discover whom in their city had left their home vulnerable to theft. The site worked by searching Twitter feeds for "check-ins" via FourSquare, a location-based mobile phone application in which users can log and broadcast their current location through Twitter. PleaseRobMe pointed out that, if people are out at a bar or a restaurant, their homes are likely to be vacant.

Ostensibly, the purpose of PleaseRobMe was to aid burglars in their criminal activity, but the creators had their tongues planted firmly in cheek when they designed the site. By satirizing the culture of constantly sharing personal information that is found on Facebook, FourSquare, and Twitter, the creators hoped to raise awareness of privacy-related issues on the internet. This strategy proved somewhat successful, as news outlets such as the BBC News and NPR reported on the site. "Think before you Tweet," wrote Dan Fletcher in a *Time* article entitled "The Dangers of Online Oversharing."

Privacy concerns aside, social media platforms such as these have been derided as superficial streams of useless, overly personal information. "How does it enhance my sense of closeness when my Facebook newsfeed tells me that Sally Smith (whom I haven't seen since high school, and wasn't all that friendly with even

then) 'is making coffee and staring off into space'?" asked William Deresiewicz of the *Chronicle Review*. *New Yorker* columnist George Packer echoed these sentiments in an editorial about Twitter, stating, "The notion of sending and getting brief updates to and from dozens or thousands of people every few minutes is an image from information hell."

Criticisms such as these are in line with historical patterns. From the printing press to the automobile, the television to the telephone, new technologies have been accused of alienating us from our relationships, our environment, and our intellects. In response to Packer's comments, *New York Times* blogger Nick Bilton points to the benefits of Twitter in circulating information swiftly, and notes that even something that today seems as quaint as the train was initially protested as a threat to society's well-being. He goes on to muse over whether a mid-nineteenth-century Packer would have ridden trains, "or if he would have stayed at home, afraid to engage in an evolving society and demanding that the trains be stopped." Do you agree with his comparison?

Sources: Nick Bilton, "The Twitter Train Has Left the Station," *New York Times: Bits Blog*, February 3, 2010; William Deresiewicz, "The End of Solitude," *The Chronicle Review*, January 30, 2009; Dan Fletcher, "Please Rob Me: The Dangers of Online Oversharing," *Time*, February 18, 2010.

money for Kraft. Instead, they cultivate a friendly, healthful, family-oriented image for Kraft food that they hope will yield purchases in supermarkets and other physical stores.

Sites Selling Products or Services

If you have ever bought anything online (and a large majority of internet-enabled individuals have) you are familiar with websites that sell products or services. This selling method has much in common with an old-fashioned catalog, except that online you sometimes have an opportunity to see a video of the products in operation. Amazon.com is a major company that sells online only; it has no physical (or brick-and-mortar) stores. Although Amazon, Zappos, and Netflix are internet-only retailers that do extremely well, it should come as no surprise that the most popular brick-and-mortar stores are among the most popular online stores; Wal-Mart, JC Penney, and Home Depot draw millions to their websites. People in the industry refer to firms with both an online and an offline sales presence as **click-and-mortar companies**. Financial analysts sometimes prefer the click-and-mortar firms over pure Web companies because the former have their warehouses and transportation services, and they have the deep pockets needed to absorb the years of losses that are likely to result from their Web operations. Analysts also suspect that consumers are more likely to be comfortable buying from the Web if they are buying brands they

click-and-mortar companies firms with both an online and an offline sales presence already know. Moreover, if something goes wrong with the products they buy online, they can take these products back to the brick-and-mortar version of the store to receive face-to-face customer service.

Content Sites Selling Subscriptions

A website that primarily shows printed or audiovisual material is called a **content site**; the company running it is called a **publisher**. Think, for example, of http://www.consumerreports.com or http://www.carfax.com. The idea of a publisher charging people subscriptions to see the content of a site may sound great, but it is one that hasn't worked very well on the Web. People who are spending hundreds, even thousands, of dollars for hardware and monthly payments to receive the internet seem to have come over the decades to expect that media content will be free or very low cost. Exceptions tend to be in the business area. Industry trade magazines such as *Variety* sometimes charge for people to get into their websites, or into substantial parts of those sites. (They may show ads, as well.) In addition, specialized information sites, such as http://www.lexis.com, charge for entry. But over the past decade consumer newspapers and magazines that have tried subscriptions have abandoned them for all but archives of their periodicals. Instead, they have turned to advertising as the way to support their online ventures.

content site sites that attempt to build revenues by attracting audiences to content provided on the site

publisher the company running a website

CRITICAL CONSUMER
FACEBOOK, MYSPACE, AND DIVERSITY

Although social media such as Facebook, MySpace, and Twitter may have been recently touted as "the great leveler," a space in which divides of race, class, and ethnicity are free to dissolve, recent findings by Microsoft's social media researcher Danah Boyd indicate that that may not necessarily be the case.

After interviewing hundreds of teenage users of social media and analyzing thousands of profiles, Boyd came to the conclusion that popular social networking sites Facebook and MySpace are strongly divided by race and class lines. MySpace, Boyd argues, is perceived as the "ghetto" of the social web, as a space for those less educated, less cultured, and predominantly for ethnic minorities.

After Facebook overtook MySpace in the number of active users in 2008, Boyd likened the migration of certain users from MySpace to Facebook to a form of virtual "white flight." "The fact that digital migration is revealing the same social patterns as urban white flight should send warning signals to all of us," says Boyd. "When people are structurally divided, they do not share space with one another, they do not communicate with one another; this canon does breed intolerance."

Boyd's provocative claims generated a swarm of controversy, yet they pointed to potential concerns for those attempting to successfully disseminate messages through social media. Instead of treating social media like a giant, digital melting pot, Boyd's research implies that marketers should be aware of and account for racial and ethnic divides on social networking sites.

Pepper Miller, a consultant in African-American marketing, echoes these sentiments. "One of the things we're seeing—and what's interesting for marketers to understand—is how people are trying to self-segregate in social media," Miller noted. "It's not this unified [social networking community] that people perceive it to be." Miller points to examples of communities of predominantly African-American communities on Twitter as evidence of the social media's racially segregated nature.

The political implications should also not be ignored. Boyd notes that politicians wanting to encourage forms of civic participation through social media should avoid excluding certain populations by recognizing the self-segregation across different sites. It may also be useful to try to figure out how to encourage ethnic and racial groups to mix in the virtual world.

Sources: Lisan Jutras, "There's Virtual Litter and Graffiti, but Is There a Real Online Ghetto?" *The Globe and Mail (Canada)*, October 12, 2009; Olopade Dayo, "MySpace to Facebook = White Flight?" *The Root*, September 16, 2009; Gillian Reagan, "In the Battle Between Facebook and MySpace, a Digital 'White Flight'," *The New Yorker*, June 29, 2009; Elaine Wong, "Why Social Media Isn't 'One Big, Happy' Space for Multicultural Marketing," *Brandweek*, February 4, 2010.

Content Sites Selling Advertisements

The bookstore, newspaper, radio, music, movie, and television sites that we have discussed throughout this text post advertisements on their websites. Sometimes the ads are for their own products. Very often, they are for other companies' goods or services, and the publishers make money for posting the ads that reach the people who visit the sites. Then there are sites such as Monster, CareerBuilder, and HotJobs that make money off the posting of classified ads.

Social Media Sites

social media site or social networking site (SNS) an online location where people can interact with others around information, entertainment, and news of their own choosing and, often, making

Social media sites are content sites that are quite different from those based on traditional media, whether based on radio or classified ads. A **social media site** (sometimes called a **social networking site (SNS)**) is an online location where people can interact with others around information, entertainment, and news of their own choosing and, often, making. Facebook, MySpace, Twitter, and LinkedIn are wildly popular social media locations that offer people quite different approaches to interacting. Twitter requires users to communicate via messages of no more than 140 characters. MySpace encourages interactions around audio and video materials. LinkedIn invites people to connect around business networks. Facebook sees itself as a way in which friends can stay connected with each other on a continuing basis. Facebook and MySpace focus on making most of their money through targeted advertising. LinkedIn sells ads, but also charges members for certain levels of networking. Twitter doesn't have a robust revenue-generating model yet. Most of its support comes from venture capitalists who expect that in the future it will generate lots of cash—most likely though an ad-based revenue model.

Many popular internet-only publishers such as YouTube and Facebook find it difficult to make profits from the internet advertising environment. One reason for this is the huge amount of available advertising space online as millions of websites compete for advertisers' money. That competition often lowers the cost of ads on some sites to $1 or less per thousand views. As a comparison, the cost-per-thousand of a large urban newspaper in 2009 hovered between $30 and $40. The concern that advertising will not be able to cover the costs of major media publishers has led executives such as News Corporation's Rupert Murdoch to insist that his holdings—including MySpace, the *New York Post*, and *The Times* of London—will find a way to charge audiences for at least some of his firm's online services. How such charges will be levied and whether consumers will go along with them are hotly debated, and their solutions will determine the fate of publishers online.

search engine websites that allow users to find sites relevant to topics of interest to them

SEARCH ENGINES   The Wikipedia online encyclopedia defines a **search engine** as "an information retrieval system designed to help find information stored on a computer system." The search engine developed out of the need of people using the Web to be able to find sites relevant to topics of interest to them. You undoubtedly have gone to Google, Yahoo, MSN, Ask, Dogpile, or another search program to find out about a person, location, or fact. Search engines work by using **Web crawlers** (also known as **Web spiders**)—programs that automatically browse the World Wide Web to create copies of all the visited pages. The search engine software will then catalog or "index" the downloaded pages so that a person searching for a word in them will find it quickly. Depending on the search engine, the spiders index more or less of the Web, but they never catalog the entire Web. Not only would it take too much time (and the crawlers have to keep doing their jobs over and over again to update their findings), there are some parts of the Web that they cannot enter because they are protected by passwords.

Web crawlers or Web spiders programs used by search engines that search the internet to retrieve and catalog the content of websites

algorithm a complex set of rules that search engines use to come up with sites that relate to your search terms

When you type in search terms, you activate a complex set of mathematically based rules, called an **algorithm**, that come up with sites that relate to your search terms. Algorithms are the "secret sauce" of search engines. It is quite well known, though, that Google's approach to search involves a particular definition of popularity: the number of websites that are linked to a site that uses the search term. So, for example, if you type "Nikon" into a Google search box, the top links that appear will be for sites with the word "Nikon" to which many other sites link. The main list of sites that you get in response to writing Nikon in the Google search box is called Google's **natural search results**. That means that the sites came up based on Google's algorithm without any influence from Nikon or any other advertiser. Yahoo and other major search engines also set their ads apart from the natural search results. This point is important because the way these search companies survive is by sending advertising to their users. If natural results were intermingled with ads, users might have a tough time knowing whether a link was placed higher because it was really relevant or because a company paid for its placement there.

The homepages of the Baidu and Google search engines

DISTRIBUTING ADVERTISEMENTS ON THE WEB Advertising of all types brought in $33.8 billion to websites in 2008; the growth rate was 14.9 percent in a bad economic environment, in which most traditional media lost lots of ad money.[2] According to the Internet Advertising Bureau and other sources, in 2008 73 percent of Web advertising flowed to the ten most popular sites on the Web. In fact, the top fifty sites grabbed 91 percent of the revenues. The remaining 5 percent is still a very large number—half a billion dollars—an amount over which many sites would want to compete. Nevertheless, those who believed that the Web would allow a great spread of ad money across a broad range of large and small sites must be disappointed by these findings.

Broadly speaking we can distinguish between two types of ads on the Web, text ads and display ads. **Text ads** typically comprise a few lines of writing about the offered product or service that link to the advertiser's website. **Display ads** add graphics and sometimes video to text and usually take up more space on a Web page. Let's look at the two types in a bit more detail.

Text Ads

The most widespread text ads on the Web are those placed by email advertising companies, advertising networks, and search engines. An email advertising company is a firm that sends commercial messages to people's email addresses. Sometimes, as in the case of Google's Gmail, text ads lie at the bottom of an otherwise normal email between two or more people. Sometimes the entire email message is an advertisement. The norm (and in some states the law) regarding email advertising is that the recipient has to agree to receive such ads or have a relationship with the firm that is sending them. That consent is called an **opt-in** rule for sending the advertising. Legitimate companies that send email ads also provide the opportunity for recipients to **opt-out**—to not continue to receive the ads. Ads that people do not want to receive are known as **spam**. The amount of spam from all over the world into people's

natural search results websites that come up based on a search engine's algorithm without any influence from any advertisers

text ads typically comprise a few lines of writing about the offered product or service that link to the advertiser's website

display ads add graphics and sometimes videos to text and usually take up more space on a Web page

opt-in a rule for sending email advertising that states the recipient has to agree to receive such ads or have a relationship with the firm that is sending them

opt-out a rule for sending email advertising that provides the opportunity for recipients to not continue to receive the ads

spam ads that people do not want to receive

ad network a collection of many websites that a company knits together in order to sell ads on them

pay-per-click (PPC) advertising a model of internet advertising in which an advertiser pays the firm that displays the commercial message only when it is clicked

contextual advertising the activity of scanning a publisher's Web page and serving ads that match the topics of the page

banners square or rectangular commercial messages that sit on the page of a website

rich media ads ads that contain animated or video presentations that activate automatically or can be activated by clicking on the ad

pop-up ads commercial messages that jump out at you (typically in square and rectangular form) when you go to a Web page or click on a picture or word

interstitial pop-up ads pop-up ads that jump out at you between page loadings

broadband technologies equipment that allows for the quick reception and transmission of a wide array of signals coming into the computer at the same time

mailboxes is so great that an industry has grown up to sell programs that attempt to filter the ads so they will not appear with legitimate mail. Many internet service providers such as Comcast and Verizon also filter the email people receive to stop spam.

An **ad network** is a collection of many websites that a company knits together in order to sell ads on them. The ad-serving company shares its revenues with the sites on which it places the ads. For example, Google has both a search engine advertising program (which it calls AdWords) and an ad network (which it calls AdSense). To make money from advertisers for its search page, it puts out bids for search words. Say, for example, that you are a camera manufacturer. You might bid on the term "digital camera"—that is, state how much you are willing to pay Google if your ad shows up and someone clicks on it. If Google accepts your bid your text ad will come up next to Google's search results when a person types "digital camera" into the search box. Google will charge you, however, only if the person clicks on the link of your text ad, thus indicating a serious interest. That model for reimbursement is called **pay-per-click (PPC) advertising**.

When an internet user clicks on an ad that shows up on Google's search page, Google alone makes the money. The situation is different with Google's AdSense network. Google computers scan the pages of the sites in the network and choose ads for products that seem to resonate with the topics on the page. So, for example, if the page discusses cameras, Google might serve up an ad for a camera to that page. This activity of scanning a publisher's Web page and serving ads that match the topic of the page is called **contextual advertising**. As with the AdWords, the advertiser pays only if the user clicks on the ad.

Display Ads

Display ads are messages that combine text and graphics. If you go to an ad-supported site, chances are you will see the two basic forms of display ads, banners and pop-ups. **Banners** are square or rectangular commercial messages that sit on a page of the website. Many of them are **rich media ads**—that is, they contain animated or video presentations that activate automatically or can be activated by clicking on the ad.

One type of ad that many people dislike is **pop-up ads**—commercial messages that jump out at you (typically in square and rectangular form) when you go to a Web page or click on a picture or word. Creators often build animated images and sell them in order to grab the attention of Web users in an environment filled with ads. In addition, increased competition for viewer attention has led advertisers to be quite creative (and sometimes annoying) with their placement of banners and, especially, pop-ups. The latest Web browsers have software that prevents pop-ups from showing up if the user chooses to eliminate them. One kind of forced viewing that remains is the **interstitial pop-up ad**. It jumps out at you, often as an entire page, as the publisher's site is loading or between the site's page loadings.

As more and more people have access to **broadband technology** in their homes and offices, display ads are adding video components. Even search and advertising network ads, which have traditionally been text-based, have been moving toward the presentation of boxed videos instead of the text links. Moreover, as publishers such as CNN and CBS put professional videos online, they incorporate commercials into the videos. These commercials are typically only fifteen seconds long, but the audience cannot move quickly past them. This forced viewing annoys many viewers, and Google has tried to find other forms of advertising for the videos it places on its YouTube site.

Web Ads, Targeting, and Data Mining

The pitch that content sites makes to advertisers is that they attract the best potential customers for their products. Because the online world is so diverse, they argue, advertisers can find sites that reach people with very specific interests. But the executives of content sites go further than that. They provide advertisers with technology that, they claim, can actually ensure that certain ads will be seen by some people on their sites and other ads will be seen by different people.

Web marketers argue that this ability to target individuals makes online advertising more "customizable" than any other mass medium in history. They call this advertising activity **mass customization**—the use of sophisticated technology to send large numbers of people messages tailored to their individual interests. So, for example, http://www.iVillage.com (owned by NBC Universal) can send different ads to a woman who says that she is in her 20s and to one who claims to be over 40, even if they are reading the same article.

Because tailoring messages in this way requires information about particular members of the audience, website owners engage in online data gathering to find out as much as they can about the individuals who visit their domains. Creating a description of someone based on collected data is called **profiling**. One straightforward method a firm can use to get data for profiling is to ask people to register to get access to a site. When you try to get into http://www.nytimes.com for the first time, for example, you will have to answer a number of questions about your work, your income, and your address before you are able to enter the site.

That information is probably not terribly reliable because you could make up everything except your email address. (The *Times* computer checks to see that that is correct.) A second profiling method (which yields different sorts of data) is to ask people what topics they want to learn about through the site. The *Times*, for example, also allows you to choose news and entertainment categories as guides to the material it sends you. A third method of profiling yields still other kinds of data: having the computer silently track your choices as you move through a particular website or across websites. These choices are stored on your computer in a tiny hidden text file called a **cookie**. Every time you visit the site, the cookie identifies you, and allows the company to record your mouse clicks, or **clickstream**, through the site. Over time, the company that created the cookie develops a profile of your interests that it can bring together with other profiles to offer to advertisers. The company can also track your behavior within its site, and many advertising networks track your

mass customization the use of sophisticated technology to send large numbers of people messages tailored to their individual interests

profiling creating a description of someone based on collected data

cookie information that a website puts on your computer's hard disk so that it can remember something about you at a later time; more technically, it is information for future use that is stored by the server on the client side of a client/server communication

clickstream computer jargon used to describe movement through websites

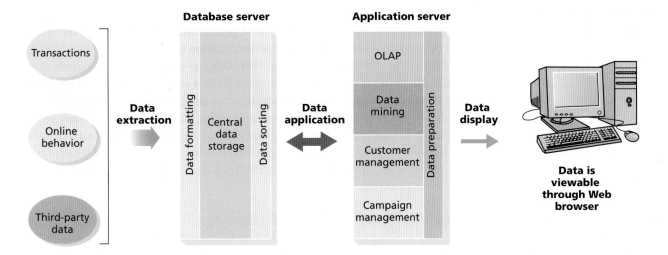

Figure 14.2 The Data-Mining Process in Action
This figure illustrates how information on individuals is "extracted" from various sources and analyzed. The database server stores the information for the application server, which takes the information and sorts it to make profiles (data mining), to create lists of types of profiles (data management), and to create Web ad campaigns and other online targeting activities. OLAP stands for online analytical processing, an activity that analyzes new and old data about an individual in real time.

behavioral targeting the process of following a person's behavior and then sending them material tailored to what was learned about them

data mining the process of gathering and storing information about many individuals—often millions—to be used in audience profiling and interactive marketing

behavior across sites. The process of following your behavior and then sending you material tailored to what was learned about you is called **behavioral targeting**.

For websites, the ideal is having all three types of data about their visitors to sell to advertisers. And even sites that don't rely on ads—such as the image-making and direct-selling sites we discussed earlier—want to know these sorts of things. They believe that very specific audience data can help them better customize their content and more persuasively encourage people to buy their products or services.

The process of gathering and storing information about many individuals—often millions—to be used in audience profiling and interactive marketing is called **data mining**. In addition to the three forms of online data just mentioned, miners try to find offline information about individuals—for example drivers' license records, mortgage information, and credit ratings—that they can link by computer to other data in the website's collection. Because of the wide interest in data gathering on the Web, an entire data-mining industry has grown up around this activity. Its goal is to help Web companies sort through the many pieces of information they have on the individuals who come to their sites so that the producers of the sites can profitably use mass customization in editorial and advertising content. Figure 14.2 illustrates this data-mining process in action.

As you can see, the Web's content is not only constantly changing, but the particular content distributed by a website may well vary with the individual. One person may see different things based on what the site knows about him or her. Sites that use cookies and sophisticated data-mining techniques to create profiles of their visitors can literally create very different sites for different personalities. Moreover, what is "produced" for any one person can change instantly, depending upon the way the person responded to material distributed to him or her an instant earlier. Offerings such as "My Yahoo!" and the options that Amazon.com encourages people to use to make its site more specific to them are examples of this sort of personalization. The truth is, though, that the great majority of sites do not have the sophisticated technology that would enable them to truly tailor news, information, and entertainment based on the profiles and real-time activities of their visitors. Most of the time, **personalization of content** does not mean writing a different story based on the known characteristics of the individual clicking on the material. Instead, it means sending one story rather than another, or sending the business section rather than the sports section.

personalization of content a strategy for providing tailored content, based upon profiles and real-time activities of a website's visitors

Web executives assert that this sort of personalization is coming soon. They point out, too, that a large amount of personalization is already taking place in Web advertising. The distribution of ads to visitors is especially critical to content sites because they depend so heavily on the revenues that advertising brings. Their claim to advertisers is that, because of their interactivity and profiling, they can reach individuals who fit the profile the advertisers are seeking more effectively than any other medium. If you are getting the feeling that these activities have the potential to violate the privacy of Web users, you are not alone. As we will note in more detail at the end of the chapter, they have led to a national dialogue on privacy in the internet age.

Exhibition in the Internet Industry

The exhibitor is the company that provides the technology through which the person can go to the site. This may seem like a basic activity, a little like picking up a wire-line telephone and making a call. Although to an extent it's like that, the potential role of exhibition firms in making decisions about the kind of sites people can visit has led to much controversy.

But before we get to the controversy, let's start with basic questions about "going" to a site: How do people "get" online? When they do get online? How do they find out about particular sites? And, equally important for media firms, how can advertisers who buy banners be persuaded that the kinds of people they are paying to meet at particular sites actually get those ads distributed to them? Let's examine these topics one at a time.

GETTING ONLINE   If you're a college student, there's a fair chance that much of your contact with the online world is through your school. In that case, the school typically picks up the tab for your email and your connections to the college's online resources (such as the library catalog), as well as to the World Wide Web. Providing this kind of access to students can cost an academic institution a lot of money, but it is considered part of the cost of educating students today.

People outside colleges are not so fortunate. They must find and pay for an **internet service provider (ISP)** individually. Broadly speaking, they have four choices for an ISP: a cable company such as Time Warner or Comcast, a phone company such as Verizon or Sprint, a packager of internet service such as Earthlink, and a mobile phone company. ISPs typically provide their customers with a browser and the ability to receive email.

If you've been online in your college or university, you've undoubtedly heard the word **WiFi**—short for **wireless fidelity**. It's a radio technology (called IEEE 802.11) that engineers designed in the late 1990s (after earlier work in Holland using a different technology) to provide secure, reliable, fast wireless connectivity. Many consumer devices use WiFi—personal computers can network to each other and connect to the internet, mobile computers can connect to the internet from any WiFi hotspot, and digital cameras can transfer images wirelessly. There are four types of WiFi—a, b, g, and n—and each provides faster connection to the Web router (see Figure 14.3). Because WiFi frequencies don't travel more than a few hundred yards, it can't be used for purposes that cover many miles. That is the purpose of **WiMAX**. It is based on a different radio technology (IEEE 802.16) and can in fact cover many miles. The U.S. cellular company Sprint Nextel announced in mid-2006 that it would invest about $5 billion in building a WiMAX technology over a few years in order to sell mobile internet users high-speed access to data[3] (see Figure 14.4).

ADDRESSING THE WEB   You probably know that you reach sites on the World Wide Web by typing a string of letters, called a **Web address**, into a browser. The structure of Web addresses is generally administered by the **Internet Corporation for Assigned Names and Numbers (ICANN)**. ICANN is a private, nonprofit

internet service provider (ISP) a company that sells access to the internet

wireless fidelity or WiFi a radio technology (called IEEE 802.11) designed to provide secure, reliable, fast wireless connectivity

WiMAX a wireless frequency that can cover many miles

Web address a string of letters that, when typed into a browser, allow you to connect to a website

Internet Corporation for Assigned Names and Numbers (ICANN) a technical coordination body for the Internet

Figure 14.3 How WiFi Works WiFi, or "wireless fidelity," technology allows an internet connection to be broadcast and received using radio waves. Technology in computers, video game consoles, cellphones, MP3 players, PDAs, and other wireless-enabled devices can pick up the signals to connect to the internet when they are within the range of a wireless network. The area in which one can connect to a wireless network is known as a hotspot. Depending upon the network provider, access to the hotspot may be available for free or restricted to subscribers and pay-as-you-go users.

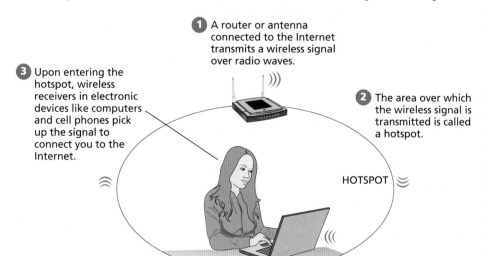

1 A router or antenna connected to the Internet transmits a wireless signal over radio waves.

3 Upon entering the hotspot, wireless receivers in electronic devices like computers and cell phones pick up the signal to connect you to the Internet.

2 The area over which the wireless signal is transmitted is called a hotspot.

HOTSPOT

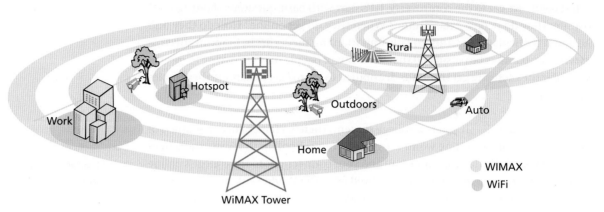

WiMAX will blanket large areas to deliver broadband internet access that moves with you beyond WiFi hotspots.

Figure 14.4 WiFi versus WiMAX

WiFi frequencies typically have a limited range of about 500 feet, but newer WiMAX (Worldwide Interoperability for Microwave Access) technology aims to provide wireless network connections over much longer distances. WiMAX uses towers similar to cellphone towers to broadcast a signal up to thirty miles. That's nearly 300 times as far! A WiMAX receiver similar to the WiFi receiver found in most computers today receives the signal that connects you to the internet. Like WiFi, WiMAX is a global standards-based technology that is being adopted in many countries around the world. Sprint Nextel launched some of the first commercial WiMAX networks in the United States in Chicago, Baltimore, and Washington, DC in early 2008.

organization that the U.S. government helped set up in 1998. More international than the previous organization that performed these tasks (and recently disconnected from formal ties to the U.S. government because of international pressures), it is a technical coordination body for the internet.

uniform resource locator (URL) internet location of a website

Web addresses are often called **URLs**, or **uniform resource locators**; they help to locate unique resources (that is, sites) on the Web. Every Web address must be unique so that the computers that connect computers on the Web can locate it. A URL has two parts, the domain name of the individual or organization, and the top-level domain (TLD).

Domain Names

domain name one word or a connected phrase with which the person or organization wants to be identified on the Web

The **domain name** is a word or connected phrase with which the person or organization wants to be identified on the Web. Routledge (this book's publisher) decided to use Routledge; it could also have used Routpub or some other identifier. As you might imagine, there are many fights over the use of domain names. Generally speaking, courts have ruled that trademark owners get to keep their names online. Only Coca-Cola can use coca_cola, for example. The issue gets more problematic if two companies in different industries have the same name. When that happens, first come, first served is typically the rule. Alternatively, one party may pay the other to bow out.

Web hosting providing space on a computer for the actual website with the domain name

Using a domain name means registering with one of the ICANN-approved registry companies that help people establish their URLs on the Web. Each registrar sets its price for registering names, and prices vary significantly. In addition, some registrars offer discounted or free registration services to those who pay for other services, such as **Web hosting**—providing space on a computer for the actual website with the domain name.

top-level domain (TLD) most general part of the domain name in an internet address. A TLD is either a generic top-level domain (gTLD), such as "com" for "commercial," "edu" for "educational," and so forth, or a country code top-level domain (ccTLD), such as "fr" for France or "is" for Iceland

Top-Level Domains

In a site's address (its URL), the domain name is connected to its **top-level domain (TLD)**, the most general part of the domain name in an internet address. The TLD is actually the first step in telling the Web computers that connect other computers on the network where to go in a search for the computer that hosts the site. Until 2001, there were only five main TLDs. They indicated whether the organization was a Web-related organization (.net), a U.S. government agency (.gov), an educational institution (.edu), a nonprofit organization (.org), or a commercial firm (.com). The U.S. military also has a suffix (.mil). With .mil, .gov, and even .edu restricted to specific types of sites, individuals and companies from all over the world began to complain that the domain names they wanted to use had already been taken in the dot-com and/or dot-net TLD. The resulting discussions led ICANN to approve other new top-level domains. So, for example, if a company finds that http://www.tires.com is taken, it might try to register http://www.tires.info or http://www.tires.biz.

Many Web addresses include top-level country names (**ccTLDs**)—for example .uk for the United Kingdom, .jp for Japan, .eg for Egypt, and .il for Israel. Until recently, an URL had to be typed in the Latin alphabet; that is changing. Now, top-level domains can now be written in other language systems. The change reflects that a large part of the non-Western world is now online.

For an individual trying to get to a website, all these behind-the-scenes activities result in the website URL that must be typed into the browser. Each URL starts with http://. That opener, **HTTP** (which stands for **HyperText Transfer Protocol**) is often followed by www. (for World Wide Web) and then by specifics about the site— its domain name and its TLD. When you know these basics, getting to some sites is often pretty intuitive. To get to ESPN's site, type http://www.espn.com. For the general Disney location, type http://www.disney.com. The White House is at http://www.whitehouse.gov. The University of Pennsylvania Web address is http://www.upenn.edu.

Of course, not all addresses are this straightforward, and so people may well need to use search engines to find them.

THE NET NEUTRALITY CONTROVERSY   Note that in mentioning the ESPN, White House, and Penn websites we assumed that everyone could go to them no matter what ISP they use. It's possible that some companies restrict their workers' ability to use the firms' computers to visit sites the companies feel will waste workers' time (game sites, for example) or embarrass other employees (pornography sites, for example). But in the United States computer users connected to the internet can typically go to any website that is open to the public. Imagine, though, if the internet service provider for your home computer began to make decisions that it would allow only certain websites to reach its clients but not others. They might do that in order to get websites to pay them to "exhibit" the sites in people's homes. Or they may tell websites that they might slow them down (thus encouraging users to go to other sites) unless they pay fees to get the fastest speeds.

As a consumer, you may think this is a terrible idea because it might make it difficult or impossible to reach certain sites. But some ISP executives argue that they should have the right to charge some sites for "exhibition" because the sites use up enormous amounts of bandwidth (by providing videos, for example) that they have to provide to their customers and for which they do not get compensated. Website executives and consumer advocates respond that the ISPs do get back that money by charging their customers for access. Moreover, they argue that the internet has become so important to society that to restrict or diminish the use of it could have unfortunate consequences for what people know and what they can share with one another.

This argument is called the **net neutrality controversy**. The term refers to the desire by websites and advocates to make sure that ISPs do not charge sites for transmission. At this point in time, no ISPs seem to do that, but the Federal Trade

HTTP or HyperText Transfer Protocol the set of rules for exchanging files on the World Wide Web

net neutrality controversy the desire by websites and advocates to make sure that ISPs do not charge sites for transmission

Video game consoles include the Sony PlayStation 3, the Microsoft Xbox, and the Nintendo Wii.

Commission (FTC) accused Comcast of violating the concept of net neutrality by slowing down the availability of certain sites that use lots of bandwidth. Comcast executives said they were doing it to make sure the great majority of their customers didn't suffer a general slowdown because of the few using those sites. Nevertheless, the company said it would not regulate its Web traffic by picking on specific sites—even as it said the FTC had no right to proclaim net neutrality and enforce it. That right, Comcast said, must come from Congress.

An Overview of the Modern Video Game Industry

The term "video game" obscures a complex industry with several different types of products and different production, distribution, and exhibition processes. They make up a big business. In the United States, video game companies of all sorts—the ones that sell consoles and accessories and the ones that sell games—brought in almost $18.9 billion in revenue in 2009—a 27.5 percent increase over the previous year.[4]

video games entertainment products powered by computer chips and displayed on monitors that require users to experience and interact with challenges in a series of tasks

Video games are entertainment products powered by computer chips and displayed on monitors that require users to experience and interact with challenges in a series of tasks. As you can infer from this definition (and from what you may know about video games), any discussion of the business has to take into consideration two key features: the hardware and the software.

Video Game Hardware

hardware the device or console on which video games are played

Hardware refers to the devices on which the video games are played, and a number of types of hardware co-exist. Games are sold for the gaming console, the desktop or laptop computer, the interactive television connection, the handheld game device, and the mobile phone. Let's dig a bit into each of these.

THE GAMING CONSOLE   Gaming consoles are optimized for the speed and graphics that many games require. You could get many of those features on a desktop or laptop computer, but you'd likely have to know a lot about ordering special components, and you'd undoubtedly pay a lot more money than if you bought a standard computer.

Three companies—Sony, Microsoft, and Nintendo—make the consoles that people associate with contemporary gaming. Before Microsoft entered the fray in 2001 the competition was between three companies—Sony, Nintendo, and Sega. Sony's PlayStation became so popular that Sega dropped out of making consoles and Nintendo was far behind. Moreover, it took a while for Microsoft to be a serious competitor. Over time, the Microsoft's Xbox and its successor, the XBox 360 (released in 2005), cut into Sony's lead. In 2007, however, Nintendo came roaring back into competition with Sony and Microsoft consoles via its Wii. The Wii represented a kind of counterprogramming to the gaming approaches of Sony and Microsoft. **Hardcore gamers**—mostly male 15- to 34-year-olds—prefer the XBox 360 platform for its superior graphics, more "hardcore" adventure titles, and strong online capabilities. PlayStation has lost market share to XBox 360 but continues to be popular among avid gamers because of its wide variety of titles. The Wii, by contrast, is a gaming platform that Nintendo purposely built for people who may be intimidated by PlayStation and Xbox controllers. Its graphics do not have as high a resolution as the other two machines, but its controller is extremely easy to use. Instead of pushing a series of buttons, the user can carry out the actions needed in the game by moving the entire device up, down, or to the side, as if the user were in the actual game. The console is particularly suited to video versions of such physical games as ping pong and racket ball. The Wii seems to have hit a nerve among so-called **casual gamers**—women and men who are older than the hardcore types and like to play less intense (though not necessarily less difficult) games than the hardcore types. By mid-2007, the Wii was the bestselling console in the United States, ahead of the XBox 360 and even further ahead of Sony's PS3. As of late 2009, Nintendo had sold 50 million Wii consoles around the world.[5]

hardcore gamers typically (75 percent) male and young (46 percent are under 18 years old) who enjoy playing complex adventures that require dexterity with hard-to-learn controls

casual gamers women and men who are older than the hardcore types and like to play less intense (though not necessarily less difficult) games than the hardcore types

THE DESKTOP OR LAPTOP COMPUTER   Like hardcore console players, the players associated with games bought to play on desktop or laptop computers are young. Computer game players also seem to prefer strategy games over the adventure games that console players tend to buy. Although games purchased to play on the computer were extremely popular in the 1990s, sales have declined as consoles became attractive to hardcore gamers and as broadband connections to internet gaming increased. Sales of new copies of entertainment software for the PC have declined every year since 2000; in that year sales reached $1.9 billion dollars, but by 2005 this had been cut to $791 million. Even more startling is the drop in educational software from a $1 billion industry in the 1990s to only a few math and reading titles still released for the kindergarten-through-6th-grade market. One summary of the PC educational software market notes that it "has almost become nonexistent" as the Web has brought new ways to access such material.[6]

Whereas buying game-playing software for stand-alone computers is falling, playing games online is rising strongly. Gambling online is illegal in the United States, though Americans do access sites elsewhere in the world to participate. Aside from gambling sites, however, you can go to many websites that offer games to play. Most fall under the casual gaming category; it is supposedly a category preferred by women aged 25 years and older. It includes puzzle, card, board, and word games, sometimes with fictional characters, and it is very popular. In fact, the Casual Games Association (http://www.casualgamesassociation.org), an industry trade group, estimates more than 200 million people worldwide play such games on the internet.[7] Pogo (http://www.pogo.com) is a website that specializes in these sorts of games, with titles such as *Mahjong Garden Deluxe* and *World Class Solitaire*. Pogo (and Yahoo Games and many other sites) also has arcade-like games and sports games. If you want to play games for free, you will see a lot of ads; some even interrupt game play. Pogo allows you to get rid of the ads by paying a fee to play, and you can join Club Pogo to play a wide range of games without ad interruptions. Zynga is another major player in this space, focusing on people who want to play games such as *Mafia Wars* and *FarmVille* on Facebook and other social gaming sites.

People interested in the more intense, complex, and often violent adventure platforms aimed at hardcore gamers can also find them, and chat rooms to discuss them, online. On http://www.gametap.com, for example, you can find games such as *Battlestations Midway*, *Shock Troopers*, and *Tomb Raider*. Some of them are free (for viewing ads) whereas others charge to play. Increasingly popular with hardcore gamers are sites for **massively multi-player online role-playing games (MMORPG)**. These are video games in which a large number of players—as many as hundreds of thousands—interact with one another in a virtual world. In an MMORPG, a player uses a client to connect to a server, usually run by the publisher of the game, which hosts the virtual world and memorizes information about the player. The user controls a character represented by an **avatar**—a character that represents the user and which can be directed to fight monsters, interact with other characters, acquire items, and so on.

MMORPGs have become extremely popular since the wider debut of broadband internet connections, now with millions of subscribers from hundreds of different countries. *World of Warcraft*, with its three expansions, is the world's most-subscribed MMORPG, with 11.5 million subscribers in 2009.[8] The newest consoles from Microsoft, Sony, and Nintendo are designed to allow large numbers of people to play their console games with others at the same time online. Microsoft and Sony, especially, see their newest consoles as potential entertainment hubs that allow connections between internet and television for movies as well as games.

HANDHELD DEVICES, MOBILE DEVICES, AND INTERACTIVE TELEVISION   **Handheld game devices** are portable machines that are primarily for game playing. During the late 2000s, the Nintendo DS dominated the market, outselling the PlayStation Portable two to one in 2008.

Also handheld, but a different sort of portable gaming platform, are **mobile phones**. The capability to use these devices for more than the most basic games with primitive graphics has grown as more Americans have been buying high-speed (3G) mobile devices with better graphics and memory capability than the phones of just a few years ago. The big video game software company Electronic Arts, for example,

massively multi-player online role-playing games (MMORPG) video games in which a large number of players interact with one another in a virtual world

avatar a character that represents the user, and which can be directed to fight monsters, interact with other characters, acquire items, and so on

handheld game devices portable machines that are primarily for game playing

mobile phones used as handheld portable gaming platforms

The gaming ability of the Apple iPhone and iPad could pose a serious challenge to established players in the video game business.

The funnest iPod ever

has a special website (http://www.eamobile.com) that sells a wide variety of games. The site sells people games that are customized to their phone carrier and specific handset. To use the game properly without corrupting the phone, you must download it directly to the phone. Prices tend to be less than $10. It's an activity that is rapidly gaining in popularity. In fact, the release of Apple's relatively speedy iPhone 3G in 2008 marked what many in the industry saw as the beginning of the mobile phone's serious competition with handheld game devices. In the first ten months of the iPhone 3G release, Apple sold 2 million copies of the twenty-seven games available from its App store. By 2010, users could download tens of thousands of games for the more powerful iPhone 3Gs—which they might also play on other platforms— games such as *Need for Speed*, *Grand Theft Auto*, and *Chinatown Wars*.

Interactive television (iTV) is another area in which games have been growing strongly. Cable, satellite, and telco operators are charging customers beyond basic fees to access the playing area. Much of the iTV gaming is done via the set-top box so that even satellite companies (whose technologies do not allow for two-way interactions with customers) can get in on the action. In 2007, for example, Dish Network was one company offering a game subscription service. Its customers could get DishGames, a collection of sixteen games including *Yahtzee* and *Scrabble*, priced at $4.99 per month.

Video Game Software

There are a huge number of video games to fit a wide variety of tastes. The major hardware makers also produce games specific to their systems; the intention is to persuade people to buy their systems because of the games exclusively associated with them. So, for example, Nintendo turns out the *Super Mario* and *Pokémon* titles, among others. Sony turns out the *Gran Turismo* racing game. Microsoft has an exclusive deal with Bungie Studios, which it used to own fully and in which it still has an equity stake, to produce the *Halo* series.

The launch of *Halo 3* illustrates the utility of this sort of exclusivity from the console-maker's standpoint. The game's global sales reached $170 million on its first day, making it the biggest launch in video game history to that point. By the end of the first week, it had reached sales of $300 million globally.[9] Not incidentally, from Microsoft's standpoint, the game has spiked sales of XBox 360, the only console on which anyone could play the game. According to initial reports from retailers worldwide, XBox 360 console sales nearly tripled compared with the weekly average before the launch of the new game.[10]

Although video games made by console and handheld manufacturers exclusively for their devices get a lot of marketing and press attention, by far the largest number of games are made by what the trade calls **third-party publishers**—companies that are unaffiliated with hardware companies. Because of their unaffiliated status, third-party publishers typically create games that work on a variety of systems. Activision is one of the most powerful third-party game publishers. Its *Guitar Hero* "rocked the house," in the words of *Variety*, generating more than $820 million in U.S. sales between fall 2007 and fall 2008.[11] Electronic Arts in another powerhouse; one of its huge hits is the *Madden NFL Football* series. Other third-party publishers on the list are THQ (*WWE Smackdown*), Eidos (*Championship Manager 2010*), and Take II Interactive (*Grand Theft Auto IV*).

third-party publishers companies that are unaffiliated with hardware companies that typically create games that work on a variety of systems

SOFTWARE GENRES As we saw in Chapter 2, creators in every mass media industry think of content in terms of categories, or **genres**. This approach helps them understand how to create in that genre; it often helps distributors and exhibitors in sending and choosing titles for certain outlets; and it sometimes helps

genres major categories of media content

consumers who are thinking about what materials they want to watch, play with, or hear. Most of the people who create video games for consoles, portables, and computers broadly categorize what they do as entertainment, meaning that the games are intended primarily for enjoyment. In fact, the variety of video games is so great that aficionados (many of whom have shared their views on the Wikipedia online encyclopedia) have developed several subgenres of entertainment to describe them, and even subtypes—subgenres of those subgenres. Below, adapted from writings about video games posted on Wikipedia, are short explanations of the ten most important entertainment subgenres.

Action Games

Action games are challenges that emphasize combat or attempts to escape being captured or killed. As a category, action games probably have the largest number of subtypes among video games. Three popular ones are shooter, competitive fighting, and platform games.

- Shooter games involve a character going through a dangerous environment hunting for bad guys. First-person shooter video games show the environment from the perspective of the character with the weapon; that character (whose full body you don't see) is controlled by the player. In third-person shooter games, by contrast, the player does see the character moving through the environment as the player uses the controls.
- Competitive fighting games emphasize one-on-one combat between two characters, one of whom may be controlled by the computer. Examples are *Virtua Fighter* and *Soul Calibur II*.
- Platform games involve travelling by running and then jumping between levels and over obstacles in order to avoid being eliminated and to reach a goal. *Super Mario Bros*, the bestselling video game of all time that was first released in 1985, is a well-known example. More recent entries are *Banjo Kazooie* and *Psychonauts*.

Adventure Games

Adventure games are characterized by investigation that focuses on exploration and a story rather than challenges that require the quick use of reflexes. One Wikipedia writer states that, "Because they put little pressure on the player in the form of action-based challenges or time constraints, adventure games have had the unique ability to appeal to people who do not normally play video games. The genre peaked in popularity with the 1993 release of *Myst*."[12] Another Wikipedia writer notes that "games that fuse adventure elements with action gameplay elements are sometimes referred to as adventure games (a popular example is Nintendo's *Legend of Zelda* series)." The writer continues that "Adventure game purists regard this as incorrect and call such hybrids action-adventures."[13]

Casual Games

Casual games are challenges with fairly straightforward rules that make them easy to learn and play. The word "casual" probably comes from the idea that a person can get into the game quickly and doesn't have to devote a major commitment of time to the idea of being a "gamer." Such commitment is often required for people who want to play adventure games and the other genres listed. Note that just because a game is deemed "casual" it doesn't mean that it is easy.

Simulation Games

Sometimes called sim games, simulation games involve players in the creation and cultivation of certain worlds that are designed to be realistic. The idea is to see whether you can excel at accomplishing a task. The task might be sprawling—for example building urban environments (*SimCity*). It might be narrower in focus, related to particular industries (*Stock Exchange, Roller Coaster Tycoon 3*). It might be even narrower still, focusing, for example, on raising pets (*Neopets*) or flying jets (*MS Flight Simulator*).

Strategy Games

Think of chess. Strategy games require a careful assessment of a situation and wise actions in order to win a competition or war. The difference between strategy and action games is that action games center almost entirely on actual combat whereas strategy games expect the player to focus on political diplomacy, the historical context, the procurement of resources, and the larger placement of troops. Two subcategories of this genre are real-time strategy (RTS) games and turn-based strategy (TBS) games. In TBS games, each player gets turns to move the units. After a user completes his or her turn, the opponent gets a chance; examples are *Poxnora* and *Silent Storm*. In RTS games, a story unfolds, participants play ongoing roles, and events of the game's story take place in real time and keep happening even if one of the players takes a break. *Company of Heroes* and *Halo Wars* are prominent examples.

Sports Games

One could argue that some sports games really belong to the category of action game and that others are a combination of action and strategy games. But producers, distributors, exhibitors, and consumers of video games consider sports-related competitions as a category unto itself. Some games focus on playing the sport (the *Madden NFL* series is an example). Others focus on the strategy behind the sport, such as *Football Manager*.

Of course, not all video games fall under the entertainment genre. A much smaller, though socially important, segment falls under the education genre. To quote a Wikipedia article on the topic, educational video games "are specifically designed to teach people about a certain subject, expand concepts, reinforce development, understand an historical event or culture, or assist them in learning a skill as they play."[14] You may be familiar with *Reader Rabbit, Zoombinis, Mavis Beacon Teaches Typing*, or *The Big Brain Academy: Wii Degree*. Actually, instead of education, some in the video game industry use the term **edutainment** to describe such teaching-oriented games. The reason is that they are designed to be a lot of fun as well as have educational outcomes for specific groups of learners.

edutainment teaching-oriented video games that have educational outcomes for specific groups of learners

Advertising Content and Video Games

It stands to reason that advertisers would be interested in a rapidly growing medium such as video games. They have been particularly interested in reaching a group that seems to gravitate to video games more than to other mass media such as television and magazines—young men. Over the years, advertisers have tried a variety of techniques to use games to reach this population segment and others with messages that would lead the target audiences to feel favorably toward the products and buy them.[15] The two most prominent ways in which they go about it are by creating custom games and by embedding ads in games.

CREATING CUSTOM GAMES   In this common activity, an advertiser links up with a game company to create a game that is exclusive to that marketer. One way to do it is to lead people to an advertiser's website to play games. The Jack's Links meat-snacks company turned a TV commercial many of its customers found funny into three Web-video games around a mythical Big Foot character who shows his angry side with allegedly comic effect—for example by swinging a big stick at animals. The company offered the potential of instant prizes for those playing the game, with a chance to enter a $50,000 grand prize drawing. During the first four months of the game during the summer of 2007, over 300,000 people played the Jack's Links games online.[16]

The classic way to do this is to distribute the game on a cartridge or disc. The Burger King fast food company did that during fall 2006. It teamed up with Microsoft in a campaign aimed at both making families feel good about the fast food chain as well as promoting the XBox 360 console, which Microsoft wanted to push beyond hardcore gamers to a more mainstream audience. The gaming firm developed two racing games and one in which users play the King and sneak up on people, as the character does in the ads. They were designed so players with XBox 360s could compete online. Burger King outlets in the United States sold the game for $3.99 with the purchase of a Value Meal.

Burger King officials judged the effort a great success. They said that outlets sold 3.2 million games, and contended that the promotion had directly contributed to a 40 percent quarterly increase in profits. "Creating your own game allows you to control every aspect of it, from the genre and characters to the tone in which the game is delivered," says Burger King's senior director, Martha Thomas Flynn. "For example, we used our own advertising characters, instead of the borrowed equity of another game's characters. We were also able to include a few surprises—something our consumers have grown to expect from us."[17]

Not all games promote commercial products and services. Some organizations create and distribute games to encourage players to adopt commercial or political beliefs through the playing of games. The U.S. Army, for example, has released multiple versions of its game *America's Army* in free CD/DVD form and for online play. In addition, the Army collaborated with the Red Storm Entertainment video game company to develop and distribute *America's Army: True Soldiers*. Released in 2007, it was created specifically for the XBox 360 and given an industry rating as acceptable for teens, the target audience for military recruitment. Clearly, the Army meant for its ideology to be built into the game. Before its appearance, the game's website noted that:

> Red Storm and the Army are working together to make sure that *America's Army: True Soldiers* game play experience is an authentic Army experience. [The game] accurately portrays the values that guide Soldiers in the U.S. Army, by specifically incorporating gameplay based on mission accomplishment, teamwork, leadership, rules of engagement, and respect for life and property. Just like in real combat, honor and respect must be earned, and in the game the Play-Lead-Recruit feature allows players to earn respect as they move up through the ranks and become a true leader.[18]

EMBEDDED ADS   Some companies or organizations don't want to go through the trouble of paying for and distributing games, but they do want to reach certain target audiences. To accommodate them, game publishers increasingly place ads or products in the action so that players will see the commercial messages or use the products in the course of their play. The game publishers realize that ad insertion adds to their profits without adding much to development costs. As the trade magazine *Advertising Age* noted, "in a low-margin business with only $3 to $5 in profit on a $50 video game, even one extra dollar per box is significant."[19] The amount invested is growing substantially; in 2008, the amount of money spent on in-game advertising passed $400 million.[20]

Embedded ads often look realistic and "natural." In racing games, for example, cars pass billboards with the names of products whose companies have paid for their presence. In fact, even the car that the player is driving may be offered because its manufacturer paid the gaming company for its presence. As this activity becomes routine, some companies are adding to it by giving people free add-ons that provide characters or more levels to the games. As an example, in summer 2007 Nissan USA, for example, sponsored add-ons for the *Forza Motorsport 2* Xbox game. It made free downloads available of a Nissan Sentra SE-R vehicle that players of the game could race in a high-performance competition that was to take place that season.[21]

But marketers and game publishers see these activities as only the beginning of a highly sophisticated process of targeting players with ads and add-ons that are specific to what the companies know about them. They realize that with increasing numbers of gamers playing online it will be possible to send them these features on-the-fly, while they are playing, and to change the ads and offer different sponsored downloads depending on their game setting and level. This activity is called **dynamic in-game advertising**, and it is drawing a lot of attention from marketers, game firms, and technology companies. In fact, Microsoft owns a video game advertising company called Massive that is one of the leaders in placing ads in games. Some studies suggest that in-game ads improve brand recall and awareness and so encourage people to buy the advertised products. Other studies, though, found gamers weren't aware of the ads in the games they played.[22] Nevertheless, the desire to reach 18- to 34-year-old males, who are thought to spend lots of times with games, has encouraged advertisers. It even led Barak Obama to appear in a paid ad in the game *Burnout Paradise* during his 2008 bid for the presidency.

dynamic in-game advertising the process of sending ads into video games while individuals are playing, and of changing the ads and offering different sponsored downloads depending on their game setting and level

Distribution and Exhibition of Video Games

There are many ways to get games to the player. As noted, some cable systems and telcos stream games to computers; the games do not remain on the computer. In the case of mobile games, the software does get downloaded and it must come directly to the phone; some of the payment is shared by the creator with the mobile phone company. Video games for consoles, PCs, and handhelds are typically distributed on disks or cartridges to stores by their manufacturers, sometimes through wholesalers, and sold through a variety of outlets. In the brick-and-mortar world, you can find collections of the top games (and consoles) in huge retailers such as Wal-Mart and toy outlets such as Toys R Us, as well as in consumer electronics stores such as Best Buy. There are also specialized video game retailers such as Gamestop that sell a wider variety of titles. In addition, you can purchase video games online at Amazon.com or many other retailers. Used games show up in Gamestop as well as on many sites, including eBay.

Although all this is pretty straightforward, selling video games isn't without controversy. That is because many games have levels of violence and sex that cause consternation among parents and civic leaders. You may remember from Chapter 3 that the industry has established the Entertainment Software Ratings Board (ESRB) as a self-regulatory mechanism to quell such concerns. Modelled after the motion picture ratings system, the **ESRB ratings** are used along with content descriptors in a way that is (according to its website) "designed to provide concise and impartial information about the content in computer and video games so consumers, especially parents, can make an informed purchase decision."[23] The six ratings (apart from "rating pending") are EC (early childhood), E (Everyone), E 101 (Everyone 101), T (Teen), M (Mature—17 and older), and AO (Adults Only). Content descriptors ran a wide gamut from "alcohol reference" to "intense violence" to "use of tobacco."

Despite this ratings system, some games have raised consternation among critics. In 2005, *Grand Theft Auto: San Andreas* was skewered by angry parents and advocacy groups as morally bankrupt. They argued that it teaches people how to engage in a crime spree with gusto. *Grand Theft Auto: San Andreas* was given an M by the ratings agency. Critics claimed that the rating and the accompanying descriptors were problematic because they didn't inform parents regarding the true level of violence and sex in the game. The controversy got hotter when players discovered that use of a certain code would unlock an explicit sex scene in the game. Even though Rockstar insisted that the sex scene and code were the work of a hacker, politicians such as Hillary Clinton and advocacy groups leaped on the company as misleading the ESRB, retailers, and parents. Rockstar pulled the game from the shelves at great cost, deleted the scene, and put it back on the market. Nevertheless, the incident served as an opportunity for groups to rail at retailers for allegedly selling games to kids as young as 9 years old.

Take 2 sparked a game-selling controversy again in 2007, with a game called *Manhunt 2*. Its central character is an inmate who escapes a mental asylum, murdering guards and prisoners. The game was banned in the United Kingdom, Ireland, and Italy, and it was given an AO rating by the ESRB. Take 2's chairman Zelnick defended the game on artistic grounds, stating that "The Rockstar team has come up with a game that fits squarely within the horror genre and was intended to do so." "It brings a unique, formerly unheard of cinematic quality to interactive entertainment, and is also a fine piece of art," he added.[24] Take 2's financial situation was precarious, however, and Zelnick knew that major retailers such as Wal-Mart would not carry a title with an AO rating. Moreover, Sony and Nintendo do not allow AO-rated games on their systems. So Rockstar toned down the sadism, and the ESRB gave it an M.

To some critics, the change was beside the point. They argued that even M ratings in stores were getting into the wrong hands, that game retailers too often sell M-rated video games to kids as young as 9 years of age. They cited research at the Harvard School of Public Health that 81 percent of M-rated games were mislabelled and had missing content descriptors, thus potentially misleading parents.[25] The ESRB replied that the researchers had exaggerated problems they found and that a long list of content descriptors on packages would be impractical. Clearly, though, the arguments surrounding video game producers, retailing, and ratings were not over.

ESRB ratings six designations that together with content descriptors provide information about the appropriateness of computer and video games for consumers of different ages

Media Literacy and the Internet and Video Game Industries

The developments regarding computers and the online world that we've just discussed are merely the surface of a huge transformation in the way mass communication is taking place. With the aim of continuing media literacy, how can we organize our understanding of the social issues that these activities raise? One way is to look at how key activities that we have described in this chapter reflect major themes that we have noted for the media in general. Another way is to look at the social controversies that the activities we have discussed are igniting. Here we'll do a bit of both. The major themes we will look at are the blurring of media boundaries and the power of conglomerates. The social controversies that we'll look at briefly relate to privacy and the filtering of content for children.

Blurring of Media Boundaries

Certainly, this book's theme of increasingly blurring boundaries between media industries applies to the internet world. The activities that we have described in this chapter are recent, and they are affecting every mass medium. The rise of dictionaries and other reference materials online, for example, has softened the market for physical versions of these works.

You may have noticed, in fact, that each of the chapters about other mass media industries in this book refers to the ways in which the industry is changing because of computers and the Web. Even media that aren't given entire chapters are changing

---

TECH & INFRASTRUCTURE
NETFLIX COMES TO WII

Joining the Xbox 360 and PlayStation 3, the Nintendo Wii is the latest in the stream of video game consoles to offer gamers the ability to instantly stream Netflix videos through their television. Yet although Wii gamers and Netflix subscribers may welcome the news, cable companies are likely to view the development much more unfavorably. It poses yet another threat to cable and satellite companies, whose consumer base is increasingly encroached upon by the capabilities provided by the internet. With more options for home entertainment through the internet comes greater competition for cable and satellite providers, and the partnership between Netflix and Nintendo is just one more thing cable companies have to worry about.

Today, full episodes of many shows are available online through the official websites of many parent networks, as well as on third-party websites such as Hulu. The game machines noted above as well as technologies such as Apple TV and Boxee are allowing movies and television accessed online to be viewed through a television set. Almost all large televisions created in 2010 have internet capabilities. At what point can the entertainment needs of consumers be fulfilled without a monthly subscription to a cable or satellite service?

Although cable and satellite firms have asserted that the number of people cutting their cable subscriptions in favor of alternatives is marginal, others in the industry have predicted that cable companies will eventually refuse to pay for carrying television networks that allow people who do not subscribe to cable or satellite services to access programs online for free.

Sources: "Boxee, Hulu Desktop Bridge the Gap between the Web, TV," *The Washington Post*, January 31, 2010; Jefferson Graham, "Tuning in to Networked TV," *USA Today*, January 7, 2010; Michael Learmouth, "Thinking Outside the Box: Web TVs Skirt Cable Giants," *Advertising Age*, January 18, 2010; Brad Stone, "Nintendo Wii to Add Netflix Service for Streaming Video," *The New York Times*, January 13, 2010.

dramatically. Consider greeting cards. With the growth of email, the greeting card industry has developed a major segment that allows people to send digital versions of cards—some of them even talking or singing—instantly across the country and around the world. It's easy to imagine that in not too many years the online method may become the preferred way of sending cards for many people. The greeting card industry, like the book industry, also relates to the internet industry.

The digital convergence not only raises questions about where one media industry begins and another ends. It even raises questions about the traditional names we give to media. When a "magazine" online and a "newspaper" online are continually updating, what is the difference between a newspaper and a magazine? When CNN, *Time* magazine, *The Washington Post*, and ABC News are posting video and audio programs, is it useful to say online that one is a cable channel, the other a magazine, the third a newspaper, and the fourth a broadcast network? Even though technologically the streaming of music online is far different from radio broadcasting, should we now talk of all streamed music as "radio"? What happens when the dominant way people access these media is through digital means (computers or handheld devices, for example)? Will these media terms still be useful? Certainly it is possible to give satisfactory answers to these questions that distinguish among media, but there is no question that the digital world messes up distinctions we long took for granted.

The Power of Conglomerates

Another theme that has followed us throughout this book has been the rise of conglomerates as the central powers in mass media industries. "Wait a minute!" you may be thinking while you read this. I understand how the biggies can keep this kind of control in traditional mass media such as television and the movies. I can also see how a few companies, such as Microsoft, can take over a huge chunk of the computer software business. I noticed how three companies control the video game console market, and how those same firms, Electronic Arts, and maybe a couple of other firms pretty well have a lock on the most popular game software. But the Web is different! Anyone can start a website—even I have one—so no one company can come in and stop people from going to the millions of sites out there. It would seem that the conglomerates would have an almost impossible time controlling cyberspace.

One might indeed think that, and at first glance it does seem that people are going to an enormous number of virtual spaces that have been created on the Web. Look a little closer, though, and we see that, to quote a *Newsweek* article, "Media consolidation has come to the internet." *Newsweek* was commenting in the summer of 2001 about a study by market researcher Jupiter Media Metrix that just four companies—AOL Time Warner, Microsoft, Yahoo!, and Napster—control roughly half of the time internet users spend online. That's down from eleven companies two years ago. Moreover, 60 percent of online time is controlled by only fourteen companies, a breathtaking plunge from 110 companies in 1999. That's "an incontrovertible trend toward online media consolidation," the authors of the report wrote.[26]

Well, times have changed. AOL Time Warner is now just Time Warner, which recently spun off AOL as a separate company. Napster no longer exists. But some would say that the consolidation that *Newsweek* identified back in 2001 has actually intensified in the commercial part of the Web. As we noted earlier, in 2008, 73 percent of Web advertising flowed to the ten most popular sites on the Web. That advertising flow reflects traffic patterns. Google, Yahoo, Microsoft, and AOL (through its Advertising.com subsidiary) control most of that advertising flow, and their decisions about what ads (and for Google and Yahoo what content) should come up in search and news have major consequences for the ways people see the world. Moreover, the major media powers have been moving to control the biggest sites. News Corporation owns MySpace (and since it bought it it has made it more far more commercial than it was at its start), Google owns YouTube, and most people assume it is just a matter of time before a media biggie (say, Microsoft) picks up Facebook. CBS, Disney, Viacom, and Time Warner are implementing internet strategies that aim to keep the huge numbers of people who made up their audiences offline coming to them online and through mobile devices. Their strategies differ, but they involve marketing muscle. They are able to drive traffic to their sites by cross-promoting these sites on cable and broadcast networks and in print through their own holdings or through joint ventures with other firms. Every time *Desperate Housewives* appears on TV, for example, the ABC network notes that the program can also be viewed online. And the sites the media conglomerates control are not necessarily few in number or with their names on them. CBS owns TV.com, for example, and NBC, News Corp, and Disney have set up Hulu as a site to attract certain target audiences to their programming. The idea is to use high-visibility programming from network television and movies to drive people to sites that fit their specific interests but which are controlled by them.

Mark Mooradian, a Jupiter vice president and senior analyst back in 2001, noted that access to the Web itself is open to everyone. But not everyone has the muscle and experience of the leading mass media firms when it comes to using the Web to grab attention. His comment is as relevant today as it was then: "Does everyone have a microphone? Yes. But are some microphones louder than others? Absolutely."[27]

The Filtering of Content

We've seen how video game violence and sex have sparked concerns in the United States and around the world. We've also looked at the tussles around the self-regulatory system that the video game industry has established. These arguments recall the struggles around content in the movies and on TV—though in the United States neither medium has shown such graphic violent and sexual images as video games. Chapter 13 discussed the V-chip filter as a legal response to parental concerns about sex and violence in certain television programs. The concept of filtering Web content that various groups consider offensive has been much more controversial.

Consider the circumstances that led to the arguments: the Web, as you probably know, is filled with images of explicit nudity and/or extreme violence that can be accessed by anyone with a Web browser. People who object to these images realize that the First Amendment prohibits the government from making such sites illegal. In fact, a federal court in Philadelphia declared unconstitutional two congressional attempts to require that such sites determine the age of visitors before letting them access the material. Looking for another way to keep this material away from children, many parents and advocacy groups have turned to Web filtering technology.

Web filters are computer programs that block objectionable sites from coming into a computer. Sites are blocked either because they have been specifically censored or because a search engine used by the filter program has detected words that indicate that there is prose (and possibly pictures) on the site that the filter's creators want excluded. Consider the situation at the Fort Worth Public Library in 2007. Debate on filters heated up there when it asked city council to give the go-ahead to install them for users younger than 17 years old. A policy against viewing adult websites and other inappropriate material was already in place. The staff was monitoring what patrons viewed, and anyone caught breaking the rules could lose his or her computer privileges. Some in the library did advocate filters, however, and the push for that on youngsters' computers started after a parent complained that her three sons had seen inappropriate images on a computer near the children's section.

Web filters computer programs that block objectionable sites from coming into a computer; sites are blocked either because they have been specifically censored or because a search engine used by the filter program has detected words that indicate that there is prose (and possibly pictures) on the site that the filter's creators want excluded

The request caused a stir that brought out the arguments on both sides. Supporters of Web filters say that they solve an important social problem and that they can be customized to the moral, religious, or political viewpoint of the person or organization installing them; liberals can use different filters from conservatives. They argue that filters should be placed on computers that children use in schools, libraries, and other public places. Many also insist that even in adult public areas, such as libraries, filters should be installed on Web computers so that other patrons don't have to see nudity and librarians don't have the embarrassing task of asking a patron to get off an offensive website.

Opponents argue that filters are not really a very good solution for Web computers in public places. For one thing, they say, filters are still fairly primitive. Some may block articles about breast cancer because the word breast was programmed in order to weed out sexually objectionable sites. Filtering technology is getting better, they concede, but it will never be 100 percent possible to ensure that filters are not systematically blocking important material. Another problem, the opponents contend, is that companies that sell filters do not as a rule reveal the sites that they block or the filtering rules that they use. They are secretive for competitive business reasons, but the result is that a person, group, or organization that uses a filter often does not really know how lenient or how strict it will be. Third, say some of the opponents to filtering, the idea that a public library or public organization would stop people from going to certain places on the Web smacks of censorship, and they are opposed to it. Parents can use filters in the privacy of their homes, and companies have a right to use them on their computer networks, but public computers should be free of filters.

Interestingly, many local librarians as well as many conservative groups support filters. Many schools have adopted filters, and a federal law ties U.S. government funding for school technology to the school's use of some philosophy or technology of filtering. But as the Fort Worth example showed, a lot of heat still exists around the subject. The controversy is likely to be around for a long time.

Privacy

So is the issue of digital privacy. Critics' concerns about the Web aren't limited to what companies deliver to people's computers via their websites and email. The concerns also extend to what the companies often try to take from people as they use their computers. At issue is the information that Web firms want about the individuals and organizations with whom they interact.

Companies aren't the only targets of these worries. Activists fear that governments—federal or state—might encourage laws that give them powers to tap into people's computers or internet activities. Officials from police agencies such as the Federal Bureau of Investigation (FBI) have already tried to prevent internet software from helping potential criminals make their email totally uncrackable by law-enforcement authorities. In the wake of the 2001 attacks on the World Trade Center and Pentagon, Congress passed laws aimed at allowing the FBI and other agencies to follow digital trails more easily than in earlier years.

In general, concerned individuals and organizations argue that we are moving into a new era when it comes to information. It is an era, they say, in which governments will be able to find out far more about citizens than the citizens want them to know. And it is an era in which companies will be able to find out far more about their customers than those customers realize. In the new digital age, the critics say, privacy must be a major social concern.

The topic has become a media issue only rather recently. As we noted in Chapter 3, in earlier decades of the century, privacy was often defined as "the right to be let alone," to use the phrase of Samuel Warren and Louis Brandeis in a famous 1890 *Harvard Law Review* article. In the twentieth century, privacy came to be a subject that people debated when they worried about governments, employers, or credit companies snooping into their personal lives.

In the past twenty years or so, concern about privacy has erupted noisily into the media realm. Most of the noise has related to corporate rather than government activities, because of a belief that laws are less strict with regard to business snooping. The first stirrings of concern began in the 1970s, when companies began to use computers to combine enormous amounts of information from public and private records about virtually everyone in the nation and sell this information to marketers. Among the largest of these companies are Experian, Equifax, Acxiom, and Choicepoint. Many marketers use these firms' universal databases (called that because they hold information on almost everyone) to find people whose profiles make them potential customers.

Acxiom, for example, maintains a storehouse of consumer information covering more than 200 million individuals and 124 million households in the United States. Drawing on its continually refreshed databases, Acxiom offers clients addresses, telephone numbers, demographics (for example age, gender, race, occupation, number of children, marital status), and past purchasing behaviors of likely direct-marketing prospects. On a section of its website titled "Targeted Advertising," the company states that "The challenge for marketers today is to understand and find their best audiences, across a growing list of media channels. With Relevance-X Display's targeting solutions you can create and deliver relevant, highly targeted audience-based advertising online, maximizing the effectiveness of every impression. Better understand your best customers—and find more like them." That involves creating predictive models of consumer behavior for identifying individuals and households that are relevant to particular marketers and those who are not.

In addition to these funds of knowledge, marketers themselves have been taking advantage of the constantly decreasing costs of computer power to create their own databases from information they learn about their customers, by asking them and by keeping records of their purchases. These storehouses of information are called **transactional databases**. A marketer that wants to learn more about the customers in its transactional database can turn to Acxiom. The company will match the names and addresses of the marketer's customers against its data on more than 124 million households. The resulting merged file could supply the marketer with a wealth of new information about each customer's purchasing behavior, estimated income, credit extended by mail-order firms, investments, credit cards, and more.

transactional database a database that stores and sorts large quantities of data that reflect transactions—such as logs of phone calls, emails, mailings, or purchases

You may already be getting nervous that your favorite department store or catalog company knows more about you than you would like. But wait!—as they say on those hard-sell TV commercials—there's more! The circulation of these data began to be a mass media issue as direct marketers increasingly used them for targeting. Members of the public got angry when advertisers used personal information to guide direct-mail advertisements and telemarketing pitches to people's homes. Until then, many Americans didn't realize that advertisers knew so much about them.

But privacy really took off as a media issue with the rise of marketing on the World Wide Web in the mid-1990s. Recall our discussion of interactive marketing and cookie technology earlier in this chapter. Interactive media firms see the ability to track the clickstreams as a great way to find out what users want and how best to serve them. It is important to point out that placing a cookie in a person's computer does not allow a marketer to learn the name, postal address, or any other so-called personally identifiable information (PII) about the person who owns the computer. Many online marketers contend that this anonymity makes following people online and creating cookie profiles about them perfectly acceptable. Critics of this viewpoint, though, point out that many ad networks and websites can easily determine PII by relating a cookie to the name or email address used when the person has registered on a site. When no registration information is available, a marketer can encourage a person with a cookie to sign up for a sweepstakes; the personal information provide then gets linked to the cookie data. But critics add that even when marketers and websites don't have personally identifiable information, they still surround individuals with ads and other content that are tailored to their understanding of what that individual is like. They are creating views of the world for a person, and giving certain people discounts that they don't give others, based on profiles they have created without people's knowledge or permission.

Rarely will media executives argue publicly that people should have no right to stop firms from collecting information about them. Under government pressures, many often concede that members of the public should have the right to know that material about them is being collected. Media executives emphasize, however, that in today's competitive media world being able to show advertisers that a medium can deliver specific, desirable types of people is crucial for their survival. Supporters of data collection also use an ingenious argument that the invasion of privacy has its positive side. They argue that the more marketers know about people, the more they will be able to send individuals materials that these individuals will find relevant to their lives. The result, they say, is that people will be unlikely to complain that they receive junk mail.

Nowadays, most Web marketers say that they understand people's desire to keep certain information private. They also insist, however, that many individuals are willing to give up information about themselves if in return they get something that they consider valuable. Many privacy advocates agree that people should have the right to decide whether they want to give up private information as part of a transaction. They disagree with the Web marketers on the way in which consumers should be informed about the data that will be collected about them, often without their knowledge.

Privacy advocates want members of the public to have to opt in when it comes to giving out information. That is, marketers should not be permitted to collect information about a person unless that person explicitly indicates it is alright for them to do so (say, by checking a box online). Marketers contend that getting opt-in permission is too difficult because people either are too lazy to give it or are concerned about their privacy when the question is put to them in that way. The marketers prefer an opt-out approach. That means that they will be permitted to collect personal information from consumers as long as they inform people of what they are doing and give them the opportunity to check a "no" box or otherwise refuse to allow it.

Chapter 3 discusses the Children's Online Privacy Protection Act (COPPA). That law requires websites to get parents' opt-in permission. Some aspects of medical privacy regulations passed by the federal government also require an opt-in approach. The government is more lax with financial organizations (banks, credit card companies). It requires them to present consumers with an opt-out choice. In some situations involving financial organizations, such as the transfer of information among affiliates within a firm, federal law gives the consumer no choice at all over the sharing of personal information. Moreover, these exceptions aside, the federal government in the early twenty-first century stayed away from imposing rules on the use of personal information by websites. The reason: to encourage Web commerce.

Yet consumer advocates, academic researchers, and lawmakers have noted increasing public concern about privacy in the digital realm. Industry representatives have kept insisting that interactive sites and marketers could regulate themselves through an opt-out norm approach, although some sites still tell their visitors nothing about the information they collect about them. Compounding all these arguments is the international nature of the issue. The European Union uses an opt-in approach, for example, and U.S. companies have to promise to accept the stricter EU rules when they deal with European, though not necessarily with U.S., consumers. This distinction riles consumer advocates, who see the European approach as the fairest one.

Note, too, that these privacy issues are not related only to the Web. What people do on mobile devices is already of interest to many advertisers; some government agencies might want to see these data, as well. The same is the case with those who plays video games, what they play, and how they play them. In fact, as home-based television viewing becomes a two-way activity, getting data about what individuals do with the medium will also interest marketers and, possibly, certain branches of government. As these types of surveillance take place, various advocacy groups will argue against them and ask for legal safeguards against the misuse and abuse of people's data. Clearly, the fight over U.S. consumer privacy in the digital age will continue.

Chapter Review
For an interactive chapter recap and study guide, visit the companion website for *Media Today* at http://www.routledge.com/textbooks/mediatoday4e.

Questions for Discussion and Critical Thinking

1 Some people say that hyperlinks lie at the center of activities of the World Wide Web. What do they mean?
2 What does tailoring refer to on the World Wide Web? How is tailoring changing the way that content is personalized on the internet?
3 What is the ESRB ratings system? Explain why some critics argue that it isn't working.
4 To what extent do the major video game genres relate to genres that also exist on other media?
5 Explain the ways advertisers have become involved in the internet and in video games.

Internet Resources

Association of Internet Researchers (http://aoir.org/)

The Association of Internet Researchers (AoIR) is an international academic organization dedicated to interdisciplinary studies of the internet. In addition to the annual AoIR conference, their mailing list provides a venue for its more than 2,000 subscribers to discuss the latest trends and issues in internet research. The "AoIR Guide to Ethical Online Research" is available online at http://www.aoir.org/reports/ethics.pdf

Digital Games Research Association (http://www.digra.org)

The website of the Digital Games Research Association (DiGRA) publishes original research on games for academics and professionals. The organization hosts a bi-annual conference for the international digital games research community.

The Electronic Frontier Foundation (http://www.eff.org/)

Founded in 1990, the Electronic Frontier Foundation is an international non-profit advocacy group with the stated aim of championing "the public interest in every critical battle affecting digital rights."

The Entertainment Software Association (http://theesa.com/)

The Entertainment Software Association (ESA), the trade association for the computer and video game industry in the United States, regularly posts press releases, research, statistics, and industry sales reports on its website.

Gamasutra (http://www.gamasutra.com/)

Gamasutra is a website aimed at game developers that posts regularly updated news, features, and job postings for the computer and video game industry. Owned by CMP Media, it is the companion website publication to the magazine *Game Developer*.

Key Terms
. . . .

You can find the definitions to these key terms in the marginal glossary throughout this chapter. Test your knowledge of these terms with interactive flash cards on the *Media Today* companion website.

Constructing Media Literacy

1 To what extent is media convergence already part of your everyday life?
2 Some observers have commented that parents in some families feel like immigrants to the United States when the family brings computers into the home for the first time. That is because, as in immigrant families, the children often "speak the language" better than the parents do. Did your experience with home computers fit this description? Do you have any friends whose experiences fit the description? Why or why not?
3 Where do you stand on the issue of net neutrality? Why?
4 If you were a parent of a 10-year-old, would you filter that child's Web content? What if you were a parent of a 15-year-old?

Companion Website Video Clips

Game Over—Video Games: The New Media
This clip from the Media Education Foundation documentary *Game Over* explores the use of realistic characters, settings, and events in the video game industry and the effects of realism on players. Credit: Media Education Foundation.

Case Study

DEVELOPING A WEBSITE

The idea It may seem easy to develop a website that can make money. In fact, it is a highly creative act that requires a lot of business sense. Apart from getting a good idea, you have to figure out how to make money.

The method Develop an idea for a profit-oriented website. Describe its target audience, its features, and its business model (that is, the way it aims to make money). To get a reality check, find a website that has a similar business model. Using a periodicals database such as Nexis or Factiva and drawing from a variety of periodicals, discuss how well it is doing and how it got to that point.

Part Five

Advertising and
Public Relations

The advertising and public relations (PR) industries play crucial and controversial roles in the media system. Advertising provides billions of dollars in support of print and electronic media. PR provides ideas, people, and sometimes technology to help mass media create content that reaches huge audiences. In exchange for these services, though, the PR and advertising industries exercise enormous influence over the media and their products.

Chapters 15 and 16 discuss these roles. In the process, they show that the largest advertising and public relations firms are controlled by a few agency-holding companies with the power of guiding the flow of resources to many media. Moreover, the boundaries of advertising, PR, and related forms of marketing communication are blurring, making it even more difficult to know when producers of mass media materials are secretly being paid to present products and ideas in particular ways.

THE CHAPTERS

15. The Advertising Industry

16. The Public Relations Industry

15 The Advertising Industry

After studying this chapter, you will be able to:

1. Sketch the history of advertising in the United States
2. Describe various types of advertising agencies and how they differ
3. Analyze the process of producing and creating ads
4. Discuss branding and positioning and explain their importance to advertisers
5. Explain the debate between advertising's critics and defenders about the industry's role in spreading commercialism and the decline of democratic participation

MEDIA TODAY

If you're like most people, you are probably aware that advertisers buy space or time in various media in order to send you messages ("advertisements") about their products or services. You might know (perhaps because you've read previous chapters of this book) that where advertisers decide to place their money can make the difference between life and death for media firms. But even if you don't know these things, it's likely that you've talked with friends about ads. Maybe you've commented about how funny or how horrible they are, or how good looking the men or women in them are.

Advertising is the activity of explicitly paying for media space or time in order to direct favorable attention to certain goods or services. Three points about this definition deserve emphasis. First, advertisers pay for the space or time that they receive. Second, advertising clearly states its presence. When you see an ad, you know what it is for, and you often know quite easily who is sponsoring it. Third, advertising involves persuasion—the ability or power to induce an individual or group of individuals to undertake a course of action or embrace a point of view by means of argument, reasoning, or emotional plea.

The aim of this chapter is to help you critically explore the quick-changing business that is behind the ads and the support of such a large part of the media. The next chapter will tackle public relations and marketing communication and examine the important links both have to advertising. Let's start by getting a sense of how the ad industry came into existence.

advertising the activity of explicitly paying for media space or time in order to direct favorable attention to certain goods or services

The Rise of the Advertising Industry

Advertising is as old as selling itself. During the time of the ancient Roman Empire, criers were paid to scream out messages about products for sale. There were "print" ads, too: archeologists have found a 3,000-year-old ad—written on papyrus—for a runaway slave in Thebes. In medieval England, shopkeepers often posted a boy or man at the entrance to their shops to shout at the top of his lungs about the goods in the store. Signs posted over shops also beckoned consumers. After the advent of the printing press several centuries later, businesses added handbills and newspapers to their advertising mix. This routine presence of advertising was transferred to the British colonies in the New World. By the time Benjamin Franklin was born in Boston in 1706, advertisements were an expected and accepted part of almost all the day's periodicals.

Franklin was one of the most successful sellers and writers of advertisements in the American colonies. Like our modern-day ads, the ads of Franklin's era shouted messages for goods, for houses for sale, for articles lost or stolen, for plays showing in local theaters, and for patented medicines. Because the colonial printing press could accommodate only the simplest drawings, ads looked more like today's stodgy classified ads than like any of the more trendy advertisements in contemporary media. Then, as now, some advertisements stirred anger and controversy. (An ad in one of Franklin's papers, for example, was accused of inciting anti-Catholic feelings.) And then, as now, intellectuals worried about the power of shrewdly worded messages to stir people to purchase too much and believe outrageous things.

From its earliest days through the 1840s, advertising involved direct negotiations between someone who wanted to advertise a product and the owner of a newspaper or magazine. Say you were the owner of a dry-goods store and you wanted to announce a new shipment of fabric. You would write the announcement yourself, and then visit the local newspaper office and pay for the space to make an announcement of your goods.

That system worked fine when only one or two newspapers were available and merchants wanted to sell goods in a relatively small area. But imagine the difficulty of buying announcements in a much greater number of papers. Say you are the producer of a horse buggy in 1840. You have heard about all the new penny-press papers that have attracted large audiences from Boston, Massachusetts, to Richmond, Virginia. Advertising your buggy in these papers would seem to be a good idea, but how can you negotiate efficiently with all of them? Sure, you could write letters, but such one-on-one correspondence with every paper would be terribly time-consuming.

The Birth of the Advertising Agency

By the 1840s, these sorts of problems led to the development of the **advertising agency**—a company that specializes in the creation of ads for placement in media that accept payment for exhibiting those ads. Volney Palmer is credited with starting the first advertising agency. Palmer was essentially a space salesman. He made money by soliciting notices from merchants or manufacturers who wanted to sell to a wide territory. He would place these notices in a group of newspapers, to which he often had exclusive space-selling rights. Though merchants were expected to write the ads, they saved time and energy by having the ad agency reach far-flung audiences. The advertising agent typically received compensation from various newspapers in the form of 15–25 percent of the payment as commission.

advertising agency a company that specializes in the creation of ads for placement in media that accept payment for exhibiting those ads

brand a name and image associated with a particular product

ad campaign a carefully considered approach to creating and circulating messages about a product over a specific period with particular goals in mind

The ad agency's function changed dramatically in the decades after the Civil War, when the United States experienced the rapid growth of manufacturing as a result of the Industrial Revolution. More and more, factory activity was based on the principle of continuous-process, or "flow", production. Conveyor systems, rollers, and gravity slides sent materials through the production process in an automatic, continuous stream. As a result, companies could transform massive amounts of raw materials into finished goods.

These new approaches changed American business. The manufacturing capacity of the United States increased sevenfold between 1865 and 1900. Cities suddenly bulged with people as workers streamed in from farms and from other countries to work in factories. Many factories created products that had been made by hand only a few years before. Other plants turned out items—toothpaste, corn flakes, safety razors, cameras—that nobody had made previously.

But the trick to making lots of money was not just in the manufacturing of these products; it was in getting stores to carry them and consumers to buy them. The large number of items available for sale encouraged competition between manufacturers of similar goods. One result was the creation of the **brand**—a name and image associated with a particular product. With brands, a company did not make just soap, it made Ivory soap or Pears' soap. To make money on a particular brand of soap or any other mass-produced item, a manufacturer had to make sure that hordes of people knew about the product and asked their local retailers—grocery and department stores—for it.

In this 1887 advertisement, Pears' Soap associates its product with family and children.

In this new environment, the advertising agency's function changed. The manufacturers and stores now needed firms to help them create ads that would stand out from the competition. Around 1910, advertising agencies started copy and art departments to create both words and images for advertisements. Along with the agency's creation of the ad came its work on the **ad campaign**, which is a carefully considered approach to creating and circulating messages about a product over a specific period with particular goals in mind. That work included early forms of research on the marketplace and on consumers, as well as on the media that claimed to reach those consumers. Entrepreneurs started research companies to meet those needs. As part of their growing research operation, in 1914 advertising agencies helped to establish an independent organization, the **Audit Bureau of Circulation**, to verify the size of a periodical's audience. Among the major agencies involved in those developments was one that still exists—J. Walter Thompson—which is today called JWT and is part of the WPP Group.

Ad agencies created jingles, artwork, and trade characters that became part of American culture. Within the industry, two broad differences in the approach to creating ads emerged, approaches that are still used today. Some practitioners used **reason-why ads**—those that listed the benefits of a product in ways that would move the consumer to purchase it. Others swore by the effectiveness of **image ads**—those that tied the product to a set of positive feelings. Advertising practitioners

Audit Bureau of Circulation an independent organization established in 1914 by advertising agencies to verify the size of a periodical's audience

reason-why ads advertisements that list the benefits of a product in ways that would move the consumer to purchase it

image ads advertisements that tie the product to a set of positive feelings

eventually agreed that some types of products were better sold through reason-why pitches, whereas others could use the push of image ads.

It wasn't long before anger about false or manipulative advertising threatened to lead to government regulation of the ad industry. To calm the population's concerns and reduce the chances of government regulation, leaders of the ad industry started organizations such as the Association of National Advertisers and the American Association of Advertising Agencies. Their purpose was to establish norms of proper ad-business behavior and to plead their industry's case with government regulators.

The Advent of Radio Advertising

Until the 1920s, virtually all of the advertising agencies' work appeared in print media. Beginning in the 1920s, however, many ad people began to turn to radio to place their ads. To help ad practitioners purchase local radio time most efficiently, **representation firms**—companies that sold time on many radio stations—came into existence. In connection with these sales, ad practitioners insisted that radio executives provide proof of their statements about the size of their audiences. A number of companies rushed in to conduct surveys of listeners in order to get this information, and the broadcast audience research (or rating) business was born.

Radio also required ad people to learn how to sell through sound rather than through text. Through the 1920s and into the 1930s, advertisers adapted tried-and-true print techniques—slogans, dramatizations, brand personalities—to the new medium. In addition, ad agencies that had large consumer goods firms as clients often coordinated the creation of weekly network radio programs. Agencies were responsible for coming up with an appropriate idea for the program, negotiating its time period and its cost with a network, and then producing the show from start to finish every week.

representation firms in radio, companies that sell time to advertisers on many radio stations

Advertising, the Post-War Era, and Television

As World War II ended and millions of soldiers came home, got jobs, and started families, production of consumer goods took off. Manufacturers and stores turned to advertising agencies to help them stir up demand for products, and by the mid-1950s the ad industry was healthier than ever.

The commercial introduction of television in the late 1940s brought a challenge to advertising practitioners that was similar to the one they had faced with radio. In fact, as we noted in Chapters 9 and 11, the large-scale movement of ad money into TV forced magazine and radio executives to make profound changes in the audiences they pursued and the content they chose. Increasingly, radio and magazines sold themselves as media that targeted particular groups that certain advertisers were chasing (young adults, for example), whereas television reached "everybody." The period clearly showed the power of the advertising industry as a whole to shape the direction of the media system.

In TV's early years, ad messages were live; as in radio, they often appeared as part of the program. Advertisers bought hour or half-hour blocks of time from the TV networks and sponsored entire shows; again, as in radio, ad agencies produced these shows for their clients. But this approach changed after a decade. By the early 1960s, advertiser interest in fully sponsoring a show diminished.

Part of the reason was that TV network executives had concluded that it was more profitable for them to shape their schedules, and sometimes own their shows, than for them to allow advertisers to do so. Advertisers had their reasons for agreeing with this approach. They wanted to reach as many people as possible with the quickly growing medium. Tying up a large amount of money in one time period every week was not the best way to achieve this goal.

As a result, advertisers scattered their time purchases across the TV schedule. With tens of millions of Americans viewing the same show at the same time, network charges for advertising on these shows skyrocketed. With the increase in charges, the length of television commercials decreased. In the 1960s, one-minute commercials were common. By the 1970s, the most common duration had dropped to thirty seconds. By the 1990s, fifteen-second TV commercials were common.

Trends in the Second Half of the Twentieth Century

The growth of television brought millions of dollars into the advertising industry for the production of audiovisual commercials, as well as for the purchase of the time to show them. An entire research industry grew up around the agencies' need to show their clients that the work they were doing was reaching large audiences and getting people to buy the products.

Proving that an advertisement causes people to make a particular purchase has never been easy, and it is sometimes impossible. Nevertheless, ad practitioners increasingly turned to a wide variety of consultants who applied **motivation research**, or used social science techniques, to learn what motivates Americans to buy certain goods. Some also studied whether **subliminal persuasion**, or quickly flashing messages, such as "buy popcorn," that reach the mind at a level below the conscious mind, in fact worked. However, whether or not these consultants' ideas about motivation research and subliminal persuasion actually did work, in the 1950s they became the subject of a number of books—notably Vance Packard's bestselling *The Hidden Persuaders*—that aroused public anger against advertising for messing with people's heads without their knowledge.

Still, the U.S. ad industry grew strongly, and two trends are most notable. The first was a shift toward a **global presence**. As American businesses expanded their operations around the world after World War II, they wanted their ad agencies to work with them on creating ads and buying media abroad. Until that time, only a few of the very biggest agencies, such as J. Walter Thompson, had had a global presence, but with the increased demand, many of the large agencies set up offices in several countries. By the 1990s, owning an "international network" was crucial to being a major player in the ad industry.

The second notable trend was the formation of advertising conglomerates—known as **agency holding companies**. These are umbrella firms that own two or more ad agencies, plus research firms, public relations consultancies, or other organizations that contribute to the business of selling products, services, or ideas. Such holding companies offer clients a range of services beyond advertising. They own more than one agency under their conglomerate umbrella to be able to serve firms that compete with one another. Traditionally, companies would not think of giving business to an agency that has such **client conflicts** for fear that confidential information might be shared among employees and get to competitors. If a totally

Frank Sinatra clowns around with spaghetti for an EKCO products commercial on the set of CBS-TV's *The Frank Sinatra Show* in 1952.

motivation research the systematic investigation of the reasons people purchase products

subliminal persuasion persuasion that works by influencing the unconscious mind

global presence having strategic offices and representatives around the world

agency holding company a firm that owns full-service advertising agencies, specialty agencies, direct-marketing firms, research companies, and even public relations agencies

client conflicts serving companies that compete with one another

CULTURE TODAY
NEGATIVE POLITICAL ADS

Politicians spend billions of dollars each election cycle trying to get themselves elected. From the election of a small-town mayor to the president and everyone in between, advertising, especially on television, is a central method by which politicians can disseminate their messages. A major goal in the advertising is to disparage their opponents. In fact, negative ads seem to make up the bulk of political advertising on television, especially during a presidential race. But are these types of commercials effective?

Professor Ken Goldstein, a political scientist with the University of Wisconsin at Madison, and John G. Geer, a professor at Vanderbilt University, argued in the *Los Angeles Times* that negative ads actually aid in improving political awareness. Professor Geer is also the author of *In Defense of Negativity: Attack Ads in Presidential Campaigns.* He contends that negative ads "are more likely than positive ads to be about the issues . . . are more likely to be specific when talking about those issues . . . are more likely to contain facts . . . and are more likely to be about the important issues of the day." Similarly, Professor Jon Krosnick of Stanford University notes that "if an ad attacks an opponent with misinformation, which engaged voters can identify [through media coverage or their own research], what

people learn from it is that this candidate is willing to lie to get ahead." Professor Krosnick also notes that "positive ads are a guy in khakis walking on the beach with his dog or sitting in front of a fireplace in a fuzzy sweater, and that simply doesn't have a lot of information."

These statements run contrary to conventional thinking, which assumes that the general public dislikes negative advertising. In fact, opinion polls from 2002 and 2004 report that "80% of voters believed that negative ads are 'unethical and damaging [to] our democracy'" according to *Newsweek* magazine. However, although the public may disapprove of the ads, the ads haven't stopped them from turning out on election day. "It's a mistake to infer that attack ads depress turnout," argues Professor Krosnick. It seems, however, that, regardless of whether you consider negative ads an informational tool or whether you just wished candidates would play nicely, negative advertising is here to stay.

Sources: Sharon Begley, with Janeen Interlandi, "Ready, Aim, Fire!; Attack Ads are Ubiquitous this Campaign Season, But They Are Not the Threat to the Electoral Process That Do-gooders Claim," *Newsweek* 152, 16 (October 20, 2008), p. 48; John G. Geer, "Those Negative Ads Are a Positive Thing," *The Washington Post,* October 12, 2008, p. B01.

different agency network is involved, though, most advertisers don't mind—even if both agencies are controlled by one firm. They accept the claim that those parts of the two businesses are kept quite separate.

Interpublic Group of Companies—recognized as the first agency holding company—was started in the late 1950s by Marion Harper. At the time, many people laughed at him for buying firms but not merging them into his existing firm. By the late 1980s, however, the agency conglomerate model had become the norm. The dominant holding companies are WPP (based in London), Omnicom (based in New York), Interpublic (also in New York), Dentsu (Tokyo), and Publicis Groupe (Paris). As Table 15.1 shows, the top eight holding companies (which are by far the biggest) have substantial business outside the United States. In fact, in 2006 only one, Interpublic, made more than half of its revenue in the United States.

Beginning in the 1980s, the multiplication of media channels as a result of cable television, satellite TV, video games, and (beginning the mid-1990s) the World Wide Web had far-reaching effects on the advertising industry. As we have discussed throughout this book, the enormous number of media outlets that were present in many homes (along with the presence of multiple TV sets) led audiences to scatter across them. That made it more challenging than ever for advertisers to reach the people they wanted as customers. The advertisers turned to their advertising agencies for help.

How did the ad agencies respond? What, in general, do ad agencies do? To answer, let's start with a broad overview of the industry and then turn to our categories of production, distribution, and exhibition.

Table 15.1 The "Big Eight" Marketing Agency Holding Companies, 2008

Holding Company	Headquarters	Worldwide Revenues	U.S. Revenue	U.S. Percentage of Total Revenue
WPP Group	London	$13.6 billion	$4.7 billion	35
Omnicom Group	New York	$13.36 billion	$6.9 billion	52
Interpublic Group	New York	$6.92 billion	$3.79 billion	55
Publicis Group	Paris	$6.90 billion	$2.95 billion	43
Dentsu	Tokyo	$3.29 billion	$110.9 million	3
Aegis Group	London	$2.49 billion	$503.6 million	20
Havas	Suresnes, France	$2.31 billion	$701.8 million	31
Hakuhodo DY Holdings	Tokyo	$1.56 billion	0	0

Source: *Advertising Age*. http://adage.com/agencyfamilytrees09 (accessed March 5, 2010).

Table 15.2 Advertising Spending By Media Industry, 2008 vs. 2003*

Industry	US$ Billions	
	2008	2003
Broadcast television	47.8	42.3
Subscription television	28.9	16.7
Newspapers	43.6	51.3
Pure-play internet**	21.8	6.6
Broadcast and satellite radio	18.0	19.6
Yellow Pages	15.4	14.8
Consumer magazines	12.9	11.5
Business-to-business magazines	11.1	9.1
Pure-play mobile	1.2	0.41
Out-of-home***	8.1	5.2
Other entertainment-based advertising****	0.96	0.20
Total	209.76	177.7

*Numbers for traditional media industries include online advertising activities within these industries.

**Includes online revenues for firms (e.g. Salon.com) with no traditional media counterpart.

***Includes billboards, kiosks, mall boards, transit ads, and other outdoor vehicles.

****Includes cinema advertising, in-game video game advertising, and advertising on film, music, video games, and consumer book websites. Does not include advergaming or product placement in video games. These are considered marketing services, not advertising.

An Overview of the Modern Advertising Industry

Advertising is a large and widespread operation, and the amount of money advertisers shell out is impressive (see Table 15.2). According to the media consultancy firm Veronis Suhler Stevenson, in 2008 advertisers in the United States spent around $77 billion in support of television programming and about $18 billion to fund radio broadcasting. In addition, the ad industry spent $43.6 billion on advertisements in newspapers (including their online and mobile versions), compared with the $10.5

MEDIA PROFILE
TOM BURRELL

An aptitude test can give more insight into one's future than you might think. At least, this turned out to be the case for 16-year-old Tom Burrell from Chicago. Burrell, now the Chairman Emeritus of Burrell Communications, took an aptitude test at the urgings of his high school teacher. The results were telling. Burrell scored highly in both his persuasive and artistic abilities—qualities that would serve him very well as a pioneering African-American executive in advertising.

Burrell continued to hone these skills while attending Roosevelt University, where he worked as a copywriter at Wade Advertising while on his way to a BA in English in 1961. As he continued to advance, Burrell moved amongst Chicago's top ad agencies before moving into a leadership position by founding Burrell Communications. The agency was particularly innovative in that it was one of the first to target African-American consumers—a previously neglected market with over $760 billion in disposable income. Burrell Communications was also the first African-American agency to win *Advertising Age*'s Multicultural Agency of the Year award. Today, with 150 employees working in offices in Chicago, Atlanta, and Los Angeles, Burrell Communications takes in approximately $23 million in marketing revenues.

Numerous well-known brands have come to Burrell for marketing consultation over the years, among them Sears, Lexus, Crest, Coca-Cola, and Pampers. However, Burrell's best-known work was with McDonalds. A 60-second spot Burrell created for the fast-food franchise, entitled "Daddy's Home," tells the story of an overworked black father who always makes time to meet his son at McDonalds. "Daddy's Home" has since found its own home in DC's Smithsonian Institution. To Burrell, the recipe for ad success returns to the elements of art and persuasion that stood out in high school. "Creative (work) is the most important element that ad agencies do," he told *Advertising Age*. "Everything else is in support of it."

Though retired, Burrell still works as a marketing consultant and recently released his new book, *Brainwashed: Challenging the Myth of Black Inferiority*. *Brainwashed* examines how media portrayals have negatively impacted perceptions of African-Americans and left them diminishing their self-worth. "By portraying it constantly on the screen and on the tube, you take the reality of one and you make it a reality for millions," said Burrell, citing *Precious*, *The Blind Side*, and the work of Tyler Perry as particularly troubling. "All of the good people, the saviors are at least half-white," said Burrell. "If it is not intentional, it is certainly insensitive."

Sources: "Burrell's Quarter Century," *Advertising Age*, June 3, 1996, p. C2; A. W. Fawcett, "Perseverance Pays Dividend at $128 Million Burrell Shop," *Advertising Age*, June 3, 1996, p. C2; "Interview with Burrell," *Advertising Age*, June 3, 1996, p. C10; Todd Johnson, "Ad Exec Tom Burrell Says America Has Been 'Brainwashed' About Blacks," *The Grio*, February 12, 2010. http://www.thegrio.com/video/ad-exec-burrell-says-america-has-been-brainwashed-about-blacks.php (accessed August 11, 2010).

billion that consumers shelled out to buy the papers. Advertisers funded consumer magazines (including their online and mobile versions) to the tune of about $13 billion, and consumers dropped a smaller $9.8 billion into the periodicals' coffers. When it came to supporting internet and mobile websites that are unattached to traditional media brands—industry people call them pure-play internet sites—advertisers put out about $11 billion to support them. The total amount is huge. As Table 15.2 indicates, Veronis Suhler Stevenson estimated that in 2008 about $210 billion was spent in the United States on all types of advertising. As you can see, that is over $30 billion more than they spent in 2003. You will also notice that the decisions by advertisers regarding what media to fund have changed as well. Newspapers have lost out, while the internet has won many advertising dollars.

Advertising Agencies

The number of companies involved in advertising is also huge. Just about every business advertises somewhere. Sometimes the executives of the business write the ads

New York City's Times Square is home to the highest density of illuminated outdoor advertising in the United States. Known as "spectaculars," the first electric sign was installed on Broadway in 1904.

themselves and then place them in newspapers and magazines. Other times—and this is particularly true of larger firms—the executives turn to companies that specialize in the creation of ads and their placement in media that accept payment for exhibiting those ads. As we said earlier, these companies are called advertising agencies. The companies that hire them and pay for their work are called advertisers. In the ad industry, when an agency takes on an advertiser's business, it is said to take on an account.

There are about 5,000 advertising agencies in the United States, and they are scattered throughout the country. The largest tend to be located in the largest cities, especially New York, Chicago, and Los Angeles. Ad agencies range from one-site operations with just a few people, to organizations with several offices and thousands of employees. The kinds of things ad agencies do also vary. We can describe them along four dimensions:

- Business-to-business agencies vs. consumer agencies
- General agencies vs. specialty agencies
- Traditional agencies vs. direct-marketing agencies
- Agency networks vs. stand-alone firms

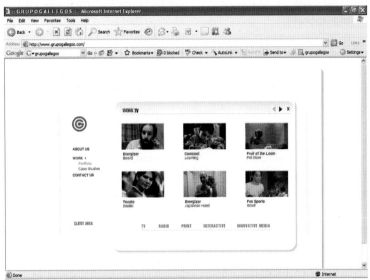

http://www.grupogallegos, the website of Grupo Gallegos, an advertising agency specializing in the Hispanic market.

business-to-business agencies advertising agencies that carry out work for companies that are interested in persuading personnel in other companies to buy from them instead of from their competitors

consumer agencies advertising agencies that carry out work for advertisers that are intent on persuading people in their nonwork roles to buy products

general ad agency an advertising agency that invites business from all types of advertisers

specialty ad agency an advertising agency that tackles only certain types of clients (or accounts)

internet agency an advertising company that promotes its expertise in understanding the technology for reaching people online, for creating the ads and websites that will lead to customer responses, and for measuring those responses

direct-to-consumer (DTC) used most effectively by the pharmaceutical industry, this type of advertising presents a prescription drug as a medical solution and encourages viewers to ask their physician to order the medicine if appropriate

traditional ad agency an advertising agency that creates and distributes persuasive messages with the aim of creating a favorable impression of the product in the minds of target consumers that will lead them to buy it in stores

BUSINESS-TO-BUSINESS AGENCIES VS. CONSUMER AGENCIES **Business-to-business agencies** work for companies that are interested in persuading personnel in other companies to buy from them instead of from their competitors. For example, a zipper manufacturer might want to inform a pants manufacturer about its great new development in the fly business. **Consumer agencies**, by contrast, work for advertisers that want to persuade people in their nonwork roles to buy products. An agency that touts a client's cereal to children and their parents is one example. Individual agencies typically do not do both.

GENERAL AGENCIES VS. SPECIALTY AGENCIES A **general ad agency** invites business from all types of advertisers, whereas a **specialty ad agency** tackles only certain types of clients. One type of specialty agency that works in both the consumer and business-to-business areas is the **internet agency**. This is a company that promotes its expertise in understanding the technology for reaching people online, for creating the ads and websites that will lead to customer responses, and for measuring those responses. A different type of specialty agency deals with healthcare advertising. A big source of clients is the pharmaceutical industry, as firms in this industry are constantly competing to persuade physicians that their prescription products are best. In recent years, pharmaceutical firms' desire to get consumers to nudge their doctors to order new prescription drugs for them has led to a specialty called **direct-to-consumer (DTC)** pharmaceutical advertising, and ad firms focusing on that business have developed. Advertising to ethnic and racial groups is also a big specialty in the consumer area. You can find agencies that claim to have particular knowledge of how to persuade African-Americans; others that tout their abilities to move Latinos to buy; others that go after Irish-Americans; still others that specialize in Asian or Russian immigrants—and the list can go on.

TRADITIONAL AGENCIES VS. DIRECT-MARKETING AGENCIES A **traditional ad agency** creates and distributes persuasive messages with the aim of creating a favorable impression of the product in the minds of target consumers that will lead them to buy it in stores. **Direct-marketing agencies** have a different mandate. Their job is not just to create a favorable image that will eventually result in purchases. Instead, they have to shape consumer mailings, telephone marketing contacts, TV commercials, and other appeals to target audiences so as to elicit purchases right then and there. Traditional advertising practitioners generally consider direct-marketing approaches more gruff, fast-talking, and even obnoxious than the traditional rhetorical tools. For their part, direct-marketing people believe that they are the only ones who really show that advertising can sell things, as the results are immediate: people either buy the product or they don't.

AGENCY NETWORKS VS. STAND-ALONE FIRMS The biggest advertising agencies tend to be traditional, consumer-oriented companies (see Table 15.3). They often have offices in a number of cities in the United States as well as in foreign countries; the trade press calls firms such as these **agency networks**. These types of agencies are different from firms that have only one location. The agency networks typically work for large national advertisers such as Procter & Gamble, Phillip Morris, General Motors, Sears, Ford, and McDonald's. Because national advertisers tend to sell many products, they will often appoint a number of ad agencies to work for them, each working on a different product or a different set of products. In 2009, for example, Procter and Gamble used the Grey, New York, agency (owned by WPP) to tout its Downey brand, Saatchi and Saatchi (also owned by WPP), New York for Pampers, and Publicis, New York, (owned by Publicis Groupe) for its oral care products.

Specialty racial and ethnic firms sometimes enter the mix. For example, in addition to relying on Saatchi and Saatchi for general advertising of Pampers, P&G called on Burrell Communications Group in Chicago for its advertising to African-American consumers. It used Conill in Miami to pitch Pampers to Hispanics.

Popular books, movies, magazine articles, and television shows encourage most people to think of a large and powerful "full service" ad agency such as JWT or Young and Rubicam when they think about the advertising industry. In today's complex marketing world, though, even large agencies such as JWT work with other organizations in the industry to carry out the three basic functions of ad work: **creative persuasion**, **market research**, and **media planning and buying**. We can explain how these three functions are carried out by exploring how they fit into our three familiar activities: production, distribution, and exhibition.

http://www.the-dma.org, website of the Direct Marketing Association, a global trade association that promotes direct marketing with more than 3,600 member companies worldwide.

Production in the Advertising Industry

It is through their work with their clients that the biggest advertising agencies channel hundreds of millions, even billions, of dollars into various media—a major source of support for American media industries. But the advertising industry does not really spend its money to support media. It spends money to persuade people to buy products, services, or ideas. How does it go about doing that?

The production of persuasive advertising messages goes on with the approval, and often the direct involvement, of executives from the client/advertiser. To ensure that its clients continually understand what the agency is doing for their products, agency heads appoint an account executive for every account. The job of the account executive is to move information between the advertiser and the agency as well as to make sure that all production, distribution, and exhibition activities take place as planned.

Production activities involve the individuals whose work relates directly to the creation of their firm's media materials; people in the ad industry call such individuals **creatives** or **creative personnel**. They include copywriters (who write the words for the ads), art directors (who guide the creation of artwork), print production personnel (who supervise the final production of magazine and newspaper ads), and TV–radio production personnel (who supervise the final production of TV and radio commercials) (see Figure 15.1).

But the work of the creatives does not take place in a vacuum. Copywriters and art directors generally do not concoct a print ad or TV commercial out of just any ideas that come to them. On the contrary, they work hard to determine which ideas will lead target consumers to purchase the product. Typically, a client does not expect that an ad will be directed toward the entire population. For example, a cosmetics company would generally expect its lipstick ads to be directed to women (not men). However, for reasons having to do with the nature of the lipstick or the company's marketing strategy, company executives may want to advertise a particular lipstick to

direct-marketing agencies agencies that focus on consumer mailings, telephone marketing contacts, TV commercials, and other appeals to target audiences so as to elicit purchases right then and there

agency networks advertising agencies with branch offices in a number of different cities worldwide

creative persuasion the set of imaginative activities involved in producing and creating advertisements

market research research that has, as its end goal, gathering information that will help an organization sell more products or services

media planning and buying a function of advertising involving purchasing media space and/or time on strategically selected outlets that are deemed best-suited to carry a client's ad message

creatives or creative personnel people whose work relates directly to the creation of their firm's media materials

Table 15.3 Top Ten Agency Networks, Ranked By 2009 Worldwide Network Revenue

Rank	Agency [Parent]	Headquarters	Worldwide Revenue ($ millions)
1	Dentsu [Dentsu]	New York	3,028
2	McCann World Group [Interpublic]	New York	2,671
3	Young & Rubicam Brands [WPP]	Tokyo	2,651
4	DBB World Communications Group [Omnicom]	New York	2,223
5	Ogilvy & Mather [WPP]	New York	1,754
6	BBDO Worldwide [Omnicom]	New York	1,671
7	TWBA Worldwide [Omnicom]	New York	1,518
8	Euro RSCG Worldwide [Havas]	New York	1,206
9	DraftFCB [Interpublic Group of COS]	New York	1,175
10	JWT [WPP]	Paris	1,119

Note that a portion of revenues of some of these firms come from divisions that carry out public relations and other activities not under the traditional definition of advertising.

Source: *Advertising Age*. http://adage.com/datacenter (accessed August 26, 2010).

market segmentation

dividing society into different categories of consumers

a few specific groups of women—say, women from 18 to 34 years, or executive women from 18 to 34 years. Dividing society into different categories of consumers is an activity called **market segmentation**. Agency creatives must understand the segments they are aiming at before they produce their ads. In fact, both when ad agency executives are competing for new business and when they are working on products

Figure 15.1 Structure of a Typical Advertising Agency

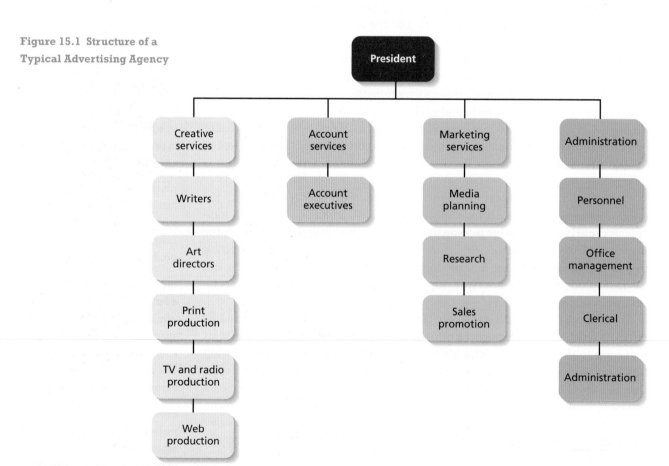

for current clients, they place a high priority on learning a lot about both the product they are seeking to represent and the audience they are trying to reach. What are the product's strengths? What do consumers think about it? What kinds of people buy it? Who are the best potential customers? Why do they—or don't they—buy the product?

Answering these questions often requires drawing on the market research function of the ad agency. Such research might involve compiling the results of previous investigations on the product or its competitors. It might involve commissioning original surveys or experiments with potential customers to check the persuasiveness of a new ad or the success of one that already has been introduced to the marketplace. It might involve joining other firms in ongoing "syndicated" studies that inquire about social trends, general product use, media habits, or other characteristics of the American population.

Through these and other approaches, researchers construct detailed portraits of the intended audience and its position within the society at large. Then creatives mix those portraits with their own sensibilities and apply the results to their work.

Creating Portraits

Portraits of society are constructed through this meeting of research facts and artistry. Whether they are developing a magazine ad that details the joys of a Ford Mustang, a TV commercial that extols Pond's cold cream, or a video game that includes the McDonald's Hamburglar in its cast, the creator's goal is to suggest the product's usefulness for the audience. Of course, to do that, the ad people must have thoughts about the audience, particularly as it relates to the product they are selling. The goal

sales pitch a presentation to a client, portraying the world of the client's intended audience and actions, to show how the client's product is valuable in that world

is to imagine the product in a social environment that is appropriate for the intended audience and its values. Armed with these imaginings, a creative team can concoct a **sales pitch**—a message that portrays the world of the intended audience, a problem in that world, and actions that show how the product can solve that problem.

The next step is to illustrate the sales pitch in stories and settings that the creatives believe the target audience will accept. Often an agency develops different campaigns for distinct audiences. Editing and casting decisions take into consideration research findings about how different audiences look at the product and the world. This approach enables agencies to create an image of the product that matches what they believe will lead various audiences to feel good about the product and to purchase it.

Creating a specific image of a product that makes it stand out in

"But gosh, Ursula, together we'd be exactly what every major advertiser is trying to reach."

the marketplace is called **branding** it. Ad practitioners consider the creation and nurturing of these product images—these brands—to be among their most important activities. The reason is their belief that people will pay more for a well-regarded brand than for a product they do not know or about which they have a bad feeling. Think about it: Which would you rather buy from your supermarket for a party—Pepsi or Coke (whichever you prefer), or something called Pop-Soda Cola? Even if your supermarket guarantees the quality of Pop-Soda Cola and says it tastes "like the big guys," and even if it's a dime less expensive, you might feel funny serv-

branding creating a specific image of a product that makes it stand out in the marketplace

ing it to your guests. Chances are you would choose Pepsi or Coke. These are brands you trust; perhaps, after years of seeing commercials, you may even think that these products belong at parties.

Advertising practitioners try to make a particular target group of consumers feel that a brand relates to their particular interests and lifestyles. Doing that is called **positioning**. To position a product, agencies call on the research and creative activities that we have already discussed. Sometimes they will settle on a broad positioning for the product and then change it somewhat when advertising to particular target markets.

positioning making a particular target group of consumers feel that a brand relates to their particular interests and lifestyles

As a brief example, consider the position of Geico Direct, the fourth largest car insurance company in the United States. An insurance industry study described its brand image in the following way: "Geico occupies unique terrain in the auto-insurance space as a relatively inexpensive carrier that is fun. State Farm and Allstate, on the other hand, occupy more traditional territory (expensive and serious)."[1] It's not hard to understand why. You've probably seen the two long-running types of television commercials created by Martin Agency that present its pitch. One series stars an earnest British gecko and another centers on self-righteous cavemen. Geico has created different versions of the commercials and also ads, many of which seem aimed at younger members of the driving public.[2]

Once the ads have been created—and sometimes while they are being created—they are tested. A variety of methods might be used, from focus groups to actually running the ads in certain areas and evaluating the results. One trial method for comparing the persuasiveness of two TV commercials is called the **split-cable test**—in which the advertiser arranges with a cable company to send one commercial to one particular neighborhood's TV sets and another commercial to a separate though similar neighborhood's TV sets during the same programs. Before the trial begins, the researchers monitor the sales of their products in stores in the two neighborhoods. After the split-cable showing of the commercials, the researchers recheck the stores to determine which commercial led to a greater increase in purchases.

split-cable test a method for comparing the persuasiveness of two television commercials

Distribution in the Advertising Industry

Creating a series of ads and spending money to test them would be totally useless if the ad agency had no idea how and where to distribute them. Deciding how to distribute ads has been affected by improvements in technology. Because of cooperation between ad agencies and media firms, ad practitioners can now actually send finished print and television ads directly to media outlets by satellite. In some cases, print ads can be sent in digital form directly to the computers of the magazines or newspapers in which they will appear. From that standpoint, distribution of ads is constantly getting easier.

Because media fragmentation has dramatically increased the number of ad vehicles, however, deciding where to place advertisements is not getting easier; instead, it is becoming more and more challenging. Making these decisions is the work of an agency's media planners. To get an idea of the challenges they face, think of where you would place Geico's TV commercials, and also Web ads that aim to convey the same message about the company to young adults.

The short answer is that planners would choose media that attract the young adult audience that Geico wants to reach with the commercials. But does this mean that any channel or website that reaches a lot of 21- to 34-year-old males is acceptable? What general criteria do ad planners use when they decide on media? The answers are important, as purchasing media can be expensive. If an ad agency uses its media-buying budget to advertise in places that do not reach the target audience, or in places that reach that audience along with many other people who are not relevant to the ads, the advertiser will be wasting a lot of money. If Martin's planners and Geico's media-planner and buyer, Horizon Media, did that and Geico executives found out about it (as they undoubtedly would), both firms would lose an important client.

To avoid such disasters, media planners track computerized data about the number and kinds of people that various media outlets (specific magazines, radio stations, or TV networks) reach. Much of this information about individual media outlets is collected in syndicated studies by audience research firms such as Nielsen (for television and cable) and comScore and Nielsen NetRatings (for the internet); the Traffic Audit Bureau and Nielsen Outdoor (for billboard advertising); Arbitron and RADAR (for local and network radio); Audit Bureau of Circulation (for newspapers and magazines); and Simmons and MRI (for magazines). Sometimes the planners pay attention to custom research findings presented to them by individual media firms that want to impress them with further details. The custom research may add to the demographic data that syndicated research provides; for example, it might explore the religious affiliations or occupations of an audience. The research might present **psychographic data**, information that links demographic categories to personality characteristics of an audience—for instance, whether they are "materialistic" or "confident" or people who want to lead rather than follow.

The research might also provide details about the lifestyles of the audience that could impress potential advertisers: how many vacations they took last year, what cars they drive, whether they play golf regularly. *Seventeen* magazine executives, for example, might commission research about how many of their teen readers have begun to use cosmetics or go to the movies each week or own cars. They would present these data to potential cosmetic, movie, and car advertisers in the hope of convincing them to include *Seventeen* in their media plan—that is, in the list of media outlets in which they advertise their products.

Outdoor and in-store media are of increasing importance for some marketers, and an insurance company such as Geico may be one. Outdoor media encompass a great variety of stationary billboards and signs as well as moving media such as buses and trains. The term **in-store media** refers to a raft of print and audiovisual ads that people see when they walk into retail spaces. In a growing number of supermarkets, a company called MediaCart sells ads on grocery carriages. Supermarkets show videos and ads at checkout too. In stores like Wal-Mart and Best Buy, PRN Corporation (owned by Thomson) sells ad space on checkout screens. Captivate Network, a

psychographic data information that links demographic categories to personality characteristics of an audience

in-store media the print and audiovisual ads that people see when they walk into retail spaces

company owned by Gannett, sets up office-building elevators with screens that run ads along with entertainment, weather, or news. AccentHealth, a company owned by Discovery Holdings, has TV screens with CNN clips and targeted ads in more than 10,000 doctors' offices across the country.[3] And supermarket firms fill their stores with the audio announcements of sales, shelf signs, floor mats with ads, and video screens showing ads at checkout. The locations for ads seem to be boundless. To hype its shows during 2007, CBS even had a company stamp 35 million supermarket eggs with its trademark "eye" logo, as well as the names and logos of the programs in its fall television line-up.[4]

In evaluating a media outlet, media planners examine syndicated and custom demographic, psychographic, and lifestyle research to decide whether the audience segment they are aiming at can be found at that outlet. If it can, the planners then ask the following questions:

- What is the outlet's reach with respect to (ad planners use the term "against") the target audience? That is, what percentage of the entire target audience (say, teenage girls) will the outlet reach?
- Considering the costs of running an ad there, how efficient is the outlet in reaching that audience compared with other outlets?

In studying *Seventeen* for a makeup client, ad planners may find that it sells 22 million copies, the overwhelming percentage of which are sold to teenage girls. Moreover, *Seventeen* provides lifestyle research that contends that many of these readers are trying makeup for the first time. Just as important, the planners learn that, although the cost of buying space for a four-color, full-page ad in *Seventeen* is similar to the cost of buying such an ad in women's magazines with larger circulations, the **cost per thousand (CPM)** of teenage girls is quite a bit lower. That is because of the selectivity of the magazine: magazines such as *Glamour* reach lots of teenage girls, but an advertiser would not be able to target an edition directly to them, and so much of the ad money would be wasted. Because *Seventeen* reaches virtually only teenage girls, the CPM of the target audience is lower.

This factor makes *Seventeen* an efficient buy compared with women's magazines, but how does *Seventeen* compare with *Teen Vogue*, for example, or with MTV? Ad planners have to study their own research, their syndicated research, and the research presented to them by the magazine and cable companies to make a decision. They might decide to see whether one or another of the teen magazines would give them a discount for the bulk of the makeup ad money. Or they might discuss the pros and cons of splitting their ad purchases equally among major teen periodicals and teen-oriented cable networks.

Considerations such as these constantly occupy media planners. They also worry about the placement of print ads, TV commercials, and Web ads. Placement concerns involve the environment of the ad as well as its visibility. **Environment** refers to the media material surrounding the ad. If you're advertising lipstick, you might want your ad placed in the vicinity of

cost per thousand (CPM) the basic measurement of advertising efficiency in all media; it is used by advertisers to evaluate how much space they will buy in a given medium, and what price they will pay

environment the media material surrounding the ad

The locations for ads are boundless. At airport security checks, the TSA now stands to save millions through a program that requires advertising companies to provide screeners with new trays and other items. Advertisers in turn target the frequent flyer demographic.

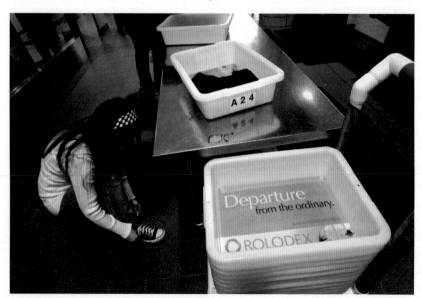

articles or TV programming that portrays good-looking people who might well be wearing makeup. You don't want it placed in the vicinity of articles celebrating a grunge look that avoids cosmetics. **Visibility** simply means putting the ad in a place where it is most likely to be seen. In a group (or **pod**) of TV commercials, the first commercial is likely to be the one that is most noticed. Similarly, the back cover of a magazine is a good place to be; a foldout from the back or front cover (called a **gatefold**) may draw even more attention.

visibility putting the ad in a place where it is most likely to be seen

pod a group of television advertisements in succession

gatefold a foldout from the back or front cover of a magazine or book

Exhibition in the Advertising Industry

The goal of the production and distribution of an ad is to exhibit it across a variety of media to a target audience. Once the media plan for an ad campaign—the entire set of advertisements using a particular theme to promote a certain product for a certain period of time—has been created, it is up to the advertisers' media buyers to carry it out. The buyers often work for separate media-buying companies. (Recall, for example, that although Martin Agency creates and produces Geico's ads, it works with Horizon Media to plan ad-placement strategy; Horizon does the actual buying.)

CULTURE TODAY
PEPSI MISSES THE SUPER BOWL

Over 100 million viewers tuned in to watch the 2010's 44th annual Super Bowl. Per Super Bowl tradition, the commercials provided a substantial part of the appeal of the game for many viewers, with the likes of Snickers, Doritos, and Budweiser all airing commercials during the Super Bowl.

However, one product was notably absent from the commercials: Pepsi. This marked the first time in twenty-three years that Pepsi did not air a commercial during the Super Bowl. Instead of spending the millions of dollars it would cost to air a thirty-second Super Bowl ad spot, Pepsi's marketing executives decided to put their efforts into a new Pepsi Refresh campaign that they felt didn't mesh with the Bowl extravaganza. Guided by the slogan "Refresh Everything," the campaign attempted to use social media to infuse the Pepsi brand with philanthropic associations. Through Pepsi's "Refresh Everything" website, members of the public were encouraged to submit proposals for charitable projects and vote on pre-existing projects. Each project was assigned a different category, such as "Food and Shelter" or "Education," and a proposed budget— from $5,000 to $250,000. Each month of the campaign, PepsiCo granted several projects from each category and expense-level funding based on the votes they received. Proposed projects ranged from shipping Girl Scout cookies to troops overseas to providing a resettlement center for North Korean refugees.

Pepsi's "Refresh Everything" campaign is one of the largest examples of cause marketing—a style of marketing that appeals to consumer's sense of social consciousness. Instead of portraying a product as socially conscious in its own right, such as promoting a product as fair trade, cause marketing partners brands with often unrelated charitable causes—for instance Yoplait's "Save Lids to Save Lives" campaign for breast cancer research. "Refresh Everything" also indicates a shift in Pepsi's advertising efforts toward interactive and social media. Ironically, though, the very absence of Pepsi from the Super Bowl may have garnered the brand more attention than a mere commercial on the sporting event would have received.

Sources: Michael Bush, "Consumers Continue to Stand By Their Causes During Downturn," *Advertising Age*, November 17, 2008, via Nexis; Chris Daniels, "Pepsi Concentrates on Social Media for 'The Refresh Project,' Bypasses Super Bowl, *PR Week*, February 17, 2010, via Nexis; Brian Morrissey, "Does Social Sell?" *Adweek*, February 15, 2010, via Nexis; Nielsen Wire, "Super Bowl XLIV Most Watched Super Bowl of All Time," February 8, 2010. http://blog.nielsen.com/nielsenwire/media_entertainment/super-bowl-xliv-most-watched-super-bowl-of-all-time/ (accessed August 11, 2010); Pepsi Refresh Project. http://www.refresheverything.com/ (accessed February 23, 2010); Natalie Zmuda, "Pass or Fail, Pepsi's Refresh Will Be a Case for Marketing Textbooks," *Advertising Age*, February 8, 2010, via Nexis.

Every mass media firm publishes its rates for space or time. It also makes a pitch for different target audiences that advertisers crave. For example, MTV's online division has organized its sales staff to sell to advertisers "against" three psychographic groups: kids/family, men/gamer enthusiasts, and youth music. The division's digital sales director noted in 2006 that the company was reaching over 30 million unique visitors per month and so could deliver the large numbers—the "online scale"—that advertisers want.[5]

For media buyers representing large advertisers, however, these charges are just the starting point. They dangle the large amounts of cash that they control as they attempt to negotiate discounts from the basic rates. Some media companies want the business of big advertisers so much that they offer inducements beyond discounts to get them to sign up. These inducements, called **value-added offers**, cover a wide gamut of activities. A newspaper firm might help the advertiser create booklets about its product and distribute them to its readers. A TV network might give the advertiser a discount for space on its internet site. A magazine company might give the advertiser access to the media firm's large database of subscribers.

It also works the other way: a television network with a popular show might tell an ad buyer that buying time in that program requires buying time in a less popular show ("Want your ads in CBS's highly-rated *CSI*? Then you'll have to run some in *Criminal Minds*.") Media firms know, too, that buyers like to follow audiences across different platforms. So, for example, Fox's *House* in 2009 created a Web page for fans to express their regrets about a character who had inexplicably committed suicide on one of the season's episodes. Similarly, NBC Universal's digital unit created a specific website aimed at "superfans'" of the sitcom *30 Rock*. The aim was to encourage marketers to place ads both on the TV series and on the sites.[6]

Eventually, with the right technology, the goal is to help advertisers track individuals across many media, so as to reach them when they are most ready to receive ads. One hint of the way that might happen relates to mobile phone companies' ability to track their customers' locations. If the customers agree, the companies can send them ads, including discount coupons, based on their geographic location. This sort of advertising, which is sure to grow, is called **location-based advertising**. Such outdoor advertising might also develop cross-platform features—for example if your phone company works with your supermarket to give you different coupons at checkout in the supermarket. The Microsoft Corporation is already carrying out a kind of location-based advertising activity in relation to gaming. Part of Microsoft's "Live Anywhere" strategy, the activity is called **cross-platform gaming** or **pervasive gaming**. It allows users to play the same game and same competitors in a variety of places. It also allows players to use one identity across platforms, as well as all-in-one scorekeeping, chat, and friend lists. All this allows Microsoft to sell ads aimed at the same people with particular demographics across all three of Microsoft's gaming areas: the XBox, its online gaming sites, and its mobile gaming platform.[7]

Of course, advertising agencies expect their work to be exhibited on the media outlets with which they have made deals. Several companies exist to help ad buyers determine whether their work did indeed get printed or aired in the appropriate way and at the appropriate time. In addition, agencies and their clients are interested in what their competition is doing. Competitive Media Reports (CMR) is one firm that provides advertisers with information about where their competitors are advertising and how much they are spending.

value-added offer a special service promised by a media firm to its most desired advertisers as an inducement to get their business

location-based advertising the process of sending commercial messages to people based on their geographic position

cross-platform gaming or **pervasive gaming** location-based advertising activity in relation to gaming that allows users to play the same game and same competitors in a variety of places. It also allows players to use one identity across platforms, as well as all-in-one scorekeeping, chat, and friend lists. All this allows ad agencies to sell ads aimed at the same people with particular demographics across all gaming areas

Determining an Advertisement's Success

After an ad campaign is exhibited, the ad agency's research division will probably be involved with the advertiser in evaluating the campaign's success. In the case of a direct-marketing campaign, this evaluation is easy. If the campaign led to the purchase of a certain number of products (or a certain dollar amount), it may be judged a success. In the case of a Web ad, evaluation depends on the nature of the response and the expectations of the marketers. If the ad is of the **click-through** sort, in which the reader can use the mouse to get to a product site and purchase the product directly, the ad's success can also be evaluated through direct purchases. Yet one can argue that the ad may be successful even if the people reading it do not click on it or,

click-through ad a Web-based advertisement that, when clicked on, takes the user to the advertiser's website

CULTURE TODAY
SUPER BOWL ADS: BEYOND THE HYPE

The Super Bowl is not only the biggest football game of the season, it is also the, well, Super Bowl for the advertising industry. Agencies launch their best ads and spend millions of dollars for thirty-second spots that air during the championship game. Many people tune into the Super Bowl, and even hold parties, for the advertisements alone. There is often a good deal of speculation surrounding the brands and commercials that will appear during the big game.

In recent years, it has become apparent that the hype around Super Bowl ads may be as beneficial as the advertisements themselves. In 2005, GoDaddy.com, a company that registers internet domain names, submitted an advertisement called "Censorship Hearing" in which a scantily-clad, boisterous woman presents herself before a Congressional Committee hearing. The advertisement was accepted and aired during the Super Bowl; however, it was deemed inappropriate and pulled before it could be aired a second time. The decision to ban the GoDaddy.com commercial received a lot of media attention and raised interest in the advertisement, which could be viewed by visiting the GoDaddy.com website.

GoDaddy.com learned from its "misfortune" and has submitted advertisements for subsequent Super Bowls with the intent of being banned and benefiting from the media coverage and speculation around the offensive advertisements. Other companies, including Budweiser and PETA, have also had Super Bowl commercials banned. Quickly, the novelty of banned commercials started to wear off.

However, in the lead up to the 2010 Super Bowl, two advertisements made headlines for their presence, or lack thereof, in the Super Bowl. ManCrunch.com is an online dating site for gay men. The company submitted

an ad for the championship game that was denied a slot. The ad showed two men, one in a Vikings jersey and one in a Packers jersey, sitting on a couch. As they reached into the chip bowl situated between them, their hands touched and, realizing their passion for each other, they engage in a raucous make-out session. Though the ad did not air during the Super Bowl, it did go viral and was widely viewed online. The decision not to include an advertisement with two men kissing sparked discussion in the media. Many criticized the decision to reject the ad as discriminatory. Others suggested that the ad itself was not worth fighting for because it mocked rather than supported the gay community.

A second ad, one that did air during the Super Bowl, also garnered a fair bit of press. It was announced weeks before the Super Bowl that Focus on the Family, a pro-life advocacy group, had paid $2.5 million for a spot. In the lead up to the Super Bowl there was much speculation about whether or not the ad would air and what the spot would look like. The decision to air a pro-life ad while rejecting the ManCrunch spot was also widely questioned. Many women's groups petitioned CBS not to air the advertisement. In the end, the Focus on the Family ad did run. It was a subtle advertisement starring former Florida football player Tim Tebow and his mother. It ended up being the least viewed advertisement during the entire game and generated little post-game discussion.

Do you think that the strategy of getting banned from the Super Bowl is an effective one?

Source: http://www.huffingtonpost.com/2010/02/11/tim-tebow-commercial-leas_n_458437.html (accessed August 11, 2010).

if they do click on it, they do not buy the product. They may buy it later, in a brick-and-mortar store or online, and that could be difficult to track.

In traditional advertising, immediate results are impossible to observe. It can be tough to determine how many teens bought lipstick as a result of the ad in *Seventeen*. Nonetheless, researchers try to find out. One way of noting the visibility of the campaign is to survey the target audience to see how many people recall the ads. Comparing the recall of those ads with the recall of other ads gives one measure of the ad campaign's ability to enter the consciousness of its targets. More directly related to the ad campaign's ability to move a product are comparisons of sales before and after the campaign. Of course, many factors, not all of them related to the campaign, can influence this comparison. But the researchers do the best they can to tease out these considerations and draw conclusions about the ads themselves.

Because the effectiveness of an advertising campaign is so difficult to measure definitively, advertisers constantly worry about whether the enormous amounts of money they are spending are worth it. Still, the revenues mass media firms collect from advertising continue to rise. A famous saying, sometimes attributed to the nineteenth-century merchant John Wanamaker, helps explain the cash devoted to the activity. "I know that half of my advertising funds are wasted," he said. "The trouble is, I don't know which half."

Threats to Traditional Advertising

The concern that companies have had about measuring the value of their ads is as old as the advertising industry. Part of that worry comes from the awareness that people may not pay attention to ads, even if they are staring right at them. As radio and television began to air commercials, advertisers also worried that many members of the audience wouldn't sit still to watch their spots. Ad practitioners imagined large segments of listeners and viewers going to the bathroom or kitchen during commercial "breaks." The challenge then becomes to make the ads interesting, funny, disgusting, or cute enough for target audiences to actually want to hear, watch, or read them. This has become an important goal of creativity in advertising.

During the past decade or so, though, advertisers have become increasingly concerned that consumers are using new technologies to help them avoid commercial messages so they don't even have to decide whether they want to attend to them. Marketers know that Americans are using digital video recorders to rush through broadcast, cable, and satellite television shows. Online, they are using email filters and pop-up killers to get rid of unwanted ads. Advertisers fear that these technologies are only the beginning of a raft of approaches that allow audiences to enjoy ad-sponsored materials with hardly any confronting of the ads.

Sometimes the ways they express their concerns verge on the hilarious. Consider the worries that Jamie Kellner, CEO of Turner Broadcasting, expressed in 2002 about DVRs. He told the magazine *Cable World* that DVR users were "stealing" television by skipping the commercials. "Your contract with the network when you get the show is you're going to watch the spots. Otherwise you couldn't get shows on an ad-supported basis. Any time you skip a commercial . . . you're actually stealing the programming." When his interviewer asked him, "What if you have to go to the bathroom or get up to get a Coke," Kellner responded: "I guess there's a certain amount of tolerance for going to the bathroom. But if you formalize it and you create a device that skips certain second increments, you've got that only for one reason, unless you go to the bathroom for 30 seconds. They've done that just to make it easy for someone to skip a commercial."[8]

Over the next few years, it became clear that DVR makers were trying to make their devices ad-friendly—for example by providing special places for advertisements on their devices and encouraging visits to advertisers' websites. Nevertheless, advertisers remained concerned. Their worries were bolstered by a 2005 survey by the Yankelovich Partners market research company that found 69 percent of American consumers "said they were interested in ways to block, skip or opt out of being exposed to advertising."[9] Fear continued that rapidly spreading technologies could make mulch of the traditional approaches to buying advertising.

Some TV executives deny that DVRs are that big an issue. They point to research that finds viewers still do remember the essential messages of brands they race through with their wands. But marketers who worry about ad skipping have come up with different tactics to get around the problem. One approach was to make advertisements more relevant to specifically targeted audiences with the hope that they would know that and not skip them. Another tactic was to make deleting or skipping the ads impossible; that's the case with in-game ads and the ads in online videos. Still another set of solutions that marketers are using involves bypassing traditional advertising altogether. To understand this last set of solutions, recall that at the start of this chapter we defined advertising as the activity of *explicitly* paying for media space or time in order to direct favorable attention to certain goods or services. From the standpoint of a marketer, the advantage of being explicit about what you are selling is that you have a lot of control over when, where, and in front of what audience your product will appear. You also have control over the message; the ad or commercial runs exactly as you intended it. The disadvantage of being explicit, though, is that the audience knows that you're trying to persuade it, and it may well try to get out of the way.

The alternative, many marketers understand, is trying to get in front of audiences through ways that don't announce their presence as persuasion. There are many ways to do that, and you've probably come into contact with all of them. You've already seen a definition for public relations, which involves the unannounced insertion of products or ideas into media materials. You've probably heard of product placement, when a brand is inserted into a TV show or movie as a result of a marketing deal. You may not have heard of viral marketing, buzz marketing, or environmental marketing. These businesses are growing tremendously—faster than the advertising business— as marketers look for a way to reach consumers in ways that will virtually force them to pay attention to their messages. We can group them under the label public relations and other marketing communications. These are important activities, critical to understanding the direction of many media today. We'll tackle them in Chapter 16: The Public Relations Industry.

Media Literacy and the Advertising Industry

Of course, advertising is here to stay—even as other forms of marketing communication come alongside it. As we have seen, companies spend more than $200 million a year on advertising. Advertising executives care about the money they allocate to the creation of ads and the purchase of ad space because this activity consumes lots of cash that could be used for other purposes. Media executives care about the money they receive from ads because it helps keep them alive. It's natural for them to be concerned, and it's natural for millions of other people to be concerned along with them because they work for companies that either spend or collect advertising money.

But what about people who are members of the larger society? What should citizens who want to live in a democratic, peaceful, thriving world think about the relationship between advertising and media? This is an important question, if only

IS IT ETHICAL?
IS IT ETHICAL TO ADVERTISE?

The question of ethics in advertising focuses on the morality of particular ads and particular types of ads, and on the basic underlying tenets of the entire business of persuasion. In regard to the latter, the Catholic Church attempted to answer that question in a thirty-five-page report titled "Ethics in Advertising." Published in 1997 by the Pontifical Council for Social Responsibility, the Church accuses advertisers of making "deliberate appeals to such motives as envy, status-seeking and lust" and urges them to avoid "manipulative, titillating and shocking ads."

Many advertising executives did not respond amiably, claiming that they should not be blamed for problems that they inherited rather than caused. One British executive responded: "[O]f course we resort to irrational motives and appeal to people's sense of status or lust or envy. That's what we are about." A decade after the Church's report, there is some evidence that the advertising industry has begun to change its stance on the applicability of ethics in marketing. The World Federation of Advertisers met in Canada in May 2007 under the banner "the ethical imperative: beyond compliance." However, critics say that this may be an attempt simply to avoid regulation and give advertisers a chance to mold ethics rather than allow ethical standards to mold them.

One of the most pertinent issues in recent years regarding ethics in advertising is that of advertising to children. Children are increasingly the target of advertising because of the growing amount of money spent on them and the influence they have over their parents—sometimes called "pester power." This is troublesome for advocates because of the vulnerable and impressionable nature of children that makes them more susceptible to messages. These messages can have negative impacts on their diet and lead to more materialistic behavior. As marketers are switching to more subtle means of advertising some governments have taken action. Both Norway and Sweden have banned advertising that targets children under 12 years of age. Both Britain and Greece have strict restrictions on the types of advertisements allowed during children's programming. More subtle tactics by advertisers and the need for governments to regulate show that such self-regulatory "ethical" initiatives commenced by groups such as the World Federation of Advertisers may indeed be all "smoke and mirrors".

Sources: Belinda Archer, "The Eighth Deadly Sin," *Africa News,* April 11, 1997; "The Vatican's Ad Ethics Report Now On-line," *Advertising Age,* April 14, 1997, p. 18; Vikki Leone, "Advertising: The Route of All Evil?," *The Age,* March 15, 2007; Simon Canning, "Ad Men Weigh into Ethical Guidelines," *The Australian,* May 3, 2007.

because advertising is all around us. Moreover, our everyday approach to ads is typically quite conflicted. We condemn the stupidity of some of them even while we hum commercial tunes and repeat commercial phrases (remember Budweiser's Whassup? ad campaign?). We hate it when ads intrude on our viewing, but we are sometimes glad when commercials appear on TV so that we can go to the kitchen or bathroom. We sometimes buy what we see in ads even while insisting that they don't affect us. In general, we accept ads as a given in our society and don't think deeply about them.

Many scholars suggest that we really ought to think deeply about them. A few writers even suggest that the future of world civilization depends on redefining society's relationship to advertising. That may sound like an extravagant claim about an industry that sells cars and candy bars. But is it really that far-fetched? See what you think as we review three issues that center on advertising, the mass media, and society. One issue—the power of advertising conglomerates in the face of blurring media boundaries—carries forward two themes that we've seen throughout this text. The others—advertising and democracy and advertising and commercialism—focus on the ad industry but also relate to the media system as a whole. As we will see, all three issues are quite interrelated.

Advertising and Commercialism

We start with commercialism because it is the term most associated with advertising and its impact on American life. **Commercialism** refers to a situation in which the buying and selling of goods and services is a highly promoted value. Many people say that the United States is a nation in which commercialism runs rampant. Everywhere we turn, we see a sales pitch.

Defenders of commercialism insist that Americans would never have the high standard of living that they now have, nor the products that they take for granted, were it not for the industrial competition that commercialism has encouraged. Detractors of commercialism question this notion of progress. They insist that many difficulties come along with making commercialism a central tenet of American society. The most common problem, they say, is leading people to purchase things that they don't really need.

From the time Americans are very young, the critics say, they are presented with a daily barrage of ads. These ads are important not primarily because they aim to sell individual products or services; sometimes they succeed at that, and sometimes they don't. Rather, the importance of the advertising barrage is that it is part of what some observers call a **hidden curriculum**—a program of study that people don't realize they are taking. Advertising critics argue that what advertising teaches, and what Americans accept as a basic lesson from the ad "course" they receive, is that society is merely a huge marketplace, and that buying products and defining oneself through them is an essential aspect of life.

Supporters of advertising say that, even if this hidden curriculum exists in as powerful a manner as its critics suggest, it is not harmful. People need to feel good about themselves, and advertising provides a vehicle—products—for doing that. Critics respond, however, that commercialism has dire side effects. Two that they especially highlight are the exploitation of children and the destruction of the global environment.

commercialism a situation in which the buying and selling of goods and services is a highly promoted value

hidden curriculum a program of study that people don't realize they are taking

THE EXPLOITATION OF CHILDREN Media critics contend that advertising to children is ethically unacceptable. They point out that children aged 2 through 12 years are often treated just like any other consumers. Ad people know that children influence their parents' spending and, as they get older, also have their own purchasing power from gifts and allowances. The critics cite scholarly research showing that the youngest children (those under age 4 or 5 years) often don't have the skills to be critical of advertisers' claims. As for the older kids, the critics contend that, by getting children hyped for toys, foods, and other products that their parents must approve, the advertisers may be encouraging family arguments. In fact, marketers and media firms that

"And so, kids, if you don't find this awesome new game under the tree you've really got to ask yourselves what you're doing there."

TECH & INFRASTRUCTURE
ADVERTISING AND VIDEO GAMES

It has become an axiom of media studies that advertising is everywhere. It is on our walks to school, on the bus, on the apple we eat as a snack, in sponsorship form, and, of course, in the traditional media of television, radio, and newsprint—not to mention the cornucopia of advertisements found on the internet. Now, however, we can add a new member of this cast: the video game.

New technologies have allowed ads to be streamed directly into a game, when players are connected to the internet through their PlayStation, Xbox, Wii, or PC. This genre of ads, known as "dynamic ads," appear in "predetermined" blank spots inserted during the creation of the game. This means that users playing *Madden* online will see different spots around the stadium depending on the deal that the advertising company has made for that time period.

In previous years, ads had to be "baked in" to the game during the creation stage. As such, they could not be changed, and companies had to pre-purchase the ad space based on a predicted number of sales. Pioneered by companies like Massive Inc., dynamic ads allow companies to purchase ad space when a game is already released. The business is predicted to grow from $54 million in 2006 to between $800 million and $1.8 billion in a few short years.

Currently, the big video game makers like Electronic Arts are leading the way with creating places to insert ads, especially with sports games in which ads can be placed on stadiums and on billboards. Supporters of the activity say it heightens the realism of the game.

Iga Worldwide—a company that inserts ads in games—argues from its research that 82 percent of respondents say that the ads don't distract from the enjoyment of the game. Of course, the problem with this study is that it was conducted by a company with a vested interest in seeing in-game ads succeed. In the end, advertisers and their agencies will have to judge

Football players Marshall Faulk, Warren Moon, and Jerry Rice attend the "Maddenoliday" launch event for the new Madden NFL video game.

whether the cost of dynamic advertising in games is worth the investment.

Sources: Matt Hartley, "Do Gamers Actually Notice Ads? Proof is at Hand," *The Globe and Mail*, June 3, 2008, Section B, p. 12; Abbey Klaassen, "Game-Ad Boom Looms As Sony Opens Up Ps3," *Advertising Age*, February 25, 2008, p. 1.

invite children into a separate channel to advertise to them are quietly setting themselves up in opposition to the children's parents—a situation that, the critics argue, is morally highly questionable.

DESTRUCTION OF THE GLOBAL ENVIRONMENT   Some critics argue that, when so many people are taught that the continual purchase of new products is the key to the good life, their resulting activities place an enormous burden on the earth's resources. The energy used to create the products they buy, the energy (and pollution) created by the use of the products, the garbage problems that are created when

CRITICAL CONSUMER
GREENWASHING

In a time when going green is just as fashionable as it is environmental, the appeal of tapping into a growing trend in eco-friendly consumerism for advertisers has led to a surge in "green marketing." This marketing approach places an emphasis on the presumably eco-friendly aspects of a product or brand, using environmental concern as a key selling point. "Greenwashing" is a pejorative term used to describe advertising that attempts to market its products or brands as environmentally friendly, but does so in a deceptive way.

Environmental marketing firm TerraChoice has made steps toward developing a taxonomy of the tactic, pinpointing what they call the sins of greenwashing. Although outright lying certainly qualifies as a greenwashing sin, so do less cut-and-dry marketing techniques, such as environmental claims that are overly ambiguous, irrelevant, or lacking in evidence to support them. When TerraChoice matched up over 1,000 consumer products against their enumerated sins, it claimed 99 percent were guilty of greenwashing in some regard.

Other organizations have also been getting involved with this issue. For example, the University of Oregon and the environmental advocacy group Greenpeace both maintain blogs wherein users can view and rate ads on their level of greenwashing—what the University of Oregon calls a "Greenwashing Index." The United States Federal Trade Commission holds the right to persecute advertisers making false or misleading claims. It is updating its environmental guidelines for the new decade.

Sources: Andrea Billups, "FTC Reviews Rules to Keep Advertisers True 'Green'," *Washington Times*, March 4, 2008; Jesse Ellison, "Save the Planet, Lose the Guilt," *Newsweek*, July 14, 2008; Dan Mitchell, "Being Skeptical of Green," *The New York Times*, November 24, 2007.

people throw away things that they could still use but that aren't fashionable—all these activities make the earth a more and more difficult place to inhabit. Supporters of advertisers counter that these problems are not really so bad, that people are living better now than ever before in history. The critics reply that the ecological disasters caused by commercialism are just beginning. As the billions of people in developing countries such as China buy into the commercialist philosophy of countries such as the United States, the pressure on the earth's environment will mount to unacceptable levels. Advertising critics such as Sut Jhally have argued that this predicament will literally lead to the end of the earth's ability to sustain human beings.

Advertising and Democracy

Writers such as Jhally extend their critique of advertising and commercialism into a critique of advertising and democracy. In doing so, they are trying to reverse a long-standing perception that advertising and democracy go hand in hand. Supporters of advertising have emphasized for decades that it is far better to have a media system that relies on advertisers for money than one that relies on the government. They point out that heads of states often try to control media in ways that preserve their power and take away the ability of citizens to understand other ways of looking at their worlds. Although outstanding examples of government-run media that encourage democratic thinking do exist (look at the British Broadcasting Corporation), many societies with government-owned media are not politically free. Because people cannot afford to foot the entire bill for their media menu, advertisers are a good alternative to government interference.

Advertising critics don't necessarily dispute the contention that government-controlled media often abuse democratic ideals. They insist, however, that advertisers

CULTURE TODAY
ADVERTISING THE CENSUS

By constitutional law, the United States government is required to perform a census every ten years. When people don't fill out the census, they are not taken into consideration when federal funding is being divided. Improper enumeration could lead to a lack of essential services, such as schools and hospitals, in certain areas. That explains the U.S. Census Bureau's focus for the 2010 census advertising campaign: community responsibility.

The message may be straightforward, but getting people who live in the United States to hear it and act on it was complex. The country is increasingly a place where many languages are spoken—and sometimes the people speaking them do not know English. To make sure that all Americans would be included in the national count, the United States Census Bureau reached out to non-English-speaking residents as well as English-speaking ones. Promotional efforts rolled out in twenty-eight languages, compared with only seventeen languages for the 2000 census. Moreover, by focusing on the benefits that the census can have for community development, the Bureau hopes to reach communities that are traditionally difficult to capture statistically.

The advertising slogans for the 2010 campaign aim to give individuals increased agency by making them feel part of the process. The themes include slogans such as "It's in your hands" and "We can't move forward until you mail it back." One television advertisement called "A March to the Mailbox" shows how, by filling out the census, one citizen can help build schools, hospitals, and parks in his community. The idea of the campaign is to show Americans how filling out the census can pave the way for changes in their community.

Although many ads aimed to reach large proportions of the population (for example via the Super Bowl broadcast), others targeted particular neighborhoods. These often featured celebrities and well-known figures prominent among particular ethnic groups being targeted, for example Dikembe Mutombo, a former basketball player particularly well known among Congolese Americans, and Luciana Gomez, the vice president and group account director of the Latino division of GlobalHue.

Do you know non-English speakers who filled out, or didn't fill out, the census? How persuasive were the campaigns for them?

Sources: Stuart Elliott, "A Census Campaign That Speaks in Many Tongues," *The New York Times*, January 14, 2010; "A March to the Mailbox" advertisement. http://www.youtube.com/watch?v=zvtHJnFgerQ (accessed August 26, 2010).

also often guide ad-supported media in ways that hinder democracy. They do this by controlling content for marketing purposes in ways that are counter to encouraging citizen participation.

Consider the situation in the United States. The First Amendment does not protect media practitioners from advertiser control, critics note. In fact, because of their importance in funding the media, advertisers actually have a lot more power over the content of media in the United States than government agencies do. What advertisers get from that power, say the critics, are media vehicles that create a friendly environment for them among the audiences they target. This relationship between advertisers and media firms hinders democracy, the critics say, because their audiences get a selective view (or no view) of certain parts of the world that they don't know from personal experience. In effect, the advertising industry's power over media screens people from learning the perspectives of certain groups in society and discourages public discussions on certain important issues.

Some critics go even further with their complaints about the effect advertisers have on the public's knowledge about, and involvement with, parts of the world that they do not experience first-hand. They say that the advertiser–media relationship has led to a situation in which much material is created primarily to get people interested so that they will see or hear commercial messages. The result, they add, is a media environment that attracts people with attention-grabbing stimuli such as sex and violence, yet puts them in a good mood when they watch, hear, or read the ads.

At its worst, say the critics, a media system driven by this mentality fosters a society of audiences, not of citizens. That is, it encourages people to pay attention to the media, but not to become actively involved in tackling the problems of the larger society, partly because the media focus so much on keeping them tuned in and entertained. Culture critic Neil Postman insisted, in fact, that because of the advertiser–media relationship we in society are "amusing ourselves to death." Postman's argument is that the stress on unchallenging, feel-good pap in so much of the U.S. media (including the news) is leading American society down the path toward a situation in which society will be too involved in entertainment to cope with serious problems, and so these problems will destroy it. Sut Jhally, with his focus squarely on advertising's role in the deterioration of the global environment, would agree.

Spiraling Clutter

During the past decade, the advertising industry has seen the same movement toward consolidation and rise of conglomerates that we have seen throughout the rest of the media system. Some of the biggest agencies in the industry were acquired mainly by the four biggest ad organizations—Omnicom Group, WPP Group, Publicis, and Interpublic Group. According to one respected industry source, these giants together accounted for about 58 percent of all the money spent on purchasing media time and space in the U.S. during 2007.[10]

Sut Jhally, a leading expert on advertising and media studies, is the founder and executive director of the Media Education Foundation. In his frequent lectures and articles, Jhally asserts that advertising constantly pushes us toward consumer goods to satisfy our needs for love, friendship, and autonomy.

Ad industry critics such as Matthew McAllister have pointed to the rise of ad agency conglomerates in an era of blurring media boundaries as signaling a deepening of the problems of commercialism and democracy. Their reasoning has two steps. First, they emphasize the power that advertisers have always had over U.S. media. Next, they note the increasing movement of all material, including advertising, across media boundaries. Third, they suggest that the agency conglomerates are working with mass media firms to turn as much space as possible into ad-friendly territory, deepening commercialism and threatening democratic dialogue even more than in the past.

The first point is one that we have seen already, in this chapter and throughout this book. Advertisers are extremely important to the survival of many U.S. media. Media executives must take the needs of potential advertisers into account when they make decisions about whom to reach and with what sorts of materials. Are women aged 25–54 years a viable audience for a fashion magazine, or would advertisers be happier with younger demographics? If the latter, what kinds of columns and covers would best attract younger readers? If you multiply these sorts of questions and their answers thousands of times, you will understand that when people read a magazine, watch a TV show, get on many websites, or use any other ad-sponsored medium they are entering a world that was created as a result of close cooperation between advertisers and media firms.

That cooperation, the critics note in their next step, increasingly involves the movement of all material, including advertising, across media boundaries. We've seen this, too, throughout our discussions of media industries. (You'll recall that Chapter 5 explains how and why this cross-media requirement developed.) The idea is to follow target audiences to as many places that they go as possible. Ad-sponsored vehicles such as ESPN and *Sports Illustrated*, for example, are no longer tied to their original media (cable and magazines, respectively). The competitors for sports audiences now follow their audiences into one another's turf and even further, appearing in print, in video, on broadcast TV, on cable, on mobile devices, on airplanes—wherever the potential fan goes.

ad clutter term used to refer to the competing messages facing Americans virtually everywhere they turn, virtually every moment of the day

With all this advertising surrounding people, ad practitioners find it more and more difficult to get people's attention. Executives commonly use the term **ad clutter** to refer to the competing messages facing Americans virtually everywhere they turn, virtually every moment of the day. Their typical solution to cut through the clutter is more ads in more and more unusual places, from supermarket floors to bathroom stalls. This, of course, merely creates more clutter and encourages ad practitioners to buy more ads, and more creatively placed ads. The ensuing clutter keeps the process spiraling, meaning, say critics, that we are all being inundated with ads. The result, say the critics, is acceleration of media clutter and, by extension, of the commercialism that deepens America's hidden ad curriculum and encourages content that is designed to keep people as audiences rather than citizens.

But the advertising industry is not alone in carrying out this process, some critics continue. The public relations industry is at least as much at fault. In addition, whereas advertising is at least visible, PR is often invisible. What is public relations, how does it work, and why should we care? To get answers, turn to Chapter 16.

Chapter Review

For an interactive chapter recap and study guide, visit the companion website for *Media Today* at http://www.routledge.com/textbooks/mediatoday4e.

Questions for Discussion and Critical Thinking

1 Why would a company hire more than one ad agency to promote the same product?
2 Explain positioning and its relation to segmentation.
3 What does it mean to say that advertisers create portraits of America?
4 How have technological innovations changed the ways advertisers reach consumers?

Internet Resources
. . . .

The Hartman Center for Sales, Advertising & Marketing History (http://library.duke.edu/specialcollections/hartman/index.html)

A Duke University site that displays thousands of old ads from the nineteenth and twentieth centuries.

Advertising Age (http://adage.com/index.php)

A major trade magazine of the advertising industry with a site that includes news, blogs, and industry data.

Mediapost.com (http://www.mediapost.com/)

This website offers to email to you, without charge, several daily bulletins about various aspects of advertising and media as well as classified job ads.

Adbusters (http://adbusters.org)

Based in Vancouver, Canada, Adbusters is a not-for-profit magazine "concerned about the erosion of our physical and cultural environments by commercial forces." The website as well as the magazine offer sharp critiques of advertising.

Key Terms
. . . .

You can find the definitions to these key terms in the marginal glossary throughout this chapter. Test your knowledge of these terms with interactive flash cards on the *Media Today* companion website.

Constructing
Media Literacy
. . . .

1 Do you agree with the notion that advertising provides a "hidden curriculum"? Why or why not?
2 How would you have responded to Jamie Kellner of Turner Broadcasting when he said that audiences have a responsibility to view ads?
3 To what extent is it possible for parents to shield their children from commercialism? Do you agree that shielding them is a good idea?
4 To what extend can you see market segmentation in the media that you use?

Companion Website
Video Clips
. . . .

No Logo—No Space: New Branded World (abridged)
This clip from the Media Education Foundation documentary *No Logo* looks at how branding by large corporations came about and its effects on the public across the globe. Credit: Media Education Foundation.

Big Bucks, Big Pharma—Branding Drugs
This clip from the Media Education Foundation documentary *Big Bucks, Big Pharma* focuses on the industry's marketing practices and how these practices shape how the public understands and relates to disease and treatment. Credit: Media Education Foundation.

Behind the Screens—Making Movies for Marketers: Cross Promotions, Merchandising and Tie-ins
This clip from the Media Education Foundation documentary *Behind the Screens* looks at how the advertising and movie industries are becoming increasingly intertwined. Credit: Media Education Foundation.

Shop 'Til You Drop
This clip from the Media Education Foundation documentary *Shop 'Til You Drop* looks at American materialism and considers the flip side of its accumulation—depletion—and how this erodes natural resources and basic human values. Credit: Media Education Foundation.

Advertising and the End of the World—How Far Into the Future Can We Think?
This clip from the Media Education Foundation documentary *Advertising and the End of the World* addresses questions about the cultural messages coming from advertising and the culture of consumption. Credit: Media Education Foundation.

Killing Us Softly 4—Ads Everywhere

This clip from the Media Education Foundation documentary *Killing Us Softly 4* explores the portrayal of women in advertising and how this affects women's views of themselves and others. Credit: Media Education Foundation.

Consuming Kids—Under the Microscope

This clip from the Media Education Foundation documentary *Consuming Kids* considers the practices of a multi-billion dollar marketing aimed at children and their parents raising questions about the ethics of children's marketing and its impact on the health and well-being of kids. Credit: Media Education Foundation.

James River Barbeque Ad

This 1960 animated advertisement for barbeque includes the use of racial stereotyping. Credit: Internet Archive/Drive-In Movie Ads.

Camel Cigarette Commercials

This clip from the Internet Archive is a compilation of Camel cigarette ads from the 1930s. Credit: Internet Archive.

Case Study

· · · · · · · · · · · · · · · · · · ·

EXPLORING ADS ALL AROUND

The issue We often don't pay attention to the many commercial messages that we see because of the clutter of advertising all around us. Knowing about this lack of attention, advertisers often send more ads our way with the aim of catching our attention, thereby increasing the clutter. The result is an everyday environment filled with ads. To see just how filled, it might be interesting to track the number of ads you see in just one part of your day.

The method Count the number of ads you see from the time you get up until the time you get to work or to class. Take care to follow your normal routines and paths. Start with the sounds you hear or see from the radio and TV; the ads on the cereal box; the commercial messages on the clothes you wear; the ones on the signs you see on your way. Keep a record of what you saw and when—and in what amount of time. Write a report of your findings, and share it with your classmates to find out how similar or different you are from one another.

16 The Public Relations Industry

After studying this chapter, you will be able to:

1 Sketch the development of the public relations industry

2 Analyze the nine areas of the public relations industry

3 Explain how public relations, advertising, and other persuasion activities are coming together to produce integrated marketing communication

4 Discuss concerns that media critics have about the persuasion industries

MEDIA TODAY

In Chapter 15, we defined advertising as explicitly paying for media space or time in order to direct favorable attention to certain goods or services. The first two elements of advertising—paying for space and explicitly advertising—are important to underscore because another persuasion industry—**public relations (PR)**—has been built on the premise that the best way to influence people through media is *not* to pay for space and *not* to announce your presence.

Recent decades have seen the fast growth of a third persuasion business—marketing communication— that mixes aspects of both advertising and public relations. All three activities have major effects on mass media. The aim of this chapter is to explain how and why that is so and to point to the growing number of circumstances in which elements of advertising and PR are mixed.

public relations (PR) information, activities, and policies by which corporations and other organizations seek to create attitudes favorable to themselves and their work, and to counter adverse attitudes

Distinguishing Between Public Relations and Advertising

You are probably much less familiar with public relations (PR) than with advertising. In fact, it wouldn't be surprising if you've never talked with anyone about a public relations campaign. Most people aren't aware that many of the media materials they read, hear, or watch are parts of a PR campaign.

That's OK with public relations practitioners. They try very hard to avoid getting public recognition for stories that appear in the press, because they believe that, for their work to be most effective, viewers and readers should not know when TV programs and newspaper articles are influenced by the PR industry. The fact is, though, that a good deal of what we see and hear in both news and entertainment material is initiated by, or filtered through, public relations specialists.

What is Public Relations?

publicity the process of getting people or products mentioned in the news and entertainment media in order to get members of the public interested in them

People sometimes talk about PR narrowly, equating it with publicity. **Publicity** is the practice of getting people or products mentioned in the news and entertainment media in order to get members of the public interested in them. Although public relations sometimes involves publicity work, it extends beyond it.

The following three examples may suggest the wide territory of the PR world:

- You're the CEO of a large chemical firm, and you're worried that state legislators will pass environmental laws that will harm your company. At the same time, you don't want the legislators or the people of the state to believe that you want to pollute the environment. You hire a PR firm to help you devise a strategy for dealing with this dilemma.
- You're the head of investor relations for a large technology firm. You are sure that the firm's stock is undervalued, but key analysts at major brokerage firms don't seem to agree. You hire a PR firm to help you change that perception.
- As CEO of a pharmaceutical firm, you learn in a late-night phone call that one of your company's over-the-counter products has allegedly poisoned five people in the Midwestern United States. Although your firm has a crisis management team for emergencies of this type, you turn to a PR firm for further suggestions about how to handle the victims and their families, the press, politicians, and federal regulators.

What do these different scenarios have in common? One expert has put it this way: public relations involves "information, activities, and policies by which corporations and other organizations seek to create attitudes favorable to themselves and their work, and to counter adverse attitudes."[1] That's a neat way of tying the examples together, and it also brings up another important issue: the relationship between public relations and mass media. If you think about the description and the three scenarios for a few moments, you'll see that they all suggest that public relations activities need not involve the technologies of mass communication. Much of the PR firm's plans for the state legislators, for example, may involve one-on-one lobbying, which is a straightforward form of interpersonal communication.

Still, in many aspects of their work, public relations practitioners do turn to the mass media—beyond simply getting good publicity for a client. For one thing, they often involve trying to counter negative media impressions of the client that were created by others. For another, media strategies typically fit into a larger PR communication strategy regarding the organization. PR work for the chemical firm, for example, may have an important mass media component, such as reaching out to reporters in the state capital with stories about the positive role the company is playing in the local economy and the care its leaders are taking with the environment. The public relations people might also believe that presenting the company in a good light to the viewing public might, in turn, encourage state politicians to believe that their constituents would applaud new laws that do not harm the firm.

Advertising differs from PR in the mass media in two major ways. First, advertisers pay for the space or time that they receive, whereas public relations practitioners typically do not. Second, advertising clearly states its presence. When you see an ad, you know what it is for, and you often know quite easily who is sponsoring it. A public relations activity, by contrast, typically hides its presence and its sponsor.

What advertising and PR have in common is that they deal in billions of dollars and play profound roles in American mass media. In fact, they are deeply involved in three important trends we have noted in media today: the movement of material across media boundaries, the rise of conglomerates, and the increase in audience segmentation and targeting. Not only do the ad and PR industries themselves reflect these trends, they encourage them in other mass media as well.

The multiplication of media and the growth of the internet and other digital outlets have led to two major developments in the advertising and public relations industries themselves. First, marketers of all types are using advertising and public relations in concert to reach audiences with persuasive messages. Second (and as a result), this concert is being orchestrated by large companies that own not just ad agencies and PR firms, but also "branding" consultancies, polling firms, and other entities that add ingredients to a symphony that goes beyond advertising alone or PR alone but is a mixture of the two for what broadly might be called marketing communication.

At this point you may be asking, "Where did public relations come from and how did it develop separately from advertising?" Not surprisingly, that's the topic of the next section.

The Rise of Public Relations

Public relations goes back a long way. In military reports sent back to the Roman Senate by generals such as Julius Caesar, historians have noted a self-aggrandizing "spin" on events that we would today associate with a masterful public relations counsel. By the time of the American Revolution, the forms of public relations clearly had a modern feel. Anti-British colonists staged the Boston Tea Party and other events to gain public attention. They used popular symbols that colonists were likely to recognize—for example the liberty tree and the minutemen—to mobilize support for their cause. In addition, writers such as Samuel Adams, Thomas Paine, Abigail Adams, and Benjamin Franklin developed messages that swayed public opinion against England. Think of the phrase Boston Massacre. As communication professor Joseph Dominick notes, what actually happened was that an angry mob got into a fight with British soldiers and a few people were killed. By calling this event a "massacre," leaders who wanted to eject the British were using inflammatory language to gain support for their position.

The Boston Tea Party took place on the night of December 16, 1773, when a group of indignant colonists, led by Samuel Adams, Paul Revere, and others, disguised themselves as native Americans, boarded three East India Company ships, and threw their entire cargoes of tea into Boston Harbor. This early "publicity stunt" helped sway public opinion against the British government and helped stir the beginnings of the American Revolution.

Early Pioneers in Advertising and Public Relations: Benjamin Franklin and P. T. Barnum

In Chapter 15 we discussed Benjamin Franklin's knack for writing advertisements in the 1700s. One historian notes that "advertising and public relations, especially self-advertising and publicity, were as natural to Franklin as his restless intelligence and curiosity. Franklin, in all his roles and on behalf of all his varied activities, was always the untiring promoter."[2] In fact, he was so successful a lobbyist and propagandist that in the 1760s he managed to persuade the British not to tax advertisements in the American colonies—even though ads were taxed in England.

Until the middle of the 1800s, people who practiced these activities (including Franklin) often didn't see them as especially separate. Many imaginative entrepreneurs touted their goods or services in a multitude of ways, some of which we would call advertising and some of which we would call PR. Phineas Taylor (P. T.) Barnum used both advertising and public relations seamlessly before the two industries developed in separate directions. You may know his name through the famous Ringling Brothers, Barnum, and Bailey Circus—only one of Barnum's many pursuits. In the 1800s, he gained fame as a result of a broad spectrum of activities that mixed advertising, public relations, and showmanship in ways that drew both scorn and respect—and a lot of money. He generated an enormous amount of media attention when he exhibited an African-American woman who, he claimed, was the 161-year-old nurse of George Washington. Barnum also garnered great publicity for such oddities and hoaxes as a "mermaid" (in reality a dummy tied to a large fish tail) and the "marriage" of two short-statured people (which took place over and over again wherever his show stopped).

Barnum didn't apologize for his tactics, arguing that his audiences liked to be fooled; he even revealed to newspaper reporters some of the tactics he had used for previous hoaxes. Everything about his work was brash; his bold, highly pictorial advertisements and his brazen promotional activities deeply influenced other show-men such as "Buffalo Bill" Cody. Barnum's expertise at getting press coverage also served as a model for railroad publicists whose job was to lure people to settle near the tracks as railroads expanded west.

The late 1800s brought growing literacy, new technologies, new organizational arrangements associated with the penny press, changes in the economy after the Civil War, and other broad social changes. Such changes gave Barnum and his cohorts a much larger readership than Ben Franklin had had 100 years before. These changes also encouraged ventures that led directly to the creation of industries devoted to public relations and advertising.

The Public Relations Industry Comes of Age

During the 1900s, PR and advertising grew into two separate industries. The new public relations practitioners emphasized a more elite role that was emerging for their profession: that of a PR "counselor" who could help guide the public images of large corporations in ways that satisfied management.

The social forces that made this sort of work lucrative—the growth of colossal companies aiming at large audiences in a national market economy—were the same ones that influenced the direction of the ad business. But whereas ad people worked to help firms get consumers to buy things, public relations practitioners gravitated to a very different corporate goal. This was an era in which the heads of large companies feared that the masses of consumers and workers might rise up against them in anger over negative articles about them that appeared in the press. Business leaders saw a major need to convince consumers and government officials not to interfere with their companies. The (often fabulously wealthy) chief executives wanted to make the case that their actions and the actions of their firms were in the best interest of the entire nation.

The job required people who could combine a Barnum-like feel for public image-making with an understanding of politics that recalled that of Julius Caesar. In the late 1800s and early 1900s, railroad firms and utility companies such as AT&T and Consolidated Edison hired PR firms to get newspapers to portray them as concerned corporate citizens as well as to coordinate lobbying activities aimed at convincing federal, state, and local government officials to preserve their monopoly positions.

Of particular note during this time was an organization called the Publicity Bureau, which was the predecessor of the modern PR agency. Its first major account,

In 1842, circus pioneer P. T. Barnum (left) hired Charles Stratton, who became world famous as "General Tom Thumb." Tom Thumb stood only twenty-five inches tall and weighed only fifteen pounds, and was thus billed as "The Smallest Man on Earth." Barnum and Thumb became close friends. During their dealings together, they traveled around the world and met various leaders and royalty, including President Abraham Lincoln and Britain's Queen Victoria and Prince Albert.

in 1906, was aimed at defeating President Theodore Roosevelt's legislation to curb abuses of power by the railroads. The bureau's tacticians wrote essays favorable to the railroads and crafted them to look like news articles written by journalists. The bureau then paid to have those articles published in newspapers around the United States. The idea was to whip up public sympathy for the railroads and against the president's bill.

Many of these early PR "counselors" would do whatever it took, even if that were shady or illegal, to take care of a client's needs. Their actions ranged from bribing lawmakers to vote in ways that helped the company to paying freelance journalists to write articles favorable to the firm. After a number of years, though, such routine ethical lapses started backfiring. Indignant journalists began exposing these practices, and then companies had to dig themselves out of even deeper public relations holes.

IVY LEE AND MODERN PUBLIC RELATIONS   One of the first individuals to help build the dignity of the corporate public relations business in the face of such embarrassments was a minister's son and former reporter named Ivy Lee. Lee cultivated a reputation of honesty among corporate leaders, government officials, and the press. In 1906, he convinced the heads of the Pennsylvania Railroad to "come clean" to journalists about their company's mistakes that had led to a rail accident. Lee argued that this sort of openness—which was unusual for its day—would lead reporters and consumers to trust the railroad for its straightforwardness.

Lee codified this view in a "statement of principles" that same year. "Our plan," he wrote, "is, frankly and openly, on behalf of business concerns and public institutions, to supply the press and public of the United States prompt and accurate information concerning subjects which it is of value and interest to know about."[3] As distinct from the press-agency approach to PR, Lee's view of the business saw the PR counselor as a kind of in-house journalist with the main purpose of disseminating factual information in order to influence public opinion. Many members of the press appreciated this perspective and turned to Lee for inside information about his clients that they could not find elsewhere.

Lee's work for John D. Rockefeller's Standard Oil Company during problems at one of the firm's plants in Ludlow, Colorado, provides an example of how Lee used his press contacts. Eighteen people, including women and children, died during violent clashes that took place when representatives of the United Mine Workers tried to organize laborers at the company. Countering statements by the union that Standard Oil had hired goons to kill striking workers, Lee put out the company's version of events, which was that the victims had died in an accident that they themselves had caused. He tried to build credibility for this version by having John D. Rockefeller Jr., who actually ran his father's company, pose in overalls with union leaders and families of the workers.

There were people both within and outside of the press who were sure that this account was false and that Lee had used his clout with journalists—and his reputation for openness—to circulate a deceitful version of the event deliberately. This criticism—that the purpose of public relations is to saturate the public with falsehoods that fit the needs of wealthy clients—is one that

Ivy Lee, a former New York City newspaper reporter, became one of the first prominent PR practitioners. He gained notoriety for carrying out damage control for the Rockefellers following the 1914 Ludlow massacre, in which eighteen people (among them women and children) were killed during an attack by the Colorado National Guard on behalf of Rockefeller mine interests in Colorado.

has dogged the business through the decades.

Public concern and awe about the alleged power of PR particularly developed when PR practitioner George Creel published his memoirs after World War I. Creel wrote of his wide-ranging campaign on behalf of the U.S. government to persuade the American people to rally around their country's entry into World War I. The Committee on Public Information, which he led, perfected many techniques that are common today—for example the wide distribution of press releases to newspapers, the use of motion pictures to evoke emotional support for a cause, and the recruitment of local "opinion leaders" to convince people in their circles of friends of the correctness of the cause. His revelations caused a lot of people to become frightened of the power of PR "propaganda." Looked at differently, the idea that PR could successfully carry out such a major campaign using so many different techniques was great publicity for the young PR industry in search of corporate clients.

Edward Bernays, a nephew of Sigmund Freud, is one of those credited with creating the profession of public relations.

EDWARD BERNAYS AND THE "SCIENCE" OF PR   Public relations professor James Grunig describes the approach to PR that both Ivy Lee and George Creel used as a "public information" model. Grunig notes that it is a **one-way model of public relations**; that is, this version of PR concentrates on sending persuasive facts that benefit the client to the press, without any attempts at systematically learning about the populations whom the client wants to persuade.

The first **two-way model of public relations** was championed by a practitioner named Edward Bernays beginning in the 1920s. A nephew of famed psychoanalyst Sigmund Freud, Bernays believed that it was essential to draw upon the social sciences to carefully shape the responses of audiences to the client's views of the world. Bernays is generally considered to be the first PR practitioner to offer all these ideas, together with a theory of how and why they would be successful. This "scientific persuader" business model is one reason PR historians call Bernays, rather than Ivy Lee, "the father of public relations." Bernays wrote the first textbook on the subject and taught the first college course in public relations, at New York University in 1923.

Borrowing from philosophers of his day, Bernays justified public relations as a profession by emphasizing that no individual or group had a monopoly on the true understanding of the world; "truth" is relative, he said, and depends upon one's perspective. In his view, the role of the professional PR counselor was to lead general or particular audiences to see the truth from the client's perspective. He angered many people both inside and outside the PR business by his blunt assertions that PR practitioners could "engineer" the "consent" of audiences for their clients by learning to push the right psychological buttons. Nevertheless, throughout his long life (he died at 103), he championed the importance of PR for organizations and cultivated a reputation for carrying out work that was based on a careful, social-scientific study of the "nature and dynamics of public opinion," as he put it.

one-way model of public relations a model of PR that concentrates on sending persuasive facts that benefit the client to the press, without any attempts at systematically learning about the populations whom the client wants to persuade

two-way model of public relations first championed by a practitioner named Edward Bernays in the 1920s, this model of PR draws upon the social sciences to carefully shape the responses of audiences to the client's views of the world

An example of this approach to PR is Bernays' decision to take into consideration children's attitudes toward soap and bathing when the Procter & Gamble company asked him to increase American families' use of Ivory Soap. His conclusion: change kids' attitudes toward bathing by promoting soap sculpture contests in schools. The idea was to get them to see Ivory Soap as a fun, friendly product that made washing and bathing inviting.

Growth and Change in the PR Industry

The work and the writings of Ivy Lee, George Creel, and Edward Bernays inspired many people to get into the public relations business. During the Great Depression of the 1930s, large corporations turned to public relations counselors to help restore them to favor in the eyes of a population that was disillusioned with and angry at big business. Companies such as Carl Byoir & Associates and Hill & Knowlton came into existence and grew in this environment. World War II gave yet another boost to public relations. During this time of national crisis, the U.S. government called upon PR practitioners to use as many techniques as necessary—interpersonal and mass media, news and entertainment—to explain the war and encourage citizens to do their part to help win it.

The number of public relations practitioners continued to grow after the war, as companies and governments increasingly realized the importance of getting and keeping the public on their side. Two types of public relations practitioners emerged. The first worked in PR companies that acted as long- or short-term counselors to a variety of organizations. The second type—far more numerous than the first— worked full time doing PR for government agencies and private organizations. The titles of these practitioners—press officer, PR specialist, communications manager— depended on their activities and where they worked.

During the 1960s, public relations practitioners felt forced to rethink their approach to their audiences. The "scientific" model that they used, although two-way, saw target audiences as groups that were to be studied so that they could be manipulated. There was little room in public relations for suggestions that the government and corporate leaders for whom the industry worked would actually change their strategies or activities in response to research on what people wanted.

Ralph Nader began to earn his reputation as a crusader taking on major corporations forty years ago when he was catapulted into the national spotlight as a young Harvard law graduate whose stinging book *Unsafe at Any Speed* challenged the safety of the Chevrolet Corvair and American cars in general.

It was in the 1960s that that attitude began to change. It was a time of resistance, fueled by the Civil Rights Movement, the war in Vietnam, and a fiery consumerism movement sparked by *Unsafe at Any Speed*, a book written by Ralph Nader that revealed major safety problems in the rear-engine Chevrolet Corvair. The press—and public—outcry that accompanied these revelations became a PR nightmare for Chevrolet's parent, General Motors.

In the years that followed, many corporations, afraid that consumer anger would lead to lost sales, beefed up their customer relations programs. Some began an even more basic re-evaluation of their public relations

strategies. Talk in the PR industry was of a more "symmetrical" two-way relationship with the public. In this approach to public relations, research would be used not only to shape messages aimed at audiences but also to figure out how the organization could position itself to most please its target audiences. The new role of public relations practitioners, in this view, would be to serve as go-betweens, as mediators between clients and the public.

Sometimes PR practitioners found that they had the attention of top management and could, therefore, follow this business model. Much of the time, however, one of the other three models—that of press agent, public information distributor, and social-scientific persuader—held sway. Moreover, all of the models raise ethical issues that people in the industry and media-literate people outside it must confront. We explore this topic soon as well. First, though, it will be useful to investigate the basic workings of the industry.

An Overview of the Modern Public Relations Industry

The number of individuals involved in public relations has risen sharply over the past few decades—from about 19,000 in 1950 to hundreds of thousands today. The U.S. Census Bureau found more than 7,000 public relations firms in the United States in 2006.[4] Apart from specific companies dedicated to public relations, PR practitioners can be found in many corporations, government bodies, healthcare institutions, military branches, professional services firms, associations, nonprofit organizations, and other public and private entities. The Veronis Suhler Stevenson media consultancy firm estimates that in 2008 companies spent about $3.6 billion on public relations.[5] Public relations in the twenty-first century is an activity in which most midsized and large companies are involved. Companies' involvement takes place in two ways, through direct involvement in corporate communication and through hiring a PR agency.

Corporate Communication Departments

Many large U.S. companies have public relations units, often called **corporate communication departments**. These departments typically have three functions: external relations, internal relations, and media relations. Let's take a look at each.

EXTERNAL RELATIONS   External relations express the company's perspective to a variety of entities outside the organization. They include community groups, government officials, officials of various countries, and various citizen advocacy groups. Public relations employees also act as lobbyists for their company. That is, they try to convince state and federal legislators to pass certain laws that will benefit the company or to eliminate rules that may hinder the firm's progress.

INTERNAL RELATIONS   Internal relations represent the voice of the company to employees, union groups, and shareholders. To that end, the external relations people may relate corporate newspapers, email notes, and (in really big companies) even television news shows about the company.

corporate communication departments public relations units that typically have three functions: external relations activities involve expressing the company's perspective to a variety of entities outside the organization; internal relations involve being the voice of the company to employees, union groups, and shareholders; and media relations handle calls with journalists, provide the answers, and coordinate the interviews with executives

MEDIA RELATIONS   Journalists call many companies on a daily basis looking for information or wanting to speak to a particular executive. Media relations employees handle these calls, provide the answers, and coordinate the interviews with executives. They may also teach executives the best ways to act on camera or with a journalist.

Public Relations Agencies

Although large companies may carry out day-to-day public relations agencies through in-house departments, they are also likely to hire "outside" PR companies for a variety of projects ranging from special lobbying to getting or controlling media exposure. Public relations companies often charge fees based on the number of hours that their employees work for a client. Sometimes clients make "retainer" deals with an agency, under which the company agrees to carry out a PR program at an agreed-upon rate per month.

Not all public relations companies do the same things. Large firms such as Fleishman-Hillard help their clients with virtually any area of communication, including teaching their top executives how to speak on TV and in front of large groups. Many smaller public relations firms, however, specialize in a particular part of their industry's work. Examples of medium-size independent agencies that specialize include Healthstar, a healthcare agency; Cerrell Associates, a public affairs and environmental agency; and Integrated Corporate Relations, a company that helps firms speak to stock analysts, institutional investors, financial media, and other corporate audiences.

The biggest public relations firms are widely considered to be Fleishman-Hillard, Weber Shandwick, Hill & Knowlton (which absorbed Carl Byoir in 1986), Burson-Marsteller, Incepta, Edelman Worldwide, BSMG Worldwide, Ogilvy PR, Porter Novelli, and Ketchum. All these companies with the exception of Edelman and Incepta are owned by one of the **agency holding companies** known as **the Big Four**: Omnicom, WPP, Interpublic, and Publicis (see Table 16.1). As we saw in Chapter 15, agency holding companies are firms that own large ad agency networks, public relations firms, and a multitude of branding, market research, and marketing communication firms. In fact, from the 1960s through the 1990s, the agency holding companies bought up twenty-one of the twenty-five largest PR firms.[6] The holding companies refuse to release data about the earnings, number of employees, or clients of the PR firms that they own. They say their policy is based on the promise of total confidentiality for their clients, but it also means that it is difficult for outsiders to know what is going on within the industry's largest and most powerful firms.[7]

This gobbling up of the largest firms should not be surprising. Consistent with what we've learned about other media industries, the PR business in the 1980s and 1990s went through a period of rapid conglomeration and globalization. Big public relations firms merged with other big ones; big firms bought smaller ones, especially specialty firms; and public relations firms were bought by ad agency

agency holding companies firms that own large ad agency networks, public relations firms, and a multitude of branding, market research, and marketing communication firms

the Big Four the largest agency holding companies, including Omnicom, WPP, Interpublic, and Publicis

http://www.fleishmanhillard. com

Table 16.1 Major PR Firms Owned by the Largest Agency Holding Companies

WPP	Omnicom Group	Interpublic
Burson-Marsteller	Fleishman-Hillard	Weber Shandwick
Hill & Knowlton	Ketchum	Golin Harris
Cohn and Wolfe	Porter Novelli	Rogers & Cowan
Ogilvy PR	Brodeur Worldwide	PMK/HBH
Carl Byoir	Clark and Weinstock	Carmichael Lynch Spong
Dai Inchi	Cone	
Dewey Square		

Sources: Holding company websites.

holding companies to create cross-industry communication firms. The number of such mergers has slowed in recent years, but the consolidation remains.

Globalization is a key to the activities of the biggest firms. Hill & Knowlton, part of the WPP holding company, reports on its website that it has seventy-nine offices and more than fifty associated PR agencies across Europe, the Middle East, and Africa.[8] It adds that it has an extensive presence throughout South America, Central America, and the Caribbean. As for the Asia Pacific, it says that, "For more than 50 years, through a network of wholly-owned offices and associates stretching from Beijing to Sydney and from Delhi to Tokyo, Hill & Knowlton has provided insights to guide clients through the opportunities and challenges of the world's fastest growing economic region."[9] In these regions, as well as in the United States and Canada, it works for local firms as well as multinational conglomerates with the need for projecting influence with consumers and governments around the world.

Major Public Relations Activities

What are the demands on any public relations campaign? Why would companies (or, in some cases, individuals such as actors or authors) pay lots of money for representation by a public relations firm? The answer is that these clients need help in explaining their actions to government regulators, companies, and members of the public in ways that will help them complete a business deal, ensure them long-term favorable treatment, or get them out of trouble. A company that can help can be worth its high cost.

At the most basic level, PR practitioners help their clients:

- Understand the challenges that face them
- Formulate objectives that they would like to reach in meeting those challenges
- Develop broad approaches—**strategies**—for meeting the objectives
- Carry out particular activities—**tactics**—that put these strategies into action

The uses for such expertise are wide. Here is how the Hill & Knowlton website describes to potential clients what the firm can do for them:

strategies broad plans or approaches for meeting objectives

tactics the particular activities that put strategies into action

> What does success look like to you?
>
> That's the first question we ask.
>
> We build up a clear picture of what you want to achieve. Then put in place whatever is needed to get that result. . . .

Does anyone feel their job is getting easier? It's doubtful. Not with the complexity, contradiction and uncertainty we all face in our lives. But the tougher it gets for brands, companies, governments and others, the bigger the prize for the smart ones who really get their message across.

And we *do* mean smart. Think of the obstacles to effective communication—fragility of reputation, media fragmentation, audience proliferation, information overload. Getting real brand and commercial results can seem an almost impossible task.

So how does Hill & Knowlton do superior quality work, even on the toughest assignments?

We start at an advantage: we have the desire to do so. We are not afraid to take on these tasks, however difficult. Because *that* is what our track record is all about, delivering real brand and business outcomes.

We are also able to do so. As a firm we are set up to meet even the most complex demands by connecting the three elements that help you leap over hurdles. Sector expertise. Practice skills. Geographic reach.

You know what you want us to achieve, what you mean by success. We put in place whatever is needed to get there.

If you think we can help, please contact us.[10]

These statements about public relations are actually quite abstract comments about the importance of a company's ability to manage its environment. The way Hill & Knowlton and other PR firms put these environment-management goals into practice is through several categories of business activities.

The most prominent public relations activities are in these areas:

- Corporate communications
- Financial communications
- Consumer and retail
- Healthcare and advanced technology
- Public affairs
- Crisis management
- Media relations

The labels indicate the broad landscape of activities in which public relations firms are involved and suggest the broad range of clients they serve. The biggest firms tackle many of these categories, though not always all of them. Moreover, some companies may combine someone or another category in organizing their expertise and personnel. As we sketch these activities below, notice that mass media are used consistently in every domain.

Corporate Communications

corporate communications the creation and presentation of a company's overall image to its employees and to the public at large

Corporate communications involves the creation and presentation of a company's overall image to its employees and to the public at large. Employers believe that, if their workers share an understanding of company goals and activities, they will be both more satisfied with their jobs and more productive. Executives also want members of the public to believe that the company is a good corporate citizen, as that image might encourage purchases and help the firm get favorable treatment from local, state, and federal governments.

In many companies, a PR firm works in conjunction with human resources departments to carry out employee-relations tasks. These companies provide their employees with company handbooks, newsletters, and magazines. Experts in this area emphasize that all forms of interaction between a firm's leadership and its rank and file—even email—are vehicles for maintaining good morale and a sense of purpose. Some organizations with widely dispersed divisions even produce news programs just for employees that are sent via satellite to offices around the world.

The other side of corporate communications involves management's concern with the images of the company that are held by consumers. Even the largest companies often hire an outside public relations firm to help with their public image. Let's say that an automobile manufacturer wants to spread the notion that it is a technologically advanced, yet socially responsible company. PR counselors might suggest a number of activities that taken together would create that image in people's heads.

The PR company might create a booklet about the auto manufacturer's recent technological achievements that dealers can distribute. PR counselors might help the firm sponsor a solar-car race on college campuses. They might send the company's engineers to speak to reporters from around the country about the firm's cutting-edge work. PR specialists in digital communication may track the discussion of the firm on the Web and try to present responses on blogs, or videos on places such as YouTube, that position the firm in a positive light. Given a high enough budget, the company might even create a movie that explains scientific innovations relating to the car for science museums. Although such a film must be carefully positioned as a science film and not an ad, it can nevertheless associate the PR agency's client with innovations by showing its name a few times during the film as well as in the sponsorship credits.

Financial Communications

Financial communications involves helping a client's interactions with lenders, shareholders, and stock market regulators proceed smoothly. Sometimes the activities center around a particular client initiative. In 1995, for example, IBM turned to the financial PR firm Sard Verbinnen to support its attempt to buy Lotus Development Company. Lotus officials initially rebuffed the offer and characterized it as an unfriendly takeover attempt. IBM's public relations goal was to get out to government regulators, investors, and Lotus employees its position that folding Lotus into IBM would help both companies. They succeeded.

Financial communications work that is more typical than such one-shot initiatives revolves around top executives' need to keep investors' interest in their company's stock high. A low share price can make it tougher for the company to raise capital or make acquisitions, since sometimes payment is made in stock. Also, lenders and new investors judge a company at least in part by the performance of its stock.

The goal of a PR firm's financial communications specialists is to design a program that helps the firm communicate its value to its target audience. The nature of this communication program will depend on the specialists' analysis of the firm's image among investors. The specialists look at such factors as the company's size, history, financial record, industry identification, national or international scope, stock distribution, past communication efforts, and stock market recognition.

The idea is to shape a message about the company that is enthusiastic, yet which falls within Securities and Exchange Commission guidelines that forbid misleading statements. Here are some of the types of work that a PR firm carries out to maximize a client's attractiveness to investors:

financial communications helping a client's interactions with lenders, shareholders, and stock market regulators proceed smoothly

- It prepares corporate and financial documents (such as annual reports) and financial fact books. Well-done photo layouts and well-turned phrases can make investors proud of their firm.
- It prepares company news releases and arranges interviews with financial journalists. When journalists, especially financial journalists, write seriously and positively about the firm, investors pay favorable attention to it.
- It coordinates shareholder meetings. A poorly run shareholder meeting can reflect badly on the ability of management to get a job done.
- It plans and arranges seminars, tours, and meetings with security analysts, portfolio managers, brokers, and professional investors. These events can help increase the visibility of the firm among the opinion leaders of the Wall Street community.

Consumer and Business-to-Business Communication

On its website, H&K boasts that it helped its Brazilian beverage client Cerveceria Rio expand into Guatemala. It did it "using an intense media relations and opinion leaders campaign" to position the company "as socially responsible, focussing on the environment and benefits like job creation, market opening and international quality brands in a market dominated by a local monopoly beer producer and distributor."[11]

The PR firm wrote in 2007 about its successful "central role" in convincing the International Olympics Committee (IOC) to choose the city of London for the 2012 Summer Olympics. H&K's website notes that the win for client London—"beating Paris, Madrid and Moscow—was one of the great sporting upsets of the past decade." How did it happen? "Through a carefully constructed international PR and lobbying campaign, H&K London, with the help of 27 global H&K offices, achieved twice as much overseas media coverage than the other 2012 bids combined." That media environment, says H&K, helped persuade the IOC.[12]

consumer communication
the process of stimulating sales from people who are in their everyday, non-employee roles

The first of these activities falls into the category of **consumer communication**, whereas the second involves **business-to-business communication**. Both activities center on using public relations, as opposed to advertising, tactics to project favorable images of the client and its products to businesspeople (the IOC) or general consumers, with the aim of getting them to buy. Advertising tactics typically involve purchasing media space or time in which to present short messages. PR practitioners, in contrast, use a wide variety of approaches to convince a client's target audience to see the client in a positive light. These approaches might range from sponsoring charities, to throwing glitzy parties for business clients, to giving away free promotional items, to instigating environmental action campaigns and providing scholarships for needy youngsters. PR staff members also work to get free media coverage of these activities. The aim is to build and maintain positive attitudes toward their client within its target audience and ultimately to pave the way for future sales.

business-to-business communication the process of stimulating sales from people in their roles as company employees

This PR work usually supplements rather than substitutes for advertising. However, PR practitioners naturally argue that their work is at least as important as paid-for commercial messages. They see the goodwill generated by such events, and the news coverage of the events, as far more credible to target consumers than traditional advertising.

HEALTHCARE AND ADVANCED TECHNOLOGY   Healthcare and advanced technology are two particularly high-profile industries for which both consumer and business-to-business PR take place. Advanced technology involves the products of computer manufacturers, silicon chip makers, and defense contractors, among others. The healthcare area includes hospitals, health-maintenance organizations, pharmaceutical firms, and provider organizations such as the American Medical Association and the American Nursing Association. Both industries have concerns related to government regulations; international sales; tensions with organizations that purchase their goods and services; and confused, angry, and even frightened members of the public. Companies in these industries hire PR firms to help them deal with these problems.

Take pharmaceutical companies as an example. They view public relations as invaluable for promoting both their products and their value to the nation. When it comes to their products, they start with the fact that prescription drugs reach the public through physicians. PR practitioners within the firm therefore work hard to establish relationships between physicians and the firm. Company representatives take physicians to lunch or dinner to explain the advantages of their products. They give doctors free samples. They send them articles from medical journals that mention the firm favorably. They may even give them medical instruments as gifts in the hope that such gestures will encourage their patronage.

Increasingly, pharmaceutical firms are also reaching out to the potential consumers of their products, hoping that they will urge their doctors to write prescriptions for these products. Some of this work is traditional advertising, carried out by ad agencies. A lot of PR work aimed at consumers goes on as well. Much of it is aimed at getting prescription drugs mentioned in newspapers and magazines and on TV programs.

Pharmaceutical companies need government approval of their drugs, and public relations employees play an important role in helping to sway government in a company's favor. Several years ago, Merck (a prominent pharmaceutical company) created a website called Merck Action Network to help its employees lobby Congress. Pharmaceutical firms also hire PR agencies for this work. One of the biggest public relations firms, Burson-Marsteller, argues it can offer companies an ability to shape the opinions of people who count in the healthcare debates. "Burson-Marsteller's global Healthcare Practice is uniquely positioned to help clients navigate this complex medical, political, social and economic landscape, and in the process create and manage perceptions that deliver positive business results."[13] To carry out this persuasion process on many levels, it offers help for companies in the following areas:

- Pre-marketing of innovative drugs
- Public health education campaigns
- Direct-to-consumer education and marketing
- Product life cycle management
- Issues management
- Regulatory and policy issues
- Public education
- Grassroots communications
- Support and counsel on payer issues
- Medical education
- Obesity

Public Affairs

As you can see by the list above, in large PR firms health units often join with public affairs specialists to achieve their government-oriented health goals. **Public affairs PR** centers on government issues. Companies that depend on government contracts or that worry about lawmakers imposing regulations that will have a negative effect

public affairs PR public relations that focuses on government issues

on them rely on public affairs experts to look out for their interests. Large firms may have their own public affairs departments within their corporate communication divisions; they may also hire outside firms to help them with this activity. Smaller companies may rely only on outside help. In both cases, the practitioners may apply their efforts in a number of directions:

communications PR sending out written materials to explain the firm's positions on various regulations

political action PR doling out money to individuals and groups that have been, or can be, politically helpful

government relations PR making sure that interactions between the firm and government officials are friendly

community involvement/ corporate responsibility PR applying corporate funds to good works with the intention of gaining favor among elected officials as well as members of the public

international relations PR ascertaining the company's strategic interests relative to governments outside the United States and soliciting the help of the U.S. government in areas of difficulty. PR agencies also help foreign companies and governments establish good relations with American officials

- **Communications PR**: sending out written materials to explain the firm's positions on various regulations
- **Political action PR**: doling out money to individuals and groups that have been, or can be, politically helpful
- **Government relations PR**: making sure that interactions between the firm and government officials are friendly
- **Community involvement/corporate responsibility PR**: applying corporate funds to good works with the intention of gaining favor among elected officials as well as members of the public
- **International relations PR**: ascertaining the company's strategic interests relative to governments outside the United States and soliciting the help of the U.S. government in areas of difficulty; PR agencies also help foreign companies and governments establish good relations with American officials

Because these activities are so important to so many companies, an enormous number of PR practitioners have gotten involved in them. In the mid-1990s, one expert estimated that there were at the time some 50,000 individual lobbyists and several hundred public relations agencies plying their trade in Washington, DC, alone.[14] There is no reason to think that the numbers are smaller today. These people exert much of their influence in the major corridors of power—the White House, the halls of Congress, and the myriad government agencies. As the Hill & Knowlton website puts it, "Commercial interests are intimately connected with and dependent on the decisions of governments and regulators. . . . Competition for such influence is now more intense than ever and no organization can afford to be silent while others dominate the debate."[15]

Public relations firms are sometimes paid to coordinate political lobbying campaigns that span nations. Take Hill & Knowlton's successful effort to help Botswana's diamond exports. With the rise of public concerns about "blood diamonds"—jewels that various armed groups in Africa used to finance their fighting—the Botswana government hired H&K to make sure that its diamonds would not be refused entry into key countries. H&K embarked on a major "information campaign" in Europe, the United States, the United Kingdom, and Japan. It "generated support among Members of Congress, U.K. Parliamentarians, Members of the Japanese Diet, and Members of the European Parliament, as well as numerous media outlets. A number of political delegations from all four regions visited Botswana to meet with President Mogae and other Government Ministers at the highest level." The result, says H&K, is "significant political support for Botswana and its diamond industry and President Bush signed into law legislation favorable to Botswana in the form of the Clean Diamond Trade Act."[16]

Crisis Management

Public relations practitioners typically assume a reasonably stable client when they submit plans for public affairs, corporate communications, media relations, or financial relations in connection with advanced technology, healthcare, or other areas of business. It doesn't always work out that way, though, because the political

CULTURE TODAY
PR AND THE TELENOVELA

Telenovelas are incredibly popular among America's Spanish-speaking population. Though telenovelas have similarities with soap operas, they are different from soap operas in that they are scripted to air for a predetermined duration.

Social messages and calls for public service are not uncommon in the telenovela. Episodes frequently tackle issues such as AIDS or alcoholism. Sometimes, the plot twists or actor's comments are written with the help of outside health or advocacy organizations in order to spread the word about such issues.

In 2009, Telemundo introduced a message into one of its telenovelas designed to help the company as well as its audience. Perla, one of the central characters in the popular telenovela *Más Sabe el Diablo* (or *The Devil Knows Best*), took a job as a census recruiter. The plotline stemmed from an informal partnership between the U.S. Census Bureau and Telemundo. The Census Bureau holds a vested interest in appearing favorable to Hispanic populations. Census officials estimate that a

quarter of a million Hispanics were not counted during the 2000 census, which they explain in part by a distrust Hispanics have over the census process. Telemundo certainly has a stake in making sure Hispanic populations do not go undercounted. Nielsen Ratings bases the number of Hispanic households included in its sampling methods on census data. The more Hispanics counted by the census, the more Hispanics that participate in Nielsen Ratings, which could mean greater clout for Spanish-language networks and higher ratings and advertising revenues.

Sources: Luis Clemens, "Plot Twists for Genre," *Multichannel News*, October 25, 2006. http://www.multichannel.com/article/81696-Plot_Twists_for_Genre.php (accessed August 11, 2010); David Montgomery, "To Engage Hispanics About Census, Telenovela Steps Up to Be Counted," *The Washington Post*, October 7, 2009, Style, p. C01; Brian Stelter, "U.S. Census Uses Telenova to Reach Hispanics," *The New York Times*, September 23, 2009, Section B, p. 1.

or economic environment surrounding a client can sometimes change drastically. At other times, unforeseen events within the client's organization can spiral out of control and create a major problem. These changes are crisis situations, and a key area of the PR industry is set up to help companies manage crises.

Crisis management refers to the range of activities that helps a company respond to its business partners, the general public, or the government in the event of an unforeseen disaster affecting its image or its products. A classic example of crisis marketing in the healthcare area was Burson-Marsteller's handling of a 1982 crisis

crisis management the range of activities that helps a company respond to its business partners, the general public, or the government in the event of an unforeseen disaster affecting its image or its products

Burson-Marsteller's handling of the 1982 Tylenol scare is considered a classic episode in crisis management.

involving Tylenol for the manufacturer Johnson & Johnson. Health officials named Tylenol as the product that had been used to kill seven people around Chicago. While law enforcement and health officials were searching for the person or persons responsible (a culprit was never found), Burson-Marsteller's mandate was to make clear to the public that its client had America's best interests in mind and would take steps to ensure that Tylenol would be absolutely safe. An obvious comparison to this case is Toyota's troubles in the late 2000s with faulty accelerators that led to death, injuries, and many recalls. As *Newsweek* pointed out, "Back in 1982, even as people in Chicago were dying of cyanide poisoning from tampered Tylenol bottles, the drug-maker's parent company, Johnson & Johnson, didn't have to worry about Internet message boards inciting panic or fueling rumors and fear-mongering. The strategy of corporate crisis management hasn't necessarily changed, but in the Google, Twitter, and Facebook era, the execution has."[17] Public relations firms have to be conversant with all these vehicles, both to monitor what people are saying about their clients and to try to head off ill will. Most experts agreed in 2010 that Toyota had not done a good job. One expert called it "the worst-handled auto recall in history in terms of the consumer anxiety that persists and the mixed messages that were being sent at the outset."[18]

Large PR firms such as Burson-Marsteller not only specialize in helping companies when a disaster arises but also teach executives how to prepare for a crisis that might happen. These PR experts perform risk analyses and set up seminars to go over various scenarios with employees. In addition, they write instruction manuals, often in different languages, to help the staff of far-flung companies come together efficiently in times of emergency to try to keep the company's image from being tarnished.

Public relations campaigns that emerge from such thinking generally involve mass media. Although advertisements are one way to reach various constituencies, PR strategists believe that influencing the news about the client that these constituencies receive is more effective. The reason is that an advertisement so obviously represents the client's position that it may not be effective in convincing skeptics. In contrast, a properly influenced reporter will often present the client's interests as one legitimate side of a debate. Receiving this sort of legitimacy in the press can help rebuild a company's battered image with stockholders, with its employees, or with government regulators.

media relations all dealings with reporters and other members of media organizations who might tell a story about a client

Toyota Motor Corp President Akio Toyoda speaks during a press conference at the company's Tokyo headquarters in Tokyo, Japan.

Media Relations

You've undoubtedly noticed that many of the PR tactics that we've discussed involve the mass media. For PR practitioners, these activities fall under the heading of **media relations**. This term covers all dealings with reporters and other members of media organizations who might tell a story about a client. In some of these dealings, journalists take the initiative—for example when reporters want to know what is going on during a company crisis. Other dealings with the media take place at the initiative of PR practitioners who want to spread the word about their clients' activities. Your university probably uses a PR staff to spread good news about research that is being carried out and about the success of its sports teams. The goal is to make both alumni and current students so proud of the institution that they will want to make financial contributions.

PR practitioners often spread news by building good relationships with relevant journalists and editors. That way, the public relations staff will have the best chance at getting its organization's desired point of view across in a media story. Getting a desired viewpoint across usually means more than just answering incoming calls and sending out information. Most media relations work is proactive. So, in addition to providing interested parties with relevant facts and information for their stories, PR staff members have to go the extra mile by doing much of the journalists' job for them—for example thinking up, selling, and sometimes even writing sample stories.

Of course, journalists have the final word on which stories they'll choose to rewrite and finally run, and they are often suspicious of their PR contacts. In addition, journalists have a large number of choices among PR-initiated stories, as so many companies are involved in media relations activities. These two circumstances create a lot of pressure on the PR practitioner. The next sections examine the public relations industry's production, distribution, and exhibition of material for the mass media in more detail.

Production in the Public Relations Industry

The most basic product of a public relations firm's attempt to influence the media is the **press release**—a short essay that is written in the form of an objective news story. Because the goal is to get a reporter or editor to write about a particular aspect of the client's activities, a successful press release finds a hook in the client's tale that the reporter can use. PR practitioners know that reporters will dismiss as propaganda stories that simply tout the views of the firm's executives or present the firm's accomplishments. The trick is to write a story with an angle that the journalist will see as interesting to her or his audience and that can also include other firms and other points of view. A press release that is too obviously self-serving will rarely get picked up.

press release a short essay that is written in the form of an objective news story

Because of the importance of knowing what attracts journalists to particular stories, PR firms and PR departments of organizations often hire former journalists as their press contacts. The Hill & Knowlton website proudly notes that:

> We have a reputation for handling complex media situations in positive circumstances as well as in times of crisis. Our media relations professionals—including former journalists, press secretaries and communications officers—have delivered results throughout the world.
>
> Using solid research and analysis, messaging, journalistic skills and close media relationships, we can deliver real business impact.[19]

As these lines suggest, writing press releases is just part of a PR firm's media duties. The company must also hire practitioners who can field questions from members of the press who come to them for stories. PR practitioners are also increasingly involved in coordinating the production of audiovisual materials that present the points of view of their companies to various constituencies. A mobile phone company, for example, might send a video to high schools to describe for students the new technologies it is using to keep rates down while providing the best service. A university might prepare a home page on the internet that gives prospective students tours of the campus. Also

TECH & INFRASTRUCTURE
TWEETING FOR PR

Social networking tools such as Twitter and Facebook are used by millions of individuals to announce their actions and opinions to friends. Over the past couple of years marketers have found that, just as these tools can be used to spread news and information, they can also be used for damage control.

Pepsi, Ford, Comcast, Amazon, and Southwest Airlines are among the many firms now employing social media directors who scan Twitter and Facebook for negative press regarding their companies. For instance, late in 2008, lawyers for Ford sent a shutdown request to TheRangerStation.com, a fan site. This action led to hundreds of online complaints against Ford. In response to the public outcry, Scott Monty, Ford's head of social media, posted on his and Ford's Twitter site that RangerStation was "selling counterfeit goods with Ford's logo." Ford didn't want to shut down the site, he insisted, just stop the illegal use of Ford's trademark. Throughout the "crisis" Monty posted constant updates, including when the site agreed to stop selling those products. He succeeded in dampening angry opinions of Ford in the Twitterverse.

PR practitioners cite the online retailer Amazon's lack of openness with social network users about a controversy as an example of what not to do. In April 2009 the firm eliminated gay, lesbian, and transgender as a search theme on its site. Quite soon afterwards, Twitter was awash with comments about this act of apparent insensitivity. Although Amazon eventually rectified the situation (blaming it on a "glitch"), the company's PR representatives did not reach out to the Twitter or Facebook audiences to try to quell the negative tweets.

In response to this silence, Tweets were instead filled with "boycott threats, petitions and caustic accusations" against Amazon. As the *Los Angeles Times* reported, this is "an outcome that suggests that the growth of social media may be driving up the cost of inaction." As communications consultant Shel Holtz observes, "social media have magnified the urgency of crisis communication." For Amazon, this was certainly the case.

While many companies are turning to Twitter to help control their reputation, some are using the social media site as a tool for generating positive publicity and lending a helping hand. After the 2010 earthquake in Haiti, MTV Networks participated in the "Hope for Haiti" telethon, which aired on network television as well as using Twitter to raise money for Haiti. The telethon raised more than $65 million for hurricane relief. The use of Twitter to help raise money seemed like a natural fit as the social media software was already being used by celebrities and everyday citizens alike to reach out for aid, locate missing friends and family, and share news of the devastation.

Sources: Sarah E. Needleman, "Theory & Practice: For Companies, a Tweet in Time Can Avert PR Mess," *The Wall Street Journal*, August 3, 2009, p. B6; David Sarno and Alana Semuels, "Tweets Are an Ally in Crisis PR; Firms that Ignore or Fail to Speedily Reply to Online Chatter about their Brands Learn that that's Not a Good Idea," *Los Angeles Times*, August 20, 2009, part B, p. 1; "The Ranger Station Fire." http://www.scribd.com/doc/9204719/The-Ranger-Station-Fire (accessed August 11, 2010); Mark Walsh, "TV Digital Heads Meet the 'Splinternet'," *Online Media Daily*, March 11, 2010.

important is the role of digital vehicles that encourage target audiences to interact with them and feel friendly toward them. PR firms help clients set up Facebook pages or Twitter feeds that inform about discounts, answer questions, quash rumors, and exude a likeable personality. Again, here's Hill & Knowlton:

> The communications world is already digital—people are online no matter when, where or how. What companies do and say online is having a profound effect on their reputation and brand. Right now, communities are communicating with businesses and brands through consumer-generated or "social" media, driving the transition to a digital world.[20]

Smart companies are already shifting their marketing focus to reflect changing media consumption habits. Others are playing digital catch up in order to remain relevant and competitive. Either way, companies need to know how to harness the power of social media by building community around an issue or a brand, driving engagement, and building strong relationships with all audiences—and all this in a way that is open, honest, and genuine.

Companies involved in consumer public relations often decide to reach people in a less-than-open way—by turning out their own TV "news" stories. For example, a computer chip manufacturer might create a short video for use on local news programs that shows how cutting-edge computer chips allow typical home users to perform an enormous number of tasks faster and make these tasks more fun. The trick to getting such a spot on the air is to make it seem like a "soft news" story created by the TV station. (See Chapter 2 for a discussion of soft news.) PR practitioners know that they should mention their client, the chip manufacturer, only in passing and show its logo only a couple of times. Subtlety is important. Overtly pushing the company and its products would be the kiss of death for a spot; a news show would never use it.

Distribution in the Public Relations Industry

Once materials for the media part of a public relations campaign have been prepared, the PR firm must distribute them to the proper publicity outlets. A **publicity outlet** is a media vehicle (for instance, a particular magazine, a specific TV interview program, a particular radio talk show) that has in the past been open to input from public relations practitioners. "Proper" in this case has two meanings: it refers to both outlets that reach the kinds of people the firm is targeting and outlets that are appropriate for the particular ideas, products, or services that the firm is trying to push.

Public relations practitioners keep lists of the publicity outlets in different areas that are appropriate for different types of products and for reaching different groups of people. When they are working on a particular campaign, they use these lists to determine which outlets to concentrate on and whom to contact. Sometimes only a press release will be sent. At other times, PR practitioners will be so familiar with the individuals involved that they will phone them directly. In fact, having good connections among media people, especially the press corps, is a crucial asset in the PR business.

Advanced distribution technologies have also become crucial to the PR industry during the past few years. PR practitioners use fax machines and email to send press releases. They pay firms to track the discussions—the buzz—about their clients on chat rooms, blogs, Facebook, Twitter, and elsewhere, and they respond by paying people to go online and insert comments that reflect the positive spin that fits the aim of the PR campaign. (They're supposed to say they represent the firm, but they don't always do that.) PR practitioners use satellite linkups to set up interviews with TV reporters from around the country and the world for their clients. They also use satellites to send video press releases to appropriate publicity outlets. These are packages of photographs, video clips, and interviews from which a reporter can choose to create a story. A video press release for a new adventure film, for example, might contain short clips from the movie, a background piece on the special effects used to make the movie, and separate as well as combined interviews with the male and female stars. Each piece would be designed to be used as a feature story on a local television newscast. The interviews will be shot in a way that allows news people in local stations to create the impression that the discussion was created exclusively for their broadcasts.

publicity outlet a media vehicle (for instance, a particular magazine, a specific TV interview program, a particular radio talk show) that has in the past been open to input from public relations practitioners

Exhibition in the Public Relations Industry

"But," you may ask, "why do TV and print journalists use this material? Haven't we learned that journalists pride themselves on their objectivity and independence?" Good question. The answer lies in the costs of news reporting in the print and electronic worlds. Costs here relate both to monetary expense and the amount of time involved. Reporting stories totally from scratch can cost a lot of money. It can also cost reporters an enormous amount of time, time that they often do not have because of deadlines.

Imagine how many reporters *The Washington Post* would have to assign to the Departments of State and Agriculture, the Treasury, and the other cabinet-level divisions of the U.S. government if there were no systematic way to find out about meetings, speeches, reports, and other materials emanating from each. The paper could not afford to ferret out all that information, but it doesn't have to do so because each department's public relations division provides it with the basic schedule. Moreover, in key parts of the government, such as the State Department, public relations representatives summarize key issues for reporters and answer their questions.

In addition to allowing news organizations to allocate fewer journalists to government agencies, these press briefings help journalists budget their time efficiently. The briefings enable journalists to gather the basic information needed to write their daily stories. They can then spend the rest of their time following up issues raised by the briefings; each journalist hopes that their stories will stand out from those of other journalists who were also at the meetings.

information subsidies the time and money that PR people provide media practitioners that helps them get their work done

As you can see, PR practitioners help the media get their work done. Communication professor Oscar Gandy calls this sort of help to media organizations and their personnel **information subsidies**. The term means that PR people's help with information is akin to advancing money and time. Faced with a beautifully done clip that is part of a video press release, a TV station's news director may genuinely believe that some of the material in that clip is interesting enough to warrant a story. She or he also knows that the low cost of putting that spot on the air will offset the extra expenses of a locally produced story.

White House Press Secretary, Robert Gibbs, serves as the official liaison between the White House and members of the press, acting as a spokesperson and PR representative for the president and delivering the daily White House briefing.

The danger of information subsidies from a client's standpoint is that they may not be used. News organizations receive many more offerings from PR firms than they have room for, and journalists can often be quite selective. The most successful, and most expensive, public relations practitioners work hard to establish strong relationships with members of the press to help grease the path to coverage. In the mid-1990s, *The New York Times* reported that Sard Verbinnen, the head of the PR agency with that name, would get pieces in the news by currying favor with journalists: giving an "exclusive" about a deal or an interview with a chief executive to one newspaper and then offering a behind-the-scenes look at a transaction to a reporter of another paper that did not get the

original exclusive. By doing that, he would be able to call on both sources to help him with coverage when he needed it.

For Verbinnen or anyone else, though, coverage doesn't always work out the way the PR practitioner wants it to. Good journalists do their own independent investigations of material suggested by a press release or some other PR initiative. Consequently, what begins as an attempt to present a favorable image of a firm or a person may backfire if the reporter finds material that contradicts the original report.

The Rise of Integrated Marketing Communication

As we have seen, public relations is potentially very useful but also unpredictable when it comes to getting a company, person, or product specific and favorable mass media coverage aimed at a particular audience. In contrast, advertising can provide quite predictable media coverage (as the advertiser pays for time or space), but it can be quite a bit more expensive than public relations work and may not be as persuasive as PR stories that appear as news.

During the past several years, the awareness that advertising and PR can complement each other has led executives to attempt to coordinate the two types of activities to get the best of both worlds. Some have dubbed this approach **integrated marketing communications (IMC)**, or sometimes simply **marketing communications**. The goal is to blend (integrate) historically different ways to communicate to an organization's various audiences and markets. Under the best of circumstances, integration means creating a campaign that sends different, yet consistent, messages around particular themes to present and potential consumers of a firm's products as well as to its employees, to the companies that sell to it and buy from it, and to government regulators.

In addition to traditional advertising and public relations, IMC often brings three related activities into its mix: branded entertainment, direct marketing, and relationship marketing. Let's take a look at each.

Branded Entertainment

Branded entertainment involves associating a company or product with media activities in ways that are not as obviously intrusive as advertisements. The word "branded" refers to linking the firm or product's name (and personality) with an activity that the target audience enjoys. The three most common forms of branded entertainment are event marketing, event sponsorship, and product placement.

EVENT MARKETING **Event marketing** involves creating compelling circumstances that command attention in ways that are relevant to the product or firm. These activities typically take place at sports and entertainment venues, by way of mobile trailers or road shows that publicize products, on college campuses, in malls, and in bars. Some of the activities are termed "grassroots." That is, companies pay nonprofessionals (say, moms who like their products) to set up parties or other meetings that promote the items. These are activities that bring the products in front of people in unusual ways. Other activities are called "guerrilla" events. An example is when a company planted blinking electronic devices around Boston in a publicity stunt for a Cartoon Network show.[21] Figure 16.1 presents the proportions of different forms of event marketing in 2008.

integrated marketing communications (IMC) or marketing communications a type of PR, the goal of which is to blend (integrate) historically different ways to communicate to an organization's various audiences and markets

branded entertainment associating a company or product with media activities in ways that are not as obviously intrusive as advertisements. The word "branded" refers to linking the firm or product's name (and personality) with an activity that the target audience enjoys. The three most common forms of branded entertainment are event marketing, event sponsorship, and product placement

event marketing creating compelling circumstances that command attention in ways that are relevant to the product or firm. These activities typically take place at sports and entertainment venues, via mobile trailers or road shows that publicize products, and in malls

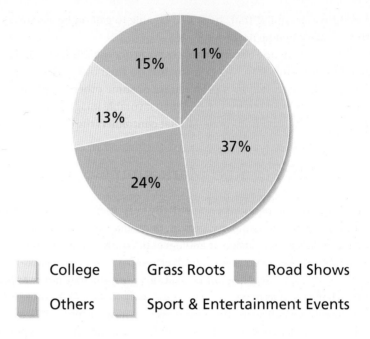

Figure 16.1 Shares of Spending on Consumer Event Marketing, 2009
Other includes mall, nightlife, and guerilla marketing. Source: Veronis Suhler Stevenson, *Communications Forecast, 2009–2013* (New York: VSS, 2009), part 3, p. 17.

College   Grass Roots   Road Shows
Others   Sport & Entertainment Events

event sponsorship situation in which companies pay money to be associated with particular activities that their target audiences enjoy or value. Examples include concerts, tours, charities, and sport

product placement agreement in which a firm inserts its brand in a positive way into fiction or nonfiction content

barter products used in movies and TV shows are provided by the manufacturer to the producers for free in exchange for the publicity

product integration the act of building plot lines or discussions for talk shows and reality TV around specific brands

Spring Break presents huge opportunities for event marketing. If you've gone to Florida or Texas for Spring Break, you may have seen companies such as Hawaiian Tropics set up bikini pageants. Often, these activities get more elaborate. In 2009, for example, the college network mtvU aired on more than 750 college campuses around the country sponsored events that framed Spring Break in Panama City, Florida. Performers included Lil Wayne, the All American Rejects, Flo Rida, Asher Roth, and Jim Jones.[22] The network also sponsored a $20,000 rock–paper–scissor tournament along with other games and giveaways. MtvU's goal was clearly twofold: first, to get viewers who hadn't traveled to Panama City to watch it on the cable net, and, second, to publicize the channel to the Panama City revelers so that they would watch the network when they got back to school and tell others about it.

EVENT SPONSORSHIP   In event marketing, the product is the focus of the activity. By contrast, **event sponsorship** occurs when companies pay money to be associated with particular activities that their target audiences enjoy or value. It happens a lot with sports, concerts, and charities. Sport has long been the largest entertainment-sponsorship category, with NASCAR and the NFL particular draws for companies. A notable concert sponsorship in 2008 was by the Clorox Company. To promote its KC Masterpiece sauces and Kingsford Charcoal, Clorox paid to support the U.S. stops of singer Keith Urban's tour.

PRODUCT PLACEMENT   **Product placement** takes place when a firm manages to insert its brand in a positive way into fiction or nonfiction content. Think of AT&T and Coca-Cola on the TV series *American Idol*, or the appearances of particular car models in movies, TV shows, and video games that you've seen. Traditionally, products used in movies and TV shows were provided by the manufacturer to the producers for free in exchange for the publicity. That is called **barter**, and it still represents the largest percentage. In recent years, paid product placement has been increasing, though observers say it still takes place less often than barter. Some marketers have paid producers of so-called reality shows and talk shows to build plot lines or discussions around their brands. The activity is called **product integration**, and

CRITICAL CONSUMER
PRODUCT PLACEMENT AND
"MOMMY BLOGGERS"

Erin Chase makes some quick notes for her blog before starting to make dinner with her two sons, Ryan, 3, and Charlie, 2, in their Dayton, Ohio, home on Monday June 1, 2009. Among the influential mother bloggers cited by Nielsen, Chase has parlayed her talents of cooking $5 nutritious dinners into http://www.5dollardinners.com.

Imagine having a job where companies send you free samples of their products, and the only thing you had to do to get them is review them for your blog. This is essentially what a lot of women—deemed "mommy bloggers" by marketers—have been doing. It should be noted that the term "mommy blogger" is one that many of these online writers don't like; they typically see themselves as helpful givers of advice about families and child-rearing—a task that frequently involves providing reviews of certain products.

Yet a few years ago, many marketers saw sending household goods and toys to women who blogged about home and kids as an inventive way for firms to promote their products. The reviewers certainly enjoyed the perks of getting more free stuff as reinforcement for favorable comments. Recently, however, the samples have amounted to lavish gifts from companies, such as cars, trips, or appliances. Some bloggers have even declared that they will only work for such extravagant compensation.

Public disclosure of these relationships has left some consumers concerned over whether the advice they

receive from what seems like an average consumer has actually been paid for by an advertiser. "I think there is a certain level of trust that bloggers have with readers, and readers deserve to know the whole truth," said Christine Young, author of the family-related blog FromDatestoDiapers.com. Though Young has often reviewed products marketers sent her for free, she insists she always discloses this connection. "Bloggers definitely need to be held accountable."

In response to growing concerns, the Federal Trade Commission (FTC) ruled in late 2009 that bloggers who review products must disclose any connection with advertisers. This includes the receipt of payment or free products by advertisers, which would make the blogger officially an endorser in the eyes of the FTC. As an endorser, bloggers are also prohibited from making false claims about a product. Penalties for bloggers can reach as high as $11,000 per violation.

The move is part of the FTC's wider efforts toward transparency in marketing, and will also apply to celebrity endorsements that may take place on talk shows or Twitter. Social media such as blogs, Facebook, and Twitter have become attractive to advertisers as a potential new avenue of marketing, as recommendations appearing to originate from an individual consumer instead of a multimillion dollar corporation exude an aura of authenticity. "Given that social media has become such a significant player in the advertising arena, we thought it was necessary to address social media as well," said Richard Cleland of the FTC's division of advertising practices. The development illustrates both the new and often surreptitious ways advertisers are finding to reach customers and the value of transparency for consumers.

Source: Stephanie Azzarone, "Mommy Blogger Backlash," *MediaPost Blogs*, July 22, 2009. http://www.mediapost.com/publications/?fa=Articles.showArticle&art_aid=110110&passFuseAction=PublicationsSearch.showSearchReslts&art_searched=Mommy%20Bloggers&page_number=0 (accessed August 11, 2010); Tim Arango, "Soon, Bloggers Must Give Full Disclosure," *The New York Times*, October 5, 2009, p. B3; Cecilia Kang, "FTC Sets Endorsement Rules for Blogs," *The Washington Post*, October 6, 2009, p. A18.

it is increasing, particularly online. In 2009, for example, ConAgra Foods bought a year-long sponsorship of the Yahoo program *What's So Funny?* The deal was that multiple ConAgra brands, including Healthy Choice, Marie Callender's, and Orville Redenbacher, would be integrated into the program's content. For example, the initial episodes featured an "Ingredients for Good Comedy" segment that combined elements of what goes into making a show funny along with visuals conveying the fresh ingredients that go into Marie Callender's Home-Style Creations.[23]

Direct Marketing

direct marketing marketing that uses media vehicles created by the marketer (phone messages, email, postal mailings) to send persuasive messages asking that the consumers who receive them respond to the marketer

Direct marketing uses media vehicles created by the marketer (phone messages, email, postal mailings) to send persuasive messages asking that the consumers who receive them respond to the marketer. Think of any of the late-night TV commercials you've watched that urge you to phone them via an 800 number; or a Web ad that asks you to click to buy a product or service. Nowadays, most direct marketing involves **databases**. These are lists of customers and potential customers that can be used to determine what those people might purchase in the future. The marketer contacts the people on these lists with advertising or PR messages. The practice of using these computerized lists is called **database marketing**.

databases lists of customers and potential customers that can be used to determine what those people might purchase in the future

Although the use of lists in marketing dates back to at least the 1800s, the past few decades have seen a huge growth in the use of computers to store information about people and their habits. This growth in marketers' ability to cross-link and retrieve huge amounts of information about people took place at the same time that the introduction of toll-free numbers, more efficient mailing techniques, and fast delivery firms made shopping from home easier than ever. These changes led to a huge increase in targeted persuasion through direct marketing.

database marketing practice of constructing computerized lists of customers and potential customers that can be used to determine what those people might purchase in the future. The marketer then contacts the people on these lists with advertising or PR messages

Relationship Marketing

relationship marketing involves a determination by the firm to maintain long-term contact with its customers through regular mailings of custom magazines, brochures, or letters or through frequent user programs that encourage repeat purchases and keep the person connected to the firm

Relationship marketing involves a determination by the firm to maintain long-term contact with its customers. This can be done by regular mailings of custom magazines, brochures, or letters or through frequent user programs that encourage repeat purchases and keep the person connected to the firm.

Agency Holding Companies

As we have noted both here and in Chapter 15, many of the major companies in each area are owned by one of the five agency holding companies that have emerged in the past twenty years to control the major advertising, public relations, and marketing communication firms around the globe. Sometimes called **marketing services companies**, these firms are deeply involved in advertising, PR, and other media activities in the United States—WPP owns the JWT agency network, for example. They are also involved in helping their multinational clients with all sorts of communication services—from media research to branding—in a multitude of countries.

marketing services companies firms that provide a spectrum of activities to help firms promote and sell their products

WPP provides an example of the scope of these firms. It has 145,000 employees, more than 2,400 offices in 107 countries, and at the end of 2008 had billings of more than $70 billion with profits of over $11 billion. Its website states that:

Within WPP, clients have access to all the necessary marketing and communications skills. [WPP] is structured as follows:

Advertising

Global, national and specialist advertising services from a range of top international and specialist agencies, amongst them Grey, JWT, Ogilvy & Mather, United Network and Y&R

Media Investment Management

Above- and below-the-line media planning and buying and specialist sponsorship and branded entertainment services from GroupM companies Mediacom, Mediaedge:cia, MindShare, Maxus and others

Information, Insight and Consultancy

WPP's Kantar companies, including TNS, Millward Brown, The Futures Company, and many other specialists in brand, consumer, media and marketplace insight, work with clients to generate and apply great insights

Public Relations and Public Affairs

Corporate, consumer, financial and brand-building services from PR and lobbying firms Burson-Marsteller, Cohn & Wolfe, Hill & Knowlton, Ogilvy Public Relations Worldwide and others

Branding & Identity

Consumer, corporate and employee branding and design services, covering identity, packaging, literature, events, training and architecture from Addison, The Brand Union, Fitch, Lambie-Nairn, Landor, The Partners, and others

Direct, Promotion & Relationship Marketing

The full range of general and specialist customer, channel, direct, field, retail, promotional and point-of-sale services from Bridge Worldwide, G2, OgilvyOne, OgilvyAction, RTC Relationship Marketing, VML, Wunderman and others

Healthcare Communications

CommonHealth, ghg, Ogilvy Healthworld, Sudler & Hennessy and others provide integrated healthcare marketing solutions from advertising to medical education and online marketing

Specialist Communications

A comprehensive range of specialist services, from custom media and multicultural marketing to event, sports, youth and entertainment marketing; corporate and business-to-business; media, technology and production services

WPP Digital

Through WPP Digital, WPP companies and their clients have access to a portfolio of digital experts including 24/7 Real Media, Schematic, BLUE and Omniture

The company states that they "encourage and enable our companies of different disciplines to work together, for the benefit of clients and the satisfaction of our people." In most cases, it seems, clients use only one or two of WPP's companies. However, the firm also notes that, "A recent development, and for a minority of clients,

WPP itself can function as the 21st century equivalent of the full-service agency, act-ing as a portal to provide a single point of contact and accountability."[24] In the case of a few, the holding company's largest clients—Ford and IBM are examples—the entire holding company works to achieve the best possible marketing communica-tion results across the gamut of new and old media.

Media Literacy and the Persuasion Industries

Using integrated communications, new media, and target marketing efficiently has for several years been a cutting-edge concern of executives and creative personnel in the persuasion industries. If we step back from their day-to-day challenges and turn our attention to what their activities mean for the larger society, we confront very different concerns regarding these aspects of mass media today. Here we will highlight three worries about the role that the persuasion industries in general, and public relations in particular, are playing in the contemporary world. Two of the issues—one on conglomerates and the other on target marketing—carry forward two themes that we've seen throughout this text. The other—on truth and the hiding of influence—centers on the persuasion industry but also relates to the media system as a whole. As you might imagine from everything you've learned in this book (we hope!), all three issues are interrelated.

Truth and Hidden Influence in the Persuasion Industries

We start with the issue of truth and hidden influence. We will review the issues together to make the point that, when a company deliberately hides the sponsor or power behind a media message, its action very much represents a problem of truth. Leading an audience to get the wrong impression of a story by encouraging it to believe that the story had one author rather than another is very close to promoting a lie.

Critics of the persuasion industries argue that their practitioners can never really be truthful because their business is to portray people, products, and organizations purposefully in ways that do not reveal problems. Advertising and PR practitioners respond that there is nothing wrong with emphasizing the positive aspects of some-thing, as long as what is emphasized is not demonstrably wrong. Their critics reply that it is possible to create an ad or public relations campaign that deceives even when the text in the ad is legally truthful. Think about all the ads you see in which men are attracted to women—or women are attracted to men—who use certain products. Technically, these ads are truthful because they never contend that using these products will automatically make you alluring. Still, the critics argue, there is a fundamental deception in photographs that imply over and over that material goods will make you sexually attractive.

A leading professor of public relations, Scott Cutlip, worries about the industry's problem with the truth. He admonishes that, "reality says . . . that the public rela-tions counselor should be seen as the advocate . . . not as a dedicated purveyor of truth to serve the public interest. Many counselors serve as advocates of institutions and causes in the same way that lawyers serve clients, to put the best possible face on the facts they can, regardless of merit or truth." He adds that, because of this, "as many PR practitioners shade the truth and deal in obfuscation as purvey accurate, useful information to the public via the news media."[25]

Executives in the persuasion industries usually shrug off such complaints. They argue that not being able to suggest that a product will bring psychological benefits or that a company has a warm personality would seriously hamper their ability to create successful advertising and public relations campaigns. When it comes to ethics they focus instead on circumstances that can hurt them legally or economically. Can the government hold them legally liable for deception in an ad or PR campaign? Are competitors making incorrect statements about their products that are likely to hurt sales? Will unscrupulous practices by competitors lessen the credibility of their industry and prompt government investigations?

To make the rules clear and to deter government regulators from intruding on their business, industry leaders have turned to self-regulation. Most notably, they have created professional associations that develop norms for the industry and write them into codes of good practice. The American Association of Advertising Agencies and the American Advertising Federation, for example, both circulate similar standards that their members promise to follow. Among their many prohibitions are misleading price claims and misleading rumors about competitors. In a similar vein, the Direct Marketing Association (DMA) compiles lists of "deceptive and misleading practices" that its members should avoid. The Public Relations Society of America also has a code of "professional standards" that includes such topics as safeguarding "the confidences of present and former clients," not engaging "in any practice which tends to corrupt the integrity of channels of communication or the processes of government," and "not intentionally" communicating "false and misleading information."[26]

Some critics contend that public relations and advertising firms violate these rules every day. Moreover, no society can force a nonmember to even pay lip service to its rules. Attempts at enforcing complaints by one member against another do exist. If, for example, one advertiser believes that another advertiser is harming its products by broadcasting misleading or inaccurate commercials, the advertiser can complain to the National Advertising Division (NAD) of the Council of Better Business Bureaus. The NAD will investigate. If it finds the advertiser's work misleading, the charge is reviewed by the National Advertising Review Board (NARB), which consists of industry practitioners. That industry body will act as a referee and make a report on its conclusion available to the public. It will also suggest how the commercial might be changed. For the sake of self-regulation, advertisers typically agree to follow these suggestions.

Although critics of advertising point out that industry disputes over accuracy are only the tip of the iceberg of problems with the truthfulness of information, they acknowledge that at least an ad is out in the open for its audience to see. A person who sees an advertisement almost always knows that it is an ad and so can be sensitive to claims and images that may be exaggerated or are unsupportable. Public relations, in contrast, is by its very nature an activity that hides its creators from public view. That, say its critics, makes it almost impossible to examine its products for accuracy as one might examine an ad. In fact, as we noted previously, this is one of the persuasive advantages over advertising that PR practitioners cite. People naturally suspect an ad, they say, whereas in the case of PR they don't even know it is taking place.

The negative social effects of public relations' hidden nature can be considerable. As we have seen, many media activities today are influenced by the information subsidies that various types of public relations agencies supply. These subsidies can be as seemingly harmless as products placed by companies into entertainment or as clearly outrageous as orchestrating fake atrocity stories to sway the news media, the public, and Congress to support a war. In all cases, though, public relations practitioners are manipulating mass media content to their clients' commercial and political benefit without letting the public know about it.

People who don't consider the impact of public relations on news and entertainment may believe what they see because they trust the news or entertainment organization that they think is the source. They may act against their best interests because they don't realize that the real source of the story is quite different from the one that they believe instigated and interpreted it. At the same time, people who are aware of the power of PR over the mass media typically will still not be able to figure out whether or not a PR organization is behind a particular story, or how or why. The result of this inability to know may be a cynical view that everything in the media is tainted by PR and therefore is not what it seems. In either case, the hidden nature of public relations may have an unfortunate, even corrosive, effect on the way people understand those parts of society that are outside their immediate reach.

Targeting and the Persuasion Industries

The past two decades have seen tremendous growth in the ways advertisers and public relations practitioners create, combine, and use lists to reach target audiences. Americans have told pollsters in growing numbers that they worry that too much information about their lives and personal preferences is being exchanged without their knowledge. It also seems clear to direct marketers that people believe that they are receiving too much junk mail and too many telemarketing calls. Moreover, both pollsters and academics predict that the growth of online services will increase worries about privacy as more ways of collecting personal information (such as cookies) are created. (See Chapter 15 for a discussion of privacy.)

Another possible consequence of targeting that deserves mention involves marketing and media firms surrounding people with content that speaks so much to their own particular interests that those people learn little, and care little, about parts of society that do not relate directly to those interests.

Critics such as Joseph Turow (yes, this book's author) point out that the ultimate aim of twenty-first century marketing is to reach consumers with specific messages about how products and services tie in to their personal lifestyles. Target-minded media help advertisers and public relations practitioners do this by building what we might call "primary media communities." These are not real-life communities where people live. Rather, they are ideas of connection with certain types of people that are formed when viewers or readers feel that a magazine, radio station, or other medium harmonizes with their personal beliefs and helps them to understand their position in the larger world.

Some media are going a step beyond trying to attract certain types of people. They make an active effort to exclude people who do not fit the desired profile. This makes the community more "pure" and thereby more efficient for advertisers. Media executives accomplish this objective simply by purposefully placing material in their medium that they know will turn off certain types of people while not turning off others (and maybe even attracting them). The message of target radio stations, cable networks, and magazines is often that "this is not for everyone."

Jackass, a coarsely funny reality program, filled this role for MTV during the early 2000s when the network was working to position itself as a young adult-oriented channel. *Dexter* and *Nurse Jackie*, Showtime series about, respectively, a likeable serial murderer and drug-addicted, adulterous, yet likeable nurse did the same for that network in 2009. These programs had so much "attitude" that they sparked controversy among people who were clearly far removed from their "in" crowds. Executives involved with scheduling the shows hoped that the controversies surrounding them would crystallize the channels' images and guarantee that the channels would be sampled by the people they wanted to attract. The executives acknowledged that they also expected these "signature shows" to turn off viewers whom they didn't want in their audience.

An even more effective form of targeting goes beyond chasing undesirables away. It simply excludes them in the first place. **Tailoring** is the capacity to aim media content and ads at particular individuals. Mass customization, clickstreams, Web cookies, and interactive TV navigators are terms we have learned that reflect an awareness that the long-term trajectory of media and marketing is toward customizing the delivery of content as much as possible. With just a little effort (habit, actually), people can listen to radio stations, read magazines, watch cable programs, surf the Web, and participate in loyalty programs that parade their self-images and clusters of concerns. With seemingly no effort at all, they receive offers from marketers that complement their lifestyles. And with just a bit of cash, they can pay for technologies that can further tailor information to their interests—through highly personalized news delivery, for example.

Customized media are still pretty expensive, so PR and advertising practitioners mostly reserve them for upscale audiences. The high cost of introducing interactive television that can customize programming for large populations has caused the process to take longer than some media firms would like. But the competition to develop interactive technologies has not faded. The momentum toward creating targeted spaces for increasingly narrow niches of consumers is both national and global.

All signs point to a twenty-first century in which media firms can efficiently attract all sorts of marketers by offering three things. One is **selectability**—the ability to reach an individual with entertainment, news, information, and advertising based on knowledge of the individual's background, interests, and habits. The second is **accountability to advertisers**—the ability to trace an individual's response to a particular ad. The third is **interactivity**—the ability to cultivate a rapport with, and the loyalty of, individual consumers.

Some companies, to be sure, will want to get their brands out to the broad population as quickly as possible and will find mass market media useful. They will support the presence of billboards, supermarket signs, and the few TV shows that still draw mass audiences, such as the Super Bowl, the World Series, and the Miss America Pageant. This kind of programming helps create immediate national awareness for a new car model, athletic shoe, or computer.

But even this material will be targeted in the future. For example, Warner Brothers Television might try to reach as many people as possible to offset the high production costs of a TV movie about a nuclear disaster. Yet it might achieve this by public relations activities aimed at targeting people's personal TV navigators with tailored plot synopses—one for people who are interested in science, and a different one for people who like the lead actor. At present, it is cheaper to customize news and information programs than to customize top-of-the-line entertainment. For instance, NBC might tailor its election coverage to viewers with different interests. Consumers who care about foreign affairs, agricultural topics, or environmental issues might be able to choose the network feed that features detailed coverage of election results in their special-interest area.

Over and over, some media critics predict, different versions of news will present different social distinctions to different people. And even when the content is the same (as in the nuclear disaster movie), producers will aim different PR and ad campaigns to different types of people or different media communities, thus encouraging the perception that the viewing experience in America is an enormously splintered one. The net result will be to push separation over collectivity.

These critics argue that it will take time, possibly decades, for the full effects of the emerging media world to take shape. Even when the new media environment does crystallize, consumers will still seek media that are not specifically aimed at them. Increasingly, though, the easiest path will be to go with the customized flow of media and marketing paraphernalia. For you and me—individual readers and viewers—this

tailoring the capacity to aim media content and ads at particular individuals

selectability the ability to reach an individual with entertainment, news, information, and advertising based on knowledge of the individual's background, interests, and habits

accountability to advertisers the ability to trace an individual's response to a particular ad

interactivity the ability to cultivate a rapport with, and the loyalty of, individual consumers

segmentation and targeting portends terrific things. If we can afford to pay, or if we're important to PR or advertising sponsors who will pick up the tab, we will be able to receive all the news, information, and entertainment we like. Who would not welcome media and sponsors that offer to surround us with exactly what we want when we want it?

A critical view of the situation would argue that, although this may benefit us as individuals, it could potentially have a harmful effect on society. Customized media driven by target-oriented advertising and PR allow, even encourage, individuals to live in their own personally constructed worlds, separate from people and issues that they don't care about and don't want to be bothered with. This kind of segmentation of the population diminishes the chance that individuals who identify with certain groups will even have an opportunity to learn about others. In a society in which immigration is increasing ethnic variation and tensions, the goal should not be to use the media to connect people. Rather, the media should encourage people to do the hard work necessary to become aware of other cultures' interests, to enjoy various backgrounds collectively, and to seek out media interactions to celebrate, argue, and learn with a wide spectrum of groups in the society.

The problem, say media critics, is that the advertising and public relations industries are working with media firms to go in the opposite direction. Their goal is to ease people into media environments that comfortably mirror their own interests so that they can be persuaded more easily. Media practitioners see nothing wrong with this approach. Media analyst Sut Jhally is among those who disagree. He argues that the tendency of the persuasion industries to play to people's self-interests rather than the larger society's interests is quite predictable. "The market," he says, "appeals to the worst in us . . . and discourages what is best in us."[27]

Conglomerates and the Persuasion Industries

The growth of mass media and advertising/public relations conglomerates is an additional development that disturbs critics of the persuasion industries who worry about what they consider antisocial uses of hidden persuasion and target marketing. They worry that these huge companies will find it productive to work together to make integrated marketing communications an even greater part of the creation of media content than it is now.

What do they mean? We saw earlier that advertising agency holding companies own several public relations agencies as well as ad agencies and research firms. The biggest of the holding companies, such as Omnicom and WPP, own hundreds of companies with offices around the world. If you go to WPP's website or the website of the other Big Four agency holding companies, you will confront a bewildering array of firms. (To get an idea, take a look at the jumble of names in Figure 16.2, which reproduces the WPP holdings search page.) As we noted earlier in this chapter, they control the great percentage of top international PR firms.

As we discussed in Chapter 15, agency holding firms funnel well over half of the money to purchase media time and space for advertising. Numbers such as these suggest that WPP, Omnicom, Publicis, Havas, and Interpublic—with their huge media-buying operations and their impressive direct marketing and branding firms—have enormous impact on the mass media. Unfortunately, however, it is very difficult to gauge their impact. They are secretive when it comes to discussing their integrated cross-media activities. The advertising, PR, and media trade press, which writes a lot about the individual advertising and PR firms that they own, rarely writes about the strategies and cross-discipline activities of the holding companies. Consequently, an area of the media business that is quite powerful is difficult to examine critically.

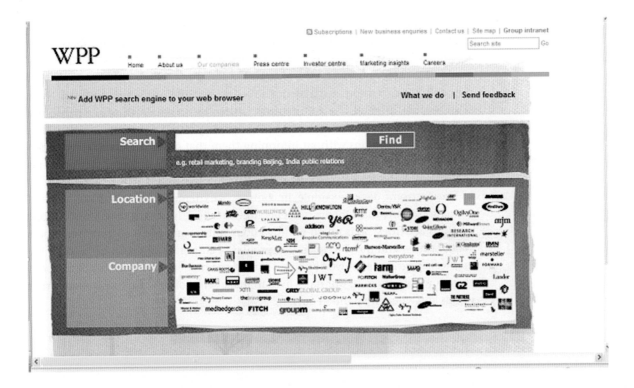

Figure 16.2 WPP's Holdings Search Page. Source: http://www.wpp.com/wpp/companies/

Realistically, it would be impossible for all the companies to work together. Nevertheless, the leaders of communications services firms emphasize that their clients will see a benefit from using a company that has general advertising, specialty advertising, general public relations, specialty public relations, media planning, media buying, and research services under one corporate umbrella. WPP puts the idea this way: "We encourage and enable our companies of different disciplines to work together, for the benefit of clients and the satisfaction of our people."[28]

The development of huge persuasion-industry conglomerates is too recent for media scholars to have published a lot on the topic. Still, we might imagine that the trend would worry critics who condemn the hidden nature of public relations and excessive target marketing. "What is going on," they would probably say, "is that the most visible media outlets, which are owned by a few companies, are increasingly working in the interests of wealthy commercial clients with PR and ad agencies that themselves are owned by just a few companies. The mutual goal of these conglomerates is to shape media environments so that they will persuade individuals wherever they go to buy products and ideas, whether they know it or not."

It should be taken as a warning to media-literate citizens to be aware of the situation when huge conglomerates have the capacity to present consumers with targeted content through media everywhere they go without the consumers knowing that they are being specifically targeted, by whom, and why. Some of the hidden persuasions may be useful—for example if a cosmetic story on a news channel customized to you is pitched to your skin color, you may like the idea and not care who is behind it. Some hidden persuasion, however, may be disturbing to your sense of honesty and your ability to navigate the world critically. Consider, for example, a magazine story or news spot about a new electronic device you are thinking of buying. The piece pretends to be open-minded but really serves the interests of a particular manufacturer. Consider, too, an editorial on a newspaper site that appears to have been sent to everyone as the voice of the paper but was really written to harmonize with the political beliefs of people like you so that you will feel good about the paper and continue to subscribe.

The example of the editorial is based on a rumor and is certainly rare, if it exists yet at all. Nevertheless, it is a development that could take place. Some publishers might argue that there is really nothing wrong with personalized editorials and that they would be great for business. Ethical concerns about not telling people directly that the editorials are customized may not be considered an impediment to this activity at all because, after all, the editorial was written by an employee of the paper, not someone from outside the organization. Others may respond that presenting readers with editorial opinions without informing them that other readers received different editorials (or an editorial on the same topic but with a different viewpoint!) is contrary to the editorial tradition of laying an opinion out for all to read or hear.

The electronic device example, in contrast, is extremely common. Much product evaluation in the mass media is deeply influenced by, if not the creation of, public relations activities. So is much writing about culture and politics, from news spots about fashion and travel to magazine profiles of corporate and political leaders. We may feel chagrined that we don't understand the hidden intentions of these stories even as we use them in our daily lives to make sense of how we think about other worlds and where we stand in ours.

Chapter Review

For an interactive chapter recap and study guide, visit the companion website for *Media Today* at http://www.routledge.com/textbooks/mediatoday4e.

Questions for Discussion and Critical Thinking

1 Why would contemporary public relations practitioners be more likely to invoke Edward Bernays than P. T. Barnum as a respected figure for their industry?

2 Explain how the consumer marketing and media relations categories of public relations activities will often overlap.

3 Why and how might a company use event marketing with respect to video games? Can you discover a situation in which that took place?

4 If reporters have as negative a view of PR as they typically say they do, why is the use of public relations output so widespread?

Internet Resources

Public Relations Society of America (http://www.prsa.org/)

Based in New York City, the PRSA calls itself the world's largest organization for public relations professionals. This website presents an overview of the association's activities, with areas dedicated to jobs, networking, professional development, and publications.

The Museum of Public Relations (http://www.prmuseum.com/bernays/bernays_1929a.html)

This is an online overview of important figures and events in the history of public relations. It includes a video of Edward Bernays reflecting on his career and on the public relations profession.

Omnicom Group (http://www.omnicomgroup.com/)

One of the Big Four agency holding companies, Omnicom has a website that illustrates the astonishing breadth of advertising, public relations, and other marketing communications firms that such conglomerates own. The site includes case studies and a map of the firm's offices around the world.

Key Terms

You can find the definitions to these key terms in the marginal glossary throughout this chapter. Test your knowledge of these terms with interactive flash cards on the *Media Today* companion website.

Constructing
Media Literacy
. . . .

1 "Product placement is a harmless way to pay for a TV program, a movie, or some other form of media content." Do you agree with this statement? Why or why not?

2 Do you agree with the argument that placing persuasive messages into entertainment, information, or news programs without telling the audience is akin to lying? Why or why not?

3 "As media increasingly become digital and interactive, advertising, PR, and marketing communications of various kinds will be used to follow individuals wherever they go and send them tailored messages." Do you agree that this can happen? Is it something to worry about? Why or why not?

4 If public relations activities are likely to be more believable to an audience than advertising, why do so many companies use advertising?

Companion Website
Video Clips
. . . .

Toxic Sludge is Good for You—Managing Crisis
This clip from the Media Education Foundation documentary *Toxic Sludge is Good for You* explores the critical issues and public concerns regarding public relations campaigns. Credit: Media Education Foundation.

Peace, Propaganda, and the Promised Land—Invisible Colonization
This clip from the Media Education Foundation documentary *Peace, Propaganda, and the Promised Land* explores the U.S. and international coverage of the crisis in the Middle East, specifically the Israeli–Palestinian conflict. Credit: Media Education Foundation.

Case Study
. . . .

EXPLORING MARKETING COMMUNICATION

The issue As this chapter and Chapter 15 note, traditional forms of public relations and advertising are two of the several approaches that marketers are using to reach target audiences. As we saw, "marketing communication" is the broad term that media and marketing personnel give to approaches that represent a wide gamut from product placement to event sponsorship and from buzz marketing to viral marketing. This case study will give you the opportunity to examine forms of marketing communication and their relation to mass media.

The method A convenient way to investigate marketing communication is to visit the website of the Big Four agency holding companies: Omnicom, WPP, Interpublic, and Publicis. Go to the website of one of these firms and explore the companies that they own that do not fall under the labels of advertising or public relations. These companies are sometimes listed as "marketing services" firms. The websites typically describe these firms and give examples of their work.

Choose two of these subsidiaries that seem to deal with a form of outreach to consumers. An example might be a company that is involved in helping marketers develop "brand" images of products. Another might be interested in using the internet to track consumers' discussions of products and decide how to react to those discussions. Still another might be involved in deciding how to use mobile media to reach customers.

For each of the two marketing communication firms describe: (1) the work the company carries out, (2) why the company says it is important, (3) in what mass media the company's activities (or the result of the company's activities) take place, and (4) in what areas of the world the firm operates. Then bring an example of each firm's activities from the website and/or from another periodical. In view of what you've learned about each firm, comment on how you think firms that carry out the two forms of marketing communication they represent are influencing the media materials audiences receive.

Epilogue

The Need For Transparency

Let us not look back in anger, nor forward in fear,
but around in awareness.

JAMES THURBER

It is easy to sit up and take notice.
What is difficult is getting up and taking action.

AL BATTISTA

As the examples we've explored throughout this text suggest, a central concern in the developing world of media today relates to people's lack of knowledge about what powers and what agendas lie behind the news, information, and entertainment that confront them across so many channels. People find it difficult to keep straight the maze of ownerships, alliances, and entanglements that affect so much of what we see and hear today. Corporate relationships within Sony affect the circulation of music and characters from video games to recordings to movies and back. Internal organizational rearrangements within Time Warner affect everything from the lineup of your local cable system to the kinds of news you get from *Time*, *Sports Illustrated*, *Entertainment Weekly*, and CNN—and how the news travels across these sources.

The easy (and understandable) reaction is to simply throw up your hands and say "It's impossible to follow these issues. All of the media world is manipulated in ways we can't understand, so I'll just distrust it all." This is the path of cynicism. It's an approach that will make you suspect everything you come across in almost every medium, even when that response isn't warranted. You'll shut yourself off from good stuff, and you won't learn to be an educated critic of what is going on in the media or the world at large.

The other, better reaction is to apply the media literacy skills that you've learned through this book in two ways. The first way is to try to keep track of the connections among the media that produce, distribute, and exhibit the materials that you use on a regular basis. What companies create these materials? Are they part of conglomerates, joint ventures, or alliances of other types? Do any of these relationships explain the kinds of content you are getting in the ways you are getting them? If so, can you figure out whether any corporate strategies might explain why these materials and not others are being released—and why one perspective and not another is being used?

The second way to apply your media literacy skills is to take action. Work with individuals or groups to convince mass media organizations to be more open about the corporate connections that go into creating their content. Demand that entertainment and news organizations routinely disclose when press releases or public relations organizations are involved in instigating or contributing to a story. Insist that media firms prominently divulge all product placements. Write to executives of public relations and "communication services" firms to demand that they work with media companies to inform the public when the products of their activities make it into print, on the air, on film, or on the Web.

It's unlikely that media executives will take kindly to such requests. It's also unlikely that the government can force these sorts of corporate disclosures, because that is probably unconstitutional. Yet consistent, insistent pressure by various public groups for openness about the ways in which marketers and PR practitioners influence twenty-first century mass media might, over time, lead corporations to provide substantially more background about the commercial and political influences behind the mass media than the public now receives. Working toward more transparency in media today might well pay off big time in terms of what we will know about media tomorrow.

Notes

Chapter 1

1 "The Apple App Store Economy," *Gigaom*, January 12, 2010. http://gigaom.com/2010/01/12/the-apple-app-store-economy/ (accessed May 19, 2010).

2 The data in this paragraph come from Paul Verna, "Recorded Music: Digital Falls Short," *Emarketer Report*, February 2007.

3 See Elihu Katz, Jay Blumler, and Michael Gurvitch, *Uses of Mass Communication by the Individual* (Beverly Hills: Sage Publications, 1974).

4 [No author], "Uzomah Barred from Seacrest for 3 Years," *UPI*, November 18, 2009, via Nexis.

5 For a summary of this work, see Lawrence Grossberg, Ellen Wartella, and D. Charles Whitney (eds.), *MediaMaking* (Thousand Oaks, CA: Sage Publications, 2005), pp. 277–297.

6 See Elihu Katz, Jay Blumler, and Michael Gurvitch, *Uses of Mass Communication by the Individual* (Beverly Hills: Sage Publications, 1974).

7 Quoted in UCLA Graduate School of Education & Information Studies, "Literacies at the End of the Twentieth Century" (Los Angeles: UCLA Graduate School of Education & Information Studies, 2000), p. 5.

Chapter 2

1 Veronis Suhler Stevenson, *Communications Industry Forecast, 2009–2013* (New York: VSS, 2009), part 1, p. 2.

2 *American Heritage Dictionary of the English Language*, fourth edition (Boston: Houghton Mifflin, 2006).

3 John Cawelti, *Six Gun Mystique* (Bowling Green, OH: Popular Culture Press, 1975).

4 See the "Bride and Prejudice" entry in the IMDB.com database. http://imdb.com/title/tt0361411/ (accessed March 6, 2008).

5 David Hinckley, "In the End Monk is TV at Its Finest," *Daily News* (New York), December 3, 2009, p. 84.

6 Veronis Suhler Stevenson, *Communications Industry Forecast, 2009–2013* (New York: VSS, 2009), part 17, p. 3.

7 Veronis Suhler Stevenson, *Communications Industry Forecast, 2009–2013* (New York: VSS, 2009), part 17, pp. 3–4.

8 Staff, "Gauging the Power of Reality in Print," *Publishers Weekly*, July 4, 2009, p. 4.

9 Rachel Deal, "Franfurt '08," *Publishers Weekly*, September 29, 2008, p. 29.

10 Veronis Suhler Stevenson, *Communications Industry Forecast, 2009–2013* (New York: VSS, 2009), part 6, p. 5.

Chapter 3

1 Guy Stern, "The Burning of the Books in Nazi Germany, 1933: The American Response," Simon Wiesenthal Museum of Tolerance website. http://motlc.wiesenthal.com/resources/books/annual2/chap05.html#4 (accessed March 6, 2008).

2 Radio Free Europe/Radio Liberty, "Uzbekistan: Government Increases its Blocking of News Websites," *BBC Monitoring World Media*, April 26, 2007.

3 [No author], "Uzbekistan Cracking Down on Dissent," Radio Free Europe/Radio Liberty, December 29, 2009. http://www.rferl.org/content/Uzbekistan_Cracking_Down_On_Dissent/1911242.html (accessed December 29, 2009).

4 *Time Inc.* vs. *Hill*, 385 U.S. 374, Supreme Court of the United States, 1967.

5 *Virginia State Board of Pharmacy et al.* vs. *Virginia Citizens Consumer Council, Inc. et al.*, 425 U.S. 748, 1976.

6 T.L. Stanley, "Heard the Latest on Gossip Girl?" *Los Angeles Times*, November 9, 2009, p. D-5.

7 Bill Katovsky and Timothy Carlson, *Embedded: The Media at War in Iraq* (Guilford, CT: The Lyons Press, 2004).

8 Paul Weidman, "Rules of Embeddedness," *The Sante Fe New Mexican*, September 10, 2004, p. 32. See also Kevin Smith, "The Media at the Tip of the Spear," *Michigan Law Review* 102, 6 (May 2004), p. 1329.

9 Julie Bisceglia, "Parody and Fair Use," *Entertainment Law Reporter*, May, 1994.

10 *The New Zealand Herald*, "Weird Al Yankovic Still Weird and White and Nerdy," March 2, 2007, via Nexis.

11 [No author], "Child and Public Advocates Urge FCC to Limit Embedded Advertising," *The White House Bulletin*, October 9, 2009, via Nexis.

12 Jim Puzzanhera, "FCC to Fine Univision $24 Million," *Los Angeles Times*, February 25, 2007, p. A20; Bloomberg News, "FCC Approves $12 Billion Sale of Univision Communications," *The New York Times*, March 28, 2007, p. C6.

13 Law quoted from "The Video Privacy Protection Act," Electronic Privacy Information Center. http://www.epic.org/privacy/vppa/ (accessed January 31, 2007).

14 http://www.ftc.gov/os/ar961/overview.shtm (accessed August 1, 2010).

15 Tricia Duryee, "Two Consumer Groups Try to Black Google's Acquisition of AdMob," PaidContent.org, December 28, 2009.

16 T. Christian Miller, "Contractors Outnumber Troops in Iraq," *Los Angeles Times*, July 4, 2007, p. A1.

17 Association of National Advertisers, "Alliance for Family Entertainment." http://paidcontent.org/

article/419-two-consumer-groups-try-to-block-googles-acquisition-of-admob/print/ (accessed December 29,2009).

18 Clifford Christians, Kim Rotzoll, and Mark Fackler, *Media Ethics*, fourth edition (White Plains, NY: Longman, 1995).

Chapter 4

1 Walter Lippmann, *Public Opinion* (New York: Harcourt Brace & Company, 1922), p. 29.

2 Walter Lippmann, *Public Opinion* (New York: Macmillan, 1922), p. 22.

3 Lawrence Grossberg, Ellen Wartella, and D. Charles Whitney, *MediaMaking: Mass Media in Popular Culture* (Thousand Oaks, CA: Sage Publications, 1998), p. 307.

4 Lawrence Grossberg, Ellen Wartella, and D. Charles Whitney, *MediaMaking: Mass Media in Popular Culture* (Thousand Oaks, CA: Sage Publications, 1998), p. 349.

5 Robert W. McChesney, *The Problem of the Media: U.S. Communication Politics in the 21st Century* (New York: Monthly Review Press, 2004).

6 Edward S. Herman and Robert W. McChesney, *The Global Media* (Washington, DC: Cassell, 1997), p. 1.

7 Lynn Spigel, "TV and Domestic Space Travels." Speech at Cornel University School of Architecture.

8 Ellen Seiter, "Television and the Internet." In J. Turow and A. Kavanaugh (eds.), *The Wired Homestead: An MIT Press Sourcebook on the Internet and the Family* (Cambridge, MA: MIT Press, 1997), p. 102.

Chapter 5

1 Ben Fritz, "Basterds Appeal is Legitimate," *Los Angeles Times*, August 24, 2009, p. B-1.

2 Cited in Joseph Turow, *Breaking Up America* (Chicago: University of Chicago Press, 1997), p. 64.

3 Simon Barker-Benfield, "Clustering Consumers not an Exact Science, but 'Generalizations Work' in Marketplace," *Florida Times-Union*. http://www.jacksonville.com/tu-online/stories/082100/bus_3737001.html. (accessed August 21, 2000).

4 Charles Pappa, "Fun Times on Business Front; Led by the Editor Who 'Gets It,' 'Fortune' Soars with Cheeky Copy," *Advertising Age*, March 12, 2001, p. S-10.

5 [No author] "MTV Networks International." http://www.viacom.com/ourbrands/medianetworks/mtvnetworks/Pages/mtvninternational.aspx (accessed December 30, 2009).

6 Elizabeth Guider, "Stars and Gripes Forever," *Variety*, November 13–19, 2006, p. 1.

7 http://www.zenithoptimedia.com/gff/index.cfm?id=73 44 0 20 7961 1000 (accessed August 2, 2010).

8 See the transcript, "Media Diversity: Minority Media Owners Conquering New Frontiers: NTIA Minority Ownership Roundtable," *National Telecommunication and Information Administration*, July 18, 2000. http://www.ntia.doc.gov/ntiahome/minoritymediaroundtable/transcript.txt (accessed March 7, 2008); also data at http://www.ntia.doc.gov/opadhome/minown98/toc.htm (accessed March

7, 2008) and http://www.ntia.doc.gov/reports/97minority/overview.htm (accessed March 7, 2008).

9 Henry Jenkins, *Convergence Culture* (New York: New York University Press, 2006), p. 23.

Chapter 6

1 Douglas Frantz and Catherine Collins, *Celebration, U.S.A.: Living in Disney's Brave New Town* (New York: Henry Holt, 1999).

2 The Walt Disney Company, *Annual Report 1999*, p. 3. http://corporate.disney.go.com/investors/annual_reports/2009/index.html (accessed August 2, 2010).

3 Craig Simons, "China Park's Rocky Debut Deflates Ambitious Disney," *Atlanta Journal-Constitution*, February 11, 2007, p. 1F.

4 Katie Allen, "Financial: Film Industry," *Guardian*, June 11, 2007, p. 27.

5 The Walt Disney Company, *Annual Report 1999*, p. 8. http://corporate.disney.go.com/investors/annual_reports/2009/index.html (accessed August 2, 2010).

6 Sharon Gaudin, "Bing Gains More Ground in Search War with Google," *ComputerWorld*, September 22, 2009. http://www.computerworld.com/s/article/9138393/Bing_gains_more_ground_in_search_war_with_Google (accessed January 8, 2009).

7 Clement James, "Google to Face AdWords Jury Trial," May 14, 2007, VNUNet.com, via Nexis; Simon Avery, "How Google is Shaking Up the Ad World," *Globe and Mail*, June 8, 2007. http://www.reportonbusiness.com/servlet/story/RTGAM.20070608.wrgoogle08/BNStory/Business/home (accessed March 7, 2008).

8 Simon Avery, "How Google is Shaking Up the Ad World," *Globe and Mail*, June 8, 2007. http://www.reportonbusiness.com/servlet/story/RTGAM.20070608.wrgoogle08/BNStory/Business/home (accessed March 7, 2008).

9 Caroline Daniel and Maija Palmer, "Google's Goal is to Organize Your Daily Life," *Financial Times*, May 23, 2007, p. 1.

10 http://www.google.com/corporate/ (accessed August 2, 2010).

11 Caroline Daniel and Maija Palmer, "Google's Goal is to Organize Your Daily Life," *Financial Times*, May 23, 2007, p. 1.

12 Richard Whitt, "Our Proposal to Build and Operate a White Spaces Database," *Google Public Policy Blog*, January 4, 2010. http://googlepublicpolicy.blogspot.com/search/label/White%20Spaces (accessed January 7, 2010).

13 Richard Whitt, "Larry Page Talk About Google's Vision of Wi-fi on Steroids," *Google Public Policy Blog*, May 22, 2008. http://googlepublicpolicy.blogspot.com/2008/05/larry-page-talks-about-googles-vision.html (accessed January 7, 2009).

14 Oo Gin Lee, "Google Unveils Rival to the iPhone," *The Straits Times*, January 7, 2010, via Nexis.

15 Dan Olds, quoted in Sharon Gaudin, "Google Risks Losing Focus Amid Expansion, Analysts Say," *ComputerWorld*, January 8, 2010. http://www.thestandard.com/news/2010/01/08/google-risks-

losing-focus-amid-expansion-analysts-say?source=nlt_daily (accessed January 8, 2010).

Chapter 7

1   Veronis Suhler Stephenson, *Communications Industry Forecast 2009–2013* (New York: VSS, 2009), Sec. 13, p. 10.

2   Veronis Suhler Stephenson, *Communications Industry Forecast 2009–2013* (New York: VSS, 2009), Sec 13, p. 10.

3   Veronis Suhler Stephenson, *Communications Industry Forecast 2009–2013* (New York: VSS, 2009), Sec 13, p. 7.

4   Bowker, "Bowker Reports U.S. Book Production Declines 3% in 2008, but 'On Demand' Publishing More than Doubles," May 19, 2009. http://www.bowker.com/index.php/press-releases/563 (accessed July 27, 2010).

5   Daisy Maryles, "Bestsellers '08," *Publishers Weekly*, January 12, 2009, p. 22.

6   David R. Kirkpatrick, "With Plot Still Sketchy, Characters Vie for Roles," *The New York Times*, November 27, 2000, p. C-1.

7   Nora Rawlinson, quoted in Judyth Rigler, "Experts Say Books Are Here to Stay," *San Antonio Express-News*, January 17, 2000, p. 1E.

8   Esther B. Fine, "Book Notes," *The New York Times*, March 3, 1993, p. C-18.

9   Lynn Andriani, "Believe It or Not," *Publishers Weekly*, June 4, 2007, p. 22.

10 Jim Milliot, "New Report Examines Book Market, Buyers," *Publishers Weekly*, July 20, 2009, p. 2.

11 Jim Milliot, "New Report Examines Book Market, Buyers," *Publishers Weekly*, July 20, 2009, p. 2.

Chapter 8

1   Quoted in "The Electric Ben Franklin." http://www.ushistory.org/franklin/courant/issue18.htm (accessed August 4, 2010).

2   Quoted in Kenneth C. Davis, Don't Know Much About History (New York: Harper Collins, 2003), p. 59.

3   National Association of Newspapers, "Number of U.S. Daily Newspapers." http://naa.org/thesource/14.asp#number (accessed March 28, 2010).

4   Veronis Suhler Stevenson, *Communication Industry Forecast 2006–2010* (New York: VSS, 2006), p. 493 and part 12, p. 4.

5   *Editor & Publisher*, "CEO of Global Free Paper Publisher Metro International Stepping Down," February 13, 2007, via Nexis.

6   *The Economist*, "This Web is Not the End of the News Industry," May 15, 2009.

7   Joshua Chaffin, "Press Ahead," *Financial Times*, August 11, 2007, p. 16.

8   *Editor & Publisher*, "McClatchy Will Pay Commissions to Shops," May 21, 2009, via Nexis.

9   Veronis Suhler Stevenson, *Communication Industry Forecast 2009–2013* (New York: VSS, 2009), part 12, p. 4.

10 Veronis Suhler Stevenson, *Communication Industry Forecast 2009–2013* (New York: VSS, 2009), part 12, p. 6.

11 Nat Ives, "Industry's Survival Plan: Unite," *Advertising Age*, May 14, 2007, p. 22.

12 Veronis Suhler Stevenson, *Communication Industry Forecast 2006* (New York: VSS, 2006), pp. 500, 502.

13 Cited in Veronis Suhler Stevenson, *Communication Industry Forecast 2009–2013* (New York: VSS, 2009), part 12, p. 12.

14 Quoted in Leslie Taylor, "Yeah, We're Going Digital—But With Dailies in Tow," *Advertising Age*, June 5, 2006, p. 4.

15 Quoted in Hamilton Nolan, "Analysis—Web Model Not Necessarily Papers' Savior," *PR Week*, March 12, 2007, p. 10.

Chapter 9

1   Nat Ives, "Moore Admits It's Not Easy, but Wants You to 'Stay Calm'," *Advertising Age*, May 28, 2007, p. 16

2   Richard Campbell, Christopher Martin, and Bettina Fabos, *Media and Culture* (Bedford: St Martin's, 2008), p. 315.

3   Advertising Age DataCenter, "US Ad Spending Totals by Medium." http://adaddge.com/datacenter (accessed February 25, 2010).

4   Hachette Fillipachi, "Custom Publishing." http://www.hfmus.com/hfmus/our_platforms/custom_publishing (accessed August 4, 2010).

5   Jack Neff, "P&G to Launch Custom Beauty Magazine Rouge in U.S.," *Advertising Age*, October 7, 2009.

6   *Smart Money* media kit. http://www.smartmoney.com/mediakit/pdf/R2.pdf (accessed October 24, 2009).

7   http://www.forbesmedia.com/events-overview (accessed October 25, 2009).

8   http://www.forbesmedia.com/properties-overview (accessed October 25, 2009).

9   Veronis Suhler Stevenson, *Communications Industry Forecast 2006–2010* (New York: Veronis Suhler Stevenson, 2006), p. 578.

10 Steve Cooper, "Start Your Own Magazine," *Entrepreneur Magazine*, June 2006. http://www.entrepreneur.com/article/printthis/160238.html (accessed August 4, 2010).

11 Robert Ames, quoted in "How Auto Mags are Turning Reviews into Digital Ad Revenue," *Advertising Age*, January 8, 2007, p. 4.

Chapter 10

1   Erik Barnouw, *A Tower in Babel* (New York: Oxford University Press, 1966), p. 129.

2   http://new.umusic.com/overview.aspx (accessed August 4, 2010).

3   RIAA, "2008 Consumer Profile." http://76.74.24.142/8EF388DA-8FD3-7A4E-C208-CDF1ADE8B179.pdf (accessed August 4, 2010).

4   RIAA, "2008 Consumer Profile." http://76.74.24.142/8EF388DA-8FD3-7A4E-C208-CDF1ADE8B179.pdf (accessed August 4, 2010).

5   RIAA, "2008 Consumer Profile." http://76.74.24.142/8EF388DA-8FD3-7A4E-C208-CDF1ADE8B179.pdf (accessed August 4, 2010).

6   [No author], "eMusic Data Shows that 72% of Sales [From Its Site] Are Albums," *Marketwire*, September 16, 2009, via Lexis.

7 ASCAP, "2008 Annual Report." http://www.ascap.com/about/annualReport/annual_2008.pdf (accessed February 26, 2010).

8 John Jurgensen, "Singers Bypass Labels for Prime-Time Exposure," *The Wall Street Journal*, May 17, 2007, p. B1.

9 John Jurgensen, "Singers Bypass Labels for Prime-Time Exposure," *The Wall Street Journal*, May 17, 2007, p. B1.

10 "MySpace Announces First Nationwide Concert Tour," August 29, 2007, via Nexis.com

11 RIAA, "2008 Year-End Shipment Statistics." http://76.74.24.142/D5664E44-B9F7-69E0-5ABD-B605F2EB6EF2.pdf (accessed August 4, 2010).

12 Ta-Nehisi Coates, "Hip-Hop's Down Beat," Time.com, August 17, 2007. http://www.time.com/time/magazine/article/0,9171,1653639,00.html (accessed September 3, 2007).

13 Voice of America News (VOA English Service), "U.S. Business, Political Leaders Target Product Piracy," August 27, 2007, via Nexis.

14 Bruce Einhorn and Xiang Ji, "Deaf to Music Piracy; Chinese Search Engines Make it Easy to Steal Net Tunes," *BusinessWeek Online*, August 31, 2007, via Nexis.

15 RIAA, "For Students Doing Reports." http://riaa.org/faq.php (accessed August 4, 2010).

16 Ryan Underwood, "UT Student Bases Internet Piracy Lawsuit on Privacy Grounds," *The Tennessean*, August 31, 2007, via Nexis.

17 RIAA, "For Students Doing Reports." http://riaa.org/faq.php (accessed August 4, 2010).

18 Steve Painter, "Wal-Mart Selling Music Online, Cheap," *Arkansas Democrat-Gazette*, August 22, 2007, via Lexis Nexis.

19 Edna Gundersen, "Moving in all Directions," *USA Today*, December 29, 2009, p. 1D.

Chapter 11

1 Arbitron, "Radio Today, 2008 edition." http://arbitron.com/downloads/radiotoday08.pdf (accessed August 4, 2010).

2 Arbitron, "Radio Today, 2008 edition." http://arbitron.com/downloads/radiotoday08.pdf (accessed August 4, 2010).

3 Veronis Suhler Stevenson, *Communications Industry Forecast 2006–2010* (New York: Veronis Suhler Stevenson, 2006), pp. 332–333.

4 Jon Coleman, quoted in Joseph Turow, *Breaking Up America: Advertisers and the New Media World* (Chicago: University of Chicago Press, 1997), p. 100.

5 "ABC Music Radio: 24-Hour Formats." http://www.abcradionetworks.com/Article.asp?id5341457 (accessed September 8, 2007).

6 [No author], "In Brief," *Crain's New York Business*, February 22, 2010, p. 2; Veronis Suhler Stevenson, *Communications Industry Forecast, 2009–2013* (New York: VSS, 2009), p. 10.

7 http://www.pandora.com/#/stations/create/ (August 18, 2010).

8 Claire Cain Miller, "Music Labels Reach Deal With Internet Radio Sites," *The New York Times*, July 8, 2009, p. 2.

9 Claire Cain Miller, "Music Labels Reach Deal With Internet Radio Sites," *The New York Times*, July 8, 2009, p. 2.

Chapter 12

1 Veronis Suhler Stevenson, *Communications Industry Forecast, 2009–2013* (New York: VSS, 2009), part 10, p. 23.

2 Dade Hayes, "Powering Up the Last Indie," *Variety*, August 27–September 2, 2007, p, 1.

3 Michael Fleming, "Bearish Biz Bites Talent Paydays," *Daily Variety*, January 21, 2009, p. 1.

4 Pamela McLintock, "Summer's Bottom Line," *Variety*, August 20–26, 2007, p. 42.

5 Lauren A.E. Schuker, "Indie Firms Suffer Drop-off in Rights Sales," *The Wall Street Journal*, April 20, 2009, p. B-1.

6 Pamela McClintock, "B.O. History Lesson," *Daily Variety*, May 26, 2009, p. 1.

7 Dade Hayes, "Powering Up the Last Indie," *Variety*, August 27–September 2, 2007, p. 1.

8 National Association of Theater Owners and Cinema Buying Group, "Reflections on the Kind of Exhibition Industry that Best Serves Movie Patrons, Makers, and Exhibitors in the Digital Era," January 2009. http://natoonline.org (accessed November 11, 2009).

9 Veronis Suhler Stevenson, *Communications Industry Forecast, 2009–2013* (New York: VSS, 2009), part 10, p. 23.

10 MPAA, "Content Protection FAQ." http://www.mpaa.org/contentprotection_faq.asp (accessed November 13, 2009).

Chapter 13

1 Veronis Suhler Stevenson, *Communications Industry Forecast, 2009–2013* (New York: VSS, 2009), part 6, p. 3.

2 Veronis Suhler Stevenson, *Communications Industry Forecast, 2009–2013* (New York: VSS, 2009), part 6, p. 3.

3 Veronis Suhler Stevenson, *Communications Industry Forecast 2006–2010* (New York: Veronis Suhler Stevenson, 2007), p. 270.

4 ABI researcher Stan Schatt, quoted in David Lieberman, "Cable Channels Undergo TV Makeovers," *USA Today*, September 11, 2007. http://www.usatoday.com/money/media/2007-09-10-cable-brands_N.htm (accessed August 26, 2010).

5 David Bauder, "Nielsen to Triple TV Sample," *Associated Press*, September 26, 2007, via Nexis.

6 Rick Kissell, "Live Viewing on Decline," *Variety*, April 27–May 3, 2009, p. 11.

7 John Dempsey, "Stations Game for Something New," *Variety*, June 25–July 8, 2007, p. 17.

8 Daisy Whitney, "Could Steve Whitfield be This Year's Rachael Ray?" *Advertising Age*, May 4, 2007, p. S12.

9 Emiliano De Pablos, "Serials Make Killing in Digital TV Universe," *Variety*, September 21–27, 2009, p. A-2.

Chapter 14

1 This brief historical sketch is based on a wide variety of articles in Wikipedia as well as on Steven Kent, *The Ultimate History of Video Games* (New York: Three Rivers Press, 2001).

2 Veronis Suhler Stevenson, *Communications Industry Forecast, 2009–2013* (New York: VSS, 2009), part 11, p. 11.

3   Sprint Nextel News Release, "Sprint Nextel Announces 4G Wireless Broadband Initiative," August 8, 2006. http://www2.sprint.com/mr/news_dtl.do?id512960 (accessed October 16, 2007).

4   Veronis Suhler Stevenson, *Communications Industry Forecast, 2009–2013* (New York: VSS, 2009), part 10, p. 17.

5   Katie Allen, "Financial: Electronics," *The Guardian* (London), September 25, 2009, p. 32.

6   Veronis Suhler Stevenson, *Communications Industry Forecast, 2009–2013* (New York: VSS, 2009), part 10, p. 22.

7   Todd Spangler, "Verizon to Put Game Face on FiOS TV," *Multichannel News*, October 3, 2007. http://www.multichannel.com/article/ca6486821.html (accessed on October 13, 2007).

8   Mike Wilcox, "A Challenge that Lets You Grow Wings," *The Age* (Melbourne, Australia), September 17, 2009, p. 24.

9   Michael Sansbury, "X-Box Outplays Rivals and Movies," *The Australian*, October 11, 2007, p. 36.

10 Langston Werz, Jr., "Video Games," *Charlotte Observer*, October 8, 2007, p. 3D.

11 Ben Fritz, "Boffo Year for Vidgame Biz," *Variety*, January 18, 2008, p. 5.

12 "Video Game Genres," Wikipedia, http://en.wikipedia.org/wiki/Video_game_genres, accessed 10/14/07.

13 "Adventure Game," Wikipedia. http://en.wikipedia.org/wiki/Adventure_game (accessed October 14, 2007).

14 "Educational Game," Wikipedia. http://en.wikipedia.org/wiki/Educational_game (accessed October 11, 2007).

15 Laurie Sullivan, "Beyond In-game Ads," *Advertising Age*, June 18, 2007, p. 1.

16 [No author], "Advergaming," *Brandweek.com*, July 23, 2007, via Nexis.

17 Robert Gray, "Play the Brand," *Marketing*, July 25, 2007, p. 33.

18 http://www.americasarmy.com/ (accessed October 15, 2007).

19 Beth Snyder Bulik, "In-game Ads Win Cachet Through a Deal with EA," *Advertising Age*, July 30, 2007, p. 8.

20 Abbey Klaassen, "Game-ad Boom Looms as Sony Opens up PS3," *Advertising Age*, February 25, 2008, p. 1.

21 Laurie Sullivan, "Beyond In-game Ads," *Advertising Age*, June 18, 2007, p. 1.

22 Veronis Suhler Stevenson, *Communications Industry Forecast, 2009-2013* (New York: VSS, 2009), part 10, p. 21.

23 ESRB, "Game Ratings & Descriptor Guide." http://www.esrb.org/ratings/ratings_guide.jsp (accessed October 14, 2007).

24 Reuters, "Banned Video Game Called 'Fine Piece of Art,' " *PC Magazine*, June 21, 2007.

25 Jonathan Silverstein, "Game Ratings Don't Always Tell the Whole Story," ABC News, April 5, 2006. http://abcnews.go.com/Technology/story?id51808712&page51 (accessed October 14, 2007).

26 Johnnie Roberts, "Chances Are, You've Only Surved a Few Sites Today," *Newsweek*, June 4, 2001. http://www.newsweek.com/2001/06/03/chances-are-you-ve-only-surfed-a-few-sites-today.html (accessed August 26, 2010).

27 Johnnie Roberts, "Chances Are, You've Only Surved a Few Sites Today," *Newsweek*, June 4, 2001. http://www.newsweek.com/2001/06/03/chances-are-you-ve-only-surfed-a-few-sites-today.html (accessed August 26, 2010).

Chapter 15

1   Myra Frazier, "Geico's $500 Million Outlay Pays Off," *Advertising Age*, July 7, 2007, p. 8.

2   Andrew Hampp, "10 Tunes in TV Spots," *Advertising Age*, December 18, 2006, p. 33.

3   Louise Story, "Away from Home, Ads Are Inescapable," *The New York Times*, March 2, 2007.

4   Louise Story, "Anywhere the Eye Can See, It's Likely to See an Ad," *The New York Times*, January 15, 2007.

5   Abbey Klaassen, "MTV Lures to Its Website Those Who Don't Buy TV," *Advertising Age*, 2006, p. 8.

6   Brian Steinberg, "Marketers Fight for the Right to Buy Shows, Not Networks," *Advertising Age*, May 18, 2009, via Nexis.

7   Beth Snyder Bulik, "Microsoft Gaming Play Lets Advertisers Buy by Dem, not Platform," *Advertising Age*, July 23, 2007, p. 20.

8   Quoted in Joseph Turow, *Niche Envy: Marketing Discrimination in the Digital Age* (Cambridge, MA: MIT Press, 2006), p. 43

9   Quoted in Joseph Turow, *Niche Envy: Marketing Discrimination in the Digital Age* (Cambridge, MA: MIT Press, 2006), p. 44.

10 RECMA, "Global Billings." http://www.recma.com/Global-Billings-2007---3-volumes.html?wpid=24036 (accessed August 11, 2010).

Chapter 16

1   Robert Oskar Carlson, "Public Relations," in *The Encyclopedia of Communication* (New York: Oxford University Press, 1989), p. 391.

2   James Playsted Wood, *The Story of Advertising* (New York: Ronald Press, 1958), p. 46.

3   Quoted in Michael Turney, "Ivy Lee Was Decades Ahead of His Colleagues." http://www.nku.edu/~turney/prclass/readings/3eras2x.html (accessed August 26, 2010).

4   Cited on the Public Relations Society of America (PRSA) website. http://media.prsa.org/prsa+overview/industry+facts+figures/ (accessed November 26, 2009).

5   Veronis Suhler Stevenson, *Communications Forecast, 2009–2013* (New York: VSS, 2009), part 3, p. 18.

6   Jack O'Dwyer, "PR Goes Marketing & Electronic," *O'Dwyer's PR Report*, August 2007, p. 3.

7   Jack O'Dwyer, "PR Goes Marketing & Electronic," *O'Dwyer's PR Report*, August 2007, p. 3.

8   Hill & Knowlton, "About Hill & Knowlton." http://www.hillandknowlton.com/about (accessed March 8, 2010).

9   Hill & Knowlton, "Asia Pacific." http://www.hillandknowlton.com/about (accessed March 8, 2010).

10 Hill & Knowlton, "Case Studies." http://www.hillandknowlton.com/casestudies; and "Getting You There." http://www.hillandknowlton.com/success/getting-you-there (accessed March 8, 2010).

11 http://www.hillandknowlton.com/index/regions/latin_america (accessed on October 28, 2007).

12 http://www.hillandknowlton.com/index/practices/marcom (accessed October 28, 2007).

13   Burson Marsteller, "Healthcare." http://www.burson-marsteller.com/Practices_And_Specialties/Healthcare/Pages/default.aspx (accessed March 8, 2010).

14   Scott Cutlip, *The Unseen Power* (Hillsdale, NJ: Lawrence Erlbaum Associates, 1996), p. 768.

15   Hill & Knowlton, "Public Affairs." http://preview.hnk-global.netcomsus.com/index/practices/public_affairs (accessed August 26, 2010).

16   Hill & Knowlton, "Debswana." http://www.hillandknowlton.com/casestudies/debswana (accessed November 27, 2009).

17   Matthew Phililips, "Toyota's Digital Disaster," *Newsweek Online*, February 3, 2010. http://www.newsweek.com/id/232962 (accessed March 8, 2010).

18   Gene Grabowski, chair of crisis and litigation practice at Levick Strategic Communications, quoted in Matthew Philipps, "Toyota's Digital Disaster," *Newsweek Online*, February 3, 2010. http://www.newsweek.com/id/232962 (accessed March 8, 2010).

19   Hill & Knowlton, "Media Relations." http://www.hillandknowlton.com/services/mediarelations (accessed November 27, 2009).

20   Hill & Knowlton, "Digital Communication." http://www.hillandknowlton.com/services/digital (accessed August 26, 2010).

21   Mark Jewell, "Legal Experts Predict Case Against Men in Boston Bomb Scare Will Be Difficult to Prove," *Associated Press*, February 2, 2007, via Nexis.

22   Jon Biltmore, "MTV Brings Big Names, Numbers to Beach," *The News Herald*, March 5, 2009, via Nexis.

23   Karlene Lukovitz, "ConAgra Sponsors Yahoo TV Clips Program," *Marketing Daily*, November 17, 2009. http://www.mediapost.com/publications/?fa=Articles.showArticle&art_aid=117534 (accessed November 17, 2009).

24   http://www.wpp.com/WPP/About/WhoWeAre/Mission.htm (accessed October 27, 2007).

25   Scott Cutlip, *The Unseen Power* (New York: Routledge, 1994), p. 252.

26   PRSA, "Preamble." http://www.prsa.org/aboutprsa/ethics/codeenglish/?utm_campaign=PRSASearch&utm_source=PRSAWebsite&utm_medium=SSearch&utm_term=the%20confidences%20of%20present%20and%20former%20clients (accessed, August 26, 2010).

27   Sut Jhally, "Advertising at the Edge of the Apocalypse." In Robin Anderen and Lance Strate (eds.), *Critical Studies in Media Commercialism* (Oxford: Oxford University Press, 2000), p. 33.

28   WPP, "Our Mission." http://www.wpp.com/wpp/about/whoweare/mission.htm (accessed August 26, 2010).

Photo Credits

Part 1

Chapter 1

Opener: ©AP/WIDE WORLD PHOTOS; © TOBIAS HASE/epa/Corbis; © Chris Whitehead/cultura/Corbis

Page 7: © Chris Whitehead/cultura/Corbis; page 8: © David Sipress/The New Yorker Collection/www.cartoonbank.com; page 10: ©AP/WIDE WORLD PHOTOS; page 19: © TOBIAS HASE/epa/Corbis; page 23: © pool ./Retna Ltd./Corbis and © ELIANA APONTE/Reuters/Corbis; page 26: © PRESTON MACK/epa/Corbis; page 28: © Scott McLane /Retna Ltd./Corbis.

Chapter 2

Opener: © Ray Stubblebine/Reuters/Corbis

Page 38: ©Michael Newman/Photo Edit; page 42: AP/WIDE WORLD PHOTOS; page 43: BET/courtesy of Photofest; page 46: © David Sipress/The New Yorker Collection/www.cartoonbank; page 49: AP/WIDE WORLD PHOTOS; page 50: www.huffingtonpost.com; page 53: AMC/courtesy of Photofest; page 62: AP/WIDE WORLD PHOTOS.

Chapter 3

Opener: ©Gary Blakeley/Shutterstock

Page 71: © Austrian Archives/Crobis; page 74: www.chinaview.cn; page 76: AP/WIDE WORLD PHOTOS; page 81: Minnesota Historical Society; page 82: © Bettmann/Corbis; page 84: AP/WIDE WORLD PHOTOS; page 87: © Henry Diltz/CORBIS; page 95: © Alfred Eisenstaedt/Time & Life Pictures/Getty Images; page 103: AP/WIDE WORLD PHOTOS, AP/WIDE WORLD PHOTOS; page 105: © Getty Images/Michael Caulfield/WireImage; page 107: © Society of Professional Journalists: www.spm.org; page 108: © The Motion Picture Association of America; page 109: www.tvguidelines.org; page 110: © Getty Images; page 111: reprinted with permission of ESRB and ESA. Please be advised that the ESRB rating icons are copyrighted works and registered trademarks owned by the Electroci Software Association and the Entertainment Software Rating Board and may only be used with their permission and authority. Under no circumstances may the rating icons be self-applied to any product that has not been rated by the ESRB.

Chapter 4

Opener: © H. Armstrong Roberts/ClassicStock/Corbis

Page 124: The Granger Collection, New York; page 127: The Granger Collection, New York, The Granger Collection, New York; page 128: © Albert Bandura; page 129: AP/WIDE WORLD PHOTOS; page 132: Do You Graphics/Still Picture Unit, National Archives and Records Administration. Photo Communication Inc.; page 133: © Peter Steiner/The New Yorker Collection/www.cartoonbank; page 134: PBS/courtesy of Photofest; page 140: photo by Ted Streshinsky page 144: CBS/courtesy of Photofest PHOTOS

Part 2

Chapter 5

Opener: AP/WIDE WORLD

Page 162: Universal Studios/courtesy of Photofest; page 163: www.adage.com; page 167: Columbia Pictures/courtesy of Photofest; page 171: AP/WIDE WORLD PHOTOS; page 181: www.moviefone.com; page 182; © Michael Crawford/The New Yorker Collection/www.cartoonbank.; page 185: © Nick Downes/The New Yorker Collection/www.cartoonbank.

Chapter 6

Opener: © Corbis

Page 196: Walt Disney Productions/courtesy of Photofest; page 201: AP/WIDE WORLD PHOTOS; page 207: AP/WIDE WORLD PHOTOS; page 208: © Getty Images; page 210: www.google.com; page 212: © Getty Images; page 217: © Getty Images.

Part 3

Chapter 7

Opener: © UWE ANSPACH/epa/Corbis

Page 229: © Bettmann/CORBIS; page 231: ©Hachette Book Group, USA; page 233: © Bettmann/CORBIS; page 244: © Bettmann/CORBIS; page 246: © Getty Images; page 248: reprinted by permission of Faithwords/Hachette Book Group; page 249: reprinted by permission of Hachette Book Group, USA; page 252: © Getty Images; page 253: © Atlantide Phototravel/Corbis; page 254: © Michael Maslin/The New Yorker Collection/www.cartoonbank.

Chapter 8

Opener: ©James Hardy/ Getty Images

Page 261: ©North Wind Picture Archives; page 262: The Granger Collection, New York; page 263: The Granger Collection, New York; page 267: The Granger Collection, New York; page 274: ©

Tom Cheney/The New Yorker Collection/www.cartoonbank; page 278: http://www.eldiariony.com; page 279: ©PhotoEdit, Inc.; page 280: © David Sipress/The New Yorker Collection/www.cartoonbank; page 283: AP/WIDE WORLD PHOTOS; page 290: © Getty Images; page 291: AP/WIDE WORLD PHOTOS.

Chapter 9

Opener: © David Brabyn/Corbis
Page 299: The Granger Collection, New York; page 301: The Granger Collection, New York; page 302: © North Wind Picture Archives; page 303: The Granger Collection, New York; page 304: © Jack Ziegler/The New Yorker Collection/www.cartoonbank; page 307: AP/WIDE WORLD PHOTOS, page 314: © PhotoEdit, Inc; page 314: © PhotoEdit, Inc; page 317: © Getty Images; page 319: © James Leynse/CORBIS.

Part 4
Chapter 10

Opener: © RAY STUBBLEBINE/Reuters/Corbi
Page 330: The Granger Collection, New York; page 331: LC-USZC2-5315 DLC Repository Library of Congress Prints and Photographs Division; page 334: The Granger Collection, New York; page 335: © Getty Images; page 339: www.universalmusic.com; page 347: www.ascap.com with permission; page 348: © Christian Simonpietri/Sygma/Corbis; page 346: AP/WIDE WORLD PHOTOS; page 358: AP/WIDE WORLD PHOTOS; page 360: © John Ricard ./Retna Ltd./Corbis.

Chapter 11

Opener: © Andi Hazelwood/Shutterstock
Page 366: The Granger Collection, New York; page 371: The Granger Collection, New York; page 372: The Granger Collection, New York; page 373: © Bettmann/CORBIS; page 389: © Mark Peterson/CORBIS; page 390: ©Lisa O'Connor/ZUMA/Corbis; page 393: © Robb Armstrong/The New Yorker Collection/www.cartoonbank; page 396: www.pandora.com; page 398: www.power.com.

Chapter 12

Opener: © ANDREW GOMBERT/epa/Corbis
Page 406: The Granger Collection, New York; page 408: The Granger Collection, New York; page 412: © Bettmann/CORBIS; page 414: 20th Centry Fox/courtesy of Photofest; page 421: AP/WIDE WORLD PHOTOS; page 423: © Sergei Karpukhin/Reuters/Corbis; page 426: © Getty Images; page 429: © Jack Ziegler/The

New Yorker Collection/www.cartoonbank; page 432: www.netflix.com; page 433: © RICK WILKING/Reuters/Corbis; page 436: © Bruce Eric Kaplan/The New Yorker Collection/www.cartoonbank; page 438: AP/WIDE WORLD PHOTOS.

Chapter 13

Opener: © DeshaCAM/Shutterstock
Page 447: © Bettmann/CORBIS; page 448: © Getty Images; page 455: www.pbs.org; page 456: www.ionline.tv; page 460: AP/WIDE WORLD PHOTOS; page 463: www.hgtv.com AP/WIDE WORLD PHOTOS; page 466: www.nielsenmedia.com; page 469: NBC/courtesy of Photofest; page 479: AP/WIDE WORLD PHOTOS.

Chapter 14

Opener: © Getty Images
Page 486: The Granger Collection, New York; page 487: The Granger Collection, New York; page 488: © Bettmann/CORBIS; page 489: image courtesy of the Computer History Museum; page 491: ©Dennis Hallinan/Getty Images; page 495: www.kraftfoods.com/jello; page 499: © BOBBY YIP/Reuters/Corbis; page 506: © Toshiyuki Aizawa/Reuters/Corbis, AP/WIDE WORLD PHOTOS, © Toru Hanai/Reuters/Corbis; page 508: AP/WIDE WORLD PHOTOS; page 513: www.pewinternet.org.

Part 5
Chapter 15

Opener: © THOMAS PETER/Reuters/Corbis
Page 529: The Granger Collection, New York; page531: ©Getty Images; page 535: © Alan Schein Photography/Corbis, www.gruopgallegos.com; page 537: www.thedma.org; page 539: © William Hamilton/The New Yorker Collection/www.cartoonbank; page 540: © Getty Images;; page 542: AP/WIDE WORLD PHOTOS; page 549: © Donald Reilly/The New Yorker Collection/www.cartoonbank.com; page 550: © Getty Images; page 553: Sut Jhally, reprinted by permission.

Chapter 16

Opener: © Dmitriy Shironosov/Shutterstock
Page 562: North Wind Picture Archives; page 563: ©Bettmann/Corbis; page 564: ©Bettmann/Corbis; page 565: © Bettmann/CORBIS; page 566: © Bettmann/CORBIS; 568: ww.Fleishmanhillard.com; page 575: ©Bettmann/Corbis; page 576: © FRANCK ROBICHON/epa/Corbis; page 580: AP/WIDE WORLD PHOTOS; page 583: AP/WIDE WORLD PHOTOS; page 599: www.wpp.com.

Index